DRAWING SENTENCES

A Guide To Diagramming

DRAWING SENTENCES

A Guide To Diagramming

Eugene R. Moutoux

Butler Books
Louisville

© 2010, 2012, 2013, 2014, 2015, 2016 Eugene Moutoux
All Rights Reserved.

No part of this book may be reproduced or transmitted in any form or by any means, electronic or mechanical, including photocopying or recording, or by any information storage and retrieval system, without permission in writing from the author or his assigns.

ISBN: 978-1-953058-66-9

Published by:

Butler Books
P.O. Box 7311
Louisville, KY 40257
(502) 897–9393
Fax (502) 897–9797
www.butlerbooks.com

To my children,

Dave, Tom, and Pam,

who, although they now live far away with children of their
own, are never far from my mind and always close to my heart.

I am grateful to Tom Moutoux for his many drawings in this book and to Joni Moutoux, Kevin Gave, and Phyllis Taylor for their proofreading, suggestions, and encouragement.

I owe a special debt of gratitude to my fifth- or sixth-grade teacher at St. Benedict's Elementary School, who introduced me to diagramming. Unlike Kitty Burns Florey, who included the name of her diagramming teacher in the title of her popular book *Sister Bernadette's Barking Dog*, I have let my teacher's name slip away into the ether of lost memories.

When I decided about twelve years ago to dig deeply into sentence diagramming, I turned to the second edition of a book entitled *Descriptive English Grammar*, by Homer C. House and Susan Emolyn Harman. I have referred to this book so often that the cover is now tattered and torn, and the pages are held together by a rubber band. Other books that have served me well are *Understanding English Grammar* by Martha Kolln and Robert Funk, *Fowler's Modern English Usage*, and three books by Alonzo Reed and Brainerd Kellogg, after whom the system of diagramming used in my book is named.

Finally, I would be remiss if I did not mention the "square-table bunch," who labored hard one evening for at least five minutes and came up with the nucleus of this book's title.

~ Contents ~

Preface   1

PART ONE: MAIN CLAUSES

Unit I: Lessons 1 - 3
Lesson 1: Subjects and Verbs   6
Lesson 2: Definite and Indefinite Articles   7
Lesson 3: Predicate Nominatives   8
Review I   9

Unit II: Lessons 4 - 6
Lesson 4: Attributive Adjectives   11
Lesson 5: Predicate Adjectives   12
Lesson 6: Possessive Pronouns   13
Review II   14

Unit III: Lessons 7 - 9
Lesson 7: Direct Objects   16
Lesson 8: Questions   17
Lesson 9: Adverbs   18
Review III   19

Unit IV: Lessons 10 - 12
Lesson 10: Commands   21
Lesson 11: Prepositional Phrases   22
Lesson 12: Nouns Used as Adjectives   23
Review IV   24

Unit V: Lessons 13 - 15
Lesson 13: Direct Address   26
Lesson 14: Prepositional Phrases (2)   27
Lesson 15: Appositives   28
Review V   29

Unit VI: Lessons 16 - 18
Lesson 16: Interjections and Possessive Nouns   31
Lesson 17: Possessive Nouns (2)   32
Lesson 18: Interrogative Adverbs and Adjectives   33
Review VI   34

Unit VII: Lessons 19 - 21
Lesson 19: Interrogative Pronouns   36
Lesson 20: Indirect Objects   37
Lesson 21: Objective Complements   38
Review VII   39

Unit VIII: Lessons 22 - 24

Lesson 22: Coordinating Conjunctions	41
Lesson 23: Adverbial Objectives	42
Lesson 24: Coordinating Conjunctions (2)	43
Review VIII	44

Exercise Solutions 45

Unit Tests 59

Test Solutions 67

PART TWO: DEPENDENT CLAUSES, VERBALS

Unit I: Lessons 1 - 3

Lesson 1: Adjective Clauses	74
Lesson 2: Noun Clauses	75
Lesson 3: Adverb Clauses	76
Review I	77

Unit II: Lessons 4 - 6

Lesson 4: Compound Sentences	79
Lesson 5: Gerunds	80
Lesson 6: Participles	81
Review II	82

Unit III: Lessons 7 - 9

Lesson 7: Infinitives	84
Lesson 8: Noun Clauses (2)	85
Lesson 9: Adverb Clauses (2)	86
Review III	87

Unit IV: Lessons 10 - 12

Lesson 10: Compound-complex Sentences	89
Lesson 11: Comparisons	90
Lesson 12: The Expletive *There*	91
Review IV	92

Unit V: Lessons 13 - 15

Lesson 13: Adjective Clauses (2)	94
Lesson 14: Phrasal Verbs	95
Lesson 15: Infinitives (2)	96
Review V	97

Unit VI: Lessons 16 - 18

Lesson 16: Unexpressed Words	99
Lesson 17: Complementary Infinitives	100
Lesson 18: Phrasal Prepositions and Conjunctions	101

Review VI 102

Unit VII: Lessons 19 - 21 104
Lesson 19: Prepositional Phrases as Predicate Adjectives ... 105
Lesson 20: Noun Clauses (3) 106
Lesson 21: Gerunds (2) 107
Review VII

109
Unit VIII: Lessons 22 - 24 110
Lesson 22: Transitional Adverbs 111
Lesson 23: Indefinite Relative Pronouns 112
Lesson 24: Bits 'n' Pieces
Review VIII

113
Exercise Solutions

135
Unit Tests

143
Test Solutions

PART THREE: REVIEW AND SUPPLEMENT

155
Diagrams and Explanations

173
Additional Diagramming Examples

Exercises

185
Exercise 1: Subjects and Verbs 185
Exercise 2: Direct Objects 185
Exercise 3: Subjective Complements (Predicate Nominatives and Predicate Adjectives)

185
Exercise 4: Definite and Indefinite Articles, Attributive Adjectives, Possessive Pronouns, Nouns
    Used as Adjectives 186
Exercise 5: Adverbs 186
Exercise 6: Prepositional Phrases

186
Exercise 7: Compounds, Coordinating Conjunctions *and or, but, both...and, either...or, neither...*
    nor, not only...but also 187
Exercise 8: Appositives, Interjections, Possessive Nouns, Vocatives (Nouns of Direct Address),
    Imperatives (Commands) 187
Exercise 9: Indirect Objects and Other Adverbial Objectives

187
Exercise 10: Objective Complements 187
Exercise 11: Adverb Clauses, Subordinating Conjunctions ... 188
Exercise 12: Adverb Clauses (2), Relative Adverbs

188
Exercise 13: Relative Clauses

Exercise 14: Noun Clauses, Indirect Questions	188
Exercise 15: Noun Clauses (2), Indirect Questrions (2)	189
Exercise 16: Participles, Objective Complements (2)	189
Exercise 17: Gerunds	189
Exercise 18: Infinitives	190
Exercise 19: Infinitives (2), Objective Complements (3)	190
Exercise 20: Expletives, Ellipses, Indefinite Relative Pronouns, Special Concessive Clauses	190
Exercise 21: Transitional Adverbs, Independent Expressions, Sentence Modifiers	190
Exercise 22: Equal and Unequal Comparisons (*as* and *than*), Other Topics	191
Exercise 23: Prepositional Phrases (2)	191
Exercise 24: *Like, Near, Different Than,* Other Topics	191
Exercise 25: Miscellaneous Topics	192
Exercise 26: Miscellaneous Topics	192
Exercise 27: Sentences from Literature	192
Exercise 28: Sentences from Literature (2)	193
Exercise 29: Sentences from Literature (3)	193
Exercise 30: Sentences from Literature (4)	193

Exercises Solutions — 195

Additional Sentences and Solutions — 257

APPENDIX: Grammatical Terms and Diagramming Symbols — 265

Index — 273

Parts One, Two, and Three of this book were published originally under the titles *A First Book of Sentence Diagramming*, *A Second Book of Sentence Diagramming*, and *A Workbook of Sentence Diagramming*, respectively.

~ Preface ~

The system of diagramming used in this book was introduced by Stephen Clark in 1847, modified by Alonzo Reed and Brainerd Kellogg some thirty years later, and expanded by Homer C. House and Susan Emolyn Harman in 1931 (*Descriptive English Grammar*, 2nd ed., Prentice Hall, 1950).

Clark's system of diagramming, explained and illustrated in his book *A Practical Grammar: in which Words, Phrases, and Sentences are Classified According to their Offices, and their Relation to Each Other*, uses tangent ovals to show how words and phrases are related to each other. Lines serve to connect clauses. Here is the sentence *She discussed the book and the movie with a friend whom she has known for many years* diagrammed using Clark's system:

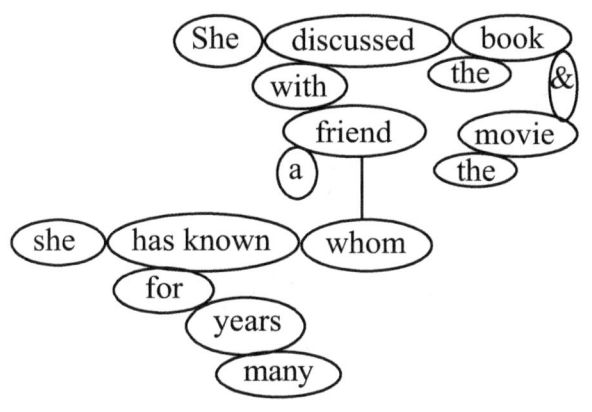

In the system of diagramming developed by Reed and Kellogg, a diagram of the same sentence looks like this:

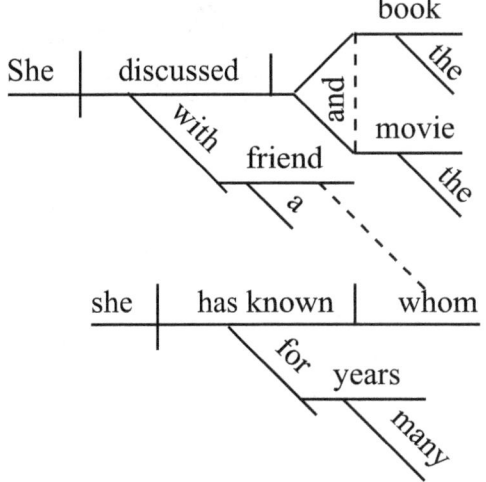

Among other books of sentence diagramming that appeared toward the end of the nineteenth century were *Harvey's Revised English Grammar* and *Hoenshel's Advanced Grammar*. Although their diagrams resembled those of Reed and Kellogg, differences are not hard to find. Compare, for example, two diagrams of the sentence *They discussed the book and the movie*, on the left a diagram using Harvey's method, on the right a Reed-Kellogg diagram:

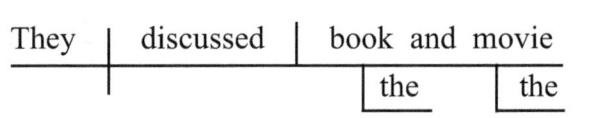

A Hoenshel diagram of the sentence *They discussed the book* is on the left, the corresponding R-K diagram on the right:

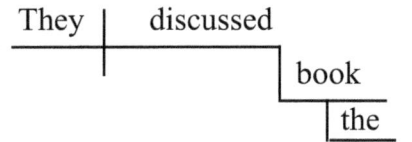 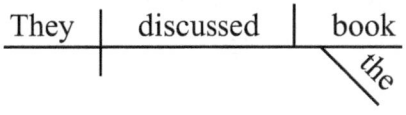

The method of diagramming preferred by most modern linguists is called tree diagramming. Tree diagramming complements a system of language analysis called transformational generative grammar. This new grammar, developed in the 1950s, highlights noun phrases and verb phrases, reduces the number of tenses from the traditional six (present, past, future, present perfect, past perfect, and future perfect) to two (present and past), and views dependent clauses as sentences within sentences, among other innovations.

Tree diagrams label sentences, main clauses, and dependent clauses with S; noun phrases with NP; and verb phrases with VP. A multi-verb string like *may have been working* carries a series of labels including VP, AUX, M, T, pres., have + en, be + ing, and V. Tree diagramming has the advantage of keeping the words of a sentence in the order in which they appear in the sentence. This advantage carries with it the disadvantage of requiring an impractical amount of space to diagram long sentences. Traditional diagramming, for its part, isn't perfect, but it is very good. It has served students well and continues to serve them well. Below are two diagrams (a tree diagram above and a traditional Reed-and-Kellogg diagram below on the left) of a relatively short, 16-word sentence, *The old woman standing on the porch has often given cookies to children whom she knows.*

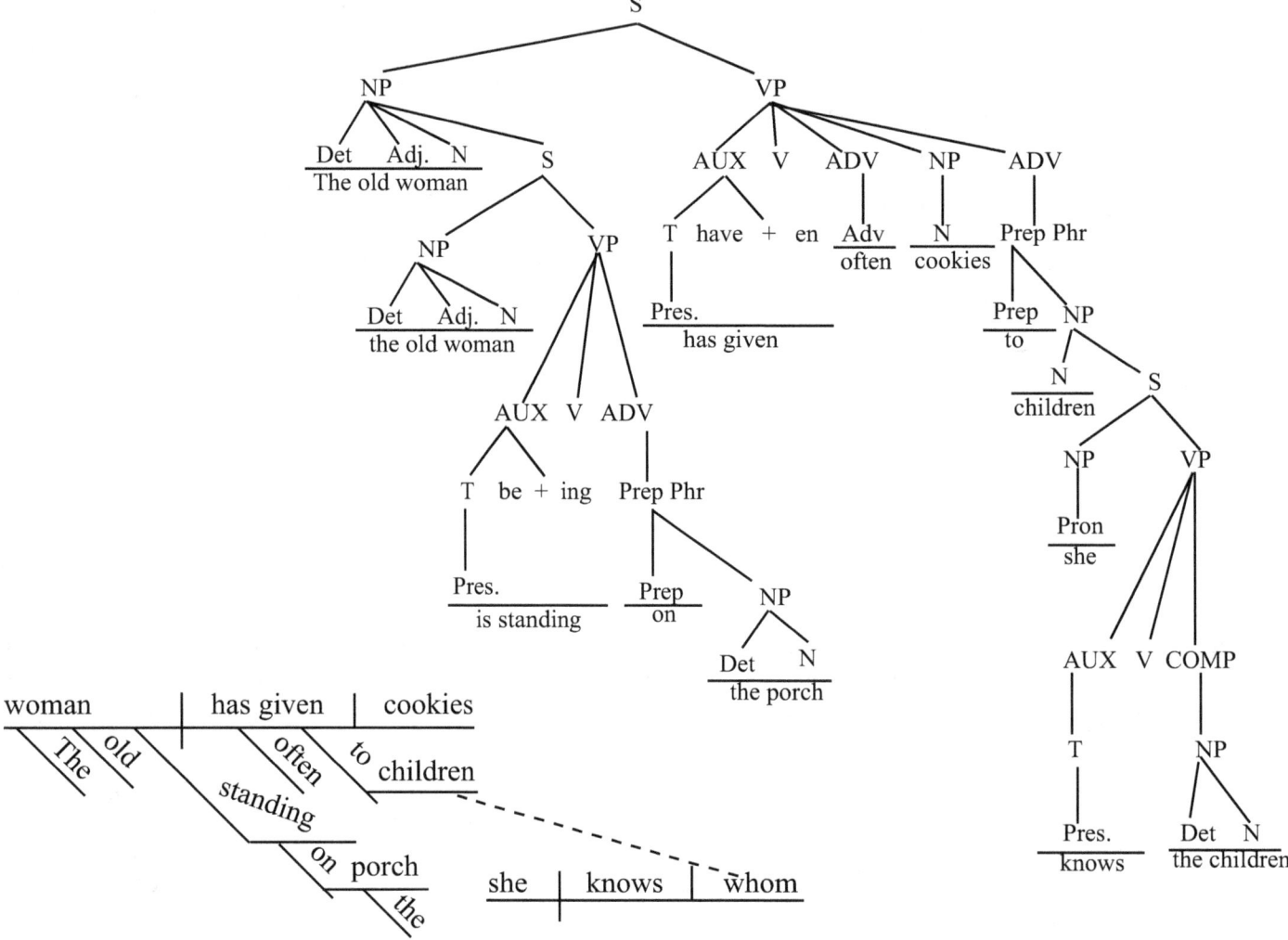

Sentence diagramming is not an end in itself; it is a means of teaching and learning grammar. You are beginning an exciting journey. Your goal is nothing less than a thorough knowledge of English grammar. I hope you enjoy each step of the way.

Part One: Main Clauses

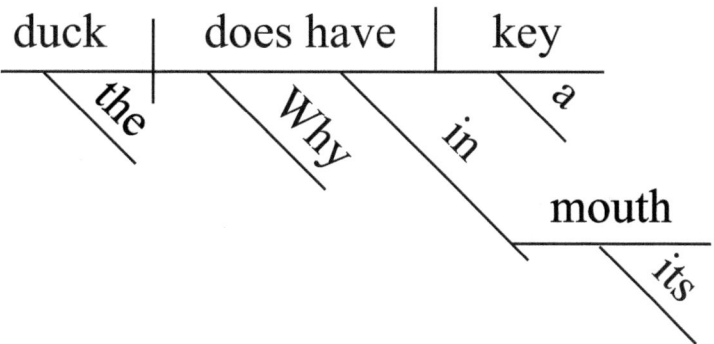

Unit I

- Subjects
- Verbs
- Articles
- Predicate Nominatives

The girl is Cinderella.

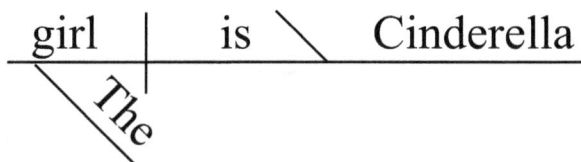

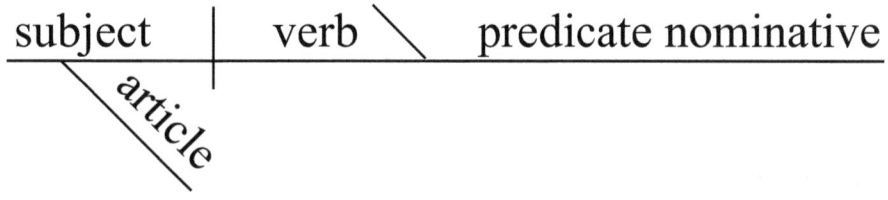

Lesson 1: Subjects and Verbs

The easiest sentence diagrams have only **two lines, a horizontal line and a vertical line**, like this:

The subject goes on the left of the vertical line, the verb on the right. To diagram a sentence like *Kids play*, we place the subject *kids* on the left and the verb *play* on the right, like this:

Kids | play

Most verbs have quite a few forms. Some of the forms of the verb *play* are *are playing, do play, played, were playing, did play, will play, will be playing, have played, have been playing, had played*, and *had been playing*. A diagram of the sentence *Kids are playing* also has **only two lines**:

Kids | are playing

In fact, if you use any of these forms of the verb *play* with a noun or pronoun subject, you need **only two lines** to diagram the sentence. This is true for all sentences that consist of only a subject and a verb.

Kids | were playing   Flags | will be waving
We | have eaten   Freinds | had been talking

The verb forms *are playing, do play, were playing, did play, will play, will be playing, have played, have been playing, had played*, and *had been playing* include the **helping verbs** *are, do, were, will, will be, have, have been, had,* and *had been*. These helping verbs are sometimes called auxiliary verbs.

There is a special group of helping verbs called **modal auxiliary verbs**. These verbs are *can, could, may, might, must, should,* and *would*. Verb forms like *can play, may be playing,* and *must have played* occupy only one position in a sentence diagram. For example, *Storms may be coming* is diagrammed like this:

Storms | may be coming

Now it's your turn to diagram some sentences.

1. Ducks waddle.

2. Rain is falling.

3. Someone called.

4. We will be listening.

5. Isabel has been working.

6. Brian must have walked.

7. Birds were singing.

8. I will wait.

9. Katie had been running.

10. Alan should be sleeping.

11. You can go.

12. She may be worrying.

Lesson 2: Definite and Indefinite Articles

The is called a **definite article**. *A* and *an* are called **indefinite articles**. Articles come before nouns, which they are said to modify. *Modify* means to change in some way. *The man* is different from *man*, and *a man* is different from *man*; moreover, *the man* and *a man* are different from each other.

To diagram an article, place it on a diagonal line under the noun it modifies, like this:

A diagram of the sentence *The farmers have been working* looks like this:

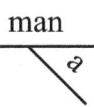

Now it's your turn to diagram definite and indefinite articles.

1. The antelope is running.

2. The parents must stay.

3. A breeze is stirring.

4. The children were crawling.

5. A letter arrived.

6. An octopus was approaching.

7. The cats had been sleeping.

8. The students should have studied.

9. A coyote must have been howling.

10. A storm could be approaching.

11. The wind had been blowing

12. The choir will be singing.

~ 7 ~

Lesson 3: Predicate Nominatives

A noun or pronoun that comes after a form of the verb *be* or *become* and repeats, identifies, or describes the subject is called a predicate nominative. In the following sentences, the predicate nominatives are underlined: *He was an officer. The women have become doctors. Anna will become a teacher. The name is Jay. A brother should be a friend.* **In a sentence diagram, a predicate nominative appears after a backslash.** Here are diagrams of the previous sentences:

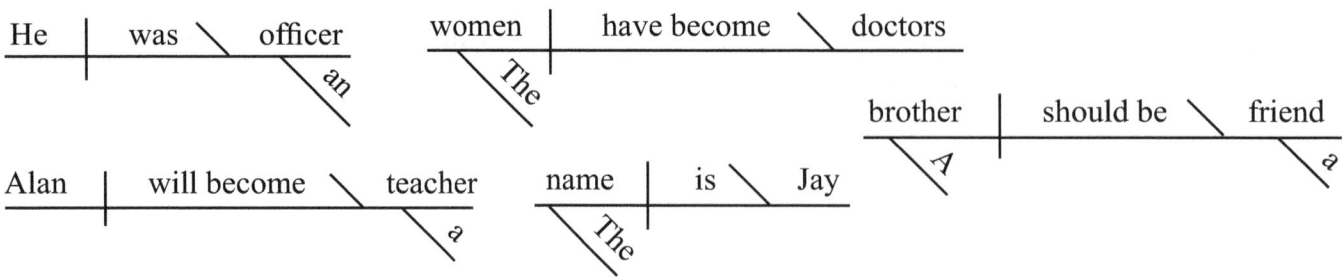

Now it's your turn to diagram predicate nominatives.

1. We are neighbors.

2. The girls are becoming friends.

3. Rembrandt was an artist.

4. I could be a lifeguard.

5. The book has become a movie.

6. The friends had been enemies.

7. The teacher may be a coach.

8. We can be friends.

9. You could become a doctor.

10. The teacher had been an engineer.

11. Tiffany was a musician.

~ 8 ~

Review I: Lessons 1 - 3

1. You should eat.

2. A girl has won.

3. The fish were guppies.

4. The moth is flying.

5. The sun is a star.

6. Anna has been thinking.

7. The baby was sleeping.

8. Mr. Kirby is a scientist.

9. Children become adults.

10. Jacob is frowning.

11. The raccoons will run.

12. Okinawa is an island.

Unit II

- **Attributive Adjectives**
- **Predicate Adjectives**
- **Possessive Pronouns**

His tiny bird is beautiful.

Lesson 4: Attributive Adjectives

An adjective is a word that modifies (changes) a noun or pronoun by describing or limiting it. We have already seen (and learned to diagram) a special group of adjectives called articles (*a, an,* and *the*). Adjectives are words like *beautiful, nice, strange, wonderful, pleasant, important,* and *attentive*. **Attributive adjectives are adjectives that come right before nouns. They are diagrammed just like articles**, that is, on diagonal lines below the nouns they modify. Here are diagrams of the sentences *The Wilsons are nice people* and *The new students are Nigerians*.

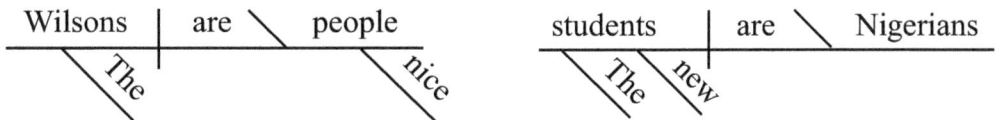

When you diagram two or more modifiers of the same noun, **start on the left and put the modifiers in the order in which they appear in the sentence.**

Now it's your turn to diagram attributive adjectives.

1. Kelly was a strong swimmer.

2. The Yankees should be the best team.

3. The big game has begun.

4. *Smithsonian* is an interesting magazine.

5. Pikes Peak is a famous mountain.

6. The same orchestra will be performing.

7. Kristen was the best jumper.

8. A tiny seed can become a huge tree.

9. The famous museum had been a palace.

10. The unhappy child became a successful adult.

Lesson 5: Predicate Adjectives

You already know how to diagram an adjective that comes before the noun it modifies; such an adjective is called an attributive adjective. **An adjective that follows a linking verb like *be* or *become* and modifies the subject of the sentence is called a predicate adjective.** The predicate adjectives in the following sentences are underlined: *They are <u>thirsty</u>. The boys are becoming <u>angry</u>. She must be <u>exhausted</u>. Your parents will be <u>proud</u>.* **Like a predicate nominative, a predicate adjective is preceded in a sentence diagram by a backslash.**

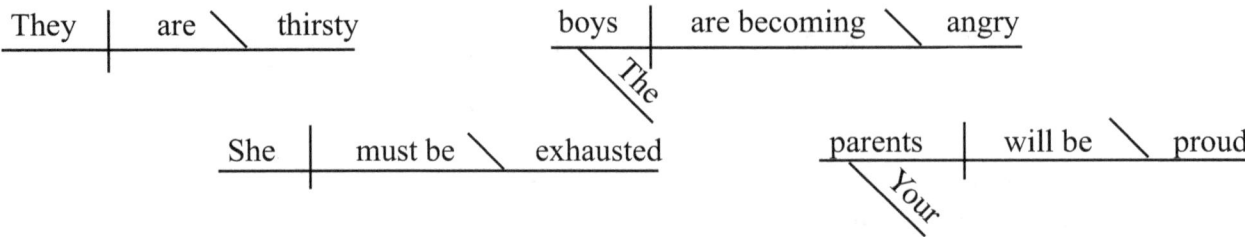

Besides *be* and *become*, verbs like *feel, taste, smell, look, sound* and *get* (when it means *become*) can also be followed by predicate adjectives. Here are examples: *The food tastes good. I feel fine. They are getting tired.*

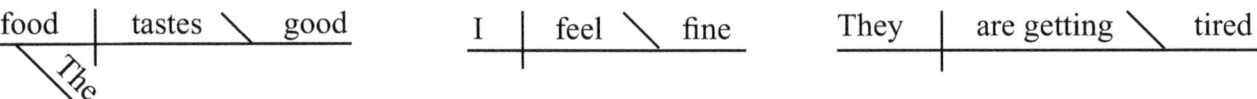

Now it's your turn to diagram predicate adjectives.

1. The flowers smell wonderful.

2. The wicked witch was ugly.

3. You should have been polite.

4. The cowardly lion became brave.

5. The children have been quiet.

6. They are becoming impatient.

7. The garden looks great.

8. Two teachers got sick.

9. We will be hungry.

Lesson 6: Possessive Pronouns

The possessive pronouns *my, your, his, her, its, our,* and *their* also modify nouns and are sometimes called pronominal adjectives. They are diagrammed exactly like other adjectives. The sentence *They are our new neighbors* is diagrammed like this:

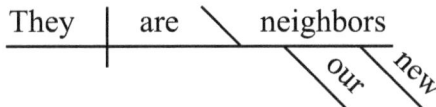

There is another set of possessive pronouns: *mine, yours, his, hers, its, ours,* and *theirs*. These possessives are always used separately from (never next to) the nouns they modify. They often appear in the predicate, as in the sentence *That book is mine*; however, they can also be subjects as in the sentence *Yours is blue*. Here are the diagrams of these sentences:

Now it's your turn to diagram possessive pronouns.

1. Their new car is a Chrysler.

2. Ours is a Nissan.

3. Your cousin has become famous.

4. His brother has been his best friend.

5. The red crayons are yours.

6. My grandfather was kind.

7. Our first president had been a successful general.

8. The gray jacket is mine.

9. Her other suitcase is blue.

10. The larger trophy will be ours.

Review II: Lessons 4 - 6

1. You must have been a beautiful baby.

2. The green glass is mine.

3. Yours looks empty.

4. A Russian baby will become his new sister.

5. Washington was a strong, intelligent man.

6. The evil Grinch became kind.

7. Theirs is the big yellow house.

8. Mary Cassat was an American painter.

9. Their favorite game is Trivial Pursuit.

10. Your home may become your castle.

11. This game is getting boring.

12. The last paper must be mine.

Unit III

- Direct Objects
- Questions
- Adverbs

Is the girl sewing the shirt patiently?

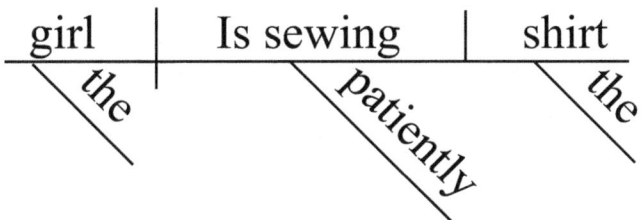

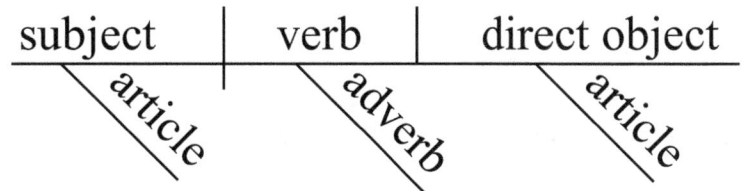

Lesson 7: Direct Objects

A noun or pronoun that receives the action of the verb directly is called a direct object. Asking *whom?* or *what?* (not *to whom?*) immediately after a non-linking verb will help you find the direct object if there is one. Take the sentence *The Johnsons have a parrot.* Ask: The Johnsons have *what?* The answer, of course, is *a parrot. Parrot* is the direct object.

Let's try another one: *Amy likes her new neighbors.* Ask: Amy likes *whom?* The answer is *her new neighbors. Neighbors* is the direct object.

Not all non-linking verbs have direct objects. For example, the sentence *He is running to the store* contains the non-linking verb *is running*; however, you get no answer when you ask *He is running whom?* or *He is running what?* Therefore, the sentence has no direct object.

In a sentence diagram, a direct object is preceded by a vertical line that stands on the horizontal line. The sentences *He likes Amy* and *She has a little brother*, in which *Amy* and *brother* are direct objects, are diagrammed like this:

```
He | likes | Amy          She | has | brother
                                      \a  \little
```

Now it's your turn to diagram direct objects. Be careful! Several sentences in this lesson have predicate nominatives, not direct objects.

1. Our new principal drinks hot chocolate.

2. My friends have visited many great places.

3. She will be the new counselor.

4. The old church should have a taller steeple.

5. His favorite movie is *Nemo*.

6. The children spotted an unusual bird.

7. Her brother had a sore throat.

8. Their daughters had become prominent chemists.

9. The inexperienced pilot made a smooth landing.

Lesson 8: Questions

Questions often begin with a verb followed by the subject. Here is an example: *Are you his brother?* When diagramming such a sentence, put the subject first even though it is not the first word in the sentence, and capitalize the verb since it is the first word in the sentence, like this:

   you | Are \ brother
                    \\his

Some questions begin with a helping verb followed by the subject. When diagramming *Do you like artichokes?* and *Have you been resting?*, **do not separate the helping verb from the rest of the verb.**

   you | Do like | artichokes   you | Have been resting

Punctuation is not included in diagrams.

Now it's your turn to diagram questions.

1. Do you have a dollar?

2. May I help you?

3. Are you a doctor?

4. Would your friend like some cake?

5. Was the baby sleeping?

6. Is that woman your mother?

7. Can we play?

8. Did anyone find a yellow folder?

9. Are you getting sleepy?

10. Does your father play chess?

Lesson 9: Adverbs

Words that modify verbs are called adverbs. The adverbs in the following sentences are underlined: *Mary can run fast. The young rider held the reins tightly. Our teacher never relaxes. Fish were jumping everywhere.* *Fast* tells how Mary can run, *tightly* tells how the young rider held the reins, *never* tells when the teacher relaxes, and *everywhere* tells where the fish were jumping. These sentences are diagrammed as follows:

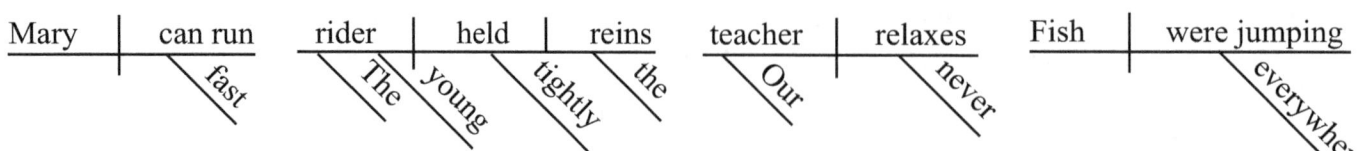

Adverbs also modify adjectives. Here are some examples: *The athletes were very tired. Our class has not read a more exciting book. This game is too boring.* *Very* tells how tired the athletes were, *more* tells how exciting the book is, and *too* tells how boring the game is. Here are diagrams of these sentences:

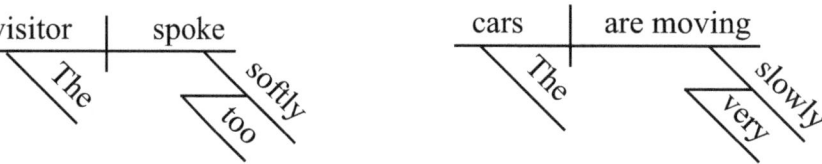

Adverbs modify other adverbs, too, as in the following sentences: *The visitor spoke too softly. The cars are moving very slowly.*

Now it's your turn to diagram adverbs.

1. A rather tall man was running very fast.

2. Did you not find an extremely old coin?

3. The refugee could finally see his terribly sick brother.

4. Does the coffee taste too strong?

5. The very steep hill was quite slippery.

6. He does not speak carefully.

7. The sensitive child talks too softly.

8. Our principal is extremely kind.

9. She should write more often.

10. Jay always addresses his parents very politely.

Review III: Lessons 7 - 9

1. Do all caterpillars become butterflies?

2. Her mother held her hand tightly.

3. Your brother sounds very angry.

4. They should finish the work quickly.

5. My parents studied the map quite carefully.

6. The very large flower smelled very bad.

7. Did you not see the old lighthouse?

8. One horse was licking my face.

9. The tiny chimpanzee was playfully chasing its much larger brother.

10. The hikers crossed the old bridge slowly.

11. Are some frogs poisonous?

12. Holly played the piano amazingly well.

Unit IV

- Commands
- Prepositional Phrases
- Nouns Used as Adjectives

Give the golden ball to the fairy-tale princess.

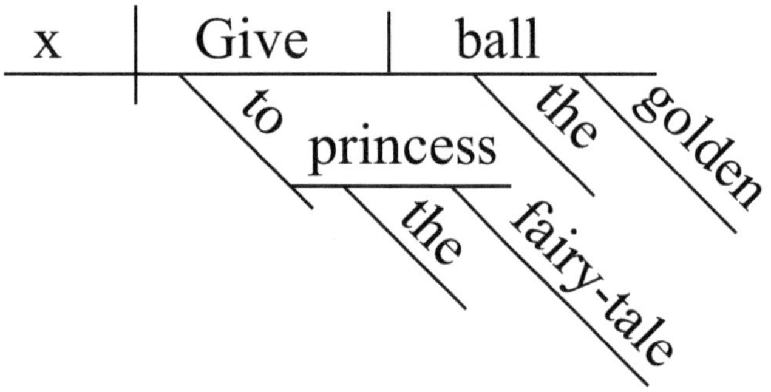

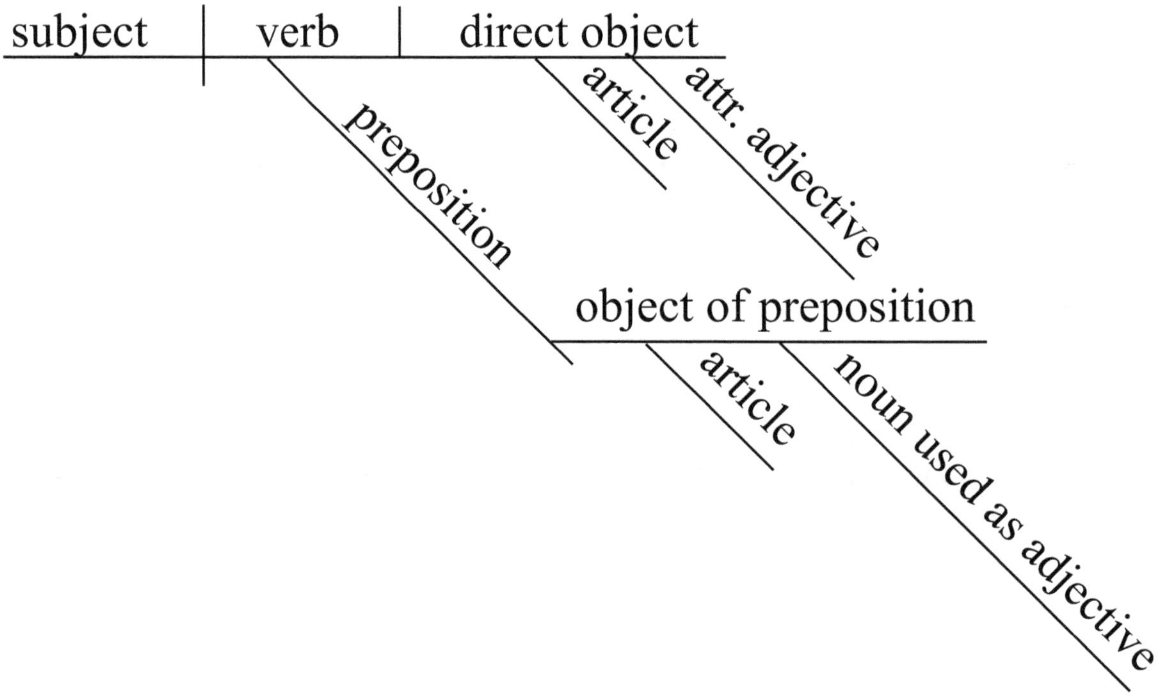

~ 20 ~

Lesson 10: Commands

A sentence that expresses a command or suggestion is called an imperative sentence. The subject of an imperative sentence is an unexpressed (understood, implied) *you.* Here are four imperative sentences and their diagrams: *Wait! Be good. Bring your CDs. Do not wear your heavy sweater.*

In diagramming, an *x* stands for an unexpressed word.

Contractions of verbs and the negative adverb *not* are not separated in diagrams. Here is an example: *Don't forget your basketball.*

Now it's your turn to diagram imperative sentences.

1. Drive carefully.

2. Read the directions.

3. Put the table here.

4. Don't shoot!

5. Sing the last line louder.

6. Don't drop the ball.

7. Be a hard worker.

8. Follow that car!

9. Don't follow too closely.

10. Get ready.

Lesson 11: Prepositional Phrases

A prepositional phrase consists of a preposition followed by a noun or pronoun that serves as its object. Most prepositions are short words. The expression "anywhere a mouse can go" will help you think of many prepositions. A mouse can go **on, in, into, to, out, over, under, around, down, up, between,** etc. Some prepositions, however, have nothing to do with direction, e.g., **at, with, without, for, after, since,** and **until**. These are not complete lists.

Remember that a preposition must have an object. In the sentence *They came down the stairs*, *down* is a preposition (its object is *stairs*), whereas in the sentence *They came down*, *down* is an adverb (it cannot be a preposition because it has no object).

Many prepositional phrases modify verbs. The prepositional phrases in the following sentences are underlined. *Take the dog <u>with you</u>. A few astronauts have flown <u>to the moon</u>. She is carrying a backpack <u>into the library</u>.*

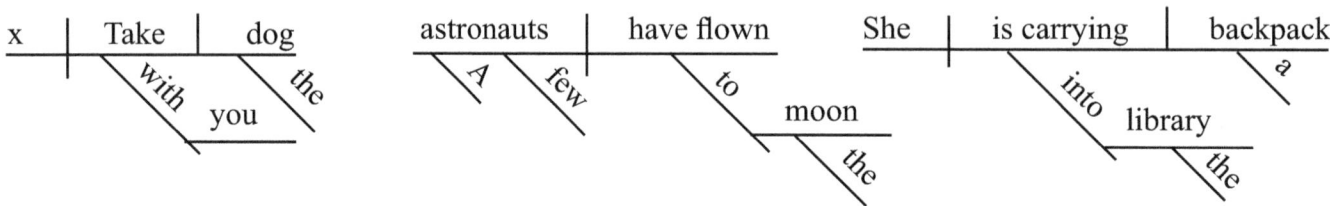

Now it's your turn to diagram prepositional phrases that modify verbs.

1. My dad put the pumpkins on the porch.

2. Can you hit a nail with a hammer?

3. The couple carried their suitcases into the airport.

4. Give the book to the teacher immediately.

5. Is Nick going to school tomorrow?

6. Stand in the corner!

7. Did you put the tickets in your purse?

8. In my dream I walked into a very large room.

Lesson 12: Nouns Used as Adjectives

Sometimes one noun can be placed before another noun, where it functions as an attributive adjective. These nouns are diagrammed exactly like other attributive adjectives. Here are some examples: *Michael Jordan was a very good <u>basketball</u> player. <u>School</u> supplies can be very expensive. On a <u>holiday</u> afternoon I walked with my mother to the <u>county</u> <u>wildlife</u> preserve.*

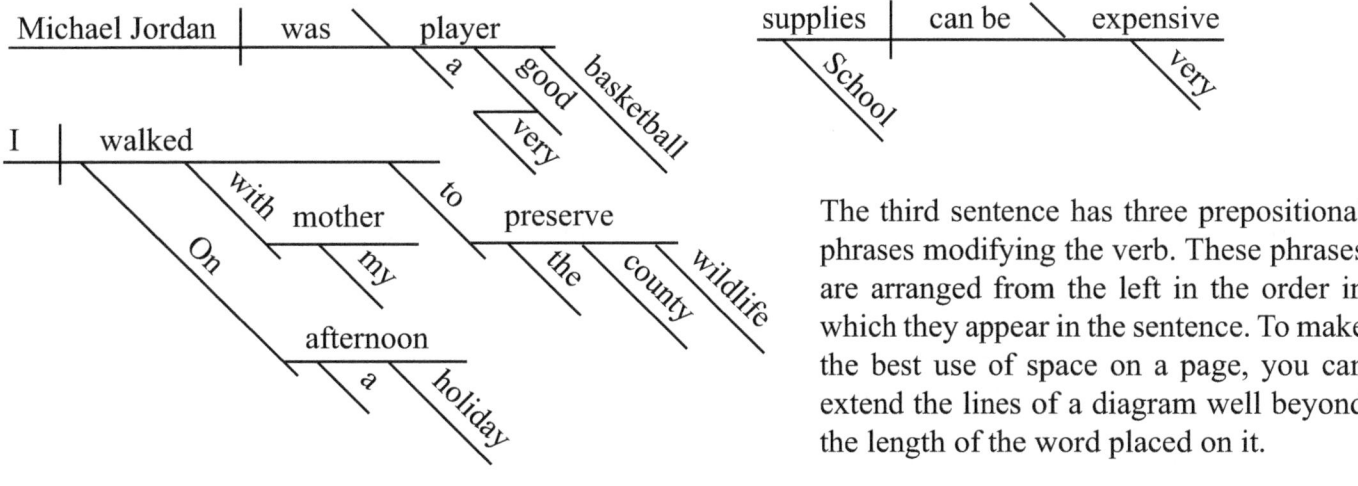

The third sentence has three prepositional phrases modifying the verb. These phrases are arranged from the left in the order in which they appear in the sentence. To make the best use of space on a page, you can extend the lines of a diagram well beyond the length of the word placed on it.

Now it's your turn to diagram nouns used as adjectives.

1. Are your parents going to the company picnic on Sunday?

2. Many children rushed to bookstores for the latest Harry Potter novel.

3. Restaurant food is becoming more nutritious.

4. Do Americans watch too many television commercials?

5. My book review is lying on the kitchen table.

6. The county champion shared her prize cake with her friends.

7. Our team won the holiday volleyball tournament.

8. The basketball fans are recovering after a miserable weekend trip.

Review IV: Lessons 10 - 12

1. The blind student must read with her fingers.

2. A good waiter serves food with a smile.

3. The German soccer fans flocked to the stadium for the big game.

4. You can't plug a lamp into a computer terminal.

5. Hold the other end with both hands.

6. The Eskimo mother carried her child on her back.

7. Holly has often skated in Central Park.

8. Take a sandwich to school for lunch.

9. Are your parents taking you to Epcot Center during the spring break?

Unit V

- Direct Address
- Prepositional Phrases (2)
- Appositives

Queen, the loveliest woman of the kingdom is Snow White, your stepdaughter.

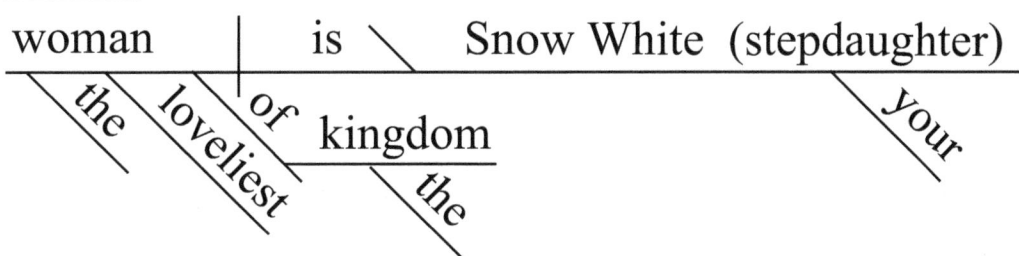

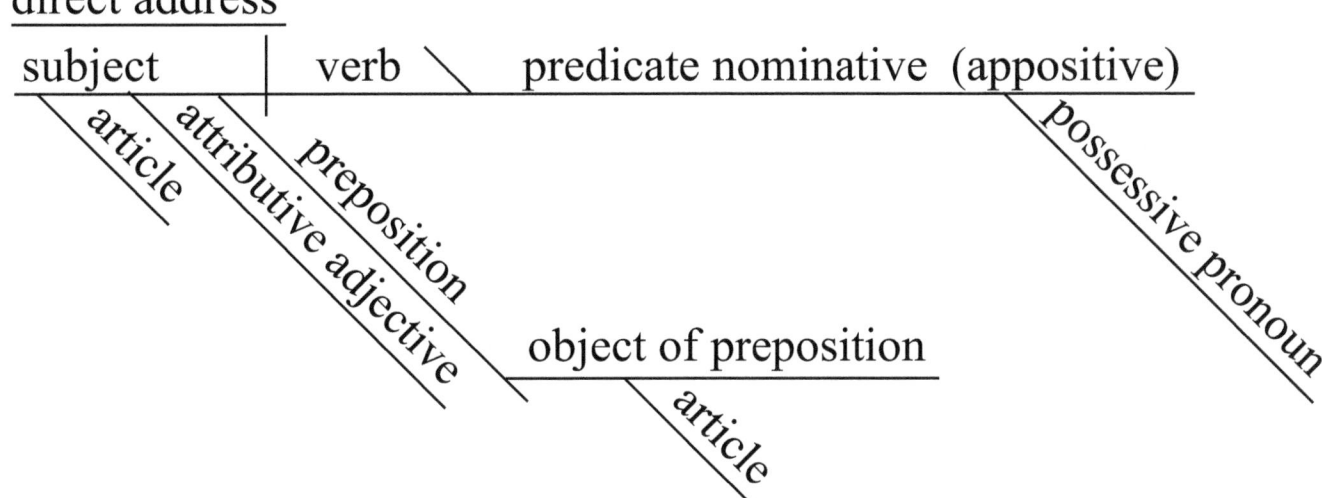

Lesson 13: Direct Address

A noun of direct address is a name of a person or thing spoken to. This name can be an actual name (Jessica, Mr. Smith, Fido), a nickname (Moose, Rocket), an expression of relationship (daughter, Mom, friend), or another identifier (men, workers, team). A noun of direct address is set off by commas. **In a sentence diagram, a noun of direct address is placed on a horizontal line above the subject of the sentence.** Here are several sentences containing nouns of direct address: *Natasha, read the first paragraph. Cole, did you get the right answer? Josh, come here now! Be a good sport, Sarah. My friend, you are right.*

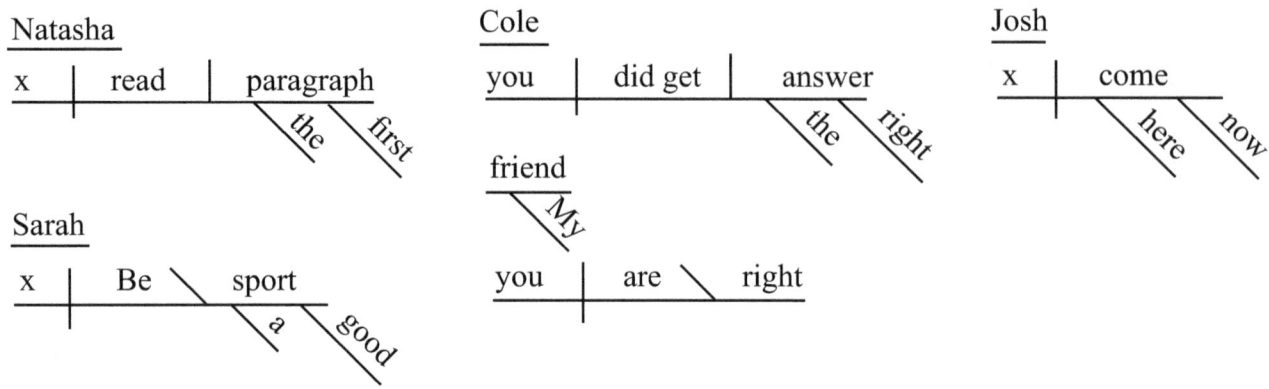

Now it's your turn to diagram nouns of direct address.

1. Grandma, can you help me with my homework?

2. Be polite, children. (Can you also diagram *Be polite children*?)

3. Tom, did you call Mother after school?

4. Boys, you are making too much noise.

5. Don't go into that old building, girls.

6. Jerry, show the pictures to your grandparents.

7. Girls, don't sit on the ground.

8. Are you writing on the desk, Susan?

Lesson 14: Prepositional Phrases (2)

Prepositional phrases that modify nouns are called adjectival prepositional phrases because they function as adjectives. Let's look at several adjectival prepositional phrases; these phrases are underlined in the following sentences: *She was carrying a bundle of books. The girl in the middle has beautiful red hair. She put the silver vase on the table in the corner. The water in the pot with the red handle is boiling.*

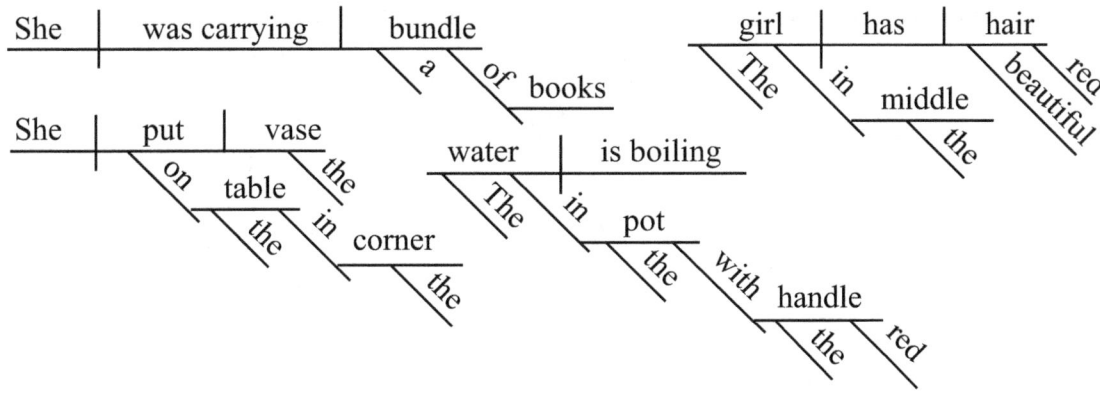

In a sentence diagram, an adjectival prepositional phrase is placed under the noun it modifies.

Now it's your turn to diagram adjectival prepositional phrases. Be careful! Some of the prepositional phrases in these sentences modify verbs, not nouns.

1. Most people really liked the picture on the cover.

2. With good weather the climbers will reach the top of the mountain in three days.

3. Brendan, do you know the weight of a gallon of water?

4. That large box under the bridge is his home.

5. This picture on the wall survived the fire of the century.

6. Most of the students did well on the first part of the test.

7. Several passengers on the small boat became seasick.

8. Today I bought ten neon tetras for the aquarium in the family room.

~ 27 ~

Lesson 15: Appositives

A noun or pronoun that comes right after another noun or pronoun and repeats or identifies it is called an appositive. In the following sentences, the appositives are underlined: *Our third President was Thomas Jefferson, a multitalented <u>man</u>. Her brother <u>Adrian</u> is sitting in the front of the canoe. For many years the Packers have had the same quarterback, <u>Bret Favre</u>. We went with our cousin <u>John</u>.* **In diagrams, appositives are placed in parentheses right after the noun with which they are in apposition.**

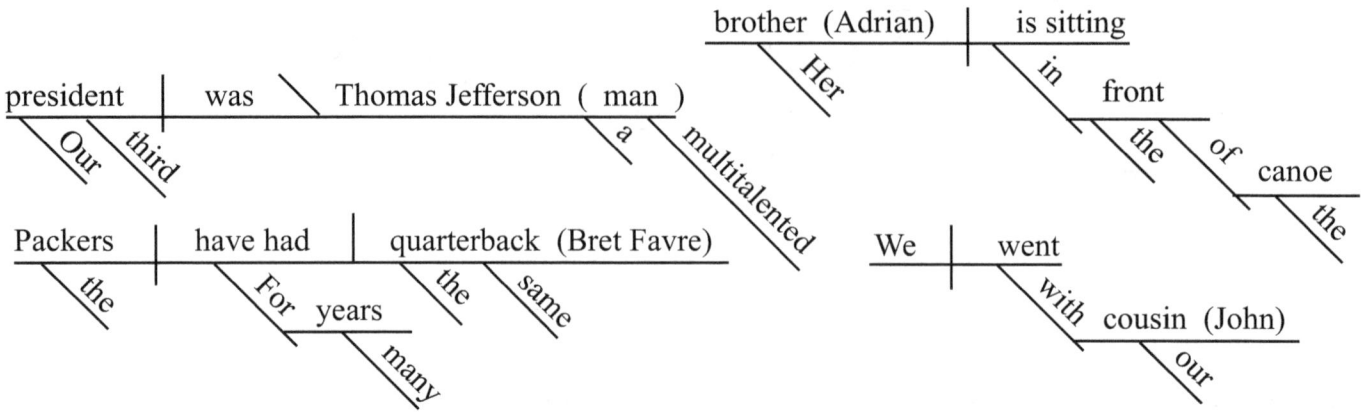

Now it's your turn to diagram appositives.

1. Mr. Jones, an animal trainer, will speak to our class tomorrow.

2. Missy Baker, a fourth grader, can throw a baseball from center field to home plate.

3. My cousin Jonathan should arrive at my house on Saturday.

4. Have you read the book *Harry Potter and the Goblet of Fire*?

5. They gave the old football to Chuckie, a neighbor.

6. Zachary Taylor, the twelfth president of the United States, died after sixteen months in office.

7. Mr. Vincent, the recreation director, hired my sister Kelsey for the summer.

8. You may give the application to Ms. Dorsey, our receptionist.

# **Review V: Lessons 13 - 15**

1. Come to the party, guys!

2. Mom, a big black cat is sleeping on the hood of our car.

3. Isn't the teacher with the big mustache your German teacher?

4. Rodrique, call your sister Liz for dinner.

5. She saw Shannon Ray, a friend of her parents, at the mall yesterday.

6. Matt, be honest.

7. Christopher, open the door for your friend Justin.

8. Did your class read the short story "The Gift of the Magi"?

9. From the top of the mountain they could see several villages.

Unit VI

- Interjections
- Possessive Nouns
- Interrogative Adverbs
- Interrogative Adjectives

Wow! Why did the boy trade his horse for the farmer's old cow?

Lesson 16: Interjections and Possessive Nouns

An interjection is a word or a phrase inserted in a sentence to show feeling or emotion, for example, *Gosh! Yippee! Great Caesar's ghost!* Interjections are diagrammed like nouns of direct address, that is, above and separate from the subject of the sentence. Here are sentences that are introduced by interjections: *Horrors! I certainly did not expect that. For Pete's sake! Can't he do anything? Oh, Timothy, come with us.* These sentences are diagrammed like this:

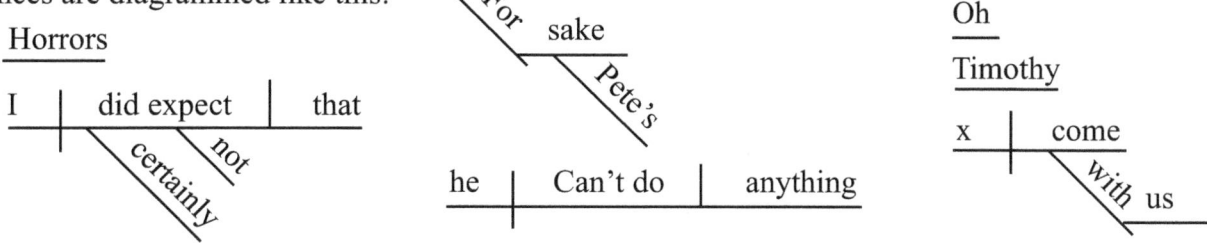

Possessive nouns are nouns ending in 's or s'. All possessive nouns function as adjectives and are diagrammed like adjectives. Here are two sentences that contain possessive nouns: *We gave the books to Jake's cousin, Katie Sullivan. You will find boys' clothes in the back of the store.* These sentences are diagrammed as follows:

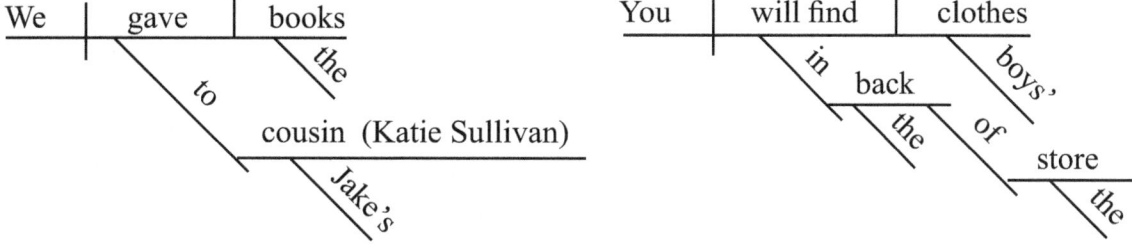

Now it's your turn to diagram interjections and possessive nouns.

1. Hurrah! Mrs. Martin's class has no test tomorrow.

2. Hey, wait for Jody's brother!

3. For heaven's sake! Don't they know our address yet?

4. Oh no! You lost Dad's car keys.

5. Good grief, Donna, did you see Mrs. Decker's purple hair?

6. Well, Miss Burnett, did Wal-Mart's employee of the month really put women's jeans in the men's section?

7. Alas, someone's child is dying at this moment.

Lesson 17: Possessive Nouns (2)

Possessive nouns can be modified by articles, adjectives, possessive pronouns, and other words. In diagramming, hook such a modifier onto the possessive noun, just as you do with adverbs that modify attributive adjectives and other adverbs. Check out these sentences and diagrams: *My mother's car is coming around the corner now. Have the old man's cows been grazing in your field? Ten children came to six-year-old Rebecca's birthday party.*

When a possessive noun has an appositive, only the appositive gets an apostrophe. Here is an example: *The couple traveled to Ohio for their daughter Emily's wedding.*

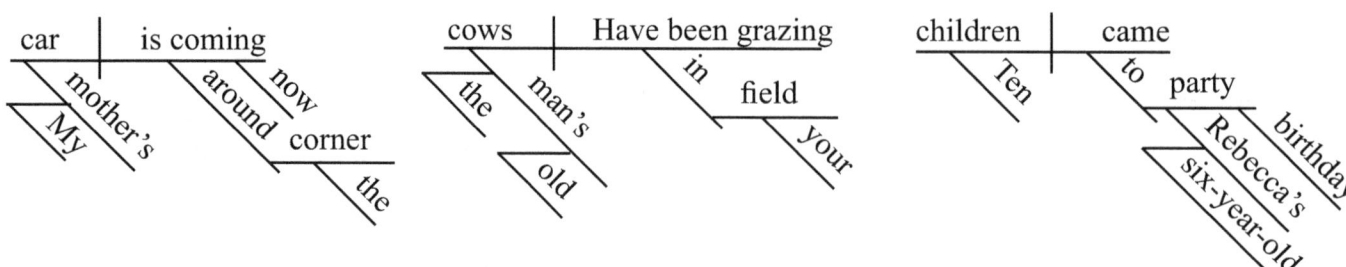

Now it's your turn to diagram modified possessive nouns.

1. Becky's older sister goes to a very famous university.

2. A large get-well card was delivered by the sick boy's friends.

3. I like the salt-water aquarium in our doctor's office.

4. Children go to their neighbors' houses on Halloween.

5. From the moon our earth's surface appears smooth.

6. Before each door lay a Christmas tree's brown skeleton.

7. We are going to my sister Gloria's house for Thanksgiving dinner.

8. The Pattersons could hardly stand the loud music of their neighbors' children.

Lesson 18: Interrogative Adverbs and Adjectives

The interrogative adverbs *how, where, when,* and *why* are used to introduce questions. In a sentence diagram, an interrogative adverb is placed on a diagonal line attached to the horizontal line under the verb. Here are some examples and diagrams: *Where do you live? How do I get there? When does the game start? Why are we going to the game?*

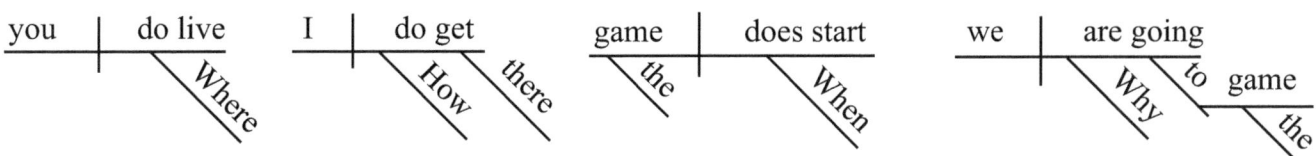

The interrogative adjectives *what* and *which* are used in asking questions like *Which CDs do you like best? What time is it? For what reason would anyone refuse your help?*

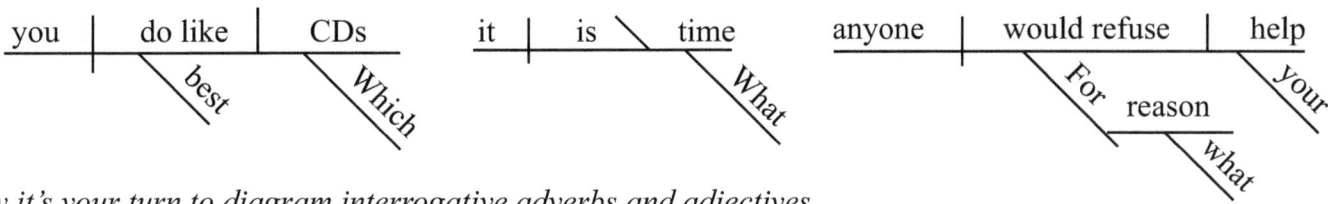

Now it's your turn to diagram interrogative adverbs and adjectives.

1. At what temperature does water boil?

2. Why does it rain so much in Seattle?

3. Mom, which shirt did I wear to school yesterday?

4. Which candle would look best on our kitchen table?

5. How can a tiny hummingbird find its way from Alaska to Mexico?

6. When did Katherine's cousin move to Florida?

7. Why have scientists not found a cure for the common cold?

8. What kinds of marine animals did you see at Sea World?

~ 33 ~

Review VI: Lessons 16 - 18

1. Hey, Robert, that is Shurita's bicycle!

2. Yikes! A snake is crawling into Mrs. Rawling's mailbox.

3. The color of my friend Eric's house is red.

4. What kind of spider has a red hourglass-shaped mark on its belly?

5. Where do frogs go in the wintertime?

6. Woops! How did that happen so quickly?

7. In my dream, Halloween skeletons were jumping on your parents' new car.

8. Which movie did you kids like best?

9. Keisha's little cousin Micah was digging for earthworms.

Unit VII

- Interrogative Pronouns
- Indirect Objects
- Objective Complements

The fish gave the man a valuable ring? Who doesn't call him lucky?

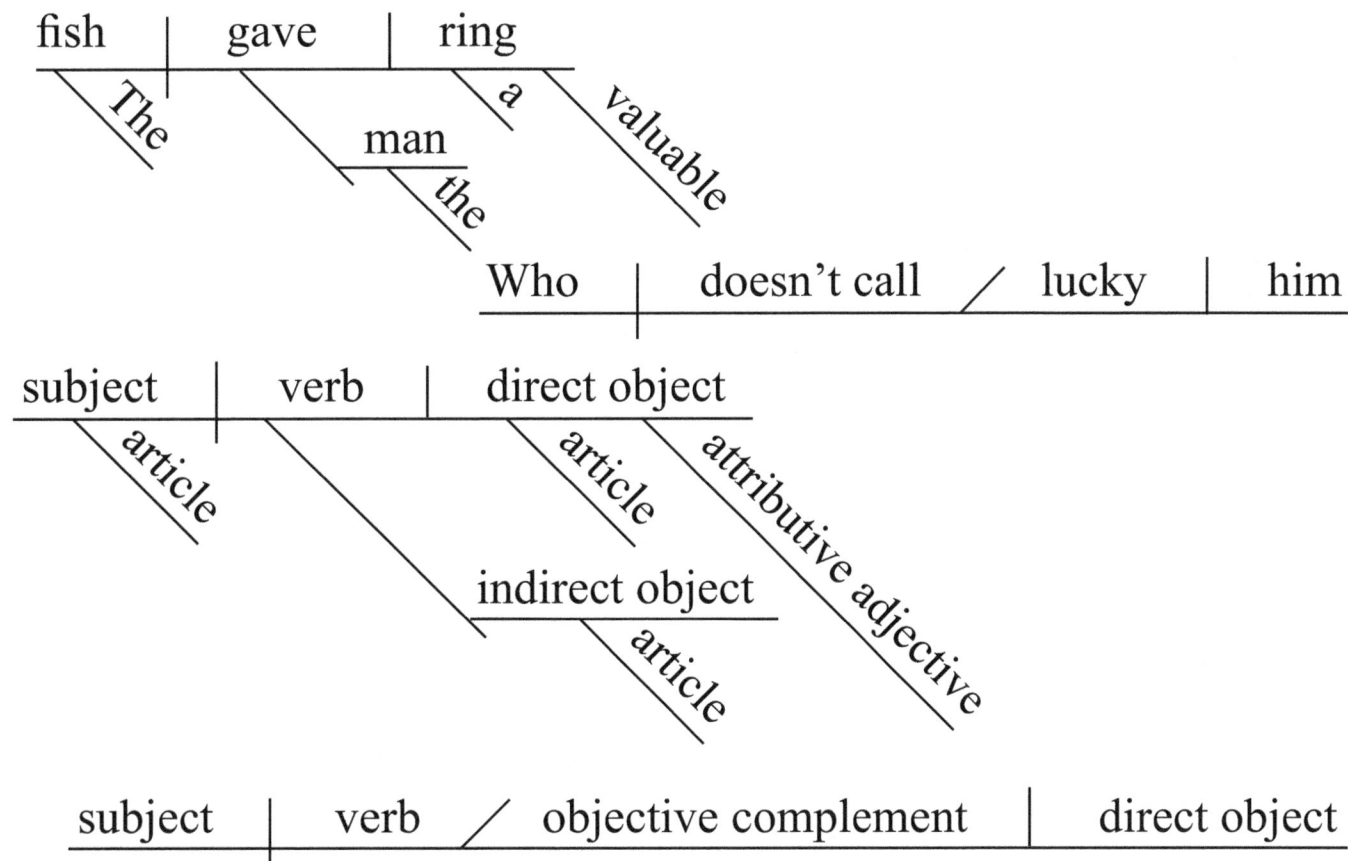

Lesson 19: Interrogative Pronouns

The interrogative pronouns are *who, whom, whose, which,* and *what*. Like all pronouns, they are diagrammed according to their function in the sentence, e.g., subject, direct object, object of a preposition. Pay special attention to the correct usage of *who* and *whom*. Here are some sentences with interrogative pronouns: *Who said that? Whom did they invite? Which of the flavors do you like best? With whom were you speaking so seriously? What did Mrs. Davis want? Whose hat is that?* These sentences are diagrammed as follows:

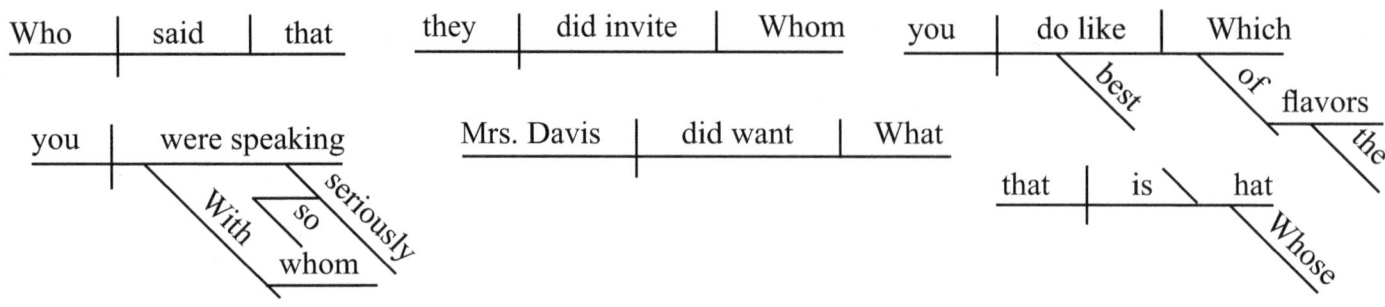

Now it's your turn to diagram interrogative pronouns.

1. Which of the two problems is harder?

2. Hey! Who took my pencil?

3. What is making that awful noise?

4. Whom did she ask?

5. To whom were the packages sent?

6. At whose house can we have the party?

7. Who am I?

8. What does he know about skateboards?

9. Whose friend are you?

10. Whom did you see there?

~ 36 ~

Lesson 20: Indirect Objects

An indirect object indicates the person or thing to whom something is given, told, or shown; it is not preceded by the preposition *to*. Here are some sentences with underlined indirect objects: *Old Mother Hubbard could not give her poor <u>dog</u> a bone. The teacher told the <u>class</u> an exciting story. Later I will show <u>you</u> some pictures from our trip to Hawaii.* Here are diagrams of these sentences:

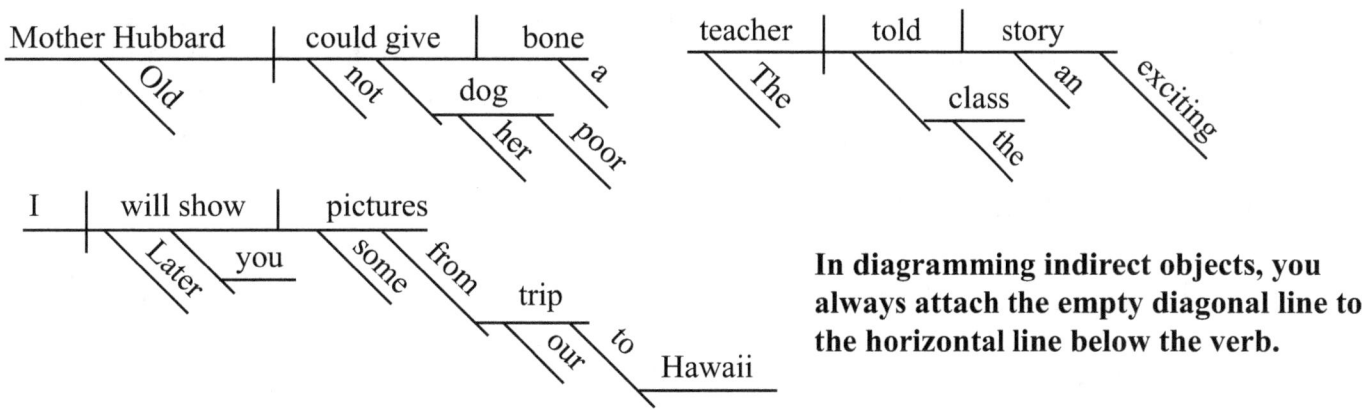

In diagramming indirect objects, you always attach the empty diagonal line to the horizontal line below the verb.

Now it's your turn to diagram indirect objects.

1. Dad, tell us the story about the big fish again.

2. That waitress never offers anyone a glass of water.

3. Mr. Jethroe, our neighborhood's newest resident, was showing everyone his new camera.

4. I wouldn't give him a penny for that piece of junk.

5. Mrs. Hardesty handed an employee her grocery list.

6. What did you give your brother for his birthday?

7. Cornelia offered me twenty-five dollars for my old bicycle.

8. Old Jim was telling the kids in the neighborhood stories about his adventures in the West.

~ 37 ~

Lesson 21: Objective Complements

A noun or adjective that completes the verb and modifies, names, or renames the direct object is called an objective complement. Objective complements are underlined in the following sentences: *They call him Chuck. Your comments made me angry. The class elected her president. The cool temperatures turned the leaves on the trees in my front yard yellow.*

There are two different methods of diagramming objective complements: 1) the traditional method, in which the objective complement, preceded by a slash, is placed before the direct object; and 2) the modern method, in which the objective complement, preceded by a backslash, follows the direct object. To demonstrate the difference, the first sentence, *They call him Chuck*, is diagrammed both ways.

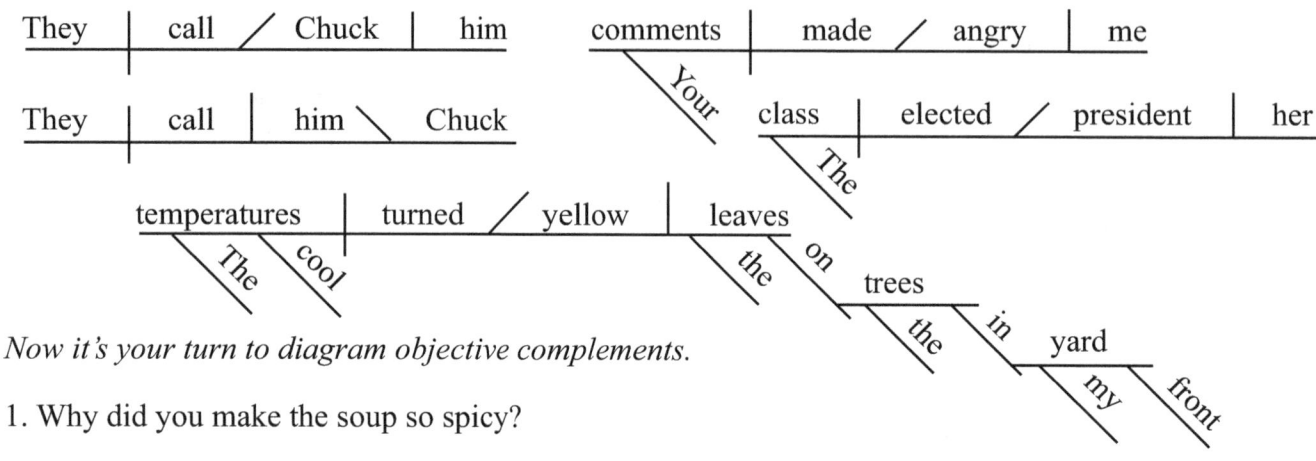

Now it's your turn to diagram objective complements.

1. Why did you make the soup so spicy?

2. Mom appointed my sister Martha keeper of the turtles.

3. Do you consider me a friend?

4. What kinds of things make your parents angry?

5. Robert, don't call people that!

6. Your questions are driving me crazy.

7. Most students consider Mr. Hardin an excellent teacher.

8. The police found the victim unconscious.

Review VII: Lessons 19 - 21

1. Who is that thoughtful person?

2. What did Little Miss Muffit sit on? (This one is tricky to diagram.)

3. How can a fourth grader spell those big words correctly?

4. The proud parents painted their baby's room pink.

5. What did she tell the clerk?

6. Some people call Michael Jordan the greatest basketball player.

7. What did you give Andrea for her birthday?

8. Most people find our cats annoying.

9. Which card should I send to Amy?

Unit VIII

- **Coordinating Conjunctions**
- **Adverbial Objectives**

All morning Hansel and Gretel walked through the forest and dropped bread crumbs on the path.

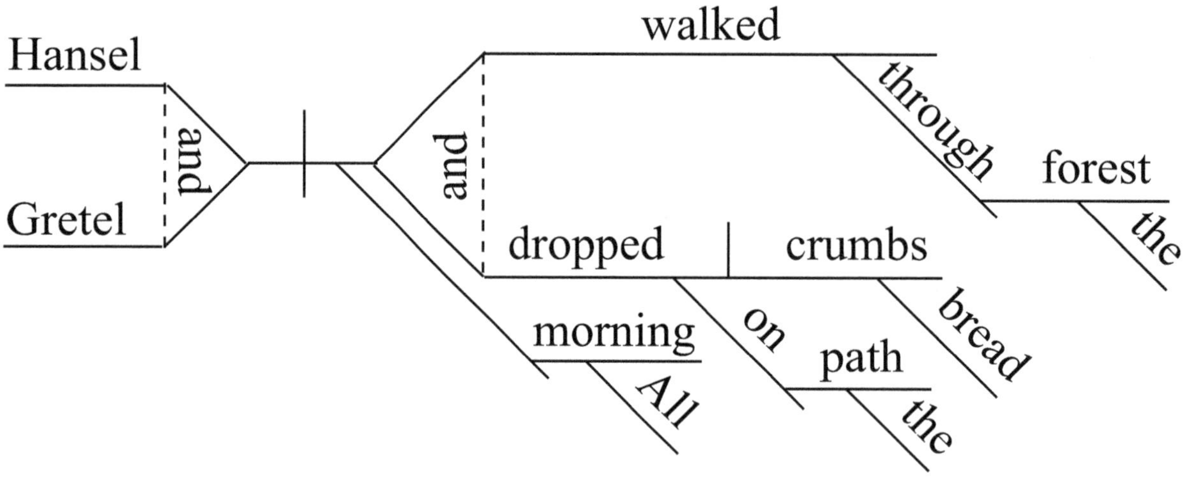

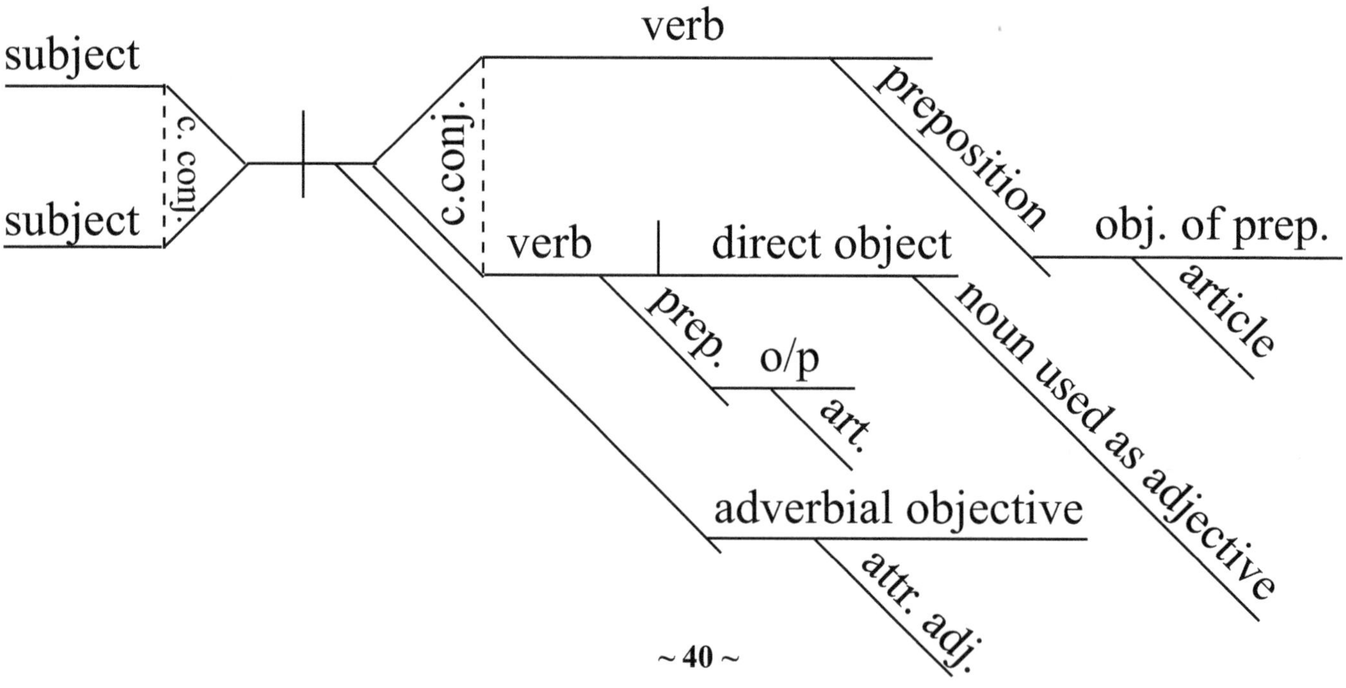

Lesson 22: Coordinating Conjunctions

The words *and, or, but, both . . . and, either . . . or,* and *neither . . . nor* are called coordinating conjunctions. They can be used to join nouns to nouns, nouns to pronouns, pronouns to pronouns, verbs to verbs, adjectives to adjectives, etc. Here are some sentences with coordinating conjunctions: *Anne and Erika are friends. Can you go with Joe and me? Children were running and playing. You can do either this or that. The water is neither hot nor cold.*

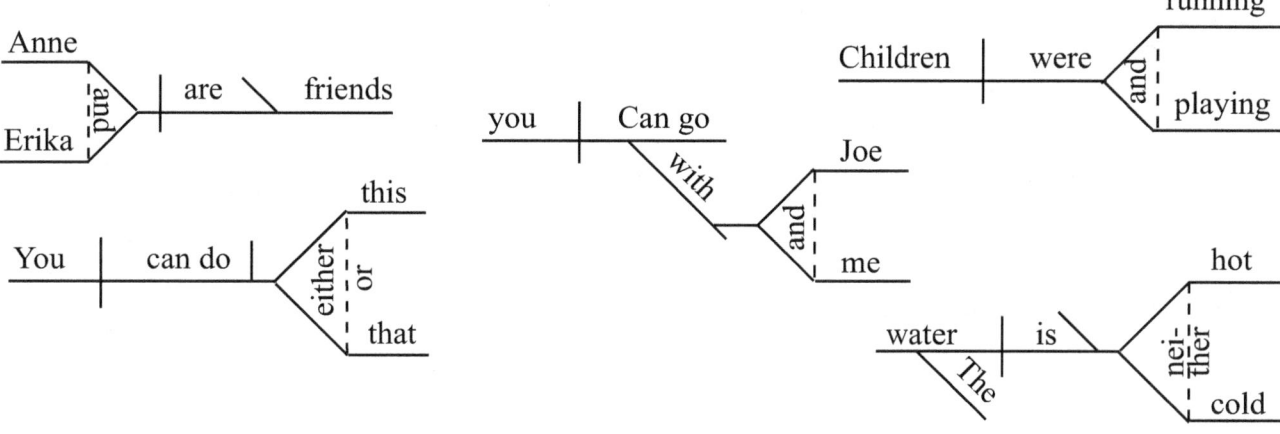

Now it's your turn to diagram coordinating conjunctions.

1. Aaron, can you carry the bread and the potatoes?

2. Good food and proper exercise make people healthy.

3. The foreign visitors can stay with either the Johnsons or the Browns.

4. I told LaTasha and Monique the news about my friend Jenny's family.

5. After two weeks at the ranch, Kendall and her family were tired but tough.

6. Mrs. Lewis, my homeroom teacher, teaches both French and Spanish.

7. In Greek mythology, gods and goddesses live on Mt. Olympus.

8. Most people in the auditorium were talking and laughing during the performance.

Lesson 23: Adverbial Objectives

Nouns used as adverbs are called adverbial objectives. They are diagrammed like indirect objects. Adverbial objectives are underlined in the following sentences: *They arrive late every <u>morning</u>. Next <u>year</u> my friends and I will organize a baseball team. Denver is a <u>mile</u> high. My mom paid four dollars a <u>pound</u> for jelly beans. We'll do it your <u>way</u> this <u>time</u>.*

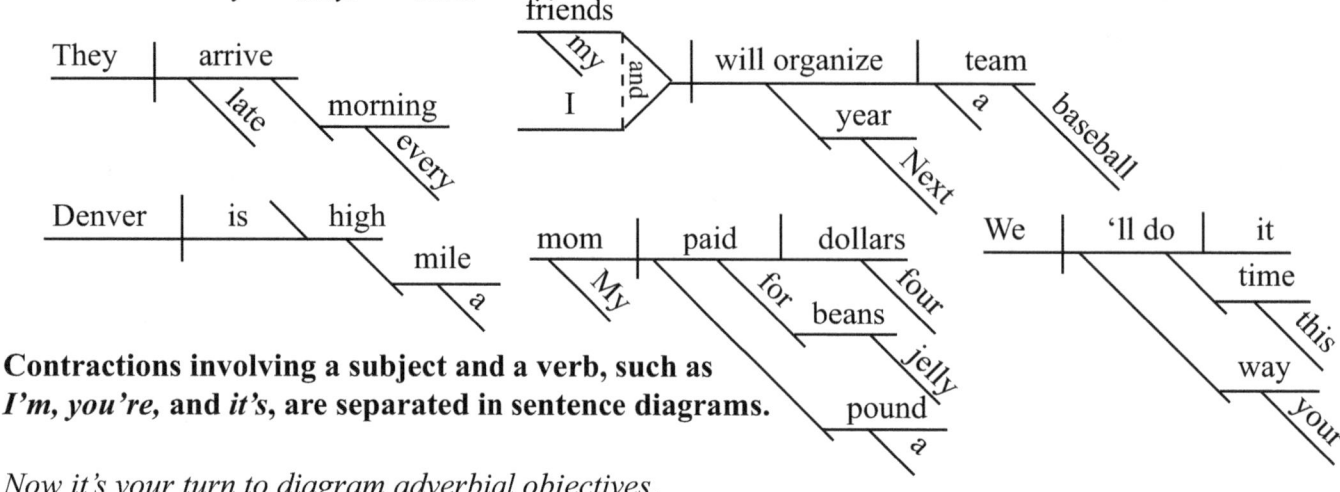

Contractions involving a subject and a verb, such as *I'm, you're,* and *it's,* are separated in sentence diagrams.

Now it's your turn to diagram adverbial objectives.

1. The old people sat and talked all afternoon.

2. Which way should we have gone?

3. Last week we played volleyball in gym class.

4. Mr. Appleton, the founder of the company, still works late every day.

5. Friday evening some friends and I went to a great restaurant.

6. One day we'll stroll together through the streets of Rome and Athens.

7. Neither Beverly nor any of her friends had ever flown first class.

8. Grammar and sentence diagrams go hand in hand.

Lesson 24: Coordinating Conjunctions (2)

Coordinating conjunctions can also join adverbs, attributive adjectives, prepositional phrases, and entire predicates. Here is an example of each: *The experienced climber reached the top quickly and easily. After a long and difficult journey, Ulysses finally arrived at his native Ithaca. They left the stadium with disappointment but without bitterness. George passed the bread and butter and took the turkey from Aunt Marie.*

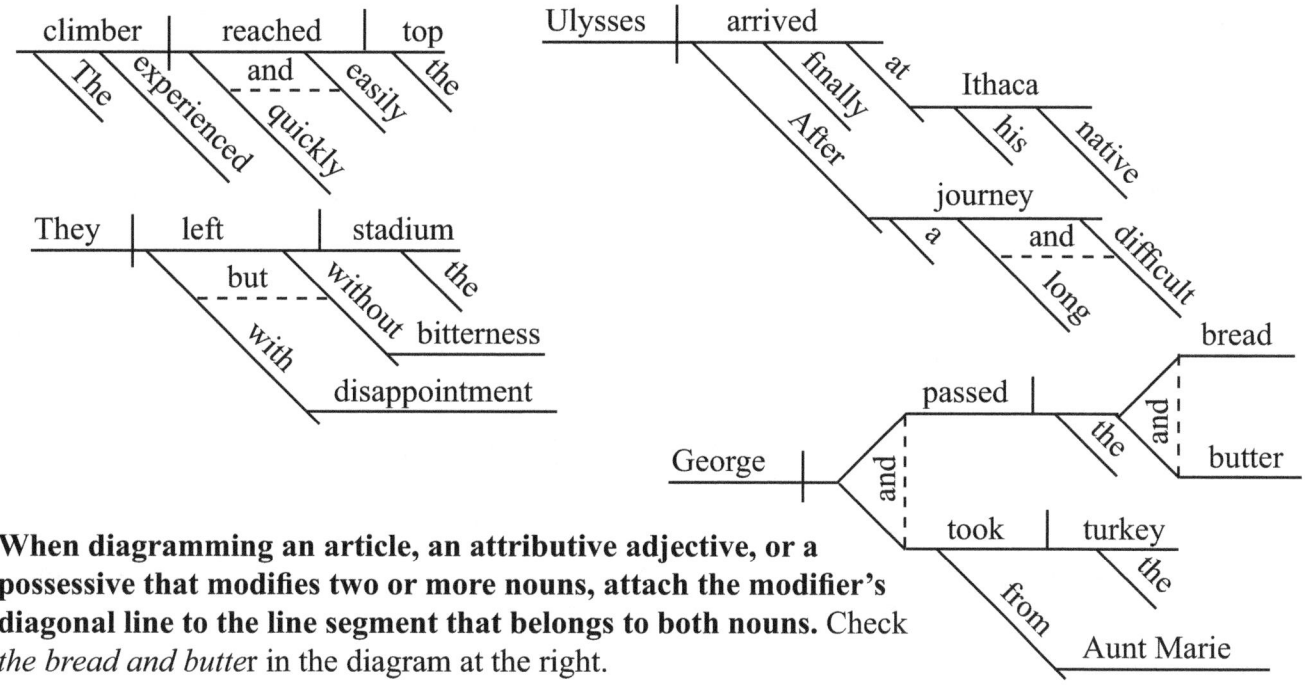

When diagramming an article, an attributive adjective, or a possessive that modifies two or more nouns, attach the modifier's diagonal line to the line segment that belongs to both nouns. Check *the bread and butter* in the diagram at the right.

Now it's your turn to diagram sentences with coordinating conjunctions.

1. Quietly and nervously they turned the key and entered the old house.

2. Every morning and afternoon she walks with Amy and Gloria.

3. They put their old furniture on the back porch and in an upstairs bedroom.

4. The Parthenon is an ancient and beautiful temple of Athena.

5. The Ramseys will stay two or three days in Munich and then travel to Salzburg or Vienna.

6. The cub scouts have been collecting used furniture and clothing every morning and afternoon of this week.

7. The children must walk in silence and in single file from their classroom to the cafeteria.

~ 43 ~

Review VIII: Lessons 21 - 24

1. Will you fly or drive?

2. Some students have neither books nor calculators.

3. Why did they go the other way?

4. Some Americans have been in Europe many times.

5. The men stood in small groups and discussed business.

6. Why did you not play soccer with Josie and Jenny this afternoon?

7. How many people would hold a fork that way?

8. May we show Kyle and Lisa our baby brother?

9. My father's company has branches in New York and San Francisco.

~ Solutions ~

Lesson 1, 1 — Ducks | waddle

1, 2 — Rain | is falling

1, 3 — Someone | called

1, 4 — We | will be listening

1, 5 — Isabel | has been working

1, 6 — Brian | must have walked

1, 7 — Birds | were singing

1, 8 — I | will wait

1, 9 — Katie | had been running

1, 10 — Alan | should be sleeping

1, 11 — You | can go

1, 12 — She | may be worrying

Lesson 2, 1 — antelope | is running \\ The

2, 2 — parents | must stay \\ The

2, 3 — breeze | is stirring \\ A

2, 4 — children | were crawling \\ The

2, 5 — letter | arrived \\ A

2, 6 — octopus | was approaching \\ An

2, 7 — cats | had been sleeping \\ The

2, 8 — students | should have studied \\ The

2, 9 — coyote | must have been howling \\ A

2, 10 — storm | could be approaching \\ A

2, 11 — wind | had been blowing \\ The

2, 12 — choir | will be singing \\ The

Lesson 3, 1 — We | are \ neighbors

3, 2 — girls | are becoming \ friends \\ The

3, 3 — Rembrandt | was \ artist \\ an

3, 4 — I | could be \ lifeguard \\ a

3, 5 — book | has become \ movie \\ The \\ a

3, 6 — friends | had been \ enemies \\ The

3, 7 — teacher | may be \ coach \\ The \\ a

3, 8 — We | can be \ friends

3, 9 — You | could become \ doctor \\ a

3, 10 — teacher | had been \ engineer \\ The \\ an

3, 11 — Tiffany | was \ musician \\ a

Review I, 1 — You | should eat

R, 2 — girl | has won \\ A

~ 45 ~

R, 3

R, 4

R, 5

R, 6

R, 7

R, 8

R, 9

R, 10

R, 11

R, 12

Lesson 4, 1

4, 2

4, 3

4, 4

4, 5

4, 6

4, 7

4, 8

4, 9

4, 10

Lesson 5, 1

5, 2

5, 3

5, 4

5, 5

5, 6

5, 7

5, 8

5, 9

Lesson 6, 1

6, 2

6, 3

6, 4

6, 5

6, 6

6, 7

6, 8

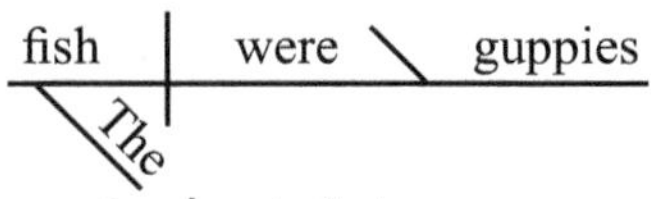

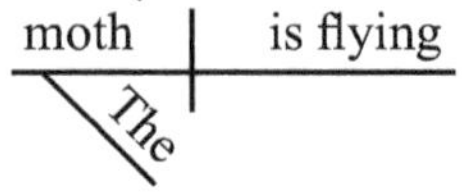

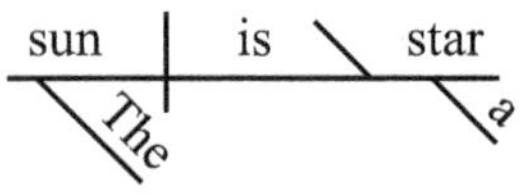

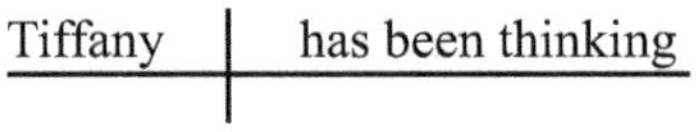

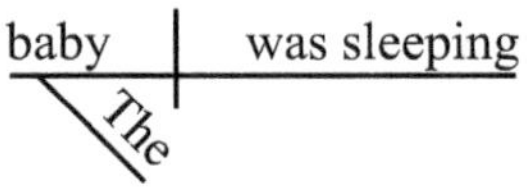

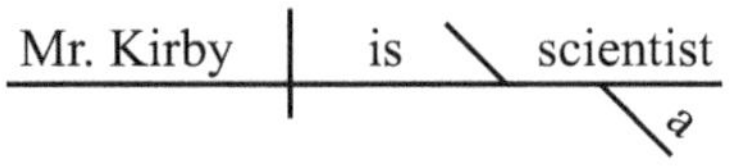

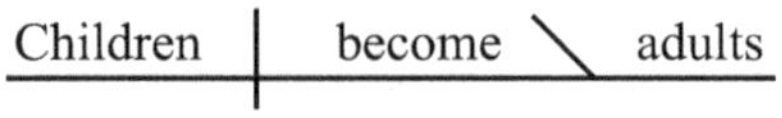

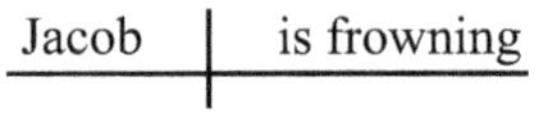

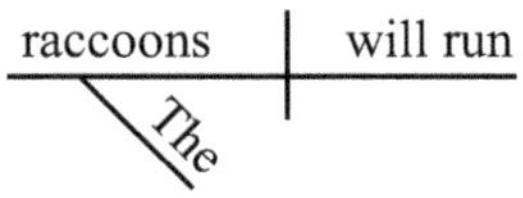

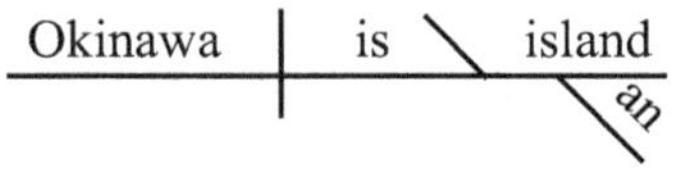

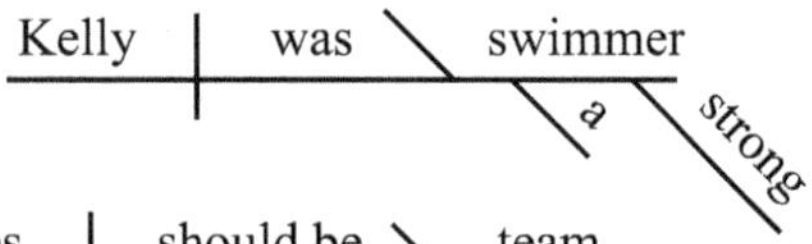

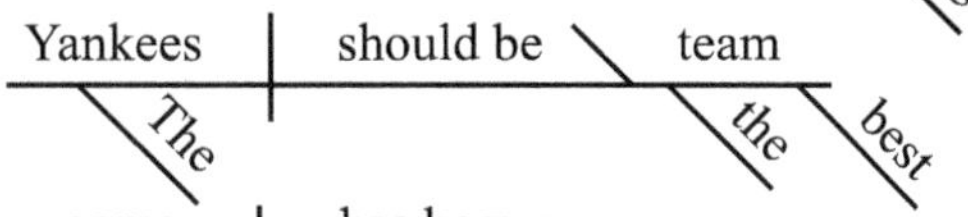

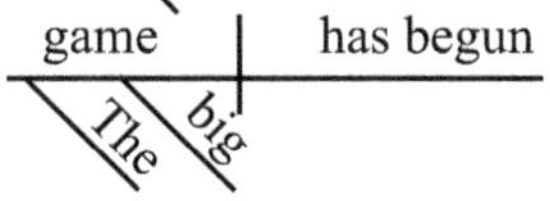

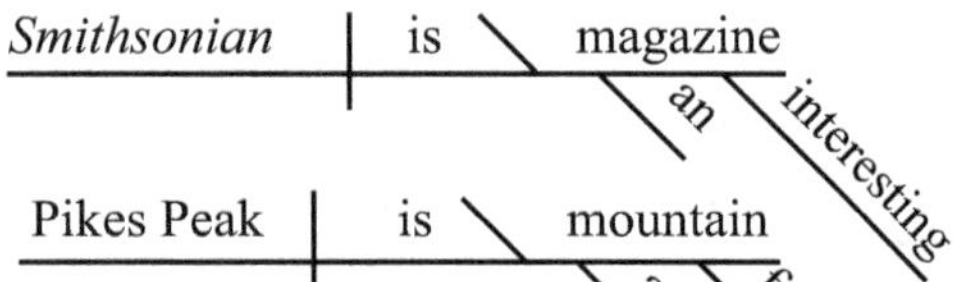

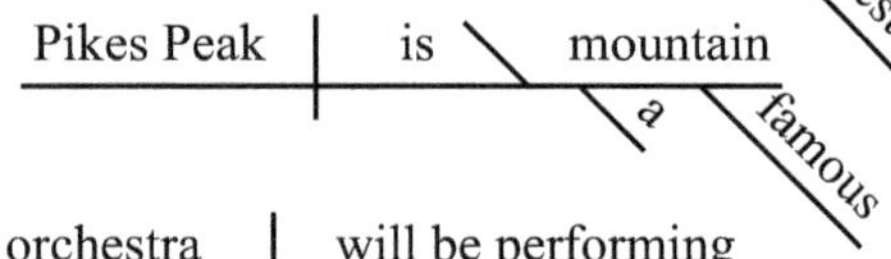

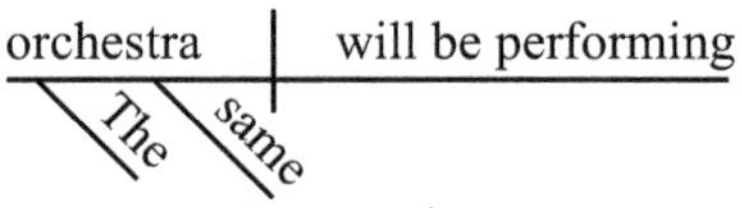

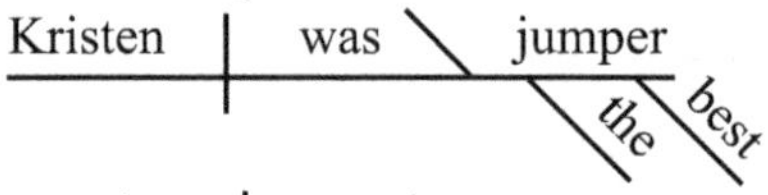

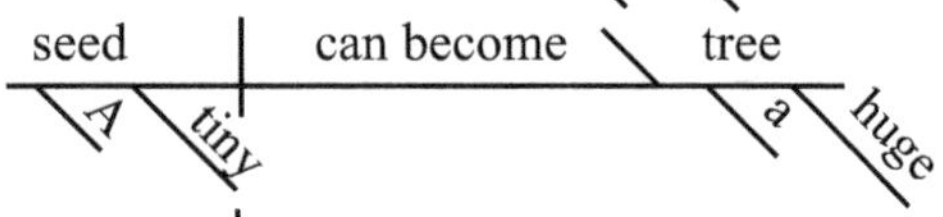

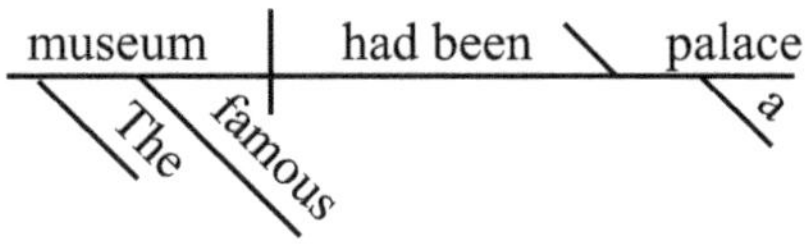

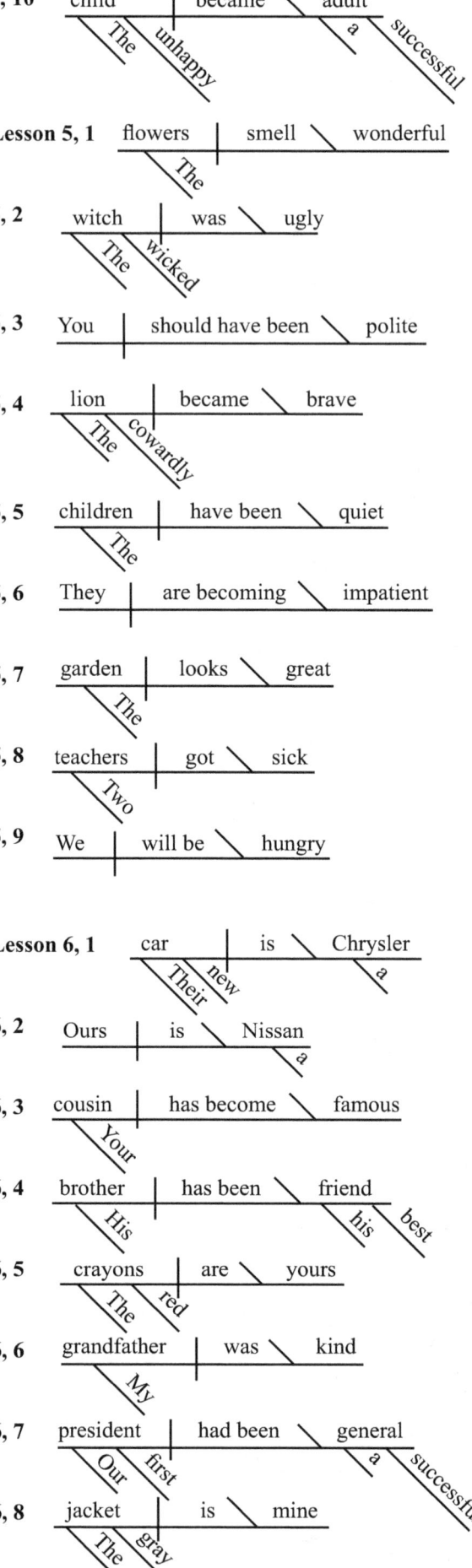

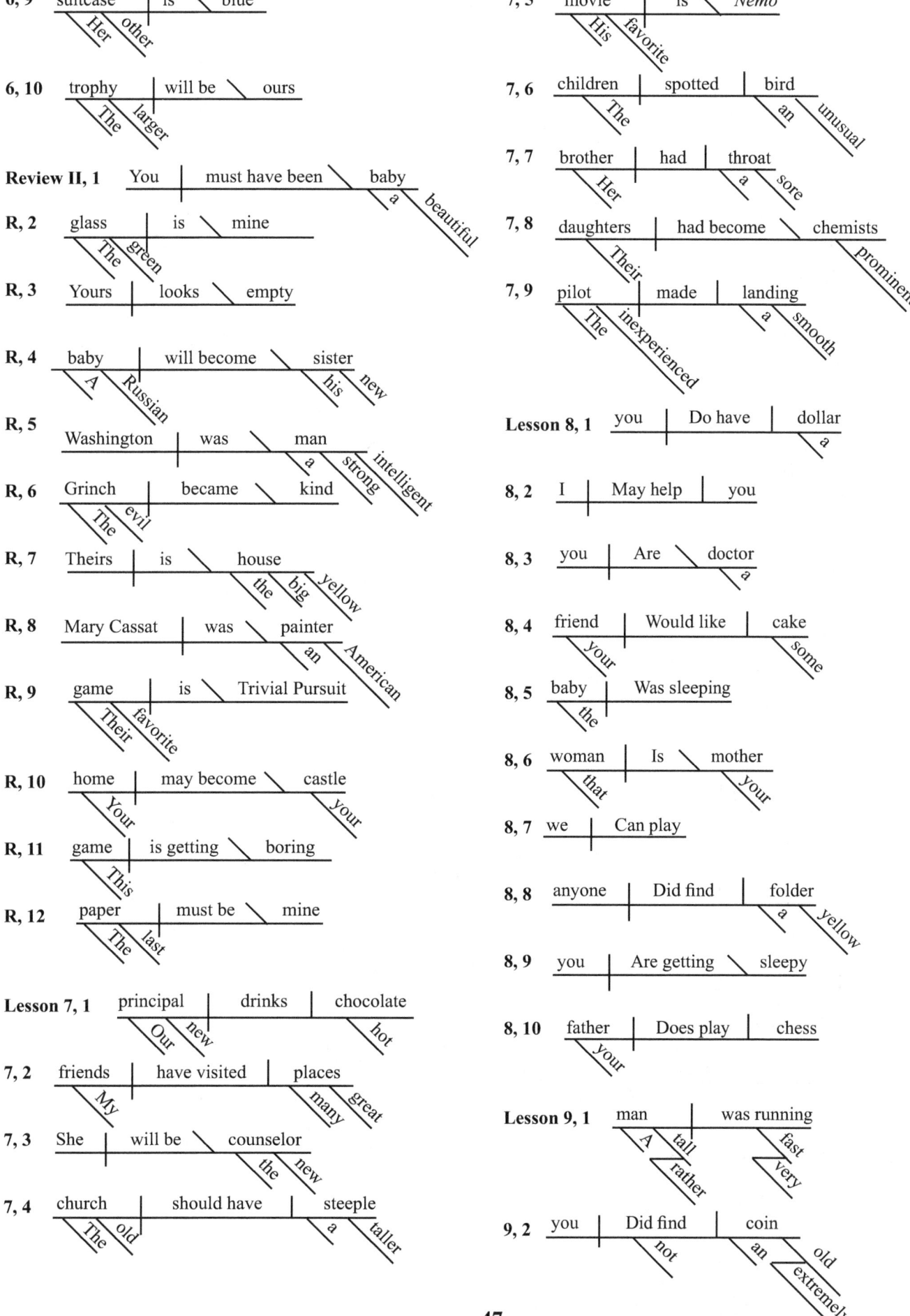

9, 3 The refugee could finally see his brother, terribly sick.

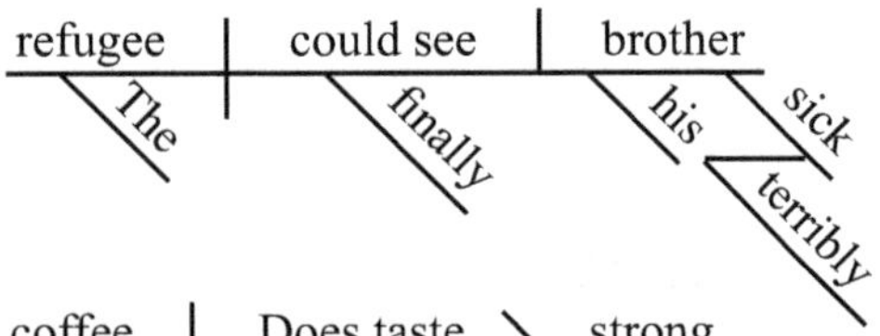

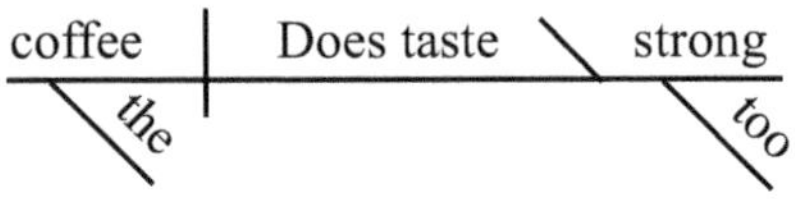

9, 4 Does the coffee taste too strong?

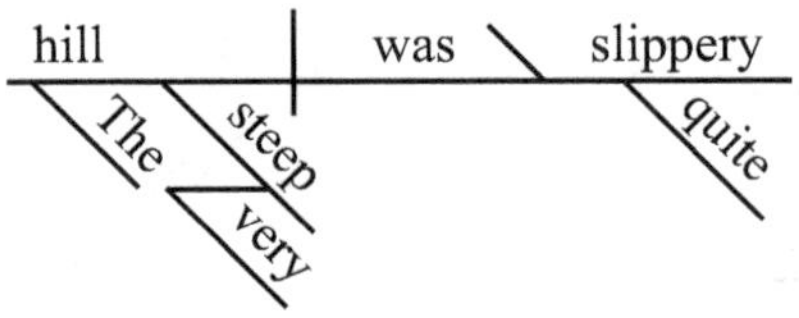

9, 5 The very steep hill was quite slippery.

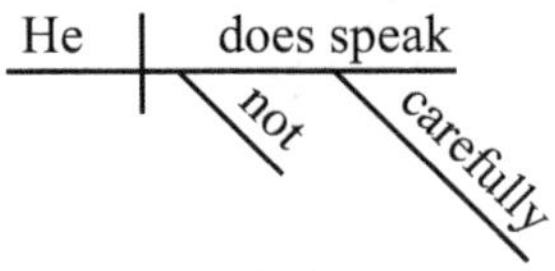

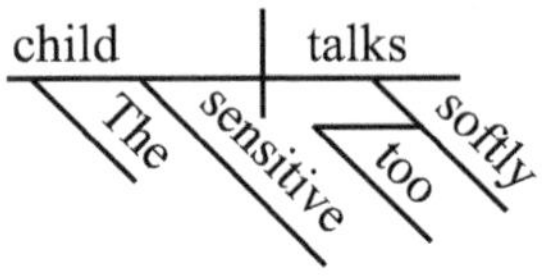

9, 6 He does not speak carefully.

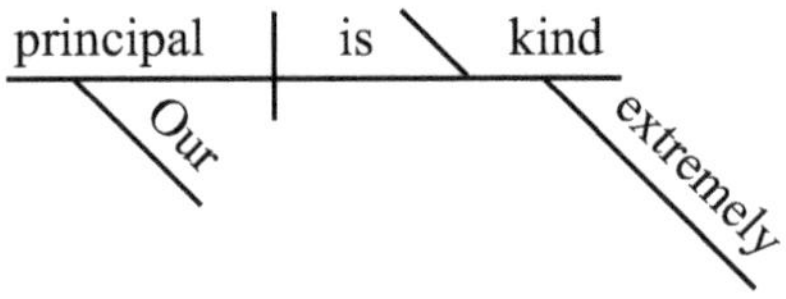

9, 7 The too sensitive child talks softly.

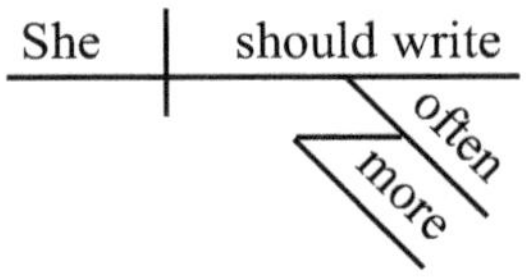

9, 8 Our principal is extremely kind.

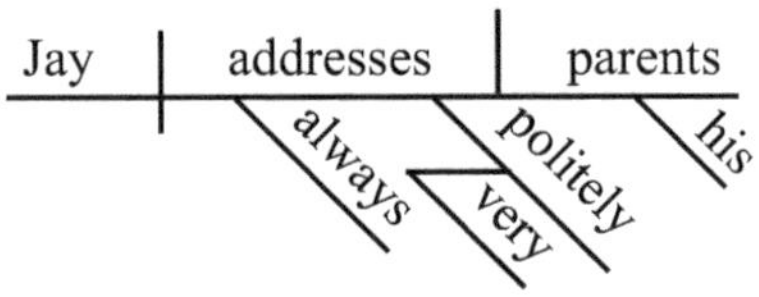

9, 9 She should write more often.

9, 10 Jay always addresses his parents very politely.

Review III, 1 Do all caterpillars become butterflies?

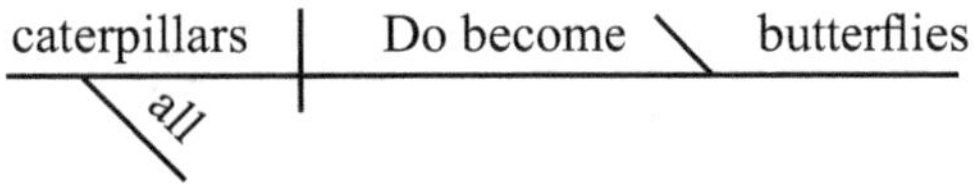

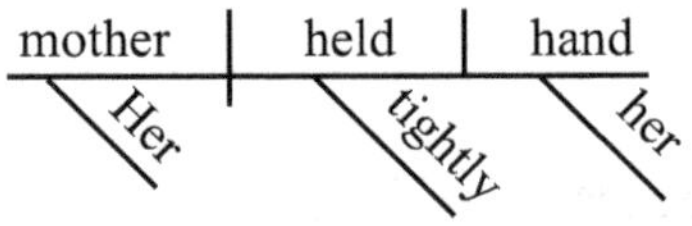

R, 2 Her mother held her hand tightly.

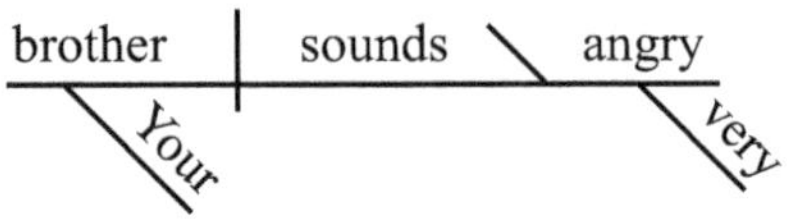

R, 3 Your brother sounds very angry.

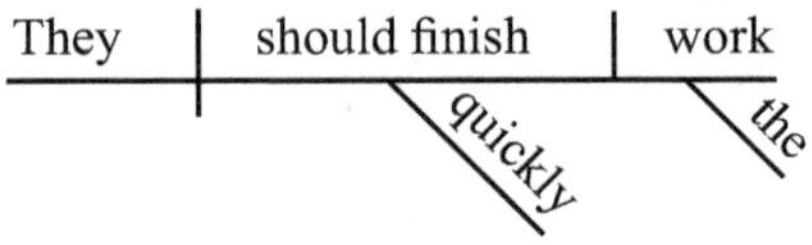

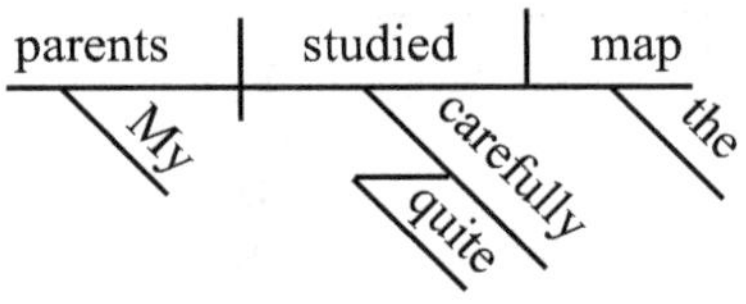

R, 4 They should finish the work quickly.

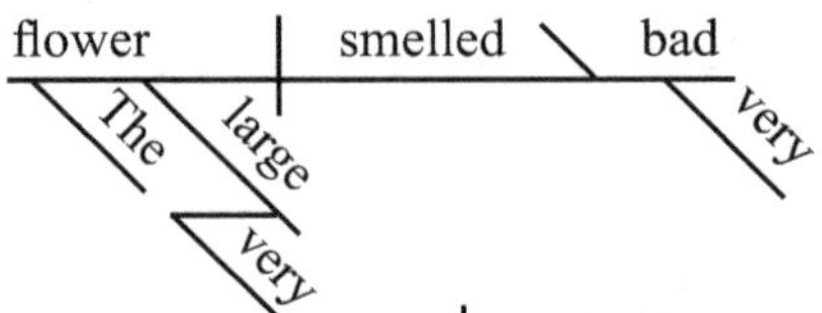

R, 5 My parents studied the map quite carefully.

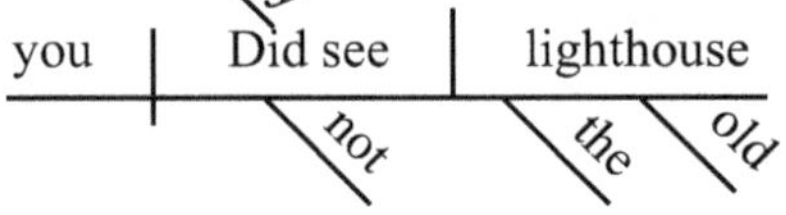

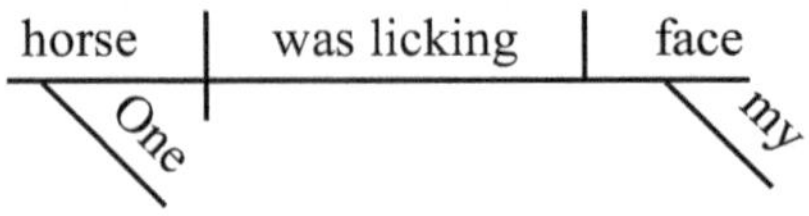

R, 6 The very large flower smelled very bad.

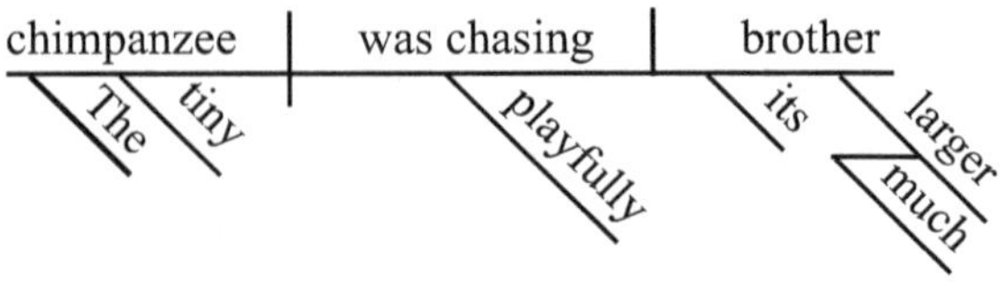

R, 7 Did you not see the old lighthouse?

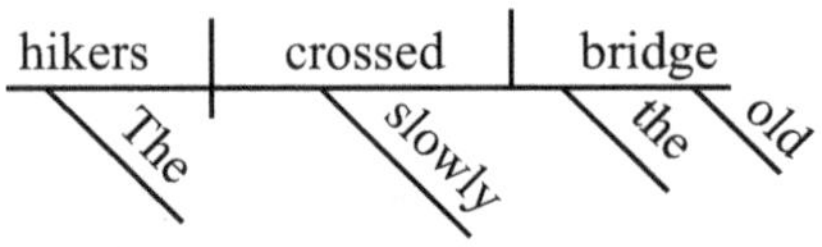

R, 8 One horse was licking my face.

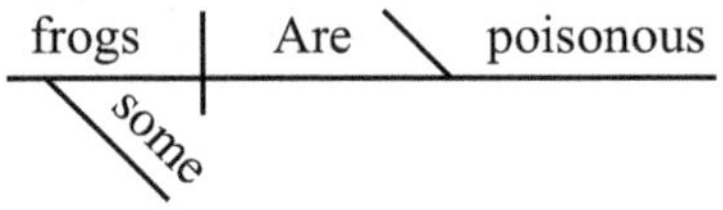

R, 9 The tiny chimpanzee was playfully chasing its much larger brother.

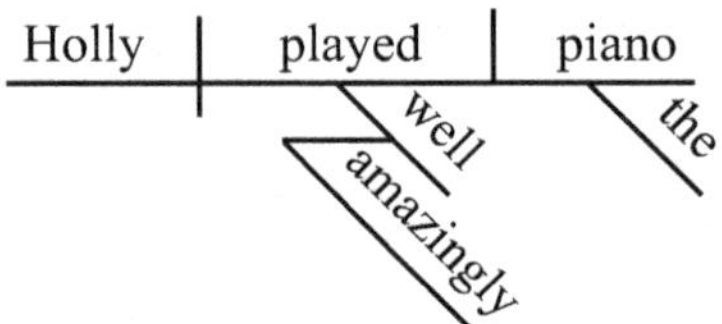

R, 10 The hikers slowly crossed the old bridge.

R, 11 Are some frogs poisonous?

R, 12 Holly played the piano amazingly well.

Lesson 10, 1 x Drive carefully.

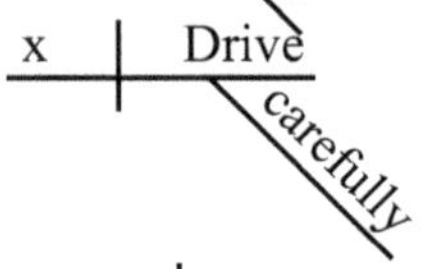

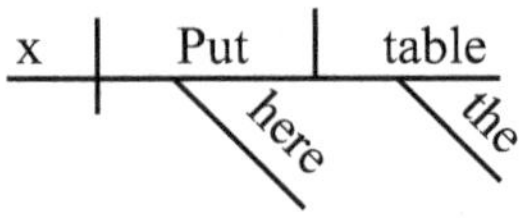

10, 2 x Read the directions.

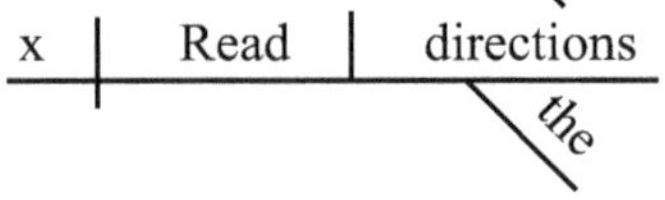

10, 3 x Put the table here.

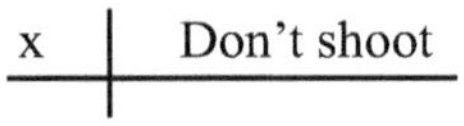

10, 4 x Don't shoot.

10, 5 x Sing the last line louder.

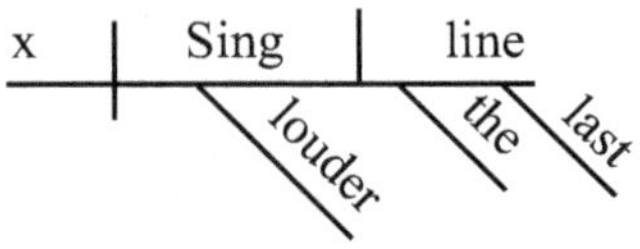

10, 6 x Don't drop the ball.

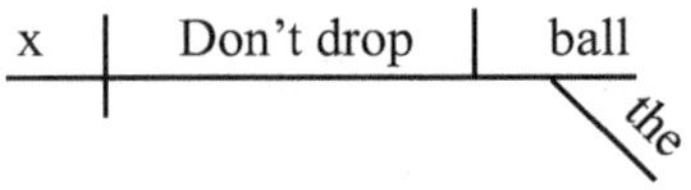

10, 7 x Be a hard worker.

~ 48 ~

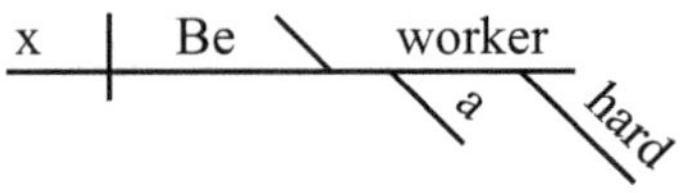

10, 8

10, 9

10, 10

Lesson 11, 1

11, 2

11, 3

11, 4

11, 5

11, 6

11, 7

11, 8

Lesson 12, 1

12, 2

12, 3

12, 4

12, 5

12, 6

12, 7

12, 8

Review IV, 1

R, 2

R, 3

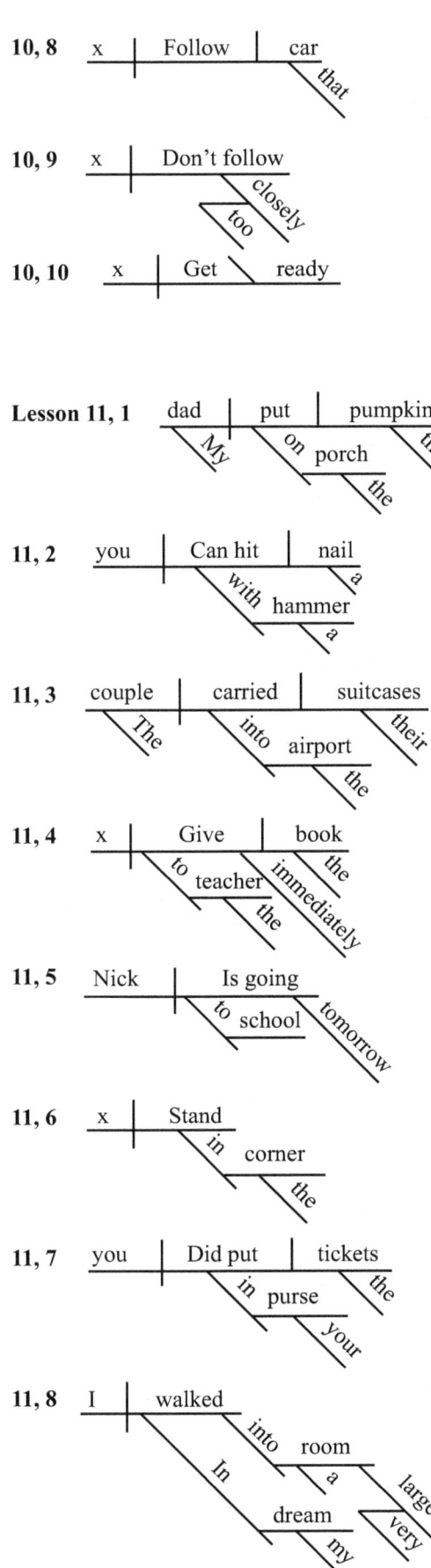

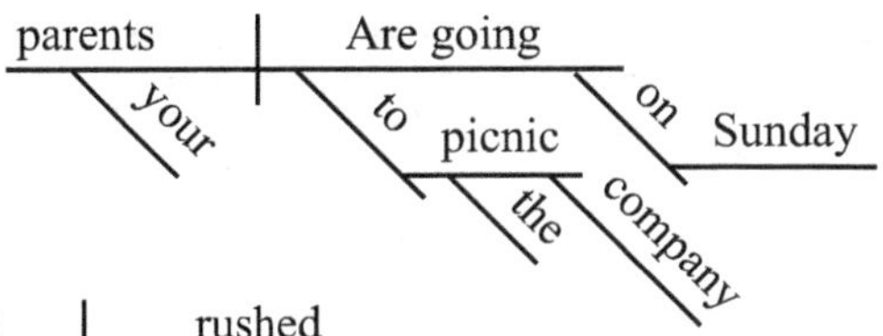

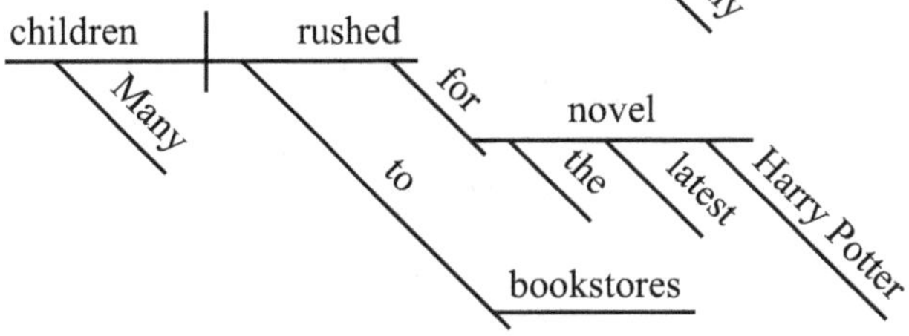

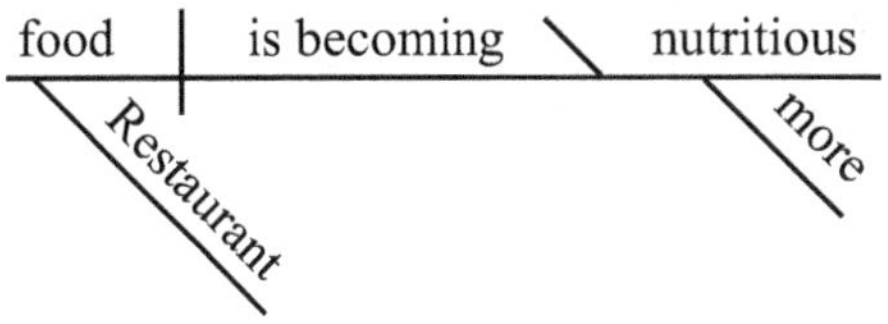

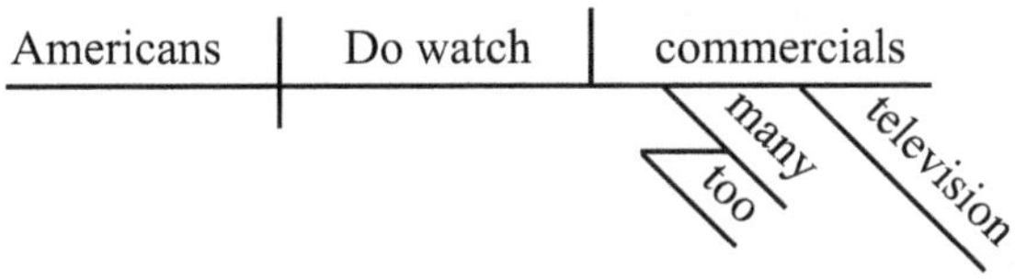

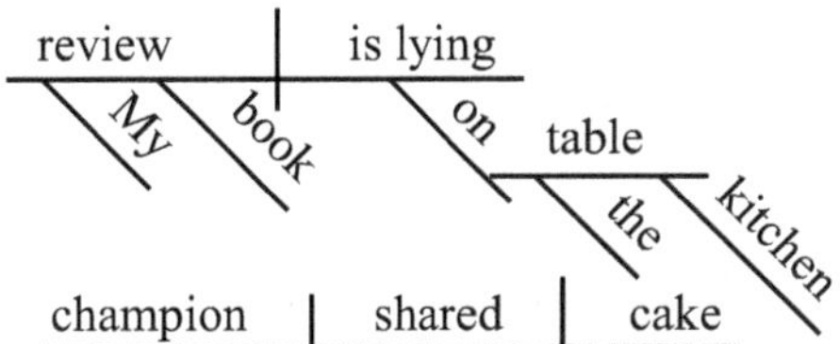

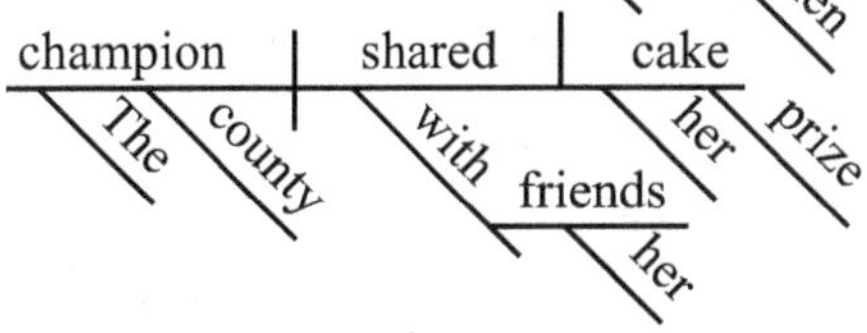

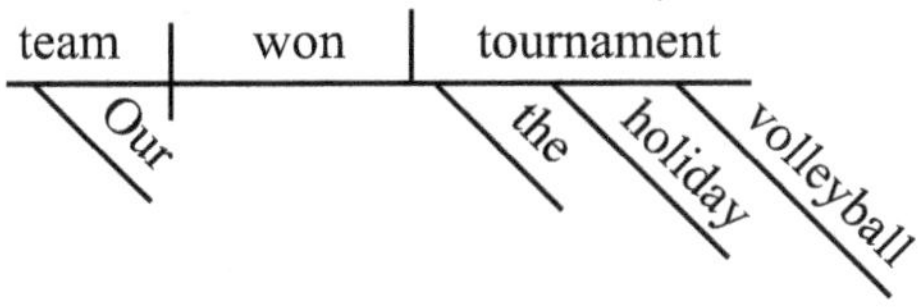

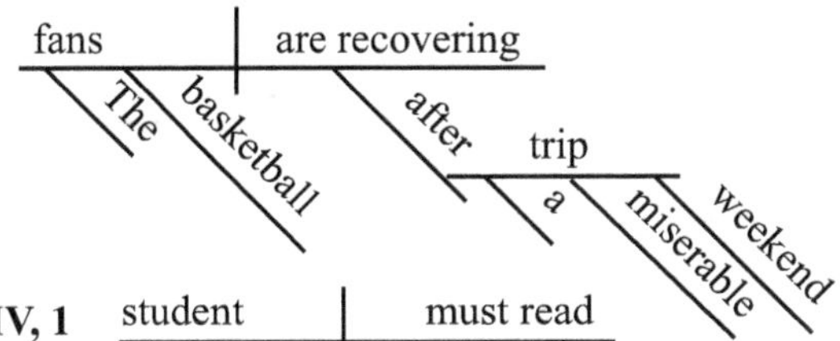

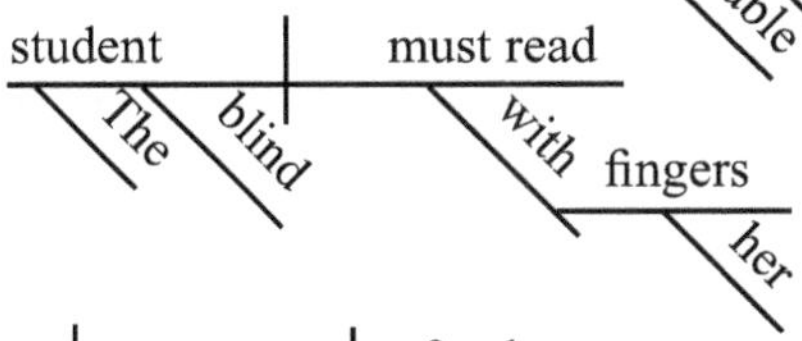

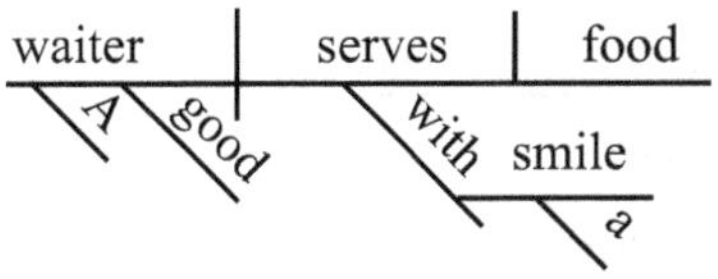

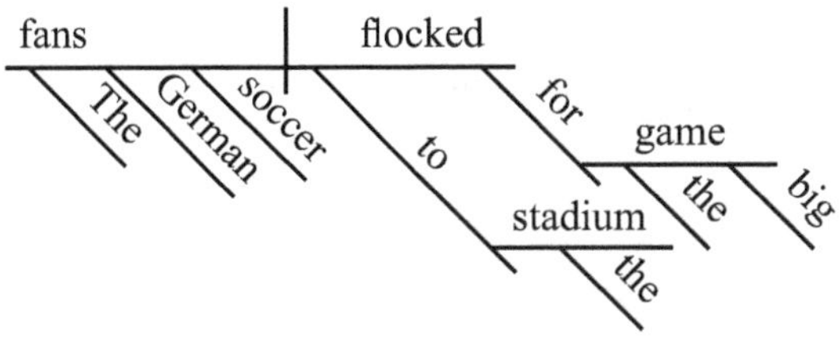

R, 4

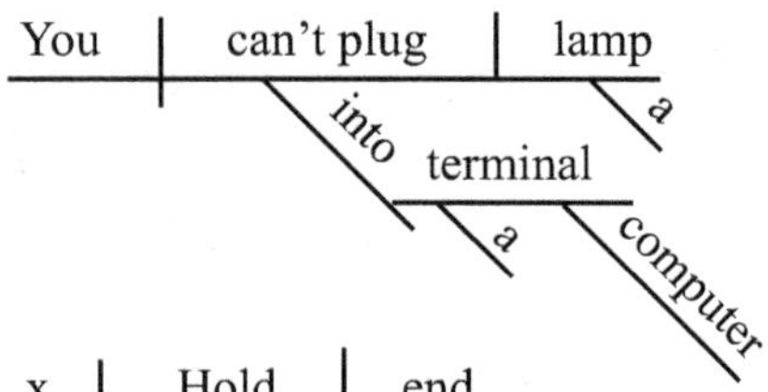

R, 5

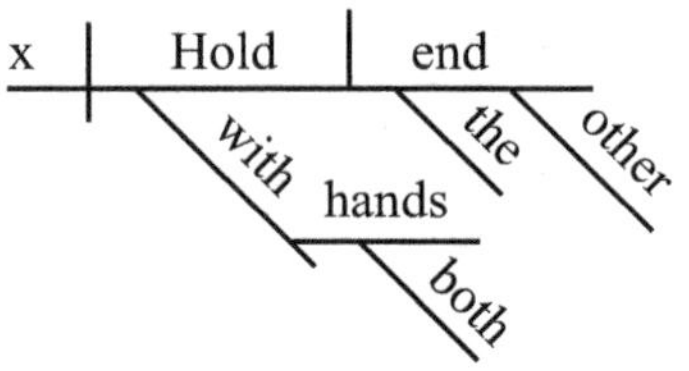

R, 6

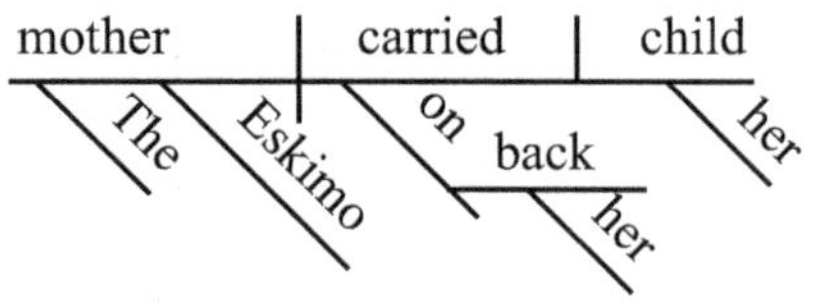

R, 7

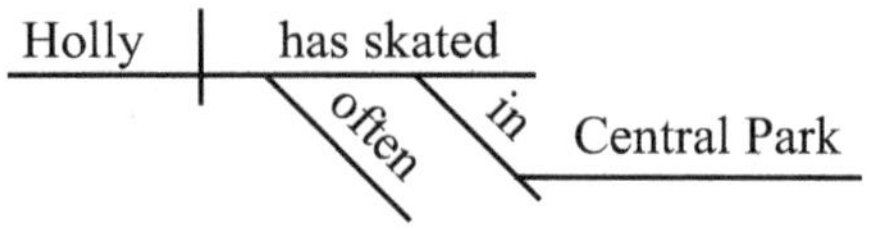

R, 8

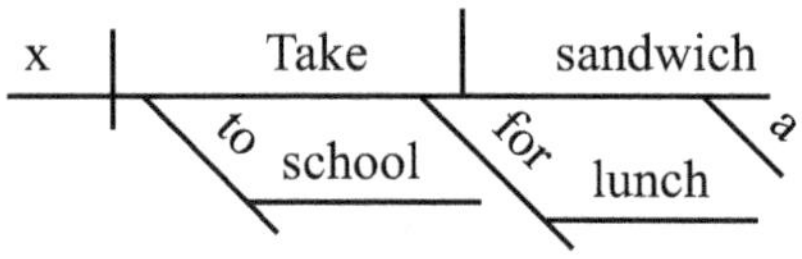

R, 9

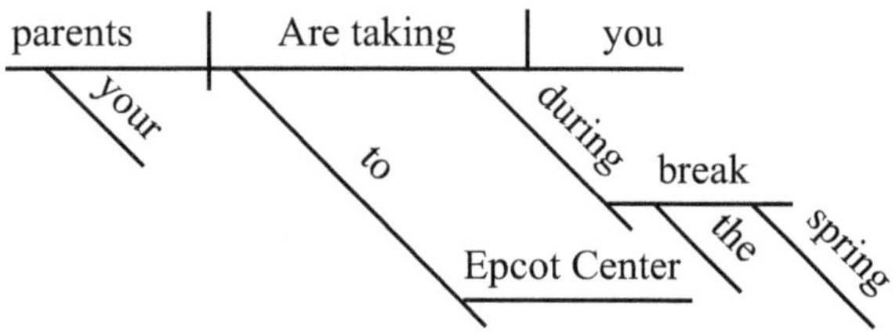

Lesson 13, 1

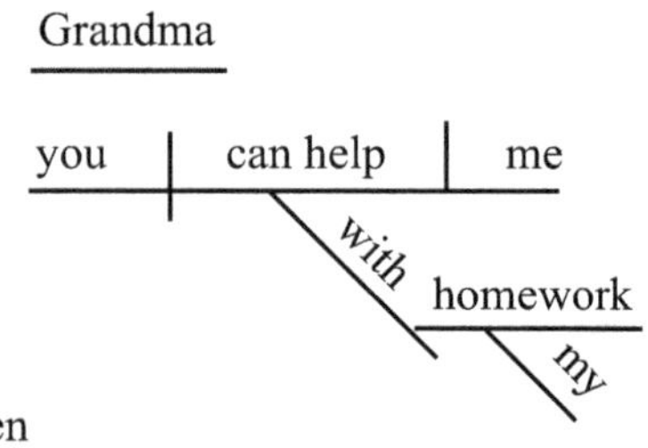

13, 2

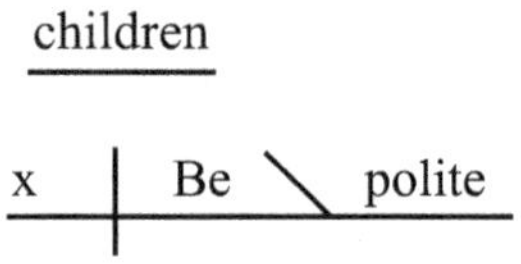

13, 3

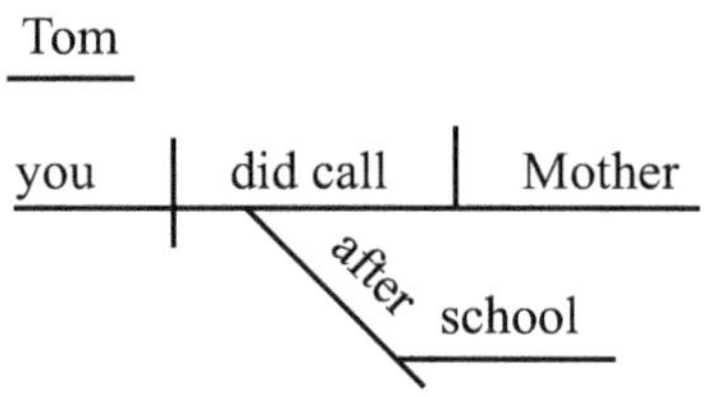

13, 4

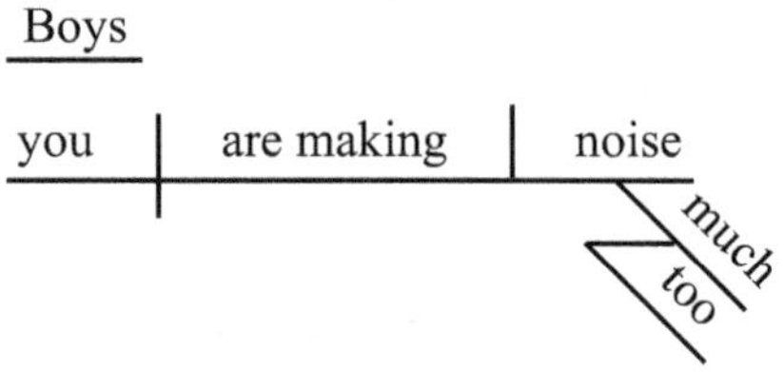

13, 5

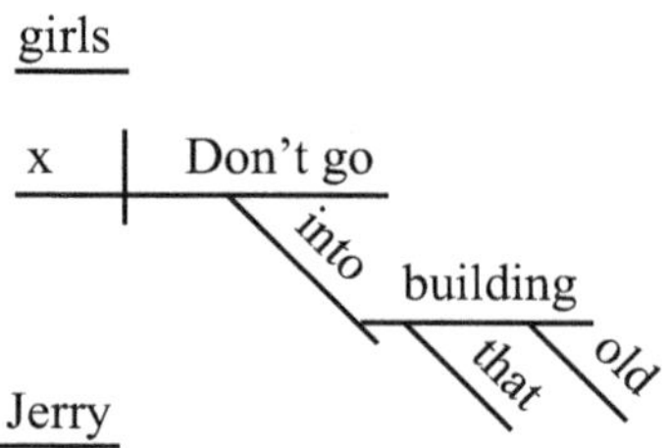

13, 6

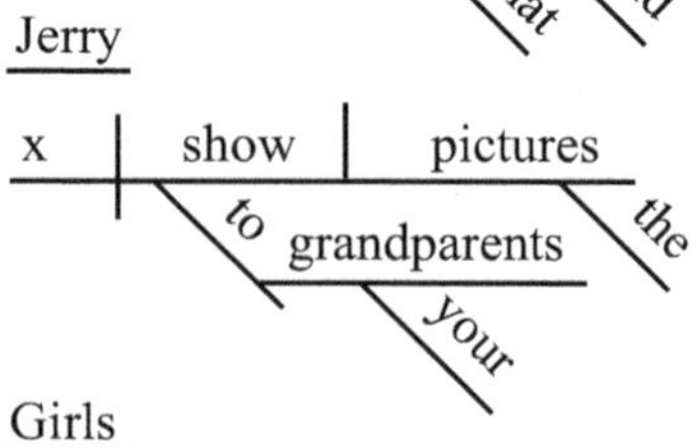

13, 7

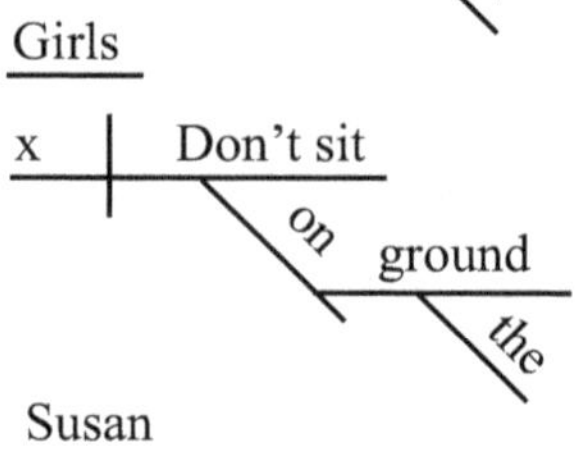

13, 8

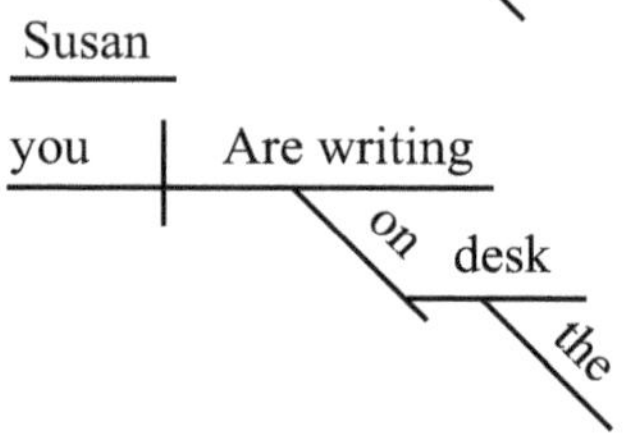

Lesson 14, 1

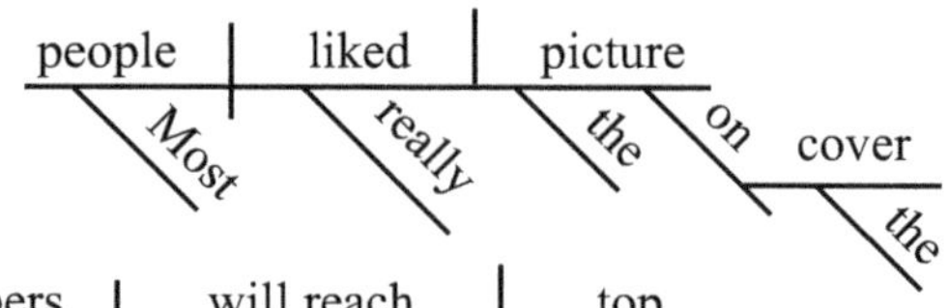

14, 2

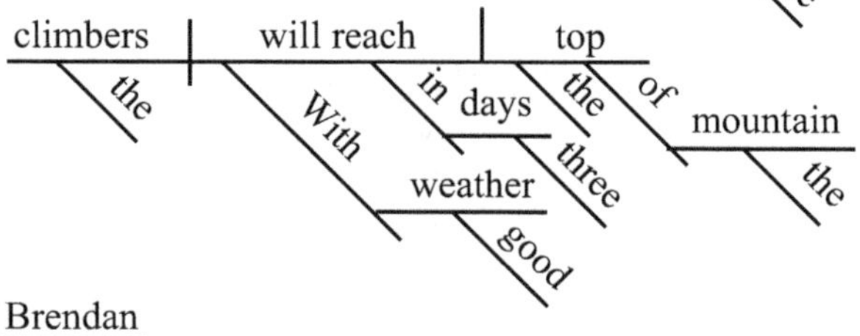

14, 3

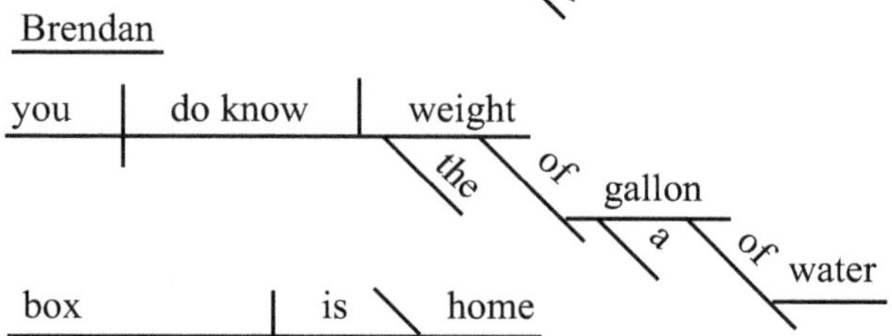

14, 4

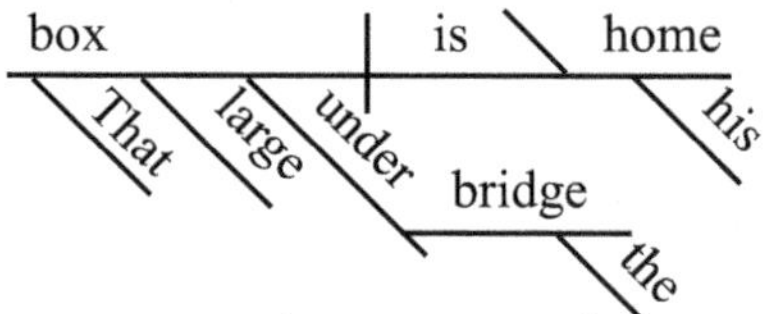

14, 5

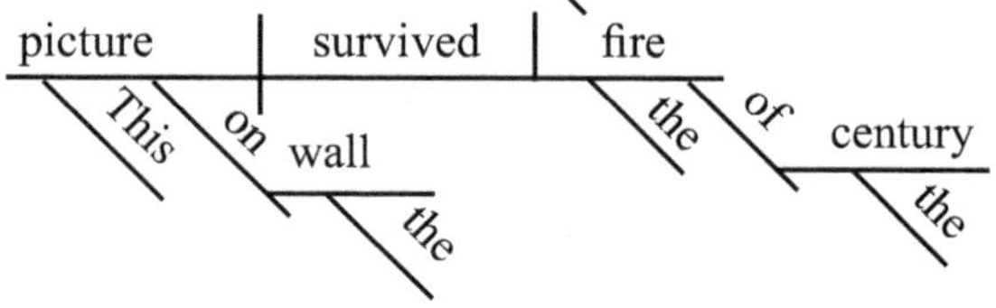

14, 6

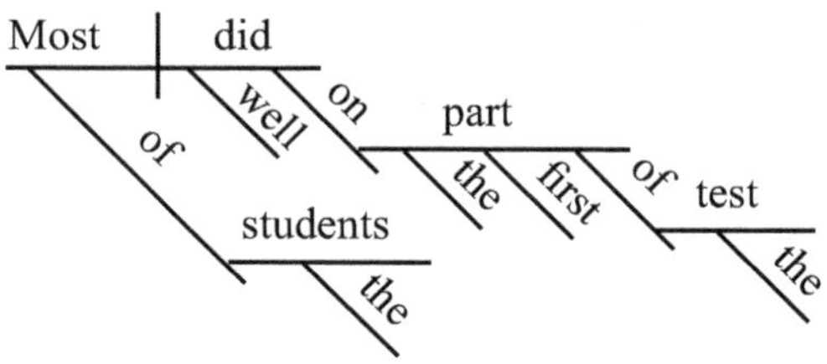

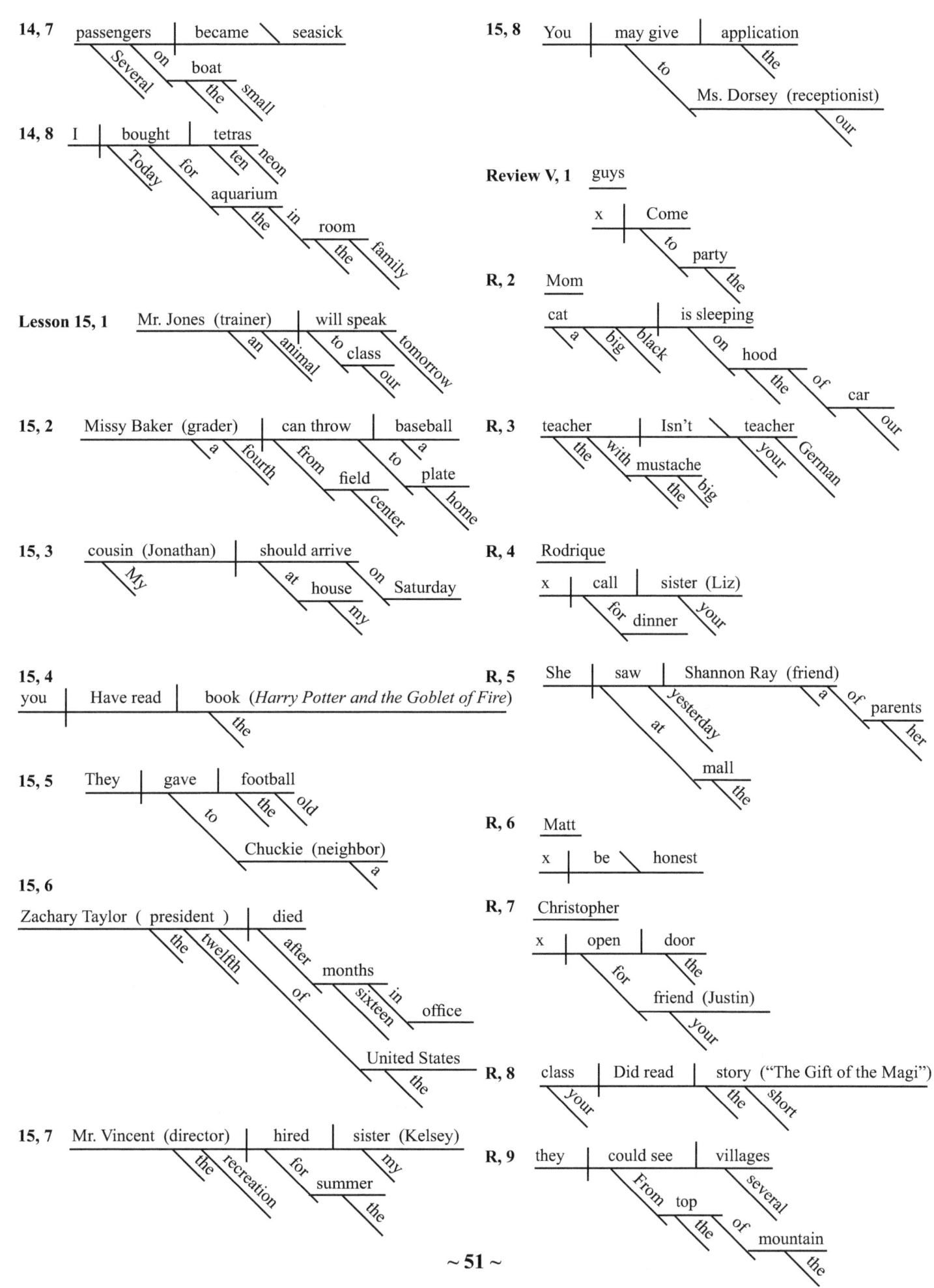

Lesson 16, 1

16, 2

16, 3

16, 4

16, 5

16, 6

16, 7

Lesson 17, 1

17, 2

17, 3

17, 4

17, 5

17, 6

17, 7

17, 8

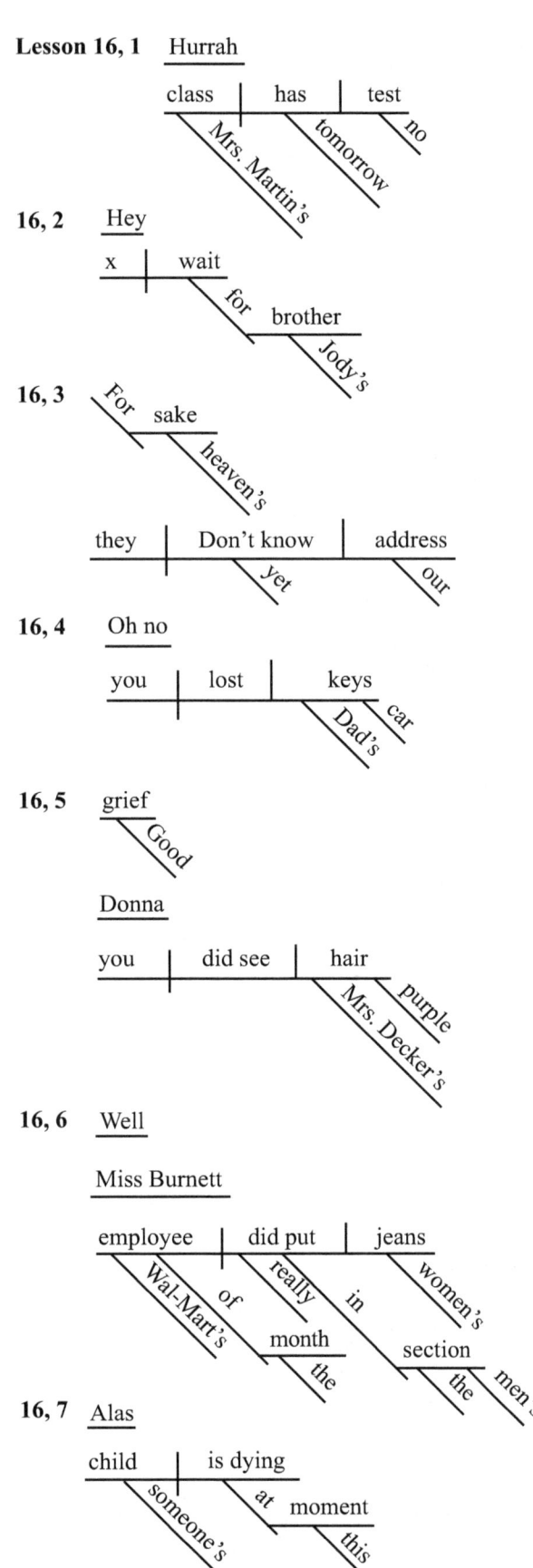

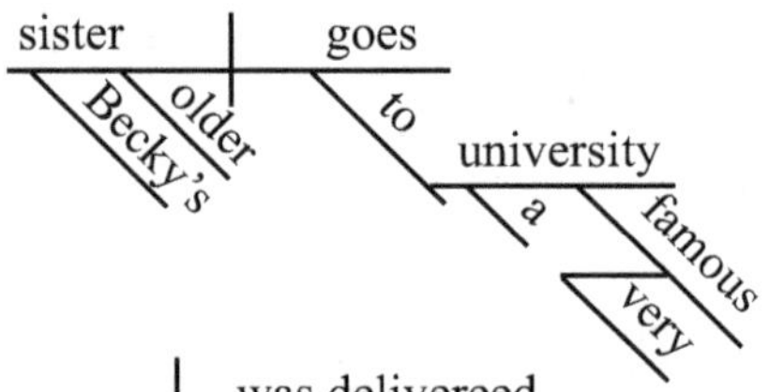

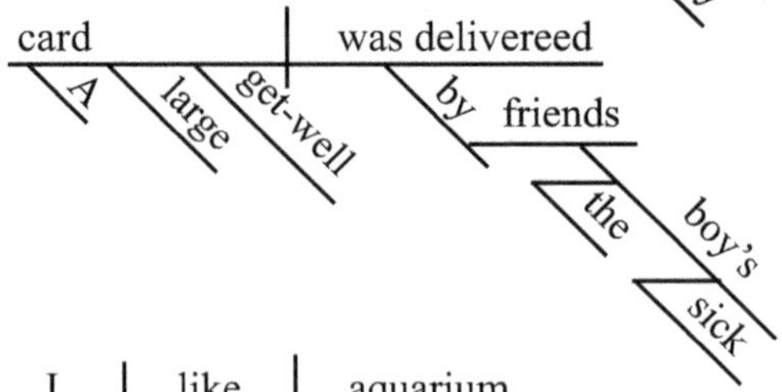

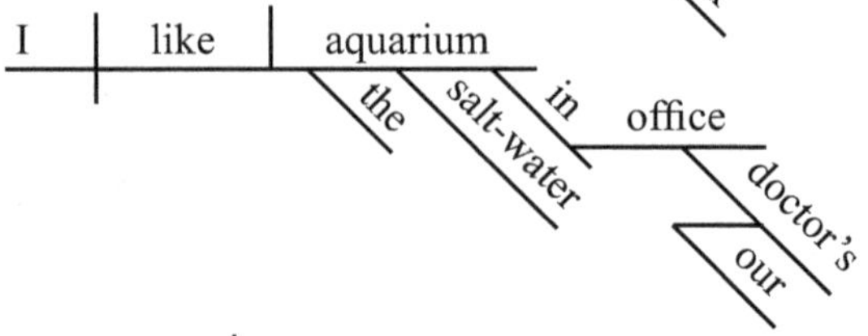

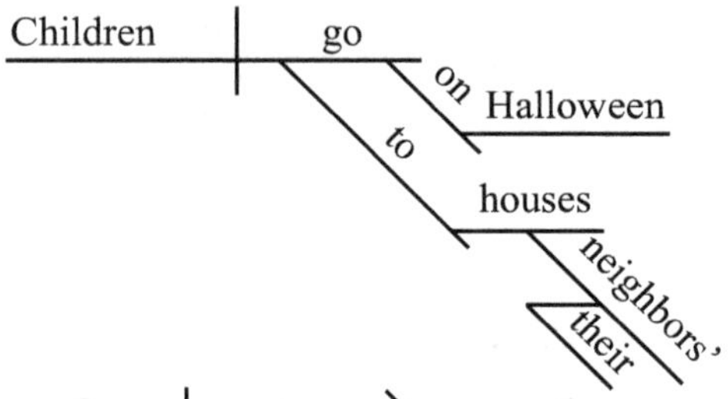

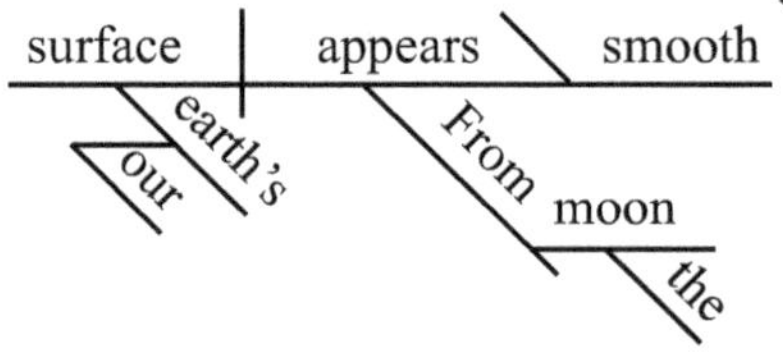

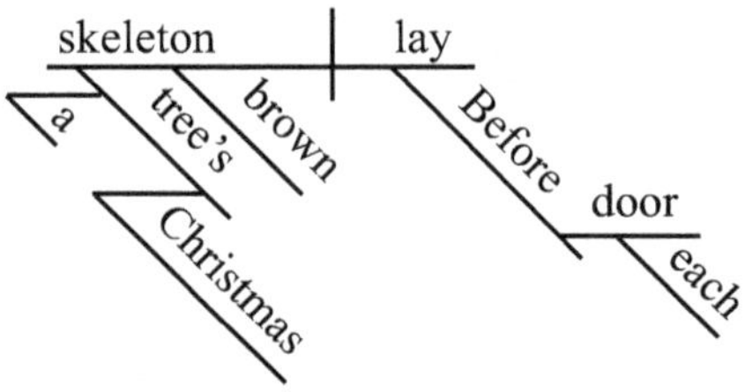

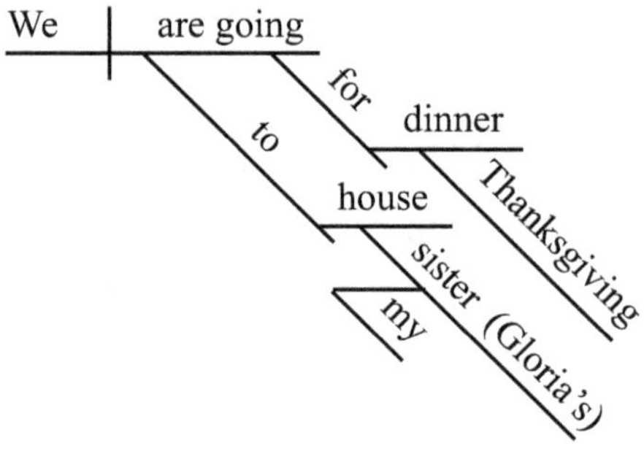

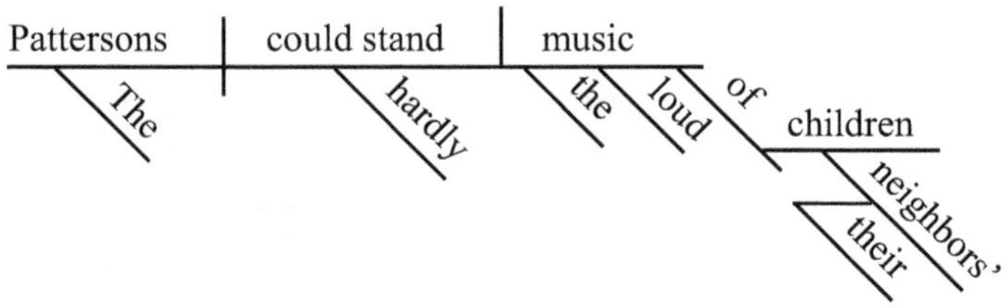

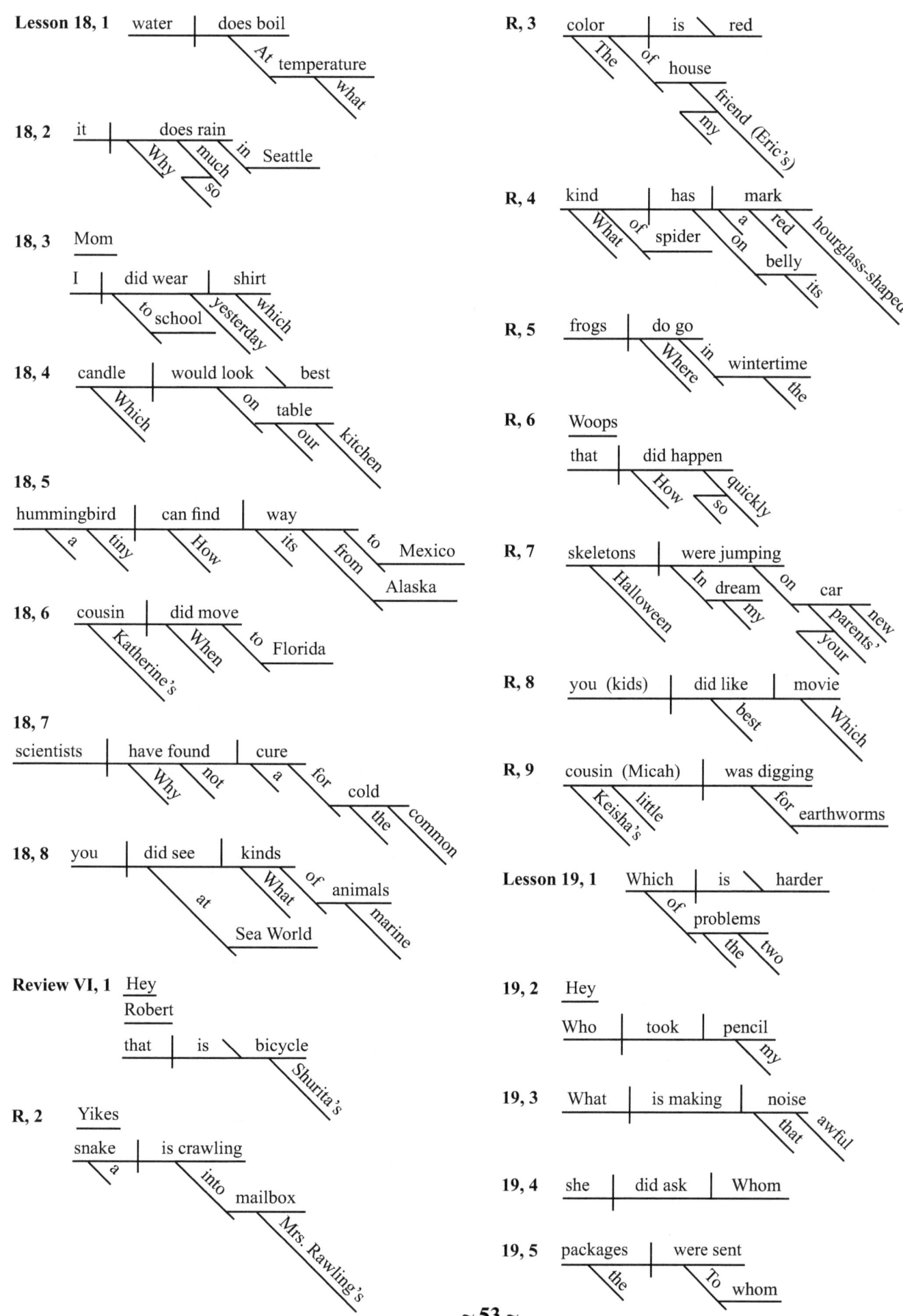

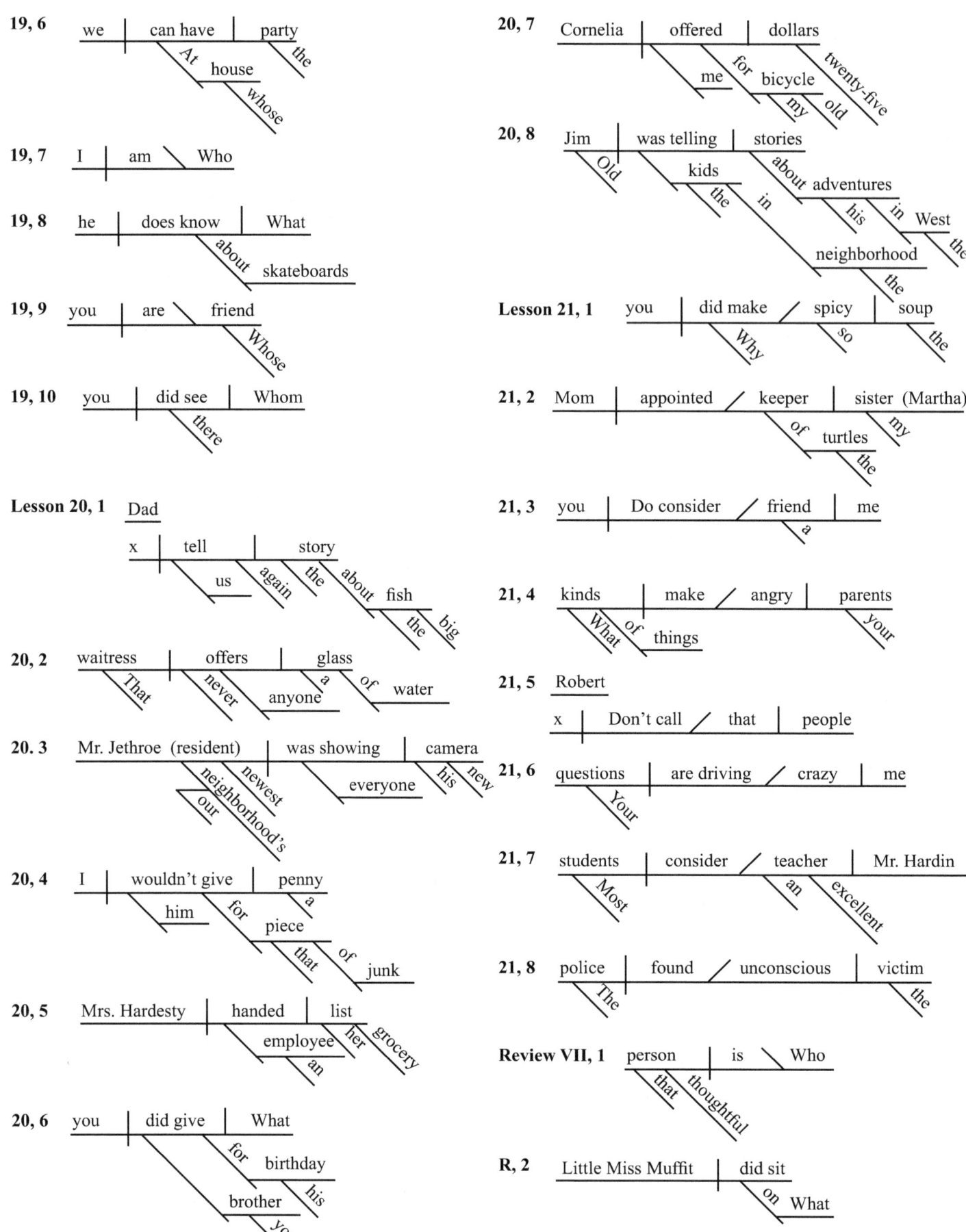

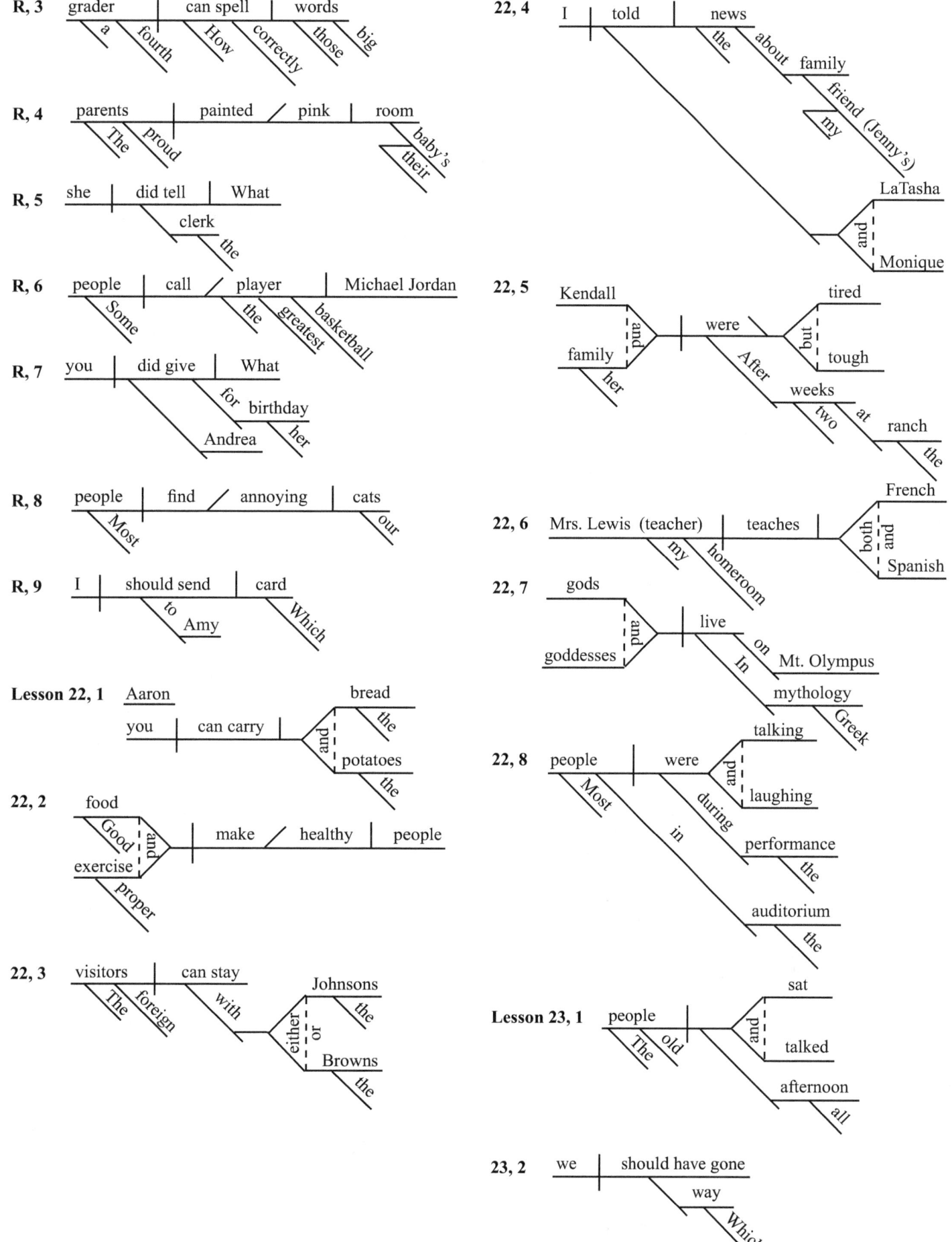

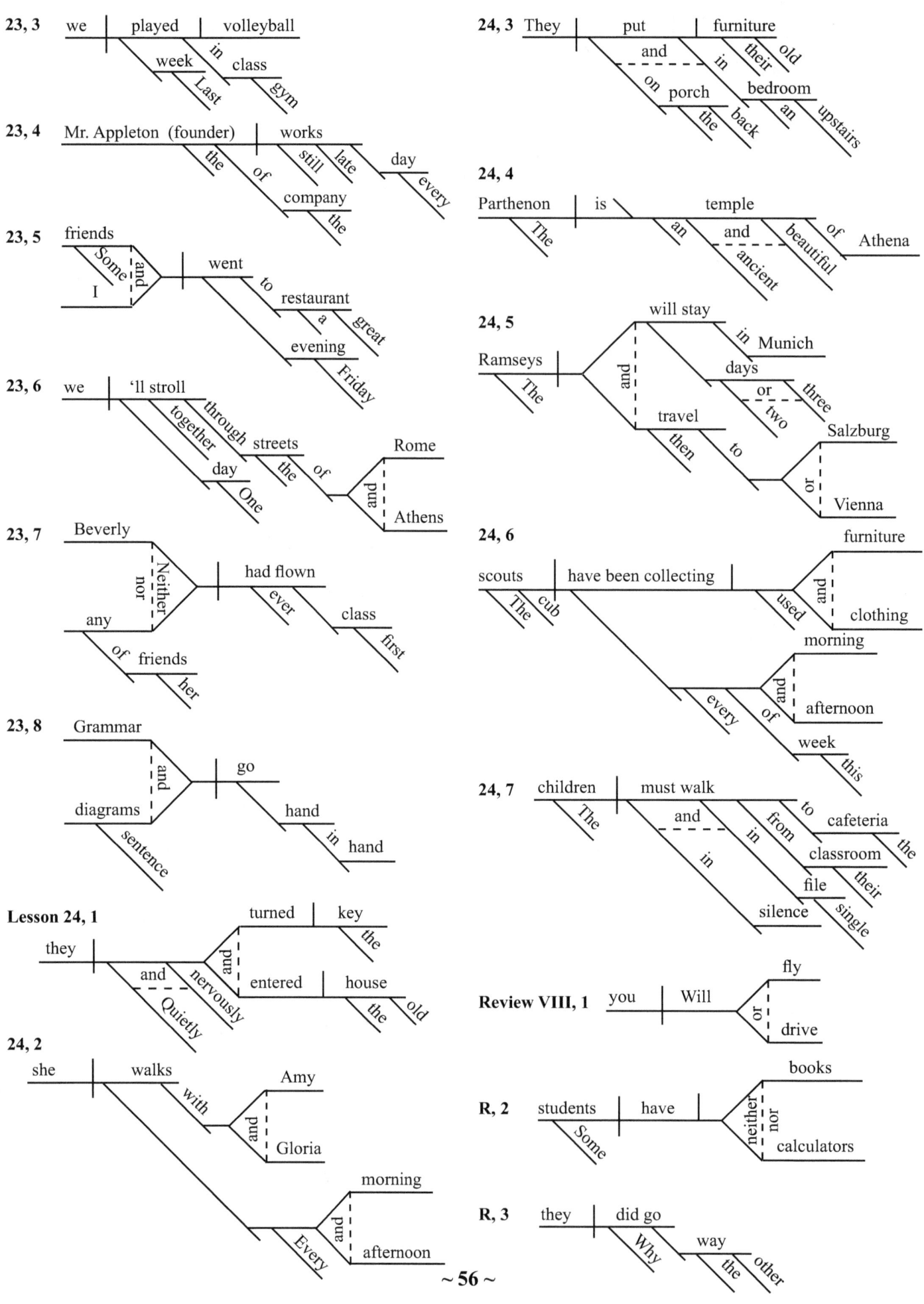

R, 4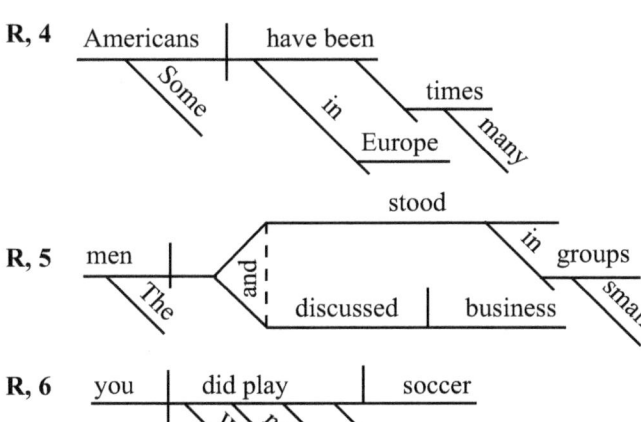

R, 5

R, 6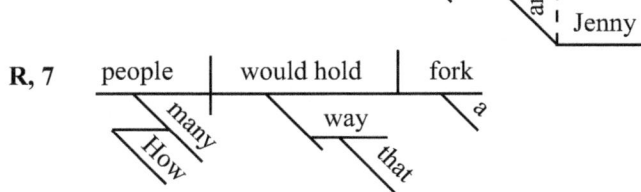

R, 7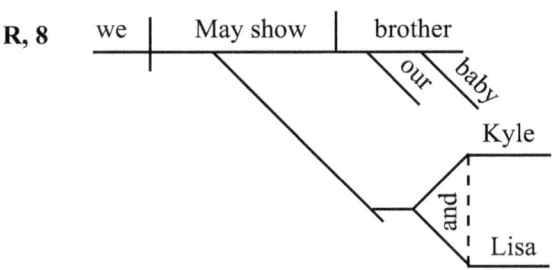

R, 8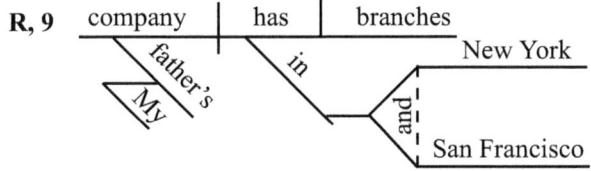

R, 9

Diagramming Test
Unit I: Lessons 1 - 3

1. The soldiers are marching.

2. They are dancers.

3. A train is coming.

4. Mr. Roberts is a carpenter.

5. She was smiling.

6. The driver is a tourist.

7. He may be working.

8. A seed can become a tree.

9. You must have hurried.

10. She had been an engineer.

11. He could become a pilot.

12. The deer has been eating.

Diagramming Test
Unit II: Lessons 4 - 6

1. Their new car is beautiful.

2. Salmon is a healthy food.

3. The white boots are yours.

4. I feel good.

5. All people should be kind.

6. Baseball is a great American pastime.

7. Your neighbors must have been shopping.

8. My poor feet are sore.

9. You may get sick.

10. That tall man is my dad.

11. Her desserts taste great.

12. Her little sister was absent.

Diagramming Test
Unit III: Lessons 7 - 9

1. Can you swim well?

2. Did she help them often?

3. That was not very nice.

4. Your brother is not wearing a jacket.

5. Did Mary really have a little lamb?

6. A roadrunner can eat a small snake.

7. The gardener has been trimming the roses.

8. The plane will land soon.

9. Am I holding your hand too tightly?

10. Didn't the cat just catch a mouse?

11. We are expecting snow tonight.

12. Have you ever gone there?

Diagramming Test
Unit IV: Lessons 10 - 12

1. Don't plant those desert flowers in the shade.

2. The young boy is standing confidently beside his father.

3. Does sauerkraut really taste good?

4. Rarely did the American tourists spot a jungle animal.

5. The huge cathedral towers over the small French town.

6. Can you find the Sears Tower in the Chicago skyline?

7. With his thumb Jack Horner pulled a plum from a Christmas pie.

8. The divers descended very slowly to the ocean floor.

9. Return to your seat immediately.

Diagramming Test
Unit V: Lessons 13 - 15

1. Our best player, Ronald Jackson, is sitting quietly at the end of the bench.

2. Children, come to the front of the room for your morning snack.

3. Aaron, the student in the middle, introduced himself to the other students.

4. Roberto Clemente, the famous baseball player, helped the poor people of Puerto Rico.

5. Daniel, have you ever seen pictures of villages in Europe?

6. Our family lived happily in a cabin on a lake in New Hampshire.

7. Bring your friends for an evening of celebration.

8. Dad, do people live in the jungles of South America?

9. Mr. Ward, the director of a local hospital, will be the guest speaker.

Diagramming Test
Unit VI: Lessons 16 - 18

1. Jeez! Why are our neighbors' raccoons making so much noise?

2. Which part of Ms. Henderson's assignment did you do first?

3. My friend Amy's cake won first prize at the fair.

4. Horrors! Why are they leaving so soon?

5. At our daughter's tea party, we ate a delicious banana bread.

6. What excuse did they give?

7. Yippee! We are going to my grandparents' house in the country for Thanksgiving dinner.

8. When are the Hudsons leaving for their vacation home in Florida?

9. The school orchestra is already planning a summer trip to Vienna.

Diagramming Test
Unit VII: Lessons 19 - 21

1. Who told you that?

2. Why do they call him the best player in the NBA?

3. Your very kind gift to the school makes us teachers happy.

4. What kind of motorcycle did your parents give your brother?

5. With whose camera did you take those pictures?

6. What do most people call her?

7. Now I must tell you my favorite story.

8. Is my face turning red?

9. Whom did you ask about the meeting after school?

Diagramming Test
Unit VIII: Lessons 22 - 24

1. Many men and women have been dancing all evening.

2. Mrs. Evans is teaching her two children about African and Asian art.

3. A walk through the woods can delight both adults and children.

4. That evening the campers held hands and danced around the campfire.

5. In the Louvre, a famous art museum in Paris, you can see both the *Venus de Milo* and the *Mona Lisa*.

6. The elderly couple walked this way and that way among the many cars.

7. The archaeologists worked quickly but carefully all day.

8. The girls ran into the house and up the stairs.

9. Once a person could walk to the corner grocery store and buy a loaf of bread for a dime.

~ Test Solutions ~

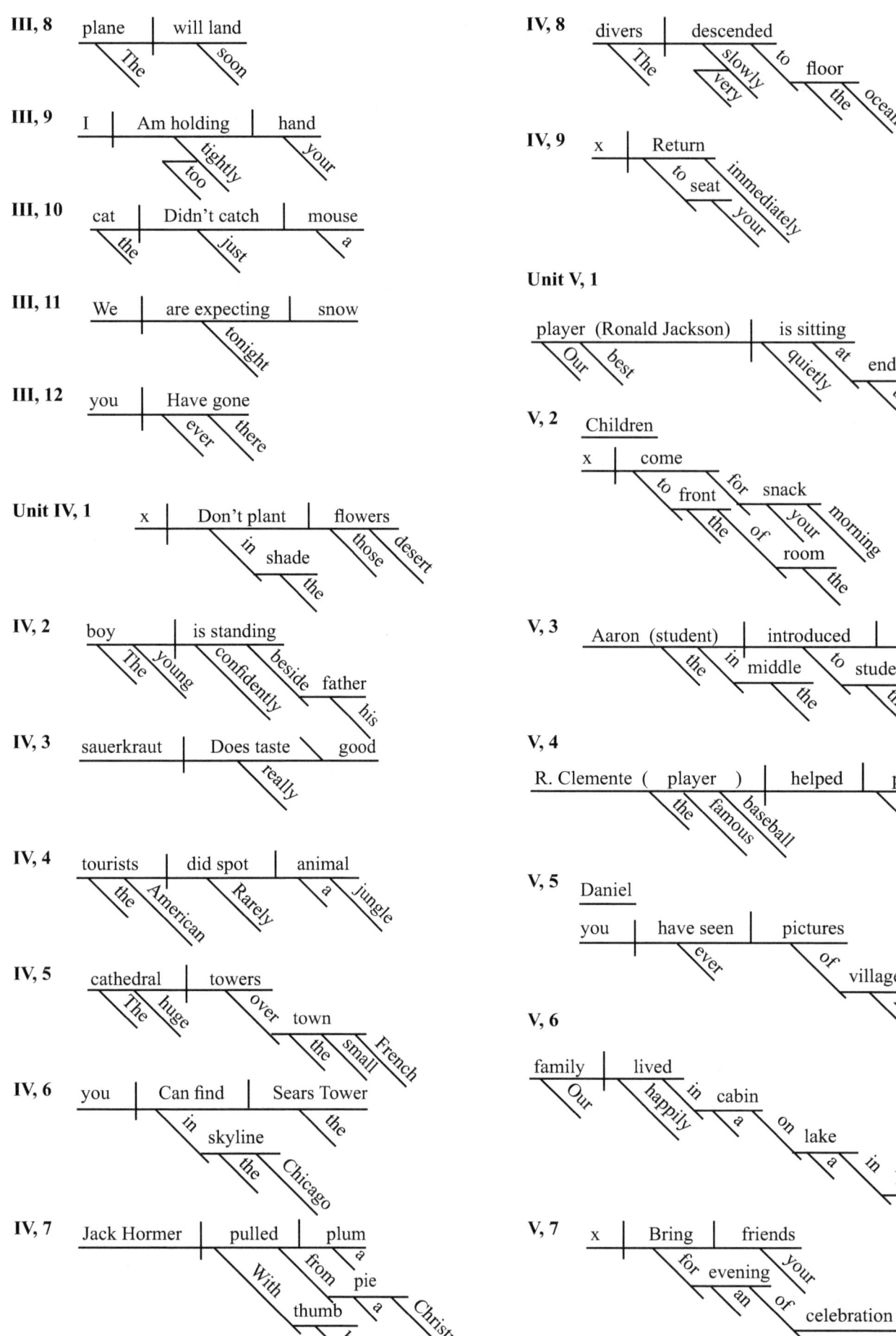

V, 8 Dad — Do people live in the jungles of South America?

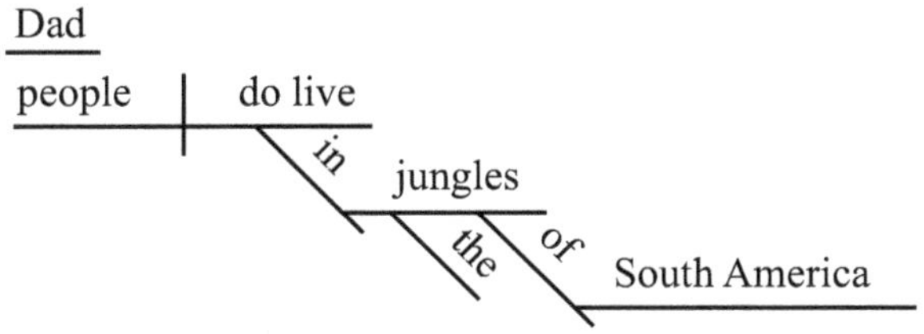

V, 9 Mr. Ward (director) — Mr. Ward, the director of a local hospital, will be the guest speaker.

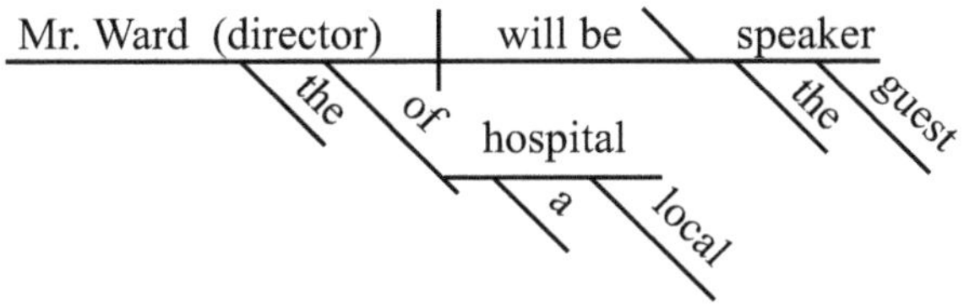

Unit VI, 1 Jeez — Why are our neighbors' raccoons making so much noise?

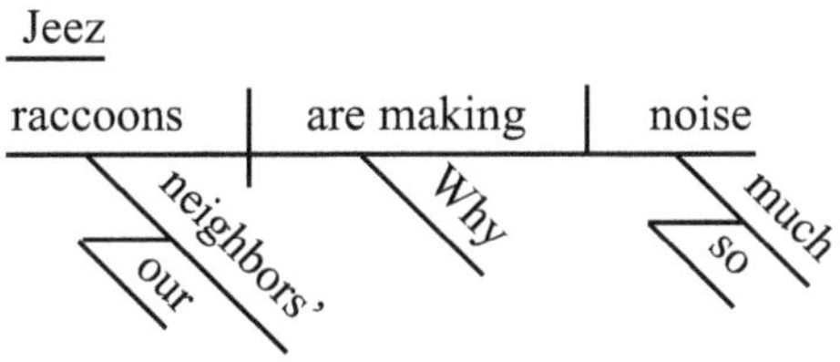

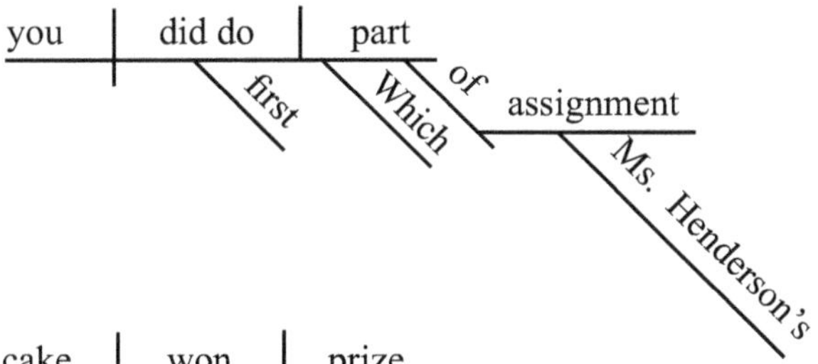

VI, 2 Which part of Ms. Henderson's assignment did you do first?

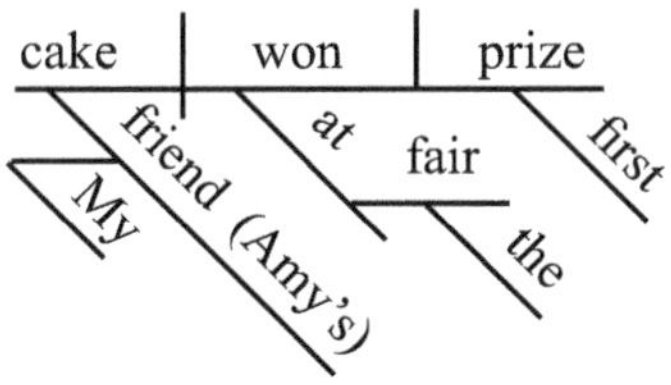

VI, 3 My friend (Amy's) cake won first prize at the fair.

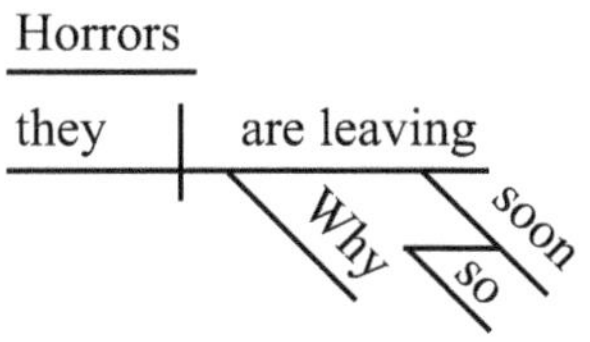

VI, 4 Horrors — Why are they leaving so soon?

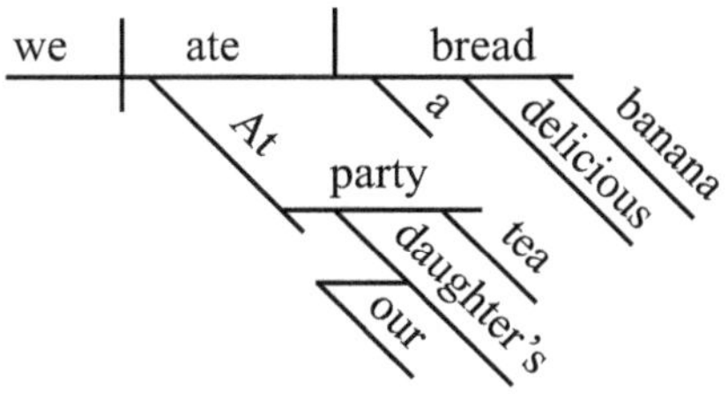

VI, 5 At our daughter's tea party we ate a delicious banana bread.

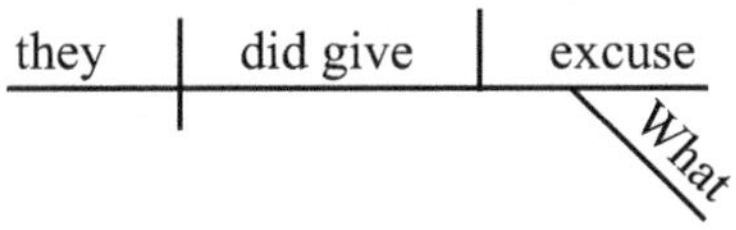

VI, 6 What excuse did they give?

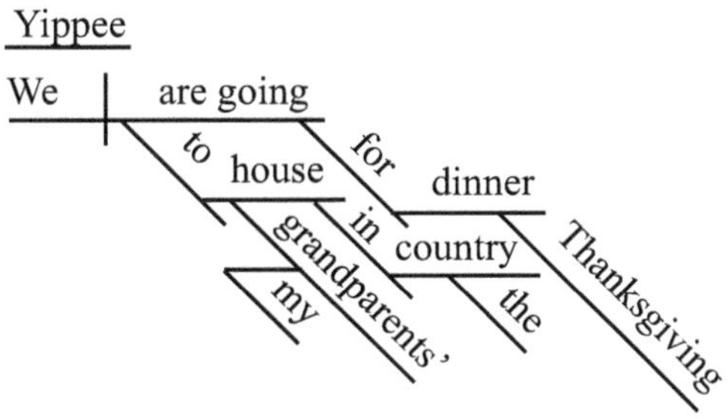

VI, 7 Yippee — We are going to my grandparents' house for dinner in the country Thanksgiving.

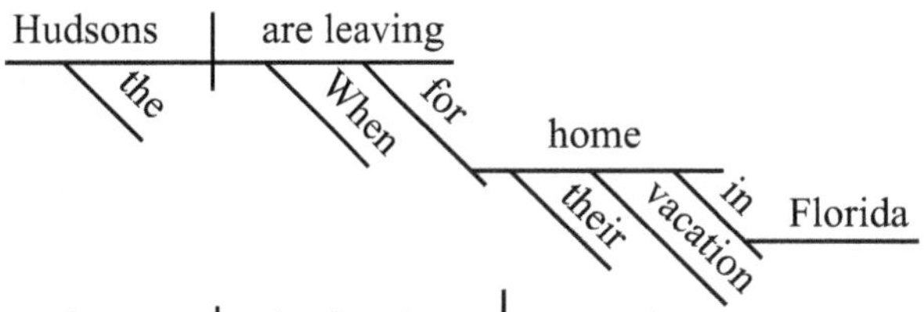

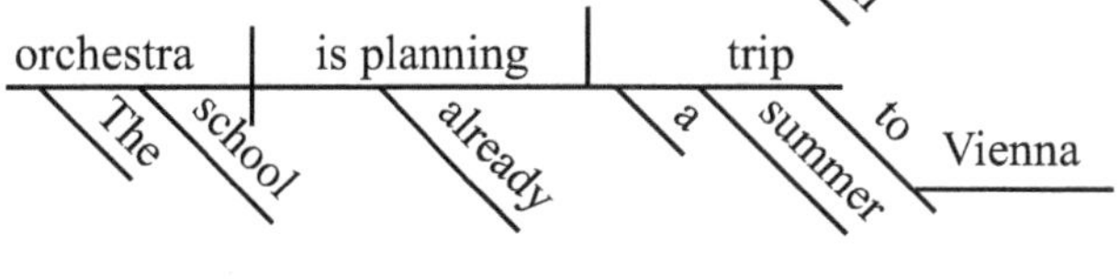

VI, 8 When are the Hudsons leaving for their home in Florida vacation?

VI, 9 The school orchestra is already planning a summer trip to Vienna.

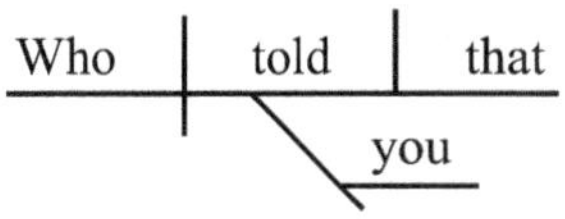

Unit VII, 1 Who told you that?

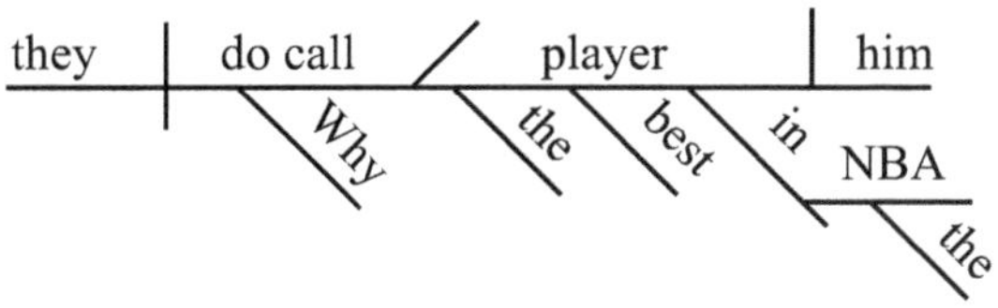

VII, 2 Why do they call him the best player in the NBA?

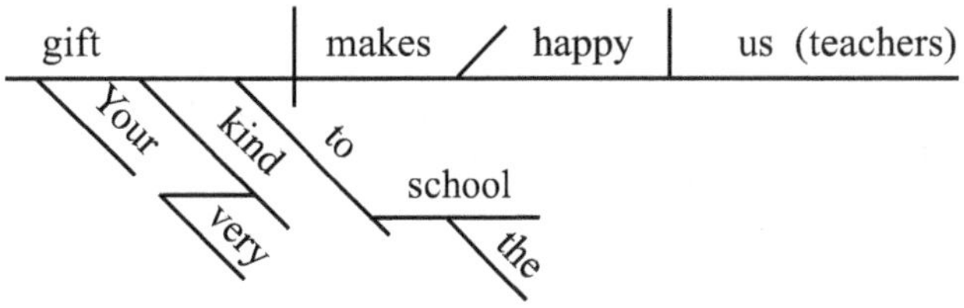

VII, 3 Your very kind gift to the school makes us (teachers) happy.

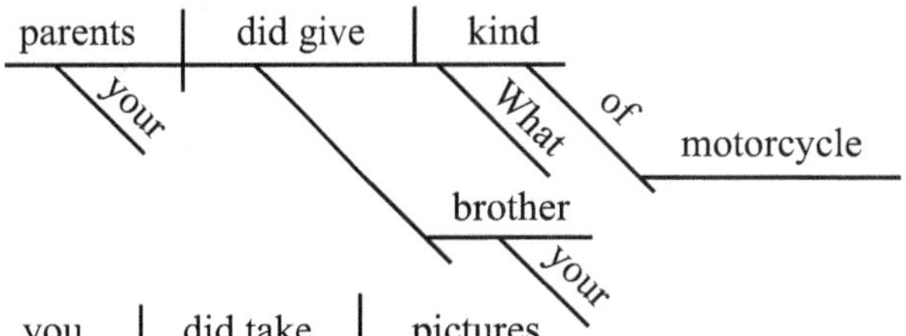

VII, 4 What kind of motorcycle did your parents give your brother?

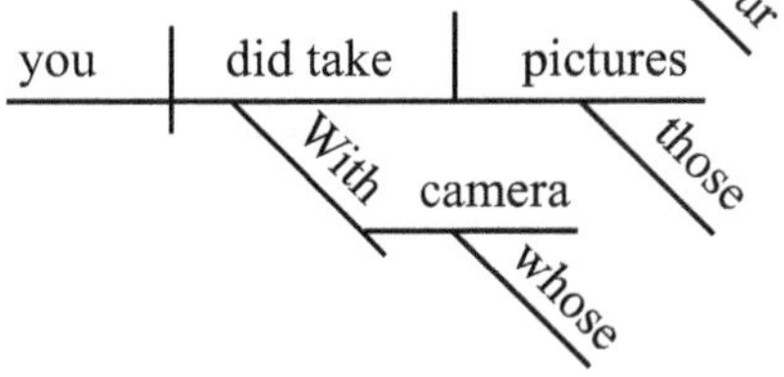

VII, 5 With whose camera did you take those pictures?

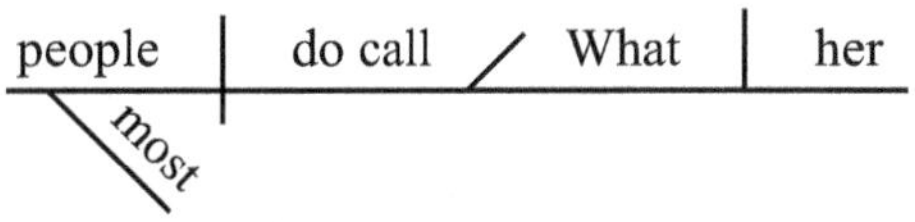

VII, 6 What do most people call her?

VII, 7 Now I must tell you my favorite story.

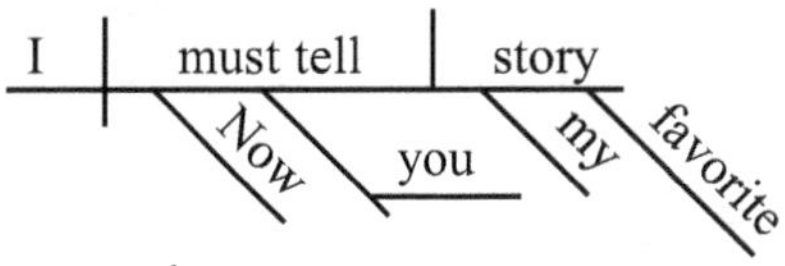

VII, 8 My face is turning red.

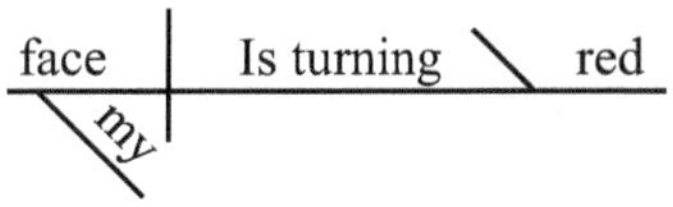

VII, 9 Whom did you ask about the meeting after school?

~ 69 ~

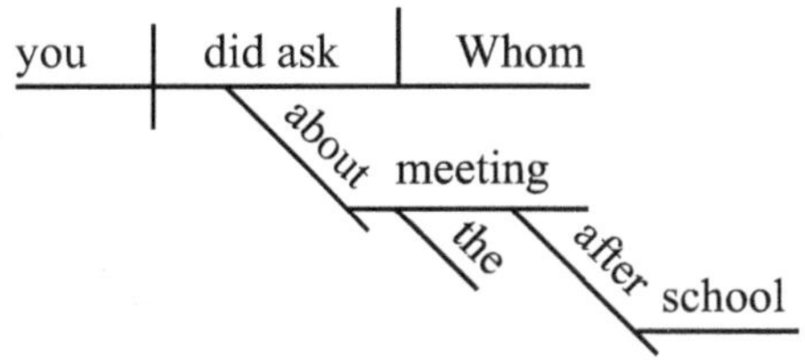

Unit VIII, 1

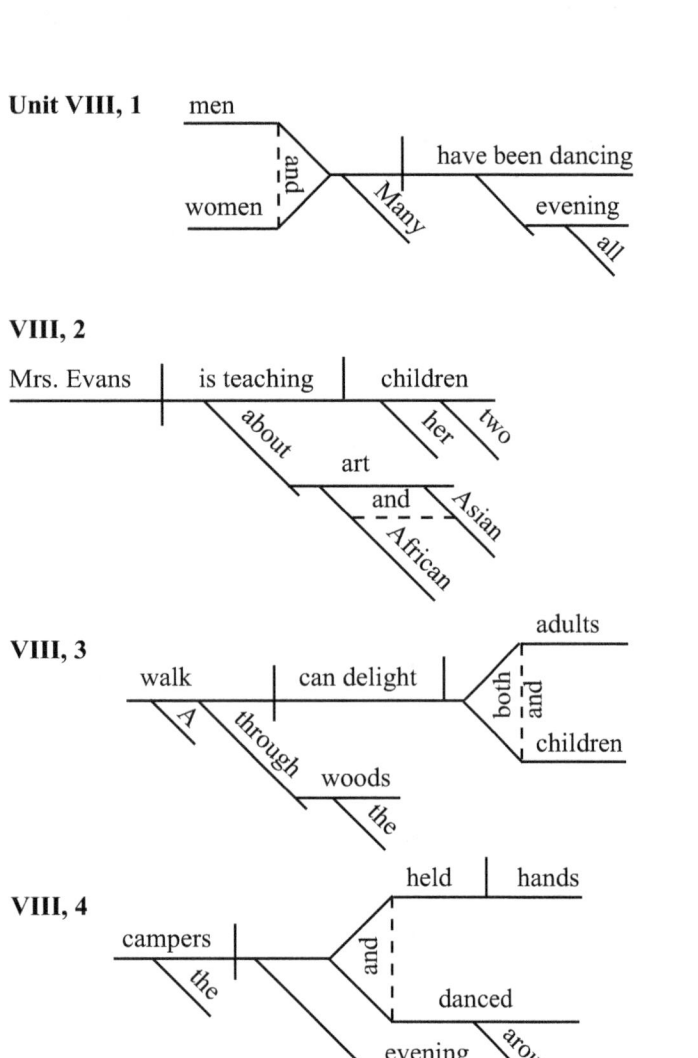

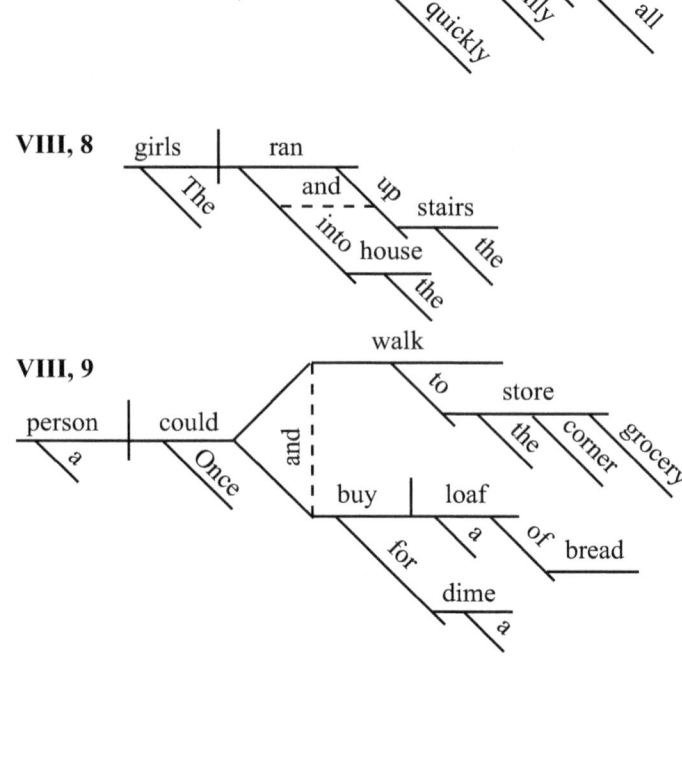

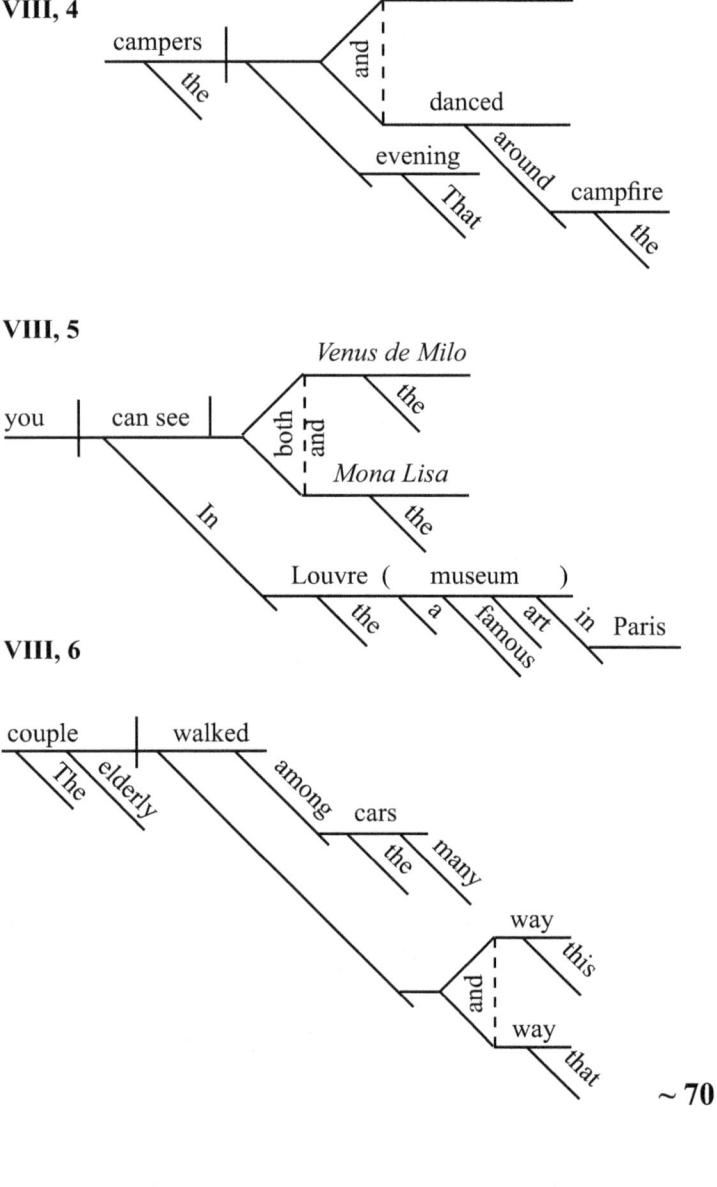

Part Two: Dependent Clauses, Verbals, and More

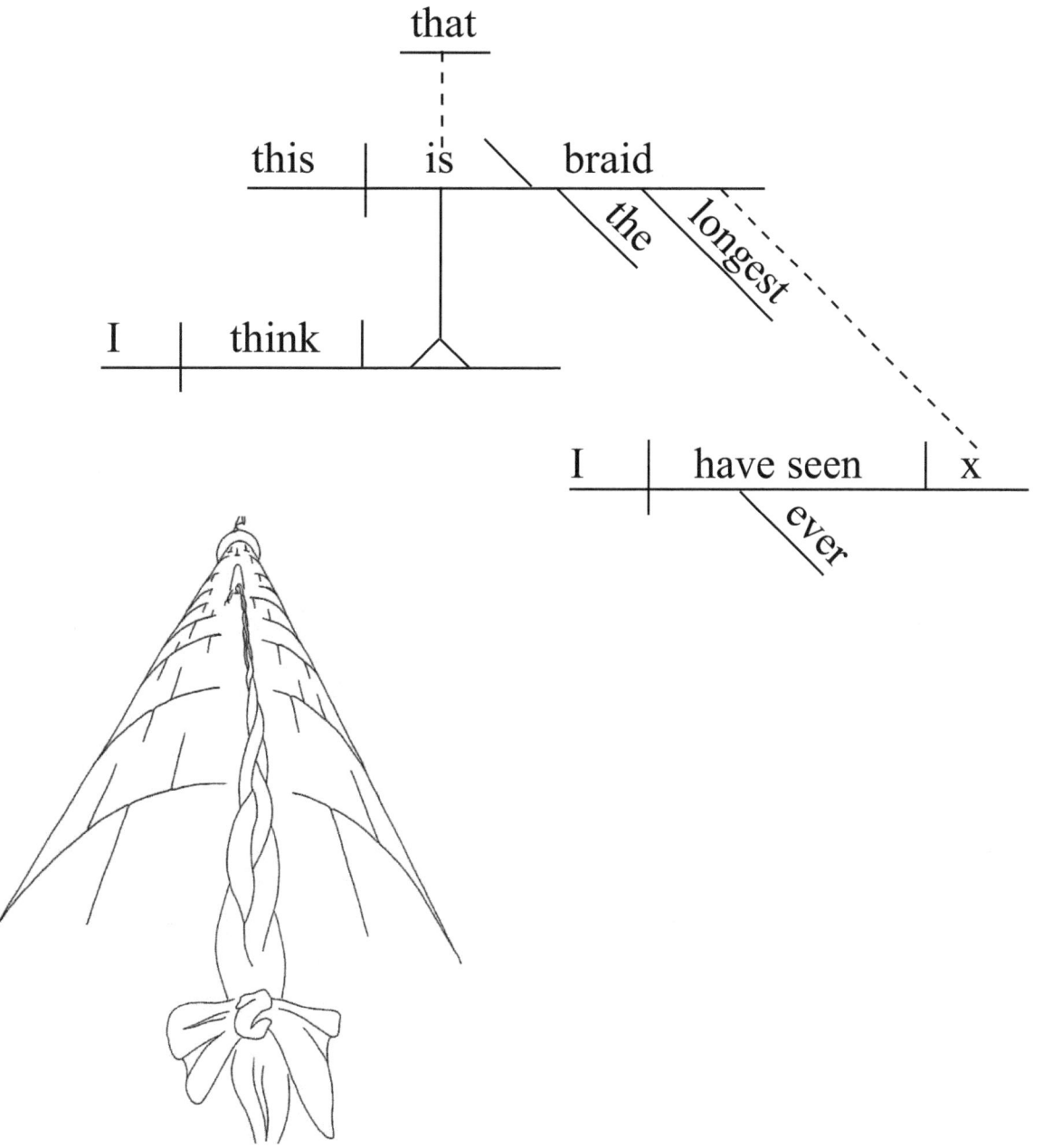

Unit I

- Adjective Clauses
- Noun Clauses
- Adverb Clauses

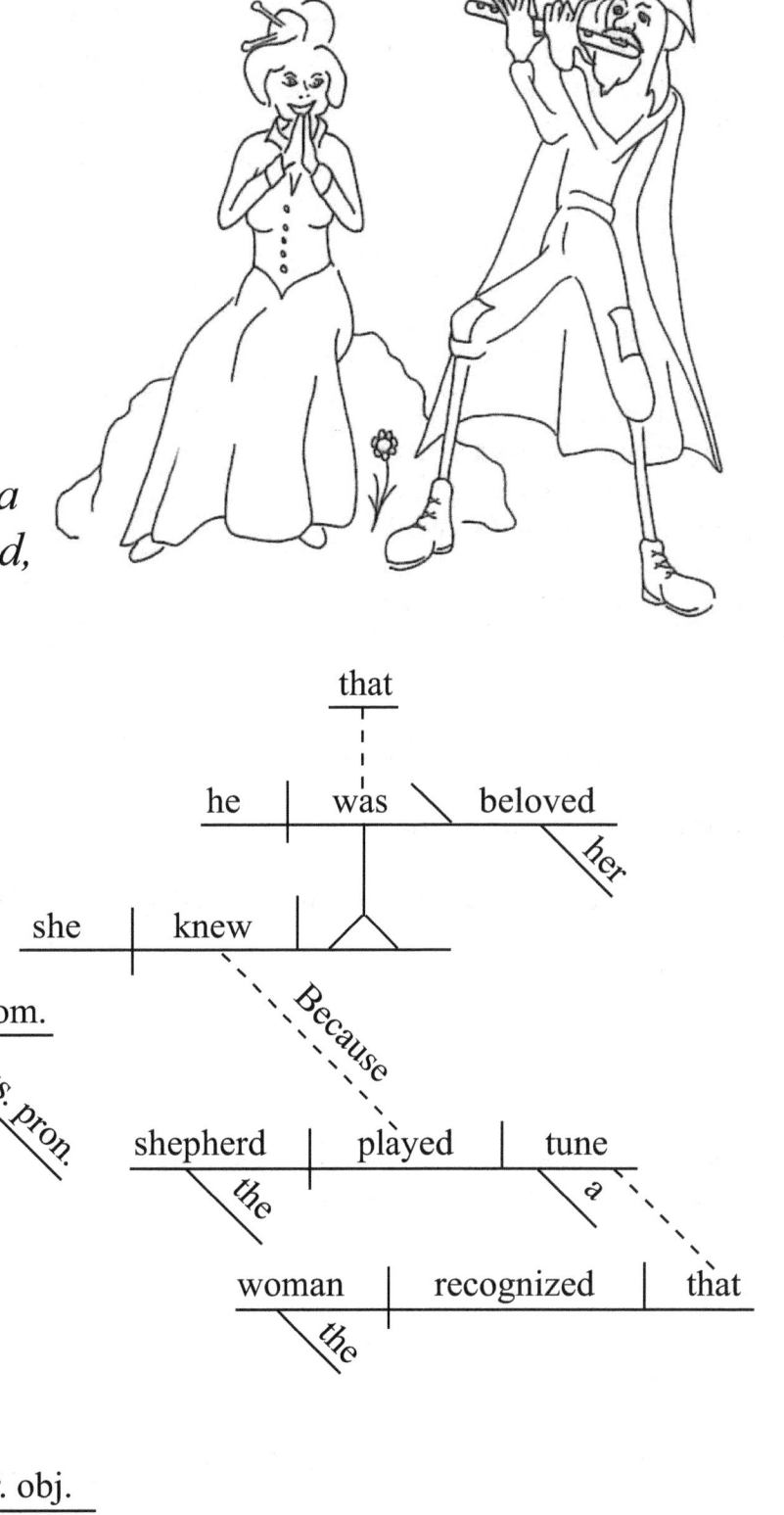

Because the shepherd played a tune that the woman recognized, she knew that he was her beloved.

~ 73 ~

Lesson 1: Adjective Clauses

Clauses that modify nouns and pronouns are called adjective clauses. There are two kinds of adjective clauses: those introduced by relative pronouns and those introduced by relative adverbs. A relative pronoun refers (or relates) to an antecedent, a word that precedes it in the same sentence. The principal relative pronouns are *who, whom, whose, which,* and *that*. Examples of relative adverbs are *when, where,* and *why*. Here are some sentences that contain adjective clauses: *Is that the guy that you saw? That is the trainer whose horse won the Derby. I told you about the friends with whom we traveled last summer. She remembers a time when life was simpler. That's the reason why I can't be there.* These sentences are diagrammed below.

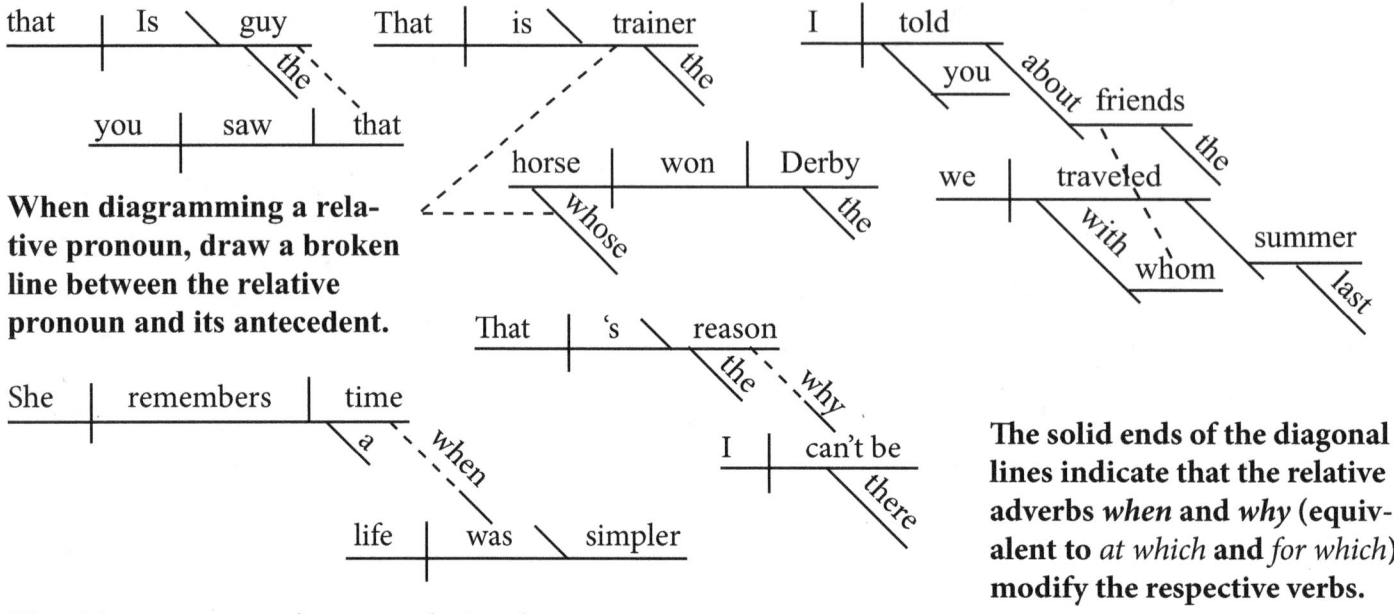

When diagramming a relative pronoun, draw a broken line between the relative pronoun and its antecedent.

The solid ends of the diagonal lines indicate that the relative adverbs *when* and *why* (equivalent to *at which* and *for which*) modify the respective verbs.

Now it's your turn to diagram relative clauses.

1. We don't even know the people who helped us.

2. She was not the only one whose clothes were muddy.

3. Isn't that the town where you once lived?

4. Will there ever be a single day when men are not fighting?

5. The charity for which the students are collecting food is called Kentucky Harvest.

6. You may be the only person in our class that I didn't see at the dance.

~ 74 ~

Lesson 2: Noun Clauses

A clause is a group of words that has a subject and a predicate. Clauses that function as nouns are called noun clauses. Noun clauses can function as subjects, direct objects, predicate nominatives, appositives, objects of prepositions, and even adverbial objectives. On this page we will consider only those noun clauses that begin with the expletive *that* (an expletive is a word that has a function but no meaning) and function as direct objects, predicate nominatives, and appositives. Here are some examples: *They said that they would hurry. Our hope is that everyone will arrive safely. The thought that it could snow that night brought a smile to her face.*

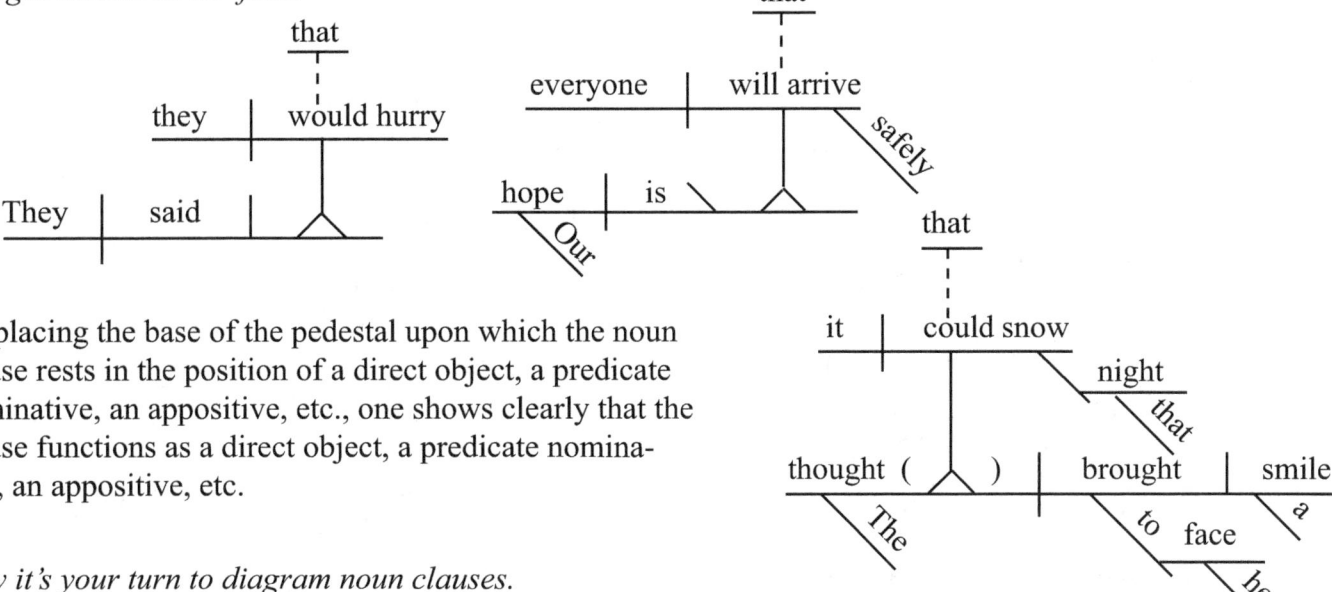

By placing the base of the pedestal upon which the noun clause rests in the position of a direct object, a predicate nominative, an appositive, etc., one shows clearly that the clause functions as a direct object, a predicate nominative, an appositive, etc.

Now it's your turn to diagram noun clauses.

1. Do you know that Alaska does not border any other state?

2. The fact that the universe has billions of stars is both strange and wonderful.

3. Their greatest fear was that they would lose their home.

4. My wife, my children, and I hope that you and your family will have happy holidays.

5. Chicken Little was haunted by the fear that the sky was falling in.

6. Foxy Woxy said that he would show Henny Penny and her friends a shortcut to the palace.

Lesson 3: Adverb Clauses

The subordinating conjunctions *because, although, if,* and *unless*, among others, introduce adverb clauses. Like adjective clauses, adverb clauses are always diagrammed below main clauses. When diagramming an adverb clause, place the subordinating conjunction on a diagonal line drawn from the verb of the main clause to the verb of the adverb clause. Here are several examples: *I cannot admit you to the theater unless you have a ticket. If you look in the wastebasket, you will find your bottle of water. Although Richard had no raincoat, he walked three blocks in heavy rain. They punished their child because they thought that a punishment would help him.*

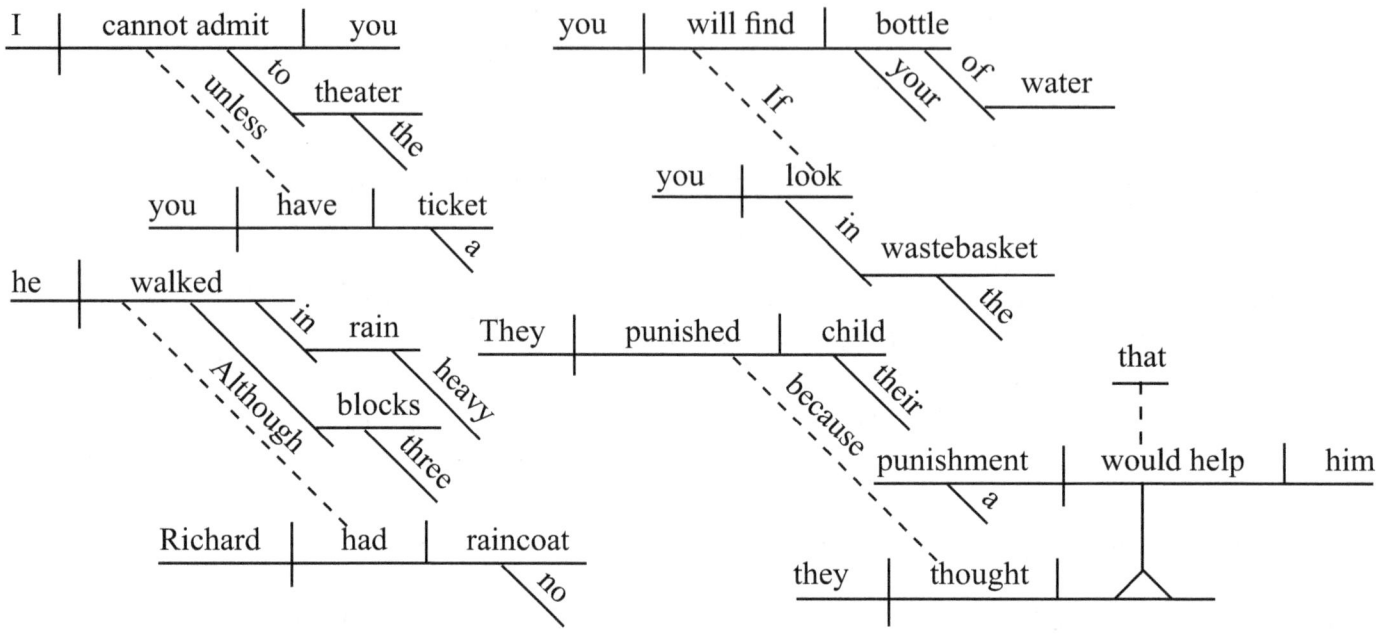

Now it's your turn to diagram adverb clauses.

1. If you don't want a disaster, don't build it that way.

2. We will not play football with you unless you ask us politely.

3. The class elected him president because he is fair and dependable.

4. She went along although she wished later that she had stayed at home.

5. If we want peace in the world, we must become messengers of peace.

6. Although they can't afford their own house, the newlyweds say that they are perfectly happy.

Review I: Lessons 1 - 3

1. The law officers thought that the James brothers had robbed the train.

2. All new cars now have air bags because air bags save lives.

3. The flight attendants were helping passengers who had been overcome by smoke.

4. If we go to the restaurant where Bruce works, I think that we should take the new bridge that was opened last week.

5. The guide told us that the man who rings the church bells every day lives under the church.

6. Although Mrs. Neal knew a man whose horse was running in the Derby, she could not get tickets.

7. Unless the Wildcats can find new energy, they will not have the kind of season that many fans anticipated.

8. Do you know that that *that* that that student pointed to is a direct object?

Unit II

- Compound Sentences
- Gerunds
- Participles

Standing one on another, the four "musicians" bellow, but bellowing is not singing.

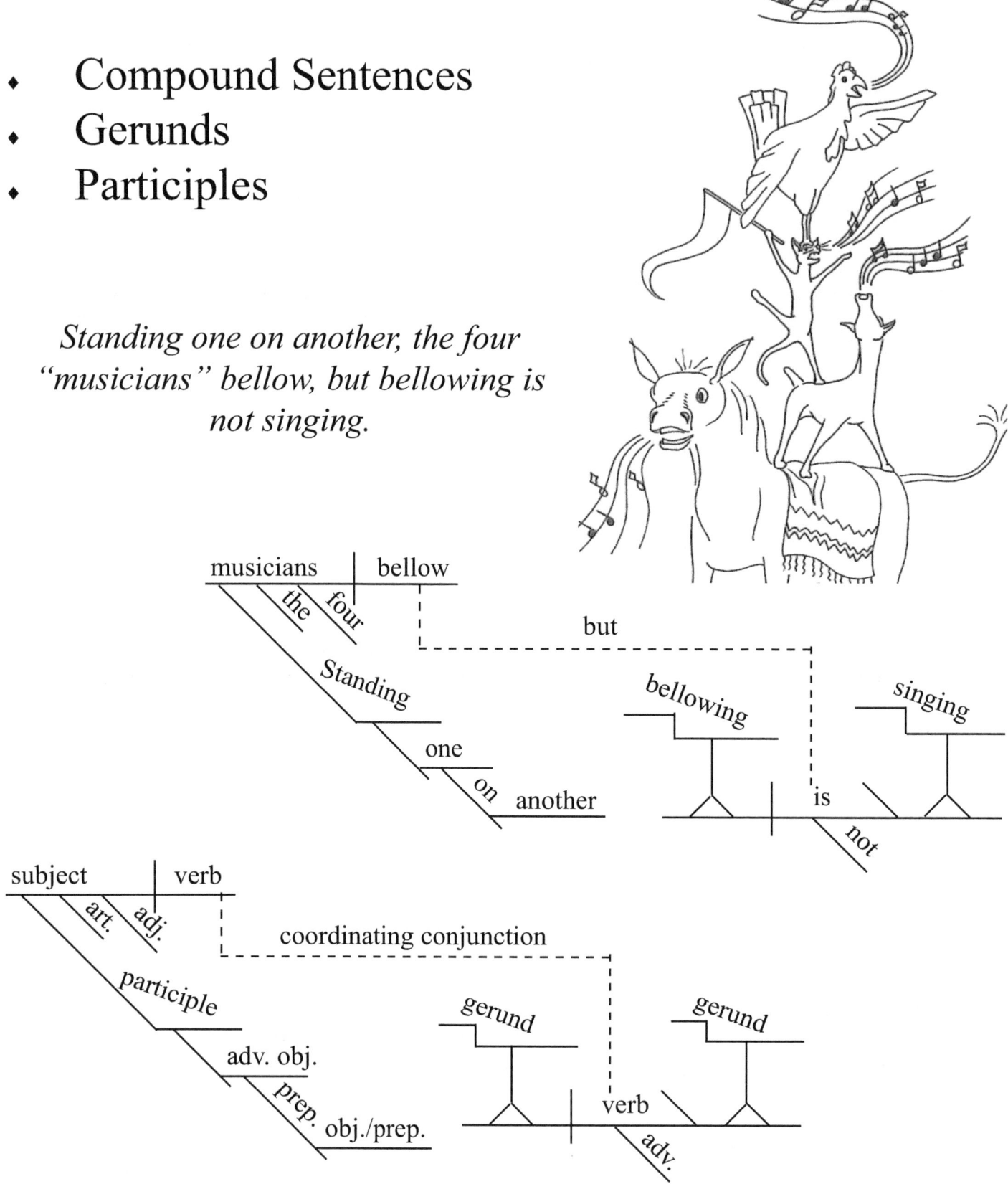

Lesson 4: Compound Sentences

Sentences that contain two or more independent clauses (main clauses) are called compound sentences. In such sentences, coordinating conjunctions such as *and, or, but,* and *either . . . or* may connect independent clauses with each other. Here are two compound sentences: *Jack and Jill went up the hill, but Jack fell down and broke his crown. Either the suspect will come out or the police will go in after him.*

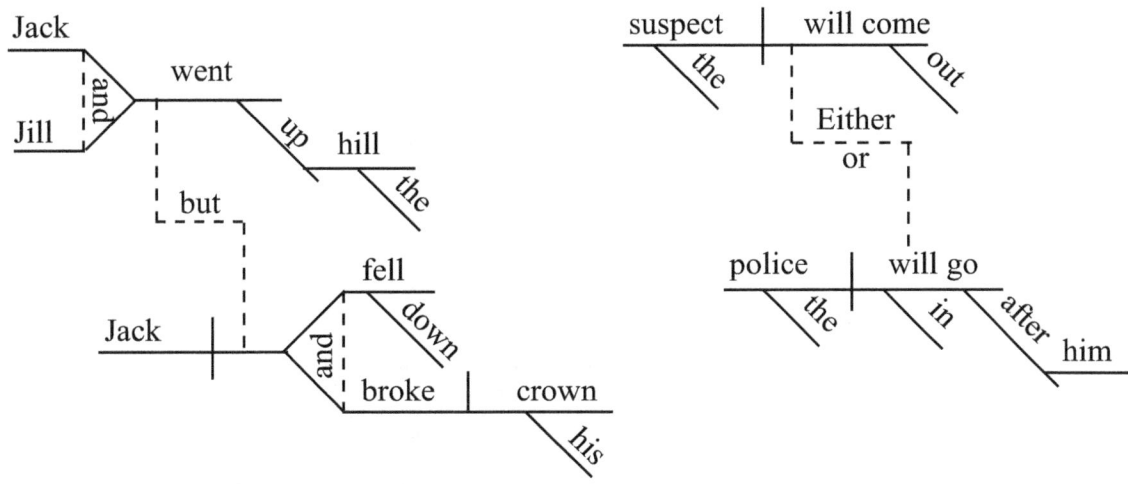

Now it's your turn to diagram compound sentences.

1. The men went outside, but the women stayed in the cabin.

2. Stephen almost never reads or watches TV, and he does not enjoy outdoor activities.

3. Either you learn algebra this year, or you must repeat the course next year.

4. Someone was sitting in my seat, and that made me angry.

5. The students collected hundreds of baskets of holiday food, but snow delayed delivery until the first week of January.

6. Either the Roths will visit us in the States, or we will travel to Germany and visit them.

~ 79 ~

Lesson 5: Gerunds

A gerund is a verbal noun. As a noun, it can be a subject, a predicate nominative, a direct object, an object of a preposition, etc. As a verb it can have a direct object, an indirect object, a predicate nominative, etc.; it can also be modified by an adverb or an adverbial prepositional phrase. All gerunds end in -ing. Here are some sentences containing gerunds: *Swimming fast is fun. Seeing is believing. How far can you run without becoming tired? They enjoy playing volleyball at the beach. She earns extra money by repairing bicycles.* These sentences are diagrammed as follows:

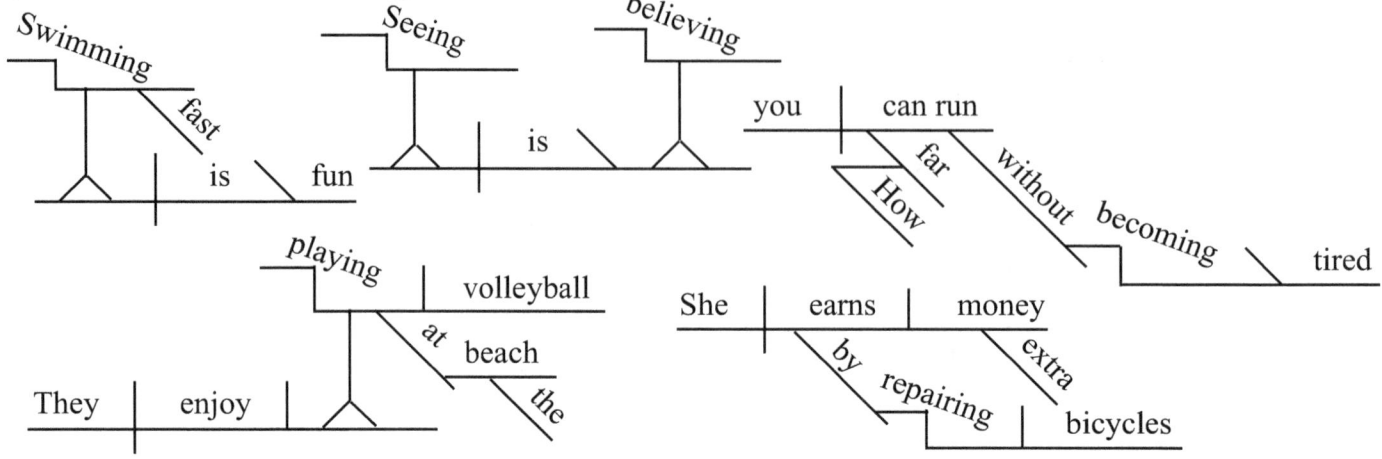

When diagramming, place all gerunds and gerund phrases on pedestals unless the gerund or the gerund phrase is the object of a preposition.

Now it's your turn to diagram gerunds.

1. Do you like taking schoolbooks home?

2. My hobby is raising tropical fish.

3. Both he and his sister have always talked about the joys of being a student.

4. She thinks that smoking in public places is impolite.

5. Flying is faster, but traveling by train has some definite advantages.

6. They may call cheating clever, but I call it hurting oneself.

~ 80 ~

Lesson 6: Participles

Participles are verbs that also function as adjectives. Transitive verbs (verbs that take direct objects) have five participles: present active (*giving*), present passive (*being given*), present-perfect active (*having given*), present-perfect passive (*having been given*), and past (*given*). Here are some sentences that use participles: *Hearing the midnight bells, Cinderella ran from the palace. His words, heard around the world, brought a message of peace and love. Having given generously to the poor, she had a very merry Christmas. Mrs. Thomas shouted at the children playing baseball in the street.* These sentences are diagrammed like this:

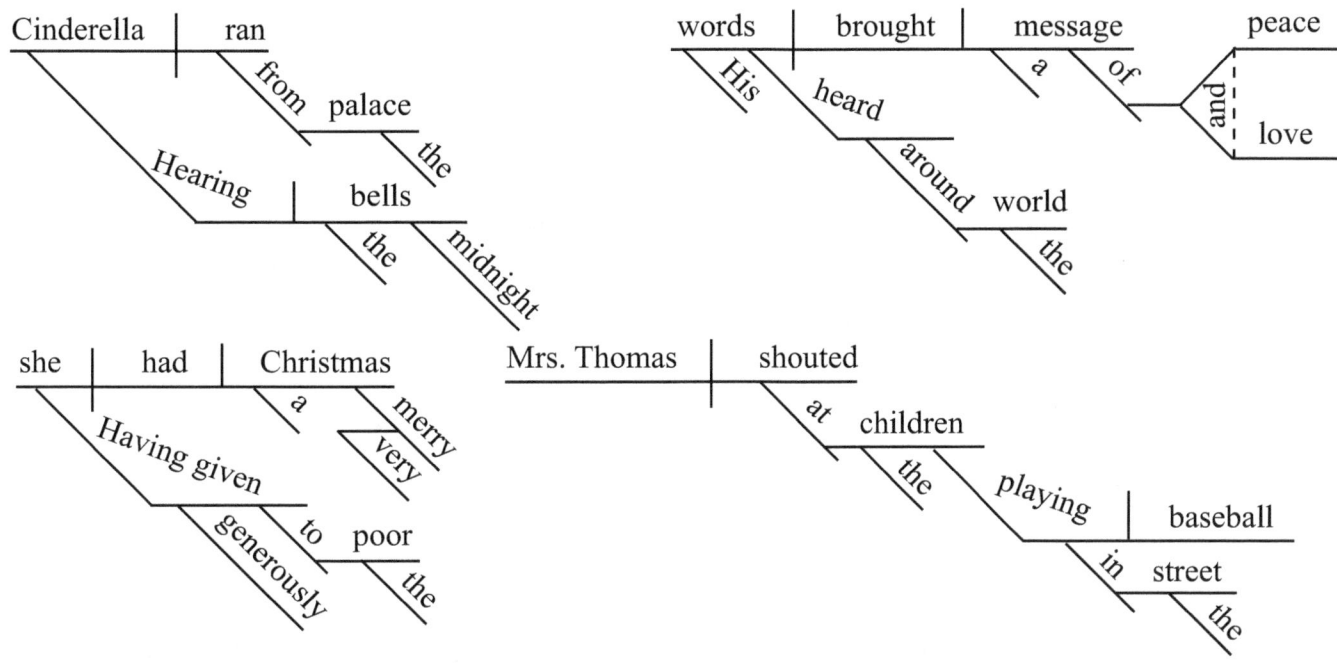

Now it's your turn to diagram participles.

1. Having touched the poison ivy, I immediately went inside and washed my hands.

2. The people waiting in the long line were becoming impatient.

3. The only beverages served at the dinner were coffee, tea, and milk.

4. Having killed seven flies with one swat, the little tailor considered himself brave.

5. A spokesman for the hospital told reporters that the coaches and players injured in Friday's bus accident are doing well.

6. Covered with mud from head to toe, the spelunkers wished that they could shower and change clothes.

Review II: Lessons 4 - 6

1. Men wearing raincoats and women carrying umbrellas rushed from store to store and bought last-minute presents.

2. William says that reading is fun, but he thinks that watching TV is a bore.

3. Working alone in her attic studio, Tara, an artist, enjoys creating things that most other people have never imagined.

4. Diagramming compound sentences is easy, but diagramming gerunds and participles is hard.

5. In the spring and summer, the kids earned extra money by cutting grass, and in the wintertime they shoveled snow.

6. Having been spotted by the police, the burglar hid in a garage owned by the mayor.

7. The exchange student from Australia is shy, but she enjoys playing in the school orchestra and working on the literary magazine.

8. If Himalayan lakes, fed by rapidly melting glaciers, burst their banks, many thousands of people will die.

Unit III

- Infinitives
- Noun Clauses (2)
- Adverb Clauses (2)

Do you know why the princess begins to clap when she sees a man carrying a goose?

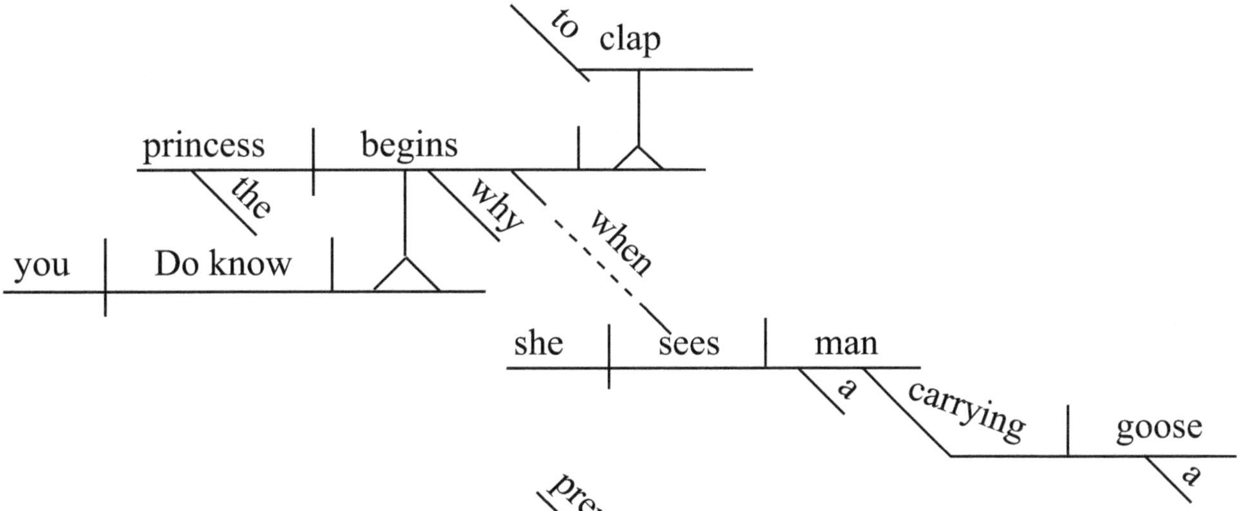

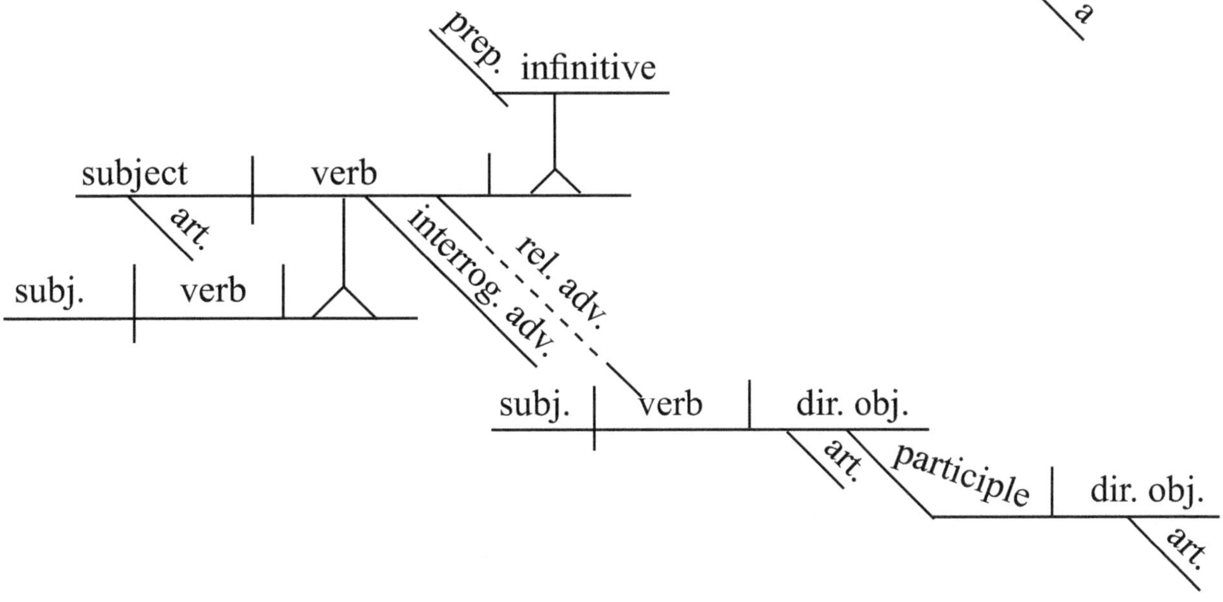

Lesson 7: Infinitives

Infinitives are verb forms that are usually preceded by the preposition *to*. Infinitives have tense (present and present perfect) and voice (active and passive): *to build* **(present active),** *to be built* **(present passive),** *to have built* **(present-perfect active), and** *to have been built* **(present-perfect passive). Infinitives can be used as nouns, adjectives, and adverbs.** On this page we will consider present active infinitives used as nouns --as subjects, predicate nominatives, direct objects, and appositives. Here are some examples: *To raise healthy, happy children is every parent's goal. Our intention was to stay until the end of the game. The girls want to play soccer or volleyball. It is a pleasure to serve you.*

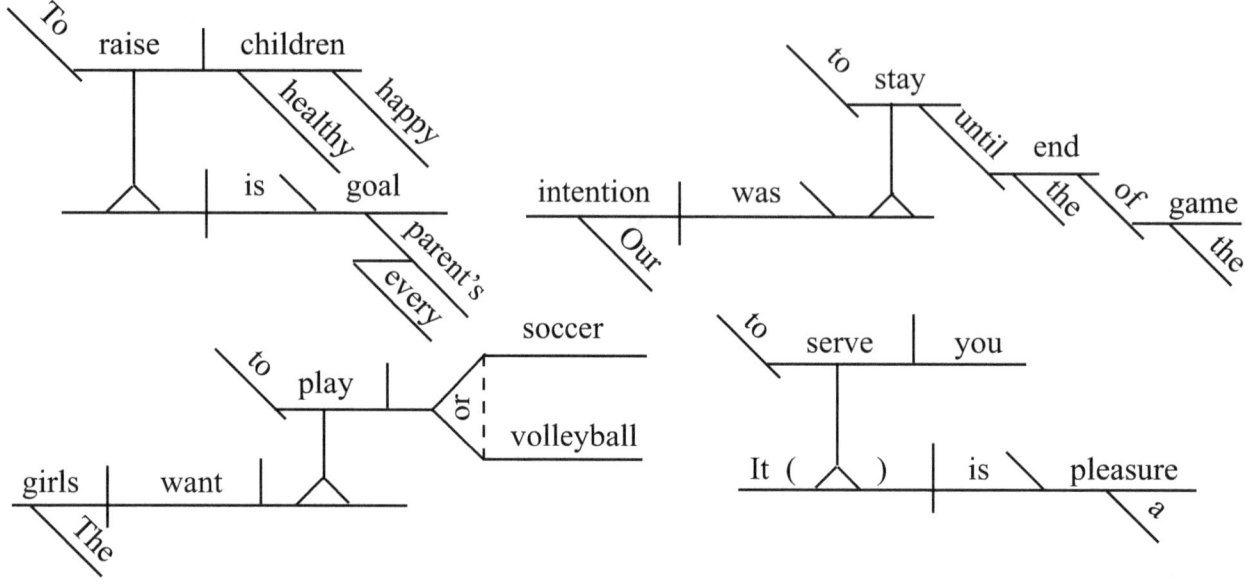

Now it's your turn to diagram infinitives used as nouns.

1. Amelie, a friend of Johanna, likes to ride horses, but Johanna likes to surf.

2. We like snow because it is fun to throw snowballs at our parents.

3. Pam's ambition is to become an astronaut.

4. Dave and Tom told me that they want to watch TV this morning.

5. Hoping to see the northern lights, Joan ventured out into the cold Minnesota night.

6. Traveling to faraway places is delightful, but it is always nice to come home.

Lesson 8: Noun Clauses (2)

Some noun clauses are introduced by the expletive *that* **(Lesson 2), while others are introduced by interrogative words like** *who, whom, whose, which, what, why, where, when,* **and** *how.* **On this page we will consider the latter clauses used as subjects, predicate nominatives, direct objects, and objects of prepositions.** Here are several examples: *How the Marlins beat the Yankees is a mystery to Yankee fans. I wonder what my dad would do. The article focuses on where wolves live. The question is which invitation I should accept.*

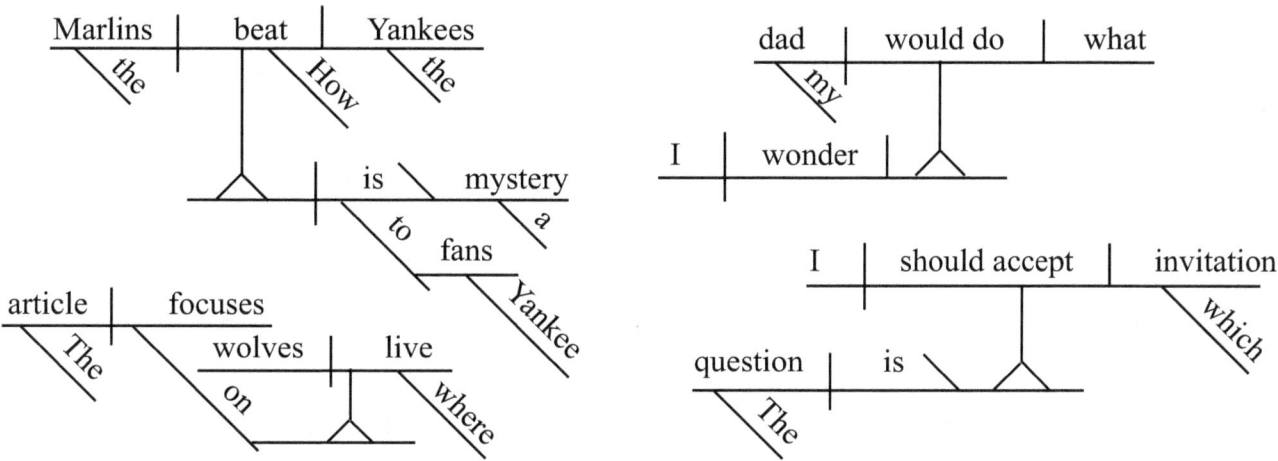

Now it's your turn to diagram noun clauses introduced by interrogative words.

1. Some friendly hikers told us how we could get to the nearest ranger station.

2. A naturalist whom we met on the trail explained why bears hibernate.

3. The three bears wondered who had eaten Baby Bear's porridge.

4. The question is where they want to have the wedding.

5. The writer was curious about why writers sometimes find writing difficult.

6. How the universe came into being is a subject that interests everyone.

~ 85 ~

Lesson 9: Adverb Clauses (2)

The relative adverbs *before, after, until, when, while*, and *as* are used to introduce adverbial clauses of time. In many books, these relative adverbs are lumped together with *since, because, although*, etc. and called subordinating conjunctions; however, I prefer to distinguish between relative adverbs and subordinating conjunctions. For a more complete explanation of relative adverbs, please refer to "Part Three" of this book.

When relative adverbs *introduce adverb clauses of time, they* are diagrammed like subordinating conjunctions, with which you are already familiar, except that both ends of the diagonal line upon which the relative adverb rests are solid, not broken. Here are two sentences with relative adverbs: *Before she came to this school, she attended a school in another state. The children stood and greeted the principal when she entered the room.*

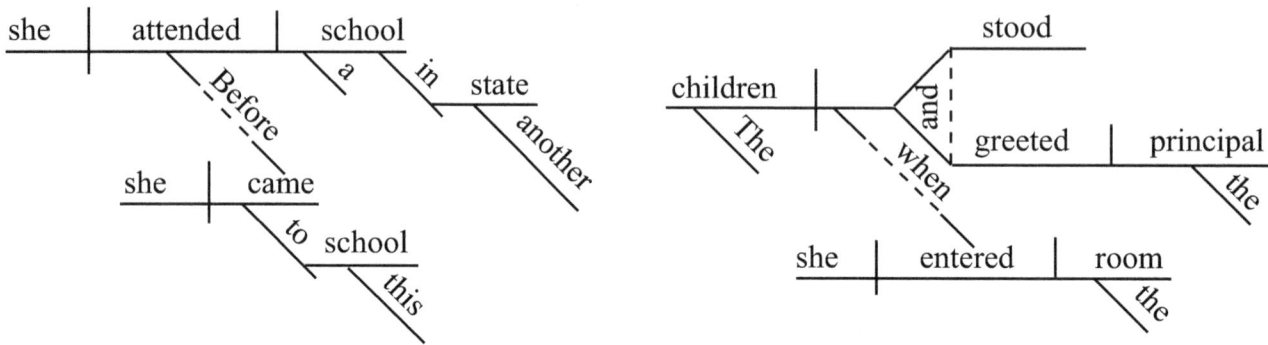

Now it's your turn to diagram relative adverbs of time.

1. Hannah promised to do that when she returns.

2. We should wait until the people who are bringing the dessert arrive.

3. While we were waiting for the bus, Beth and Jenny drove by and waved.

4. As you leave, don't forget to greet the people sitting by the door.

5. After the couple had spent two weeks in southern India, they decided to travel to Sri Lanka, a nearby island country.

6. It has been said that we will not have peace among nations until we have peace among individuals.

Review III: Lessons 7 - 9

1. His job is to decide how the company can improve its public image as it moves into the twenty-first century.

2. Josh said that he would begin working before I could count to a million.

3. As our country struggles against an epidemic of obesity, it is unclear why some schools continue to sell junk foods.

4. When bicyclists wanted to bike on popular mountain trails, hikers said that the paths were too narrow.

5. The speaker, a forest ranger, explained why it is not a good idea to keep a wolf in the house.

6. After she had stared at the question for a long time, the youngster finally remembered how one converts Fahrenheit to Celsius.

Unit IV

- Compound-complex Sentences
- Comparisons
- The Expletive *There*

There are seven dead flies, and the little tailor thinks that he is braver than others because he killed them with one blow.

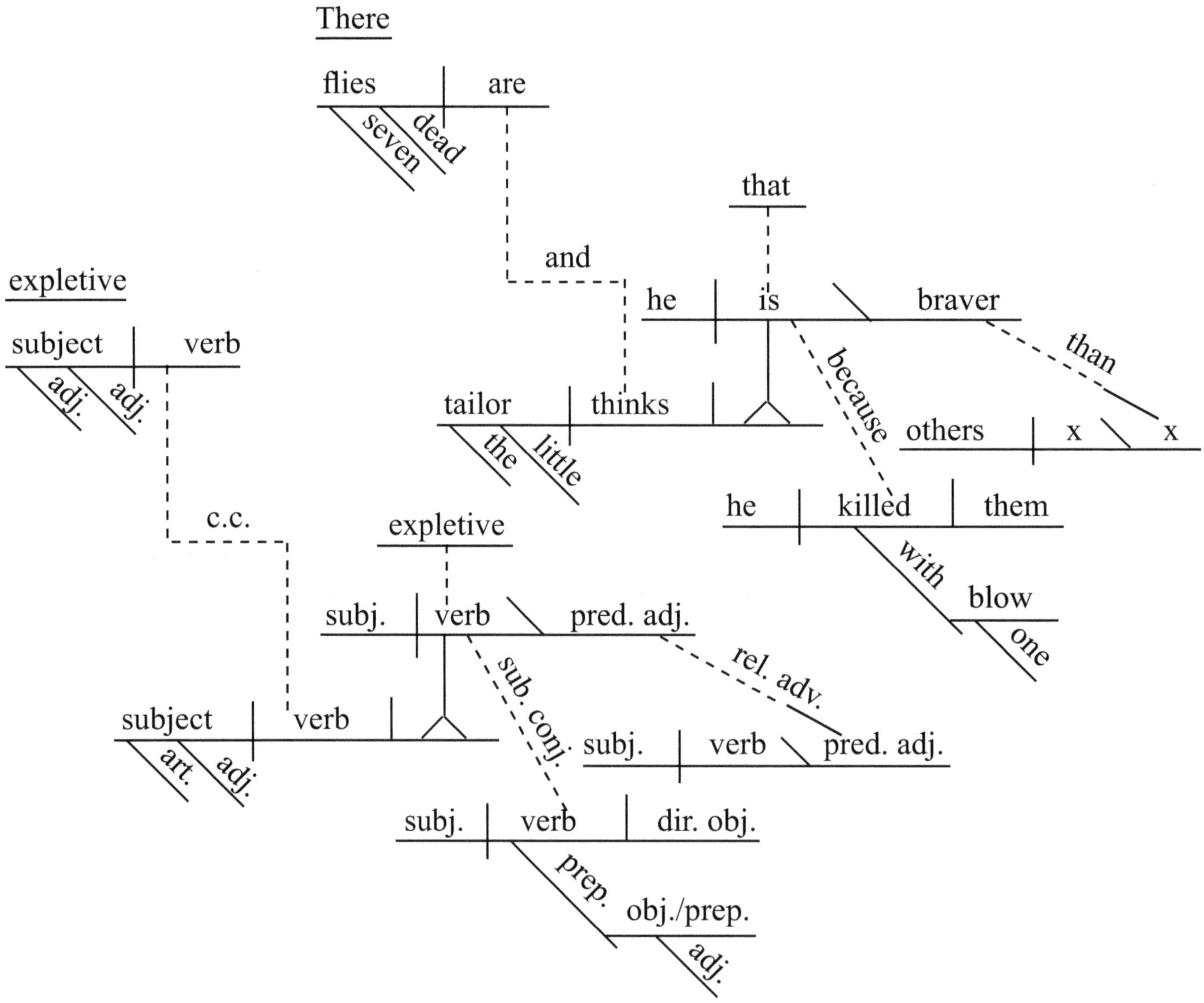

Lesson 10: Compound-complex Sentences

Sentences that contain at least one dependent (subordinate) clause are called complex sentences. Complex sentences that contain two or more independent clauses are called compound-complex sentences. Adverb clauses, adjective clauses, and even noun clauses are all dependent clauses. Here are two examples of compound-complex sentences: *If we go, I can drive, and if we stay home, you can make some popcorn. Before we begin building a soapbox car, you boys must clean the garage, and Sandy must get the wood that we will need.*

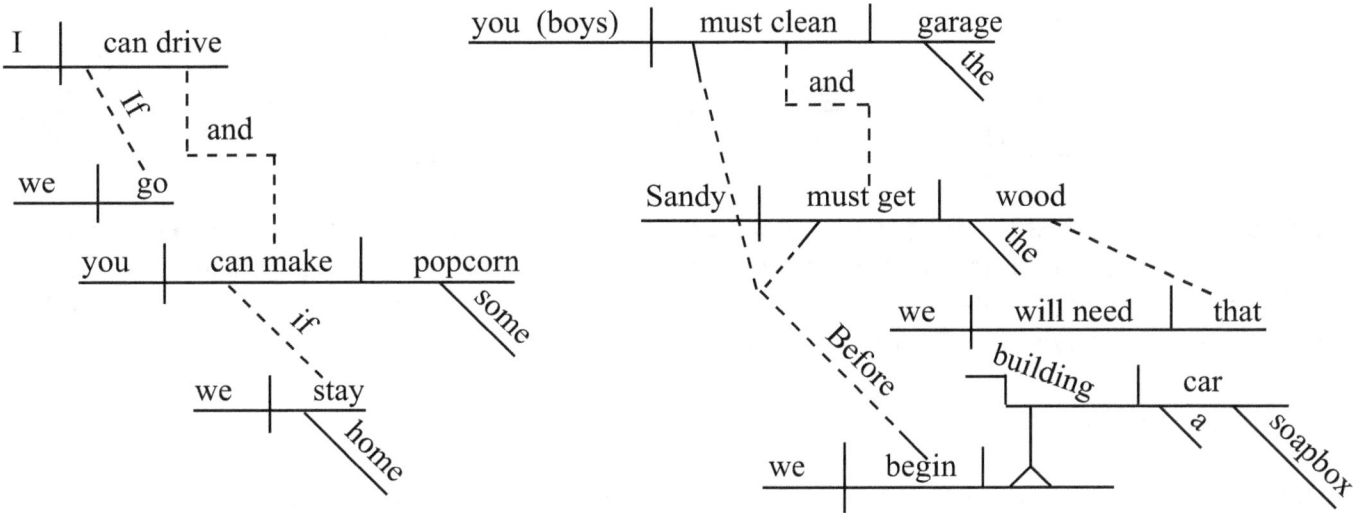

Now it's your turn to diagram compound-complex sentences.

1. Did we buy an expensive camera while I wasn't looking, or did the Alveys forget to take their Nikon with them?

2. Children, if you want to have a party, I will bring cookies and drinks, and you must throw all scraps in the trash.

3. Give the pencil to the person to whom it belongs, or I must insist that you stay after school.

4. If we really want to have peace among individuals and among nations, you must want peace, and I must want it, too.

5. We will go outside and play soccer if the sun shines, but we will stay inside and work on our art project if it rains.

Lesson 11: Comparisons

There are two kinds of comparisons: equal comparisons and unequal comparisons. Here are four examples (two of the former and two of the latter): *She is as fast as he. I can jump as high as you. He is taller than she. They have traveled more than most people.* These sentences are diagrammed as follows:

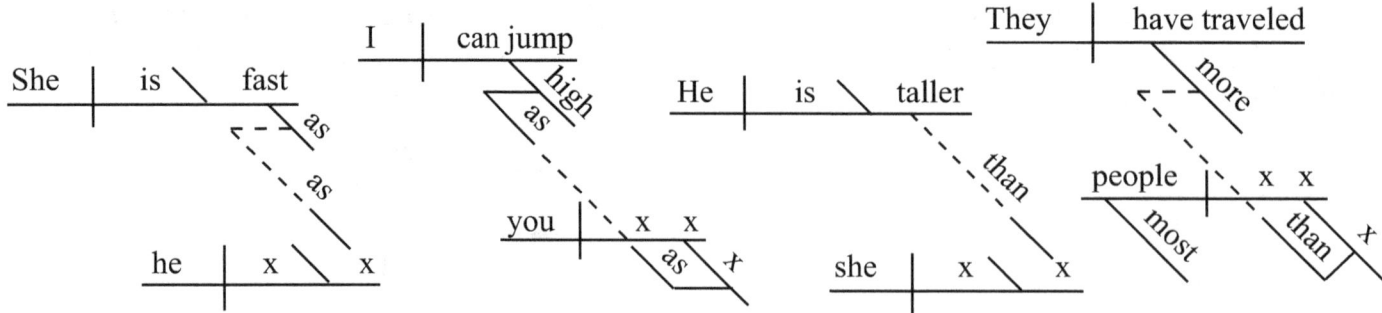

The second *as* in the first two sentences and *than* in the third and fourth sentences are relative adverbs. The x's stand for unexpressed (but understood) words. In the first sentence they stand for *is fast*, in the second for *can jump high*, in the third for *is tall*, and in the fourth for *have traveled much*. For more information about relative adverbs, see "Part Three" of this book.

Now it's your turn to diagram equal and unequal comparisons.

1. This canyon is deeper than that one.

2. You can work as hard as anyone.

3. Some of my friends know José, who is a better shortstop than Miguel.

4. Although Danielle is my friend, I must admit that she talks more than anyone.

5. She likes him more than me.

6. Your friend is not as friendly as you.

7. If you want to be healthy, you must eat more vegetables than sweets.

~ 90 ~

Lesson 12: The Expletive *There*

The word *there* is an expletive (a word with a function but no meaning) in the sentences *There is someone at the door* and *There is a good reason for not smoking*. The subjects of these sentences are *someone* and *reason*, as you can see from these diagrams:

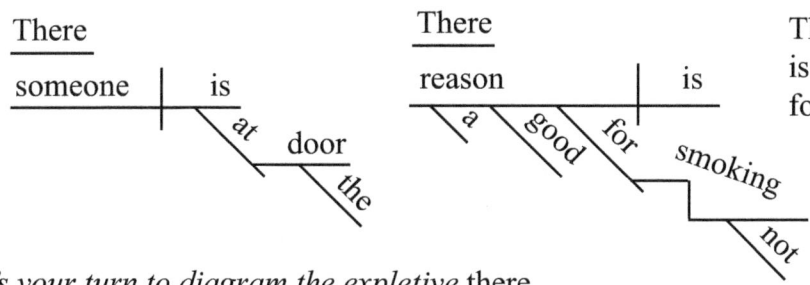

The function of the expletive *there* is to announce that the subject will follow the verb.

Now it's your turn to diagram the expletive there.

1. There will be many people there.

2. Waiter, there is a fly in my soup.

3. Why are there so many people who have so little food?

4. Is there nothing faster than the speed of light?

5. The child complained because there was no dessert.

6. There are those who like the Cardinals, and there are those who like the Wildcats.

7. Look carefully at the words on the board, and you will see that there is no *there* there.

Review IV: Lessons 10 - 12

1. Matt is taller than his father, but his sister Maggie is taller than he.

2. There are people who like to lead, and there are people who like to follow.

3. Mile for mile, driving is more dangerous than flying, and there is ample statistical evidence for this.

4. There are some students who enjoy studying, but most students find that it is more enjoyable to play video games than to do homework.

5. There is someone in this room who is older than you, or I am a monkey's uncle.

6. There are not many marathoners who play football, but running a marathon takes as much courage as playing football.

Unit V

- Adjective Clauses (2)
- Phrasal Verbs
- Infinitives (2)

The hungry wolf says that he is eager to help out Grandmother, which Red Riding Hood foolishly believes.

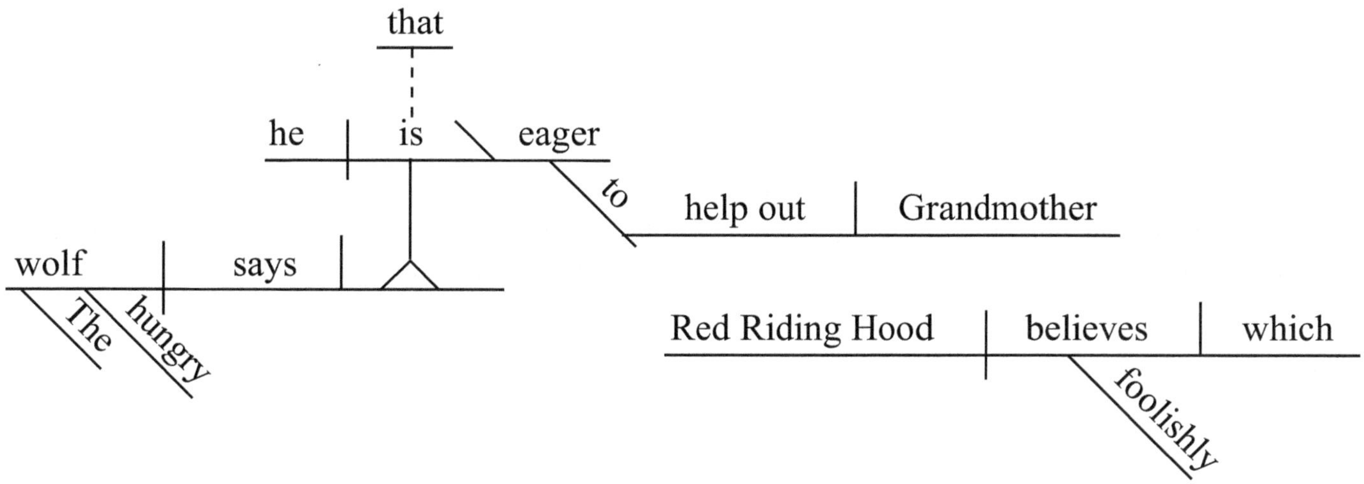

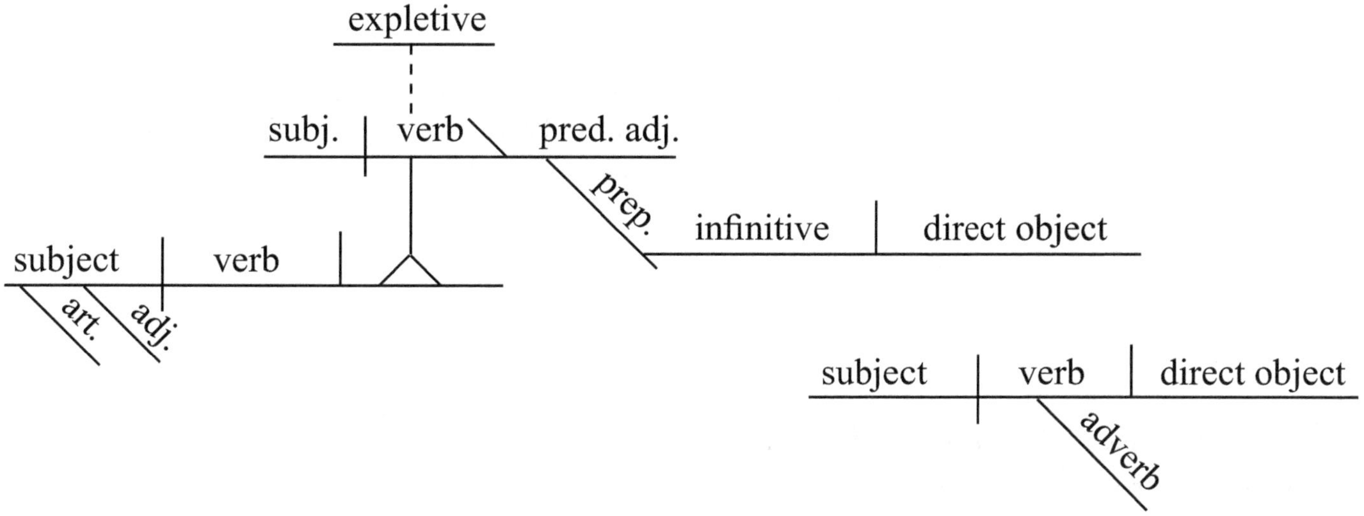

~ 93 ~

Lesson 13: Adjective Clauses (2)

Sometimes the relative pronoun *which* has an entire clause as its antecedent. When this is the case, one draws no line at all between the relative pronoun and its antecedent. Here is an example: *Mom and Dad promised to take Christina and me along, which made us very happy.*

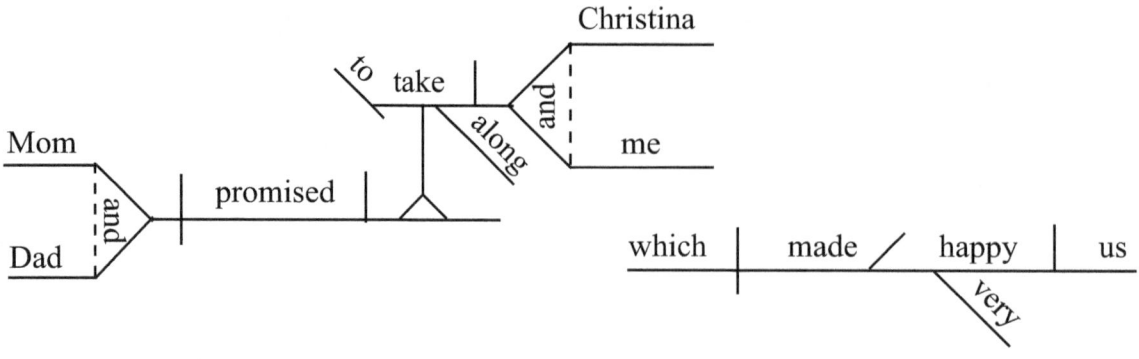

Now it's your turn to diagram relative pronouns with clausal antecedents.

1. Chris continuously taps his pencil on his desk, which annoys me greatly.

2. It snowed yesterday and the schools canceled classes, which made the students happy.

3. The dog ate my book, which meant that I couldn't do my homework.

4. News came of the birth of a grandson, which brightened the old man's day considerably.

5. Sophia played hard defensively and took open shots, which is all that her coach had asked of her.

6. Antarctica is becoming warmer, which explains why a Delaware-sized ice shelf recently separated from the continent.

7. A Thai woman pictured in *National Geographic* can hold a king cobra's head in her mouth, which amazes tourists.

Lesson 14: Phrasal Verbs

A phrasal verb is a verb whose meaning cannot be known from the separate meanings of the words that comprise it, for example, *look up* in the sentence *I must look up that word in a dictionary* and *pick up* in the sentence *Mrs. Collins picks up her children each day after school.* The particle *up* is part of each verb as the following diagrams show.

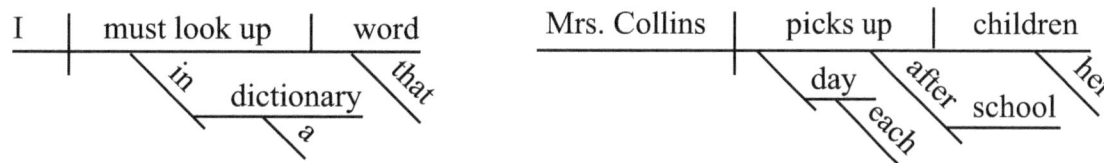

If *up* were an adverb in the first sentence, one would be able to rephrase the sentence as *Up I looked the word.* If it were a preposition, one could say *Up the word I looked* without changing the meaning of the sentence. Since both tests fail, *look up* in this sentence is a phrasal verb. Of course, *look up* is not a phrasal verb in all sentences. *Up* is an adverb in the sentence *I looked up and saw an airplane* and a preposition in the sentence *The child looked up the chimney to see if Santa was coming down.*

Now it's your turn to diagram phrasal verbs.

1. While Angie was standing in line, she passed out.

2. He no longer wore the gloves that he had worn out.

3. Brittany and Scott argue sometimes, but they always make up quickly.

4. The tired campers ate early and turned in before sunset.

5. They tried not to give in to temptations.

6. The unconscious player came to on the way to the hospital.

7. The ambassador asserted that he would carry out the mission that the president had entrusted to him.

8. Excited by the thought of seeing Simon and Garfunkel in person, thousands of fans turned out for the free concert in Central Park.

Lesson 15: Infinitives (2)

Infinitives and infinitive phrases can function not only as nouns (Lesson 7) but also as adjectives and adverbs. As adjectives, they modify nouns; as adverbs, they modify verbs, adjectives, and adverbs. Two sentences that use infinitives as modifiers of nouns are *There was nothing to do* and *She had no desire to fly*.

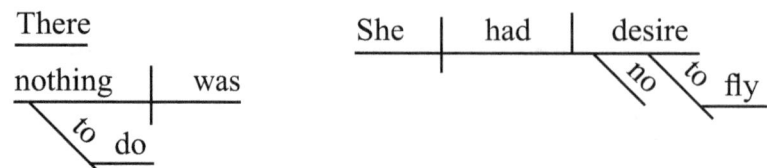

Infinitive phrases modify a verb, an adjective, and an adverb, respectively, in the sentences *They drove to California to see the giant redwoods*, *That is hard to say without lisping*, and *He arrived too late to shop carefully*.

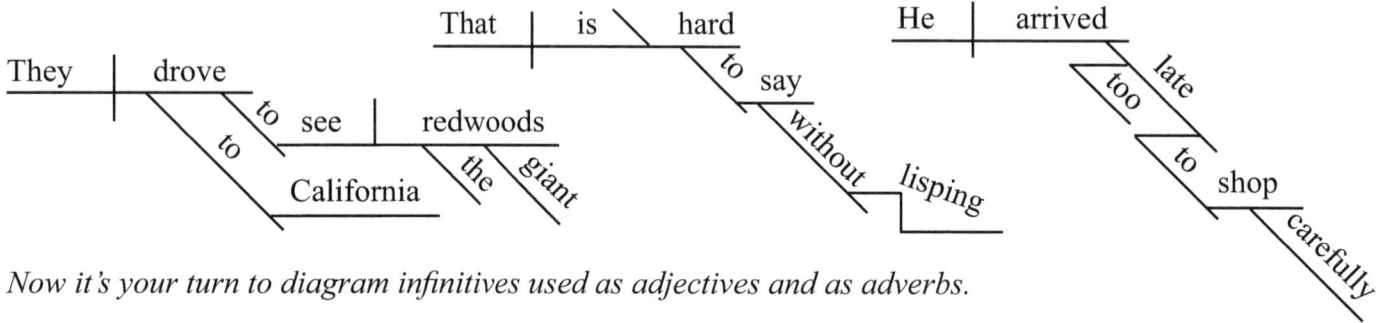

Now it's your turn to diagram infinitives used as adjectives and as adverbs.

1. The question is easy to understand but hard to answer.

2. I prefer to stay home this evening because I have no reason to go anywhere.

3. The jets flew too low to be seen by radar. (The infinitive in this sentence is in the passive voice.)

4. Highway workers put fences along some highways to protect them from high drifts of snow.

5. The accordion hanging on the wall is the one that my grandfather bought in New York to celebrate his arrival in America.

6. Some musical instruments are easy to play, but all are hard to play well.

Review V: Lessons 13 - 15

1. Both officials called the foul incorrectly, which angered both the coaches and the spectators.

2. We arrived too early to enter the stadium, which gave us time to look up a friend who was living in the vicinity.

3. A flood of cool water shot from the fire hydrant, which made us kids happy on a hot summer afternoon.

4. Stace has worked out regularly for two years, which has made him a much better athlete.

5. In 1932, Amelia Earhart became the first woman to fly alone across the Atlantic, which gave encouragement to other women interested in flying.

6. Kristen, an amateur mushroom hunter, set out to find mushrooms for dinner, but I hoped that she would find nothing.

Unit VI

- **Unexpressed Words**
- **Complementary Infinitives**
- **Phrasal Prepositions and Conjunctions**

So that the fish he had caught would change his cottage into a palace, the fisherman had to release the fish instead of eating it.

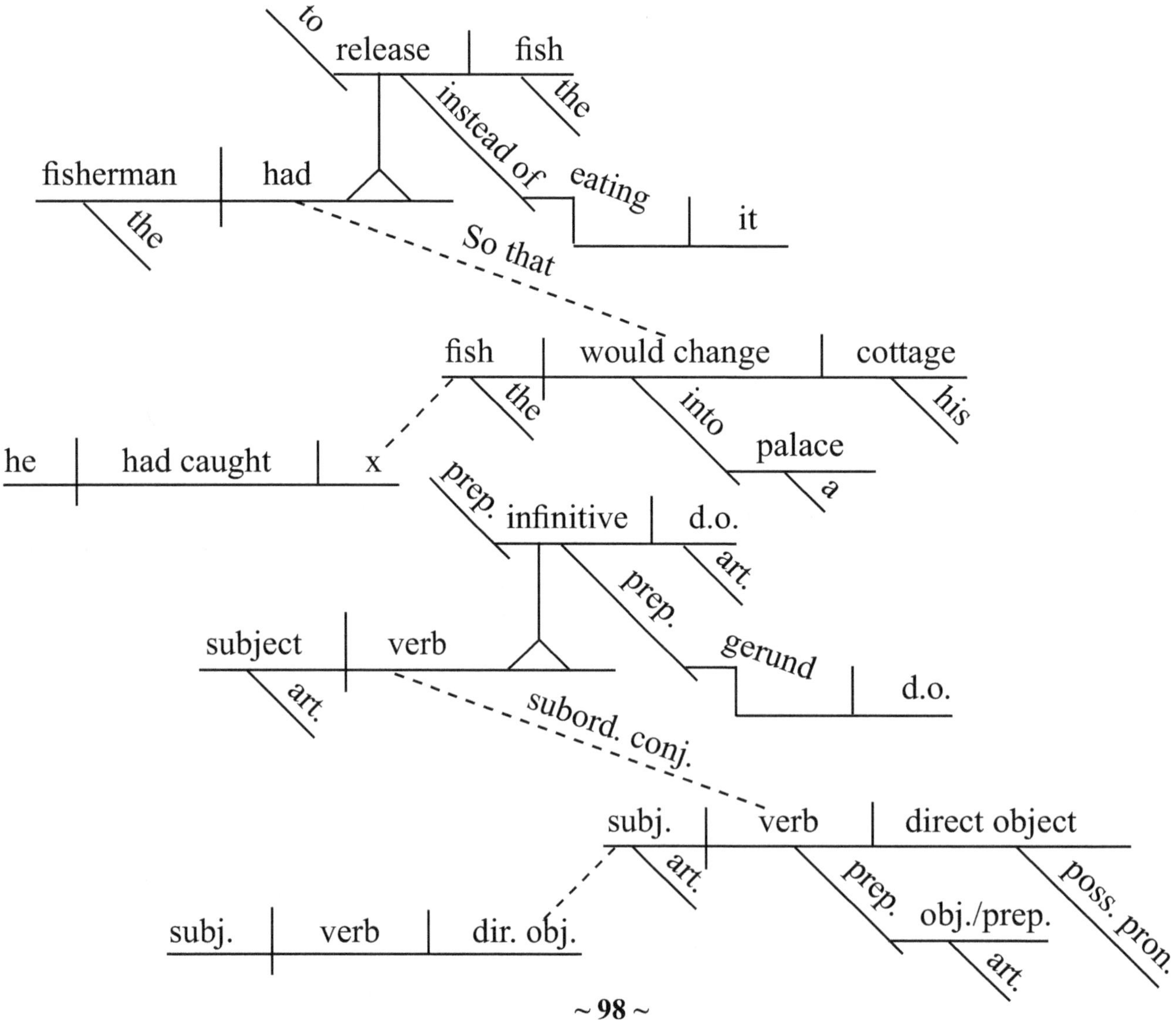

Lesson 16: Unexpressed Words

The expletive *that* and the relative pronouns *whom* and *that* are sometimes unexpressed. An unexpressed expletive or relative pronoun is represented in a diagram by an x. The sentence *I didn't know you were here* has an unexpressed expletive, and the sentence *The girl you met is Joey's sister* has an unexpressed relative pronoun. These sentences are diagrammed as follows:

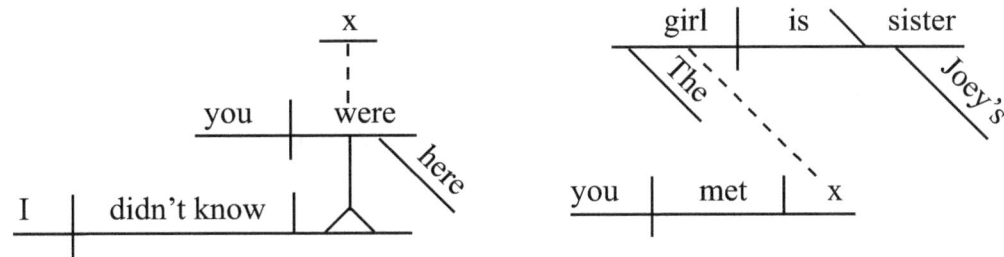

Now it's your turn to diagram the unexpressed expletive that *and unexpressed relative pronouns.*

1. That is the person I was talking about.

2. I didn't know they lived in this part of town.

3. The people we talked to just now were childhood friends of mine.

4. By talking to the woman Mr. Evans works for, she found out he is planning to retire soon.

5. He said he hoped you would find a job that you like.

6. Tara said she knows why you didn't call.

7. The poor princess knew the king intended to marry her off to the first bachelor he encountered.

~ 99 ~

Lesson 17: Complementary Infinitives

Infinitives in phrases like *are to read, am going to study, have come to think, used to enjoy, have to stay,* and *ought to listen* are so closely associated with the accompanying verbs that, in diagrams, no line separates the two. These infinitives are called complementary infinitives. Here are two examples: *You ought to study. We are going to sit here and talk.*

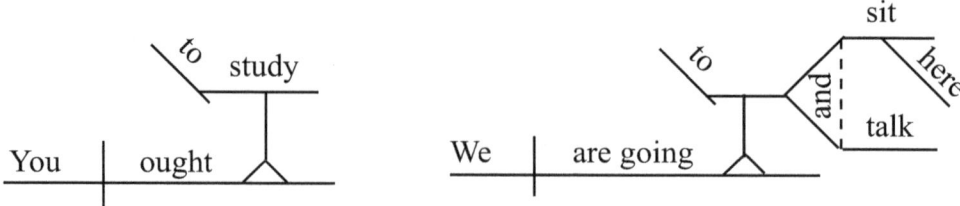

Now it's your turn to diagram complementary infinitives.

1. Greg used to eat pancakes every morning, but now he prefers Wheaties.

2. Kathleen is to catch the first train in the morning and travel directly to Gloucester.

3. Who knows when we are to board the busses?

4. The principal said the students don't have to go to school if it snows a lot.

5. The thing you have to remember is to treat everyone kindly.

6. Noticing that the wobbly old lady wanted to cross the street, Wesley thought he had to help her.

7. Theodore knows he ought to say home, but he is going to go out with his friends.

Lesson 18: Phrasal Prepositions and Conjunctions

Phrasal prepositions and conjunctions consist of more than one word. Some phrasal prepositions are *out of, because of, instead of, as for, along with,* **and** *in spite of.* **Some phrasal conjunctions are** *so that, in order that, as if,* **and** *as though.* Of the following sentences, the first has a phrasal preposition, the second a phrasal conjunction: *The drowsy bear came out of its den and looked around. It is fun to give money so that poor children will receive Christmas presents.*

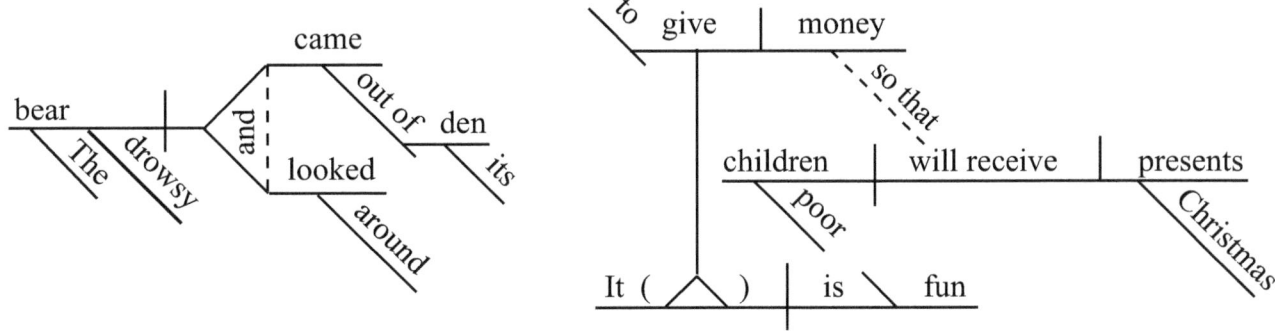

Now it's your turn to diagram phrasal prepositions and phrasal conjunctions.

1. Elka practices the violin as if her life depended on it.

2. Instead of walking to school, Derrick rode the new bicycle that Santa had given him.

3. In spite of her caution, Brandy jumped out of the pan and into the fire.

4. Mrs. Hagan brought along some carrots so that her children might feed the camels and goats.

5. Along with the traditional turkey and dressing, Grandma served peas, fried apples, and pumpkin pie.

6. I know a teacher who took up knitting so that she wouldn't sleep in faculty meetings.

7. Because of the personal nature of his decision, Mr. Lewis avoided telling his students why he had decided to retire.

Review VI: Lessons 16 - 18

1. I think you ought to put off the work you don't like and go to the mall with me.

2. Lindsey used to have to ask her parents for the money she needed to eat out.

3. In order that the Pierces might go to their favorite restaurant, they had to convince their friends of its merits.

4. Because of their desire to visit ten countries in two weeks, the tourists are going to buy the pass recommended by their travel agent.

5. They acted as if they didn't know they were to read the next chapter for today.

6. The victorious boxer stepped out of the ring and into the arms of the fans he had counted on for support.

Unit VII

- Prepositional Phrases as Predicate Adjectives
- Noun Clauses (3)
- Gerunds (2)

One could ask if the duck's pulling the witch into the water means that the duck is in a bad mood.

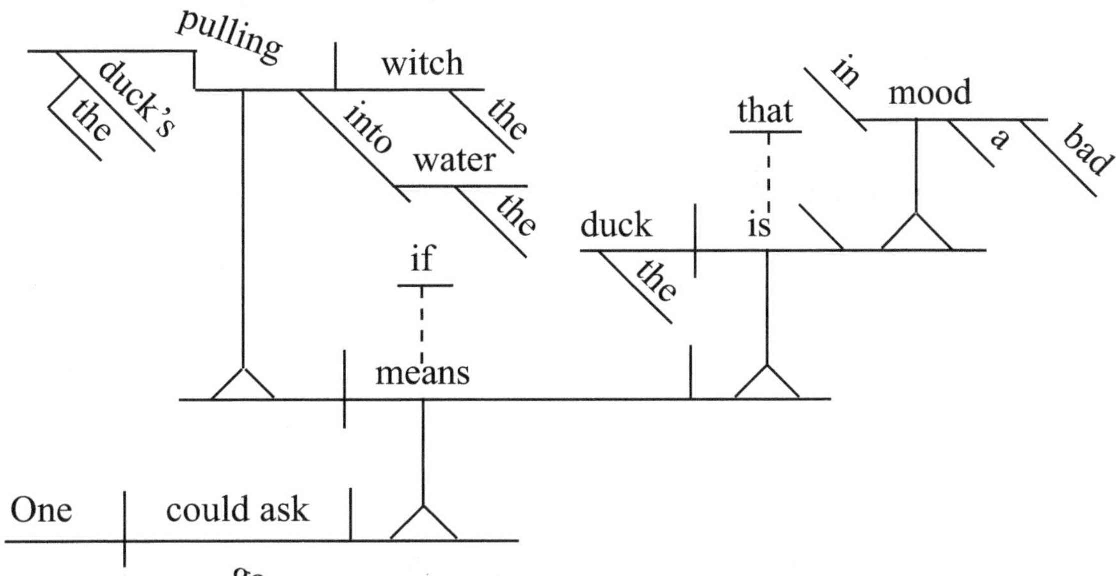

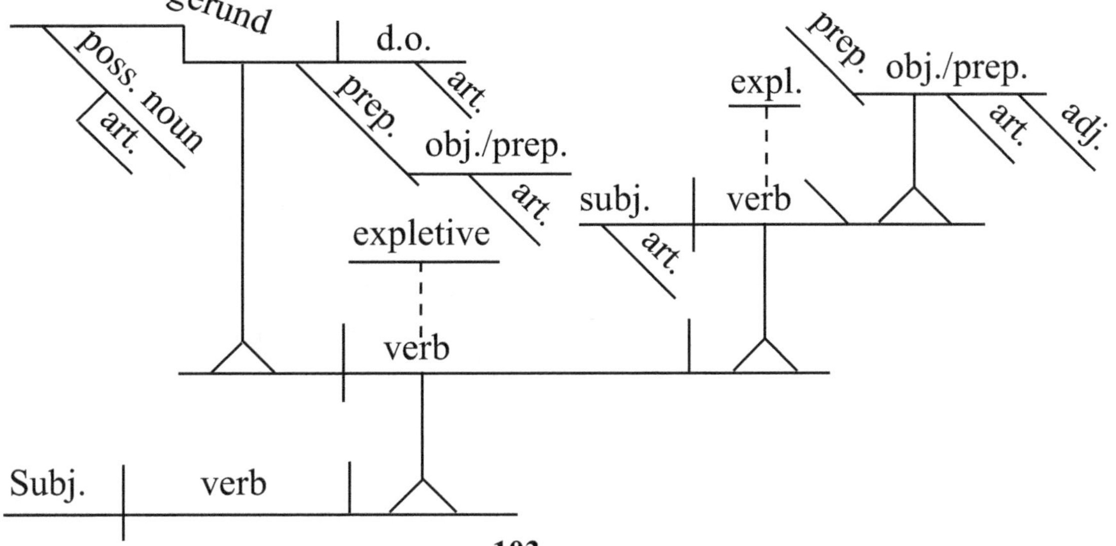

Lesson 19: Prepositional Phrases as Predicate Adjectives

Prepositional phrases that follow linking verbs and describe someone or something function as predicate adjectives. Here are examples: *Grandpa was in a good mood. Theresa thinks that she is without a friend in the world. Last year I started exercising regularly, so that I'd be in better shape.*

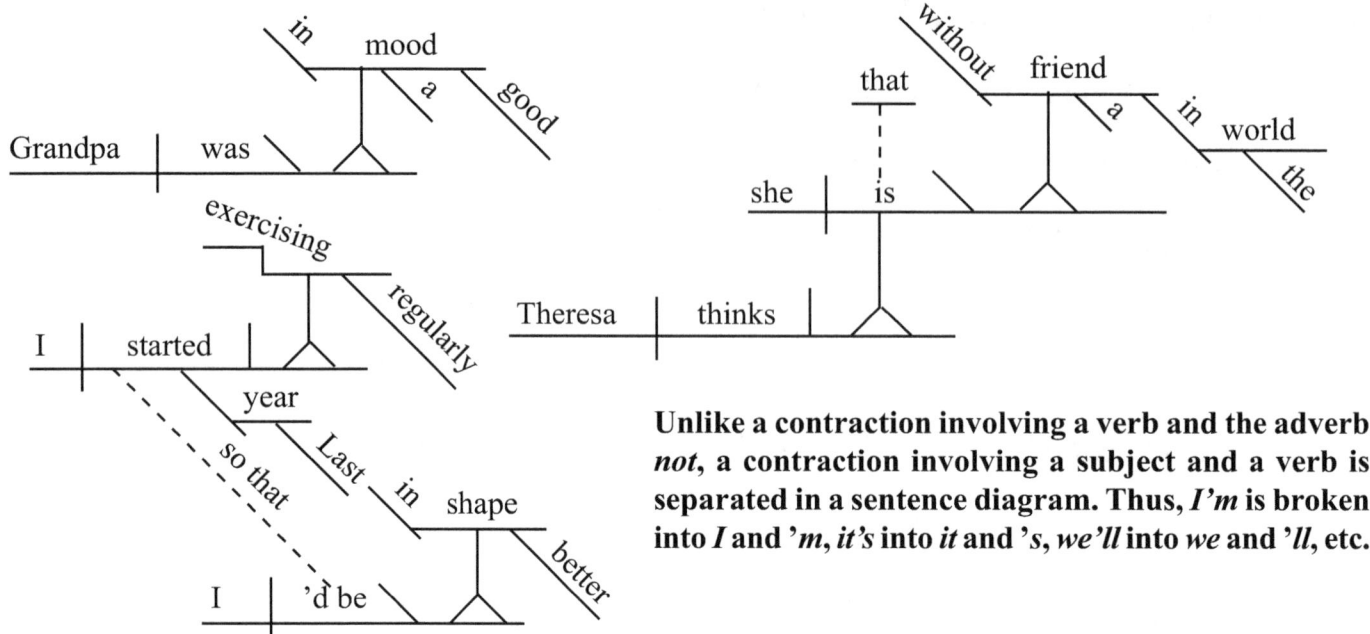

Unlike a contraction involving a verb and the adverb *not*, a contraction involving a subject and a verb is separated in a sentence diagram. Thus, *I'm* is broken into *I* and *'m*, *it's* into *it* and *'s*, *we'll* into *we* and *'ll*, etc.

Now it's your turn to diagram prepositional phrases used as predicate adjectives.

1. The parents were against a change in the student dress code.

2. I used to think you were out of your mind, but now I think you're crazy.

3. The knobs, handles, and hinges are of the same color and texture.

4. I'm sorry to hear that you are under the weather.

5. Although Victor's journal entries, essays, and worksheets show only average talent, his tests are out of the ordinary.

6. Sitting behind the wheel of his Alfa Romeo, Jayce tries to give the impression that he is above everyone else.

Lesson 20: Noun Clauses (3)

Noun clauses can be introduced also by the expletives *whether* and *if* (when *if* means *whether*). These two words introduce indirect questions which, if expressed as a direct questions, could be answered with yes or no. Here are three examples: *The waiter asked whether we wanted a salad. Melissa wondered if Richard had a sister. Their question was whether or not they had enough time.*

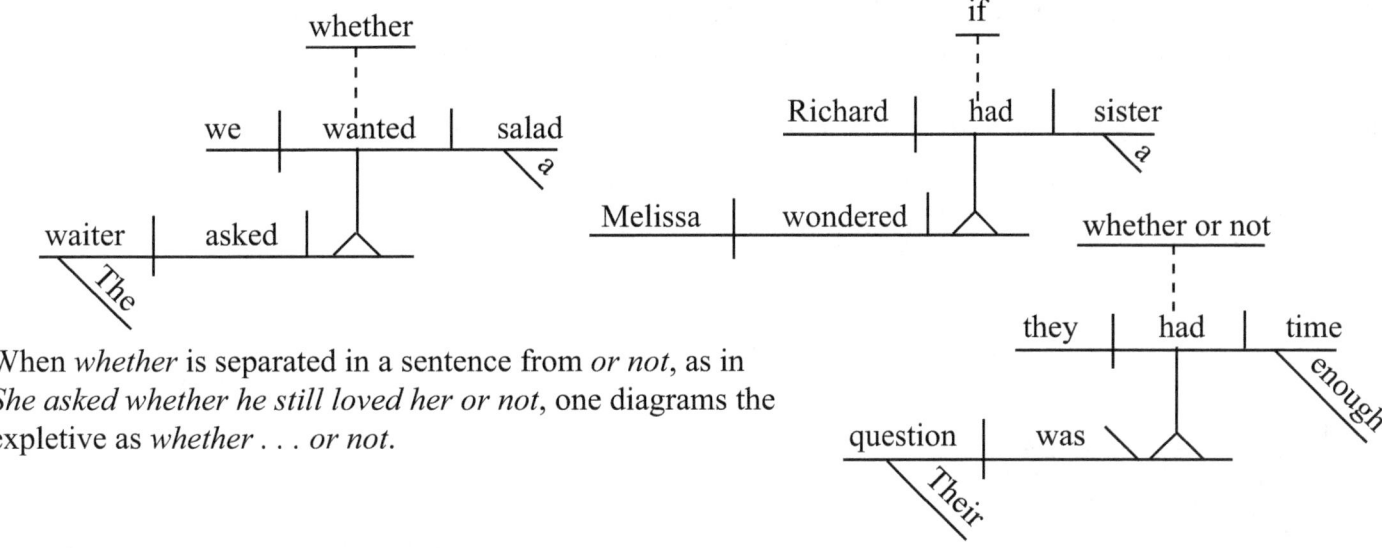

When *whether* is separated in a sentence from *or not*, as in *She asked whether he still loved her or not*, one diagrams the expletive as *whether . . . or not*.

Now it's your turn to diagram the expletives *whether* and *if*.

1. Arriving after midnight, they wondered whether their elderly parents had already gone to bed.

2. Having missed the big game, Joan asked if her favorite team, the Vikings, had won.

3. Heather was worried about whether or not she had remembered to turn off the stove.

4. As the snow fell, the only question on most students' minds was whether or not they would have school the next day.

5. I wonder if the man who changes the light bulbs on the antenna of the Empire State Building enjoys his job.

6. Whether there is intelligent life on other planets is still unknown.

Lesson 21: Gerunds (2)

In Lesson 5, you saw that gerunds can be modified by adverbs and adverbial prepositional phrases. **Since gerunds are verbal nouns, they can be also be modified by adjectival modifiers such as articles, adjectives, possessive nouns, and possessive pronouns.** You will recall that, when diagramming an adverbial modifier of a gerund, you attach its diagonal line to the lower of the two horizontal lines on which the gerund rests. On the other hand, **when the modifier is adjectival, you attach its diagonal line to the upper horizontal line of the gerund.** Here are sentences that contain gerunds modified by adjectival modifiers: *That employer subjects each job applicant to a thorough questioning. Lauren's whistling in class annoyed her classmates. The Lions' victory in the final game made up for their having played poorly in recent weeks.*

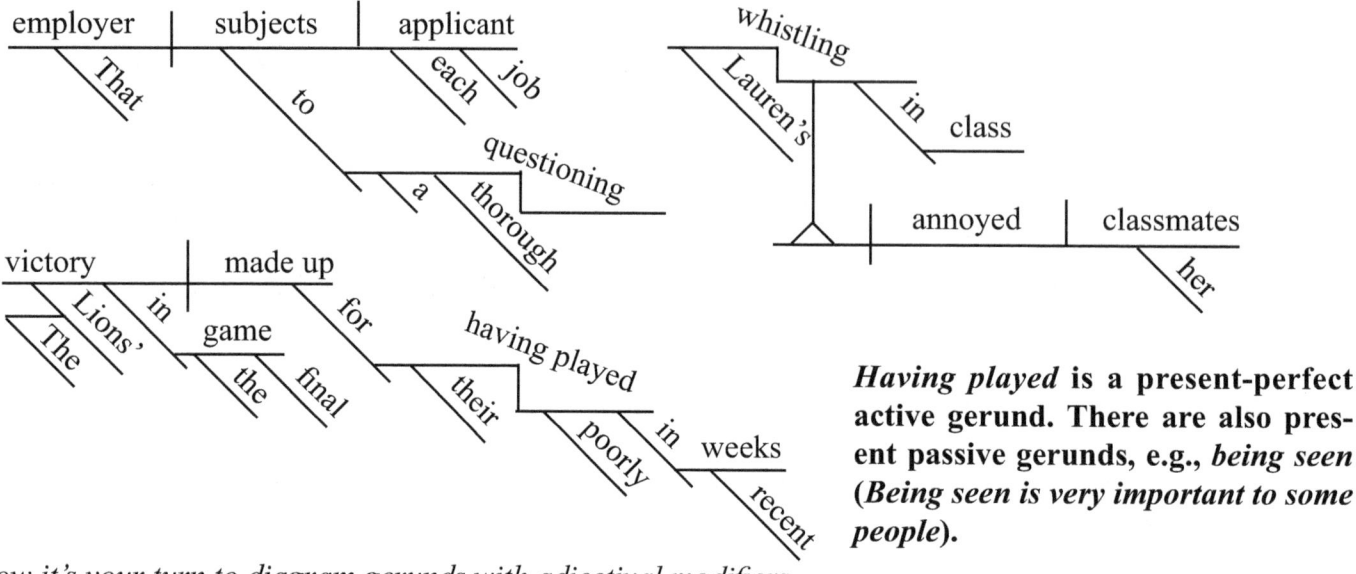

Having played is a present-perfect active gerund. There are also present passive gerunds, e.g., *being seen* (***Being seen** is very important to some people*).

Now it's your turn to diagram gerunds with adjectival modifiers.

1. The decathlete's jumping improved, but his throwing stayed the same.

2. Desperately needing to sleep longer, they awoke to the banging of trash cans.

3. Mr. Malone attributes the success of his business to his having hired Latoya, the best worker in town.

4. Jaclyn doesn't see how her singing can give anyone a headache.

5. The employees' constant idling finally became too much for the owner, and he sold the business.

6. What mother has not had to tell her children that she would appreciate their closing the door quietly?

Review VII: Lessons 19 - 21

1. Knowing that the endless waiting was over, Captain Swann was in great spirits as he got ready to leave the plane.

2. The band members wondered if the director, who looked out of sorts, had been embarrassed by their playing.

3. Because of her compulsive gambling she is without a penny to her name.

4. Jetting off to yet another race, the marathoner wondered if his running was out of control.

5. Scientists did not know if the collision of a huge comet with Jupiter would cause a rippling of the planet's atmosphere.

6. The meteorologist was unable to say whether it would snow on Christmas or not.

Unit VIII

- Transitional Adverbs
- Indefinite Relative Pronouns
- Bits 'n' Pieces

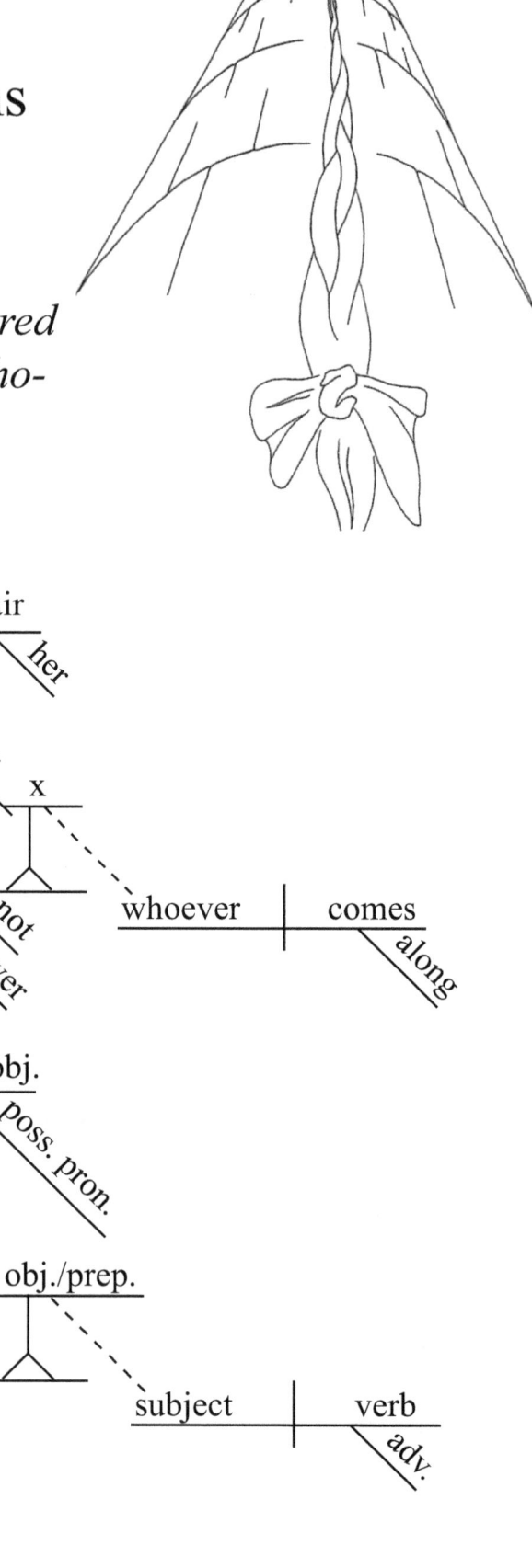

Rapunzel has lovingly braided and lowered her hair; however, her love is not for whoever comes along.

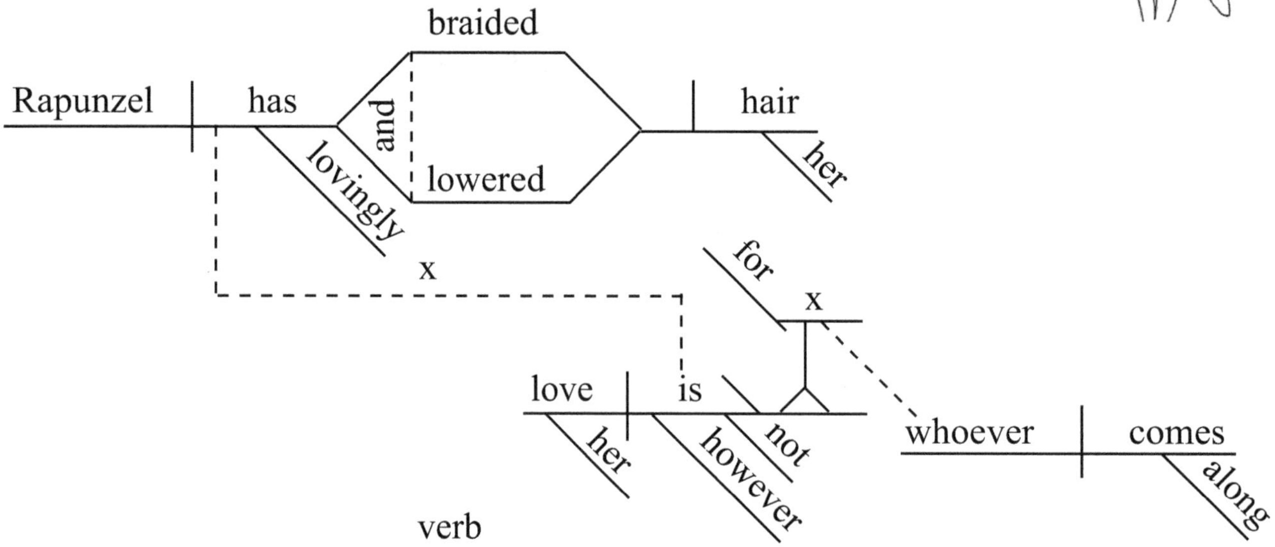

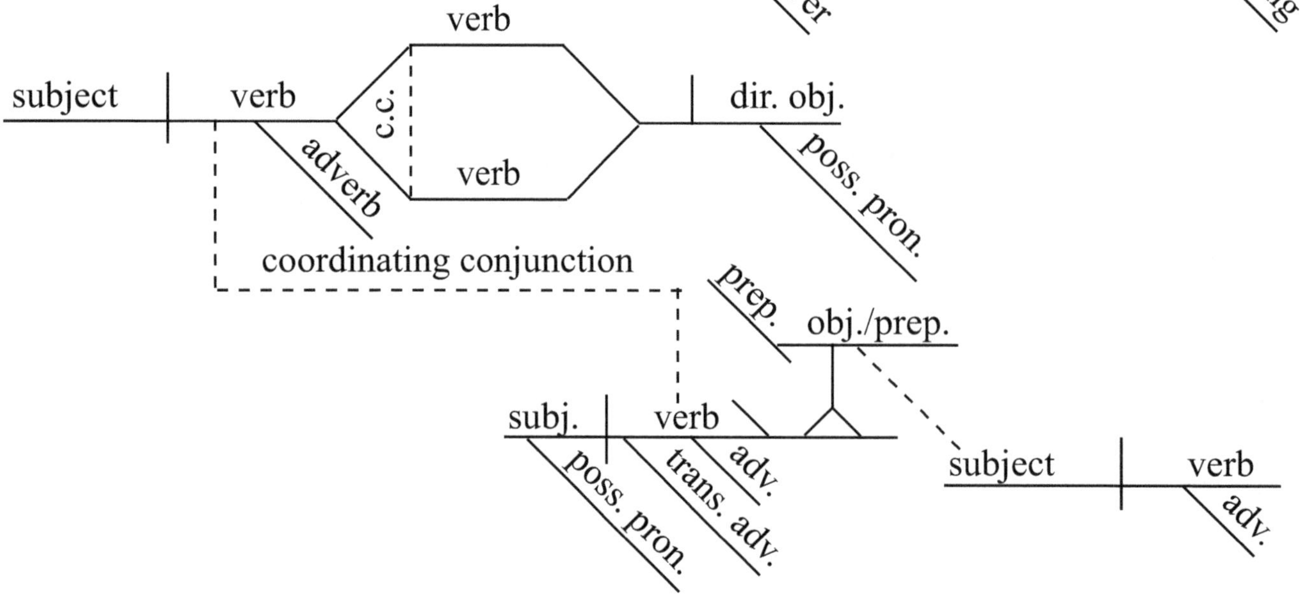

Lesson 22: Transitional Adverbs

Transitional adverbs--words like *however, moreover, nevertheless,* and *therefore*--function both as adverbs and as conjunctions. *Also, now, so, then, still,* **and** *yet* **are sometimes used as transitional adverbs. When transitional adverbs follow semicolons (as they often do), an** *x* **(representing an unexpressed coordinating conjunction) is placed on a horizontal broken line between the clauses, and the transitional adverb is diagrammed as a modifier of the main verb of the clause in which it appears.** Here are two examples: *Having arrived late, Sherona sprinted to the gate of her connecting flight; however, the plane had already departed. Three days had passed since the earthquake devastated the area; still, rescuers did not abandon hope of finding survivors.*

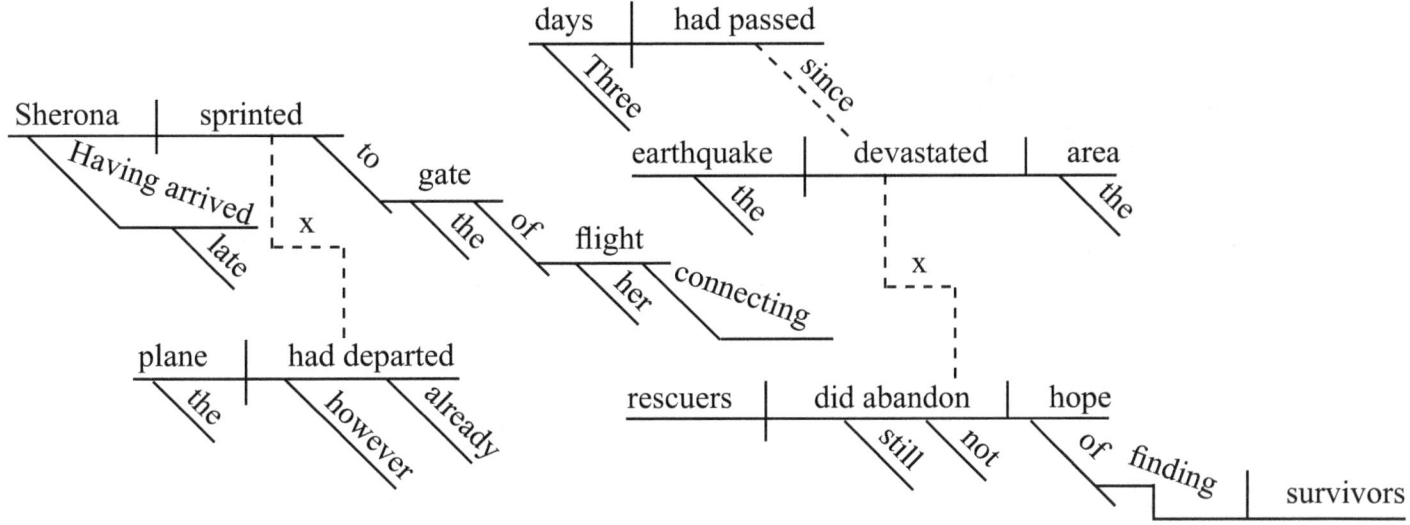

Now it's your turn to diagram transitional adverbs.

1. Rosa Parks refused to give up her seat to a white passenger; therefore, she was arrested, and the civil rights movement began.

2. The weather had turned frigid; nevertheless, the carolers continued their musical stroll through the neighborhood.

3. Heidi had been putting money aside to remodel her kitchen; also, she hoped to buy a used car for her daughter, Kristina.

4. The family had spent six wonderful years in California; nevertheless, when opportunity knocked, they packed up without complaint and moved to Ohio.

Lesson 23: Indefinite Relative Pronouns

The most important indefinite relative pronouns are *whoever, whomever, whosever, whichever, whatever,* and *what*. Also worth noting are *whosoever, whomsoever,* and *whatsoever*. An indefinite relative pronoun has an unexpressed antecedent, which is represented in a sentence diagram by an *x*. Here are several sentences that contain indefinite relative pronouns: *Do whatever she tells you. Each day the teacher gives a piece of candy to whoever works hardest. I will ask whomever I want to ask. You can have whichever you choose.*

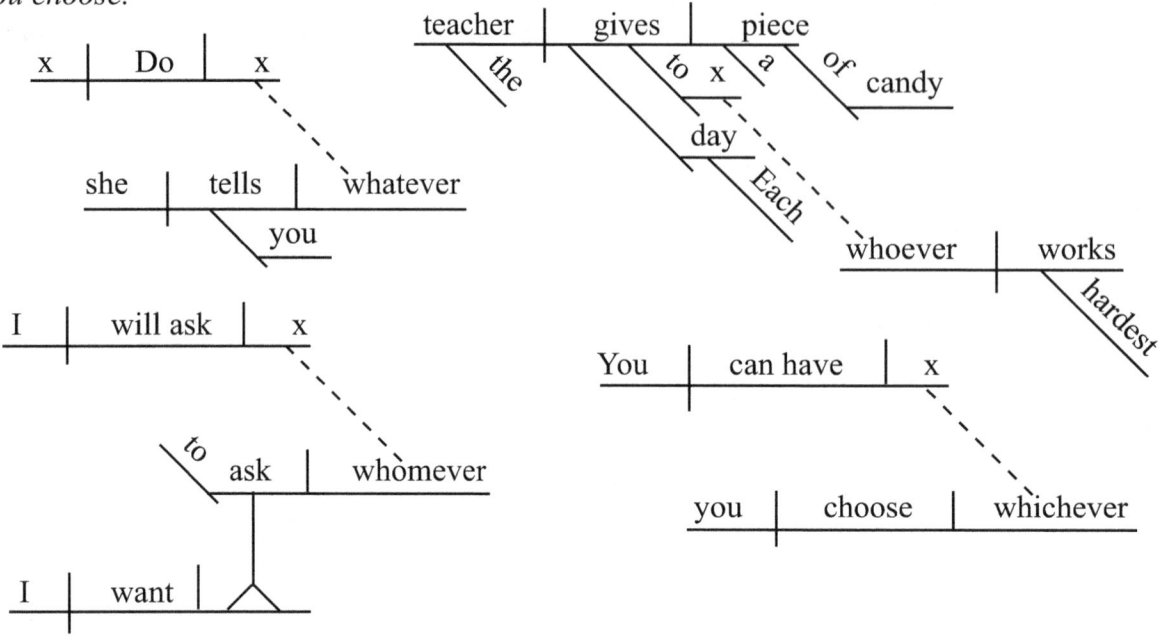

Now it's your turn to diagram indefinite relative pronouns.

1. Son, one cannot always have whatever one's heart desires.

2. Lying, he said that he would marry whoever walked into the room next.

3. The repairmen didn't do what they said they would do.

4. Whomever I call should come to the front of the auditorium to receive a prize.

5. The princess told the frog that she would give him whatever he wanted if he would retrieve the ball she had lost.

6. At the conference, the delegates had to converse for thirty minutes with whomever they met as they left the cafeteria.

Lesson 24: Bits 'n' Pieces

In the following diagram of the sentence *Amelia herself carved and painted the statue*, notice how one diagrams **the direct object of two verbs**.

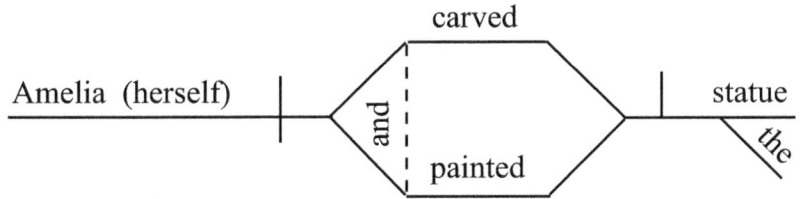

Herself is an intensive pronoun in this sentence. Other intensive pronouns are *myself, yourself, himself, itself, ourselves, yourselves,* and *themselves*. **Intensive pronouns are appositives.**

Infinitives and participles can function as objective complements, as they do in the sentences *You made me fall* and *We saw you running*, respectively.

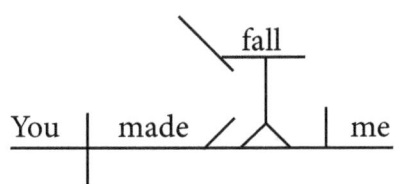

Most infinitives are preceded by *to*. In this sentence, *fall* is **a "to-less" infinitive.**

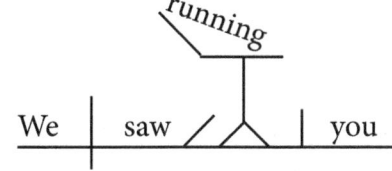

Now it's your turn to diagram sentences that have the characteristics discussed above.

1. Darin called his friends Mark and Richard to find out about the party he had missed.

2. Little Tammy insisted that she had both seen and heard Santa himself.

3. With the help of her two employees, Patrice and Blake, my aunt Laura buys and sells used books.

4. The head chef himself baked and iced the cake and then brought it to the guest of honor.

5. On his way into the house, he saw the carpenters --Mr. Stone and his son Bill--leaving.

6. Mrs. Gentry had been unable to get out of bed that morning; therefore, she had Laurel wash a load of clothes before she left for school.

~ 111 ~

Review VIII: Lessons 22 - 24

1. The French still find and detonate thousands of World War II shells annually.

2. The prize will be awarded to whoever gets the correct answer first; therefore, it is important to work fast.

3. I saw Nora go into the library with her friends Tyler and Regina; however, Jenna is still not here.

4. We are to tell whoever calls that Claire has to wash and dry her hair.

5. Waikiki Beach is heavenly; nevertheless, Paul wasn't at peace with himself there.

6. Some people think millions of dollars can buy whatever the heart desires; however, money can't buy two important things: peace and love.

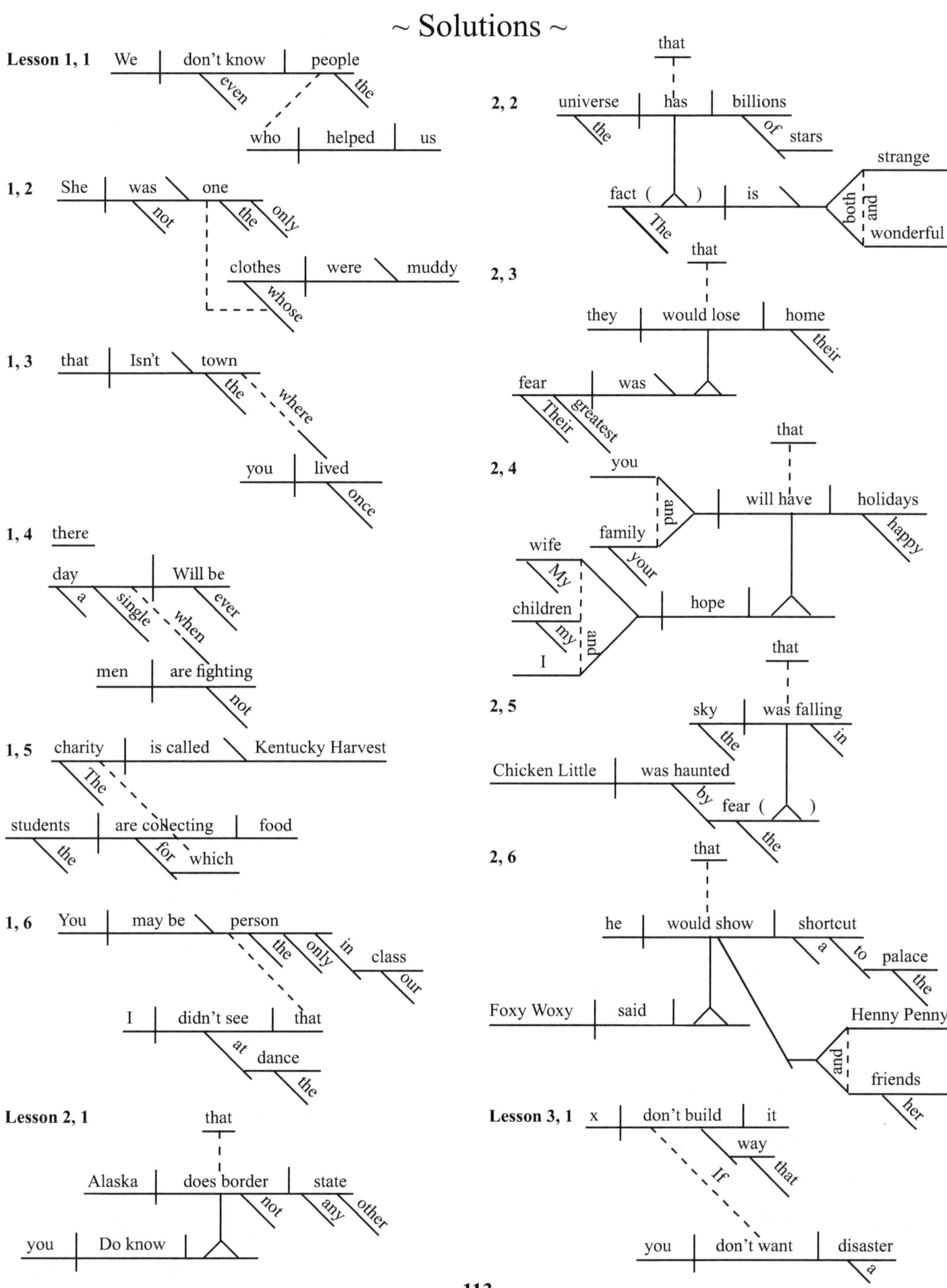

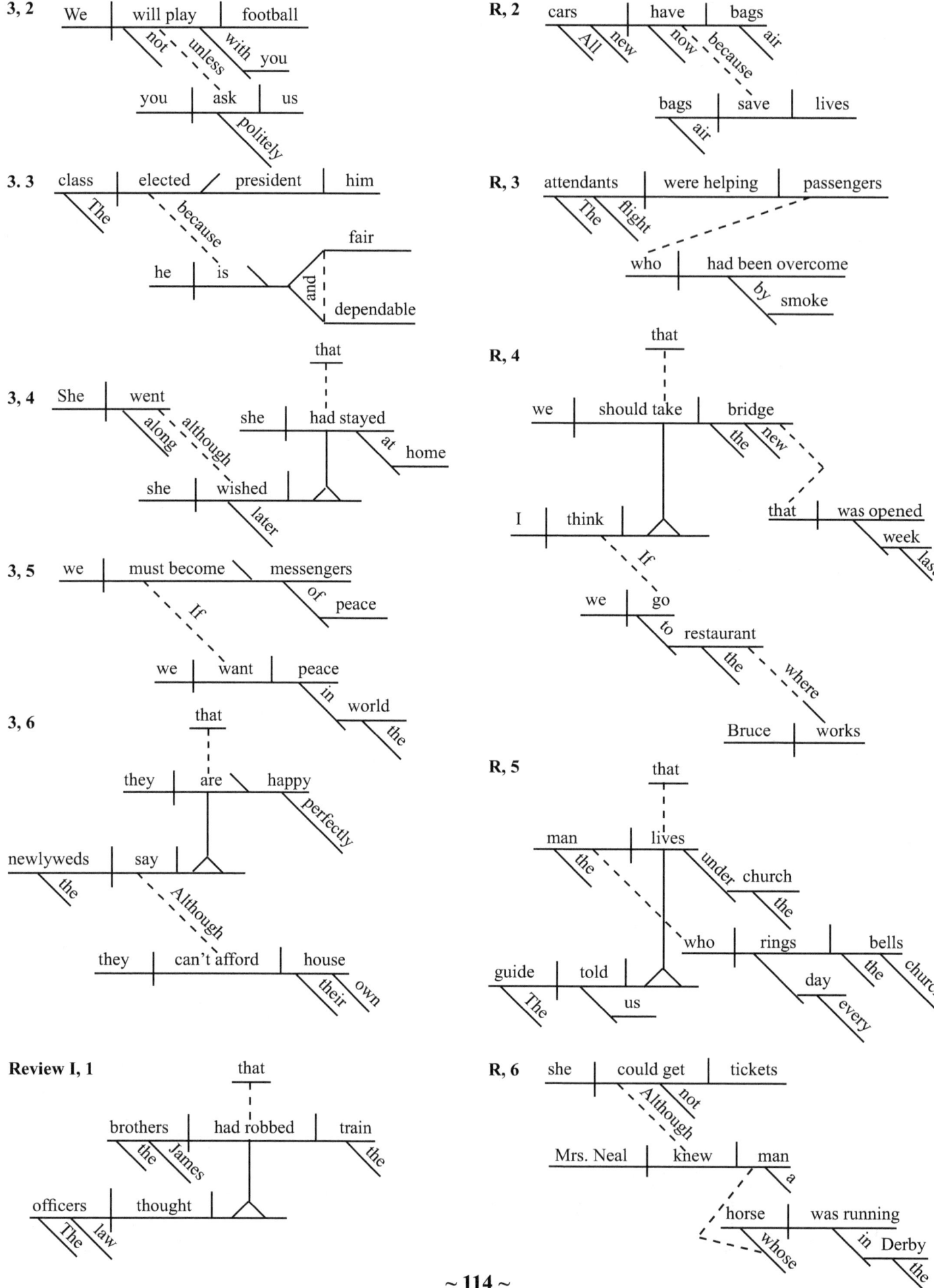

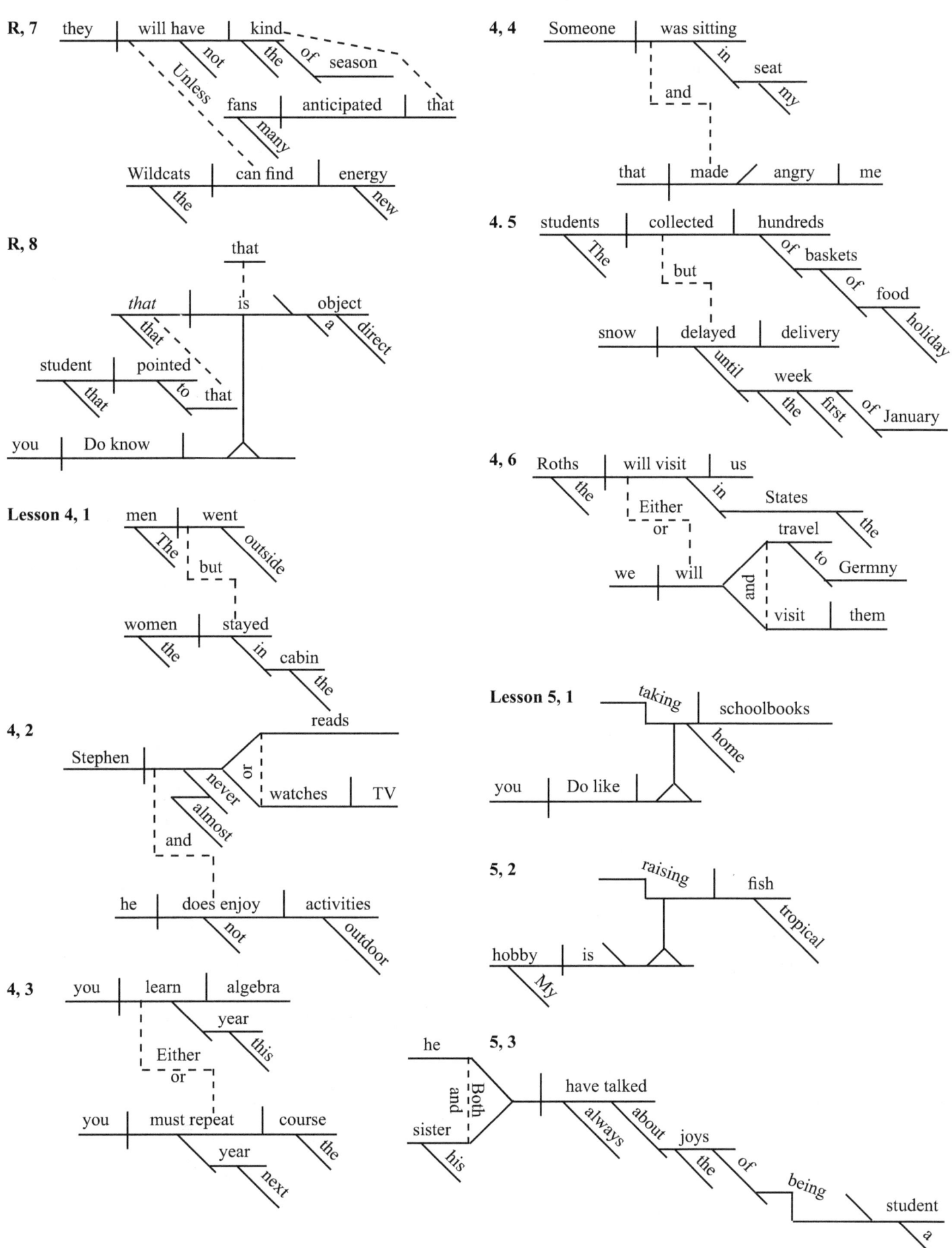

5, 4

5, 5

5, 6

Lesson 6, 1

6, 2

6, 3

6, 4

6, 5

6, 6

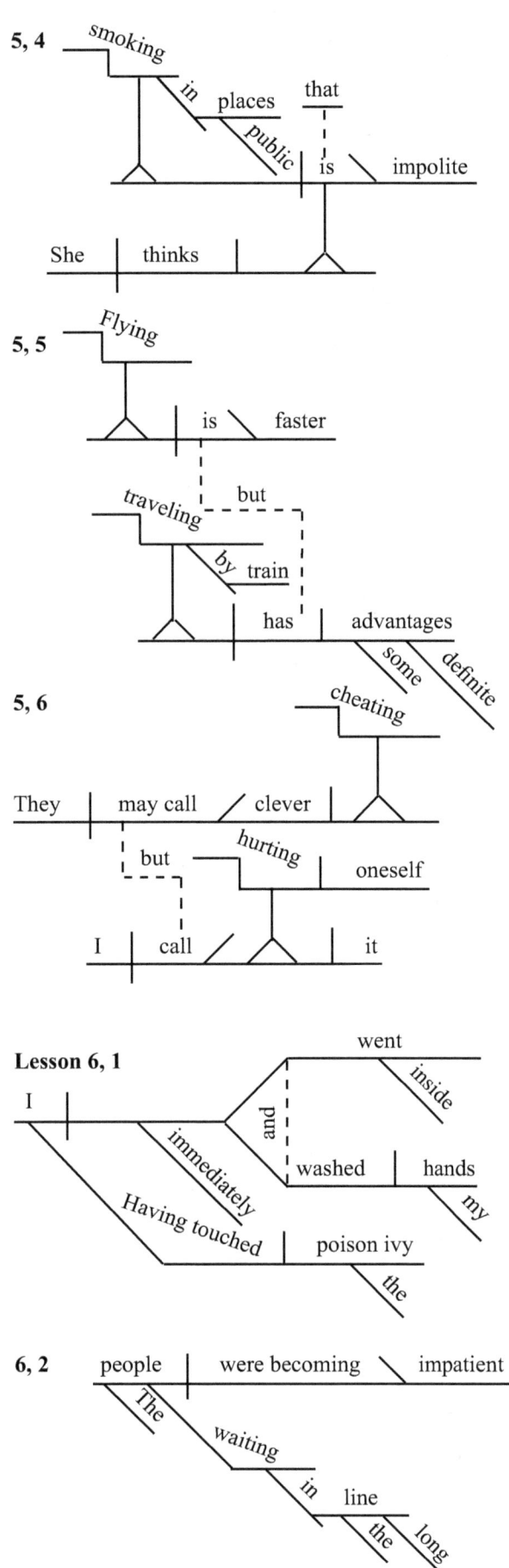

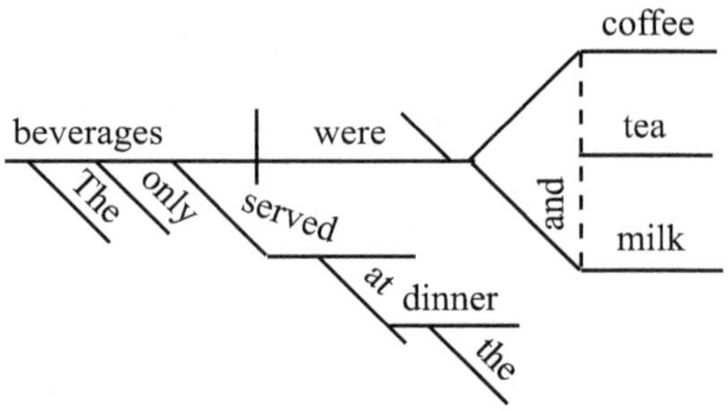

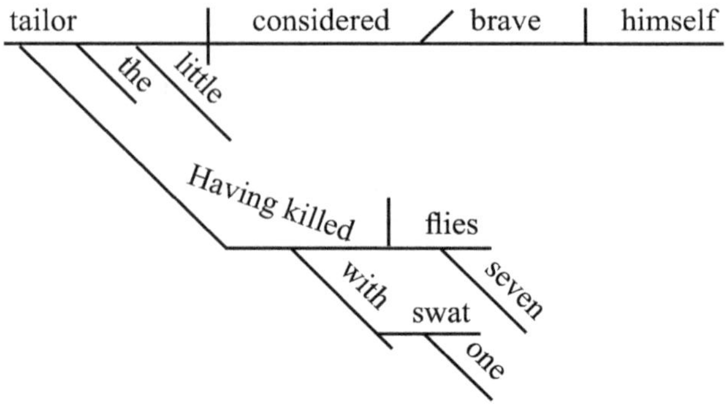

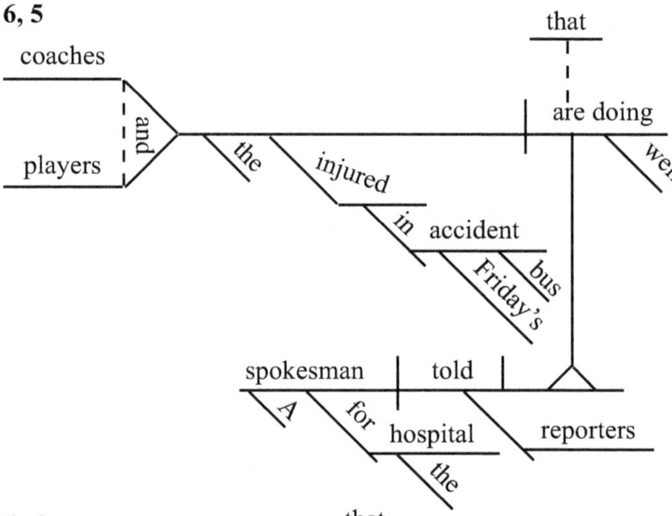

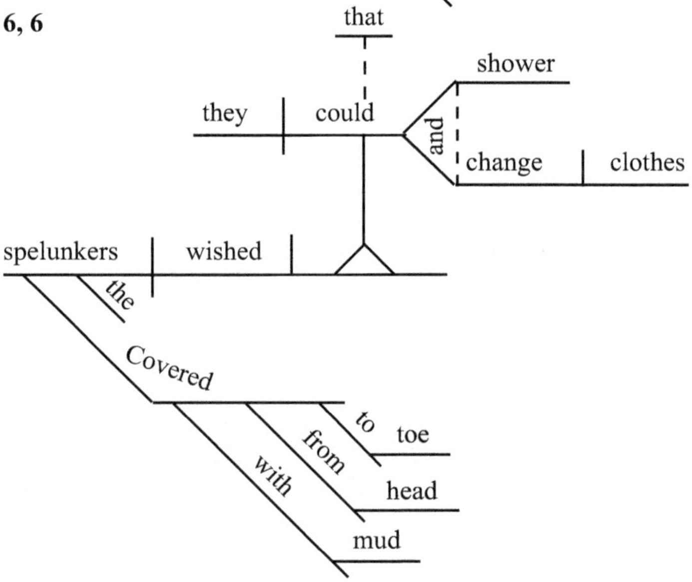

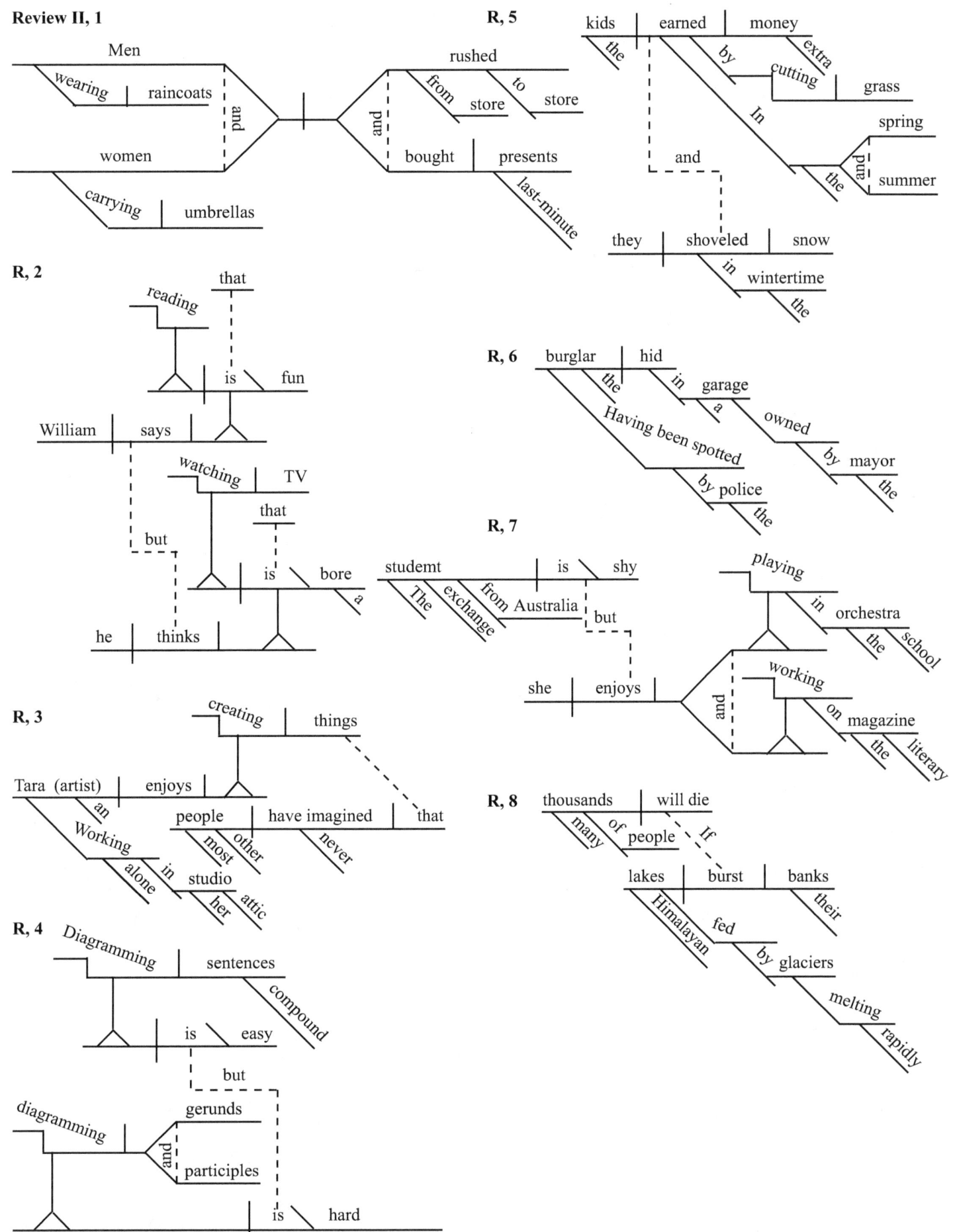

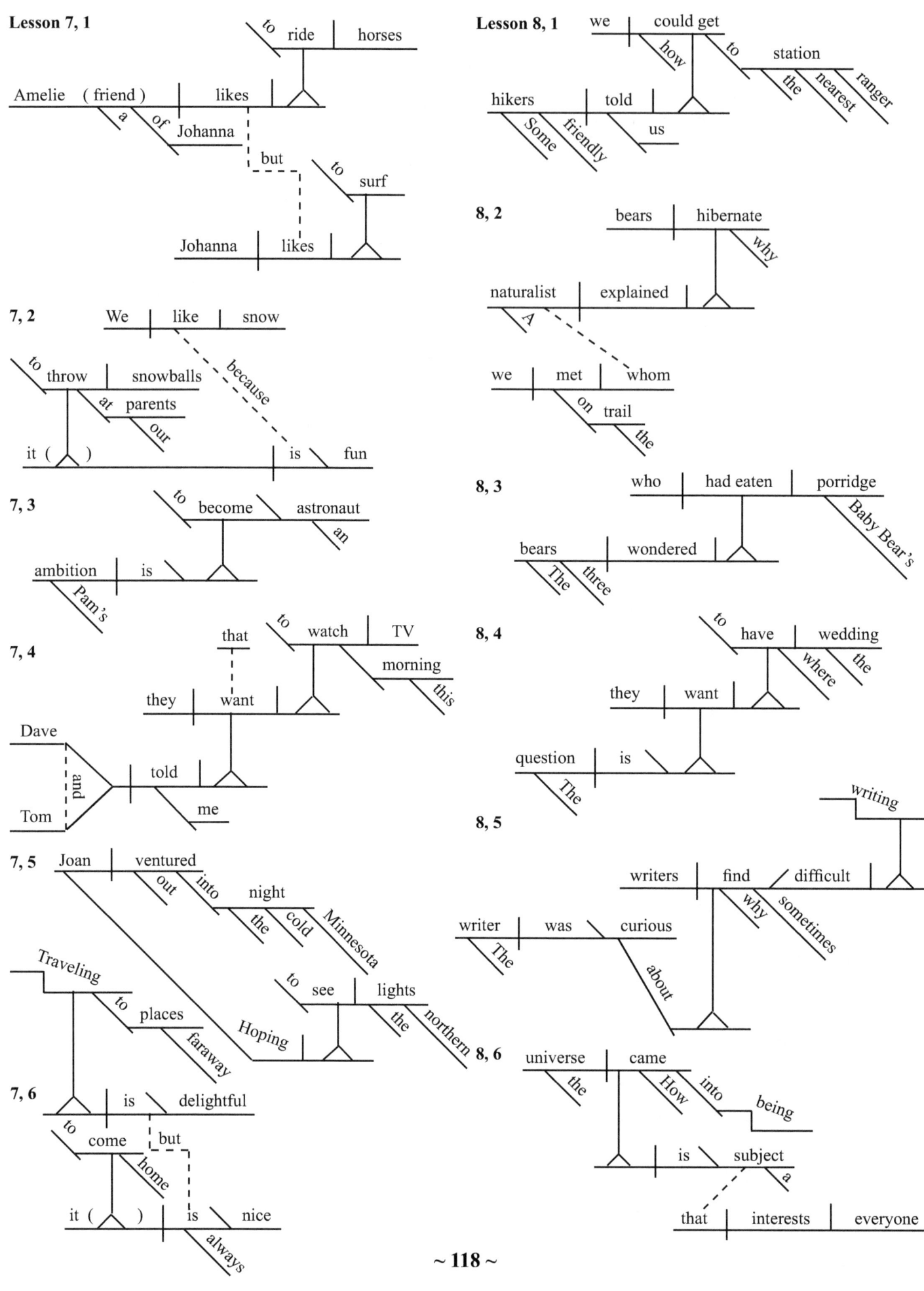

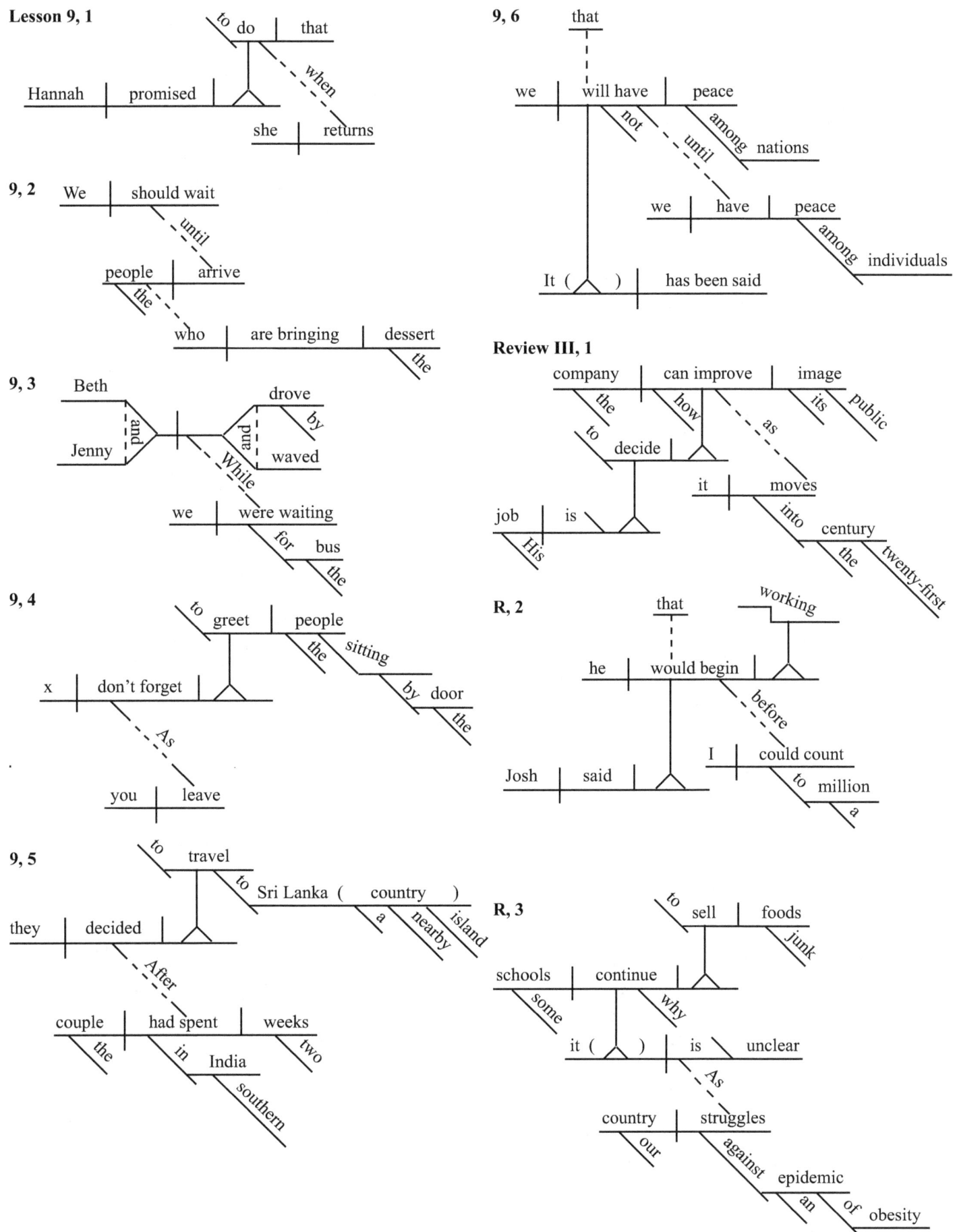

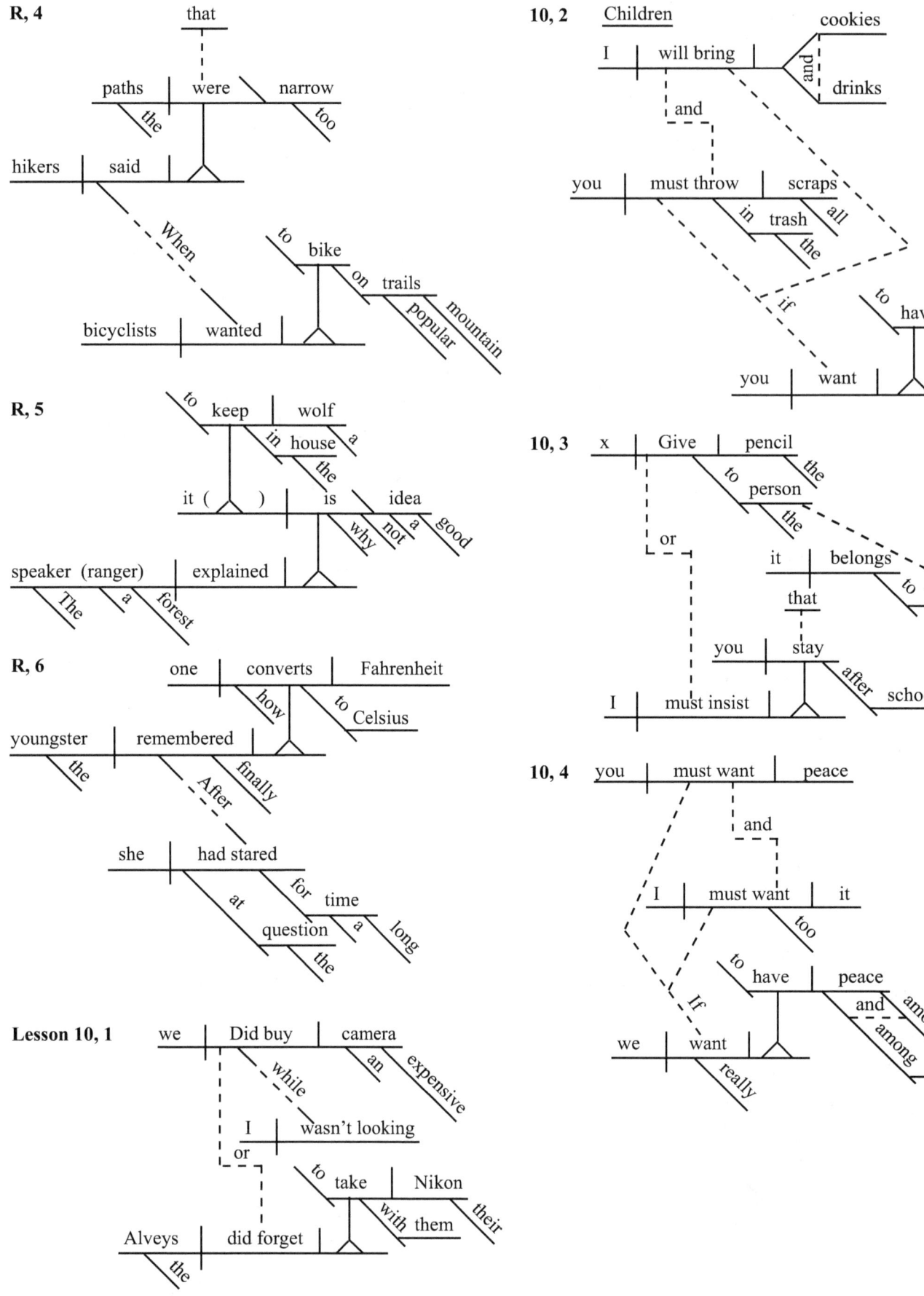

10, 5

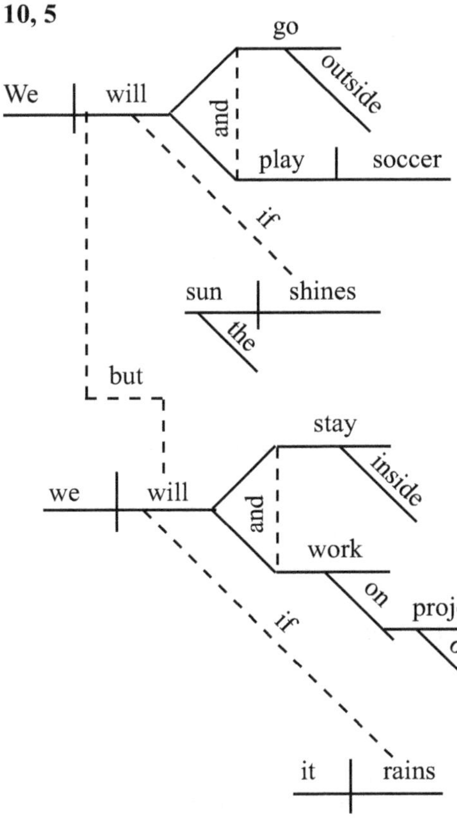

Lesson 11, 1

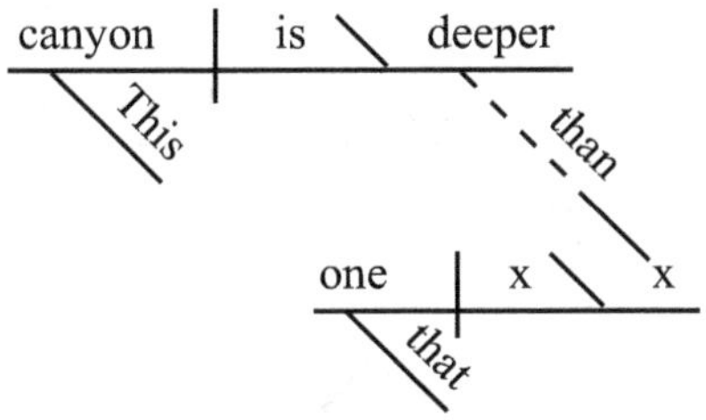

11, 2

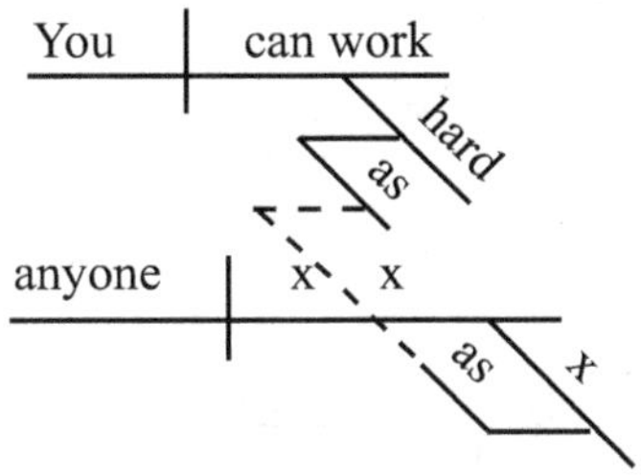

11, 3

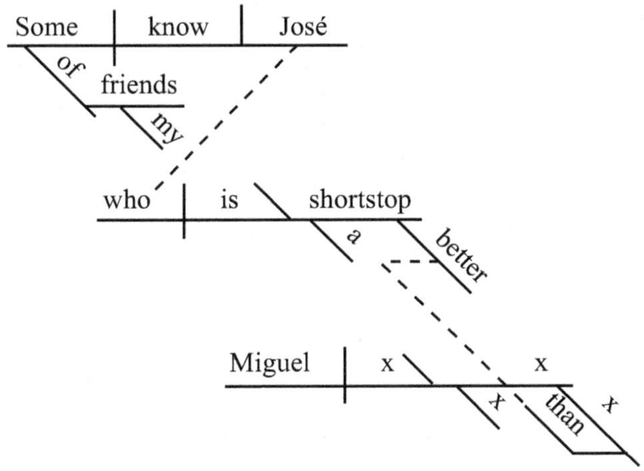

11, 4

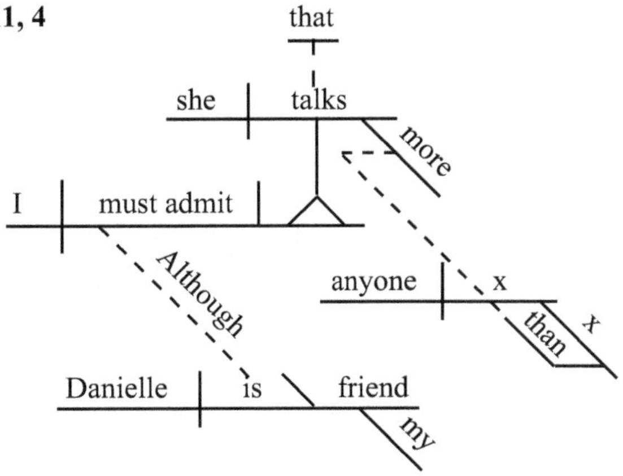

11, 5

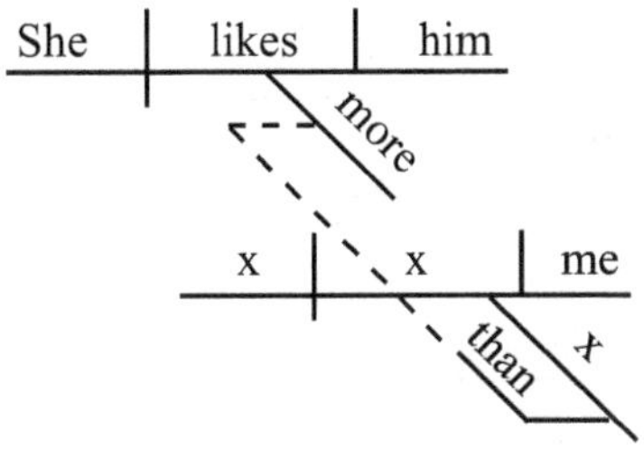

11, 6

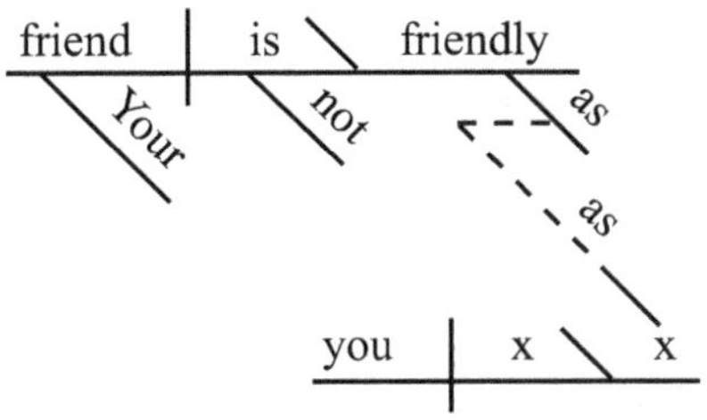

11, 7

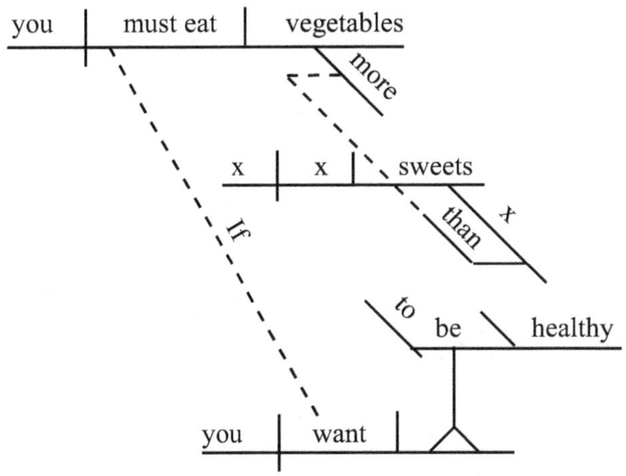

Lesson 12, 1

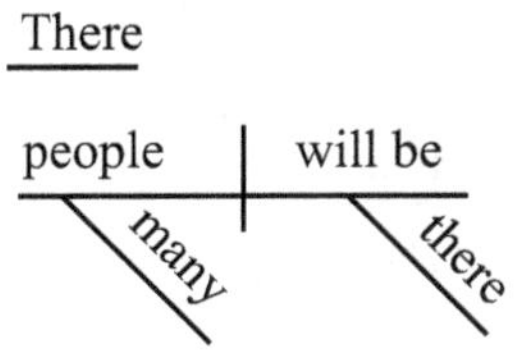

12, 2

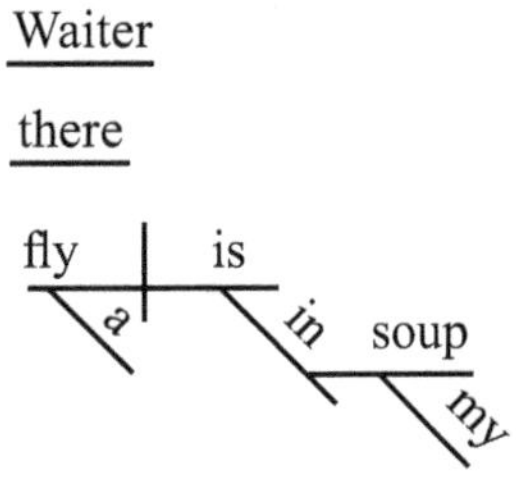

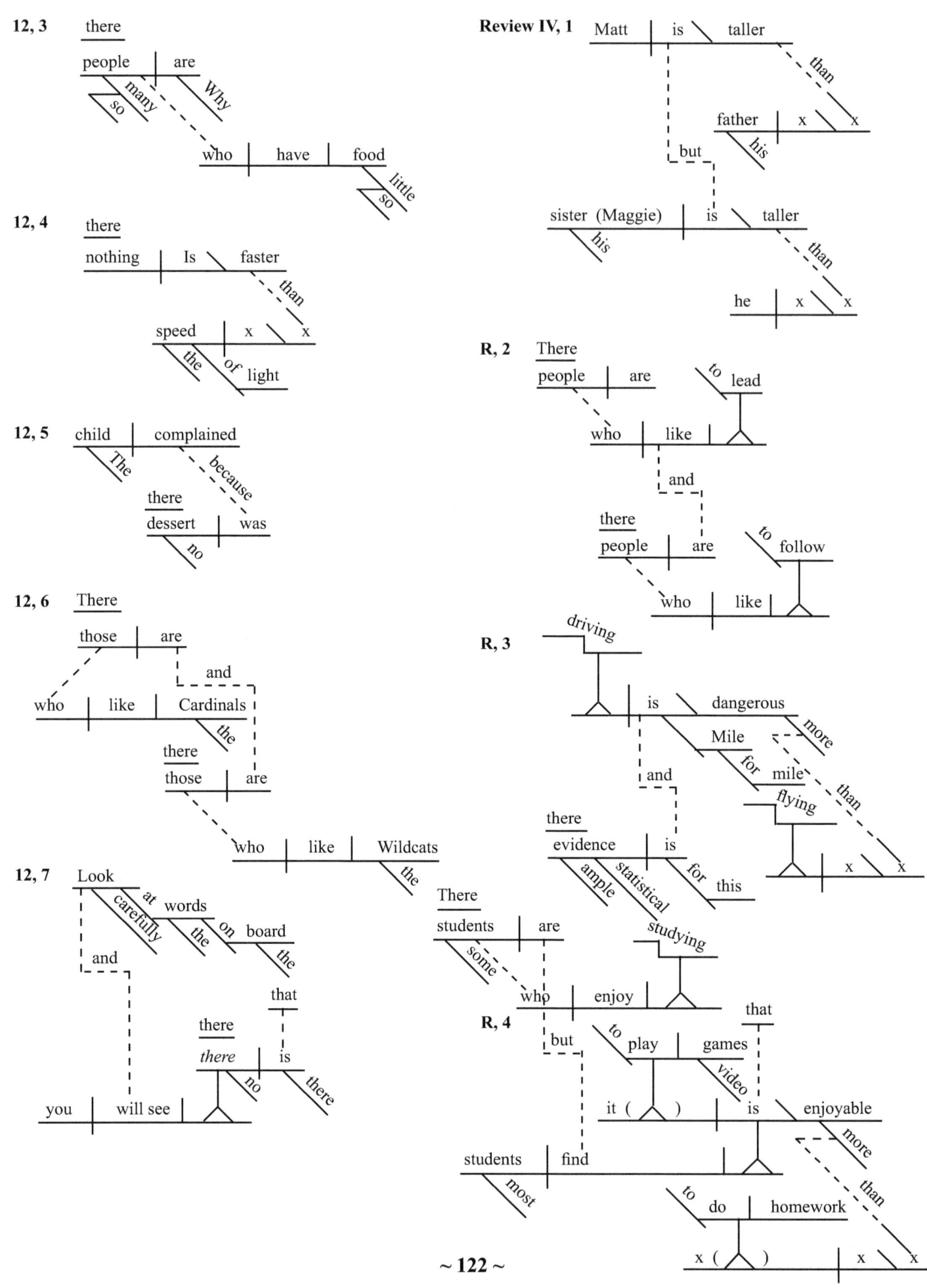

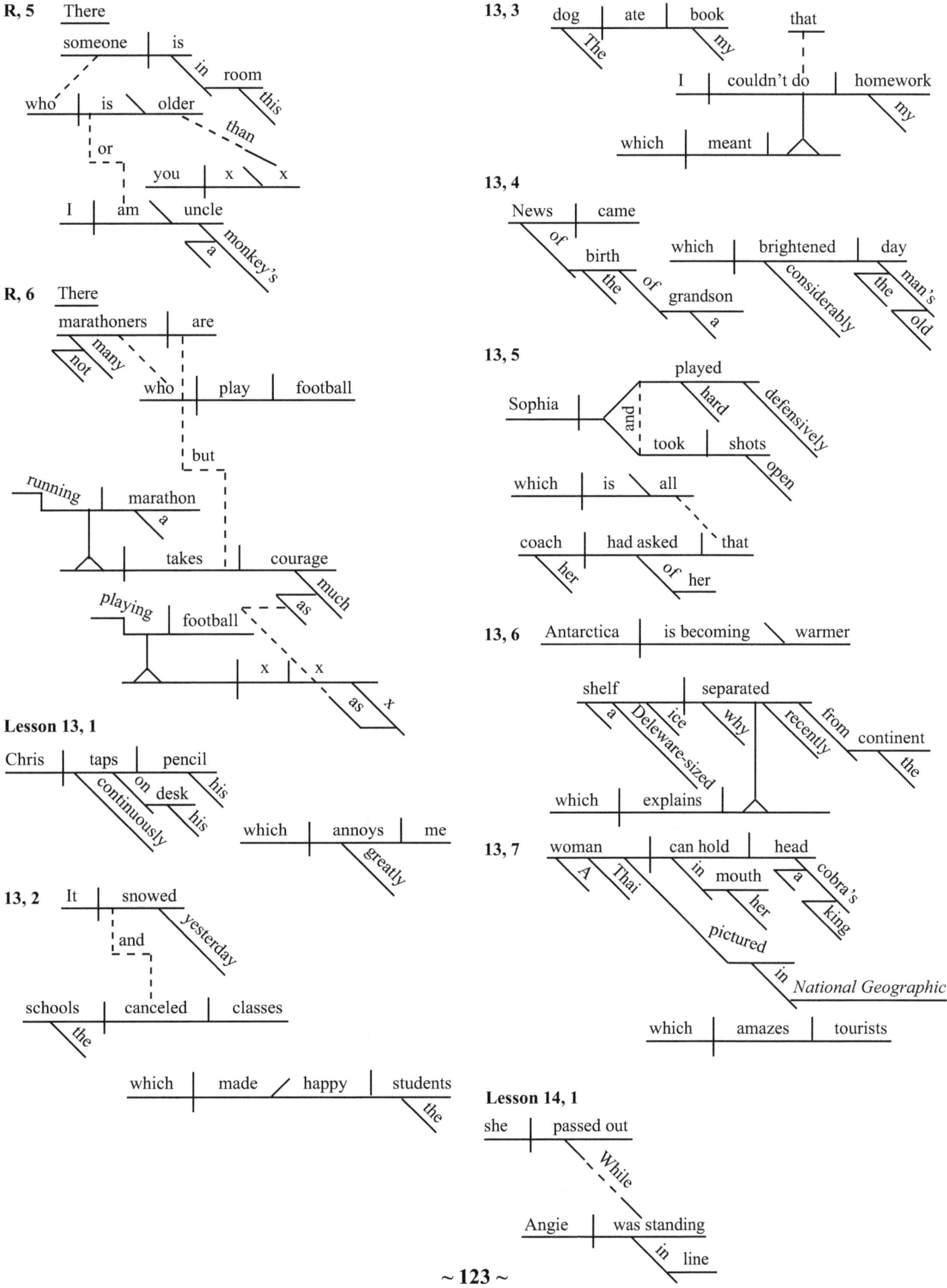

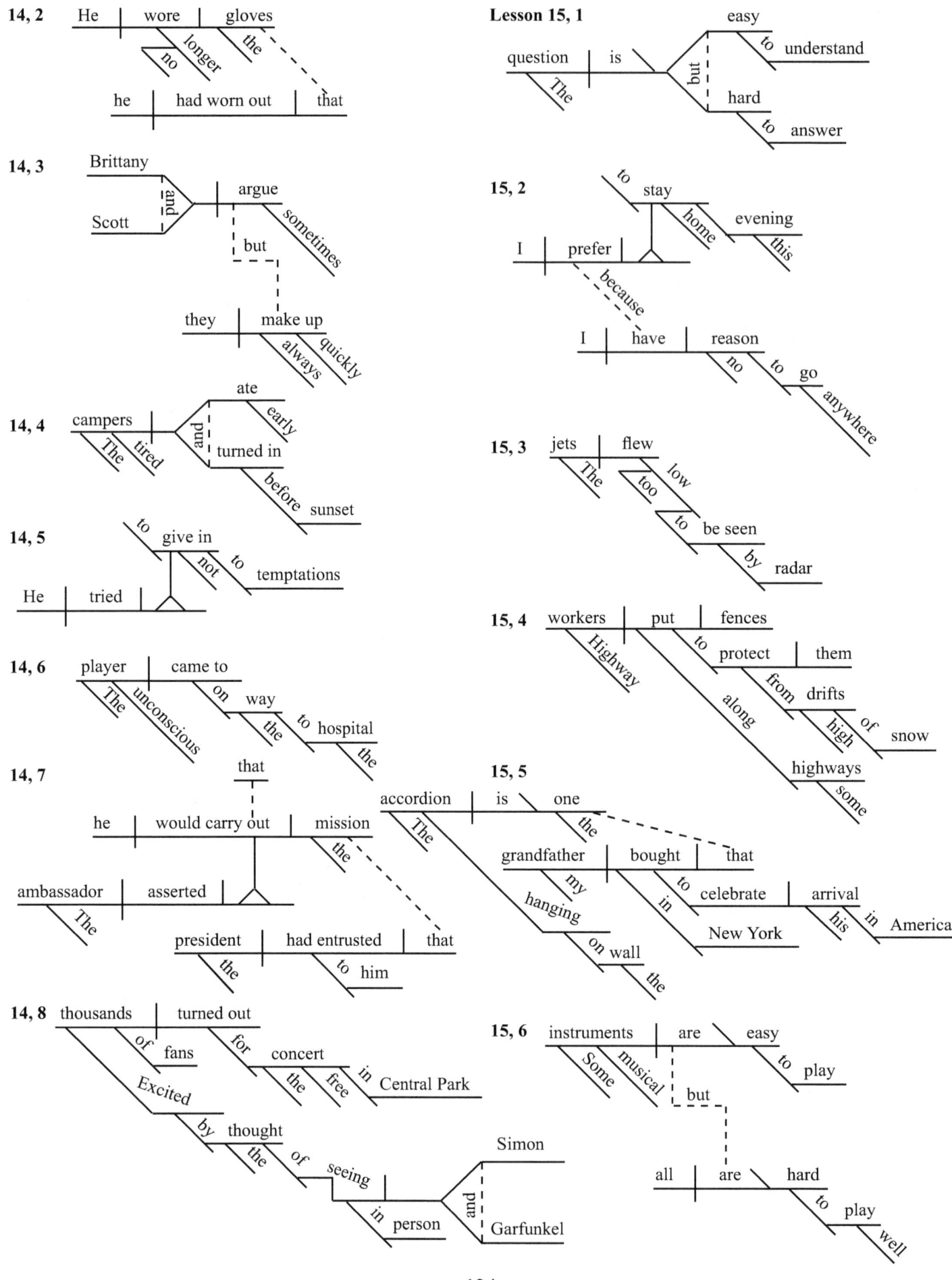

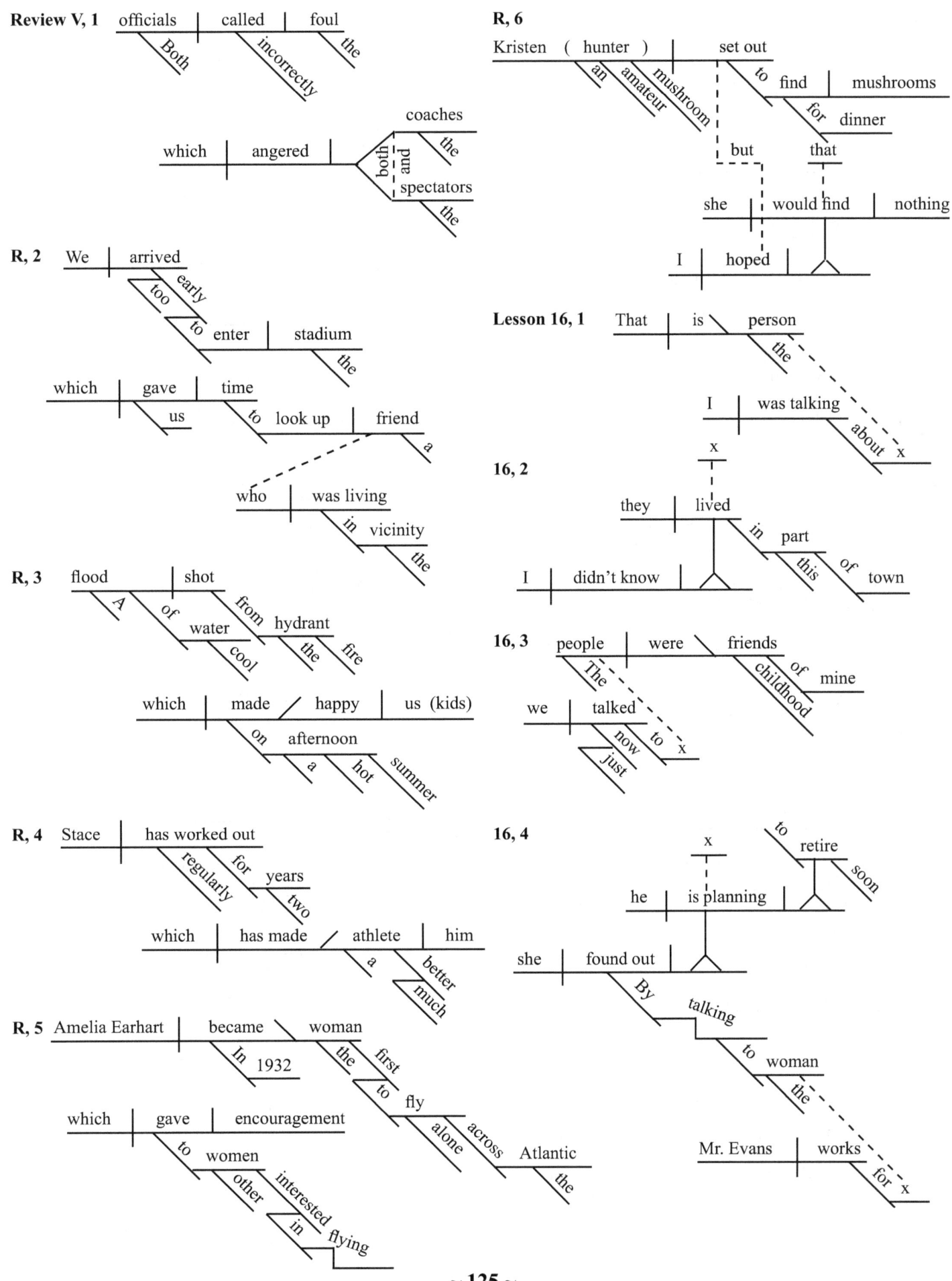

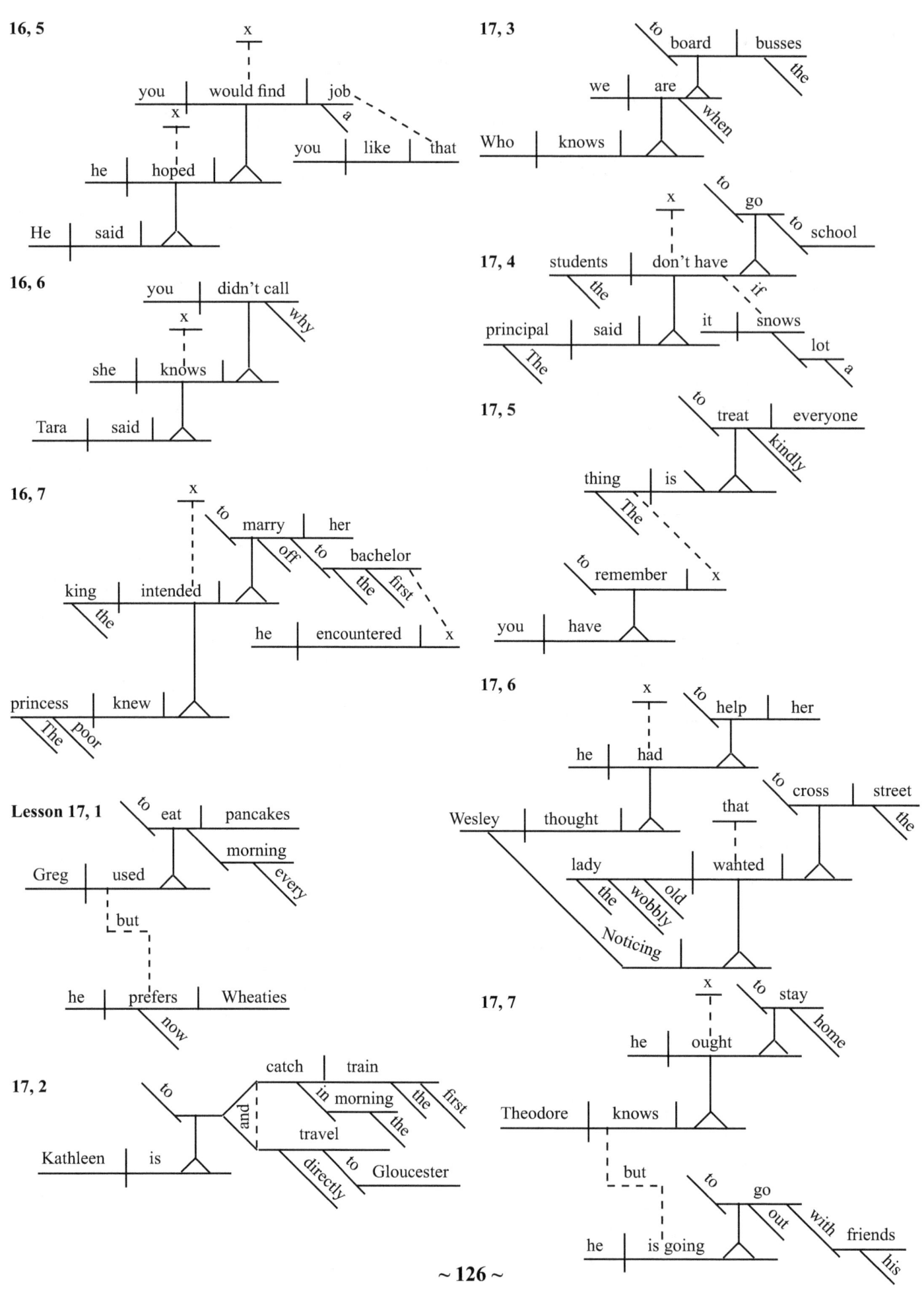

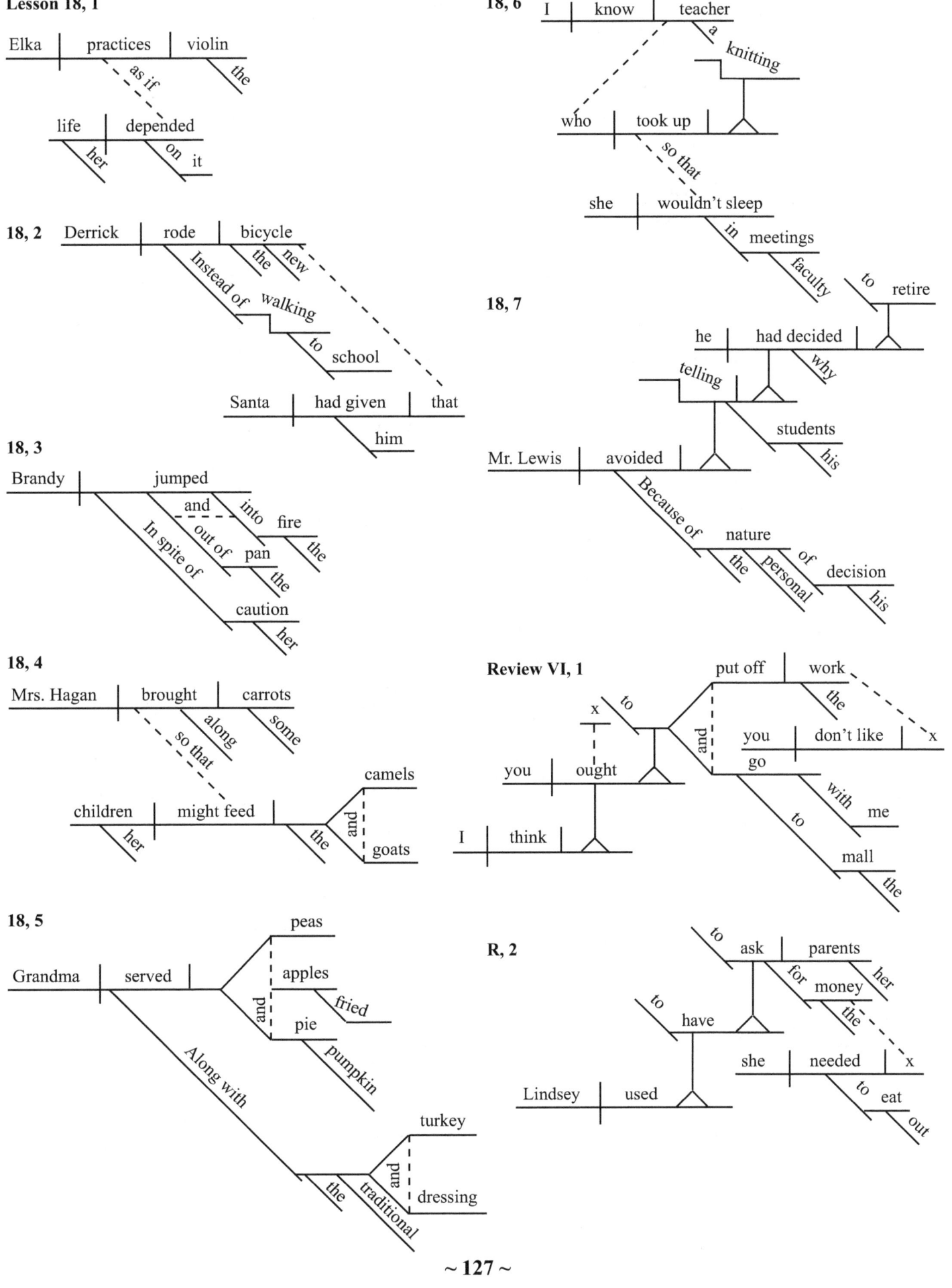

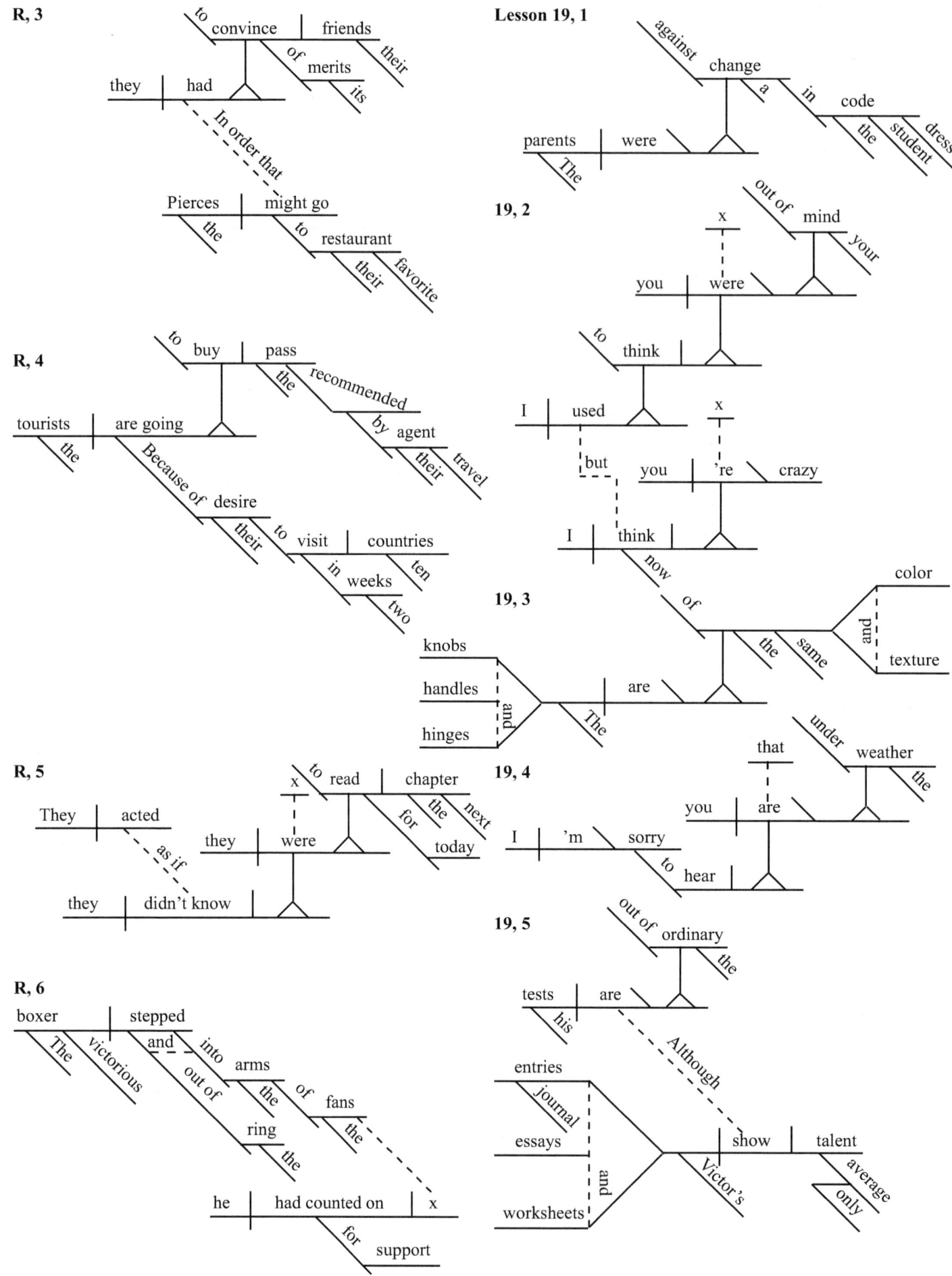

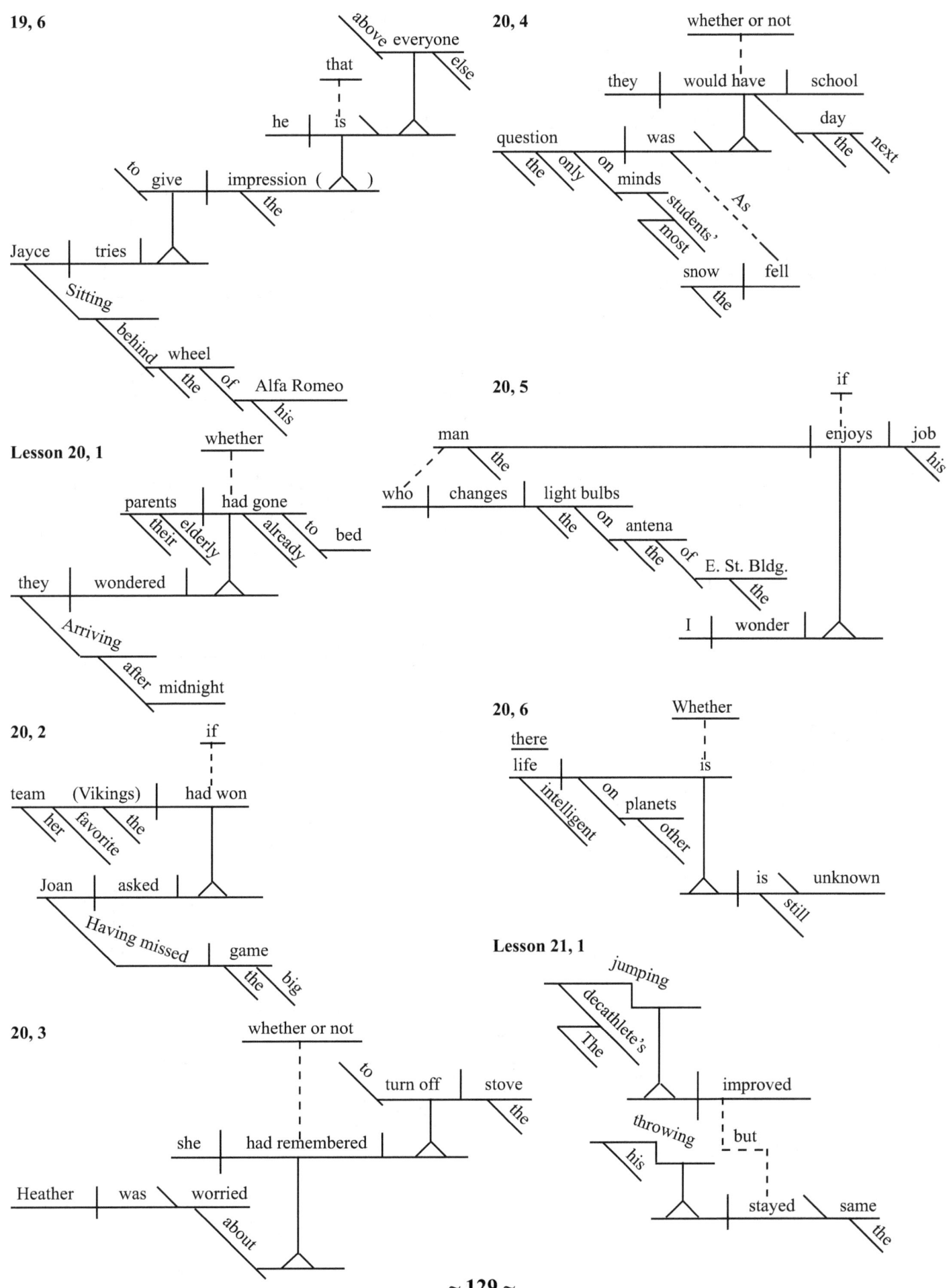

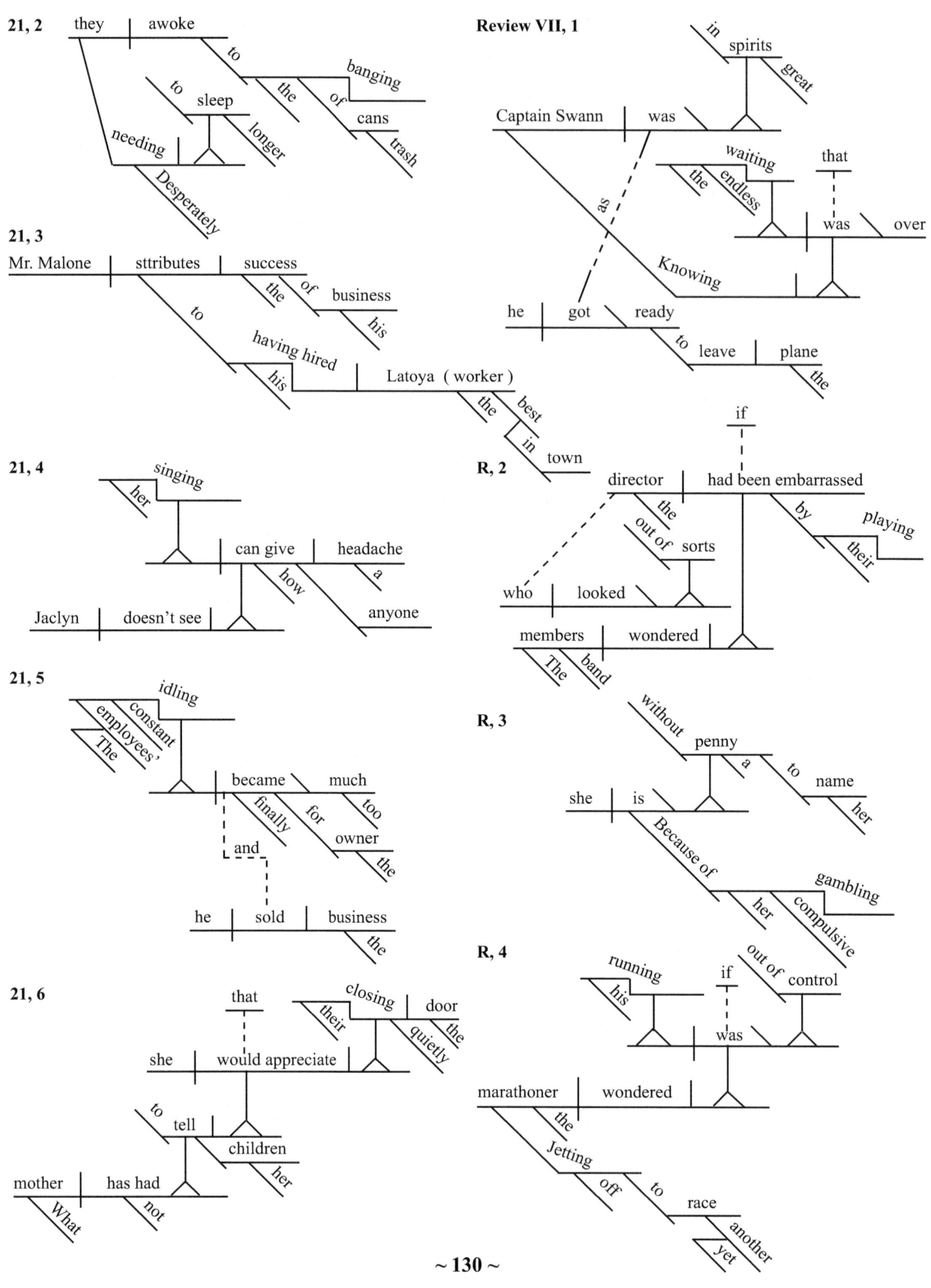

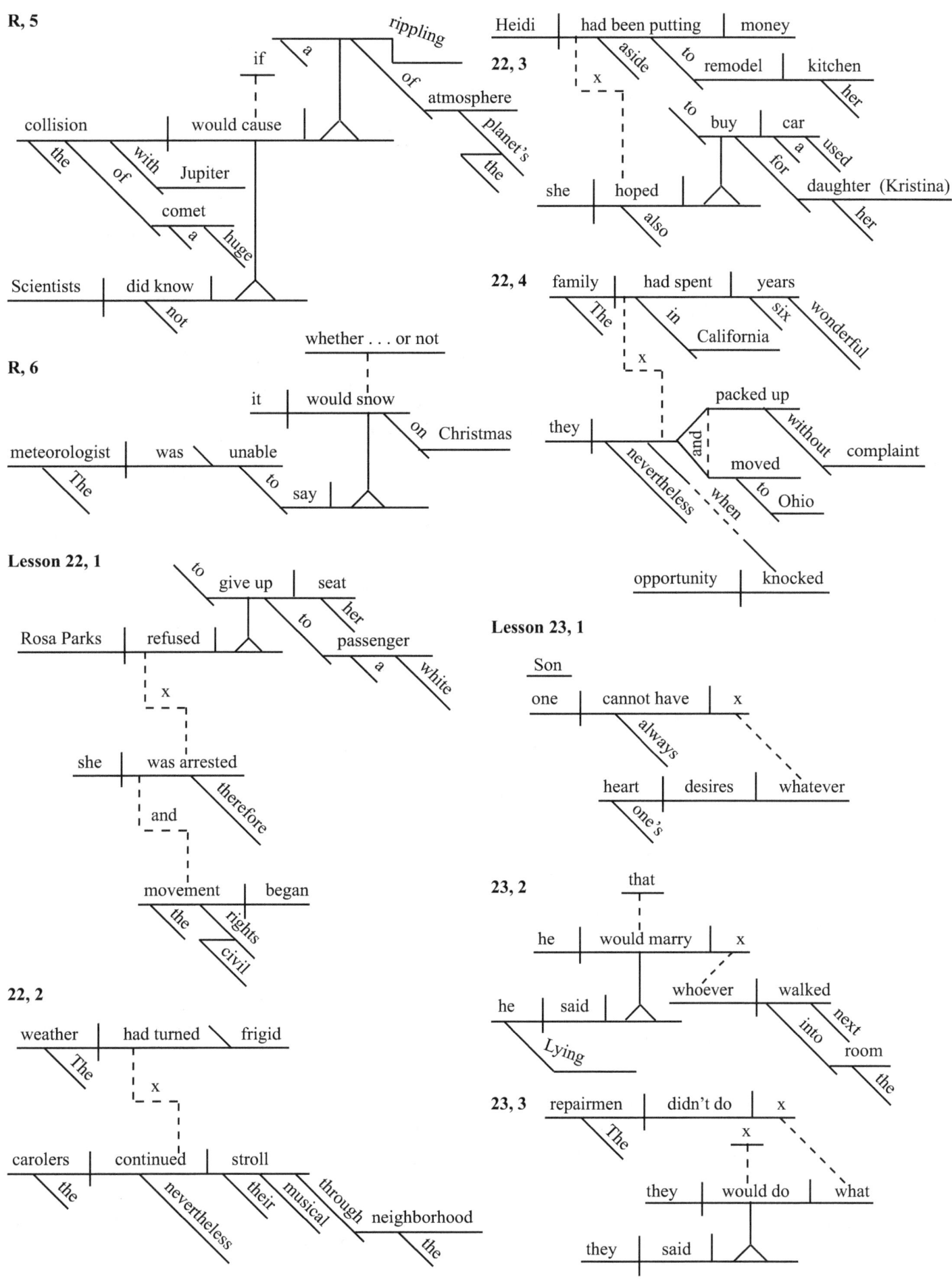

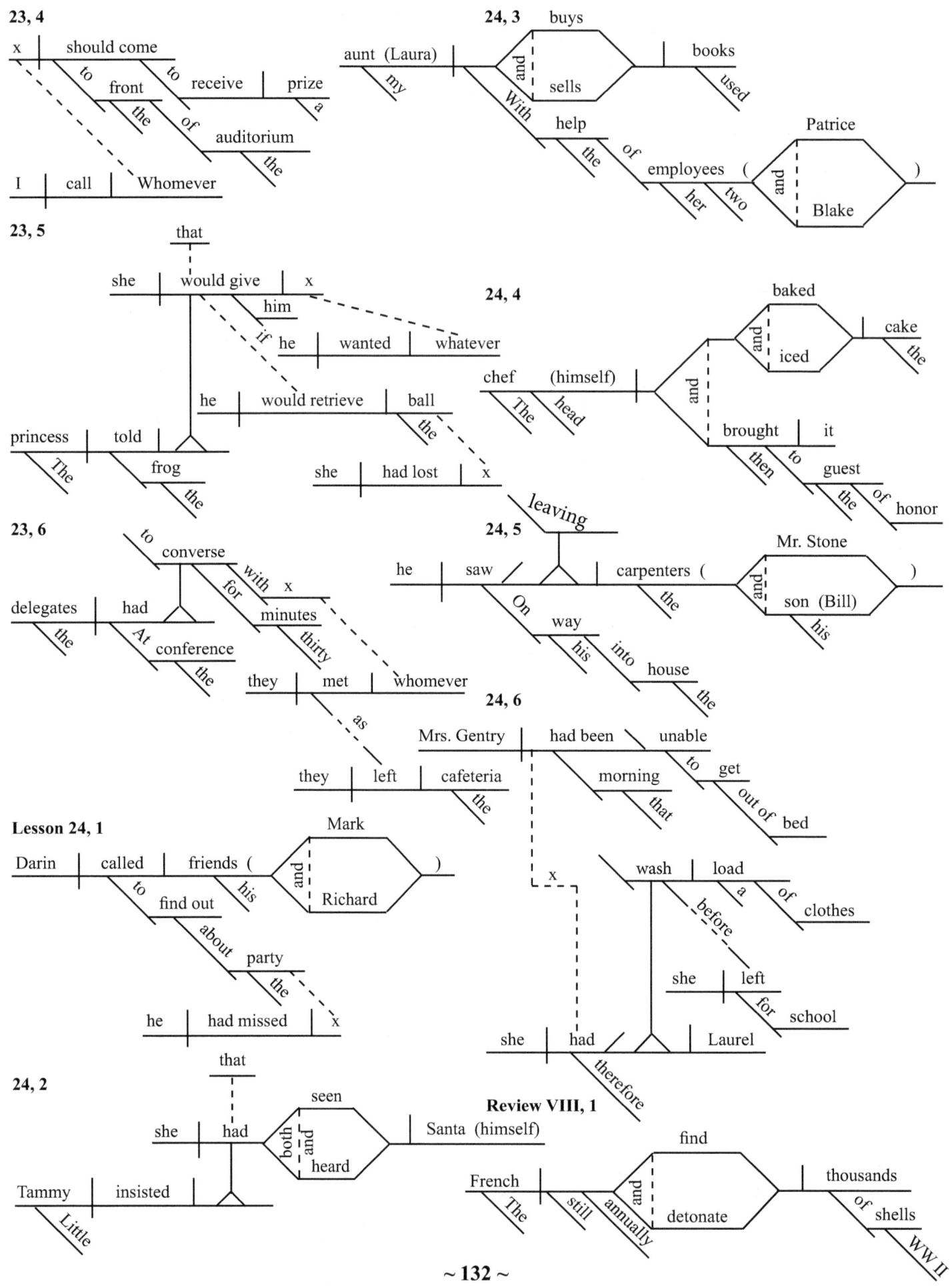

R, 2

prize
will be awarded
The
whoever
gets
answer
to
first
the
correct
x
to
work
fast
it (
)
is
important
therefore

R, 3

go
into
with
friends (
Tyler
and
Regina
)
her
library
the
I
saw
Nora
x
Jenna
is
however
still
not
here

R, 4

to
wash
and
dry
hair
her
that
Claire
has
to
tell
whoever
calls
We
are

R, 5

Waikiki Beach
is
heavenly
x
at
peace
with
himself
Paul
wasn't
there
nevertheless

R, 6

x
millions
can buy
x
of
dollars
heart
desires
whatever
the
people
think
Some
x
peace
money
can't buy
things (
and
love
)
however
two
important

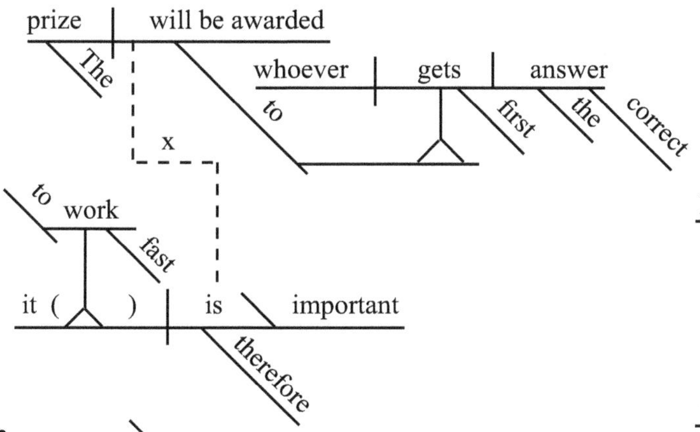

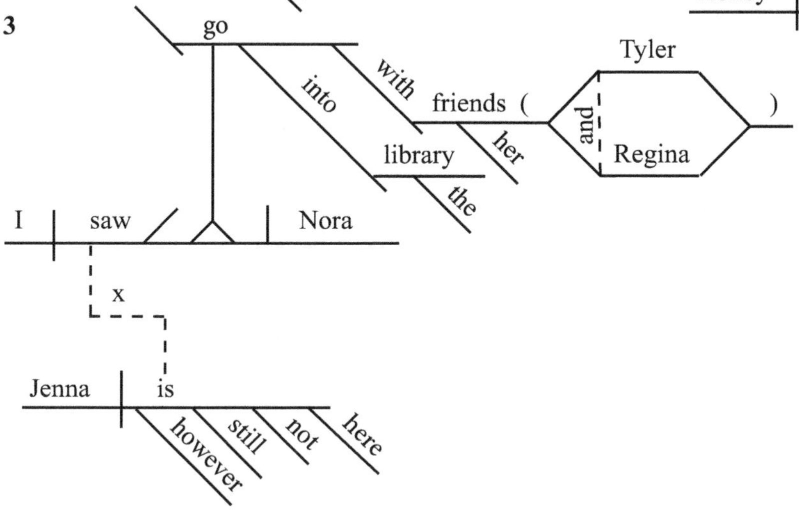

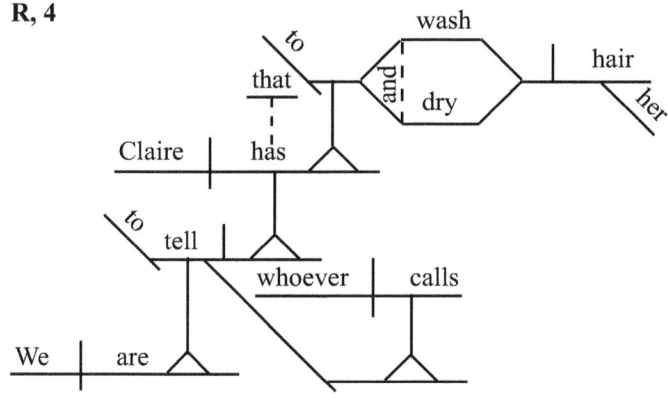

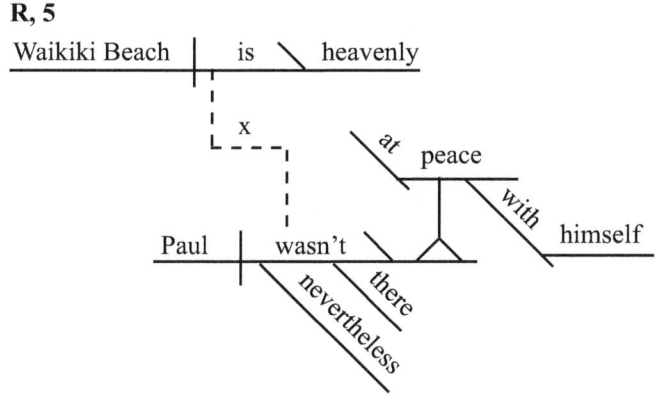

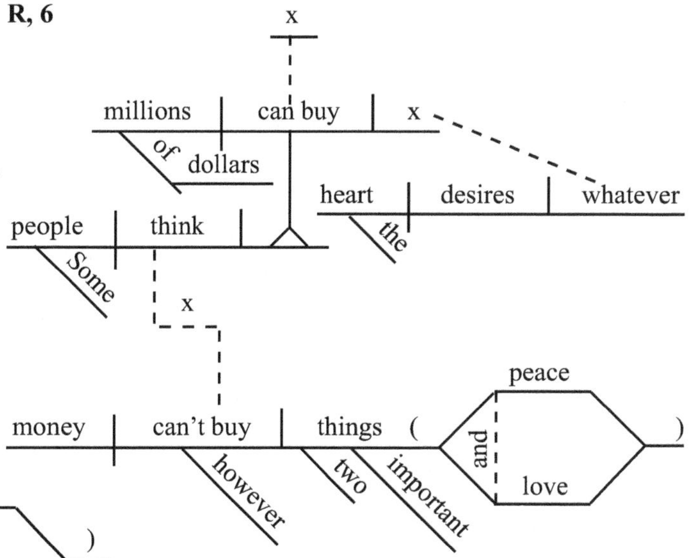

Diagramming Test
Unit I: Lessons 1 - 3

1. Ray Tomlinson, a computer engineer who in 1971 invented e-mail, derives great pleasure from solving hard problems.

2. Armina joined a book club because she could get the first five books for one dollar.

3. The people whose house burned down say that they will build another house in the same location.

4. The magic mirror, which always told the truth, told the queen that Snow White was the fairest of all.

5. Do you know the reason why we tell our children that Santa will bring them presents if they are good?

6. Although she misses the warmth of the coastal sun, she misses especially the evening fog, which frequently enveloped their old neighborhood.

7. Do you think that the Gypsies who travel around Europe and sell products that they make deserve their bad reputation?

8. Although old Mrs. Alvey died in the early summer, the flower garden that she planted behind her house is blooming lavishly.

Diagramming Test
Unit II: Lessons 4 - 6

1. It may rain or snow tomorrow, or the sun may appear and warm the earth.

2. He says that he can beat you in a race without trying at all.

3. Patas monkeys are the fastest primates, but cheetahs are the fastest land mammals.

4. Lying in bed that evening, Peter Rabbit realizes that going into Mr. McGregor's garden was foolish.

5. Lending money at interest was taboo in ancient and medieval times, but it is commonplace in the modern world.

6. Dressed in her best Sunday clothes and shaking with fright, Reyona approached the personnel manager's office.

7. Convinced that reading is a vital skill, the Broyles read to their young children every evening at bedtime.

8. For children, playing games with others is important, because they learn social skills that they will need throughout their lives.

Diagramming Test
Unit III: Lessons 7 - 9

1. Everyone was asking where the game would be played.

2. Do you want to stay here until your parents call?

3. Lucas, tell the class how you solved the problem without using a calculator.

4. Do you know which president liked to listen to the song "Camelot" before he went to bed at night?

5. Scratching his bald head, Grandpa asked how it could be so hard to eat rice with chopsticks.

6. In the old photo, Mom and Dad are standing by their 1955 Ford while Billie and I play in the foreground.

7. When Clayton returned from Blockbuster, he immediately asked when he should start the video.

8. Do you want to know why the Grinch who stole Christmas did not return Christmas when he returned the Whos' presents?

Diagramming Test
Unit IV: Lessons 10 - 12

1. When the lunar module had landed, Neil Armstrong stepped onto the surface of the moon, and Buzz Aldrin followed.

2. There is a time for working and a time for playing, but little Joe can't do either today because he is sick.

3. Kevin says that blue whales are larger than elephants, and he is sure of that.

4. Although Cookie Monster is not as big as Big Bird, he can eat more cookies than Big Bird.

5. Although Zeus was mightier than the other Greek gods, he was not all-powerful, and he certainly had his faults.

6. There are people in the world who have never seen a book, a car, or a telephone, and anthropologists enjoy visiting them.

7. There once was a fox who tried to reach some grapes, but when he did not succeed, he said that they were sour.

8. When the first group had finished breakfast, they returned to their rooms, and the staff quickly prepared the tables for the second group.

Diagramming Test
Unit V: Lessons 13 - 15

1. Psyche was prettier than Venus, which made the goddess jealous of Psyche.

2. Mindy said that she would be happy to help, but she gave up after a few minutes and went home.

3. Finally the rain let up, which gave us a chance to finish cleaning out the gutters.

4. There can be no love where there is no trust, which is why Cupid flees from Psyche.

5. Many people use their credit cards to run up huge debts.

6. To stick up for his little brother, Marvin fought his best friend, which was a brave but stupid thing to do.

7. The thieves took too much time to hold up the bank, which gave the police an opportunity to intercept them.

8. Old Mrs. Harkett set out for the market to get her poor dog, whose name is unknown, a bone.

Diagramming Test
Unit VI: Lessons 16 - 18

1. We are going to identify the pictures we no longer like and take them out of the collection.

2. Because of their desire to finish the project on time, they began working ten hours each day.

3. Some Floridians say the state ought to restrict boat traffic in waters inhabited by manatees, an endangered species.

4. Do you think Jordan acts as if he had the weight of the world on his shoulders?

5. The building you asked about, the Empire State Building, used to be the tallest building in the world.

6. In spite of its reputation for immensity, St. Peter's in Rome is not as large as Ta Som, a Buddhist temple in Cambodia.

7. Over the years, the old teacher has come to realize that he has to be patient so that his students learn patience.

8. Instead of using a mechanical device to lift the heavy statue, engineers contacted a group of weightlifters, who were happy to do the job.

Diagramming Test
Unit VII: Lessons 19 - 21

1. Lenora's friends couldn't tell whether she was in a bad mood or not.

2. Alexandra's sewing draws praise from young and old, and her knitting is above average.

3. Because of his relentless striving for perfection, Austin thinks he always has to be at his best.

4. Mrs. Ridge wondered if she should tell Mr. Ridge that his loud snoring was out of this world.

5. He says he doesn't know if his gambling is out of control, but everyone else knows.

6. I won't ask if this is your second or third citation, but this speeding has to stop.

7. The question is whether your chattering will make you hoarse.

8. Listening to the happy chirping of the birds, Carrie wonders if they are without a care in the world.

Diagramming Test
Unit VIII: Lessons 22 - 24

1. Identical twins Bonnie and Connie are picky eaters when they eat out; however, at home they eat whatever is served.

2. All Muslims possess and treasure the Quran; moreover, many Muslims learn the entire text by heart.

3. My cousins Emily and Melissa save their quarters and give them to whoever is in need.

4. Rodney reads and speaks German two hours a day; nevertheless, he still has much to learn.

5. The Cardinal basketball team is without two key players, Garcia and Dean; still, I can imagine them winning tonight's game.

6. The parents hope and pray that their son will benefit from what the new school offers.

7. Two friends, Jack and Jill, went up a hill to fetch a pail of water; however, Jack fell and let the pail tumble down the hill.

8. Whoever writes and speaks English correctly understands the importance of grammar; still, vocabulary and creativity are important, too.

~ Test Solutions ~

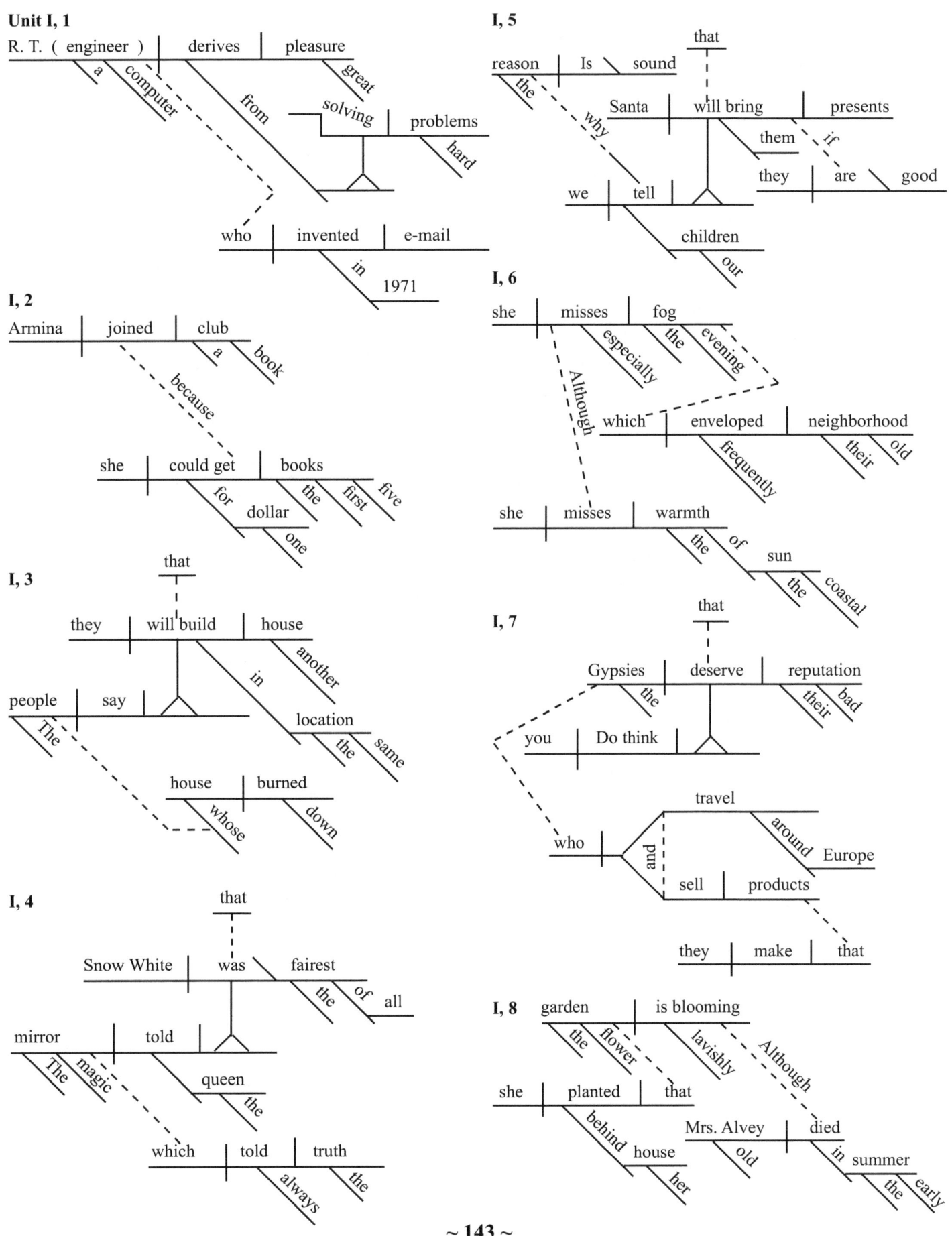

Unit II, 1

II, 2

II, 3

II, 4

II, 5

II, 6

II, 7

II, 8

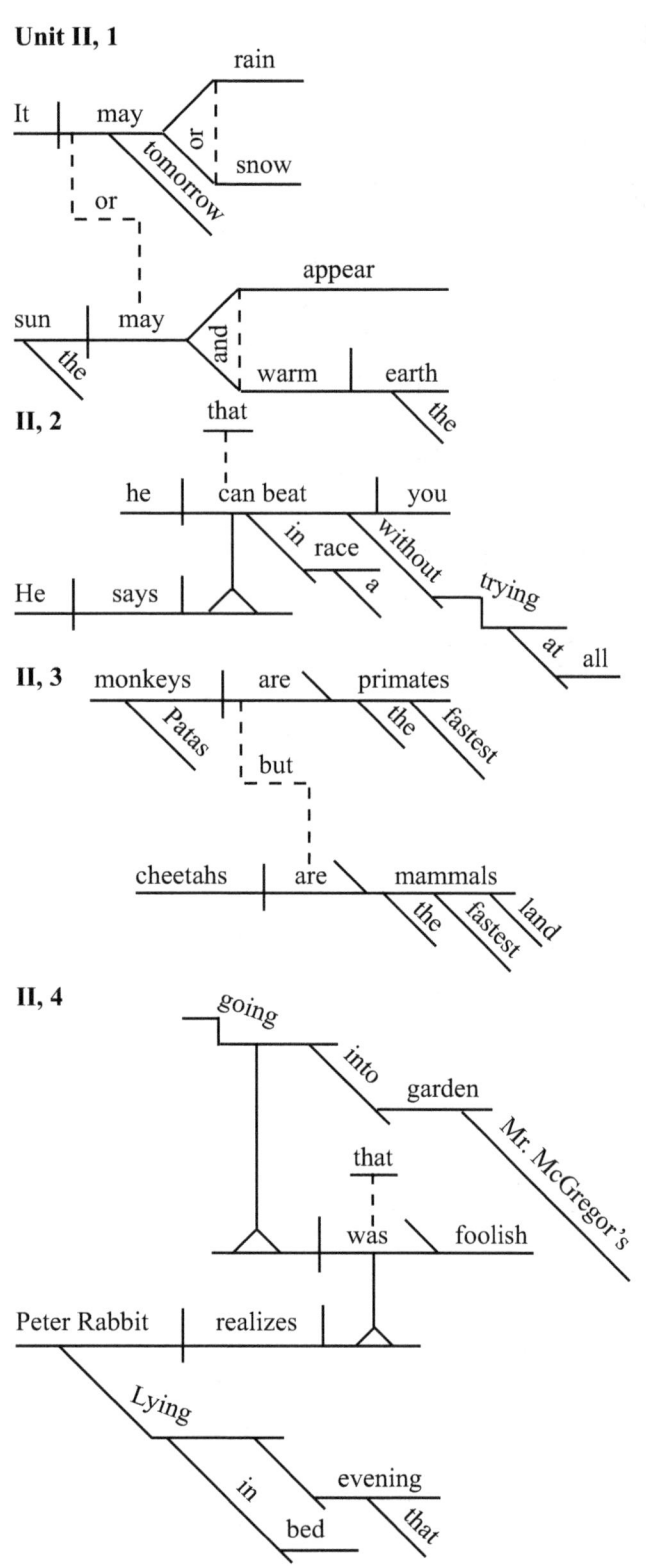

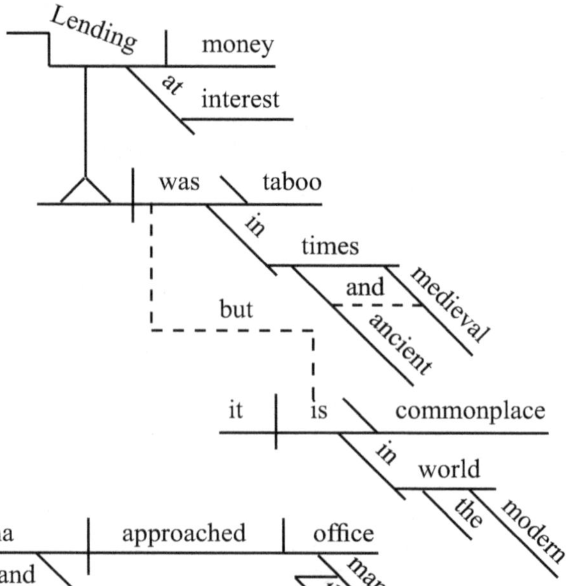

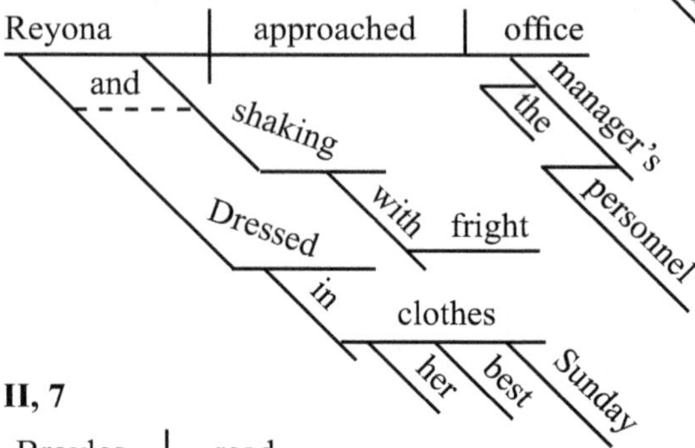

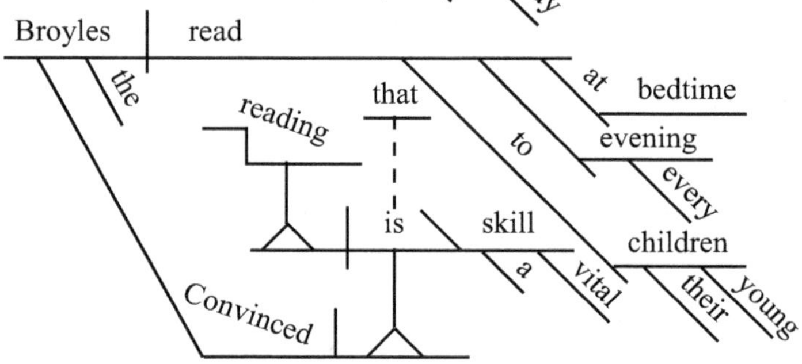

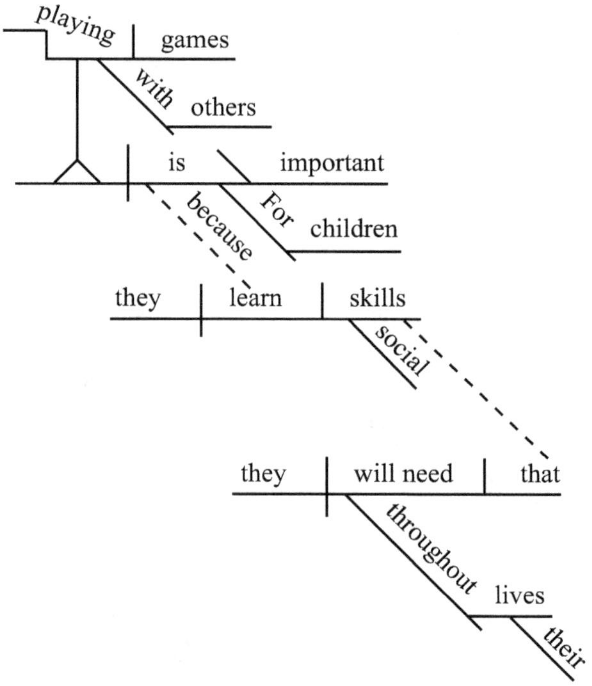

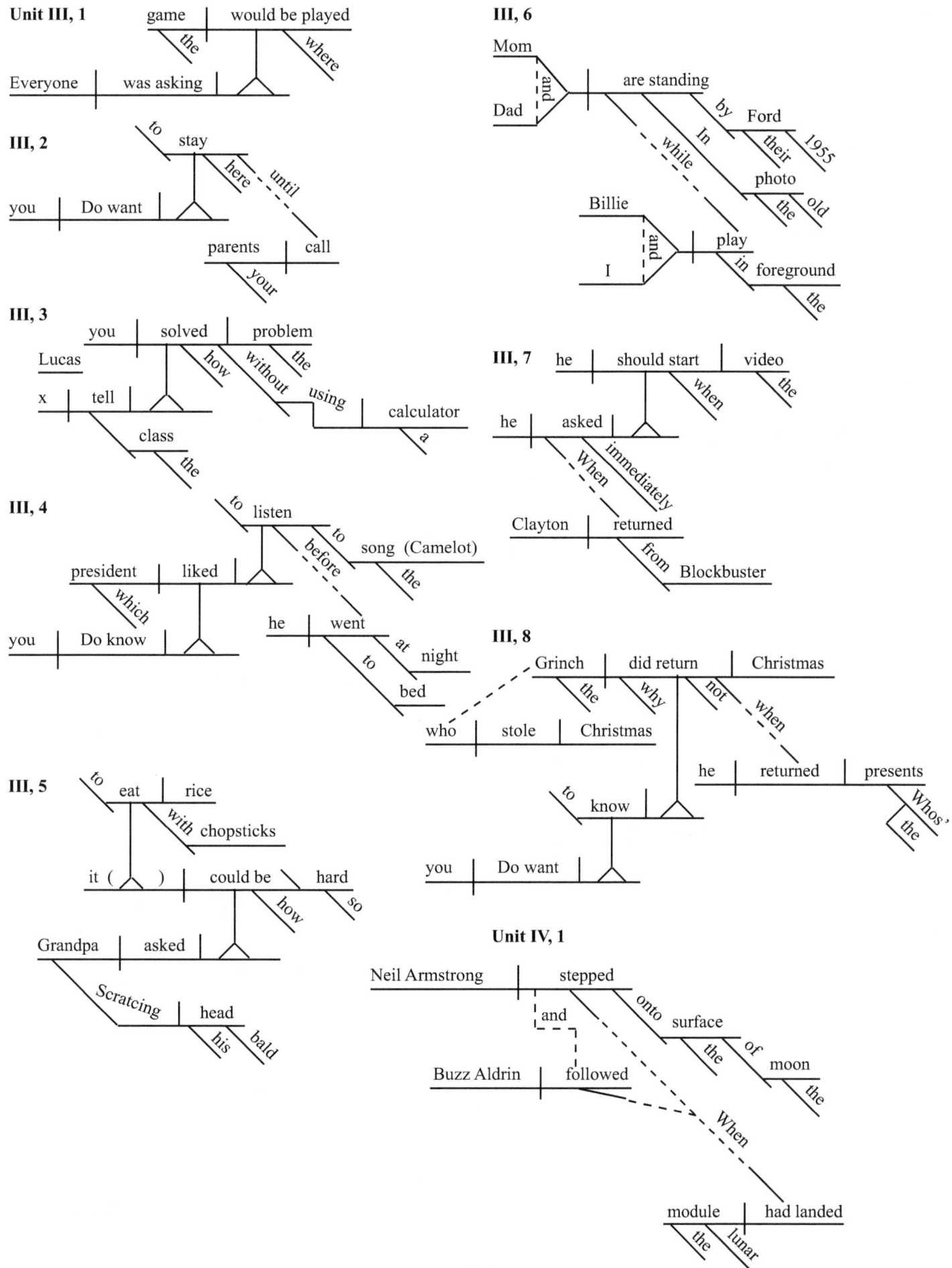

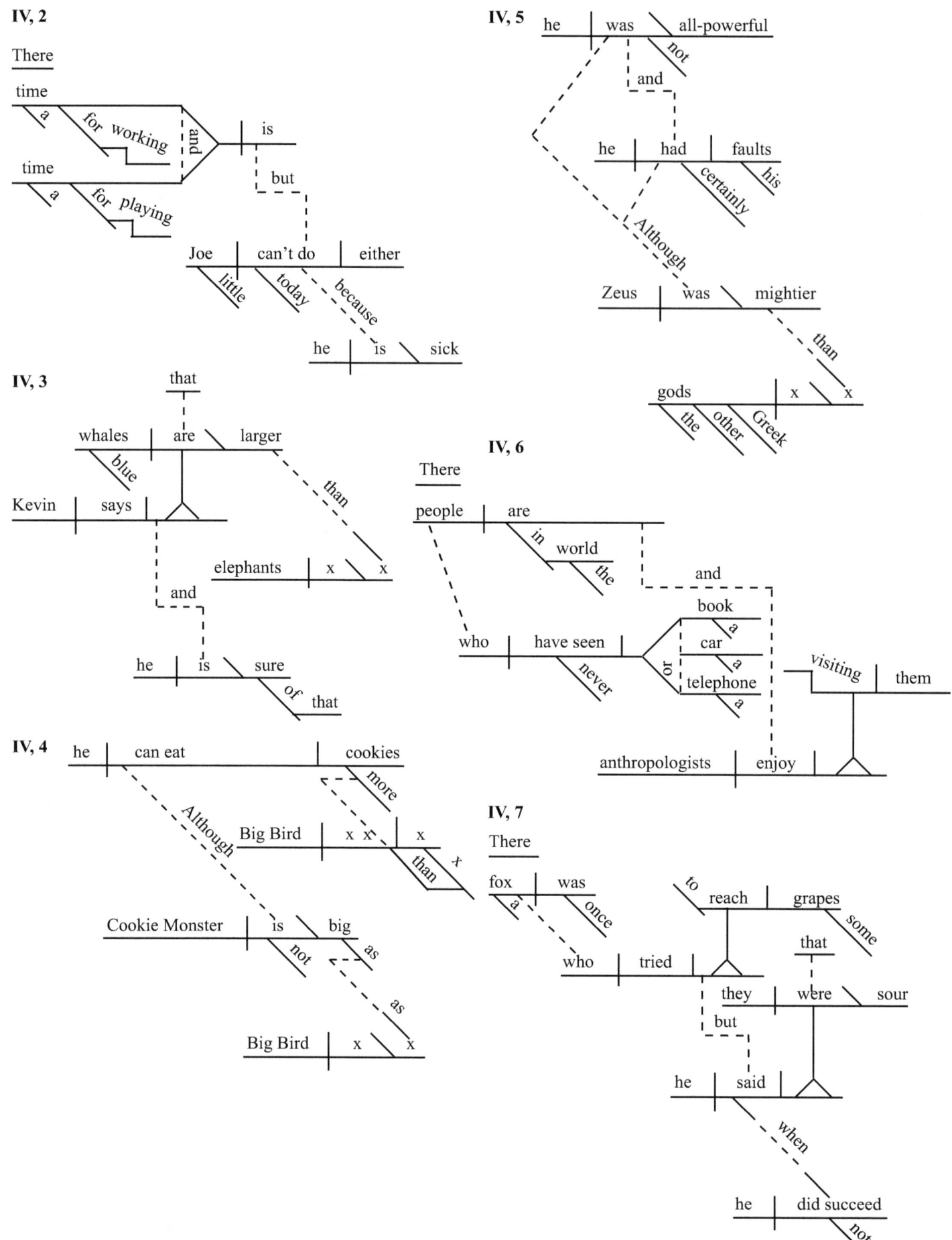

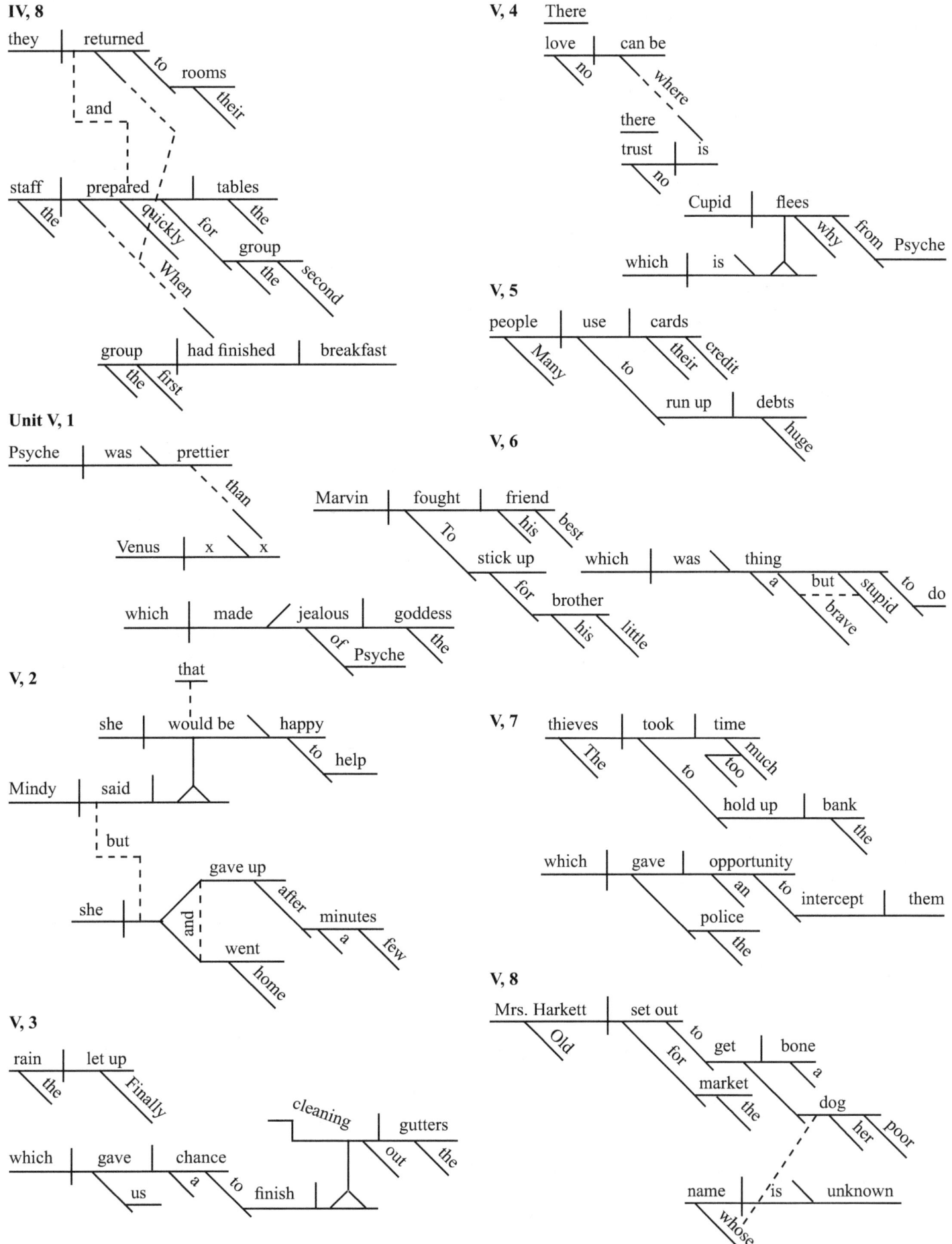

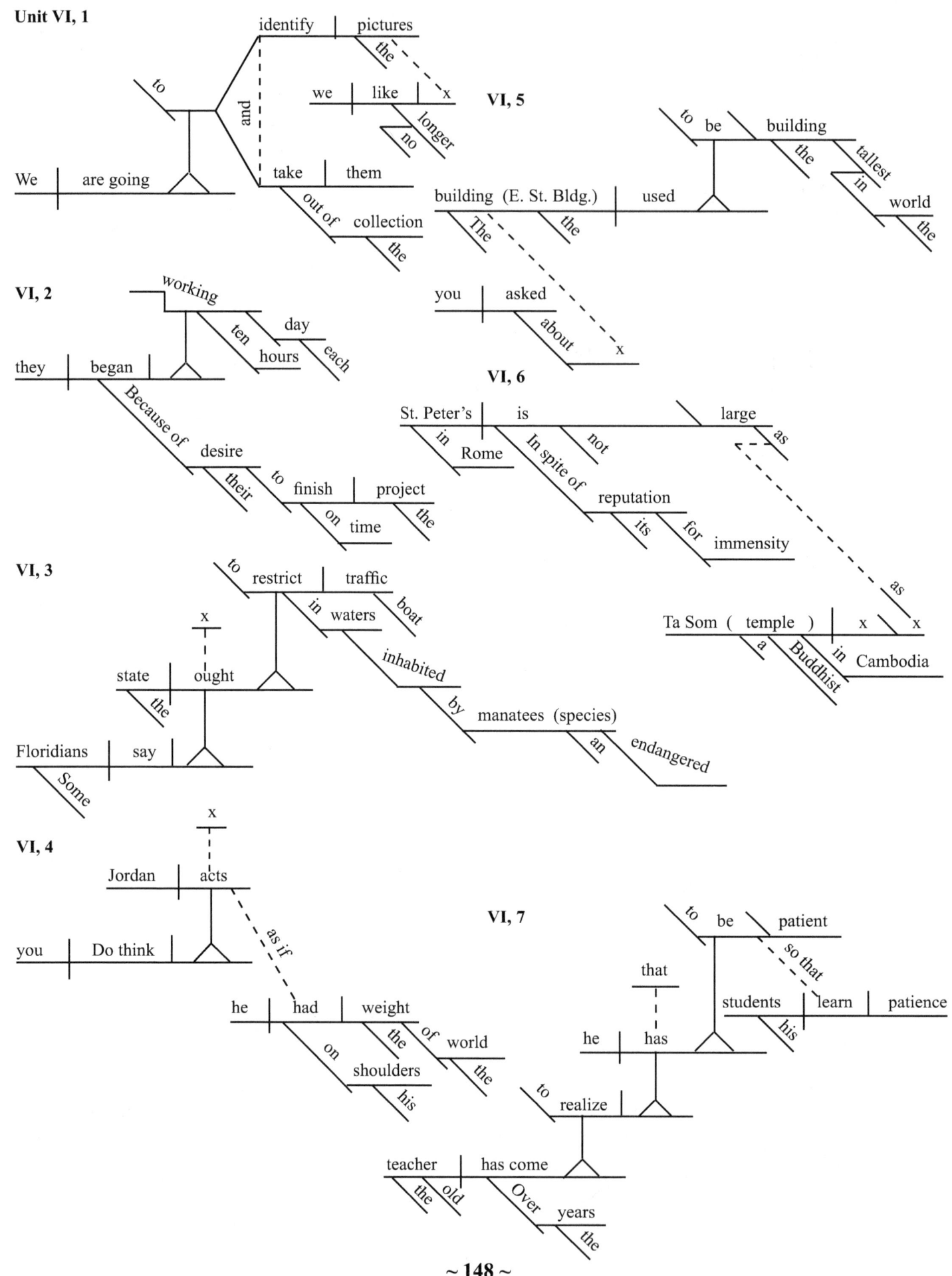

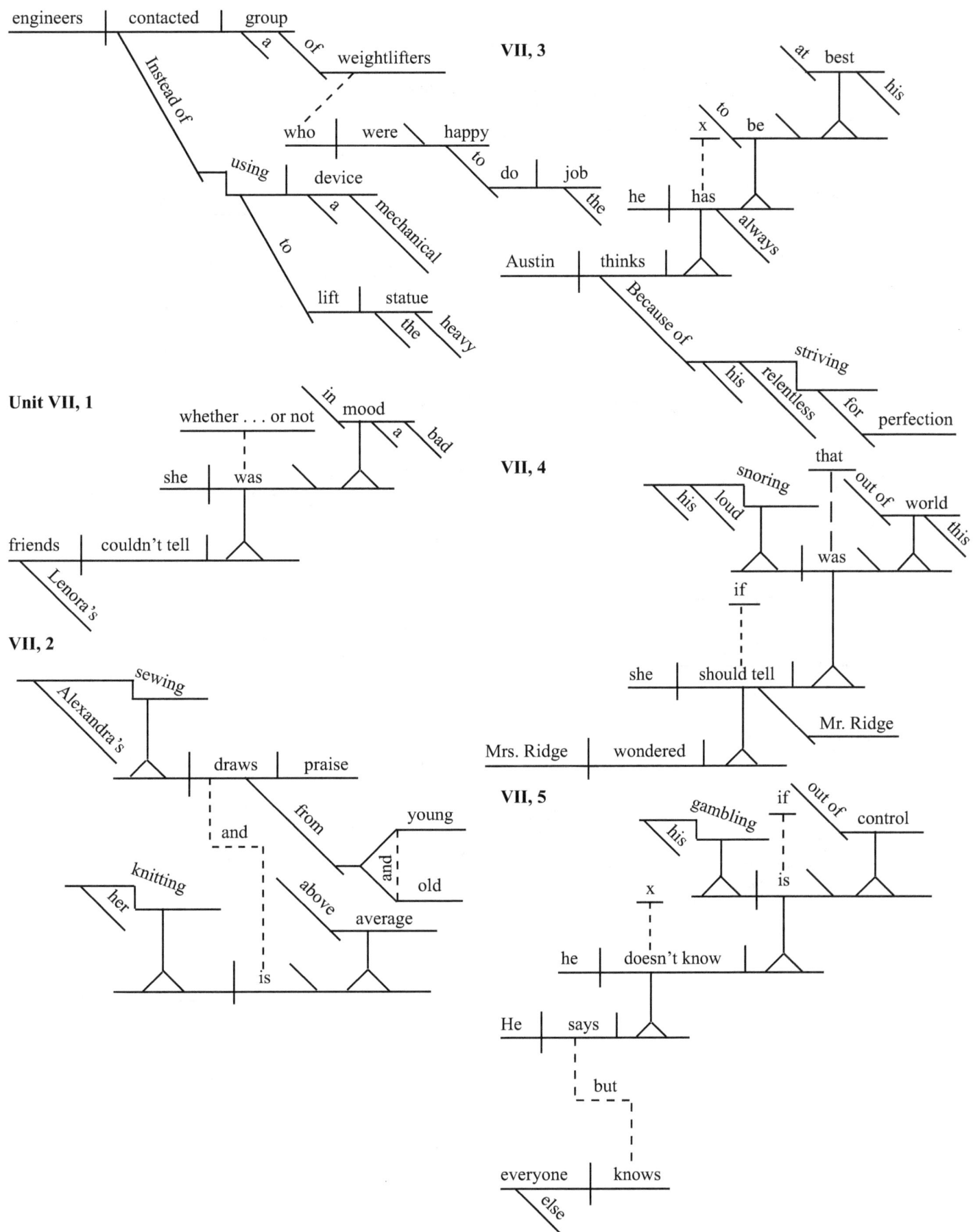

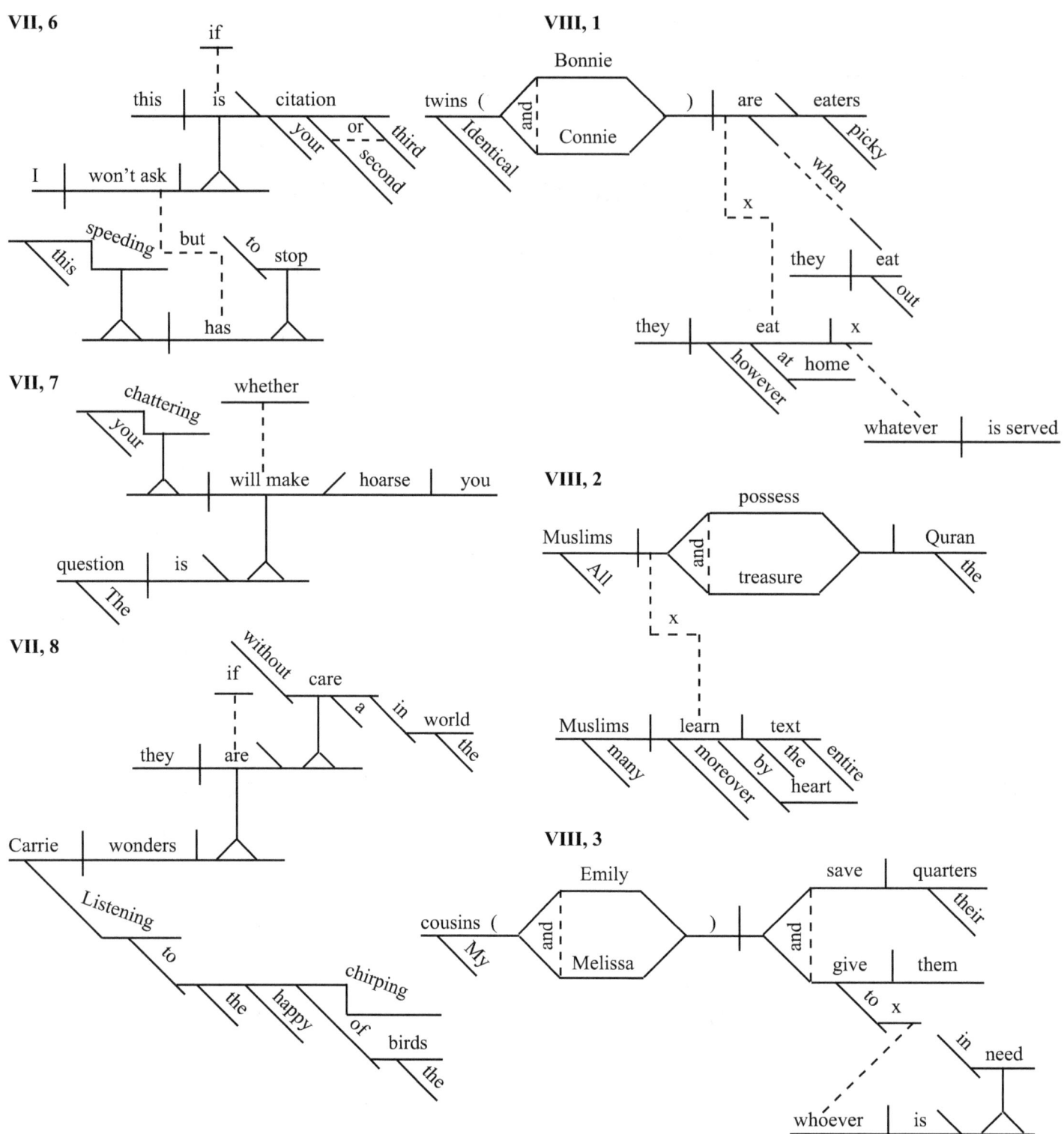

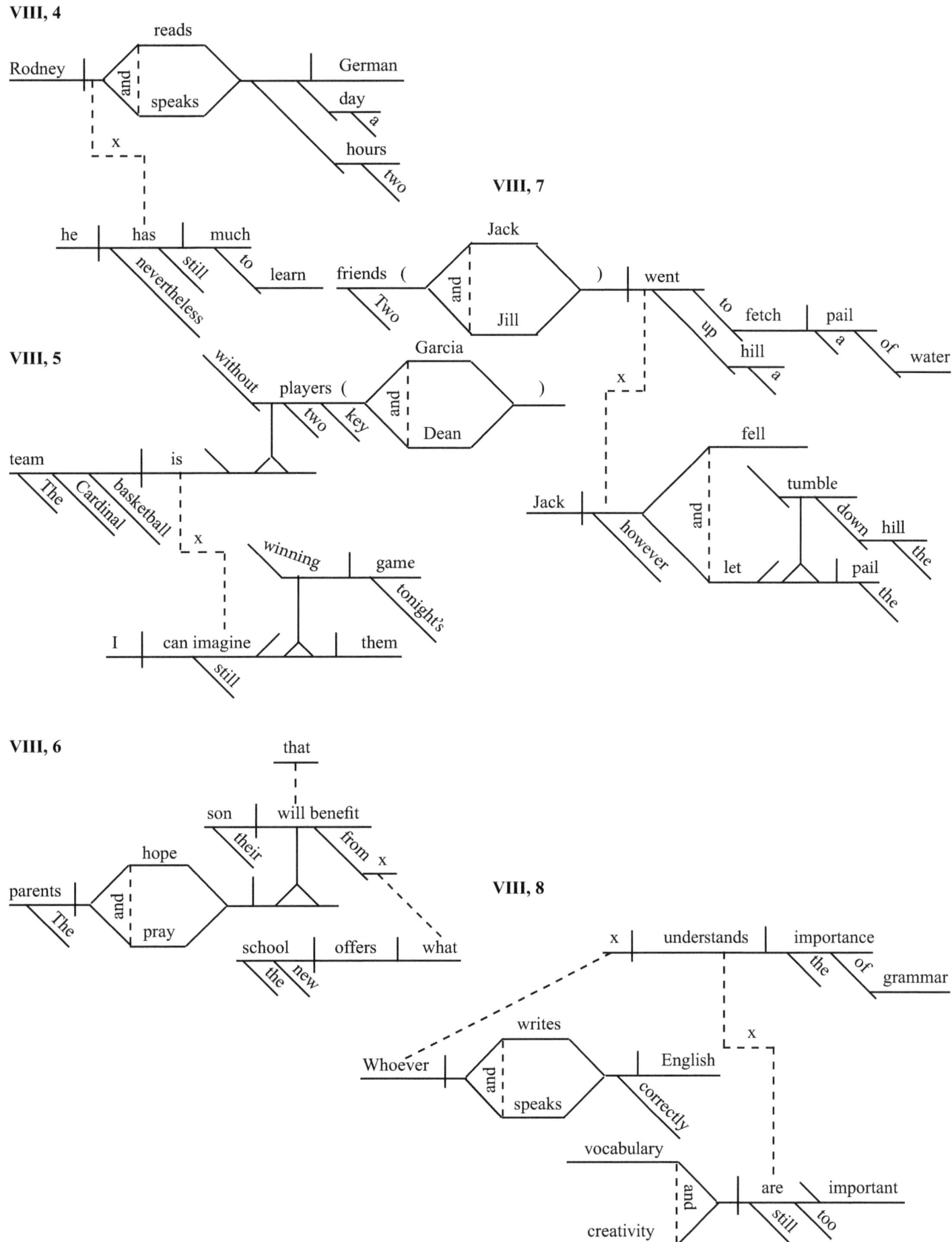

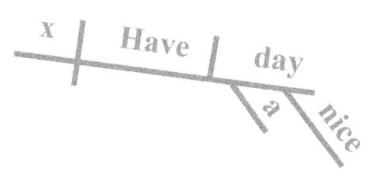
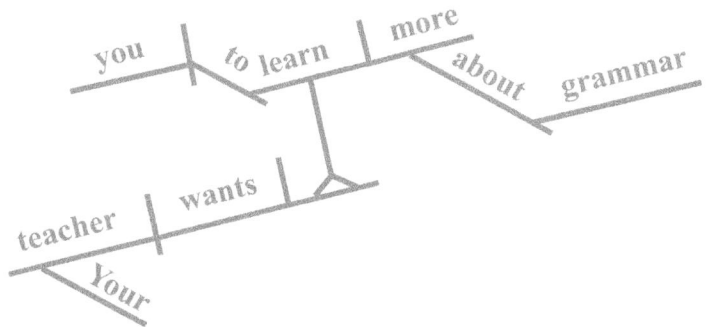

Part Three:
Review and Supplement

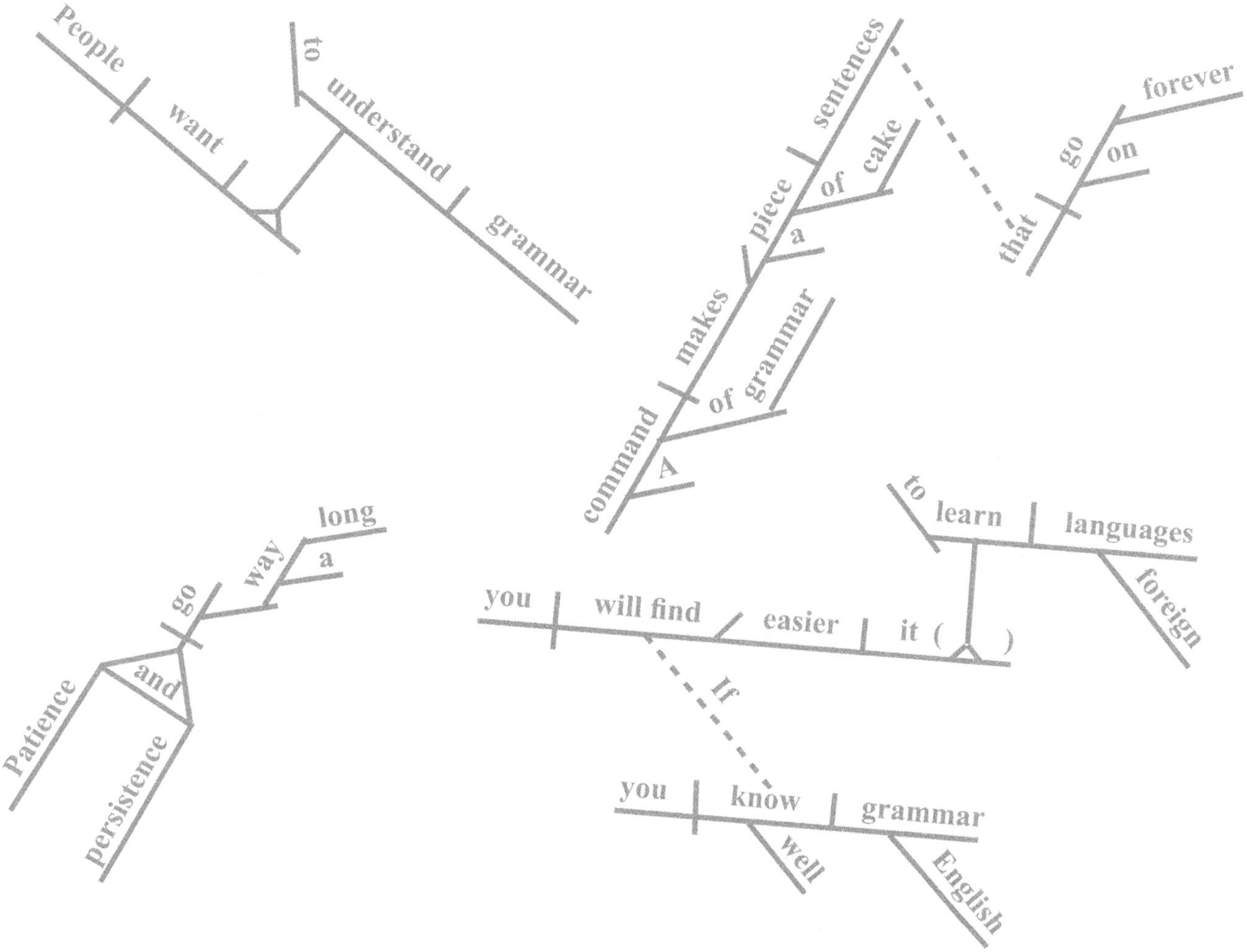

~ Diagrams and Explanations ~

Sentence 1: *She waved.*

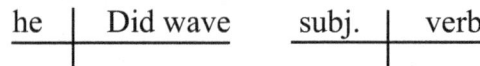

The **personal pronoun** *she* is the **subject** of the sentence. The **verb** *waved* is in the past tense. In diagramming, the subject is separated from the verb by a vertical line that passes through the base line.

Sentence 2: *She was waving.*

The personal pronoun *she* is the **subject** of the sentence. The **verb** *was waving* is past progressive.

Sentence 3: *Did he wave?*

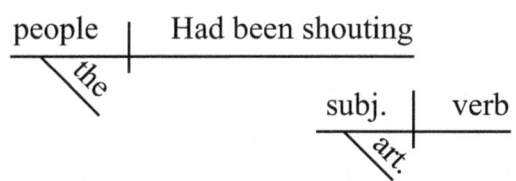

The **subject** of the sentence is the personal pronoun *he*. The **verb** *did wave* is past emphatic. *Did* is capitalized in the diagram to show that it is the first word of the sentence.

Sentence 4: *A boy shouted.*

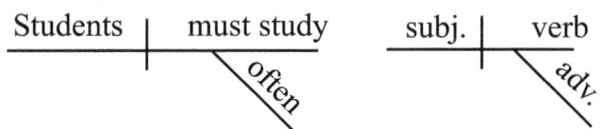

The subject of the sentence is the noun *boy*. It is modified by the **indefinite article** *a*. The verb *shouted* is in the past tense.

Sentence 5: *Had the people been shouting?*

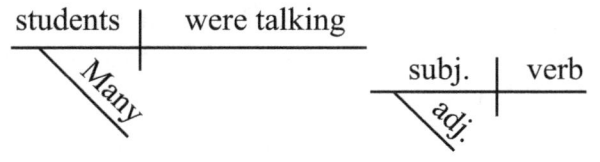

The subject *people* is modified by *the*, a **definite article**. The verb is the past-perfect progressive *had been shouting*. Even if parts of a verb form, like *had* and *been shouting*, are separated in a sentence, they are placed together in a sentence diagram.

Sentence 6: *Students must study often.*

The noun *students* is the subject of the sentence, and the verb is *must study*. *Should, would, can, could, may, might,* and *must* are called **modal auxiliary verbs**. The **adverb** *often* modifies the verb *must study*.

Sentence 7: *Many students were talking.*

The subject of the sentence, *students,* is modified by the **attributive adjective** *many*. An attributive adjective is placed on a diagonal line under the noun it modifies. The verb *were talking* is past progressive.

Sentence 8: *All students should have been listening.*

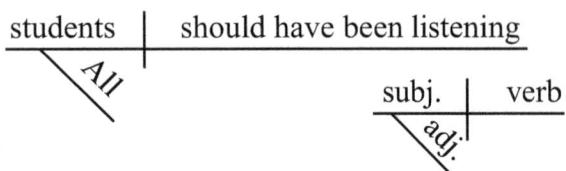

The subject *students* is modified by the **attributive adjective** *all*. The verb consists of the modal auxiliary *should* with the present-perfect progressive of *listen*.

Sentence 9: *My best friend will be skiing.*

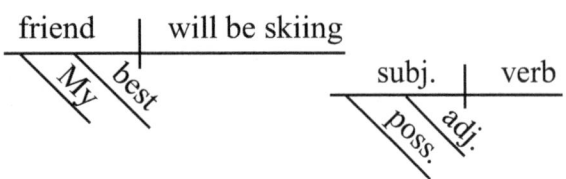

Friend, the subject of the sentence, is modified by the **possessive pronoun** *my* and the attributive adjective *best*. The verb *will be skiing* is future progressive. In diagramming, multiple modifiers of the same word are lined up from left to right according to their sequence in the sentence.

Sentence 10: *Her friend is a ski instructor.*

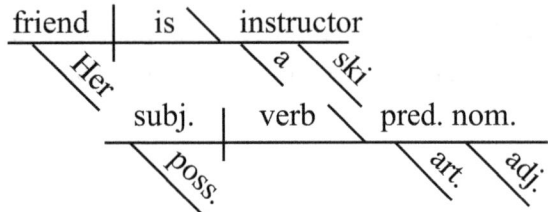

The possessive pronoun *her* modifies the subject *friend*. The verb *is* is a **linking verb**. *Instructor*, a **predicate nominative**, is modified by the indefinite article *a* and by *ski*, a **noun used as an adjective**. In a diagram, a predicate nominative is preceded by a backslash. FYI: When the verb *be* means *exist*, it is a non-linking verb.

Sentence 11: *Has he been an instructor long?*

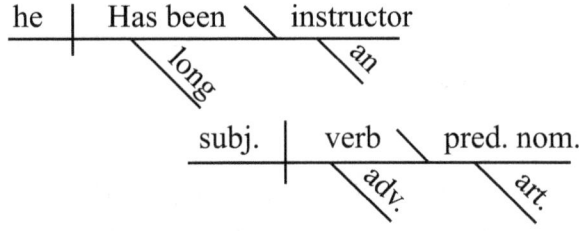

The personal pronoun *he* is the subject of the sentence. The **linking verb** *has been* is in the present-perfect tense. *Instructor*, a **predicate nominative**, is modified by the indefinite article *an*. *Long* is an **adverb** modifying the verb.

Sentence 12: *He looks extremely handsome.*

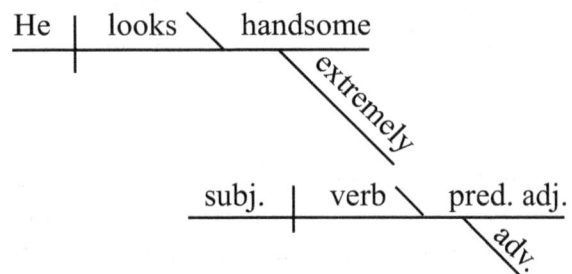

He, a personal pronoun, is the subject of the sentence. *Looks* is a **linking verb**, and *extremely* is an **adverb** modifying the **predicate adjective** *handsome*. A predicate adjective, like a predicate nominative, is preceded by a backslash.

Sentence 13: *Maybe we can become very good skiers.*

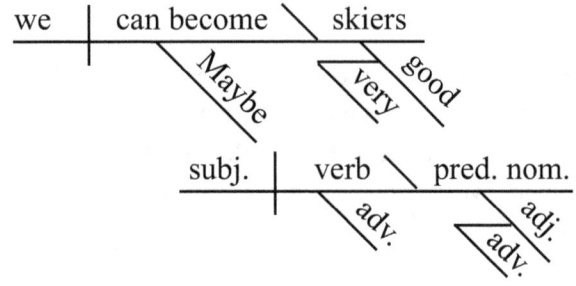

The personal pronoun *we* is the subject. *Can become* is a **linking verb**; it is modified by the adverb *maybe*. The predicate nominative *skiers* is modified by the **attributive adjective** *good*, which in turn is modified by the **adverb** *very*. If an adverb modifies an attributive adjective or an adverb, it is "hooked onto" the diagonal line of that word.

Sentence 14: *My French teacher is not always friendly.*

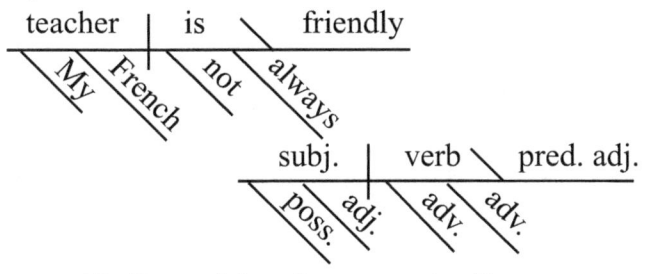

The subject *teacher* is modified by *my*, a possessive pronoun, and by *French*, a **noun used as an adjective**. The linking verb *is* is modified by the adverbs *not* and *always*. *Friendly* is a **predicate adjective**.

Sentence 15: *Doesn't he often seem tired?*

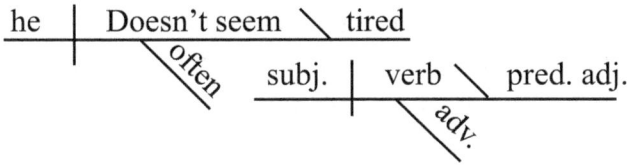

The subject of the sentence is *he*, a personal pronoun. *Does seem*, a linking verb, is modified by the adverb *often*. *Tired* is a predicate adjective. When diagramming, one does not separate **negative contractions** such as *doesn't, can't, aren't, won't,* etc.

Sentence 16: *He cannot be getting any younger.*

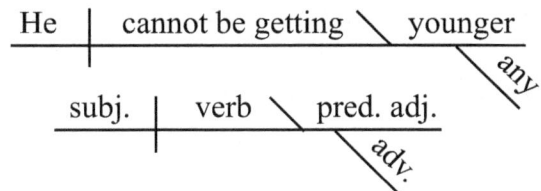

The personal pronoun *he* is the subject, *can be getting* (present progressive) is a **linking verb**, and *younger* is a predicate adjective. **Cannot** is not separated in a sentence diagram. *Any*, usually an adjective, is an adverb here.

Sentence 17: *I feel too lazy today.*

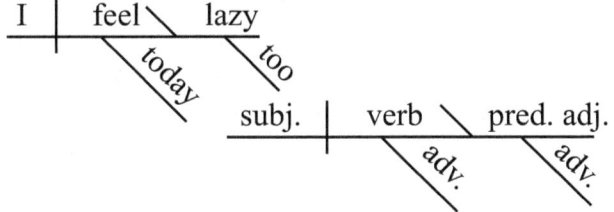

The personal pronoun *I* is the subject of the sentence. The **linking verb** *feel* is modified by the adverb *today*. *Lazy*, a predicate adjective, is modified by the adverb *too*.

Sentence 18: *You may need more sleep.*

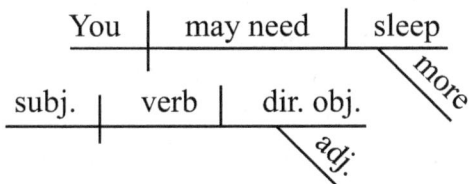

Sleep is a **direct object**; it is modified by the adjective *more*. Direct objects answer the question *whom?* or *what?* when asked immediately after a non-linking verb. In a diagram, a direct object is preceded by a vertical line that rests on the base line.

Sentence 19: *Why do you think that?*

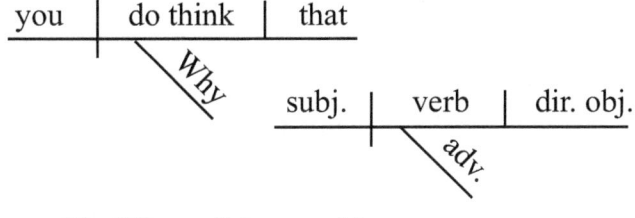

The **demonstrative pronoun** *that* is a **direct object** in this sentence. *Why* is an **interrogative adverb.**

Sentence 20: *Whom did you ask?*

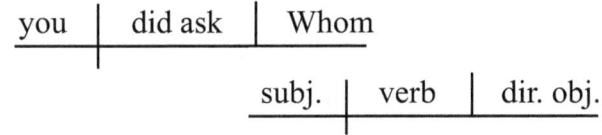

The **interrogative pronoun** *whom* is a **direct object** here.

Sentence 21: *My extended family includes two small, sleepy nephews.*

The subject *family* is modified by the possessive pronoun *my* and the adjective *extended*. The verb *includes* has a **direct object**, *nephews*, which is modified by three adjectives.

Sentence 22: *When did you read the newspaper?*

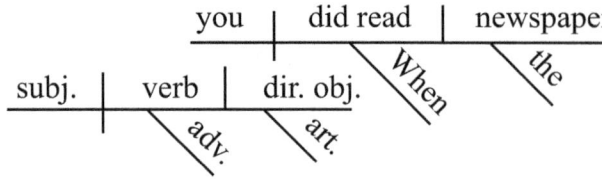

The subject of the sentence is the personal pronoun *you*, and the verb is the past-emphatic *did read*. The **direct object** *newspaper* is modified by the definite article, *the*. *When* is an **interrogative adverb**.

Sentence 23: *Who won the game?*

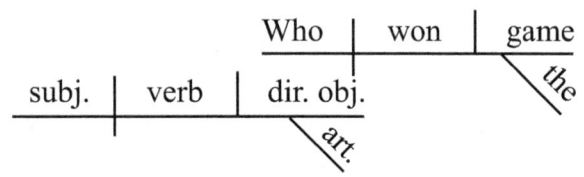

Who, an **interrogative pronoun**, is the subject of the sentence. *Won* is the verb. *Game*, a **direct object**, is modified by the definite article, *the*.

Sentence 24: *There are still several teams in the gym.*

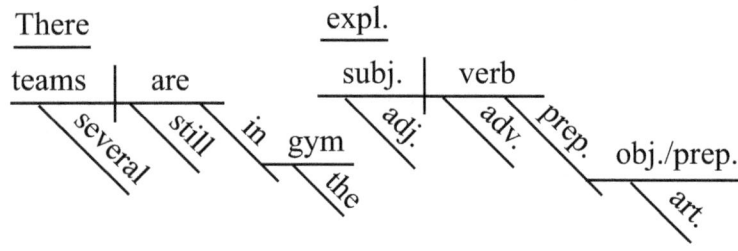

There is an **expletive**. Expletives have a function but no meaning. As an expletive, *there* announces that the subject will follow the verb. *In the gym* is a **prepositional phrase**; *in* is the **preposition** and *gym* is its **object**. In this sentence, *are* does not function as a linking verb.

Sentence 25: *My team will definitely be playing in the final game.*

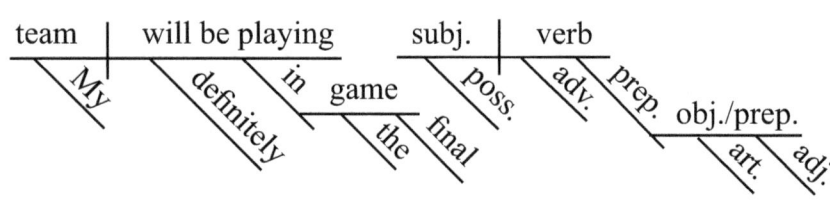

The subject of the sentence, *team*, is modified by the possessive pronoun *my*. The future-progressive verb *will be playing* is modified by the adverb *definitely* and by a **prepositional phrase**.

Sentence 26: *Brad's team was beaten soundly in the first game of the tournament.*

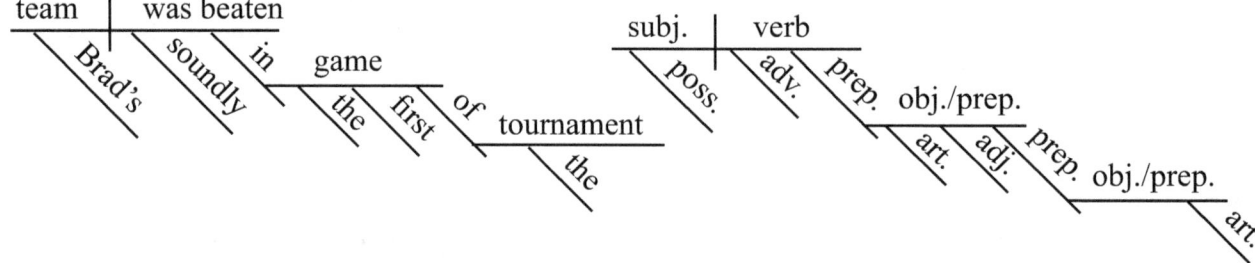

The subject *team* is modified by the **possessive noun** *Brad's*. The first **prepositional phrase**, *in the first game*, is adverbial (since it modifies the verb) and the second, *of the tournament*, is adjectival (since it modifies a noun). The verb *was beaten* is in the past tense, passive voice.

Sentence 27: *Long ago the octogenarian found the secret to a long life.*

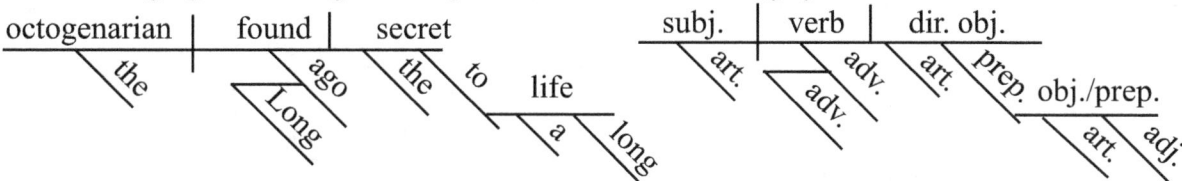

The adverb *ago* is modified by the adverb *long*. The prepositional phrase *to a long life* modifies the direct object *secret*.

Sentence 28: *Jessica, open your book.*

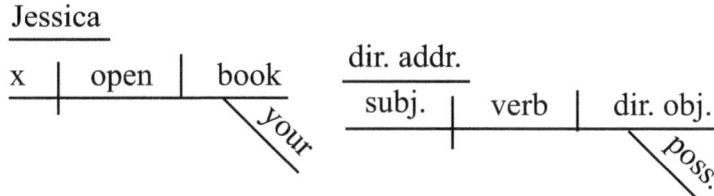

Jessica is a noun of **direct address**; it indicates the person spoken to. The subject of the sentence is an **unexpressed you**. An unexpressed (understood) word is represented in a diagram by an *x*.

Sentence 29: *Turn to page 16.*

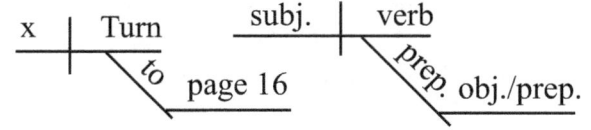

Page 16 can be construed as a **phrasal noun**. The **unexpressed subject** is *you*.

Sentence 30: *Children, write the answers to the first exercise.*

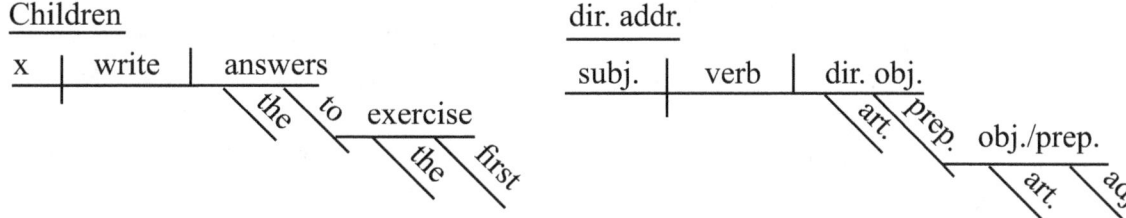

Children is a noun of **direct address**. The subject of the sentence is an **unexpressed you**, represented in the diagram by an *x*. *Answers*, a direct object, is modified by the prepositional phrase *to the first exercise*.

Sentence 31: *Teacher, tell us a story.*

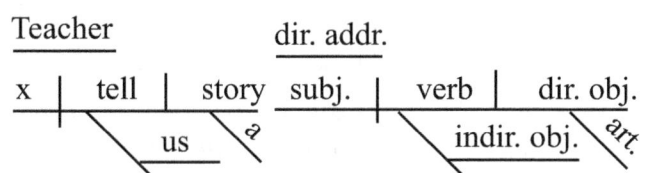

Story is a direct object, and *us* is an **indirect object**. An indirect object, which is a particular kind of **adverbial objective** (a noun used as an adverb), indicates the person or thing to whom something is given, said, or shown. It is diagrammed like an object of a preposition.

Sentence 32: *Each year we visit neighbors at Christmastime.*

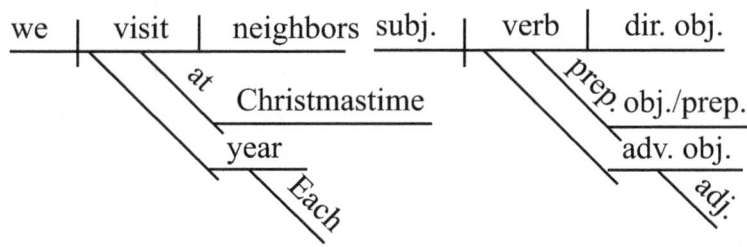

The personal pronoun *we* is the subject of the sentence, *visit* is the verb, and *neighbors* is a direct object. *Year* is an **adverbial objective**. *At Christmastime* is an adverbial prepositional phrase.

Sentence 33: *We always give them some Christmas cookies.*

The subject is the personal pronoun *we*. The adverb *always* modifies the verb *give*. *Them* is an **indirect object**. The direct object *cookies* is modified by the adjective *some* and by a noun used as an adjective, *Christmas*.

Sentence 34: *Last year we were given a jug of apple cider.*

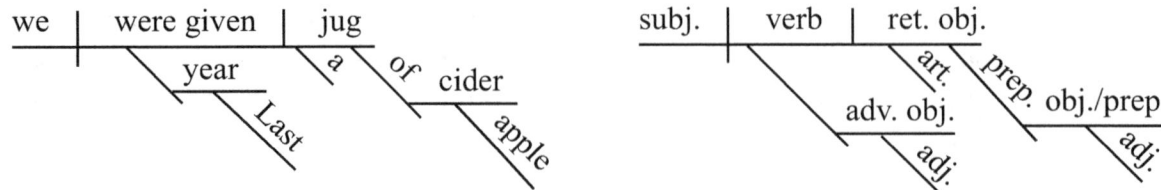

Normally a verb in the passive voice does not have a direct object; however, if the subject of a passive sentence (in this case, *we*) can be expressed as an indirect object (*us*) in a corresponding sentence in the active voice (*Last year someone gave us a jug of apple cider*), the direct object (in this case, *jug*) is retained when the active sentence becomes passive. Such an object is called a **retained object**.

Sentence 35: *Mr. Edwards, a lifelong non-smoker, attributes his longevity to a healthy lifestyle.*

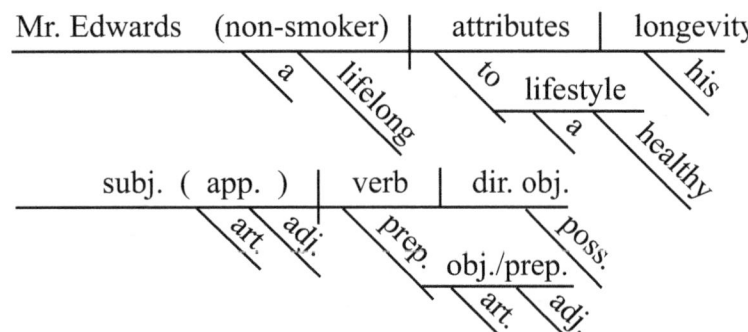

Non-smoker is in **apposition** with the subject of the sentence, *Mr. Edwards*. Like most appositives, *non-smoker* is a noun; however, other parts of speech (verbs, adjectives, etc.) can also be appositives, as can phrases and clauses. *To a healthy lifestyle* is an adverbial prepositional phrase. *Longevity*, a direct object, is modified by the possessive pronoun *his*.

Sentence 36: *Grandma and grandpa sent their grandchildren, Suzy and Shirley, some toys and clothes.*

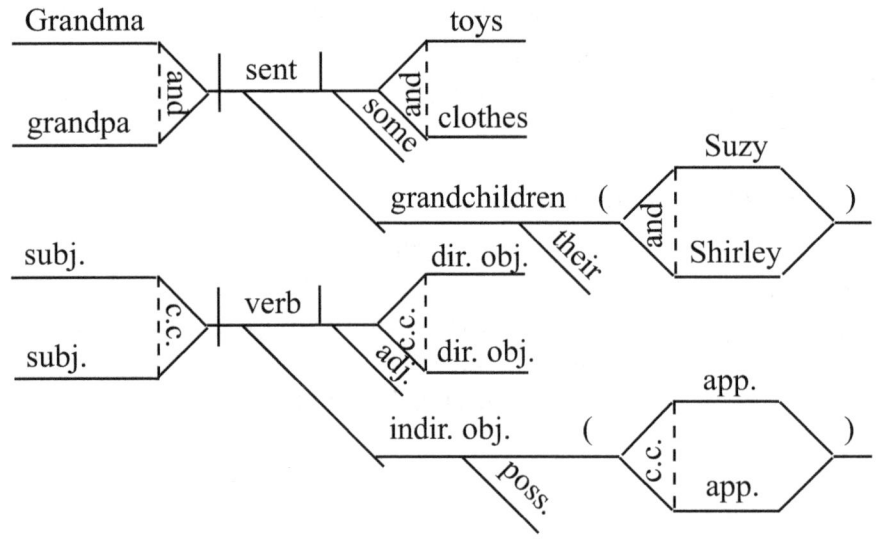

This sentence has a **compound subject** (*grandma and grandpa*), a **compound direct object** (*toys and clothes*), and a **compound appositive** (*Suzy and Shirley*). An **appositive** is diagrammed in parentheses, next to the noun or pronoun with which it is in apposition. *And* is a **coordinating conjunction**. Branching is used to diagram compound words and phrases. *Some* modifies both *toys* and *clothes*.

Sentence 37: *He walks every day for an hour, eats low-fat foods, and sleeps eight hours every night.*

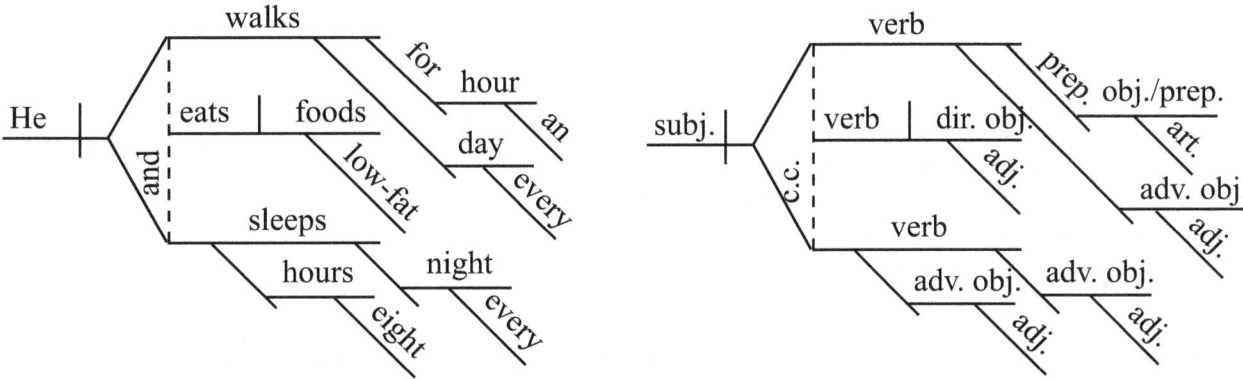

This sentence has a **tripartite predicate**; all three verbs (*walks, eats,* and *sleeps*) share the same subject, the personal pronoun *he*. The coordinating conjunction is *and*. There are three **adverbial objectives**: *day, hours,* and *night*.

Sentence 38: *They put the dishes in the dishwasher and washed the sticky pots and greasy pans by hand.*

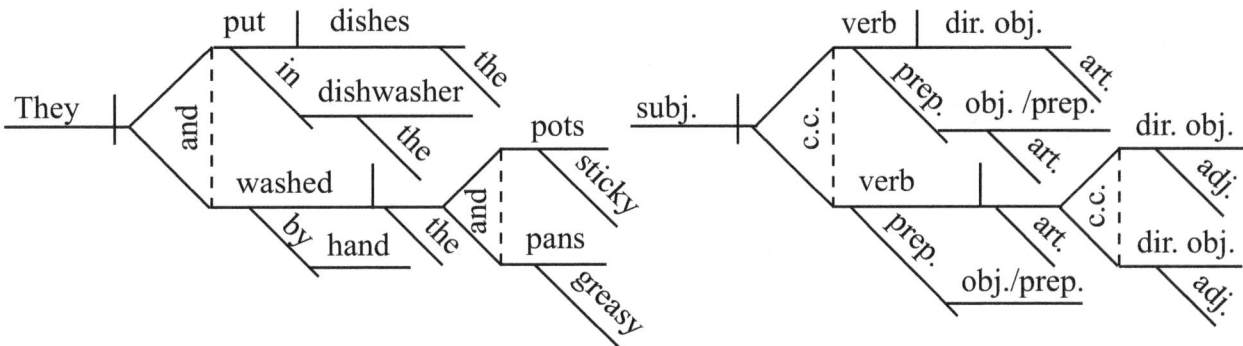

The second predicate of the **compound predicate** contains a **compound direct object**. Notice that *the* modifies both *pots* and *pans*, whereas *sticky* modifies only *pots* and *greasy* modifies only *pans*. *And* is a coordinating conjunction.

Sentence 39: *The men sat outside and talked about sports and politics, but we women watched our favorite TV program.*

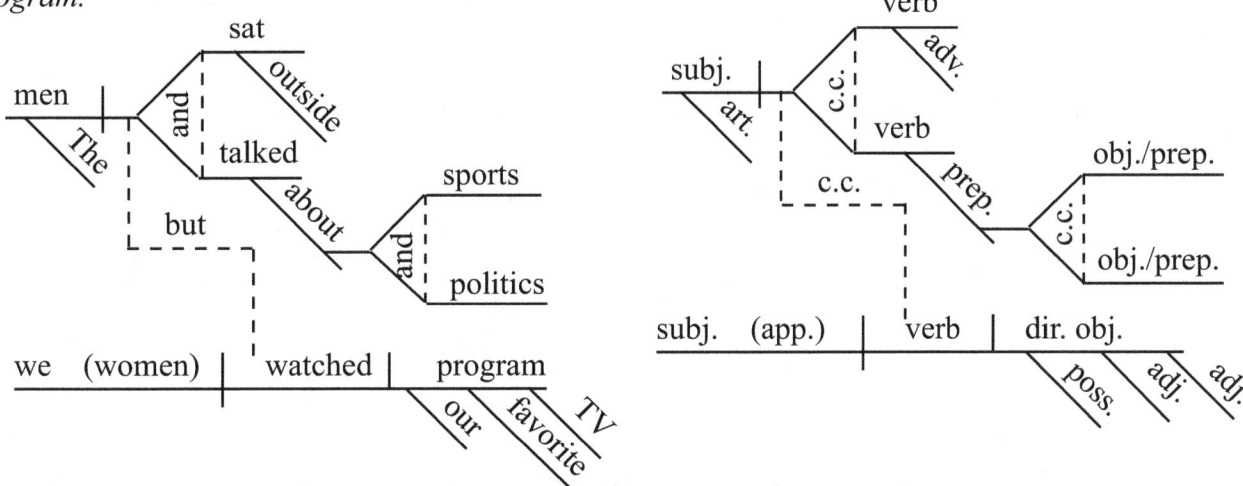

This is a **compound sentence**; it has two main clauses joined by the coordinating conjunction *but*. The first main clause has a **compound predicate** containing a **prepositional phrase with a compound object**. In the second main clause, *women* is in apposition with the subject *we*. *TV*, a noun, is used here as an adjective.

Sentence 40: *I like cake and cookies, but my favorite dessert is either strawberry pie or ice cream.*

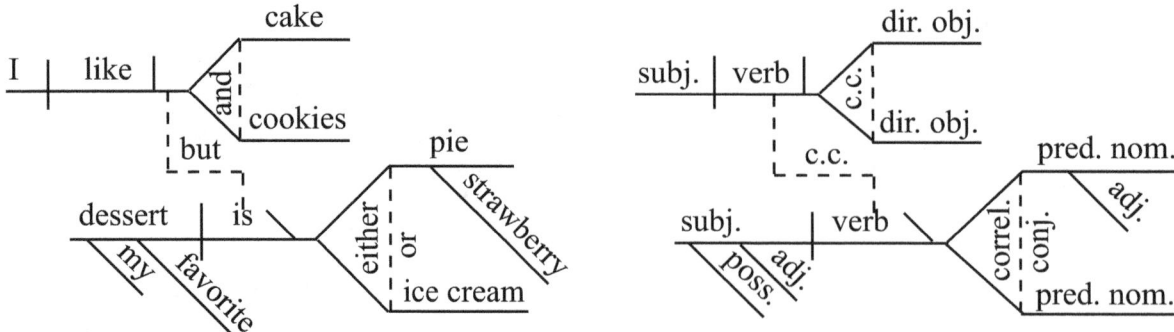

In this **compound sentence**, the first main clause has a **compound direct object** and the second a **compound predicate nominative**. When a noun and its modifier are so closely associated that they can be found as a single entry in a dictionary, they can be diagrammed together, like *ice cream*. *Either* and *or* are **correlative conjunctions**. Other such conjunctions are *both . . . and* and *neither . . . nor*.

Sentence 41: *We can't go with you tonight because the teachers assigned enough homework for two days.*

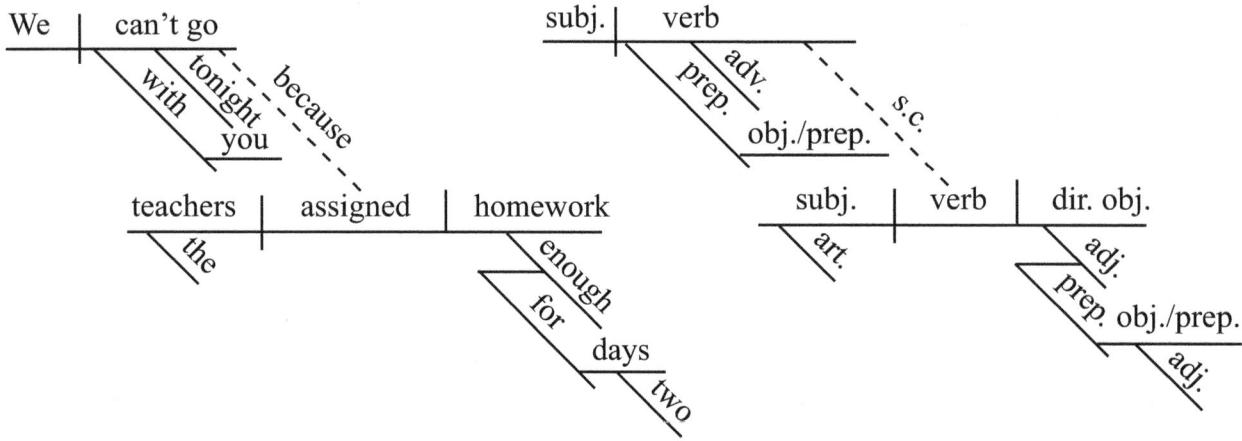

Sentences that have one or more **subordinate clauses (dependent clauses)** are called **complex sentences**. In this sentence, the subordinate clause is introduced by the **subordinating conjunction** *because*. The word *tonight*, often a noun, is an adverb in this sentence. The prepositional phrase *for two days* modifies the adjective *enough*.

Sentence 42: *Although there were still many unanswered questions, the committee selected a site and hired an architect.*

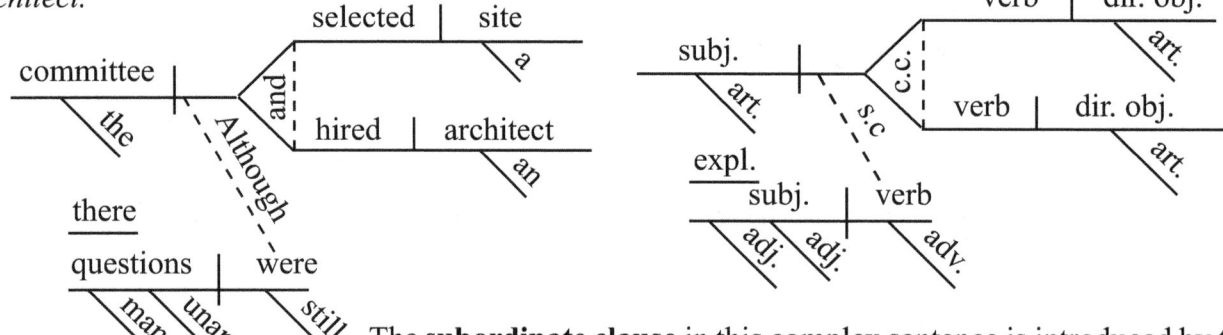

The **subordinate clause** in this complex sentence is introduced by the **subordinating conjunction** *although*. *There* is an **expletive**, whose function is to announce that the subject will follow the verb. The **main clause** has a **compound predicate**.

~ 162 ~

Sentence 43: *Sue left school early because of a persistent headache, but she returned later and picked up her books.*

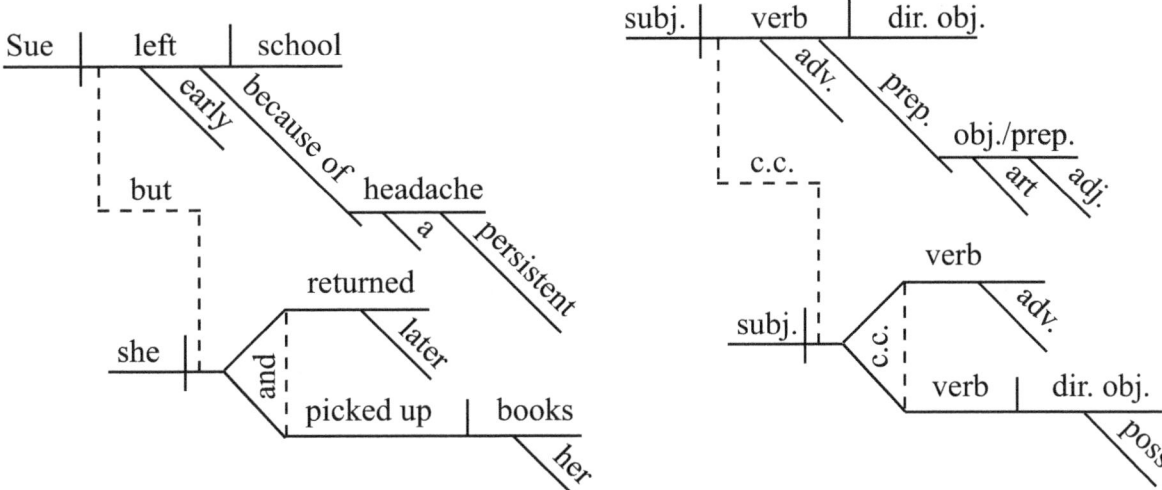

This is a compound sentence; its two main clauses are joined by the coordinating conjunction *but*. *Because of* is a **phrasal preposition** (a preposition consisting of more than one word). In the second main clause, which has a compound predicate, one of the verbs is *picked up*, a **phrasal verb** (a verb-particle combination whose meaning cannot be deduced from the separate meanings of the verb and the particle).

Sentence 44: *The freshmen elected Missy vice-president.*

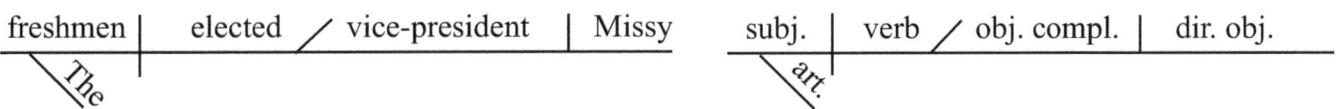

Vice-president, a noun that completes the action of the verb and in a way repeats the direct object, is an **objective complement.**

Sentence 45: *The same students chose Scott as class secretary.*

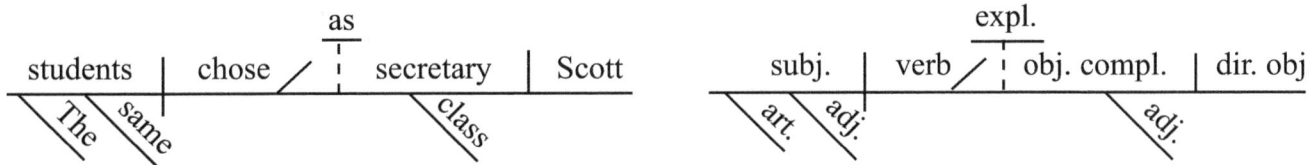

Secretary is an **objective complement**. It is preceded by the **expletive *as***, whose function is to introduce the objective complement. *Class* is a noun used as an adjective.

Sentence 46: *The results of the election made them happy, and their parents were made proud.*

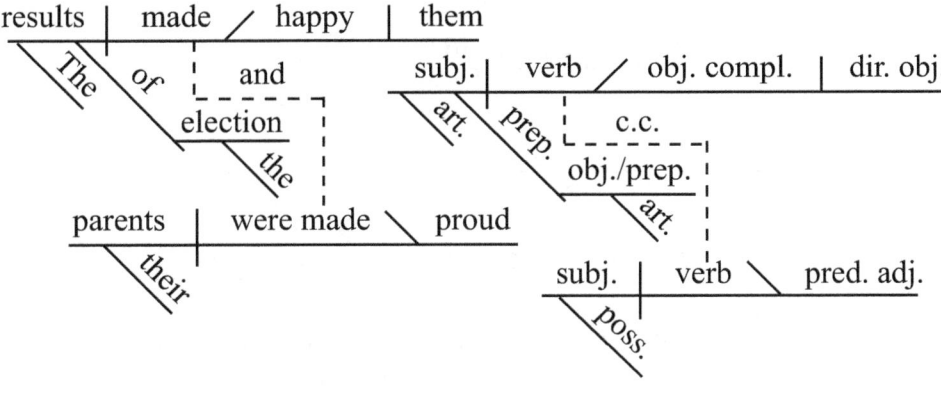

The verb *made* is in the active voice, and the adjective *happy* is an **objective complement**. The verb *were made* is in the passive voice; it functions as a **linking verb**. *Proud* is a **predicate adjective** (subjective complement).

Sentence 47: *No one greeted the people who arrived late.*

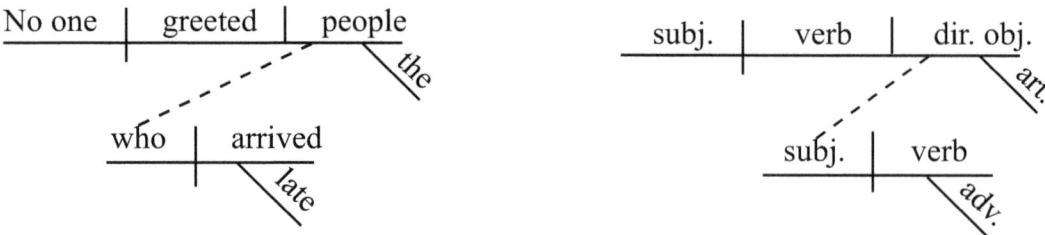

The **relative pronoun** *who* is the subject of the **relative clause**. A relative pronoun must have an **antecedent**, i.e., a preceding word to which it refers. In this sentence, the antecedent is *people*, a direct object.

Sentence 48: *Of course, the host and hostess greeted only the people whom they had invited.*

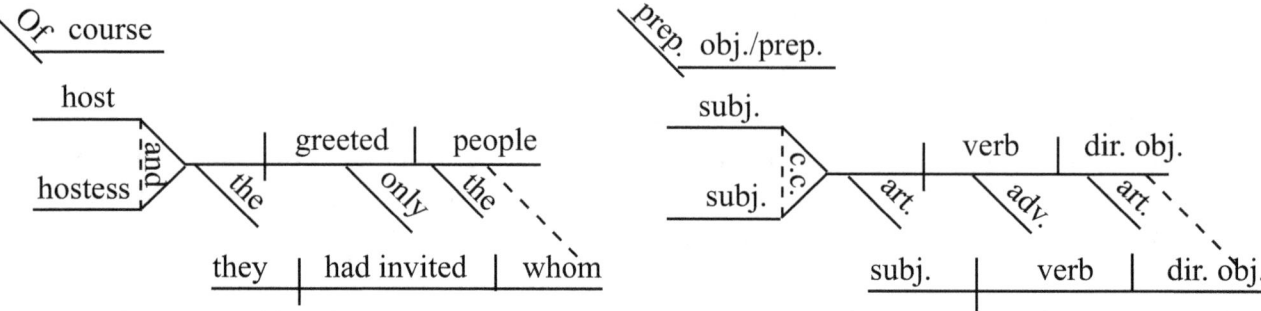

Of course is a prepositional phrase used as a **sentence modifier**. The **relative pronoun** *whom*, a direct object in its clause, has the direct object *people* as its **antecedent**. A relative pronoun takes its **case** from its use in its own clause, not from the case of its antecedent.

Sentence 49: *The customer whose name had just been announced left the store in a hurry.*

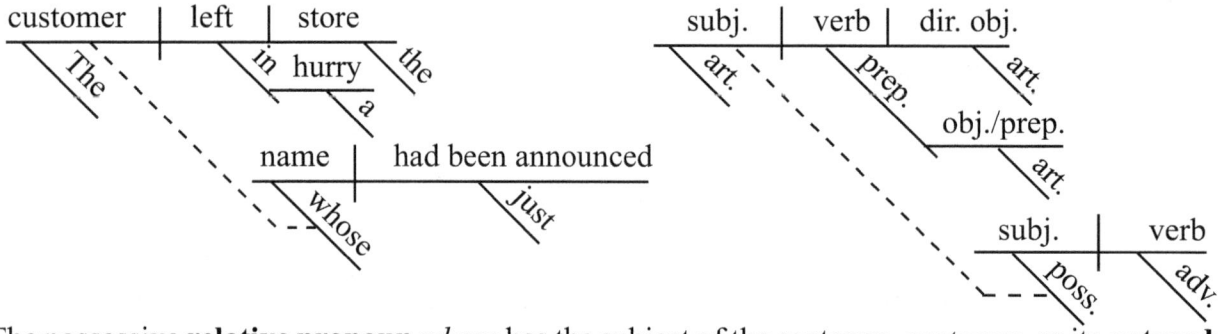

The possessive **relative pronoun** *whose* has the subject of the sentence, *customer*, as its **antecedent**. The verb in the **relative clause**, *had been announced*, is in the past-perfect tense, passive voice.

Sentence 50: *You mean the man to whom the management had issued a warning, don't you?*

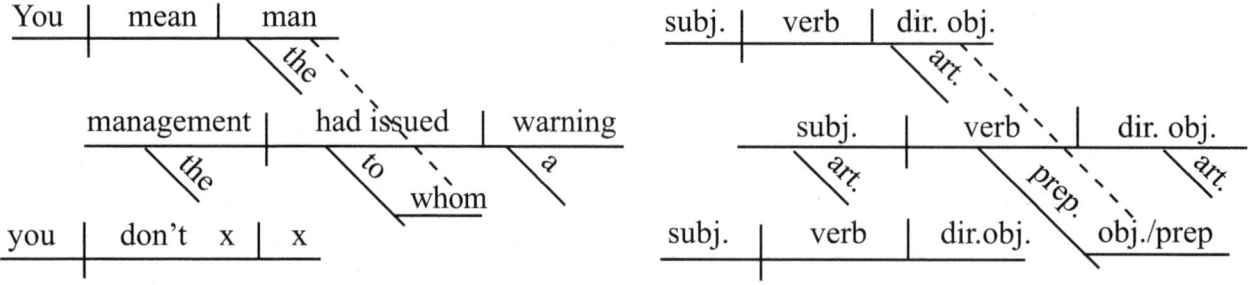

The **relative pronoun** *whom* is the object of the preposition *to*; its **antecedent** is the direct object *man*. The **independent clause** *don't you?* is an **elliptical clause**. The *x*'s stand for the words *mean him*.

Sentence 51: *Yes, that is the person I mean.*

Yes is an adverb used as a sentence modifier. The demonstrative pronoun *that* is the subject of the main clause. *Person*, a predicate nominative, is the antecedent of the **unexpressed relative pronoun** *that*, which is a direct object in the relative clause; it is represented in the diagram by an *x*.

Sentence 52: *Is that what you asked?*

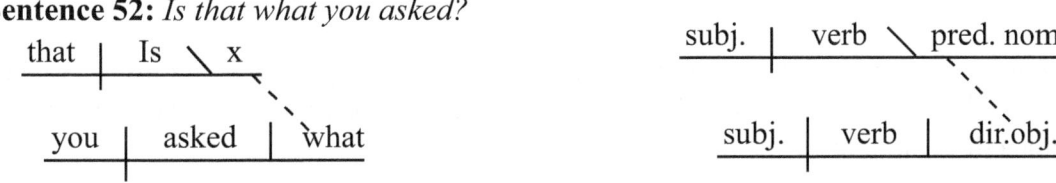

This sentence has an expressed relative pronoun (the direct object *what*) and an **unexpressed antecedent** (the predicate nominative *that*), represented in the diagram by an *x*.

Sentence 53: *Don't tell me that you are going to the lake again.*

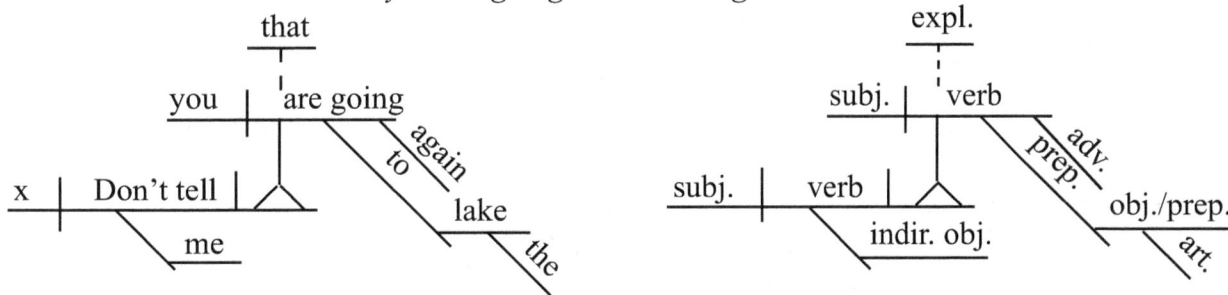

The subject of the sentence is an unexpressed *you*. *Me* is an indirect object. The **noun clause** *that you are going to the lake again* functions as a direct object. The function of the **expletive** *that* is to introduce the noun clause.

Sentence 54: *Didn't I tell you this was the lure that caught the big fish?*

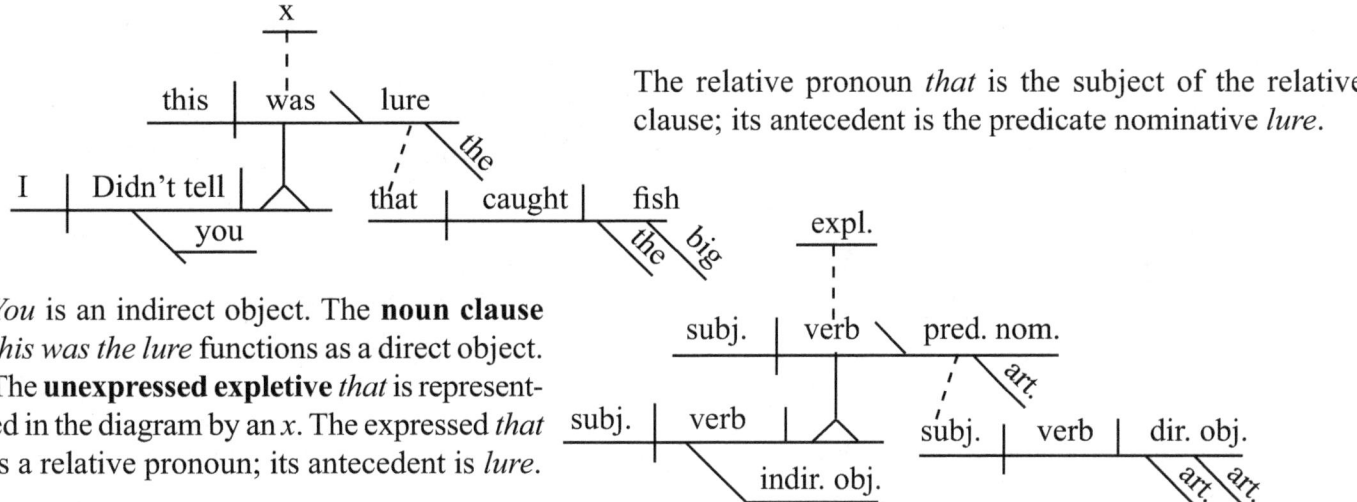

The relative pronoun *that* is the subject of the relative clause; its antecedent is the predicate nominative *lure*.

You is an indirect object. The **noun clause** *this was the lure* functions as a direct object. The **unexpressed expletive** *that* is represented in the diagram by an *x*. The expressed *that* is a relative pronoun; its antecedent is *lure*.

Sentence 55: *I know that it was a bass and that it weighed five pounds.*

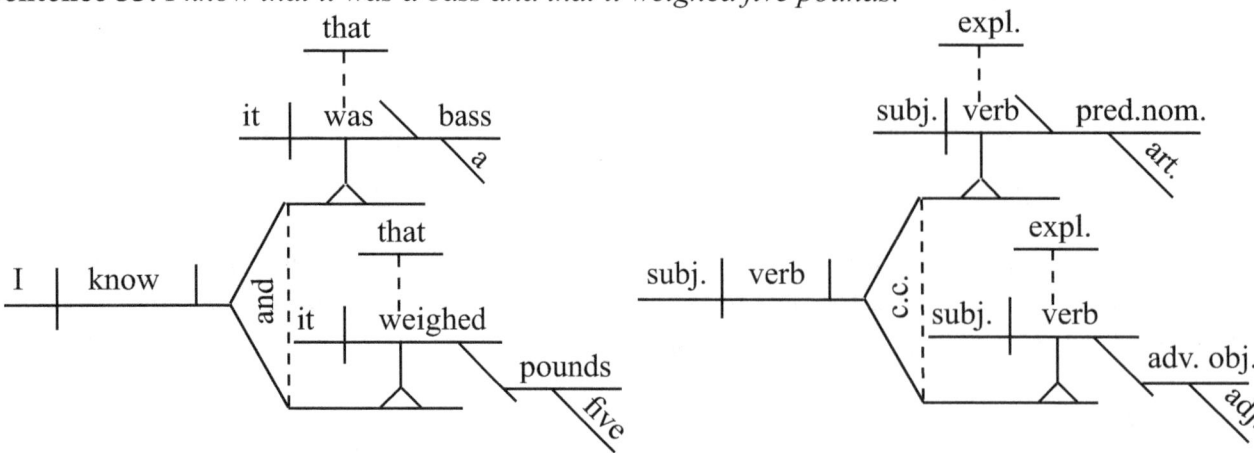

This sentence has a compound direct object whose components are not nouns or pronouns but **noun clauses**. Each noun clause is introduced by the expletive *that*. *Five pounds*, which tells how much the bass weighed, is an **adverbial objective**, not a direct object.

Sentence 56: *Having read extensively about the possibility of life on Mars, she wrote an excellent portfolio piece for her science class.*

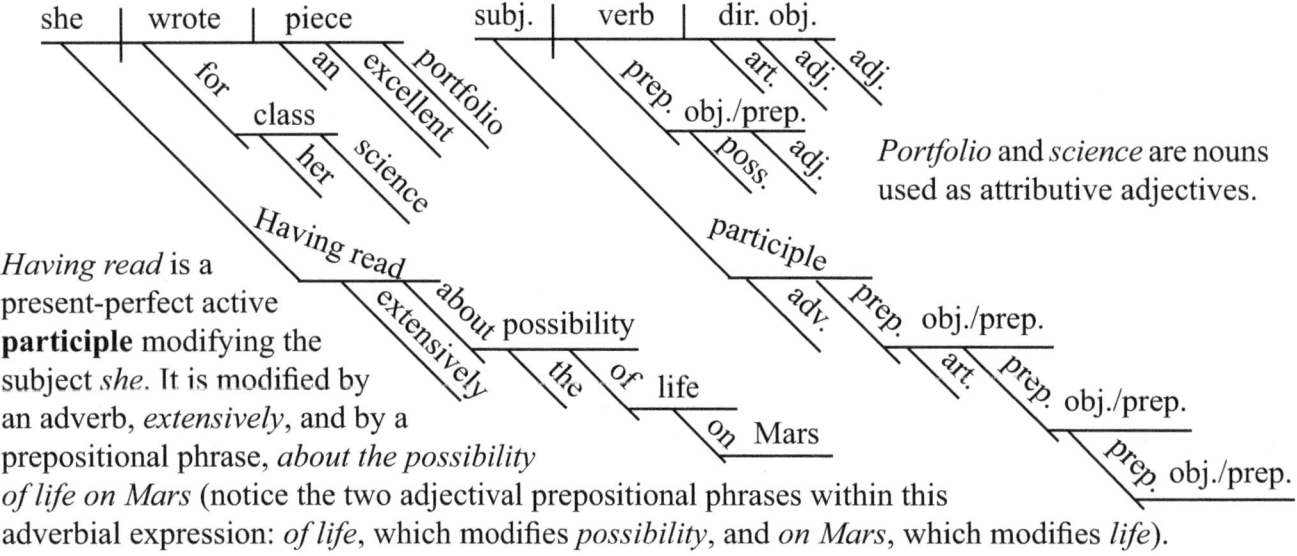

Portfolio and *science* are nouns used as attributive adjectives.

Having read is a present-perfect active **participle** modifying the subject *she*. It is modified by an adverb, *extensively*, and by a prepositional phrase, *about the possibility of life on Mars* (notice the two adjectival prepositional phrases within this adverbial expression: *of life*, which modifies *possibility*, and *on Mars*, which modifies *life*).

Sentence 57: *Strolling through the woods in the fall, we saw on the ground leaves of every imaginable size, shape, and color.*

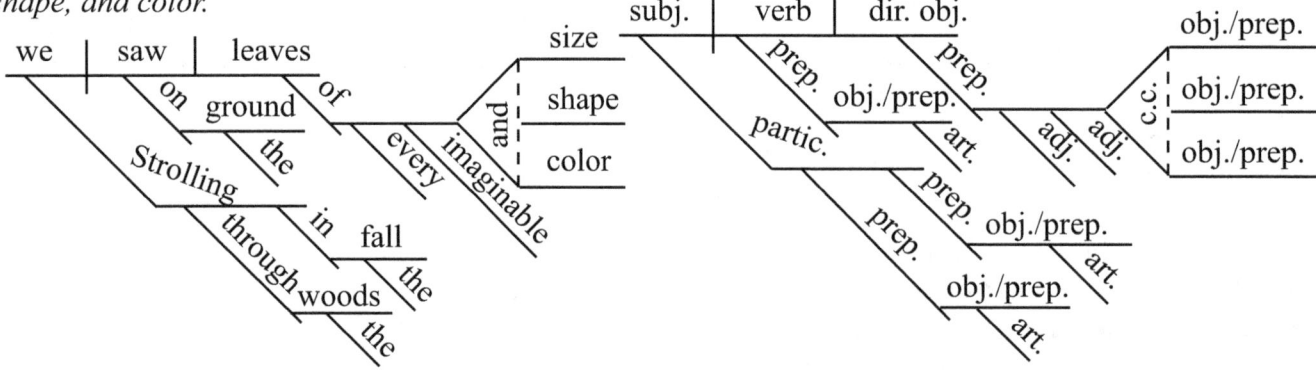

The present active **participle** *strolling* modifies the subject *we*. *Size, shape,* and *color* comprise a tripartite object of the preposition *of*. The adjectives *every* and *imaginable* modify all three nouns (*size, shape, color*) and so are attached to the prepositional-object line at points shared by the three objects.

~ 166 ~

Sentence 58: *We walked out onto the ice and saw fishermen dressed in heavy clothes and shivering nevertheless.*

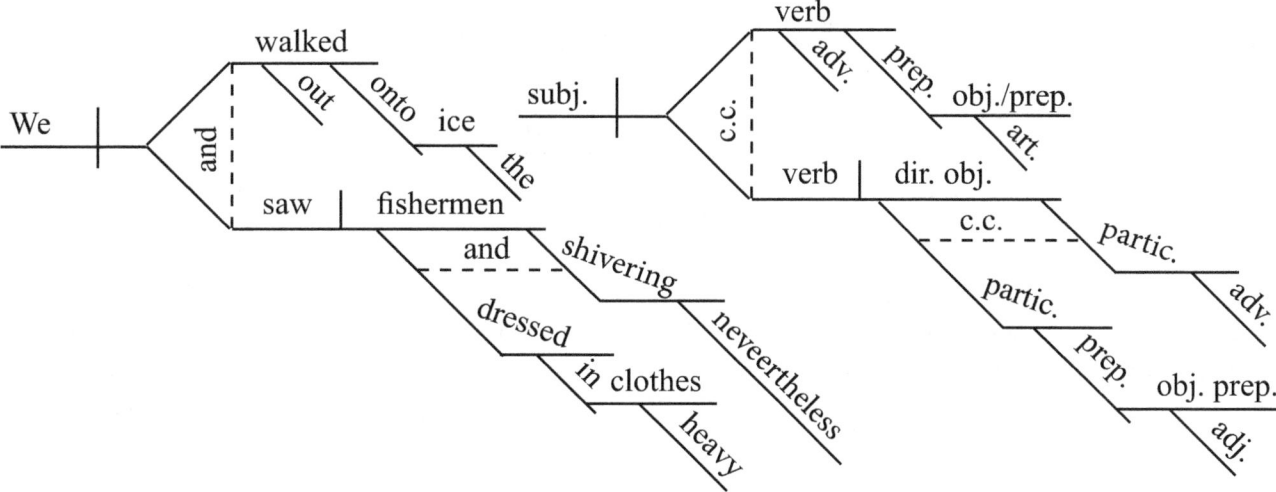

This sentence features a compound predicate and a **compound adjectival modifier** consisting of **two participial phrases**: *dressed*, a past participle, and *shivering*, a present active participle.

Sentence 59: *Some students do not enjoy diagramming sentences.*

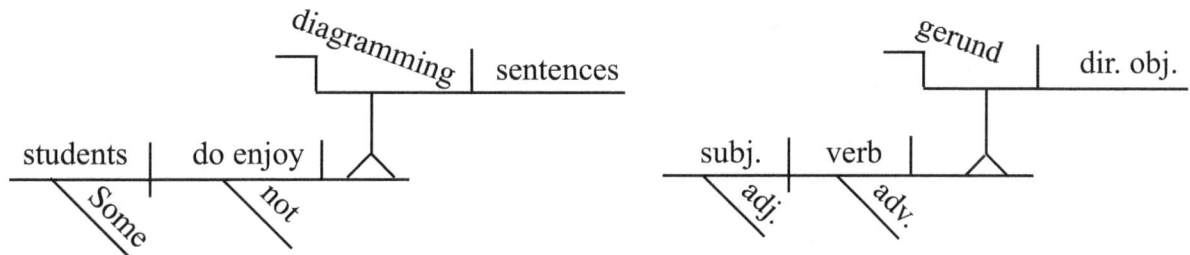

The **gerund phrase** *diagramming sentences* is a direct object in this sentence. **Gerunds** are verbal nouns. Like finite verbs, gerunds (some, not all) can take a direct object. In this sentence, *sentences* is the direct object of the gerund *diagramming*.

Sentence 60: *Trying hard helps.*

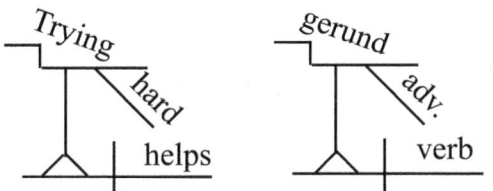

The subject of the sentence is the gerund phrase *trying hard*. As a verb, a gerund can be modified by an adverb (in this sentence, *hard*).

Sentence 61: *Doctors recommend eating moderately and exercising regularly.*

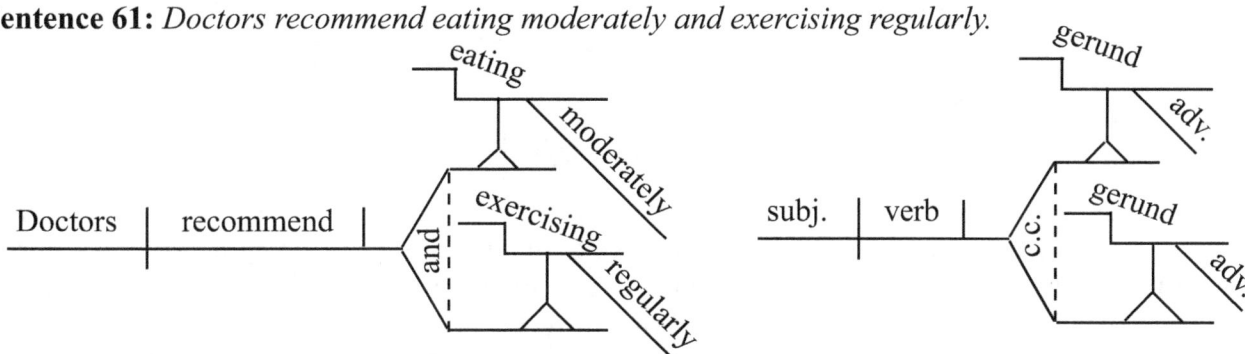

The compound direct object consists of two gerund phrases. *Eating* and *exercising* are gerunds; *moderately* and *regularly* are adverbs.

Sentence 62: *They were kept awake all night by the loud celebrating in the next room.*

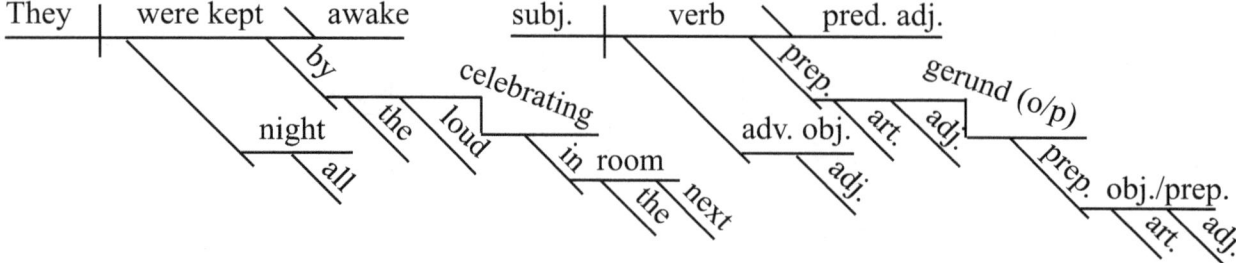

The passive verb *were kept* functions as a **linking verb**; *awake* is a **predicate adjective**. The gerund *celebrating* is the object of the preposition *by*. As a noun, *celebrating* is modified by the article *the* and the adjective *loud*; as a verb, it is modified by the prepositional phrase *in the next room*. **Adjectival modifiers of gerunds** are attached to the upper step on which the gerund rests, while **adverbial modifiers of gerunds** connect to the lower step.

Sentence 63: *For completing all assignments promptly and accurately, she was given a commendation.*

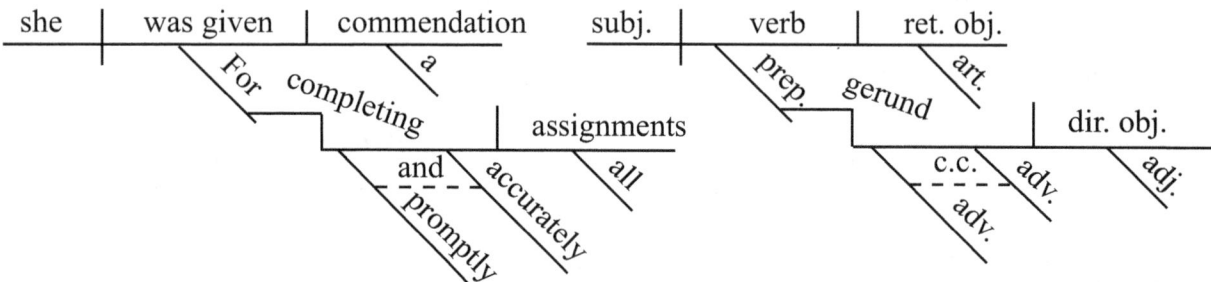

The direct object of a verb in the passive voice is called a **retained object** because it is retained when the indirect object of a corresponding sentence in the active voice (in this case, *Someone gave her a commendation*) becomes the subject when the sentence is expressed in the passive voice. The object of the preposition *for* is the **gerund phrase** introduced by the **gerund** *completing*. *Assignments* is a direct object of the gerund. *Promptly and accurately* is a **compound adverbial modifier.**

Sentence 64: *She wants to have it framed, which is what I would do if I were she.*

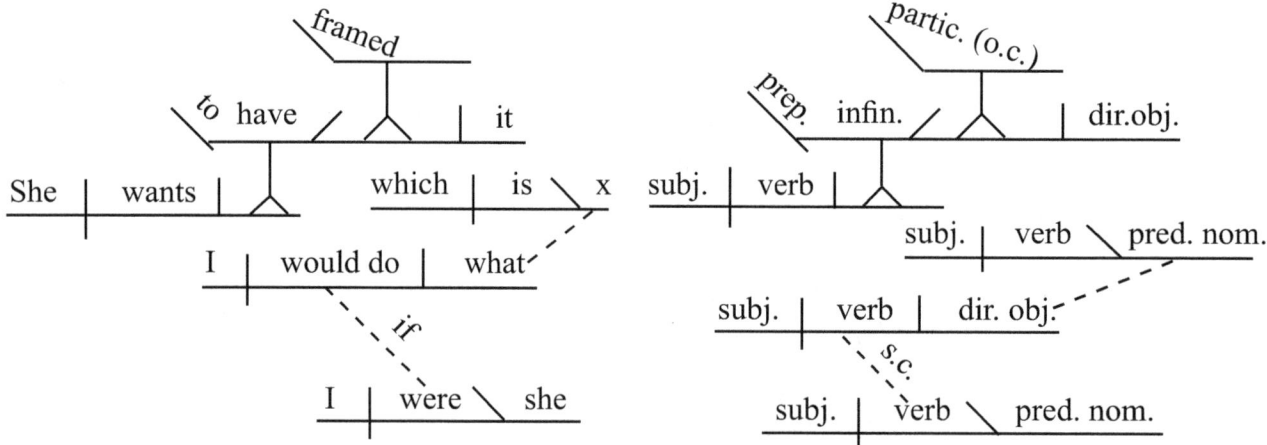

The direct object of the verb *wants* is the **infinitive phrase** *to have it framed*. In this phrase, the past **participle** *framed* functions as an **objective complement**. The **relative pronoun** *which* has the entire infinitive phrase as its **antecedent**; thus, the broken line that usually connects a relative pronoun with its antecedent is not used here. *What* is also a relative pronoun; it has an **unexpressed antecedent**, which is represented in the diagram by an *x*. The **subordinating conjunction** *if* introduces the **subordinate clause** *if I were she*.

Sentence 65: *It is fun to walk to the park and throw a Frisbee back and forth.*

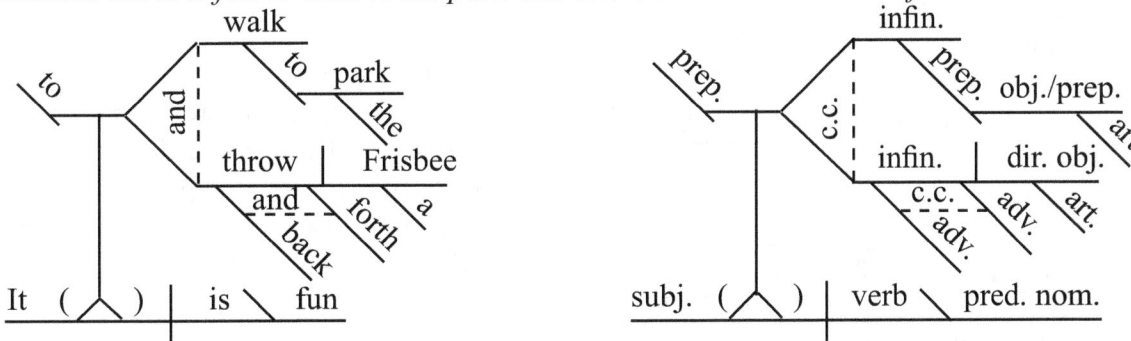

The **compound infinitive phrase** *to walk to the park and throw a Frisbee back and forth* is in **apposition** with the subject of the sentence, *it*. *Back and forth* is a compound adverb. The coordinating conjunction in both compounds is *and*. *Fun*, a noun in this sentence (it is an adjective only when used colloquially in an expression like *a fun thing to do*), functions as a predicate nominative.

Sentence 66: *They said they were too tired to study for the test.*

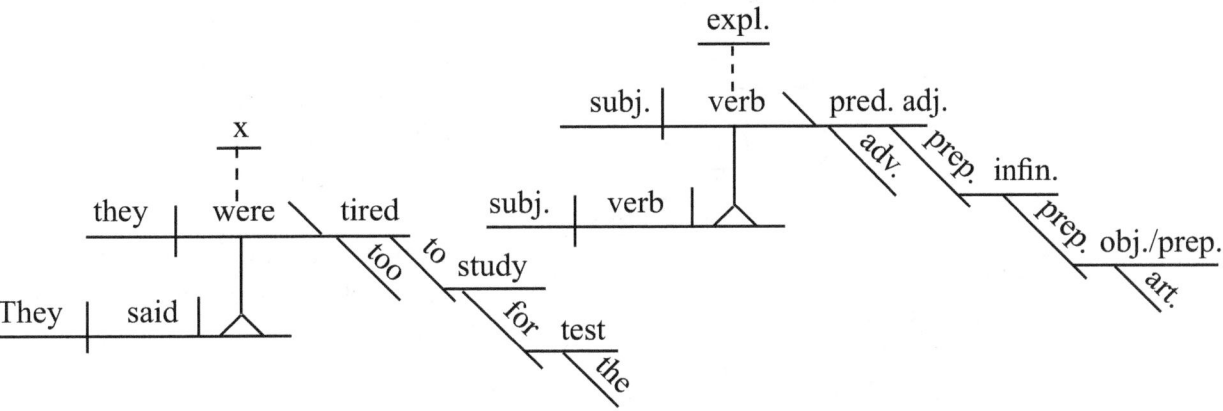

The **noun clause** *they were too tired to study for the test* is the direct object of the verb *said*. The introductory expletive *that* is unexpressed. The **infinitive phrase** *to study for the test* modifies the predicate adjective *tired*.

Sentence 67: *His injured friend hopes to be able to come outside and play soon.*

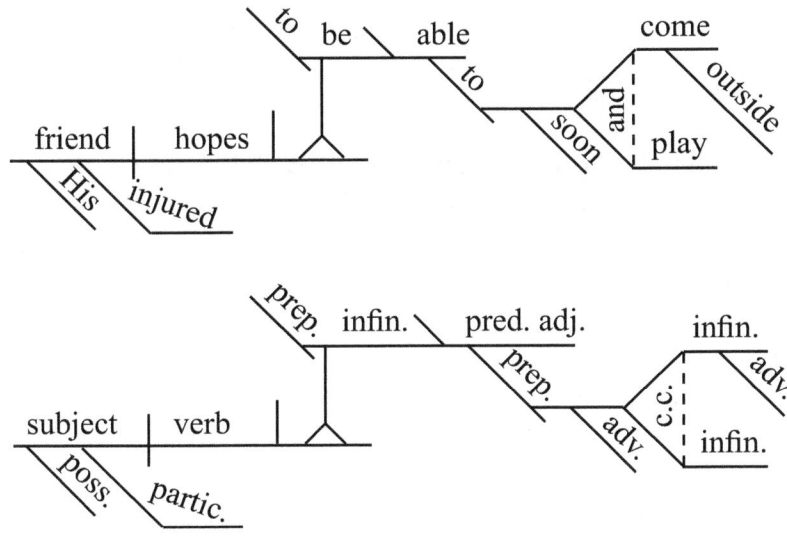

The **infinitive phrase** beginning with the infinitive *to be* and extending to the end of the sentence is the direct object of the verb *hopes*. *Able* is a predicate adjective. It is modified by the **compound infinitive phrase** *to come outside and play soon*. *Soon*, a modifier of both infinitives, is attached to a line segment common to both. *Injured* is a past participle.

Sentence 68: *They are confident they will learn to diagram well.*

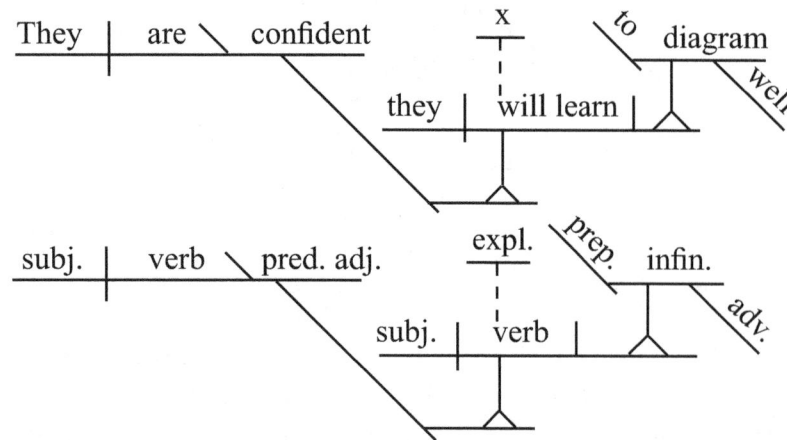

The **noun clause** *they will learn to diagram well* functions here as an **adverbial objective**. The *x* in the diagram stands for the unexpressed expletive *that*. The **infinitive phrase** *to diagram well* serves as the direct object of the verb *will learn*.

Sentence 69: *We ought to leave now in order to arrive at the theater by 7:30.*

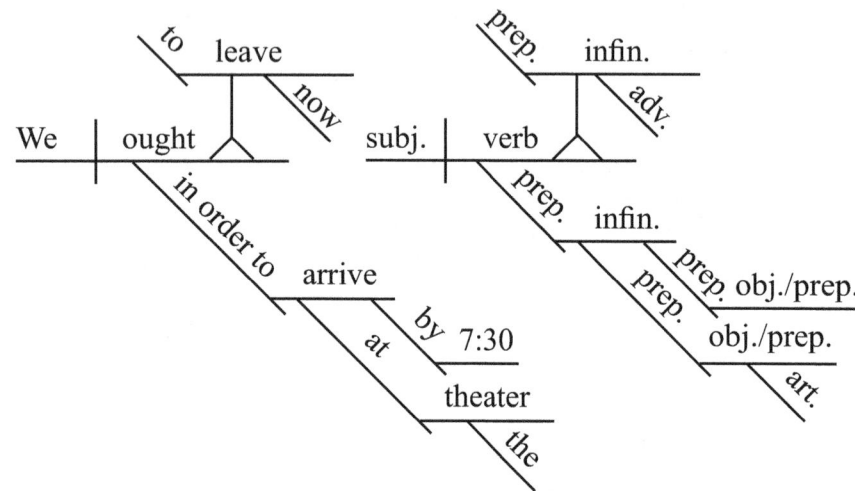

In this sentence, the infinitive *to leave* is associated very closely with the verb *ought*; indeed, *ought to leave* means nearly the same thing as *must leave* or *should leave*. Such an infinitive is called a **complementary infinitive** and is diagrammed on a pedestal next to the verb with no intervening line. *In order to*, a **phrasal preposition**, introduces an infinitive phrase that ends with *7:30* and modifies *ought*.

Sentence 70: *He asked if they could help him push his car.*

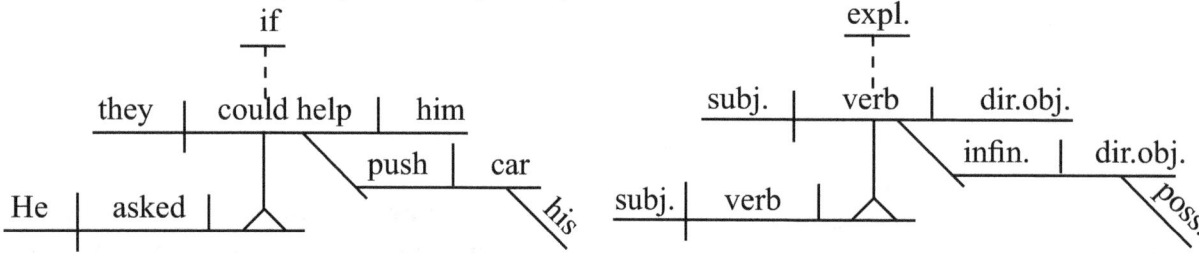

In this sentence, *if* is an **expletive**; when so used, its function is to introduce an **indirect question** expecting a yes or no answer. The infinitive phrase introduced by the **"to-less" infinitive** *push* functions here as a modifier of *help*; it tells *how* they could help, not *what*.

Sentence 71: *They had nothing to do but watch TV.*

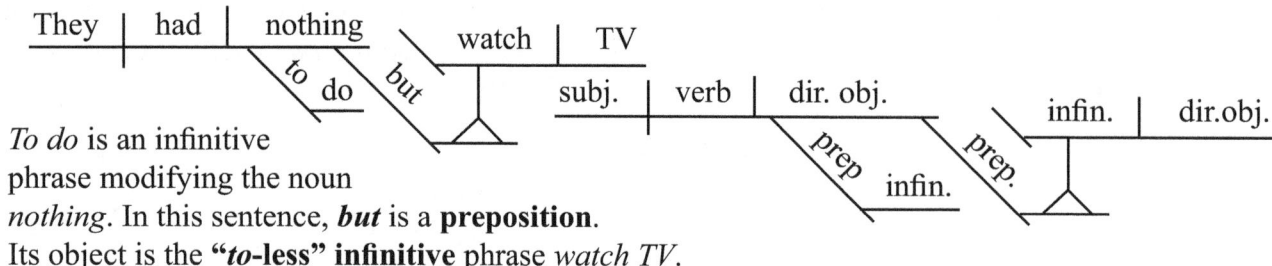

To do is an infinitive phrase modifying the noun *nothing*. In this sentence, *but* is a **preposition**. Its object is the **"to-less" infinitive** phrase *watch TV*.

Sentence 72: *They wondered whether they should play football when the temperature was close to zero.*

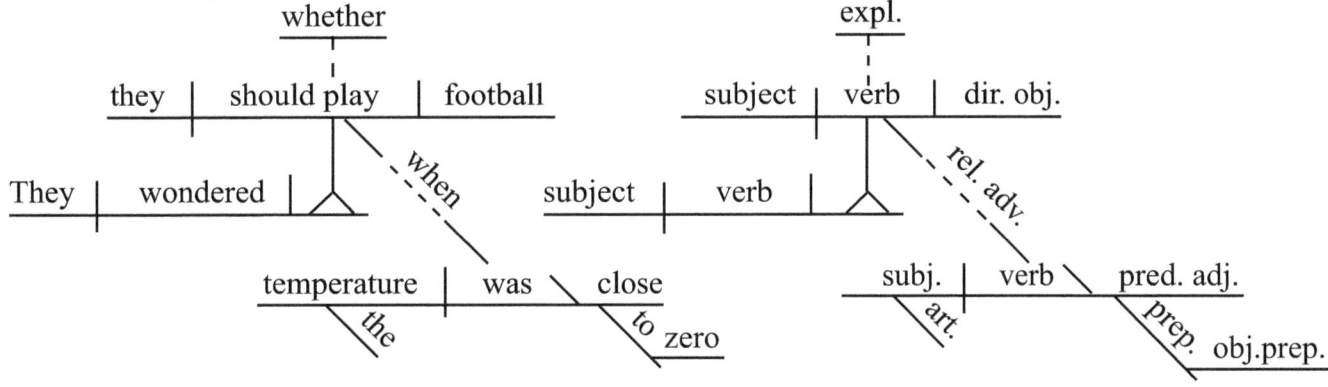

Whether they should play football is a noun clause, more specifically, an **indirect question** expecting a yes or no answer. *Whether* is an expletive. The **subordinate clause** *when the temperature was close to zero* is introduced by the **relative adverb** *when* (*at the time at which*).

Sentence 73: *"That depends on how much candy you will give us for helping," they answered.*

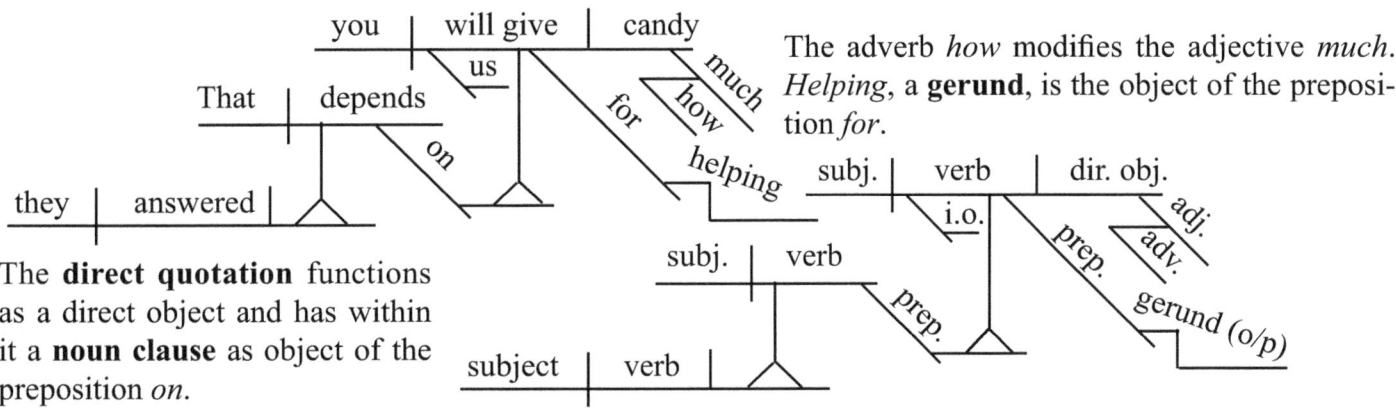

The adverb *how* modifies the adjective *much*. *Helping*, a **gerund**, is the object of the preposition *for*.

The **direct quotation** functions as a direct object and has within it a **noun clause** as object of the preposition *on*.

Sentence 74: *I forgot to tell you that Eric is taller than James.*

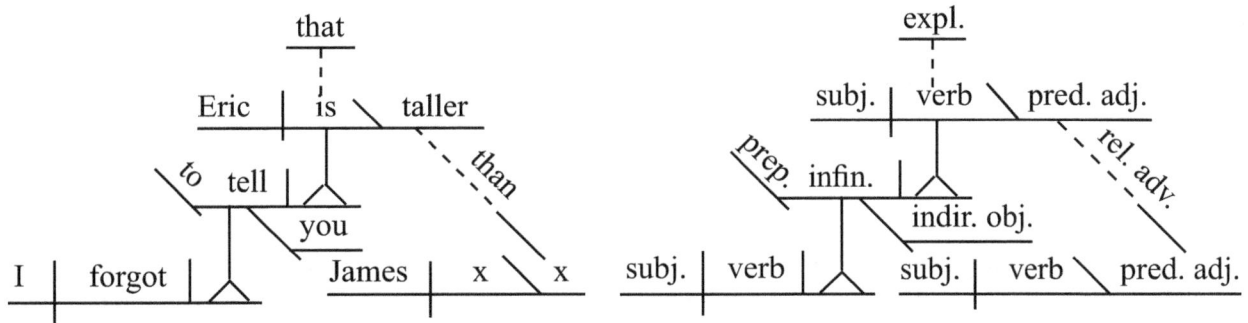

The direct object of *forgot* is an **infinitive phrase**, and the direct object of *tell* is a **noun clause**. *Than* is a **relative adverb**. *Taller than James* is equivalent to *tall beyond the degree in which James is tall.*

Sentence 75: *Rachel got as many A's as Hannah.*

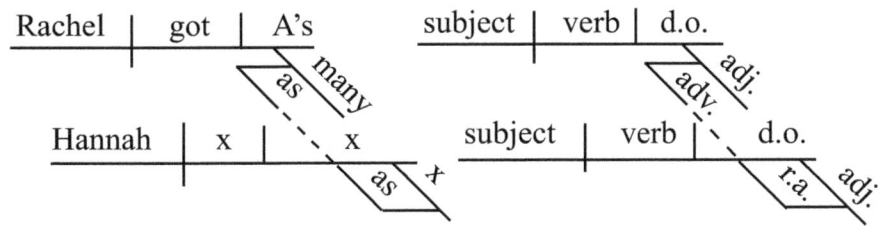

As and *as* are **correlative adverbs**. *As many A's as Hannah* is equivalent to *many A's in the amount in which Hannah got many A's.*

~ Additional Diagramming Examples ~

1. I see them.

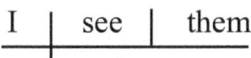

The **personal pronouns** *I* and *them* are **subject** and **direct object**, respectively. *See* is a **verb**.

2. Whom do you see?

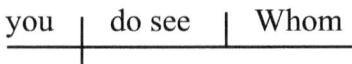

The subject of the sentence is the **personal pronoun** *you*. The **interrogative pronoun** *whom* is a direct object. It is capitalized in the diagram because it is the first word of the sentence. *Do see* is a present-tense **emphatic form** of the verb *see*. This form is often used, without emphasis, in questions.

3. I see my friends Allison and Jennifer.

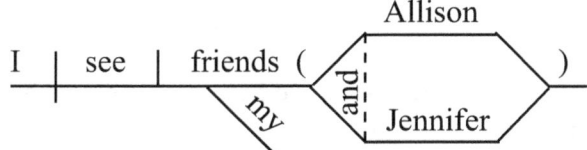

The **compound appositive** *Allison and Jennifer* is in apposition with the direct object *friends*. *My*, a **possessive pronoun**, modifies *friends*. *And* is a **coordinating conjunction**.

4. Where are they?

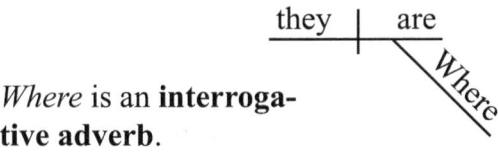

Where is an **interrogative adverb**.

5. They are standing in front of the school.

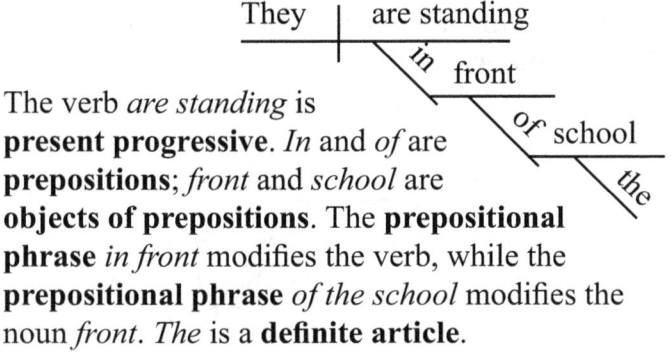

The verb *are standing* is **present progressive**. *In* and *of* are **prepositions**; *front* and *school* are **objects of prepositions**. The **prepositional phrase** *in front* modifies the verb, while the **prepositional phrase** *of the school* modifies the noun *front*. *The* is a **definite article**.

6. Which girl is Allison?

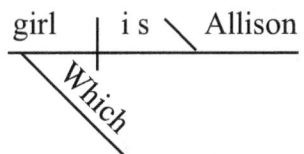

Allison is a **predicate nominative**. *Which* is an **interrogative adjective**.

7. She is the one who is wearing the baseball cap.

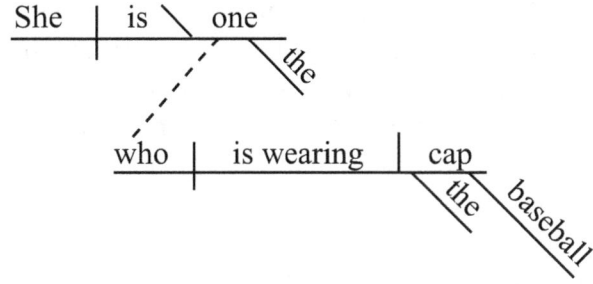

The **relative pronoun** *who* is the subject of the **relative clause**. The **antecedent** of *who* is the pronoun *one*, a predicate nominative. The noun *cap* is modified by a **noun used as an adjective**, *baseball*.

8. Both girls look very pretty.

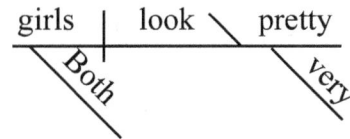

Both is an **attributive adjective** modifying the subject *girls*. The **adverb** *very* modifies the **predicate adjective** *pretty*.

9. They are nice and extremely bright.

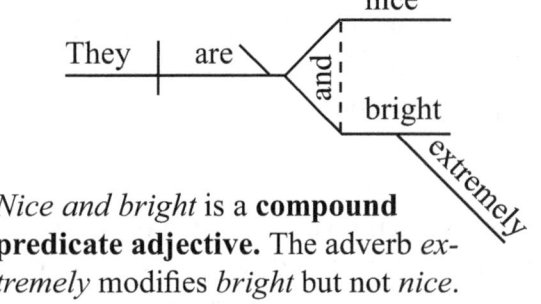

Nice and bright is a **compound predicate adjective**. The adverb *extremely* modifies *bright* but not *nice*.

10. Come along, and I will introduce them to you.

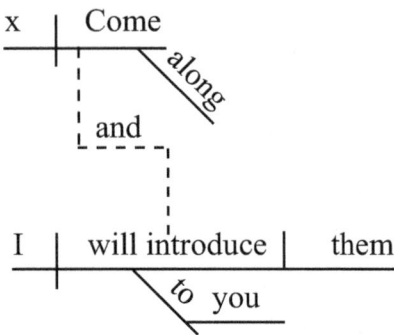

The verb *come* is an **imperative** (command) form. The **unexpressed subject** *you* is represented in the diagram by an *x*. The coordinating conjunction *and* joins **two main clauses**. A sentence with two or more main clauses is called a **compound sentence**. The verb in the second clause, *will introduce*, is in the future tense. *To you* is a prepositional phrase; *to* is the preposition, and *you* is its object.

11. John, do you drink coffee?

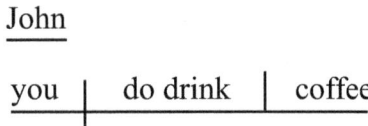

John is a noun of **direct address**.

12. I prefer to drink water or juice with my breakfast.

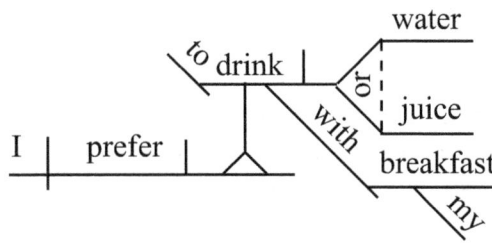

The **infinitive phrase** *to drink water or juice with my breakfast* functions here as a direct object. *Water or juice* is the **compound direct object** of *drink*. *Or* is a coordinating conjunction. *With my breakfast* is an adverbial prepositional phrase.

* * * * *

On the right is an equally valid diagram of Sentence No. 15, in which *mother* is understood as an indirect object and the noun clause as a direct object.

13. Caroline and her sister will bring you something to eat.

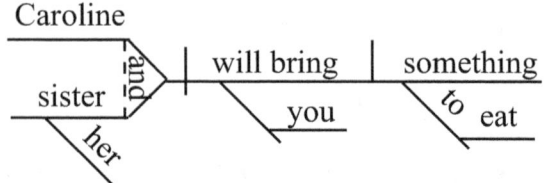

Caroline and her sister is a **compound subject**. *Her* is a possessive pronoun. *You* is an **indirect object**. The infinitive *to eat* modifies the direct object *something*.

14. Do you know what we will do after breakfast?

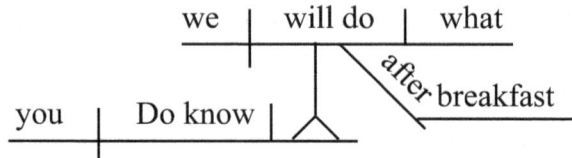

The **noun clause** *what we will do after breakfast*, an **indirect question**, is the direct object of the verb *do know*. The **interrogative pronoun** *what* is the direct object of *will do*.

15. Caroline, ask mother if we can go to the beach this morning.

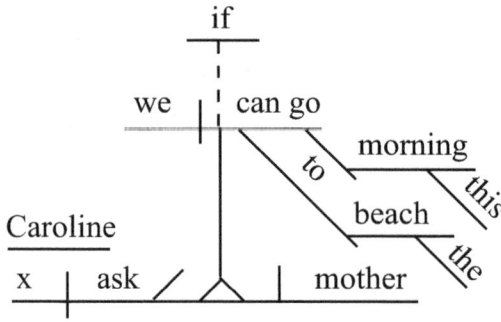

The expletive *if* announces an **indirect question** expecting a *yes* or *no* answer. The indirect question functions here as an **objective complement**. *Caroline* is a noun of direct address. The *x* represents the understood subject of the sentence, *you*. *This morning* is an **adverbial objective**.

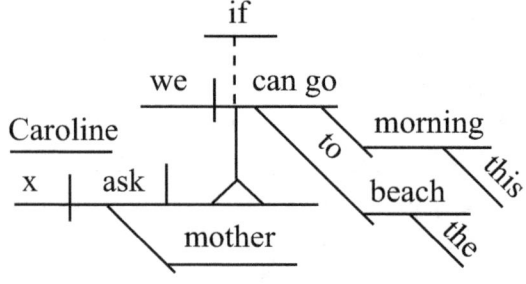

16. The beach is out of the question because the weather turned cold overnight.

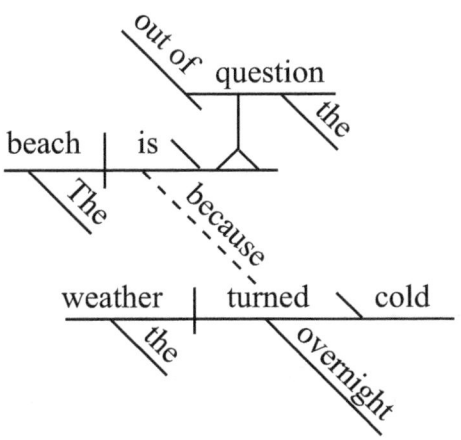

Out of the question is a **prepositional phrase used as a predicate adjective**. *Out of* is called a **phrasal preposition**. The second clause, a **subordinate clause**, is connected to the main clause by the **subordinating conjunction** *because*. In this sentence, *turned*, like *is* in the main clause, is a **linking verb**; thus *cold* is a predicate adjective. *Overnight* is used here as an adverb.

17. That is a problem we did not anticipate; however, I'm sure we will think of something as exciting as swimming.

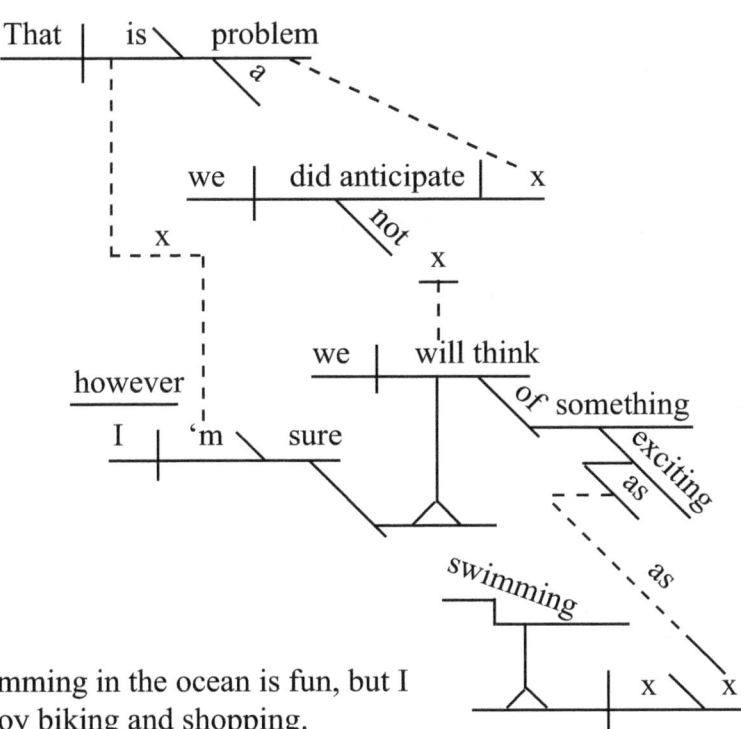

In the relative clause [*that*] *we did not anticipate*, the relative pronoun *that* is unexpressed; *x* stands for this unexpressed word, whose antecedent is *problem*. *However* is a **transitional adverb**; this one doesn't modify a particular word but the entire clause. The noun clause that begins with the words *we will think* is used as an **adverbial objective**. It is introduced by the unexpressed expletive *that*. The second *as* is a **relative adverb** (*as . . . as* is equivalent to *to the degree to which*). *Swimming*, a **gerund**, is the subject of its clause. The unexpressed verb and predicate adjective in the **elliptical clause** are *is* and *exciting*, respectively. These two words are represented in the diagram by *x*'s.

18. Swimming in the ocean is fun, but I also enjoy biking and shopping.

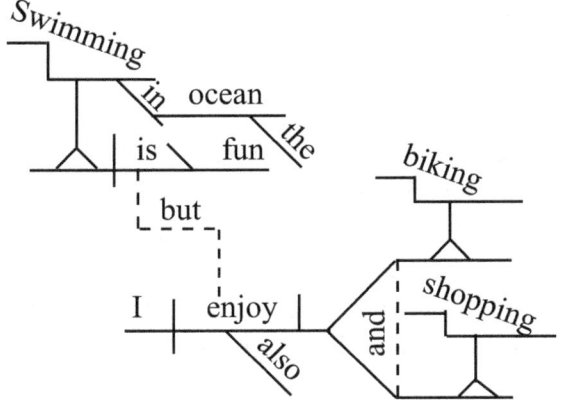

Three gerunds dominate this sentence. The first, *swimming*, introduces a **gerund phrase** that functions as the subject of the first main clause; the second and third **gerunds**, *biking* and *shopping*, constitute a **compound direct object** in the second main clause. The coordinating conjunction *but* connects the two main clauses.

19. Not knowing whether it would be wise to go biking or not on such a cold and cloudy day, we decided to do some shopping at the mall.

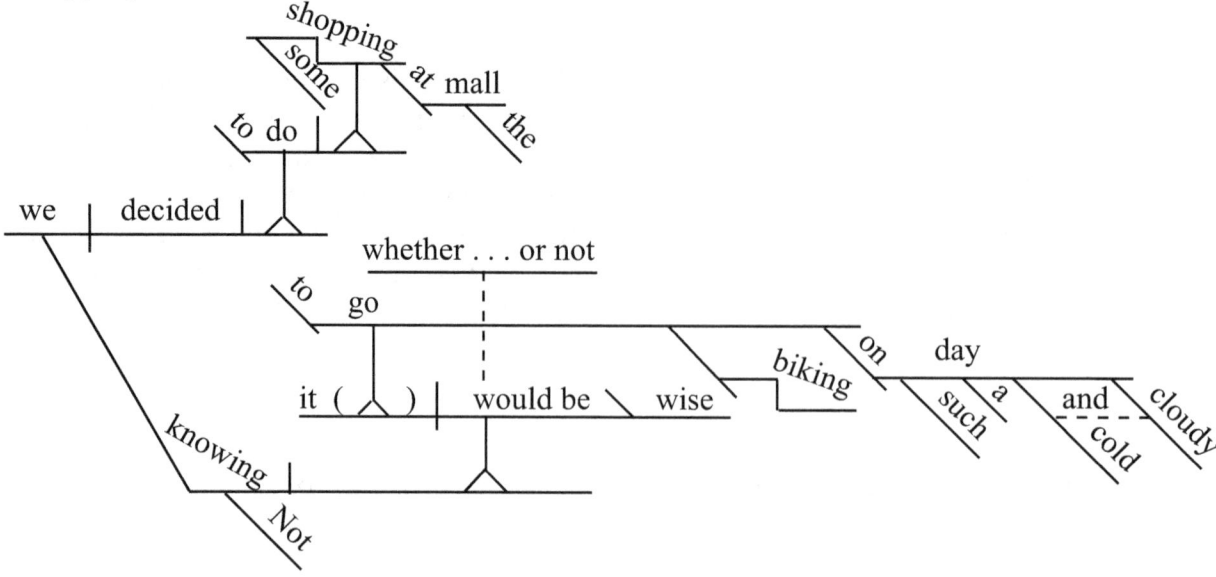

The infinitive phrase *to do some shopping* is the direct object of the verb *decided*. The gerund *shopping* is a direct object of the infinitive *to do*. As a noun, *shopping* is modified by the adjective *some*; as a verb, it is modified by the prepositional phrase *at the mall*. When diagramming, place **adjectival modifiers of gerunds** under the upper step and **adverbial modifiers of gerunds** under the lower step. A case can be made for regarding *shopping* as a mere noun; after all, it is listed in dictionaries as a noun. On the other hand, the fact that it cannot be made plural argues in favor of it being regarded as a gerund. The noun clause (indirect question) introduced by the expletive *whether* and ending with the word *day* is the direct object of the **present participle** *knowing*. The infinitive phrase that begins with *to go biking* and ends with *day* is in **apposition** with the subject of the noun clause, *it*. *Biking* is a gerund used as an **adverbial objective**.

20. After a long but rewarding morning of the best shopping ever, we went to a food court, where I ordered a grilled chicken sandwich, a spinach salad, and a glass of milk.

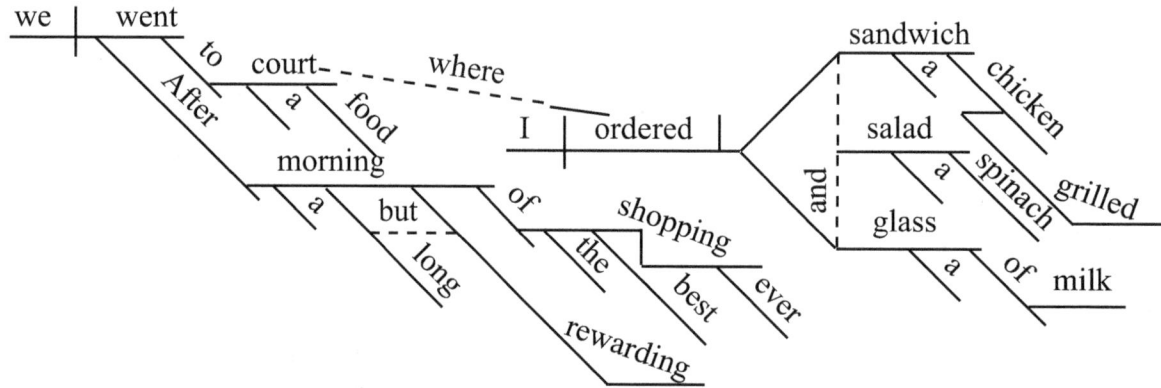

Of the four prepositional phrases in this sentence, two are adjectival and two are adverbial. The article *the* and the adjective *best* modify the gerund *shopping* as a noun, while the adverb *ever* modifies it as a verb. *Where* is a **relative adverb**; it has the force of *at which*. The clause it introduces is called a noun clause because it modifies the noun *court*. The solid portion at the right end of the line on which *where* rests indicates that the relative adverb modifies the verb *ordered*. The dependent clause features a **tripartite direct object**. The coordinating conjunction *and* is placed in the diagram between the second and third parts of the series, which is where it appears in the sentence.

21. One day we looked out the window and saw a deer eating apples from our apple tree.

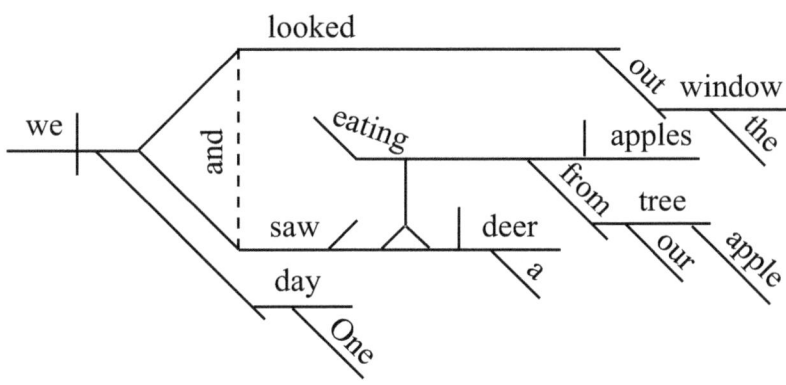

This sentence has a **compound predicate**. The **participial phrase** introduced by the present participle *eating* serves as an **objective complement**. *Day* is an **adverbial objective**. Since one can say *From our apple tree a deer was eatng apples* without changing the meaning of the clause, it seems that the prepositional phrase *from our apple tree* is adverbial.

22. Well, it being late summer, many apples on the tree were almost ripe.

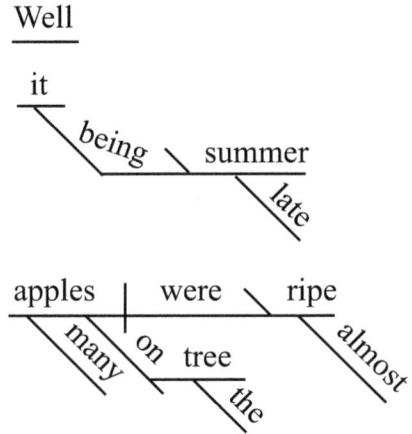

Well and *it being late summer* are both **independent elements**, the former an **independent adverb**, the latter an **absolute phrase** known as an **nominative absolute**. *Almost* is an adverb modifying the predicate adjective *ripe*.

23. Standing at the window, we watched silently and intently as the deer ate the apples.

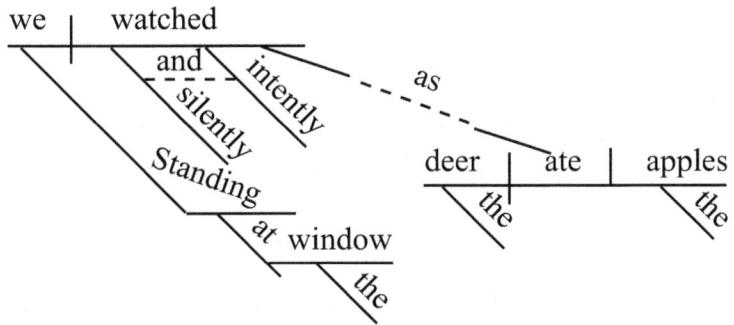

Standing is a present participle modifying the subject *we*. The coordinating conjunction *and* joins the adverbs *silently* and *intently*. *As* is a **relative adverb**; it has the force of *at the time at which*.

24. The deer was eating only the apples that hung on the lower branches because she could not reach the upper branches even by standing on her hind legs.

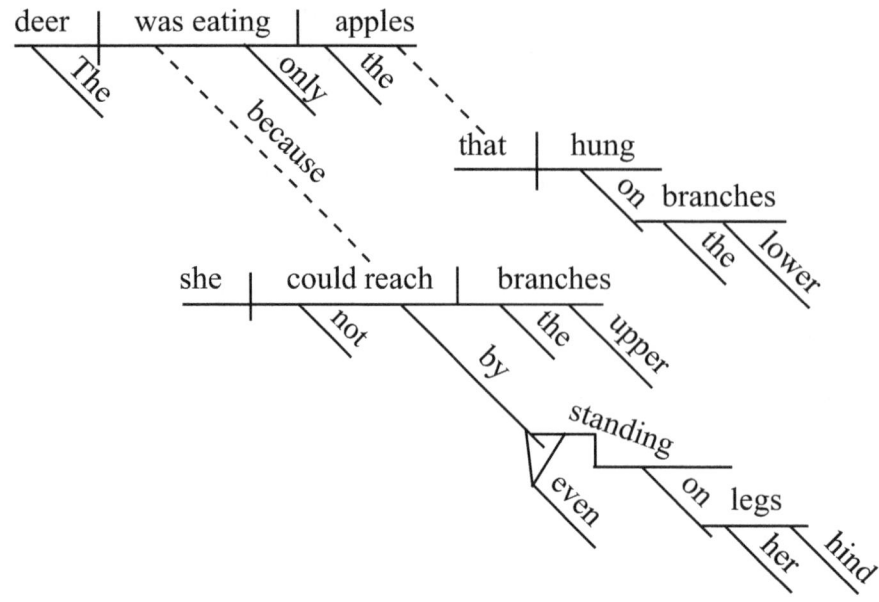

That is a relative pronoun whose antecedent is *apples*. The **adverb** *even* **modifies the prepositional phrase** *by standing*, not just the preposition *by*; thus, in the diagram, lines connect *even* to both *by* and *standing*. *Because* is a subordinating conjunction.

25. Ben, my little brother, called the deer a moose.

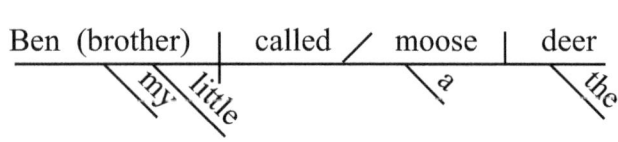

Brother is in **apposition** with the subject of the sentence, *Ben*. *Moose* is an **objective complement**.

26. "Ben, that is not a moose," I said.

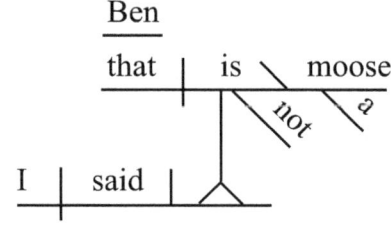

The quotation is the direct object of the sentence. *Ben* is a **noun of direct address**.

27. I wanted to show him that he was wrong, but I knew he would never believe me.

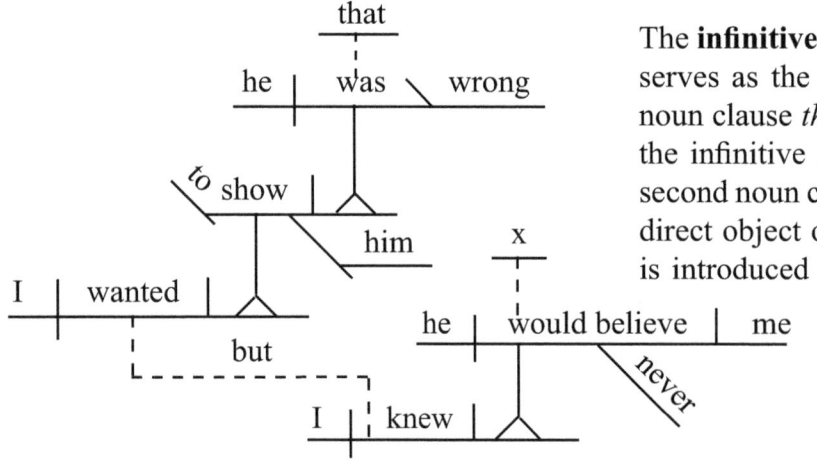

The **infinitive phrase** *to show him that he was wrong* serves as the direct object of the verb *wanted*. The noun clause *that he was wrong* is the direct object of the infinitive *to show*. *Him* is an **indirect object**. A second noun clause, *he would never believe me*, is the direct object of the verb *knew*. The first noun clause is introduced by the expletive *that*, while the second omits the expletive (hence the *x* in the diagram). The coordinating conjunction *but* connects the two main clauses.

28. I wanted him to learn the difference between a deer and a moose.

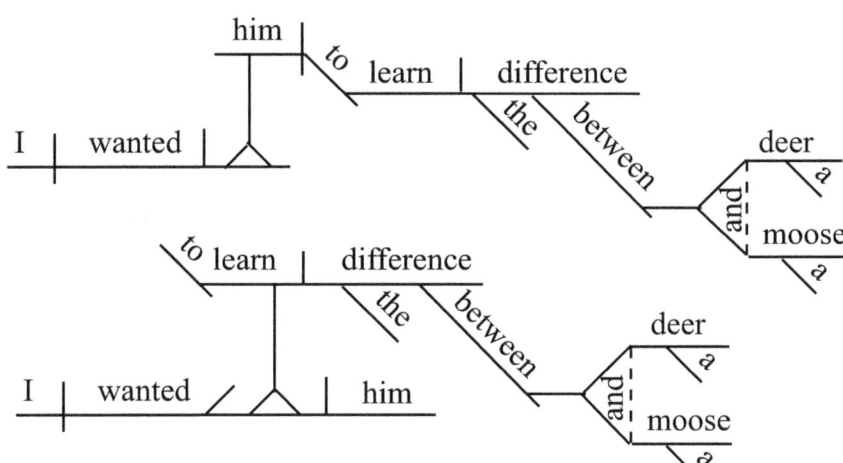

In the top diagram, the direct object of *wanted* is the remainder of the sentence, in which the objective-case *him* acts as the **subject of the infinitive** *to learn*. Alternatively, the infinitive phrase can be understood as an objective complement (cf. lower diagram). *A deer and a moose* is the **compound object of the preposition** *between*.

29. Luke and Adam, friends of Ben, came to the rescue by taking a very large book about animals from a shelf and showing Ben pictures of both deer and moose.

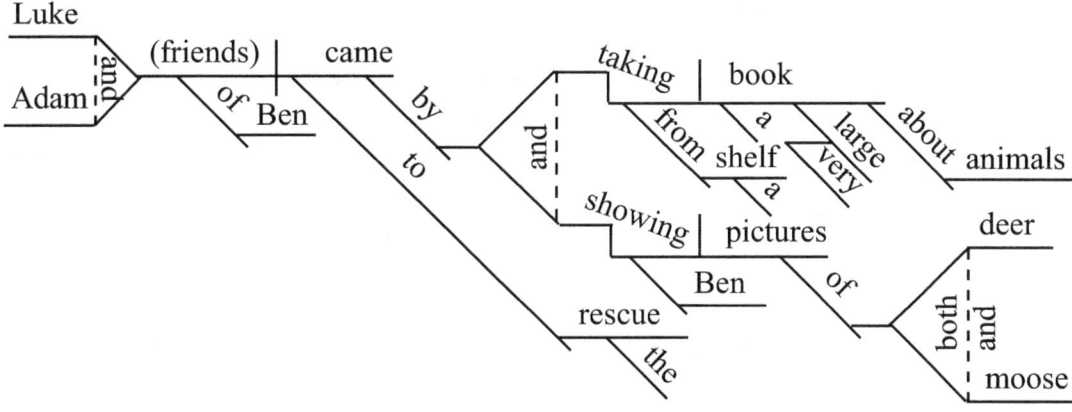

In this sentence, we have a compound subject and two compound objects of prepositions, the first of which consists of two **gerund phrases** introduced by the gerunds *taking* and *showing*. There are four additional prepositional phrases, two adverbial and two adjectival. The second time *Ben* is used, it is an indirect object. *Friends* is an appositive. *Very* is an adverb modifying the adjective *large*. *Both . . . and* are **correlative coordinating conjunctions**.

30. Don't waste your time telling Ben that it's easy to believe what your brother tells you.

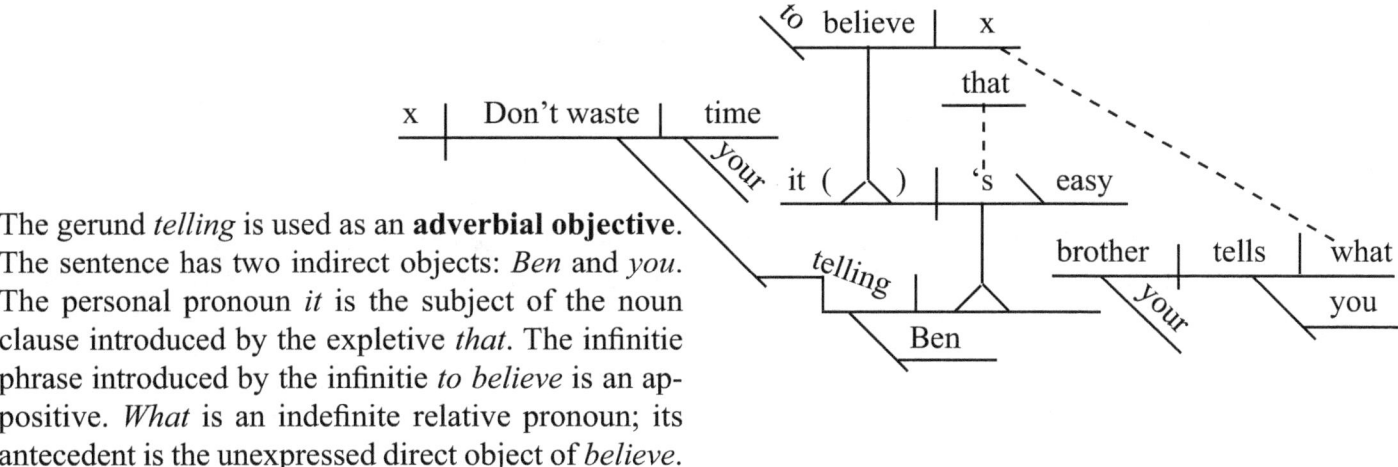

The gerund *telling* is used as an **adverbial objective**. The sentence has two indirect objects: *Ben* and *you*. The personal pronoun *it* is the subject of the noun clause introduced by the expletive *that*. The infinitive phrase introduced by the infinitive *to believe* is an appositive. *What* is an indefinite relative pronoun; its antecedent is the unexpressed direct object of *believe*.

31. What would you do if you were driving through a desert and your car had a flat tire?

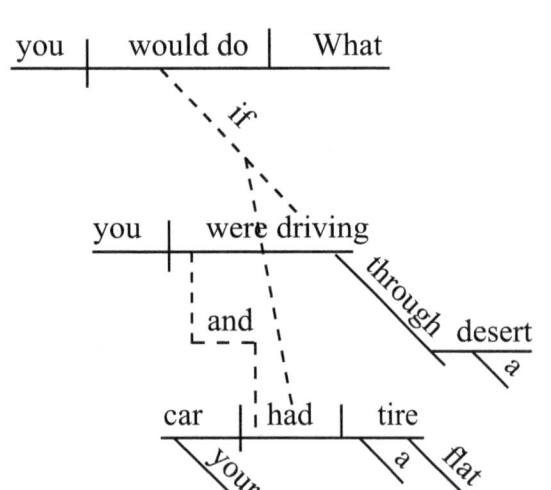

The subordinating conjunction *if* introduces a **compound subordinate clause**. This kind of subordinate clause is called a conditional clause.

32. At first I would just wonder what to do because I don't know anything about repairing flat tires.

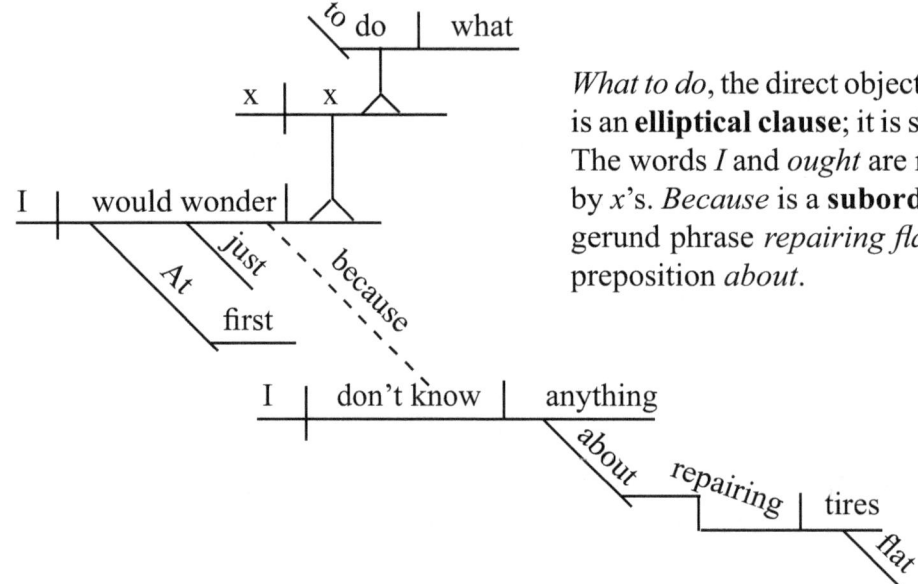

What to do, the direct object of the verb *would wonder*, is an **elliptical clause**; it is short for *what I ought to do*. The words *I* and *ought* are represented in the diagram by *x*'s. *Because* is a **subordinating conjunction**. The gerund phrase *repairing flat tires* is the object of the preposition *about*.

33. As the owner of a car manual, you can read, can't you?

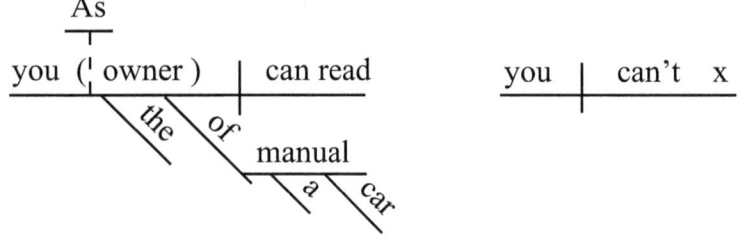

Owner is an appositive. Like many appositives, it is introduced by the expletive *as*. *Can't you* [*read*] is an independent element; when diagrammed, it must be kept separate from the rest of the sentence. *Car* is a noun used as an adjective.

34. Yes, but since you didn't stipulate that I am traveling alone, I would like to assume that I have a passenger who repairs cars for a living.

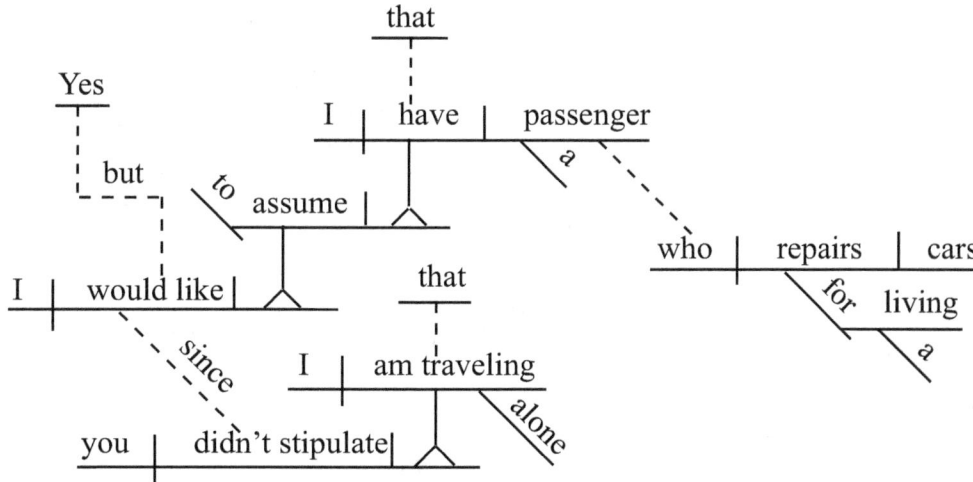

For the most part, coordinating conjunctions join elements of the same grammatical kind. One wonders, therefore, how the single word *yes*, an adverb, can be connected by the coordinating conjunction *but* to a main clause; the elements are different grammatically. The reason is that *yes*, when it stands alone, expresses an affirmative response; thus, in this sentence, *yes* means *I can read*. The sentence also includes an infinitive phrase used as a direct object, two noun clauses used as direct objects, and two other dependent clauses: a relative clause introduced by the relative pronoun *who* and an adverbial clause introduced by the subordinating conjunction *since*.

35. I will allow you to have a passenger, but it is unacceptable for him or her to know more about car repair

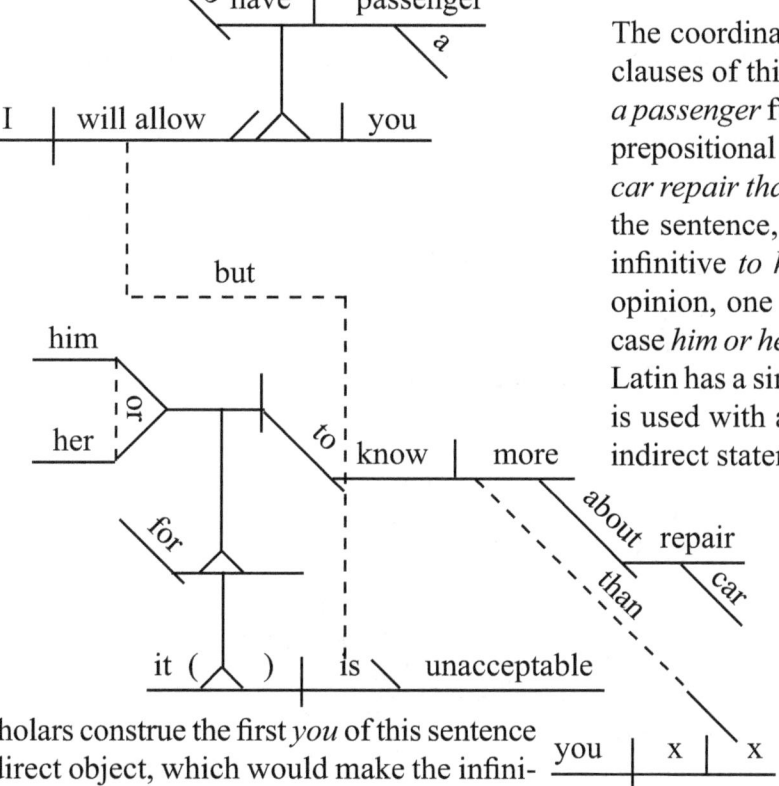

The coordinating conjunction *but* joins the two main clauses of this sentence. The infinitive phrase *to have a passenger* functions as an objective complement. The prepositional phrase *for him or her to know more about car repair than you* is in apposition with the subject of the sentence, *it*. House and Harman would make the infinitive *to know* a modifier of *him* and her. In my opinion, one should regard the compound objective-case *him or her* as the **subject of the infinitive** *to know*. Latin has a similar phenomenon in which the infinitive is used with an accusative-case subject to express an indirect statement. In the expression *more than*, *more* can be restated as *an amount beyond the degree*, and the relative adverb *than* means *to which*. *Much* is an adjective functioning as a noun. *Than* is a relative adverb. To show that *than* modifies *much* in the elliptical clause *you know much*, the right end of the slanted line upon which *than* rests is made solid.

Some scholars construe the first *you* of this sentence as an indirect object, which would make the infinitive phrase *to have a passenger* a direct object. I believe this analysis merits serious consideration.

36. Furthermore, you haven't said what season of the year and time of day it is; how much food, water, and gasoline we have; and whether the region is so remote that other cars cannot be expected to pass by.

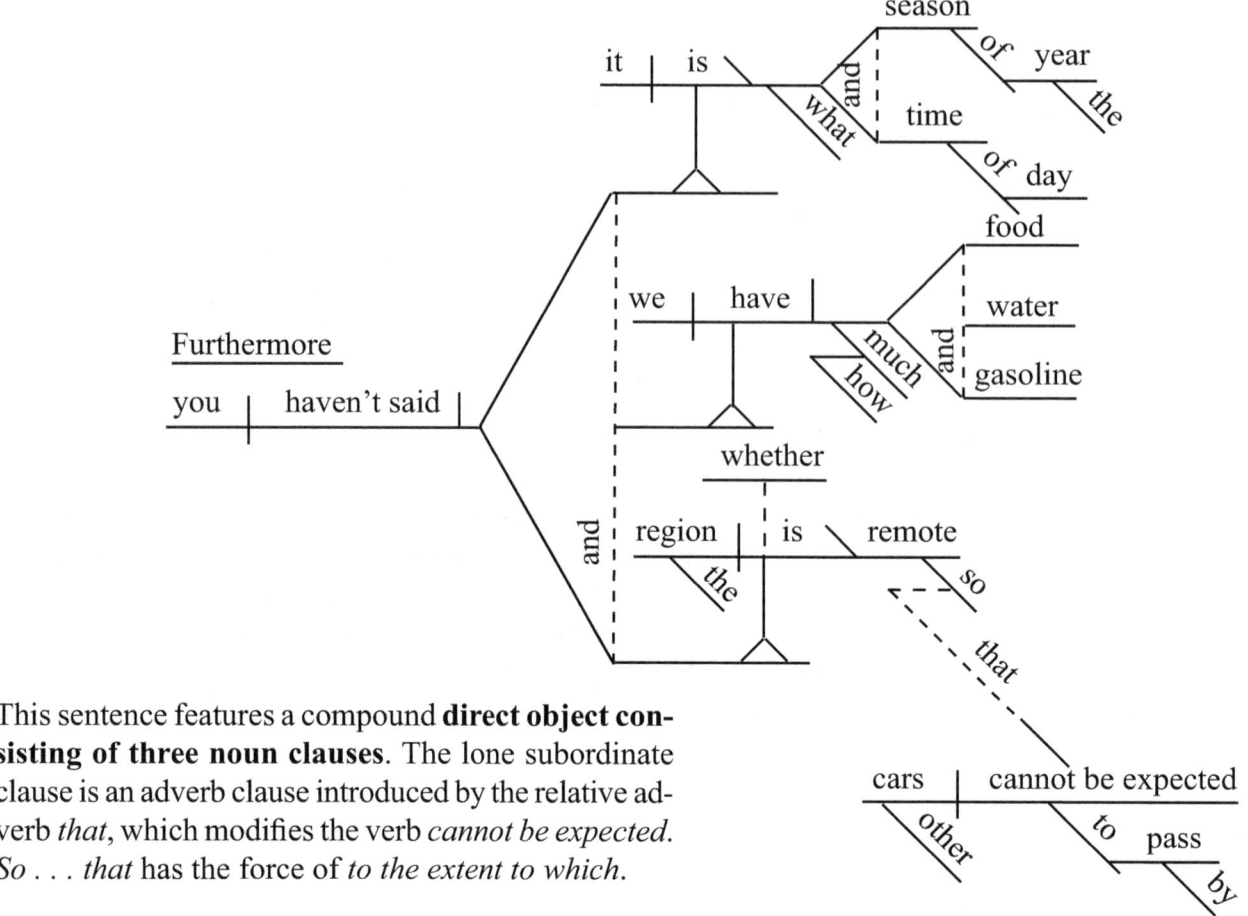

This sentence features a compound **direct object consisting of three noun clauses**. The lone subordinate clause is an adverb clause introduced by the relative adverb *that*, which modifies the verb *cannot be expected*. So . . . *that* has the force of *to the extent to which*.

37. It is four o'clock on a summer afternoon, and you have nothing but two Snickers bars, a large bag of potato chips, and about a gallon of water.

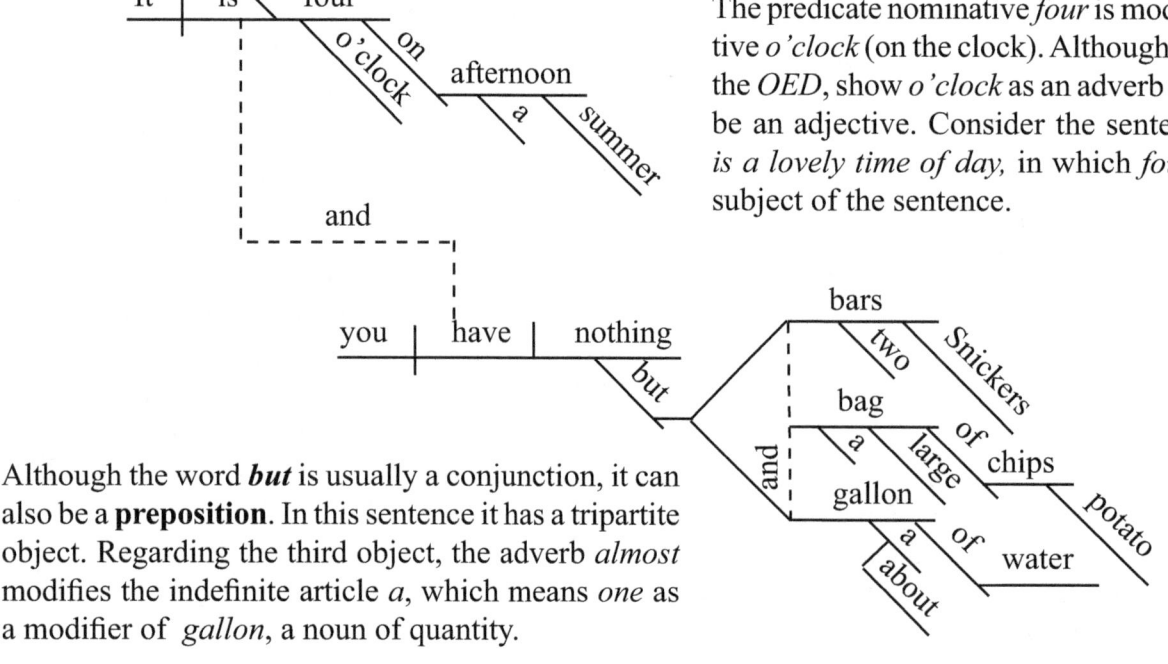

The predicate nominative *four* is modified by the adjective *o'clock* (on the clock). Although dictionaries, even the *OED*, show *o'clock* as an adverb only, it can clearly be an adjective. Consider the sentence *Four o'clock is a lovely time of day,* in which *four* is certainly the subject of the sentence.

Although the word **but** is usually a conjunction, it can also be a **preposition**. In this sentence it has a tripartite object. Regarding the third object, the adverb *almost* modifies the indefinite article *a*, which means *one* as a modifier of *gallon*, a noun of quantity.

~ 182 ~

38. I can't stand the thought that we haven't been given any Cokes or Pepsis.

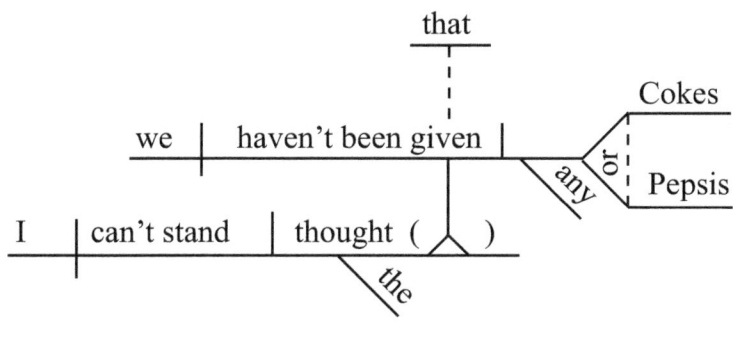

In general, verbs in the **passive voice** do not have direct objects; however, there is an exception. If a sentence in the active voice is made passive in such a way that the indirect object of the former sentence becomes the subject of the latter, the direct object is retained as direct object. Such an object is called a **retained object**. In this sentence, the retained object is *Cokes or Pepsis*. The noun clause introduced by the expletive *that* is in **apposition** with the direct object *thought*. The adjective *any* modifies both *Cokes* and *Pepsis*.

39. However painful the thought may be, you'll just have to get used to it.

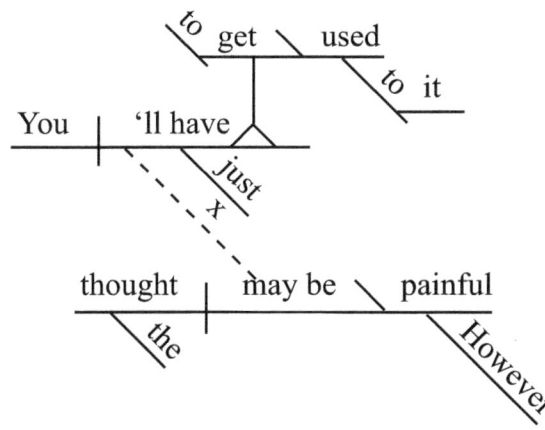

To get is a **complementary infinitive**. In this sentence, *get* is a linking verb (it means *become*) and takes a predicate adjective. The clause introduced by *however* is actually a **concessive clause** (*x* stands for the **unexpressed subordinating conjunction** *although*); *however* is an adverb.

40. Having been raised by loving parents, who would never have subjected me to such deprivation, I have decided to end this discussion.

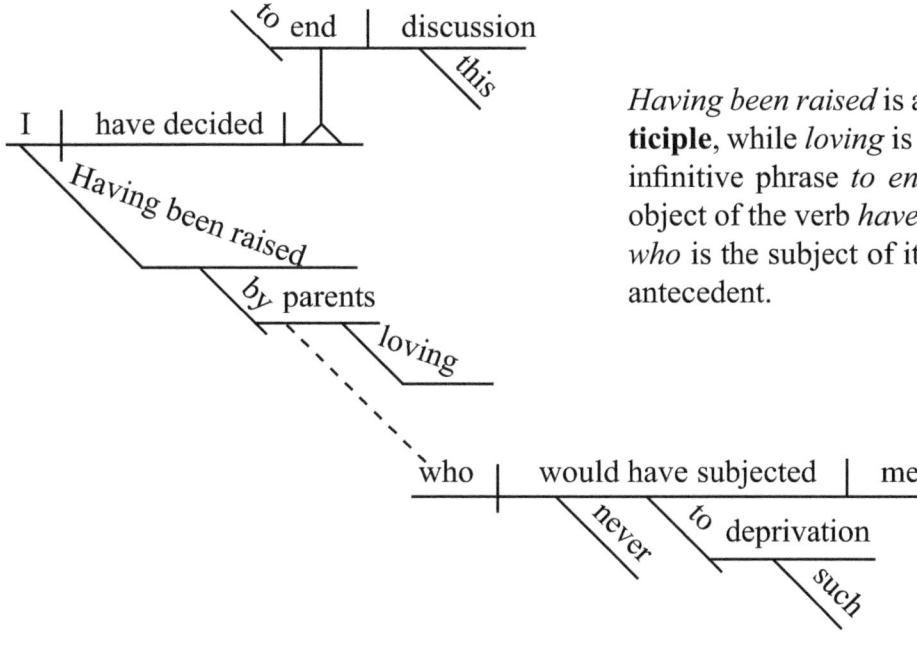

Having been raised is a **present-perfect passive participle**, while *loving* is a present active participle. The infinitive phrase *to end this discussion* is the direct object of the verb *have decided*. The relative pronoun *who* is the subject of its relative clause; *parents* is its antecedent.

~ Exercises ~

Exercise 1: Subjects and Verbs

1. Birds fly.
2. Fish are jumping.
3. Do people fly?
4. Can you jump?
5. What is happening?
6. I must know.
7. Students are being tested.
8. Were parents informed?
9. Has everyone arrived?
10. We should have been told.

Exercise 2: Direct Objects

1. Lizards lay eggs.
2. Who is playing volleyball?
3. Motorcyclists must wear helmets.
4. Do you have pets?
5. We could donate time.
6. Someone may ask you.
7. Will they bring presents?
8. She had visited relatives.
9. Shoppers were pushing carts.
10. Kindness can change things.

Exercise 3: Subjective Complements (Predicate Nominatives and Predicate Adjectives)

1. We are friends.
2. They are being good.
3. Has he been sick?
4. Parents must be teachers.
5. I feel tired.
6. Everyone became quiet.
7. Who will be elected president?
8. Did Jeff get angry?
9. She had been absent.
10. Must we be enemies?

Exercise 4: Definite and Indefinite Articles, Attributive Adjectives, Possessive Pronouns, Nouns Used as Adjectives

1. The baseball hit our new car.
2. A young boy had thrown that baseball.
3. Do many new cars have baseball dents?
4. July 4th is a national holiday.

5. All giraffes have long necks.
6. That old, spooky house has been demolished.
7. Is that girl a new student?
8. My best friend was elected class president.
9. Did you see those big horses?
10. These three books will be my constant companions.

Exercise 5: Adverbs

1. The new neighbors are not very friendly.
2. They waited patiently.
3. Sprinters run quite fast.
4. They are very fast runners.
5. An exceedingly beautiful young lady slowly entered the room.
6. That unusually quiet boy is a most intelligent student.
7. Must you be so aggressive?
8. He likes her very much.
9. Does she also like him?
10. These perfectly normal children don't want too much homework.

Exercise 6: Prepositional Phrases

1. Most people do not hike in this remote region without a guide.
2. In the morning we skied on the bunny slope.
3. With determination you can open doors to the objects of your dreams.
4. Yesterday it was raining in the southern part of the state.
5. After the meeting she spoke informally with several club members.
6. Do you have the key for the file cabinet in the corner?
7. Because of the exceptionally heavy rainfall, many houses along the river had been inundated by several feet of water.
8. After the show they went with some friends to the new Italian restaurant in the mall.
9. With one of the smallest recorders in the world, she secretly recorded every word of the industrial spy.
10. During the storm, the family across the street used flashlights instead of candles.

Exercise 7: Compounds, Coordinating Conjunctions *and, or, but, both . . . and, either . . . or, neither . . . nor, not only . . . but also*

1. Jack and Jill went up the hill.
2. Miss Muffet was eating her curds and whey.
3. Either Jack Horner or Tom Thumb put in his thumb and pulled out a plum.
4. Do these characters come from fairy tales or from nursery rhymes?
5. After the test, Jennifer and Kristy were tired but relieved.
6. Both Paul and Seth walked through the park and along the beach, but Adam stayed at home.
7. They wandered for many hours over hill and dale.
8. We have food, clothes, and shelter, but they have neither food nor shelter.
9. Each employee not only knew his or her particular assignment but also worked amiably and efficiently with the other members of the department.
10. How much money did you have, and to whom did you give it?

Exercise 8: Appositives, Interjections, Possessive Nouns, Vocatives (Nouns of Direct Address), Imperative Sentences (Commands)

1. Ted Smith, captain of our 1960 football team, died today.
2. What does the word *nascent* mean?
3. Hurrah! Helen finally bought her favorite antique car, a 1957 turquoise and white Chevy.
4. Danielle's twin brothers, Cory and Rory, belong to the debate team.
5. Each student must analyze (separate into constituent parts and examine critically) five poems or short stories.
6. Kathy, have you read *The Universe in a Nutshell*, a new book by Stephen Hawking?
7. We sent a Christmas present to each of their five children, Jean, Jeff, Jill, Jerry, and Joe.
8. Do you know my brother Pete's sister-in-law Nancy?
9. Heavens! Close the door quickly.
10. Class, open your books and read silently.

Exercise 9: Indirect Objects and Other Adverbial Objectives

1. Why didn't you tell me that last week?
2. Come this way, and I will show you the prettiest flowers of all.
3. John bought Mary an ugly lamp, and Mary passed it on to her cousins Joy and Shirley.
4. At that time gold cost only thirty dollars an ounce.
5. Two weeks after graduation from college she found a great job.
6. The child showed everyone (friends, relatives, and passers-by) his treasure, a jar of lightning bugs.
7. Her son brought her home from the hospital on Tuesday, but she suffered a relapse the next day and returned to the hospital.
8. Mt. Everest is five and one-half miles high, and the Mariana Trench is almost seven miles deep.
9. "Give me liberty, or give me death." (Patrick Henry, *Speech in the Virginia Convention*, 1775)
10. I myself showed the latest proposal to at least five other people.

Exercise 10: Objective Complements

1. The class elected her vice-president.
2. Architects and artists make our surroundings beautiful.
3. Some of the guests called him a great cook, but others called him lucky.
4. The President appointed him Ambassador to France.
5. Many in the audience thought her arrogant and boring.
6. Just go away and leave me alone.
7. You are driving me crazy.
8. She found her largest angelfish dead.
9. The drought turned the grass brown.
10. I consider her an honest person and a good friend.

Exercise 11: Adverb Clauses, Subordinating Conjunctions

1. If you work hard, you can succeed.
2. We succeeded because we worked hard.
3. His friends call him Moose, although he prefers the name Clifford.
4. Bring some soft drinks and chips unless you hear otherwise.

5. The All-Star Game ended in a tie in the eleventh inning because both teams had used all their pitchers.
6. Something must be changed so that that does not happen again.
7. While many people eat immoderately large quantities of pizza and hamburgers with short-term impunity, people with high cholesteral must severely restrict their intake of such foods.
8. Since one family could not arrive until midafternoon, the traditional Christmas dinner was moved from noon to the evening.
9. We will be there even if we must walk all day.
10. Although our next-door neighbors' dog looks tough and barks threateningly, we do not fear him.

Exercise 12: Adverb Clauses (2), Relative Adverbs

1. Does it really pour when it rains?
2. As the parishioners leave the church, the priest stands on the front steps and greets them.
3. Whenever the children visit the farm, they explore the old barn from top to bottom.
4. The campers stayed in their tent until the sun was high in the sky.
5. A few band members left the practice field before the director dismissed the band.
6. Does he not act as if he had been elected emperor by a landslide?
7. Every morning he carefully places the newspapers where they will stay dry even if it rains.
8. Girls, wait until your mother gets here.
9. After she had worked in the garden all afternoon, she stood back, looked at the tomato and cucumber plants, and gave herself a mental pat on the back.
10. They stay wherever they feel comfortable.

Exercise 13: Adjective (relative) Clauses

1. Do you remember the time when our teacher brought along candy bars, which she gave it to the students who worked hardest that day?
2. Cindy showed me the shells that she had found in Florida.
3. While the wealthy CEO, who has enough money for ten lifetimes, is paid a fortune, some of his employees, whose bank accounts hover around zero, earn a pittance.
4. Marlon Brando starred with Rod Steiger in *On the Waterfront*, a 1954 film that won seven Academy Awards.
5. Is that not the boy whom we saw at the party last week?
6. The flowers were not delivered to the house of the person for whom they were intended.
7. The guest speaker talked about the German airship *Hindenburg*, which exploded in May of 1937 in Lakehurst, New Jersey, where it had just arrived.
8. Have your parents never met the guy you love?
9. Is that the party of four whose table is ready?
10. Those are the people I told you about.

Exercise 14: Noun Clauses, Indirect Questions

1. Anyone can see that you are a bright person.
2. I know you will not disappoint your parents and teachers.
3. It is possible that several prisoners will be released next month.
4. Do you ever wonder if all people of the world can live together in peace?
5. Can you tell me whether or not we have school next Friday?
6. The problem is that we have too much homework or too little time.
7. I am afraid that it rained very little while we were away.

8. On the way to Florida, they talked about whether they should visit an aunt who was living in St. Augustine.
9. I know that you know that they know the answer.
10. Our hope that the stock market would rebound soon was diminished by disclosures of fiscal fraud by several very large companies.

Exercise 15: Noun Clauses (2), Indirect Questions (2)

1. The question is why they didn't act sooner.
2. They asked which seats belonged to them.
3. The future of our company depends on how well its present employees work together.
4. Authorities still do not know how many people were killed or injured when the bridge collapsed.
5. Have you considered why they stole the money or what they did with it?
6. Why they did what they did will probably never be known.
7. In Shakespeare's *Hamlet*, Polonius speaks these words: "Neither a borrower nor a lender be."
8. The interviewer wondered what books the applicant had read recently.
9. Scientists do not yet know why general relativity and quantum mechanics are incompatible with each other.
10. If you are interested in superstrings, you should ask where you can get a copy of Brian Greene's book *The Elegant Universe*.

Exercise 16: Participles, Objective Complements (2)

1. Having reached the top of the mountain, we thought that we could see four states.
2. When the people standing in the rear of the theater saw that several members of the audience had gotten up, taken their coats, and left the theater, they moved into the empty seats.
3. Buffeted by gale-force winds and 15-foot waves, the small vessel broke apart and sank.
4. Alarmed by the recovery of Carthage, which had been defeated by the Romans in the first two Punic Wars, the Roman statesman Cato the Elder ended every speech with the words, "Carthage must be destroyed."
5. She sat down, closed her eyes, and felt her muscles relaxing.
6. One could see the wounded and dying being placed on stretchers.
7. Having been seen in the vicinity of the victim's house at the time of the crime, he was brought in by the police for interrogation.
8. Lying on the floor was a letter addressed to her ex-husband.
9. Having heard the unmistakable sound of their mother's voice calling them to dinner, the children came flying.
10. Some just kept staring at the collapsing building, while others were running away.

Exercise 17: Gerunds

1. Running is rewarding.
2. Because we enjoy swimming, we built a pool in our backyard.
3. Watching soccer is fun for those who understand the game.
4. The teacher does not appreciate the children's screaming in the classroom.
5. Nothing will be accomplished by their being punished so severely.
6. He calls his cutting corners shrewd business, but his former customers call it cheating.
7. He commented briefly on his having been chosen for the award but then spoke of other things.
8. That movie is worth seeing a second time.
9. When all is said and done, one thing seems most important: being kind to others.
10. She said that she succeeded in life by working hard and standing tall.

Exercise 18: Infinitives

1. To travel to Europe is her dream.
2. Children and ducks like to play in the rain.
3. To diagram or not to diagram, that is the question.
4. Since they had not had a chance to visit Fisherman's Wharf, they decided to stay in San Francisco one more day.
5. If you are in Rome and have nothing to do, it is a good idea just to walk and look.
6. Be sure to make reservations, unless you want to wait at least an hour.
7. Her ambition was to play the piano, but she hated to practice.
8. You used to understand why it is necessary to study.
9. It is not too early to plant lettuce, peas, and spinach.
10. Although more people want to and ought to ride a bicycle to work, our city puts little effort or money into constructing bicycle lanes and paths.

Exercise 19: Infinitives (2), Objective Complements (3)

1. They let the visitors feed the camels and the goats.
2. I'm sorry if I made you cry, but you make me want to scream.
3. Although we asked them to extend their visit, they were able to stay only one day.
4. I am going to have a large garden this year, and I want you to feel free to pick tomatoes and squash for your family.
5. Sometimes I want nothing but to be left alone.
6. You are to meet your parents at the station and travel with them to Ohio for the weekend.
7. We must shop quickly because the store is about to close.
8. His mother said that she had a box for him to carry.
9. Since the new concepts were difficult, it was necessary for the teacher to explain them carefully.
10. The student complained that his advisor had forced him to takes courses that he neither wanted nor needed.

Exercise 20: Expletives, Ellipses, Indefinite Relative Pronouns, and Special Concessive Clauses

1. Hey, you don't have to exercise, but you will be healthier if you do.
2. People are not allowed to do whatever they want to.
3. While staying at our house, please turn off the lights when you leave a room.
4. If necessary, the authorities, namely, the local police and other law-enforcement officers, will use force to keep the demonstration from becoming unsafe.
5. Our team, though young and inexperienced, somehow managed to win.
6. Hush! Jerry had to work overtime last night, and he needs to get some sleep.
7. I would like for you to give this money to whoever needs it most.
8. However hard they try, they never seem to be able to make ends meet.
9. Whatever happens, they will not be caught unprepared.
10. Whatever he says, she says the opposite.

Exercise 21: Transitional Adverbs, Independent Expressions, and Sentence Modifiers

1. Yes, the Dawsons now have a large pantry and a large freezer; therefore, they no longer have to shop every week for canned goods and frozen foods.

2. Well, I must say that I enjoy shopping for groceries.
3. That having been said, we can move on to a different subject.
4. Treat other people as you would want them to treat you--Morality 101.
5. To make a long story short, the princess did not kiss the frog but threw it against a wall; nevertheless, they married and lived happily ever after.
6. Speaking of unexpected twists of fortune, my cousin Ambrose, who forgot his lines in the school play last year, landed an acting job in New York City.
7. In conclusion, there is no need to panic--unless, of course, the stock market doesn't recover.
8. Without being told to do so, the children took out their math books and began working, which delighted their teacher.
9. Great Caesar's ghost! I'm sure I paid that bill two months ago.
10. There, that's enough.

Exercise 22: Equal and Unequal Comparisons (*as* and *than*), and Other Topics

1. Are you taller than your father?
2. I know that I will arrive earlier than you.
3. Since you give me a choice, I must say that I would rather stay here and watch TV than see a mediocre movie that I've already seen twice.
4. She is as considerate as anyone we know.
5. I am thinking of something that is larger than a mailbox but not so large as a sofa.
6. There is good reason to believe that she is older than you.
7. Perhaps the game will start earlier than you think.
8. Even when she was sleepier than her children, she always found the energy to read them a book.
9. Speaking of a time and place for optimism, the current situation in the Near East must not be regarded as hopeless.
10. Given the longstanding animosity between the two countries, it is to be expected that, whatever opportunities present themselves for a rapprochement, their leaders will continue to find excuses for prolonging the fighting.

Exercise 23: Prepositional Phrases (2)

1. Karen finds it easy to be nice to other people when she is in a good mood.
2. I understand that you need to use the phone, but ours is out of order.
3. When the circus was in town, the kids were in a state of high expectation.
4. It is frightening to be without food and money.
5. The arrival of a package from home put him in good spirits.
6. He was small in size but large in personality.
7. In accordance with the wishes of the employees, and in spite of the sweltering weather, the company picnic will take place outdoors as planned.
8. She is a friend of his and a neighbor of ours.
9. The ships were sailing just below the horizon and could be seen only from the air.
10. For all we know, an alien space ship could be traveling at this very moment from a distant galaxy towards the Earth, the third planet from a star of moderate size, one of billions of stars that comprise the universe.

Exercise 24: *Like, Near, Different Than,* and Other Topics

1. If you were more like her, you wouldn't pay five dollars a pound for meat.
2. He wore his brother Will's tux to the prom, and he looked like a million dollars.

3. He eats like a horse, runs like a deer, and sleeps like a baby.
4. The game was different than they had expected.
5. This tastes like the homemade ice cream that my grandfather used to make.
6. I made it myself, but I hurt myself in the process.
7. His journey having taken him to an exceedingly old and ugly village, he took the scrap of paper from his pocket to see if he had perhaps misread or misremembered the name.
8. In 1905, while working as a patent examiner, only five years after he had graduated from the Swiss Polytechnic Institute, Albert Einstein published four papers that reshaped physics.
9. We are near the school, nearer than you think.
10. Salesmen are expected to be honest; however, unscrupulous salesmen use "bait and switch" to ensnare the unsuspecting--an old story.

Exercise 25: Miscellaneous Topics

1. She works downtown as a sales representative for a computer company and uses the bus as her principal means of transportation to and from work, which both helps the environment and allows her to put money aside for a new house.
2. She began working there nine years ago; during her tenure with the company, she has been given several promotions along with generous increases in pay.
3. The old professor's desk contained the usual items: pictures and letters, clippings and notes, pens and staples, mints and gum.
4. It's no wonder they don't want to go along.
5. Regarding the matter we discussed when you were here last, I'm afraid I'm unable to tell you what you want to hear.
6. His brothers and sisters came too late to see the best part of the movie.
7. The students were told that no one would be permitted to leave the room except to use the restroom.
8. All of us were uncertain as to whether or not the design for the new bridge was the same as the design that had been presented to and approved by the bridge committee.
9. Kids have a great time playing the same games their parents used to play.
10. Some people just took a place on the lawn, where they remained all afternoon and evening.

Exercise 26: Miscellaneous Topics

1. The well-worn 1970 World Book Encyclopedia, which from year to year had taken up more and more shelf space as one by one yearbooks had been added to the set, and which, one fine day, Harvey stacked in four large boxes that he carried to the attic, has been replaced by a CD.
2. I am afraid that for him to go along we would need a second vehicle, and that is out of the question.
3. When they do their part, then we will do ours.
4. Until the 1936 presidential election, people used to say, "As Maine goes, so goes the nation."
5. Well, only one other state, Vermont, went as Maine went in that election.
6. Did you know that he acted as if he were sick so that his mom would keep him home from school?
7. I'll be in my room; should he call, please tell me.
8. I'll help you tomorrow if the world doesn't end in the meantime and if I still feel like it.
9. Before junior-league football games, his father used to try to give him courage by saying, "The bigger they are, the harder they fall."
10. "Either the dog goes or I go," had become her almost daily threat; how could he be sure that she didn't mean it this time?

Exercise 27: Sentences from Literature

1. Dost thou love Life, then do not squander Time, for that is the Stuff Life is made of. (from *Poor Richard's Almanack*, by Benjamin Franklin)
2. Early to bed, and early to rise, makes a Man healthy, wealthy and wise. (from *Poor Richard's Almanack*, by Benjamin Franklin)
3. I should have no objection to a repetition of the same life from the beginning, only asking the advantages authors have in a second edition to correct some faults of the first. (from Benjamin Franklin's *Autobiography*)
4. I grew convinced that *truth, sincerity* and *integrity* in dealings between man and man were of the utmost importance to the felicity of life; and I formed written resolutions (which still remain in my journal book), to practice them ever while I lived. (from Benjamin Franklin's *Autobiography*)
5. One paper, which I wrote for Mr. Kinnersley on the sameness of lightning with electricity, I sent to Dr. Mitchel, an acquaintance of mine, and one of the members also of that society, who wrote me word that it had been read, but was laughed at by the connoisseurs. (from Benjamin Franklin's *Autobiography*)

Exercise 28: Sentences from Literature (2)

1. For as in absolute governments the king is law, so in free countries the law *ought* to BE king, and there ought to be no other. (from *Common Sense*, by Thomas Paine)
2. I have as little superstition in me as any man living, but my secret opinion has been, and still is, that God Almighty will not give up a people to military destruction, or leave them unsupportedly to perish, who have so earnestly and so repeatedly sought to avoid the calamities of war, by every decent method which wisdom could invent. (from *The American Crisis*, by Thomas Paine)
3. The heart that feels not now is dead; the blood of his children will curse his cowardice, who shrinks back at a time when little might have saved the whole, and made *them* happy. (from *The American Crisis*, by Thomas Paine)
4. Not all the treasures of the world, so far as I believe, could have induced me to support an offensive war, for I think it murder; but if a thief breaks into my house, burns and destroys my property, and kills or threatens to kill me, or those that are in it, and *"to bind me in all cases whatsoever"* to his absolute will, am I to suffer it? (from *The American Crisis*, by Thomas Paine)

Exercise 29: Sentences from Literature (3)

1. Called upon to undertake the duties of the first executive office of our country, I avail myself of the presence of that portion of my fellow-citizens which is here assembled, to express my grateful thanks for the favor with which they have been pleased to look towards me, to declare a sincere consciousness that the task is above my talents, and that I approach it with those anxious and awful presentiments which the greatness of the charge and the weakness of my powers so justly inspire. (opening sentence from Thomas Jefferson's *First Inaugural Address*)
2. It has been frequently remarked, that it seems to have been reserved to the people of this country to decide, by their conduct and example, the important question, whether societies of men are really capable or not, of establishing good government from reflection and choice, or whether they are forever destined to depend, for their political constitutions, on accident and force. (from Thomas Jefferson's *The Federalist No. 1*)

Exercise 30: Sentences from Literature (4)

1. It is remarkable that the visionary propensity I have mentioned is not confined to the native inhabitants of the valley, but is unconsciously imbibed by every one [sic] who resides there for a time. (from Washington

Irving's "The Legend of Sleepy Hollow")

2. During the whole of a dull, dark, and soundless day in the autumn of the year, when the clouds hung oppressively low in the heavens, I had been passing alone, on horseback, through a singularly dreary tract of country, and at length found myself, as the shades of evening drew on, within view of the melancholy House of Usher. (from "The Fall of the House of Usher," by Edgar Allan Poe)

3. A person who watched the interview between the dead and the living, scrupled not to affirm, that, at the instant when the clergyman's features were disclosed, the corpse had slightly shuddered, rustling the shroud and muslim cap, though the countenance retained the composure of death. (from "The Minister's Black Veil," by Nathaniel Hawthorne)

~ Solutions ~

1, 1.

$$\text{Birds} \mid \text{fly}$$

The noun *birds* is the **subject** of the sentence. *Fly* is the **verb**. In every sentence diagram, a vertical line passing through the base line separates the **subject** from the **verb**.

1, 2.

$$\text{Fish} \mid \text{are jumping}$$

The noun *fish* is the **subject** of the sentence, and *are jumping* is the **verb**. Whereas the **verb** *fly* in Sentence 1 is **simple present**, the **verb** *are jumping* is **present progressive**. Progressive forms consist of forms of the **auxiliary verb** *be* (*am, are, is, was, were, will be*, etc.) plus the **present participle**.

1, 3.

$$\text{people} \mid \text{Do fly}$$

The noun *people* is the **subject**, *do fly* the verb. *Do* is capitalized in the diagram because it is the first word in the sentence. Regardless of position in a sentence, the **subject** precedes the **verb** in a sentence diagram. The **verb** *do fly* is **present emphatic** (often used in questions).

1, 4.

$$\text{you} \mid \text{Can jump}$$

You, a personal pronoun, is the **subject** of the sentence. The **verb** *can* is called a **modal auxiliary verb**. Other **modal auxiliary verbs** are *could, may, might, should*, and *would*.

1, 5.

$$\text{What} \mid \text{is happening}$$

What is an interrogative pronoun. It functions as the **subject** of this sentence. The **verb** *is happening* is **present progressive**.

1, 6.

$$\text{I} \mid \text{must know}$$

The personal pronoun *I* is the **subject** of the sentence. The verb is *must know*. *Must*, like *can*, is a **modal auxiliary verb**.

1, 7.

$$\text{Students} \mid \text{are being tested}$$

The **subject** of the sentence is the noun *students*. *Are being tested* is a **present-progressive verb** in the **passive voice**. The **passive voice** is used to show that something is being done to the **subject** of the sentence.

1, 8.

$$\text{parents} \mid \text{Were informed}$$

Parents, a **noun**, is the **subject** of the sentence. *Were informed* is in the **simple past tense, passive voice**. Only **transitive verbs** (that is, **verbs** that can take direct objects) can have **voice**.

1, 9.

$$\text{everyone} \mid \text{Has arrived}$$

The indefinite pronoun *everyone* is the **subject** of the sentence. The **verb** *has arrived* is in the **present-perfect tense**. Verbs in this tense have *have* or *has* as an **auxiliary verb**. *Arrive* is an **intransitive verb**.

1, 10.

$$\text{We} \mid \text{should have been told}$$

The **subject** is the personal pronoun *we*. *Should* is a **modal auxiliary verb**. *Should have been told* is in the **present-perfect tense, passive voice**.

2, 1.

```
Lizards | lay | eggs
```

Lizards is the subject of the sentence. *Lay* is a transitive verb; its **direct object** is *eggs*. In sentence diagrams, a **direct object** is preceded by a vertical line that meets, but does not pass through, the base line.

2, 2.

```
Who | is playing | volleyball
```

Who, an interrogative pronoun, is the subject of the sentence. *Is playing* is a present-progressive verb, and *volleyball* is a **direct object**.

2, 3.

```
Motorcyclists | must wear | helmets
```

Motorcyclists is the subject. *Must* is a modal auxiliary verb. *Helmets* is a **direct object**.

2, 4.

```
you | Do have | pets
```

The personal pronoun *you* is the subject of this sentence. *Do have* is present emphatic. *Pets* is a **direct object**.

2, 5.

```
We | could donate | time
```

The subject of this sentence is the personal pronoun *we*. The verb *could donate* is in the subjunctive mood. The subjunctive mood is used for ideas or thoughts that are not or may not be realized; its opposite, the indicative mood, is used for facts. *Time* is a **direct object**.

2, 6.

```
Someone | may ask | you
```

The indefinite pronoun *someone* is the subject of the sentence. *May* is a modal auxiliary verb. *You* is a **direct object**.

2, 7.

```
they | Will bring | presents
```

The subject is the personal pronoun *they*. *Will bring* is in the future tense, active voice. *Presents* is a **direct object**. In general, only active verbs can take **direct objects**.

2, 8.

```
She | had visited | relatives
```

The personal pronoun *she* is the subject of the sentence. *Had visited* is in the past-perfect tense. *Relatives* is a **direct object**.

2, 9.

```
Shoppers | were pushing | carts
```

The noun *shoppers* is the subject. *Were pushing* is **past progressive**. *Carts* is a **direct object**.

2, 10.

```
Kindness | can change | things
```

The subject of the sentence is the noun *kindness*. *Can* is a modal auxiliary verb. *Things* is a **direct object**.

3, 1.

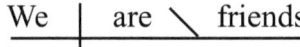

The subject of the sentence is the personal pronoun *we*. *Are* is a present-tense form of the linking verb *be*. *Friends* is a **predicate nominative**. A **predicate nominative** is a noun or pronoun that comes after the verb and identifies or further explains the subject.

3, 2.

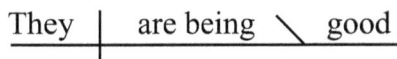

Are being is a present-progressive form of the linking verb *be*. *Good* is a **predicate adjective**. A predicate adjective appears in the **predicate** after the verb (usually a linking verb) and modifies (describes or limits) the subject.

3, 3.

he | Has been \ sick

Has been is a perfect-tense form of the linking verb *be*. *Sick* is a **predicate adjective**.

3, 4.

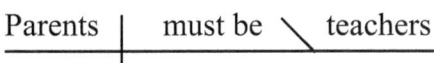

Must is a modal auxiliary verb. *Teachers* is a **predicate nominative**.

3, 5.

I | feel \ tired

Feel is a linking verb. *Tired* is a **predicate adjective**. Some additional linking verbs are *be, become, appear, seem, taste, look, grow, keep,* and *remain*.

3, 6.

Everyone | became \ quiet

Became is a simple-past form of the linking verb *become*. *Quiet* is a **predicate adjective**.

3, 7.

Who | will be elected \ president

The subject *who* is an interrogative pronoun. The verb *will be elected* is in the future tense, passive voice. Passive forms of verbs like *elect, appoint, designate, choose,* and *make* are often followed by a **predicate nominative**.

3, 8.

Jeff | Did get \ angry

Did get is the past emphatic form of the verb *get*. When *get* means *become*, as it does here, it is a linking verb. *Angry* is a **predicate adjective**.

3, 9.

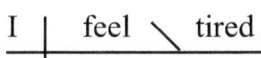

Had been is a past-perfect form of the verb *be*. *Absent* is a **predicate adjective**.

3, 10.

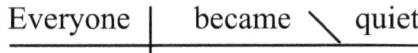

The subject is the personal pronoun *we*. *Must* is a modal auxiliary verb. *Enemies* is a **predicate nominative**.

4, 1.

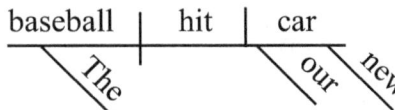

The **definite article** *the* modifies the subject of the sentence, *baseball*. The **possessive pronoun** *our* and the **attributive adjective** *new* modify the direct object *car*. An **attributive adjective** comes before the noun it modifies. *The* is the only **definite article** in the English language.

4, 2.

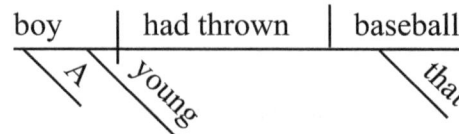

The **indefinite article** *a* and the **attributive adjective** *young* modify the subject *boy*. *Had thrown* is in the past-perfect tense. The **demonstrative adjective** *that* modifies the direct object *baseball*. **Demonstrative adjectives** and demonstrative pronouns have the same forms: *this, that, these, those*. **Indefinite articles** are *a* and *an*.

4, 3.

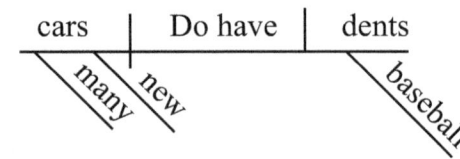

The subject *cars* is modified by the **attributive adjectives** *many* and *new*. *Do have* is present emphatic. In this sentence, *baseball* is a **noun used as an attributive adjective** modifying the direct object *dents*.

4, 4.

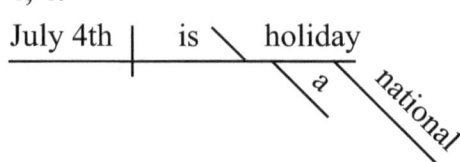

The **indefinite article** *a* and the **attributive adjective** *national* modify the predicate nominative *holiday*.

4, 5.

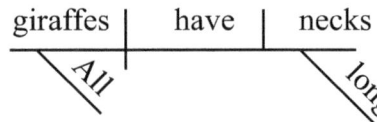

The **attributive adjectives** *all* and *long* modify the subject *giraffes* and the direct object *necks*, respectively.

4, 6.

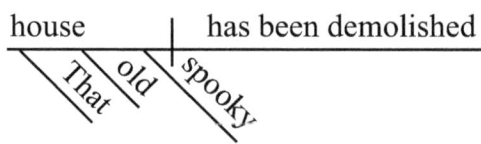

The **demonstrative adjective** *that* and the **attributive adjectives** *old* and *spooky* modify the subject *house*. *Has been demolished* is in the present-perfect tense, passive voice.

4, 7.

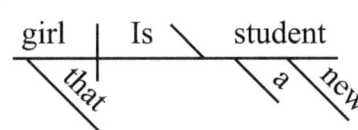

The **demonstrative adjective** *that* modifies the subject *girl*, while the **indefinite article** *a* and the **attributive adjective** *new* modify the predicate nominative *student*. *Is* is capitalized because it is the first word in the sentence.

4, 8.

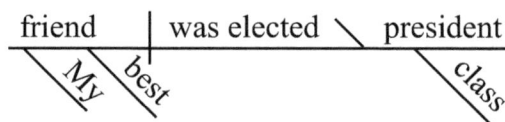

The subject *friend* is modified by the **possessive pronoun** *my* and the **attributive adjective** *best*. *Was elected* is a past-tense form in the passive voice; it functions here as a linking verb. *President* is a predicate nominative; it is modified by the noun *class*, which is used here as an **attributive adjective**.

4, 9.

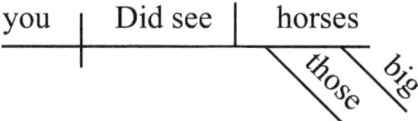

Did see is past emphatic. The direct object *horses* is modified by the **demonstrative adjective** *those* and the **attributive adjective** *big*.

4, 10.

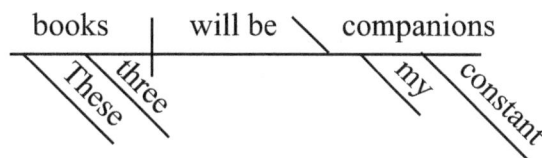

The **demonstrative adjective** *these* and the **attributive adjective** *three* modify the subject *books*. *Will be* is in the future tense. The **possessive pronoun** *my* and the **attributive adjective** *constant* modify the predicate nominative *companions*.

5, 1.

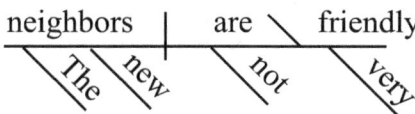

Not and *very* are **adverbs**. *Not* modifies the verb *are*, while *very* modifies the predicate adjective *friendly*. **Adverbs** modify verbs, adjectives, and adverbs, as well as prepositions, conjunctions, phrases, clauses, and entire sentences.

5, 2.

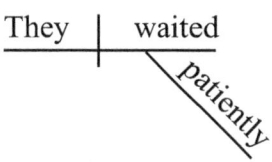

The **adverb** *patiently* modifies the past-tense verb *waited*.

5, 3.

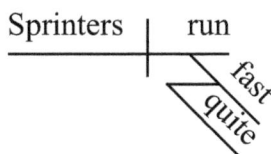

Quite and *fast* are both **adverbs**. *Fast* modifies the verb *run*, and *quite* modifies the **adverb** *fast*.

5, 4.

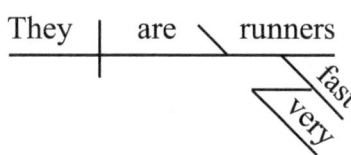

Whereas *fast* is an **adverb** in Sentence 3, in this sentence it is an adjective. It modifies the predicate nominative *runners* and is modified by the **adverb** *very*.

5, 5.

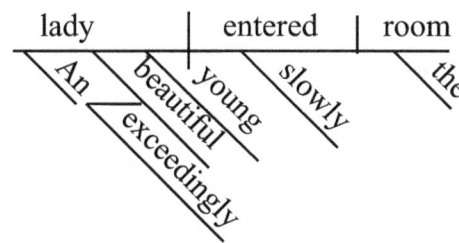

The subject *lady* is modified by the indefinite article *an*, and the attributive adjectives *beautiful* and *young*. *Beautiful*, in turn, is modified by the **adverb** *exceedingly*. The **adverb** *slowly* modifies the verb *entered*. *Room* is a direct object.

5, 6.

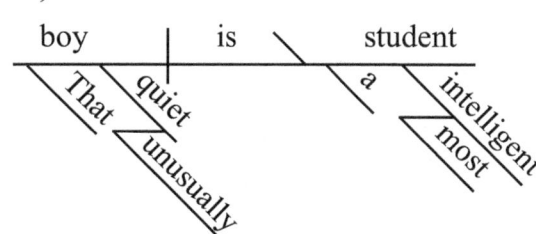

The **adverb** *unusually* modifies *quiet*, an adjective modifying the subject *boy*. The **adverb** *most* modifies the adjective *intelligent*, which modifies the predicate nominative *student*.

5, 7.

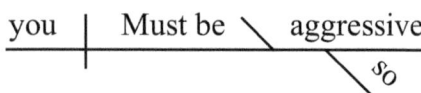

The **adverb** *so* modifies the predicate adjective *aggressive*.

5, 8.

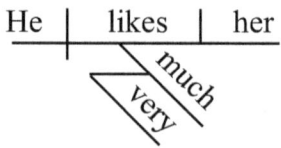

Much is an **adverb** modifying the verb *likes*, and the **adverb** *very* modifies *much*. The personal pronoun *her* is the direct object. It is said to be in the objective case. Other objective-case forms of personal pronouns are *me, you, him, it, us,* and *them*.

5, 9.

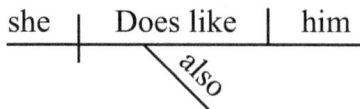

The **adverb** *also* modifies the verb *does like*. The personal pronoun *him* is in the objective case; it functions here as a direct object.

5, 10.

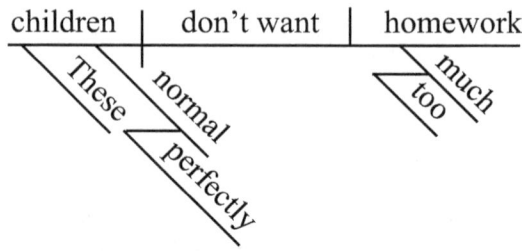

These is a demonstrative adjective. Contractions, like *don't*, that involve the **adverb** *not* are diagrammed in their contracted form. The **adverbs** *perfectly* and *too* modify the adjectives *normal* and *much*.

6, 1.

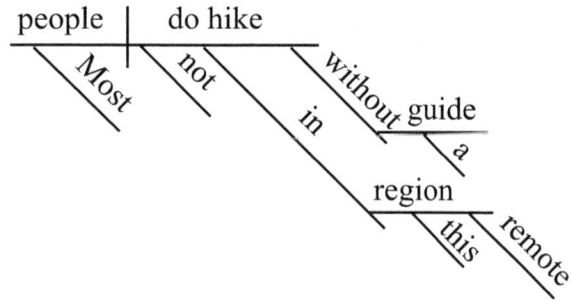

The adjective *most* modifies the subject *people*. *Not* is an adverb. Both **prepositional phrases**, *in this remote region* and *without a guide*, are adverbial; they modify the verb *do hike*.

6, 2.

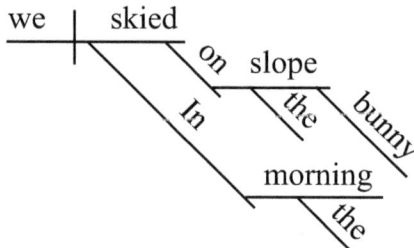

In the morning and *on the bunny slope* are **prepositional phrases**, and both function as adverbial modifiers of the verb *skied*.

6, 3.

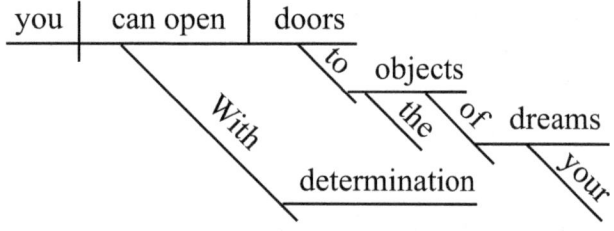

With, to, and *of* are **prepositions**; they have the objects *determination, objects,* and *dreams,* respectively. The **prepositional phrase** *with determination* is adverbial; the other two **prepositional phrases** are adjectival.

6, 4.

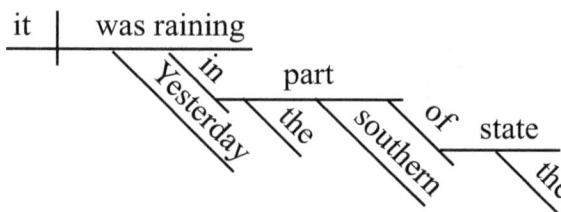

The **prepositions** *in* and *of* have as their objects *part* and *state*, respectively. A **prepositional phrase** consists of a **preposition** and its complete object (object with modifiers). The first **prepositional phrase** is adverbial, modifying the verb, while the second is adjectival, modifying a noun.

6, 5.

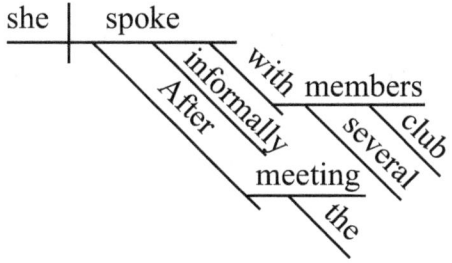

The subject of the sentence is the personal pronoun *she*. *After* and *with* are **prepositions**. Both **prepositional phrases** modify the simple-past verb *spoke*. *Spoke* is modified also by the adverb *informally*.

6, 6.

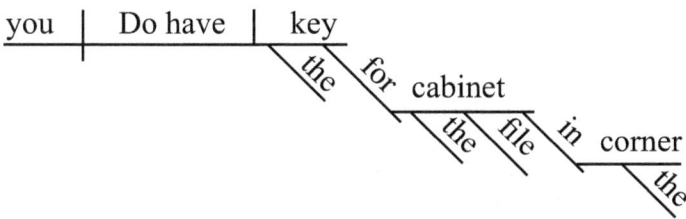

The subject of the sentence is the personal pronoun *you*. The verb *do have* is present emphatic. *For* and *in* are **prepositions**. The **prepositional phrase** *for the file cabinet* modifies the direct object *key*. *Cabinet*, in turn, is modified by the **prepositional phrase** *in the corner*.

6, 7.

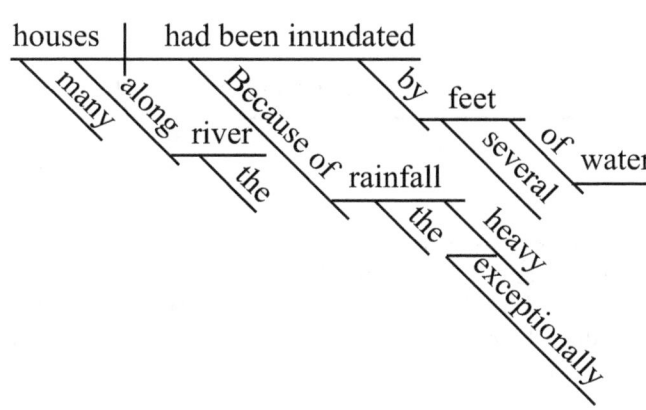

The verb *had been inundated* is in the past-perfect tense, passive voice. The sentence includes the **prepositions** *along, because of* (a **phrasal preposition**, so called because it consists of more than one word), *by*, and *of*. Of the four **prepositional phrases**, two are adverbial (*because of the exceptionally heavy rainfall* and *by several feet of water*) and two are adjectival (*along the river* and *of water*).

6, 8.

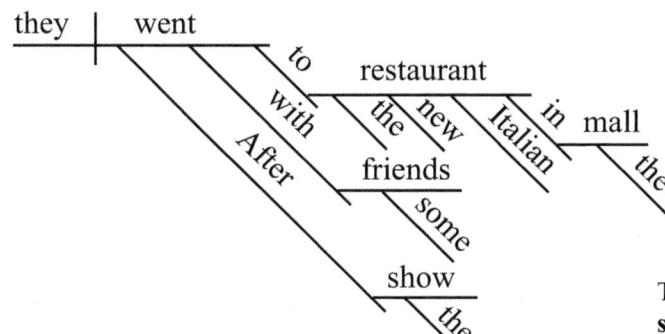

The **prepositions** are *after, with, to,* and *in*. Three of the **prepositional phrases** modify the verb *went*, and one modifies the noun *restaurant*.

6, 9.

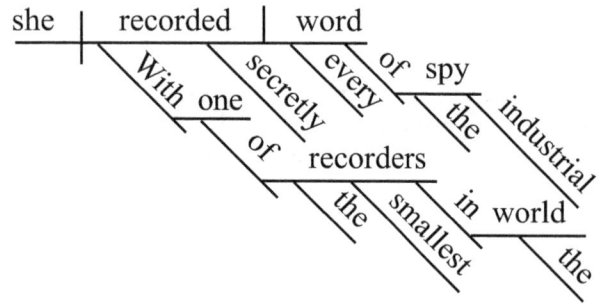

This sentence has four **prepositions**: *with, of, in,* and *of*. Three of the **prepositional phrases** are adjectival, and one is adverbial. *Word* is a direct object.

6, 10.

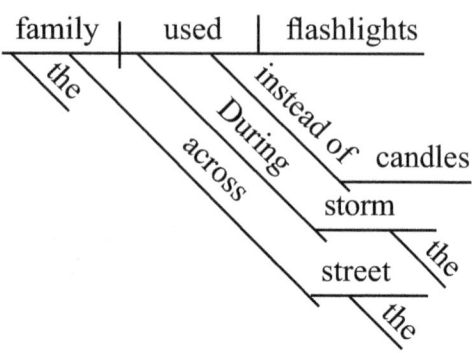

Across is a **preposition**; *across the street* is a **prepositional phrase** modifying the subject of the sentence, *family*. *During* and *instead of* are likewise **prepositions**, the latter **phrasal**. The **prepositional phrases** *during the storm* and *instead of candles* modify the verb *used*. *Flashlights* is a direct object.

7, 1.

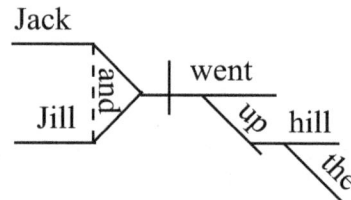

Jack and Jill is a **compound subject**; the **coordinating conjunction** *and* joins the two nouns. The verb *went* is the simple past of *go*. In this sentence, *up* is a preposition (prepositions have objects; adverbs do not). In the sentence *they went up*, *up* is an adverb.

7, 2.

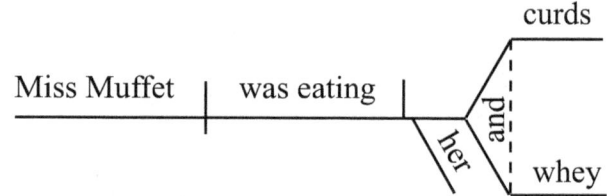

Titles are not separated from names in diagramming; thus, *Miss* is not separated from *Muffet*. The verb *was eating* is past progressive. *Curds and whey* is a **compound direct object**. Because *her* modifies both *curds* and *whey*, its diagonal line is connected to a part of the direct object line that pertains to both objects.

7, 3.

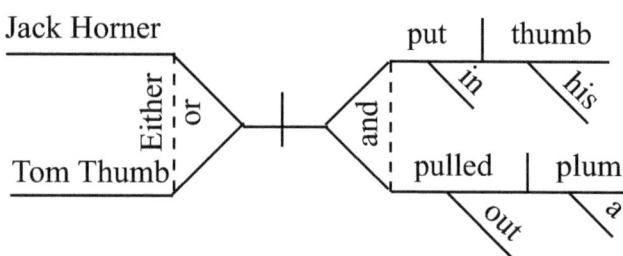

This sentence has a **compound subject** and a **compound predicate**, predicate being the name for everything that is not part of the subject and not an independent element. The **coordinating conjunctions** *either . . . or, neither . . . nor,* and *both . . . and* are sometimes called **correlative conjunctions**. The words *in* and *out*, which are often used as prepositions, are adverbs in this sentence. If one tries to read them as prepositions, as *in his thumb* and *out a plumb*, the sentence loses all meaning.

7, 4.

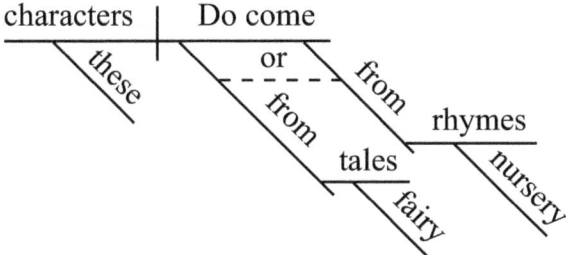

The demonstrative adjective *these* modifies the subject *characters*. The verb *do come* is present emphatic. It is modified by a **compound adverbial modifier** consisting of two prepositional phrases connected by the coordinating conjunction *or*.

7, 5.

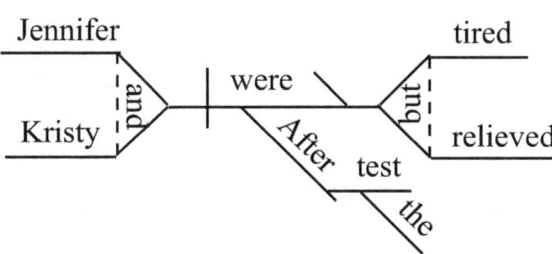

And and *but* are **coordinating conjunctions**. *Jennifer and Kristy* is a **compound subject**; *tired but relieved* is a **compound predicate adjective**. *After the test* is an adverbial prepositional phrase, i.e., a prepositional phrase that functions as an adverb.

7, 6.

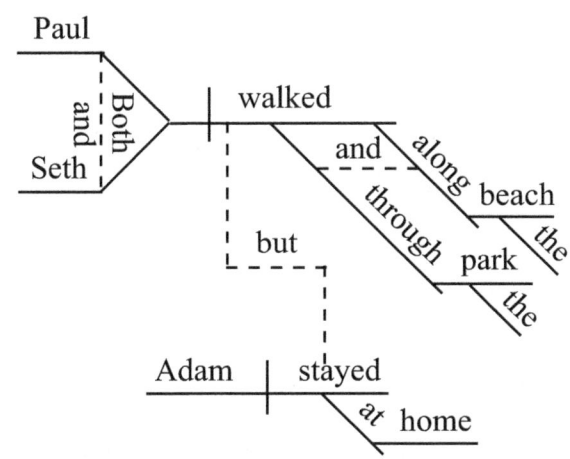

Both Paul and Seth is a **compound subject**, and *through the park and along the beach* is a **compound adverbial modifier**. The **coordinating conjunction** *but* connects the two independent (or main) clauses. An independent clause is a group of words with a subject and a predicate that can stand alone as a complete sentence. A sentence with two or more independent clauses is called a **compound sentence**. Notice that the broken-line connection between the two clauses is drawn from verb to verb. *At home* is a prepositional phrase.

7, 7.

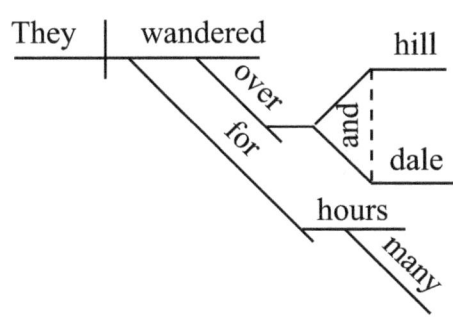

Hill and dale is a **compound object of a preposition**. Both prepositional phrases, *for many hours* and *over hill and dale* are adverbial.

7, 8.

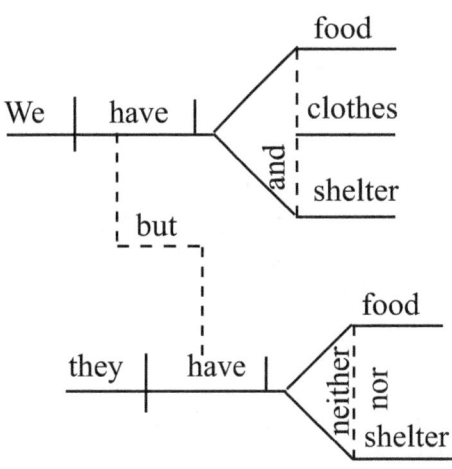

Each independent clause in this **compound sentence** contains a **compound direct object**. Notice that the placement of *and* in the diagram corresponds to its placement in the series.

~ 203 ~

7, 9.

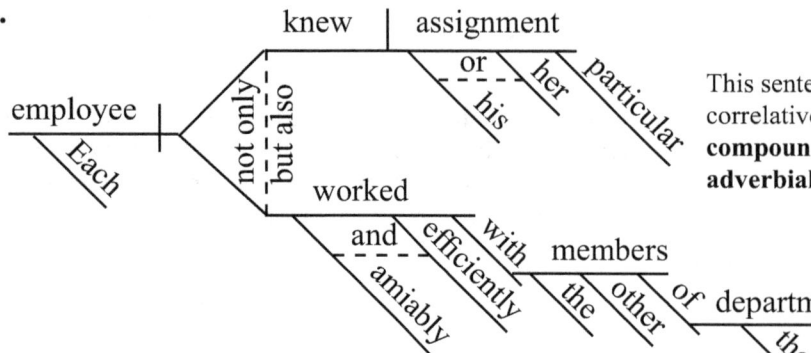

This sentence has a **compound predicate** (connected by the correlative conjunctions *not only . . . but also*) as well as a **compound adjectival modifier** (*his or her*) and **a compound adverbial modifier** (*amiably and efficiently*).

7, 10.

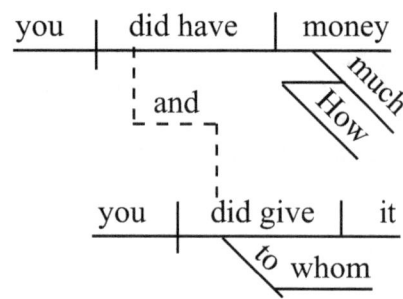

Each independent clause of this **compound sentence** has the personal pronoun *you* as subject, a past emphatic verb, and a direct object (*money* and *it*, respectively). In the first clause, the adjective *much* modifies the noun *money*, and the adverb *how* modifies *much*. In the second clause, the object of the preposition *to* is the interrogative pronoun *whom*.

8, 1.

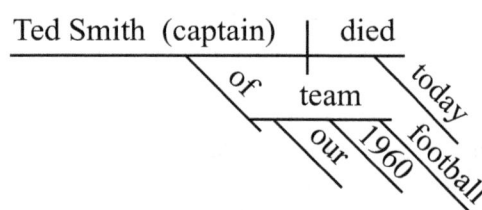

The word *captain* is an **appositive**. It is in **apposition** with the subject of the sentence, *Ted Smith*. In this sentence, *today* is an adverb. In the sentence *Today is the tomorrow I was so worried about yesterday*, both *today* and *tomorrow* are nouns, whereas *yesterday* is an adverb.

8, 2.

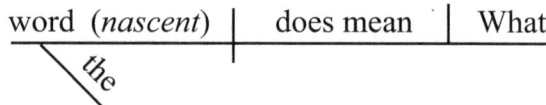

Nascent is an **appositive**; it is in **apposition** with the subject of the sentence, *word*. *Does mean* is present emphatic, and the interrogative pronoun *what* is a direct object. In a sentence diagram, an **appositive** appears in parentheses next to the word(s) with which it is in **apposition**.

8, 3.

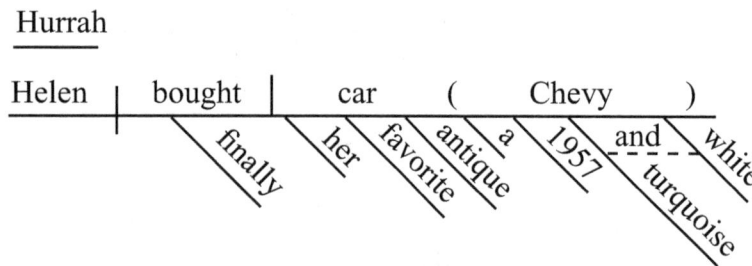

Hurrah is an **interjection**. **Interjections** are diagrammed above, and apart from, the rest of the sentence. *Chevy* is in **apposition** with the direct object *car*. Notice that the adjectives modifying the word *car* (*her, favorite,* and *antique*) are situated in the diagram below the part of the base line that pertains to *car*, while the adjectives modifying *Chevy* are positioned below the section of line delimited by the parentheses of the **appositive**.

8, 4.

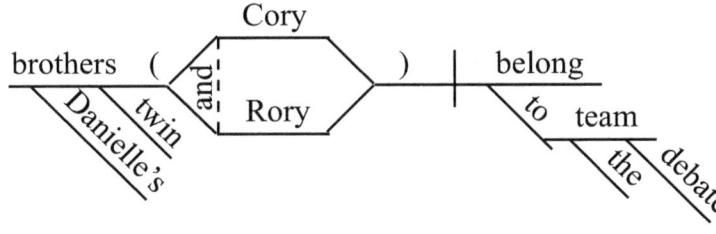

The phrase *Cory and Rory* is a **compound appositive**; like other **appositives**, **compound appositives** are placed in parentheses in a sentence diagram. *Debate* is a noun used adjectivally to modify the noun *team*.

8, 5.

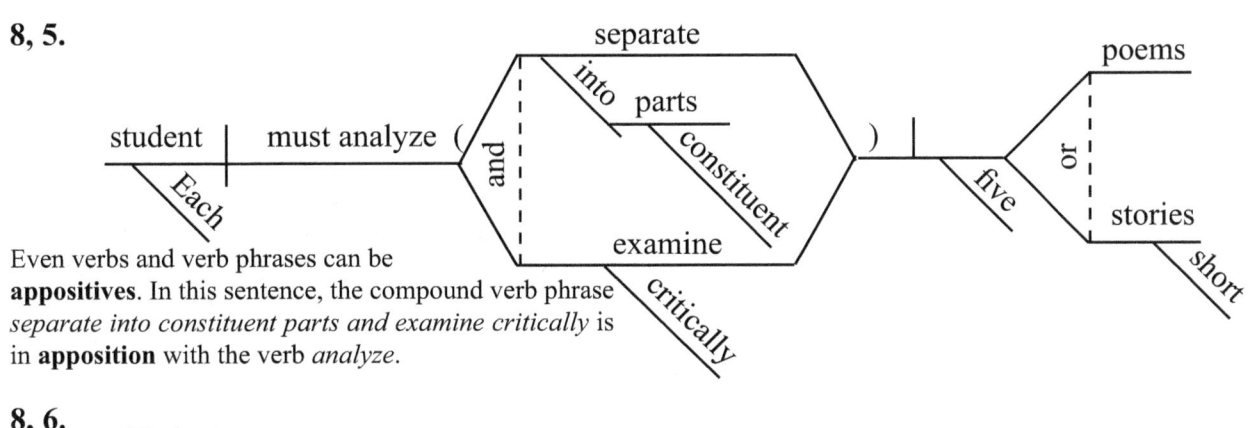

Even verbs and verb phrases can be **appositives**. In this sentence, the compound verb phrase *separate into constituent parts and examine critically* is in **apposition** with the verb *analyze*.

8, 6.

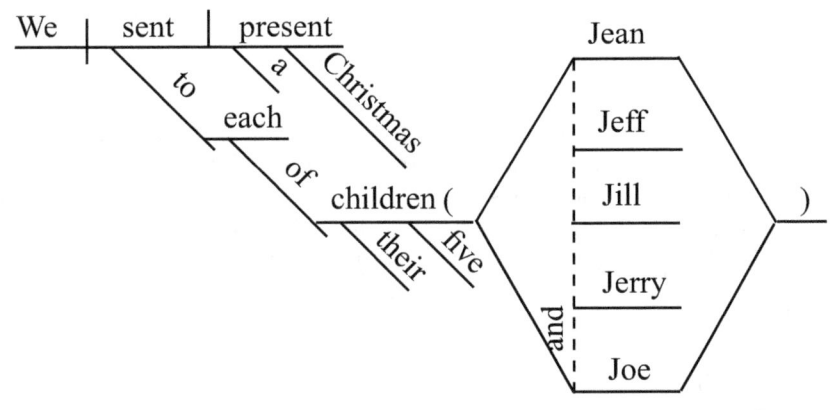

Kathy is a **noun of direct address**. Such nouns are diagrammed above and separately from the rest of the sentence. The direct object of the verb *have read* is *The Universe in a Nutshell*, whose **appositive** is *book*. Proper names, titles of books, movies, etc. are diagrammed as single entities.

8, 7.

The **compound appositive** *Jean, Jeff, Jill, Jerry, and Joe* is in **apposition** with *children*, the object of the preposition *of*. The noun *Christmas* is used here as an adjective to modify the noun *present*.

8, 8.

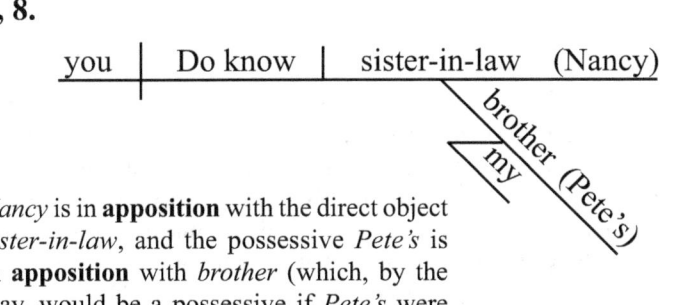

Nancy is in **apposition** with the direct object *sister-in-law*, and the possessive *Pete's* is in **apposition** with *brother* (which, by the way, would be a possessive if *Pete's* were omitted).

8, 9.

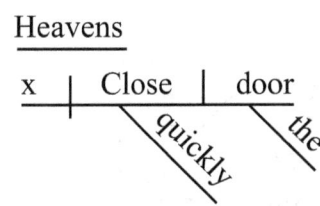

Heavens is an **interjection**. The *x* in the diagram stands for the unexpressed *you*.

8, 10.

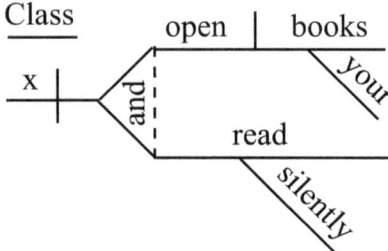

Class is a **noun of direct address**. The *x* stands for the unexpressed subject *you*. *Silently* is an adverb.

9, 1.

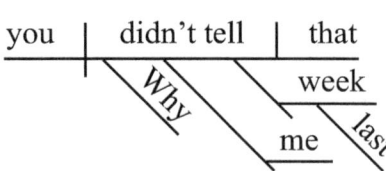

Why is an interrogative adverb. *Me* is an **indirect object**. An **indirect object** is a noun or a pronoun that tells to whom something is given, said, or shown; it is not the object of a preposition. You can identify an **indirect object** by asking *to whom?* or *for whom?* after the direct object. *Week* is an **adverbial objective**. An **adverbial objective** is a noun or a pronoun used as an adverb.

9, 2.

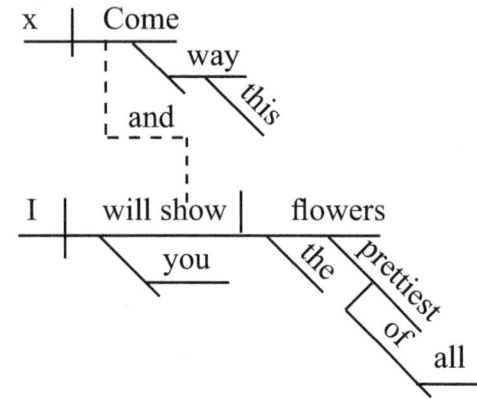

This is a compound sentence; the coordinating conjunction *and* connects the two independent clauses. The noun *way* is used here as an adverb; it is an **adverbial objective**. The personal pronoun *you* is an **indirect object**. The prepositional phrase *of all* modifies the superlative adjective *prettiest*.

9, 3.

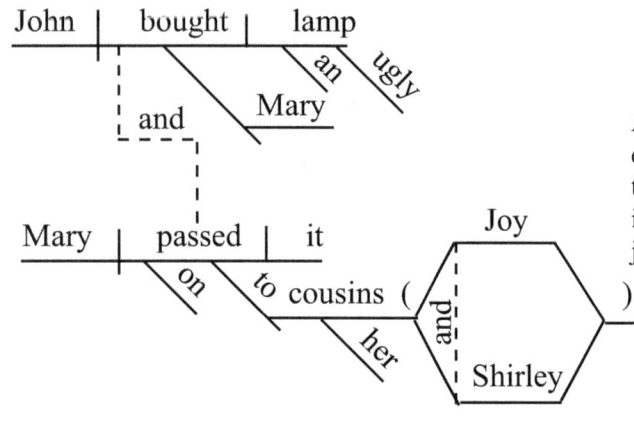

Mary and *cousins* both tell to whom something was given; however, *Mary* is an **indirect object**, while *cousins* is the object of the preposition *to*. The compound appositive *Joy and Shirley* is in apposition with *cousins*. *And* is a coordinating conjunction joining two independent clauses.

9, 4.

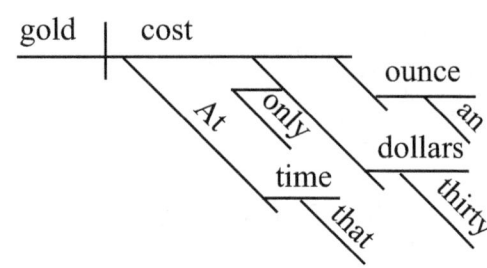

According to several American dictionaries, the verb *cost* is transitive. According to the *Oxford English Dictionary* and *Descriptive English Grammar* (House and Harman), it is intransitive. I agree with the latter sources. In my opinion, not only *ounce*, but also *dollars* (which some would call a direct object) are **adverbial objectives**. It should be noted that one cannot say, *Thirty dollars was cost by the gold*. The adverb *only* does not modify *thirty* alone but the complete **adverbial objective** *thirty dollars*.

9, 5.

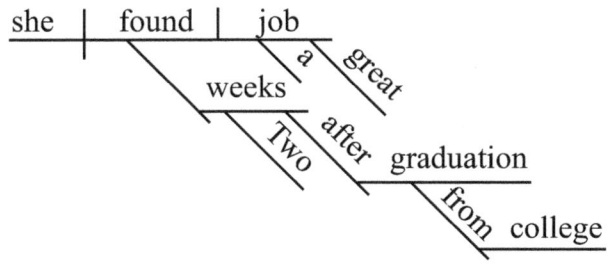

The personal pronoun *she* is the subject of the sentence. *Found* is a verb in the simple past. Its direct object is *job*. *Weeks* is an **adverbial objective**. *After graduation* and *from college* are prepositional phrases; both are adjectival because they modify nouns.

9, 6.

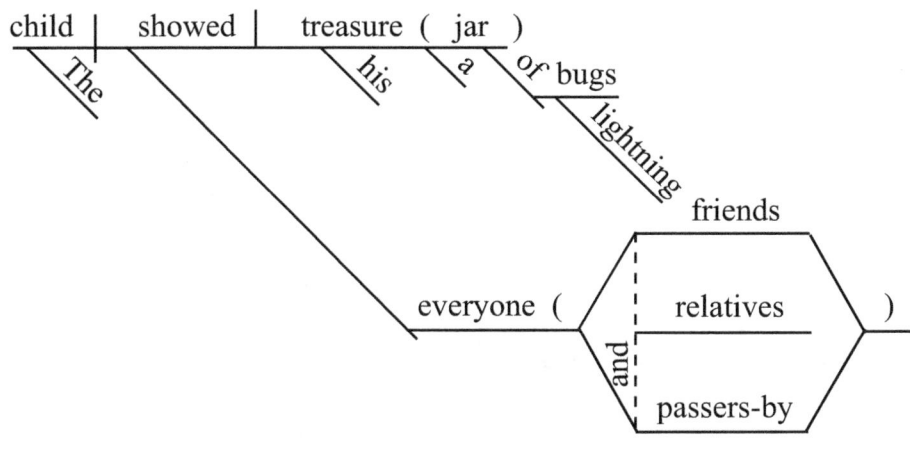

Everyone is an **indirect object**. It has a compound appositive, *friends, relatives, and passers-by*. There is no grammatical significance to the length of lines in a diagram. Sometimes lines must be made longer than usual to avoid an unpleasant bunching together of words. *Jar* is also an appositive; it is in apposition with the direct object *treasure*.

9, 7.

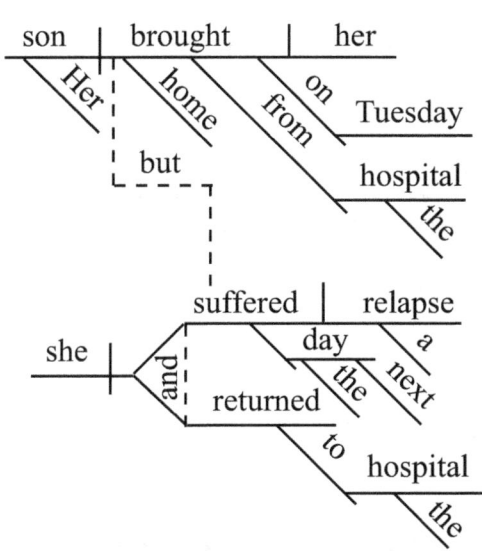

This compound sentence consists of two independent clauses, the second of which has a compound predicate. I see no reason to call *home* an **adverbial objective**, since the dictionaries I consulted label it both noun and adverb; however, *day* definitely is an **adverbial objective**.

9, 8.

Miles is an **adverbial objective** in each of these parallel independent clauses. *And* is the coordinating conjunction that joins the two clauses. *Almost* is an adverb modifying the adjective *seven*. *High* and *deep* are predicate adjectives.

9, 9.

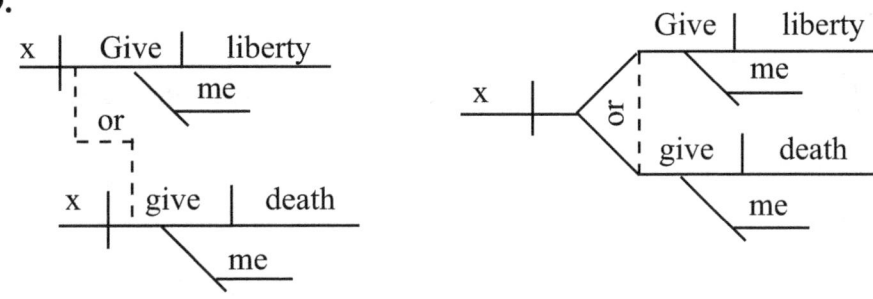

This sentence can be construed as a compound sentence (see the diagram on the far left) or as a sentence with a **compound predicate** (see the diagram on the immediate left). The *x*'s represent the unexpressed subject *you*. The personal pronoun *me* is an **indirect object** in each clause; it represents the person (Patrick Henry) to whom liberty or death is to be given.

9, 10.

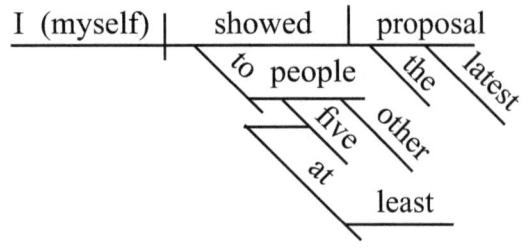

In this sentence, *myself* is an **intensive pronoun**. It is in **apposition** with the subject of the sentence, *I*. The prepositional phrase *at least* modifies the adjective *five*.

10, 1.

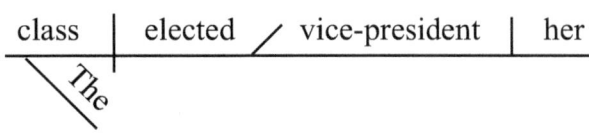

Vice-president is an **objective complement**. One sometimes sees objective complements diagrammed as follows:

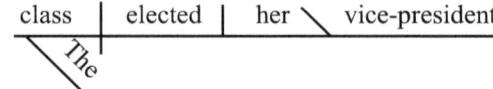

10, 2.

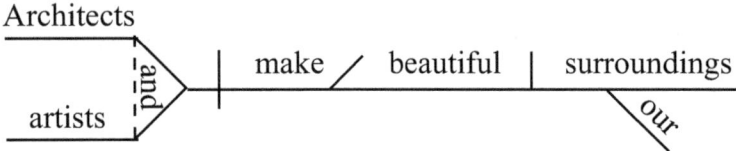

Architects and artists is a compound subject. *Beautiful* is an adjective used as an **objective complement.**

10, 3.

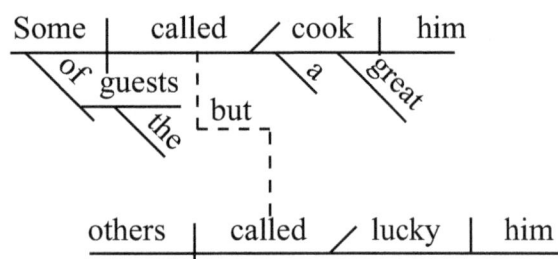

This compound sentence features two **objective complements**, one a noun (*cook*) and the other an adjective (*lucky*).

10, 4.

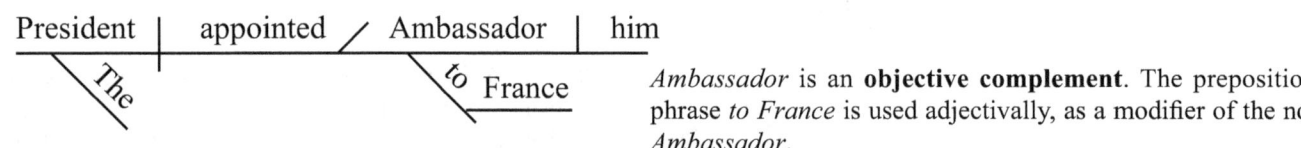

Ambassador is an **objective complement**. The prepositional phrase *to France* is used adjectivally, as a modifier of the noun *Ambassador*.

10, 5.

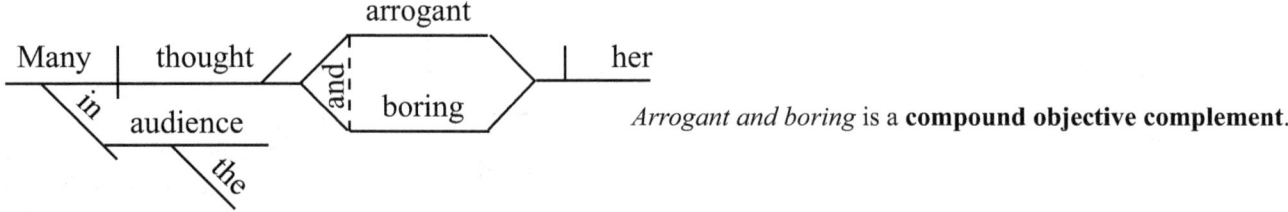

Arrogant and boring is a **compound objective complement**.

10, 6.

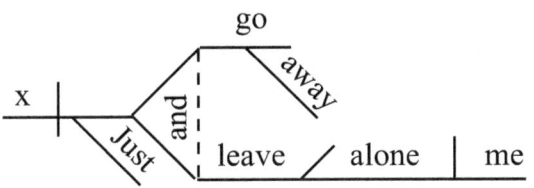

The *x* represents the unexpressed subject *you*. *Just* and *away* are adverbs. *Just* modifies both verbs, and *away* modifies only *go*. *Alone* is an **objective complement**.

10, 7.

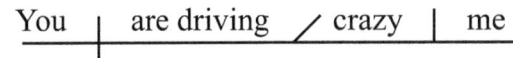

Crazy is an **objective complement**. *Are driving* is a present-progressive form of the verb *drive*.

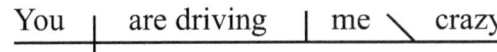

10, 8.

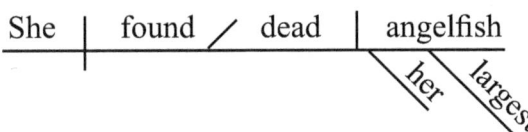

The adjective *dead* is an **objective complement**.

10, 9.

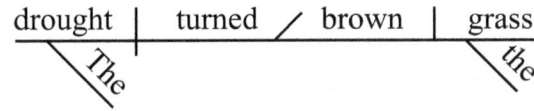

The adjective *brown* is an **objective complement**.

10, 10.

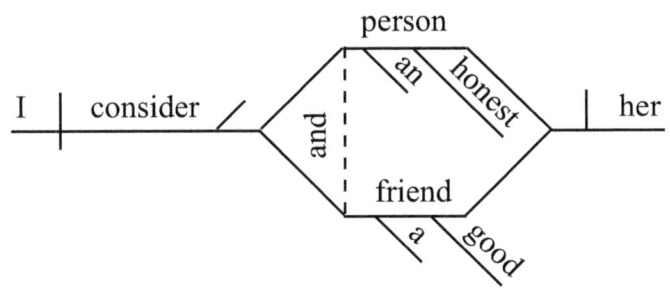

An *honest person and a good friend* is a **compound objective complement**.

11, 1.

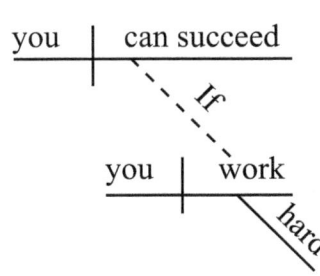

The **adverb clause** *if you work hard* is introduced by the **subordinating conjunction** *if*.

11, 2.

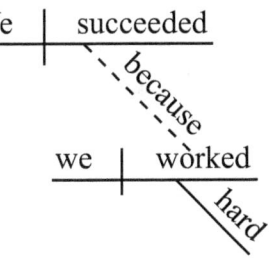

The **adverb clause** *because we worked hard* is introduced by the **subordinating conjunction** *because*.

11, 3.

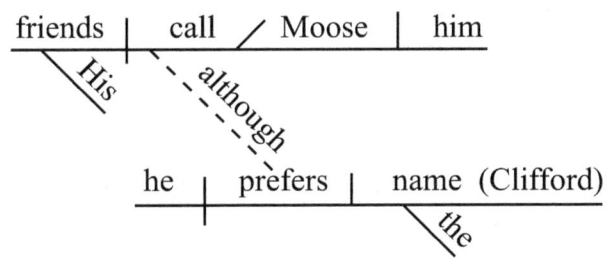

The **adverb clause** *although he prefers the name Clifford* is introduced by the **subordinating conjunction** *although*. *Moose* is an objective complement. *Clifford* is an appositive; it is in apposition with the direct object in the **subordinate clause**, *name*.

11, 4.

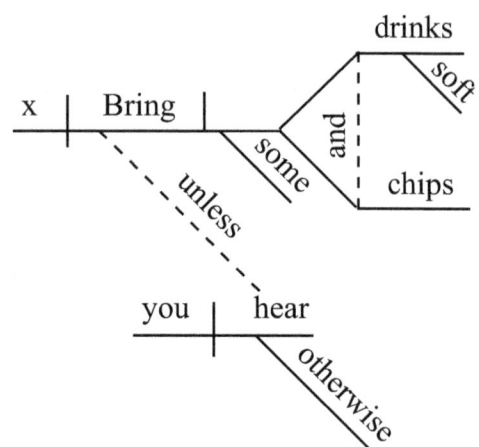

The *x* represents the unexpressed subject *you*. The adjective *some* modifies both *soft drinks* and *chips* and is connected, therefore, with a part of the direct-object line common to both objects. The **adverb clause** *unless you hear otherwise* is introduced by the **subordinating conjunction** *unless*.

11, 5.

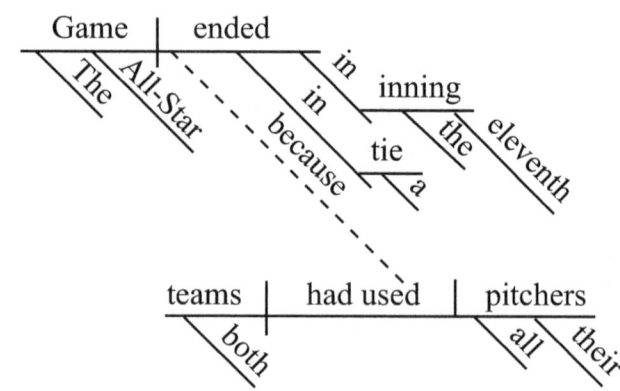

The **adverb clause** *because both teams had used all their pitchers* is introduced by the **subordinating conjunction** *because*.

11, 6.

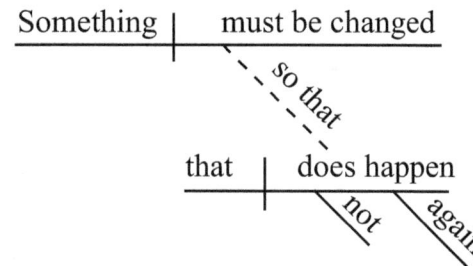

The **adverb clause** *so that that does not happen again* is introduced by the **phrasal subordinating conjunction** *so that*. The second *that* of this sentence is a demonstrative pronoun.

11, 7.

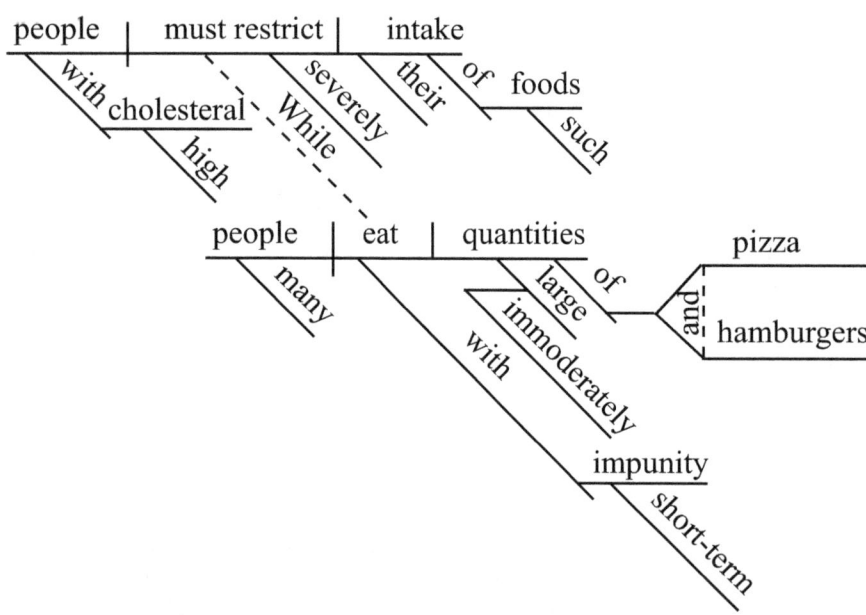

The **adverb clause** *while many people eat . . . with short-term impunity* is introduced by the **subordinating conjunction** *while* (used here in the sense of *although*). The adverb *immoderately* modifies the adjective *large*.

11, 8.

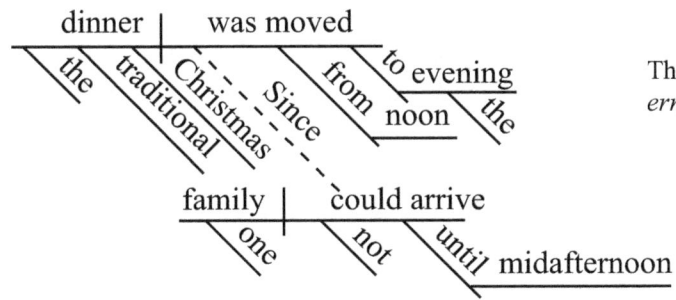

The **adverb clause** *since one family could not arrive until midafternoon* is introduced by the **subordinating conjunction** *since*.

11, 9.

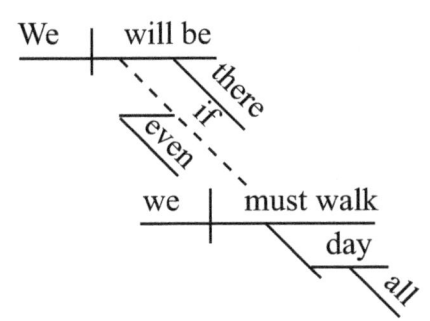

The **adverb clause** *even if we must walk all day* is introduced by the **subordinating conjunction** *if*. *Even* is an adverb modifying the conjunction *if*. *Day* is an adverbial objective.

11, 10.

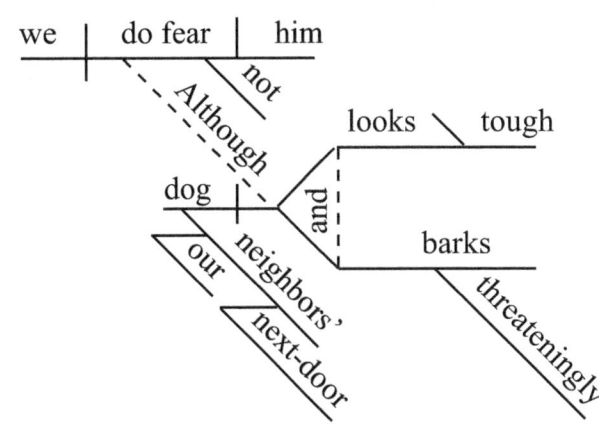

Neighbors' is a possessive noun. The possessive pronoun *our* and the adjective *next-door* modify it. *Although* is a **subordinating conjunction**.

12, 1.

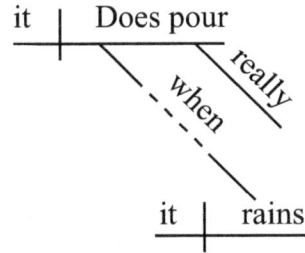

When is a **relative adverb**. It is equivalent to two prepositional phrases, *at the time* and *at which*. If one were to substitute these prepositional phrases for *when*, the former would modify *does pour* and the latter would modify *rains*. *When* has the same relationship to these two verbs, and the line on which it rests in the diagram is made solid at both ends to show this relationship.

Whenever is a **relative adverb** equivalent to *at any time at which*.

12, 2.

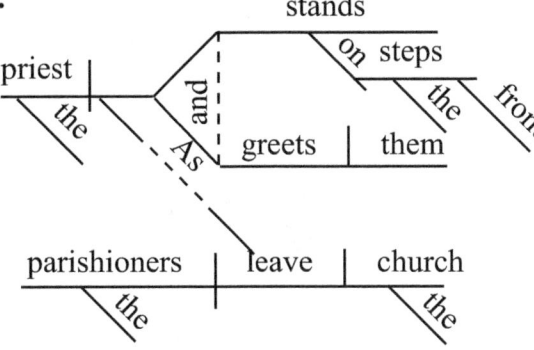

As is a **relative adverb** equivalent to *at the time at which* or *during the time in which*. The main clause has a compound predicate.

12, 3.

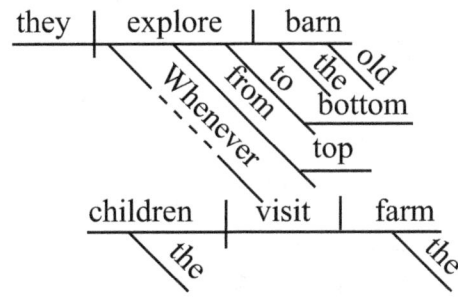

12, 4.

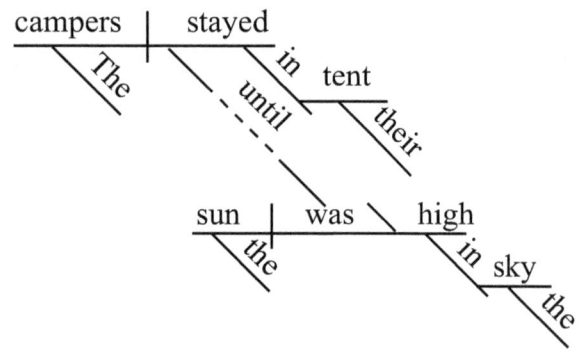

Until is a **relative adverb**; it is equivalent to *until the time at which.*

12, 5.

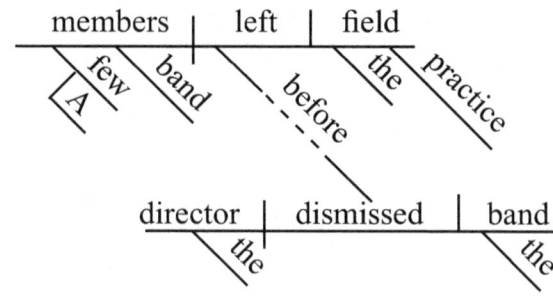

Before is a **relative adverb**; it is equivalent to *before the time at which.* Few and band are nouns used as adjectives. A modifies *few*, not *members*.

12, 6.

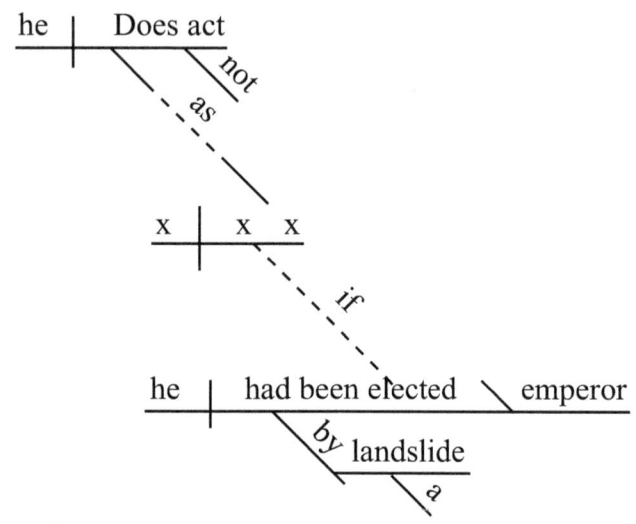

This is an elliptical sentence, the full version of which is *Does he not act as he would act if he had been elected emperor by a landslide?* With the sentence in this expanded form, one can see that **as** is a **relative adverb** equivalent to *in the manner in which*. *If* is a **subordinating conjunction**. The x's represent the unexpressed words *he would act*.

12, 7.

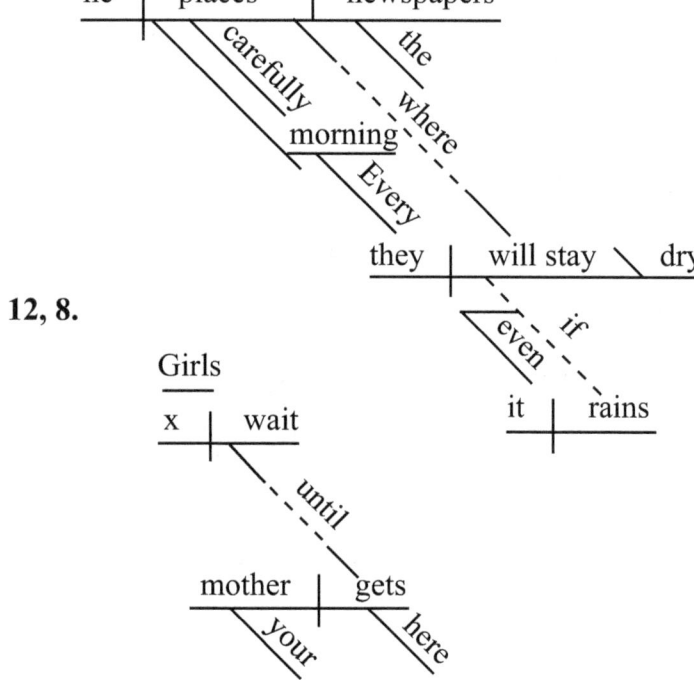

Where, a **relative adverb** equivalent to *in a place in which*, introduces the **adverbial clause** *where they will stay dry*, while the **subordinating conjunction** *if* introduces a second adverbial clause, *even if it rains*. Morning is an adverbial objective. Dry is a predicate adjective.

12, 8.

Girls is a noun of direct address. Wait, an imperative form, has no expressed subject; x stands for the unexpressed subject *you*. The **relative adverb until** introduces the **adverb clause** *until your mother gets home*; it is equivalent to *until the time at which*.

~ 212 ~

12, 9.

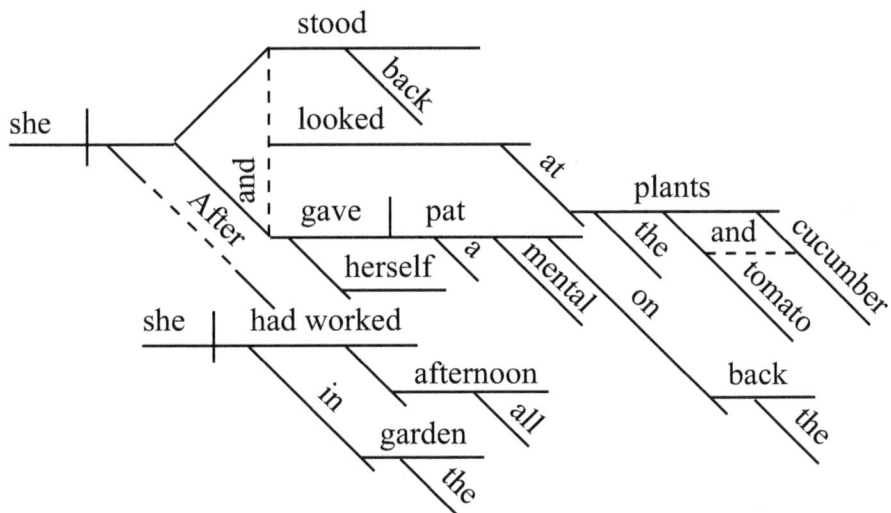

After is a **relative adverb** equivalent to *after the time in which*. This sentence has a tripartite predicate. All verbs in the sentence have adverbial modifiers of one sort or another. *Stood* is modified by the adverb *back*, *looked* by a prepositional phrase, *gave* by the indirect object *herself*, and *had worked* by a prepositional phrase and by the adverbial objective *afternoon*. Of the four verbs, only *gave* has a direct object. *Tomato* and *cucumber*, nouns used as adjectives, are connected by the coordinating conjunction *and*. It is possible to defend the position that *looked at* is a phrasal verb whose direct object is *plants*, for one can make *plants* the subject of the passive sentence *The plants that were being looked at were tomatoes and cucumbers*.

12, 10.

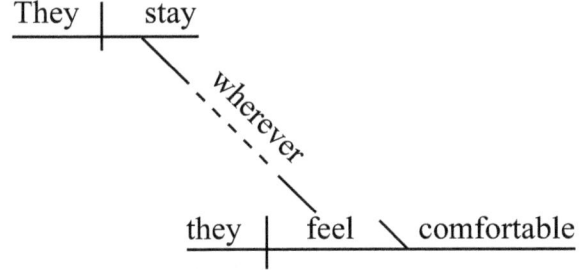

Wherever is a **relative adverb** equivalent to *at any place in which*. *Comfortable* is a predicate adjective.

13,1.

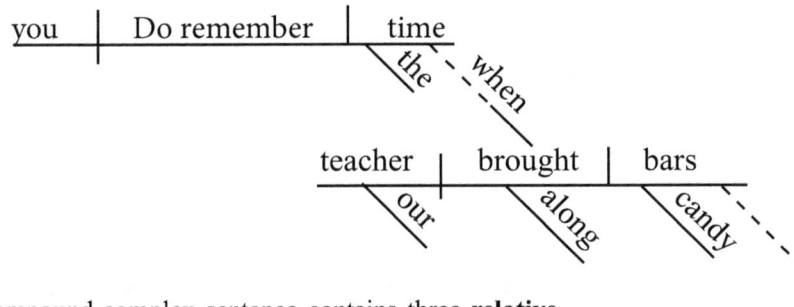

This compound-complex sentence contains three **relative (adjective) clauses**. The first is introduced by a **relative adverb**, the other two are introduced by **relative pronouns**. The **relative adverb** *when* (equivalent to *at which*) modifies the verb *brought*; its clause modifies the noun *time*. The **relative pronoun** *which* is the direct object of the verb *gave*; its **antecedent** is *bar*. The **relative pronoun** *who* is the subject of its **relative clause**; its **antecedent** is *student*, the object of the preposition *to*. *Day* is an adverbial objective. *Along* is an adverb.

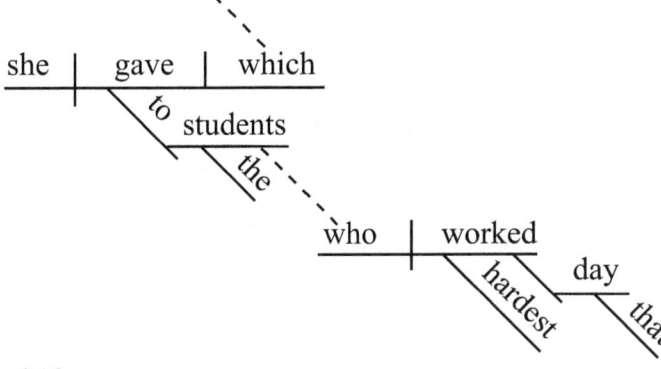

13, 2.

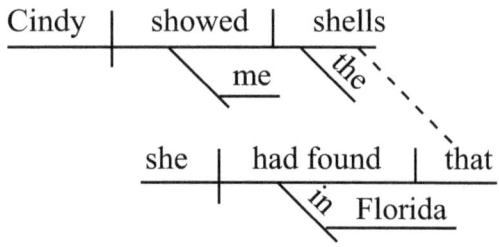

The **relative pronoun** *that* is the direct object in the **relative clause**; its **antecedent** is *shells*, the direct object in the **main clause**.

13, 3.

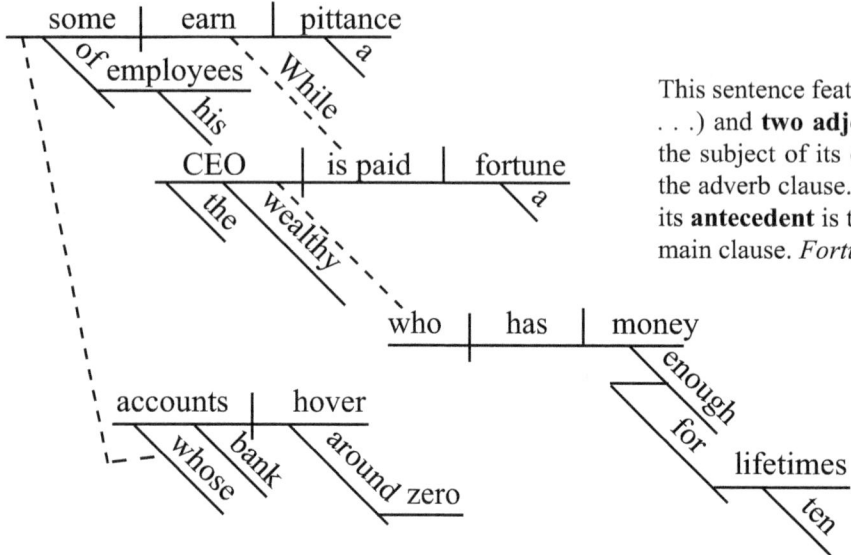

This sentence features an adverb clause (*while the wealthy CEO . . .*) and **two adjective clauses**. The **relative pronoun** *who* is the subject of its clause; its **antecedent** is *CEO*, the subject of the adverb clause. The **relative pronoun** *whose* is a possessive; its **antecedent** is the indefinite pronoun *some*, the subject of the main clause. *Fortune* is a retained object.

13, 4.

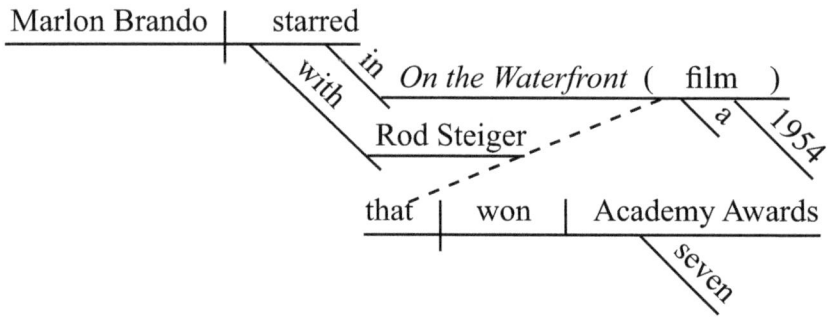

The **relative pronoun** *that*, the subject of its clause, has as its **antecedent** the word *film*, which is in apposition with *On the Waterfront*, the object of the preposition *in*.

13, 5.

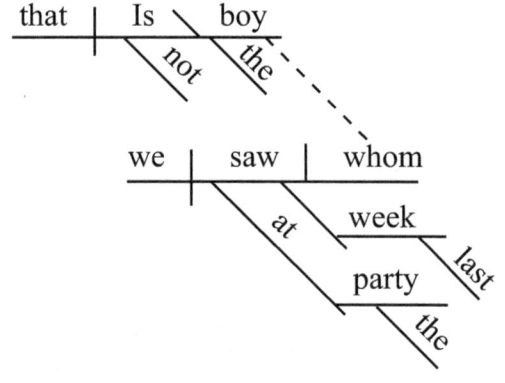

The **relative pronoun** *whom*, the direct object of the verb *saw*, has as its **antecedent** *boy*, a predicate nominative. *Week* is an adverbial objective.

13, 6.

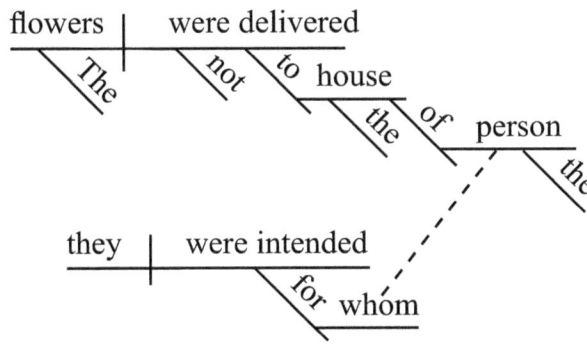

The **relative pronoun** *whom* is the object of the preposition *for*; its **antecedent** is *person*. Both the main verb, *were delivered,* and the verb in the **relative clause**, *were intended*, are in the passive voice.

13, 7.

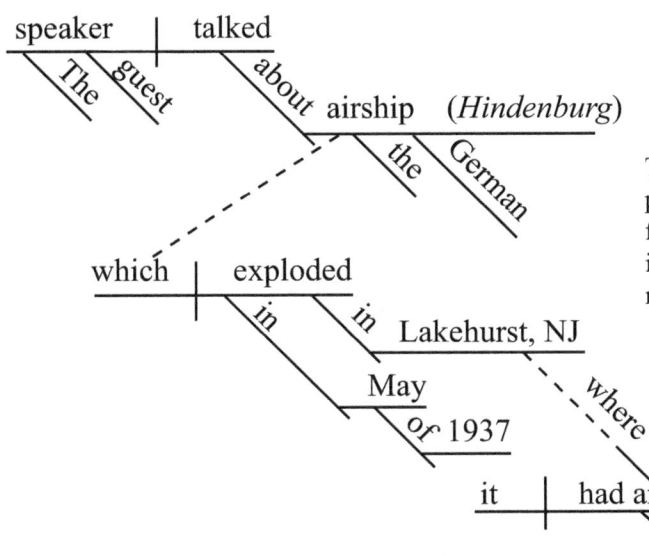

This sentence has two relative clauses: one introduced by a relative pronoun a **relative pronoun**, the other by a **relative adverb**. In the former, the **relative pronoun** *which* is the subject; its **antecedent** is *airship*. The latter modifies the proper noun *Lakehurst, N.J.* The relative adverb *where* is equivalent to *at which*.

13, 8.

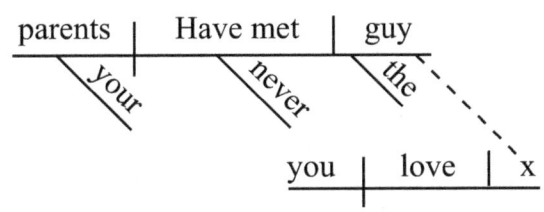

In the diagram, *x* represents the **unexpressed relative pronoun** *whom* or *that*. The **antecedent** is *guy*.

13, 9.

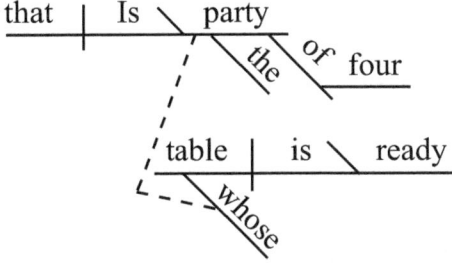

The **relative pronoun** *whose* (possessive form) has as its **antecedent** the predicate nominative of the main clause, *party*.

13, 10.

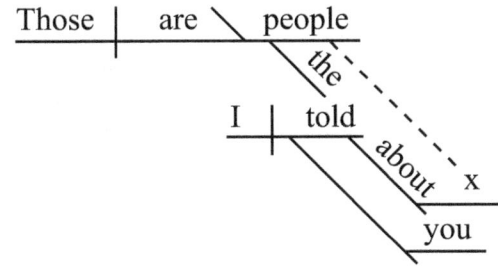

The **unexpressed relative pronoun** *that* or *whom* is represented in the diagram by an *x*. The **antecedent** is *people*. *You* is an indirect object.

14, 1.

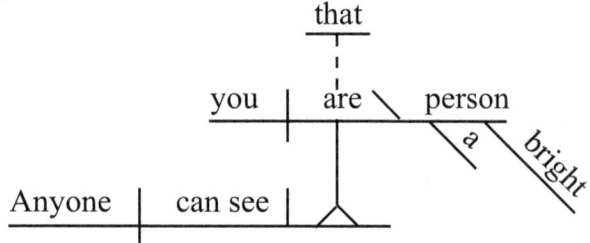

The **noun clause** *that you are a bright person* is the direct object of the verb *can see*. *That* is an expletive. It has a function (to introduce the noun clause) but no meaning.

14, 2.

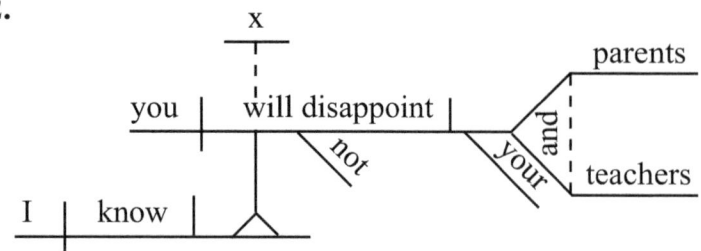

The **noun clause** *you will not disappoint . . . teachers* is the direct object of the verb *know*. The *x* indicates the omission of the expletive *that*. The verb *will disappoint* has a compound direct object, *parents and teachers*. *Your* modifies both of these nouns.

14, 3.

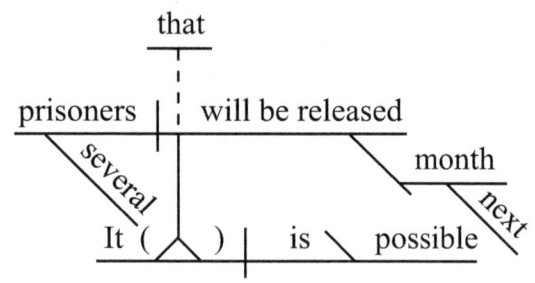

The **noun clause** *that several prisoners will be released next month* is in apposition with the subject of the sentence, *it*. *Month* is an adverbial objective.

14, 4.

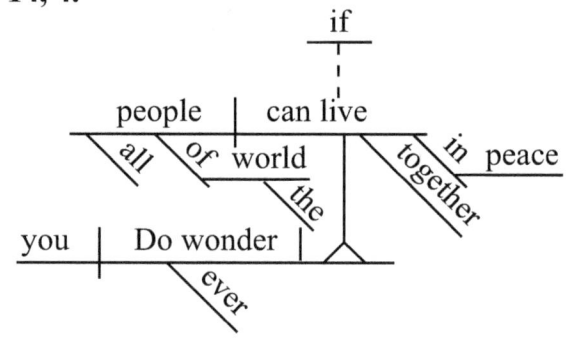

The **noun clause** *if all the people . . . in peace* is the direct object of the main verb *do wonder*. In this sentence, *if* is an expletive whose sole function is to introduce an **indirect question** that expects a yes or no answer.

14, 5.

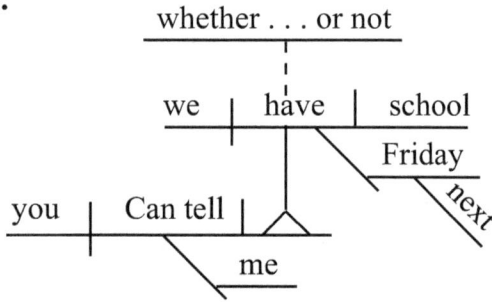

The **noun clause** *whether or not we have school next Friday* is an **indirect question** that acts as the direct object of the main verb *can tell*. *Me* is an indirect object, *Friday* an adverbial objective, and *whether* an expletive. *Or not* is a correlative of *whether*.

14, 6.

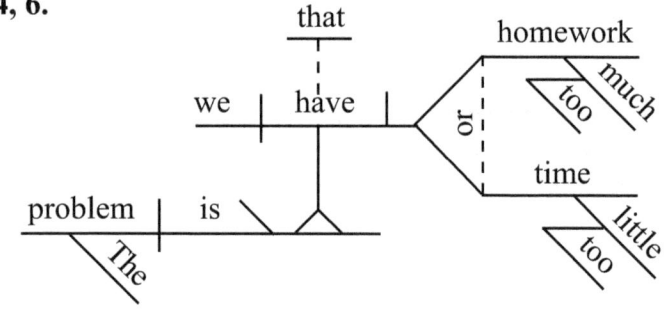

The **noun clause** *that we have too much homework or too little time* is a predicate nominative. *That* is an expletive. The adverb *too* is used twice, each time to modify an adjective.

~ 216 ~

14, 7.

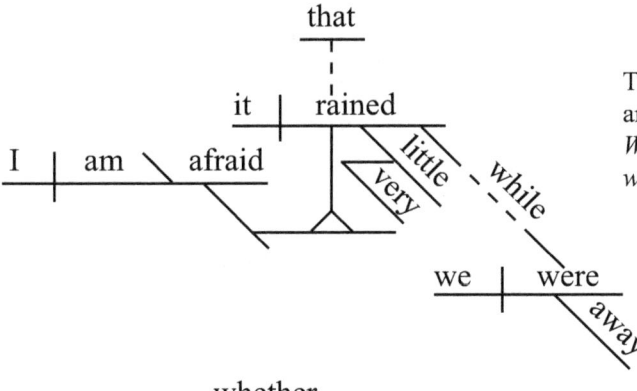

The **noun clause** *that it rained very little while we were away* is an adverbial objective modifying the predicate adjective *afraid*. *While* is a relative adverb; it is equivalent to *during the time in which*.

14, 8.

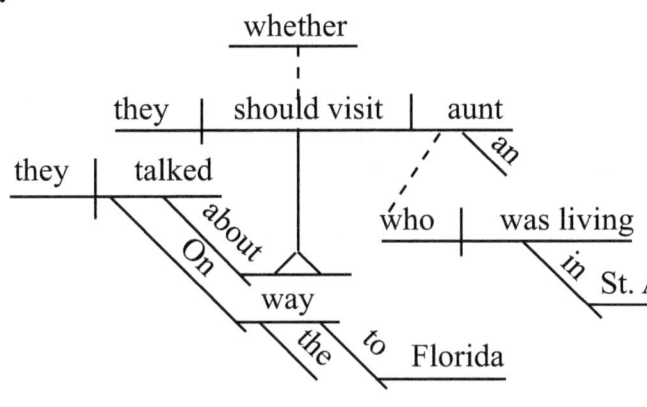

The **noun clause** *whether they should visit an aunt* is an **indirect question** that functions as the object of the preposition *about*. The relative clause *who was living in St. Augustine* modifies *aunt*, the direct object of the verb *should visit*.

14, 9.

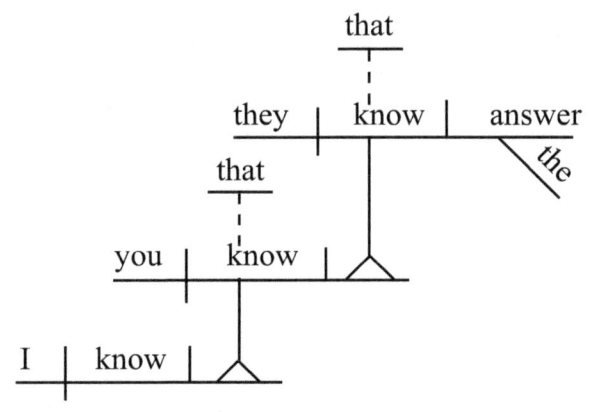

The **first noun clause**, *that you know . . .* , is the direct object in the main clause and has as its direct object a **second noun clause**, *that you know the answer*. *That*, used twice in this sentence, is an expletive both times.

14, 10.

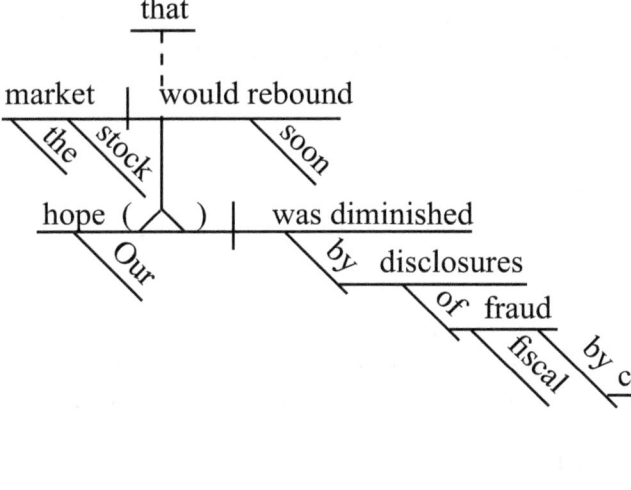

The **noun clause** *that the stock market would rebound soon* is in apposition with the subject of the sentence, *hope*. *That* is an expletive.

15, 1.

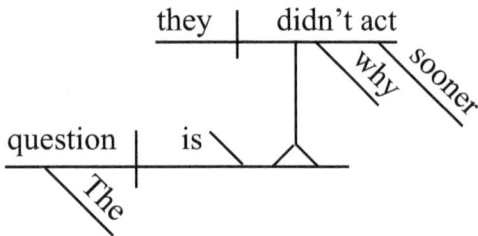

The **noun clause** introduced by the **interrogative adverb** *why* is a **predicate nominative**.

15, 2.

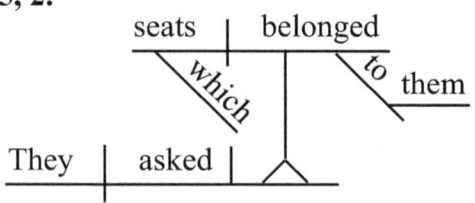

The **noun clause**, an **indirect question** introduced by the interrogative adjective *which*, is a direct object.

15, 3.

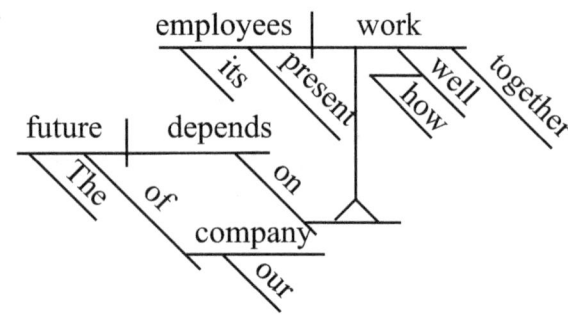

The **noun clause** introduced by the interrogative adverb *how* is the object of the preposition *on*.

15, 4.

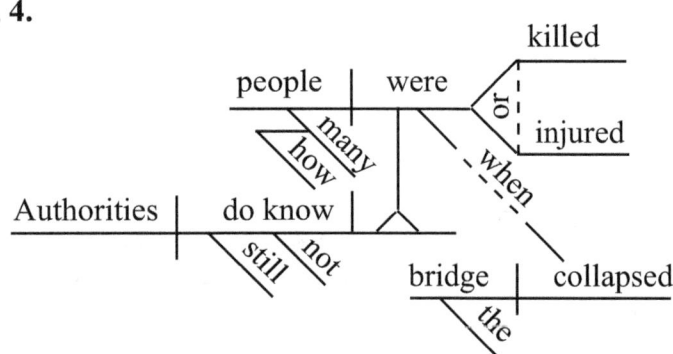

The **noun clause**, an **indirect question** introduced by the interrogative adverb *how*, is a direct object. The relative adverb *when* introduces the adverb clause *when the bridge collapsed*.

15, 5.

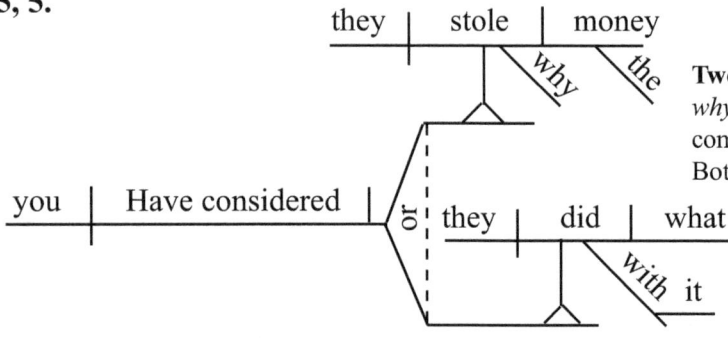

Two noun clauses, the first introduced by the interrogative adverb *why* and the second introduced by the interrogative pronoun *what*, comprise the compound direct object of the verb *have considered*. Both noun clauses are **indirect questions**.

15, 6.

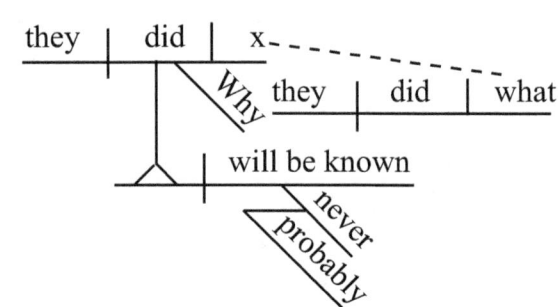

The **noun clause** introduced by the interrogative adverb *why* is the subject of the sentence. In the adjective clause *what they did*, *what* is a relative pronoun meaning *that which*. The unexpressed antecedent is represented in the diagram by *x*. *Probably* and *never* are both adverbs.

15, 7.

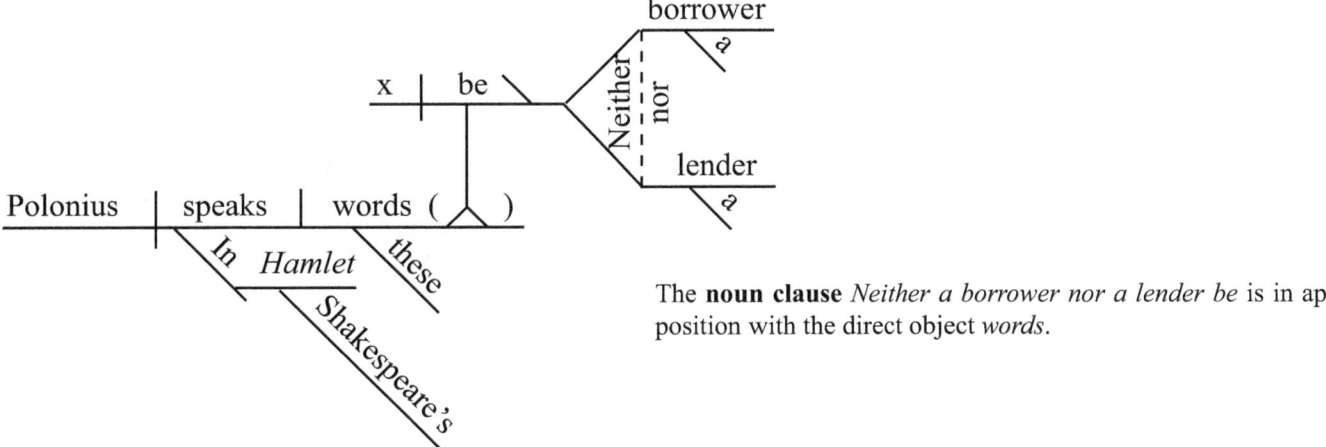

The **noun clause** *Neither a borrower nor a lender be* is in apposition with the direct object *words*.

15, 8.

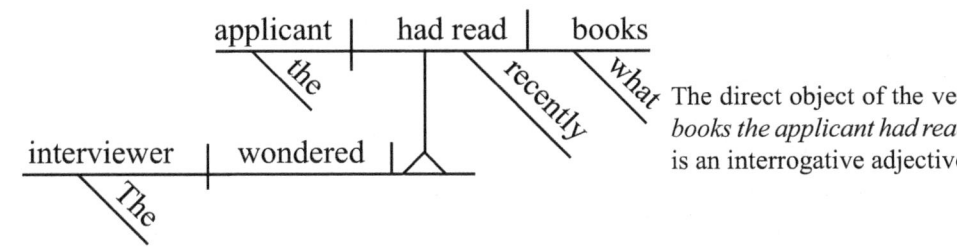

The direct object of the verb *wondered* is the noun clause *what books the applicant had read recently*, an **indirect question**. *What* is an interrogative adjective.

15, 9.

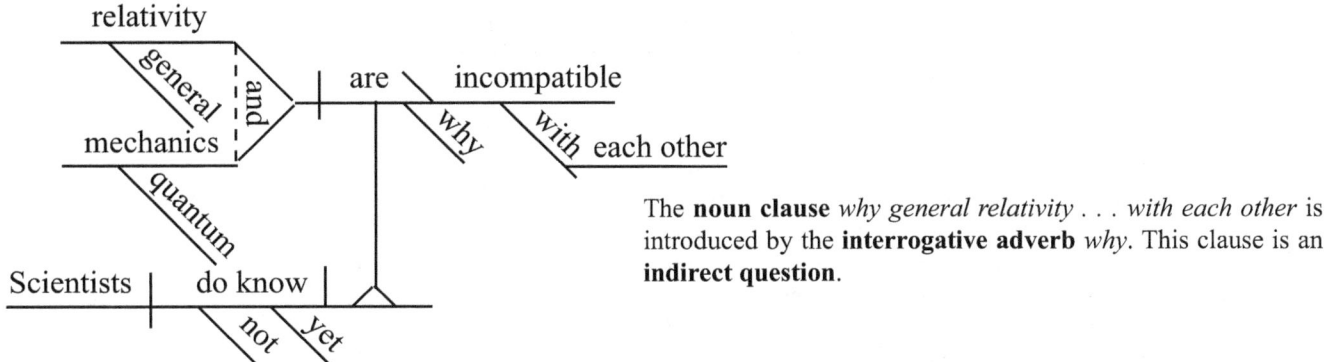

The **noun clause** *why general relativity . . . with each other* is introduced by the **interrogative adverb** *why*. This clause is an **indirect question**.

15, 10.

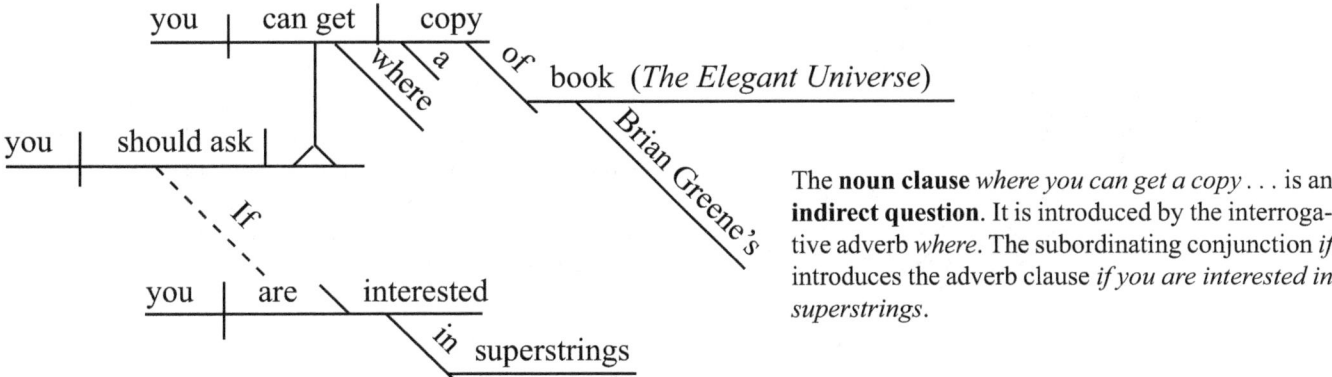

The **noun clause** *where you can get a copy . . .* is an **indirect question**. It is introduced by the interrogative adverb *where*. The subordinating conjunction *if* introduces the adverb clause *if you are interested in superstrings*.

16, 1.

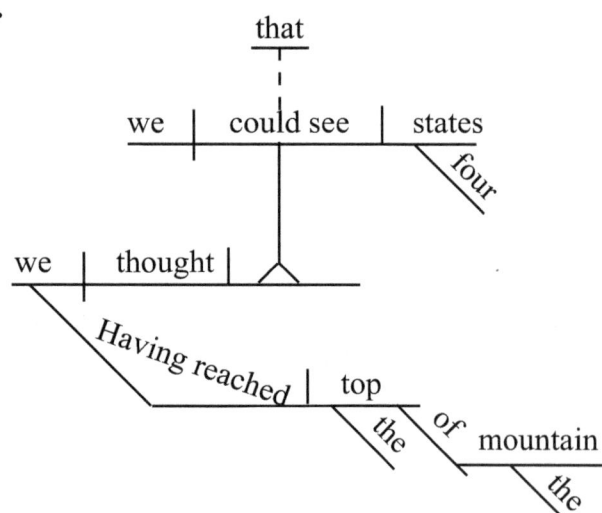

Having reached is a **present-perfect active participle** modifying the subject of the sentence, the personal pronoun *we*. The direct object of the participle is *top*. The noun clause *that we could see four states* is the direct object of the verb *thought*.

16, 2.

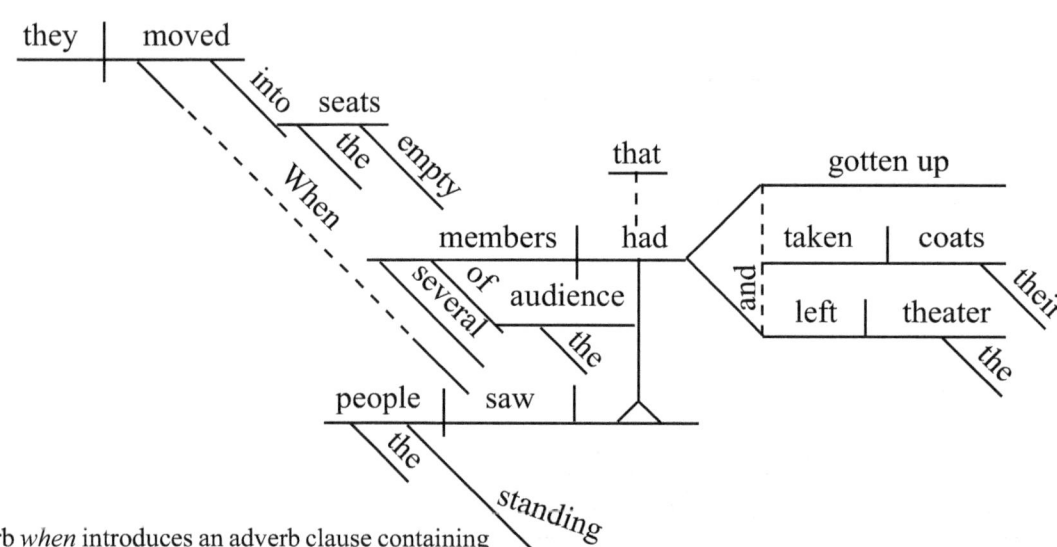

The relative adverb *when* introduces an adverb clause containing as its direct object a noun clause introduced by the expletive *that*. The noun clause has a tripartite partial predicate (the division into three parts begins after the helping verb *had*, which is part of the predicate). *Gotten up* is a phrasal verb. The main clause is *they moved into the empty seats*. *Standing* is a **present active participle** modifying the noun *people*.

16, 3.

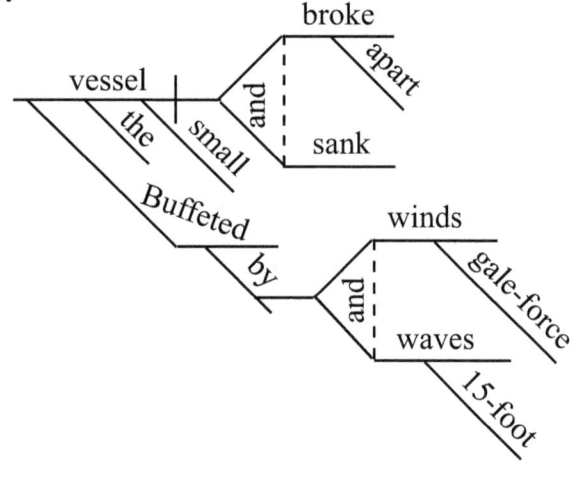

The **past participle** *buffeted* modifies the subject of the sentence, *vessel*. Past participles of transitive verbs are almost always in the passive voice (exceptions are the past participles *risen* and *fallen*, among others). The main clause has a compound predicate, *broke apart and sank*. The preposition *by* has a compound object, *gale-force winds and 15-foot waves*.

16, 4.

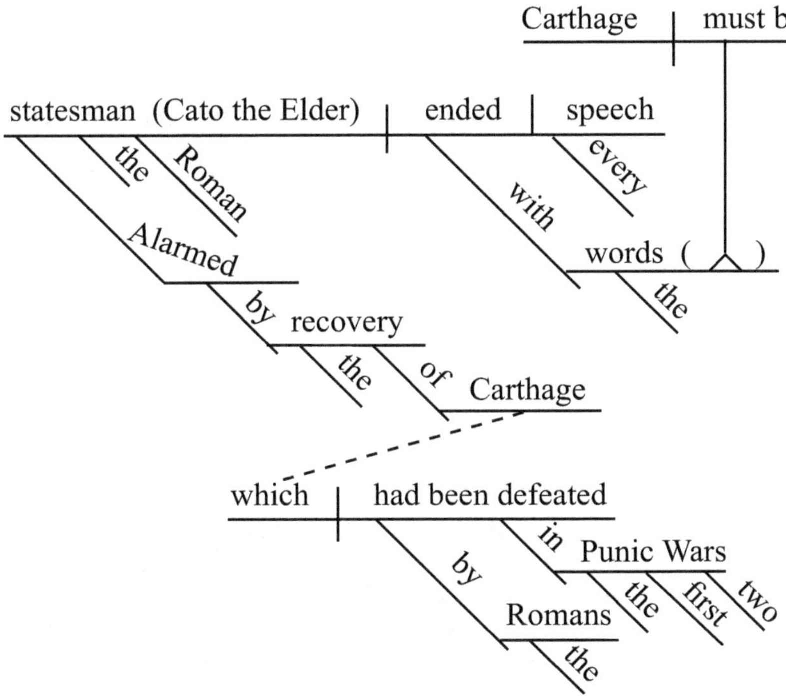

The **past participle** *alarmed* modifies the subject of the sentence, *statesman*. *Cato the Elder* is in apposition with *statesman*. The noun clause *Carthage must be destroyed* is in apposition with *words*, the object of the preposition *with*. The adjective clause *which had been defeated . . .* is introduced by the relative pronoun *which*; its antecedent is *Carthage*. The verb *had been defeated* is in the *past-perfect tense, passive voice*.

16, 5.

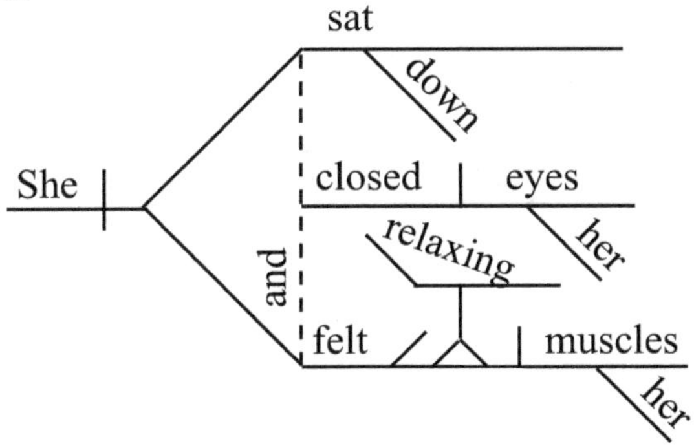

This sentence has a tripartite predicate. In the third part of the predicate, the **present active participle** *relaxing* is used as an **objective complement**.

16, 6.

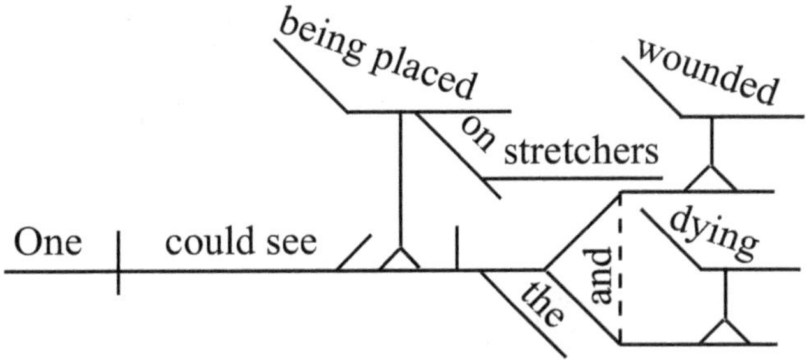

Wounded is a **past participle** and *dying* is a **present participle**. Both are used here as nouns. *Being placed* is a **present passive participle**. It is used in this sentence as an **objective complement**. The definite article, *the*, modifies both *wounded* and *dying*.

16, 7.

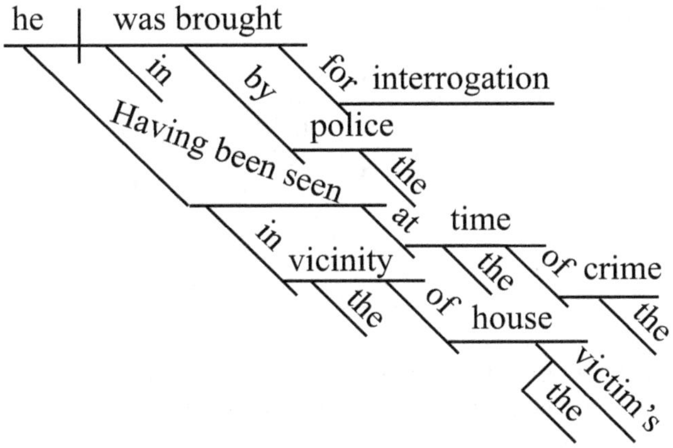

Having been seen is a **present-perfect passive participle**. It modifies the subject of the sentence, the personal pronoun *he*. The particle *in* is often used as a preposition and, in fact, is used in a prepositional phrase in this sentence (*in the vicinity*); however, in the expression *brought in*, *in* is an adverb. There are six prepositional phrases in this short sentence. *The* modifies *victim's*, not *house*. You can test that by replacing *the* with a possessive adjective like *his*; it's his victim but not his house.

16, 8.

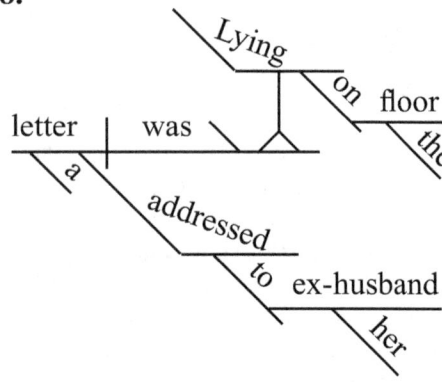

In this sentence, *lying*, a **present participle**, does not function as the participial component of a past-progressive form, but as an adjective. The **past participle** *addressed* modifies *letter*, the subject of the sentence.

16, 9.

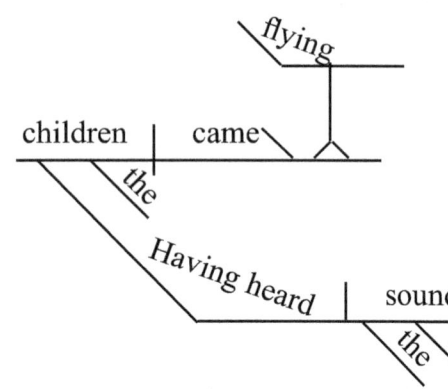

Even though *came* is not a linking verb, the **present participle** *flying* functions here as a predicate adjective. *Having heard* is a **perfect active participle**. The possessive noun *mother's* is modified by the possessive pronoun *their*. *Calling* is a present active participle. Both *having heard* and *calling*, being transitive verbs, take direct objects.

16, 10.

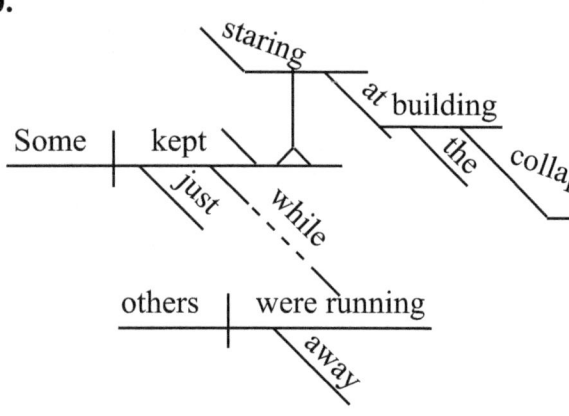

In this context, *kept* is a linking verb. The **present participle** *staring* introduces a **participial phrase**, which functions as a predicate adjective. The verb *were running* is past progressive in form. *While* is a relative adverb.

17, 1.

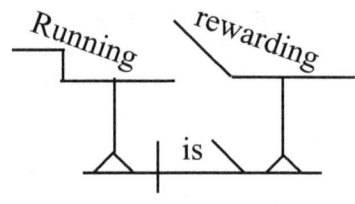

The subject of the sentence is *running*, a **gerund**. The present active participle *rewarding* is a predicate adjective.

17, 2.

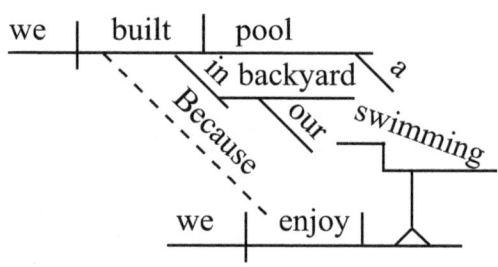

The subordinating conjunction *because* introduces an adverb clause. The **gerund** *swimming* is a direct object in the subordinate clause.

17, 3.

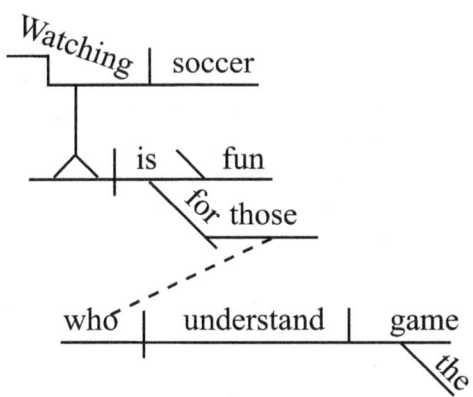

The **gerund phrase** *watching soccer* is the subject of the sentence. The relative pronoun *who* has as its antecedent the demonstrative pronoun *those*.

17, 4.

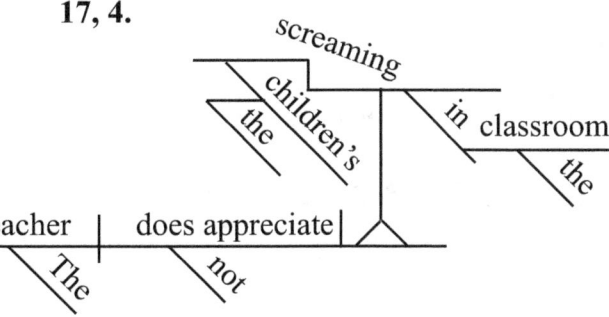

The **gerund phrase** *the children's screaming in the classroom* is the direct object of the verb *does appreciate*. That *the* modifies *children's* and not *screaming* can be seen by substituting *my* for *the* and imagining you are the parent of the children; they are your children, but it's not your screaming.

17, 5.

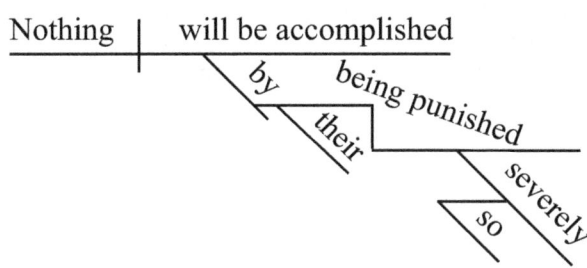

The passive **gerund** *being punished* is the object of the preposition *by*. The possessive pronoun *their*, an **adjectival modifier**, is attached to the upper segment of the gerund's step-down structure, while *severely*, an adverb, is placed under the lower segment.

17, 6.

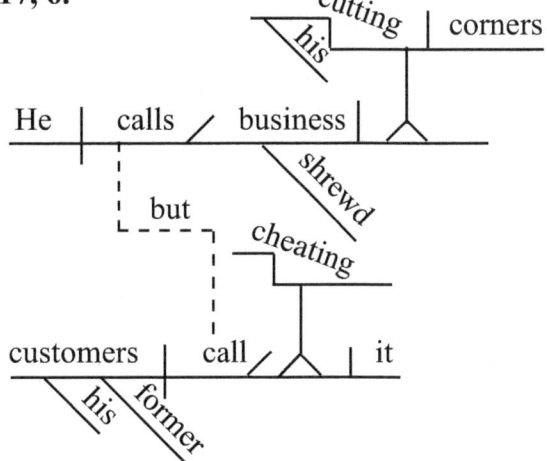

The **gerund phrase** *his cutting corners* is a direct object in the first main clause, and the **gerund** *cheating* is an objective complement in the second.

17, 7.

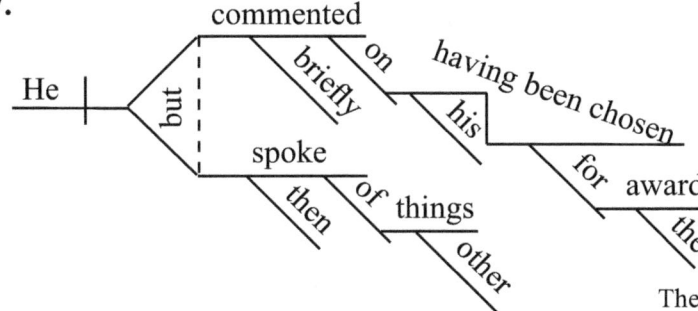

The **present-perfect passive gerund** *having been chosen* is the object of the preposition *on*. The sentence has a compound predicate.

17, 8.

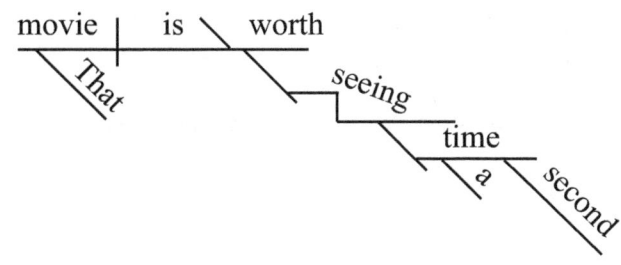

The **gerund** *seeing* and the noun *time* are both adverbial objectives. *That* is a demonstrative adjective, and *worth* is a predicate adjective.

17, 9.

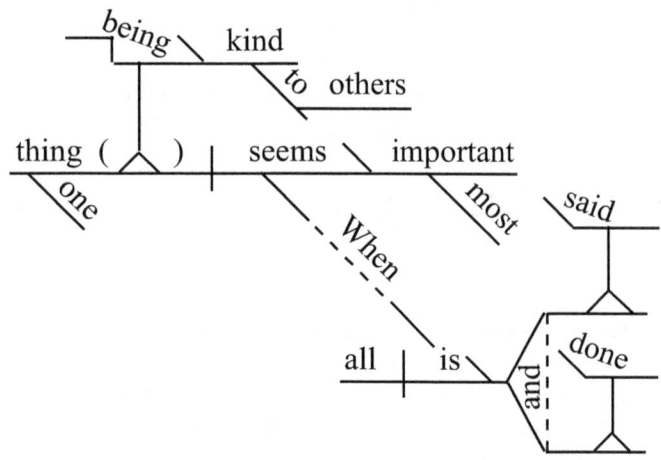

The **gerund phrase** *being kind to others* is an appositive; it is in apposition with *thing*, the subject of the main clause. *Kind* and *important* are predicate adjectives. *When* is a relative adverb, equivalent to *at the time at which*. Since, according to the sentence, all has been said and done before one thing seems most important, the phrase *is said and done* is not a passive voice form in the present tense; instead, the past participles *said* and *done* function as predicate adjectives; they form, together with the verb *is*, what is sometimes called a statal passive. Consider this example: *During class, the classroom door is always closed* (statal passive); *it is closed by the teacher at the beginning of each period* (true passive).

17, 10.

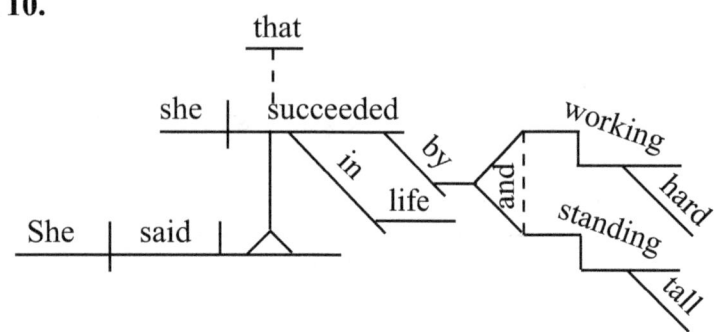

The noun clause *that she succeeded . . . standing tall* is a direct object. *That* is an expletive. The preposition *by* has a compound object, *working hard and standing tall*. *Working* and *standing* are **gerunds**. *Hard* and *tall* are adverbs.

18, 1.

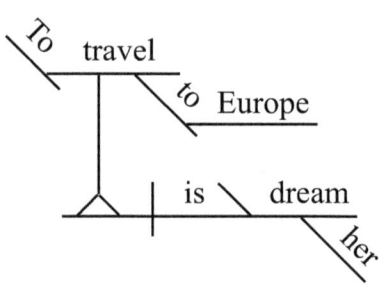

To travel is an **infinitive**. The **infinitive phrase** *to travel to Europe* is the subject of the sentence. *Dream* is a predicate nominative.

18, 2.

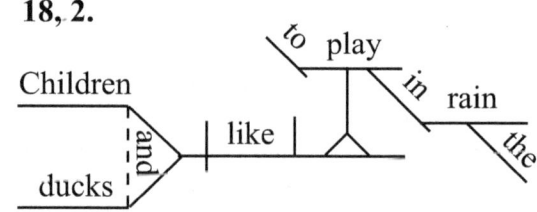

Children and ducks is a compound subject; *and* is a coordinating conjunction. *To play* is an **infinitive**. The **infinitive phrase** *to play in the rain* is a direct object.

18, 3.

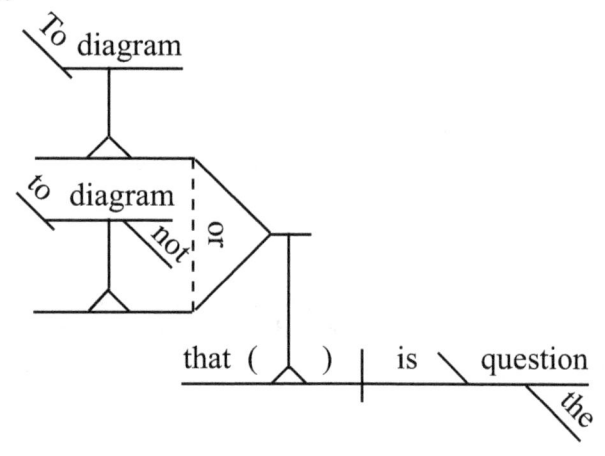

Two **identical infinitives**, *to diagram*, the second modified by the adverb *not*, comprise a compound appositive. It is in apposition with the subject of the sentence, *that*, a demonstrative pronoun. *Or* is a coordinating conjunction. *Question* is a predicate nominative. (Not all authorities would agree that *to diagram or not to diagram* is an appositive. House and Harmon, using Longfellow's sentence *The smith, a mighty man is he* as an example, diagram *the smith* as an independent element, not as an appositive.)

18, 4.

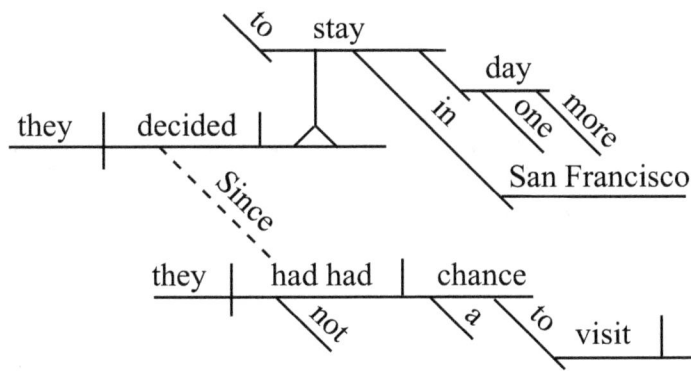

The **infinitive phrase** *to stay in San Francisco one more day* is the direct object of the verb *decided*. *Day* is an adverbial objective. *Since* is a subordinating conjunction. *To visit Fisherman's Wharf* is an **adjectival infinitive phrase**; it modifies the noun *chance*.

18, 5.

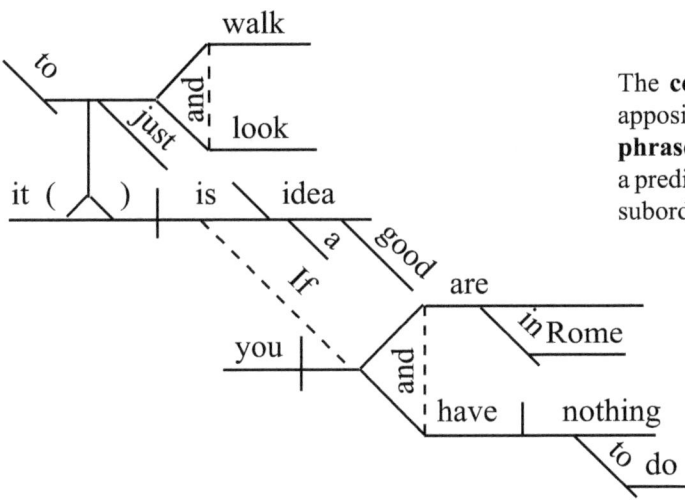

The **compound infinitive phrase** *just to walk and look* is in apposition with the subject of the sentence, *it*. In the **infinitive phrase**, the verbs *walk* and *look* share the preposition *to*. *Idea* is a predicate nominative. The subordinate clause introduced by the subordinating conjunction *if* has a compound predicate.

18, 6.

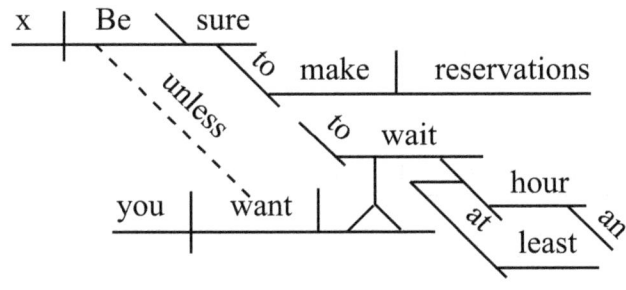

The **adverbial infinitive phrase** *to make reservations* modifies the predicate adjective *sure*. *Unless* is a subordinating conjunction. The **infinitive phrase** *to wait at least an hour* is the direct object of the verb *want*. The prepositional phrase *at least* modifies the adverbial noun phrase (complete adverbial objective) *an hour*.

18, 7.

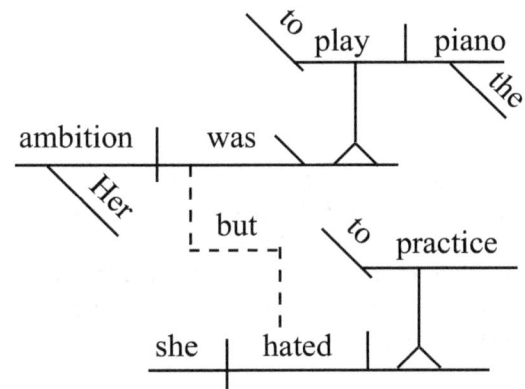

This compound sentence uses the **infinitive phrase** *to play the piano* as a predicate nominative and the **infinitive** *to practice* as a direct object. *But* is a coordinating conjunction.

18, 8.

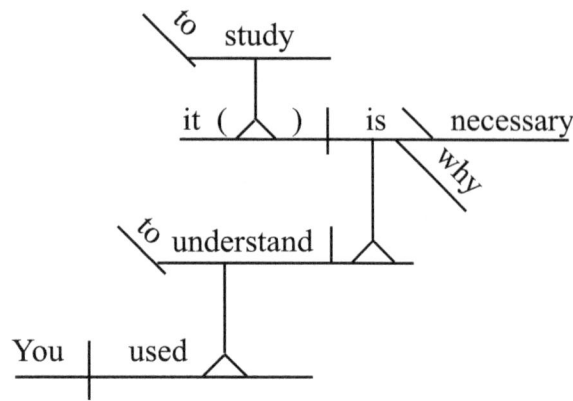

When *used to* means *were accustomed to*, it is followed by a **complementary infinitive**; *to understand* is such an **infinitive**. The remainder of the sentence is an indirect question. The infinitive *to study* is used as an appositive.

18, 9.

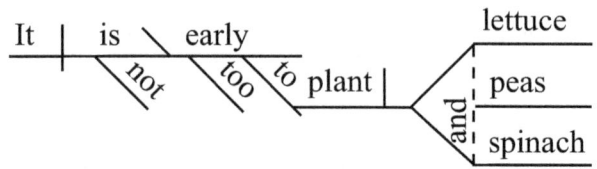

The adverb *too* and the **infinitive phrase** *to plant lettuce, peas, and spinach* are modifiers of the predicate adjective *early*.

18, 10.

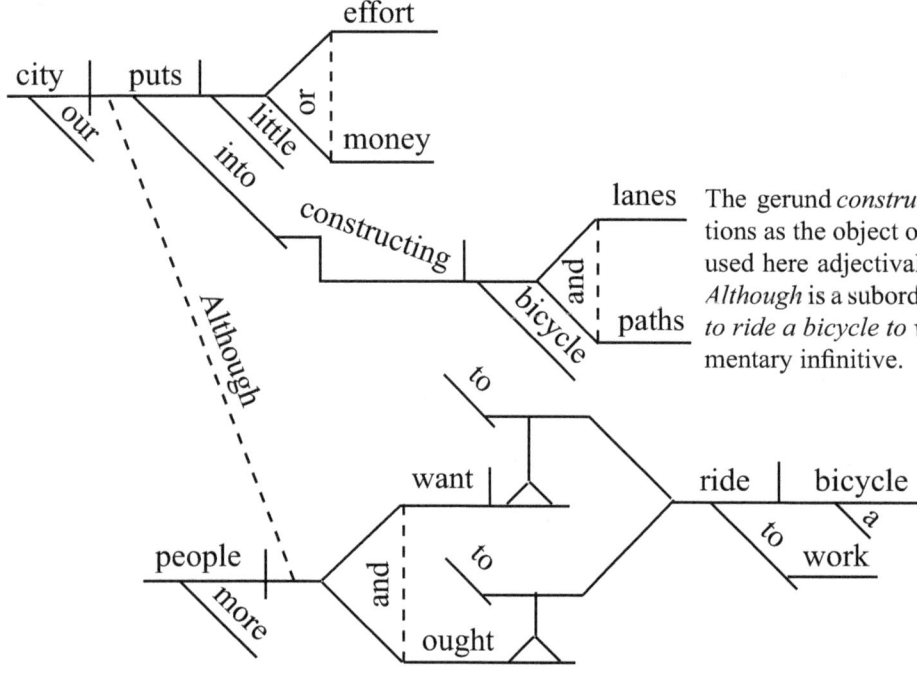

The gerund *constructing* introduces a gerund phrase that functions as the object of the preposition *into*. The noun *bicycle* is used here adjectivally as a modifier of both *lanes* and *paths*. *Although* is a subordinating conjunction. The **infinitive phrase** *to ride a bicycle to work* is both a direct object and a complementary infinitive.

19, 1.

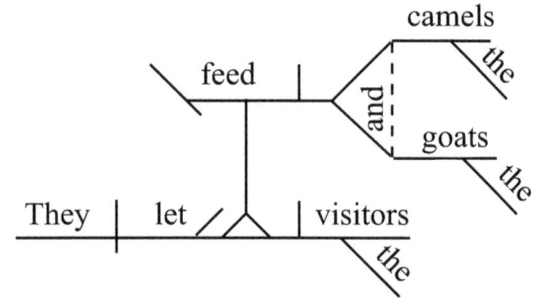

The **infinitive phrase** *feed the camels and the goats* serves as an **objective complement**. **Infinitives** used as **objective complements** after *let* are not preceded by the preposition *to*. It seems equally valid to construe *visitors* as an **indirect object**, in which case the infinitive phrase is a direct object. There are gray areas in grammar analysis.

19, 2.

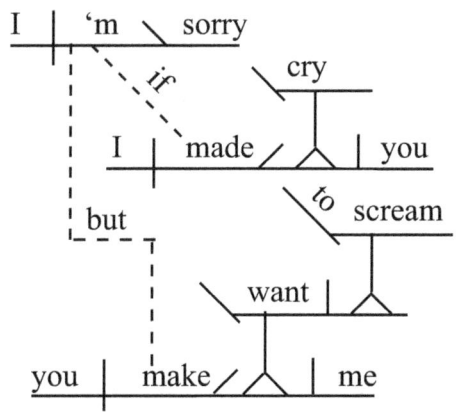

While contractions involving verbs and the adverb *not* (e.g., *don't, can't, won't*) are not separated when diagramming, contractions of verbs with personal pronouns used as subjects (e.g., *you're, I'll, I'm*) are separated. When an **infinitive** is used as an **objective complement** after a form of the verb *make*, it is not preceded by *to*; thus, *cry* and *want* are "*to*-less." The **infinitive** *to scream* is the direct object of the verb *want*. *If* is a subordinating conjunction, *but* a coordinating conjunction.

19, 3.

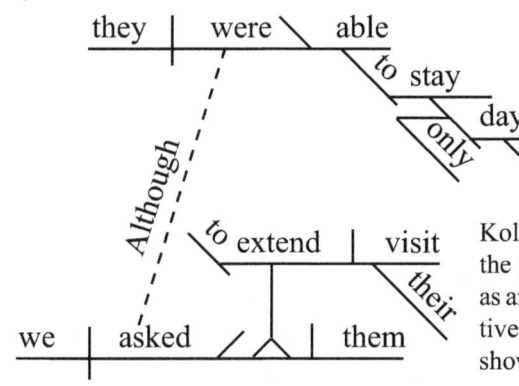

To stay only one day is an **adverbial infinitive phrase** modifying the predicate adjective *able*. *Only* is an adverb modifying the adverbial noun phrase (complete adverbial objective) *one day*. *Although* is a subordinating conjunction. In the subordinate clause, the **infinitive phrase** *to extend their visit* is used as an **objective complement**.

Kolln and Funk would diagram the subordinate clause with *them* as an indirect object and the infinitive phrase as the direct object, as shown on the right.

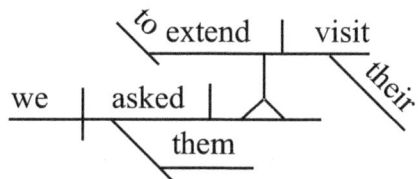

19, 4.

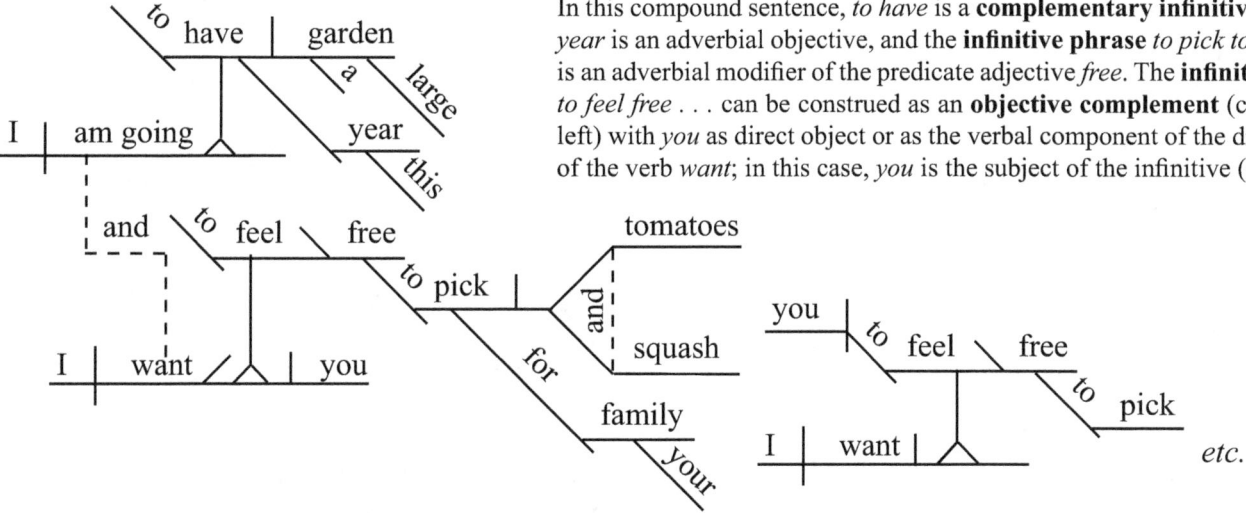

In this compound sentence, *to have* is a **complementary infinitive**, the noun *year* is an adverbial objective, and the **infinitive phrase** *to pick tomatoes . . .* is an adverbial modifier of the predicate adjective *free*. The **infinitive phrase** *to feel free . . .* can be construed as an **objective complement** (cf. diagram, left) with *you* as direct object or as the verbal component of the direct object of the verb *want*; in this case, *you* is the subject of the infinitive (cf. below).

19, 5.

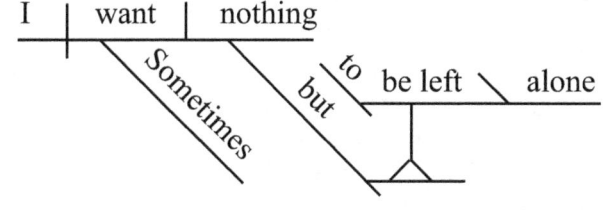

In this sentence, *but* is a preposition. Its object is the **infinitive phrase** *to be left alone*. Certain passive verbs such as *be called, be made,* and *be found* can take predicate adjectives; *be left* is such a verb, and *alone* is a predicate adjective.

19.6.

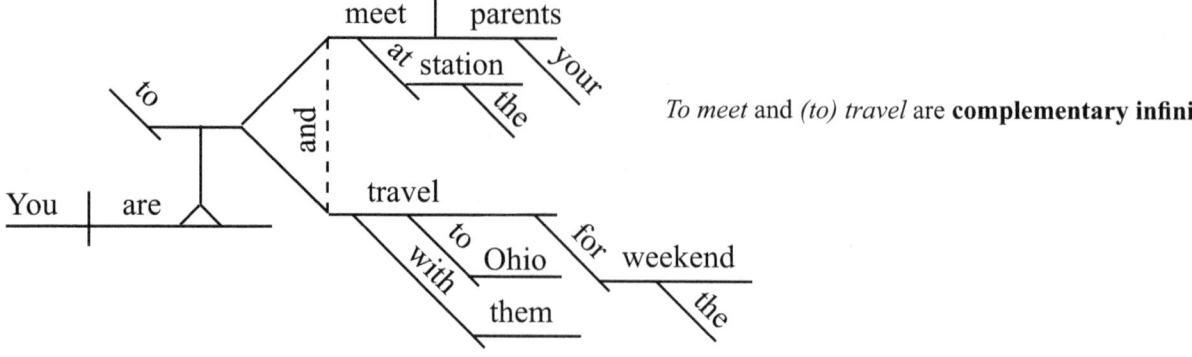

To meet and *(to) travel* are **complementary infinitives**.

19, 7.

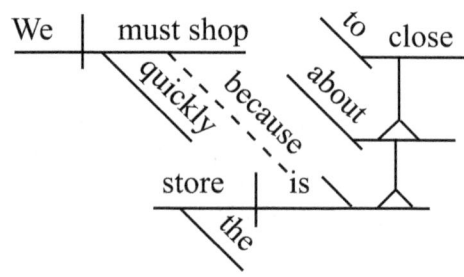

The prepositional phrase *about to close* is used as a predicate adjective. The object of the preposition *about* is the **infinitive** *to close*. *Must* is a modal auxiliary verb.

19, 8.

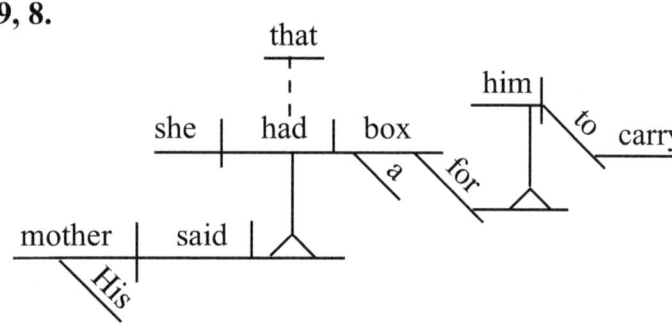

The noun clause introduced by the expletive *that* is the direct object of the main verb, *said*. The object of the preposition *for* is not just *him*, but *him to carry* (he should carry the box). The objective-case *him* is the subject of the infinitive *to carry*. House and Harman would diagram this prepositional phrase as follows:

19, 9.

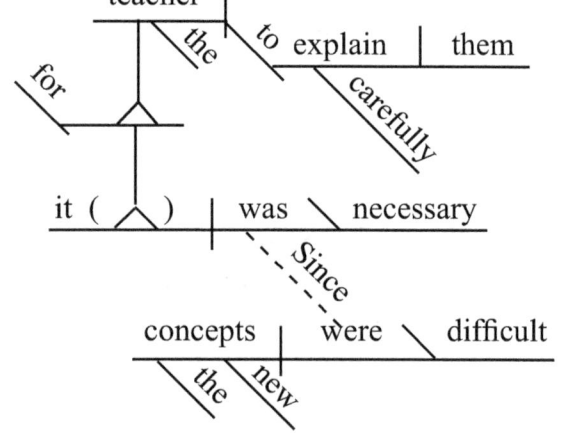

19, 10.

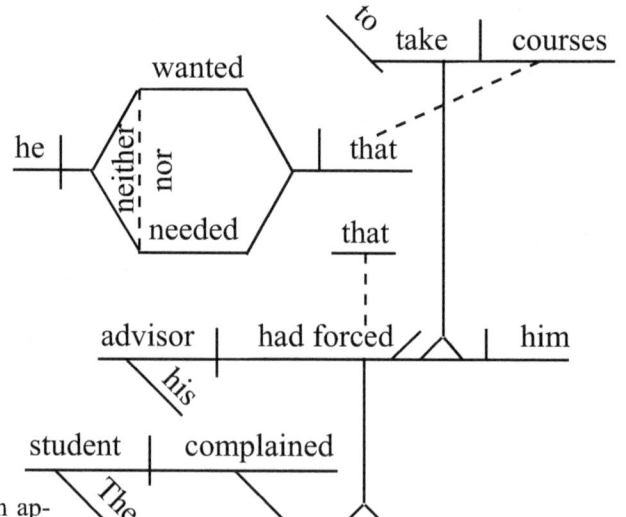

The phrase *for the teacher to explain them carefully* is an appositive. Idiomatic, it is diagrammed as a prepositional phrase although *for* has little or no meaning. What was necessary was a careful explanation by the teacher, not <u>for</u> a careful explanation by the teacher. *Teacher* is the subject of the infinitive *to explain*. *Since* is a subordinating conjunction.

The noun clause *that his advisor had forced him . . .* functions as an adverbial objective. The **infinitive phrase** *to take courses . . .* is an **objective complement**. The first *that* is an expletive; the second is a relative pronoun whose antecedent is *courses*.

20, 1.

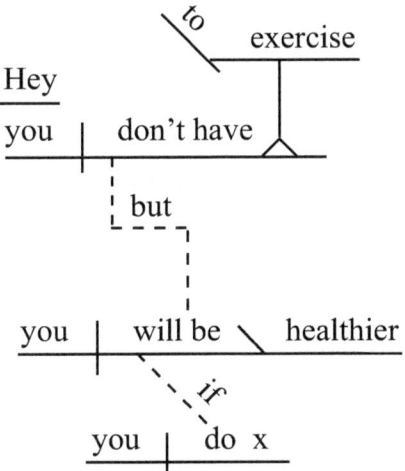

In this compound-complex sentence, *but* is a coordinating conjunction and *if* is a subordinating conjunction. *Hey* is an **interjection**. *To exercise* is a complementary infinitive. The *x* after *do* stands for the **unexpressed verb** *exercise*.

20, 2.

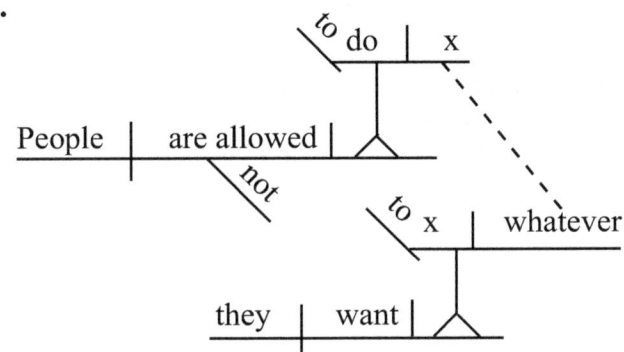

Whatever is an **indefinite relative pronoun** and as such does not have an expressed antecedent. Since indefinite relative pronouns are equivalent to relative pronouns with indefinite pronoun antecedents (*whatever* is equivalent to *anything that* and *whoever* is equivalent to *anyone who*), the traditional manner of diagramming indefinite relative pronouns is to use an *x* to show where its antecedent would be if it were expressed. The first x in the diagram at the left does just that. The second *x* stands for the **unexpressed verb** *do*.

20, 3.

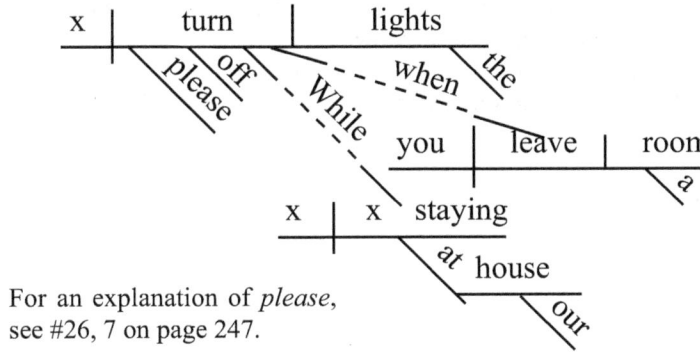

For an explanation of *please*, see #26, 7 on page 247.

While (equivalent to *during the time at which*) and *when* (equivalent to *at the time at which*) are relative adverbs. Since *while* is not a preposition, *staying* cannot be a gerund. Indeed, it must be the participial portion of the present-progressive verb *are staying*, which means that *while staying at our house* is an **elliptical dependent clause**. Each of the first two *x*'s in the diagram stands for the **unexpressed subject** *you*; the third stands for the **unexpressed auxiliary verb** *are*.

20, 4.

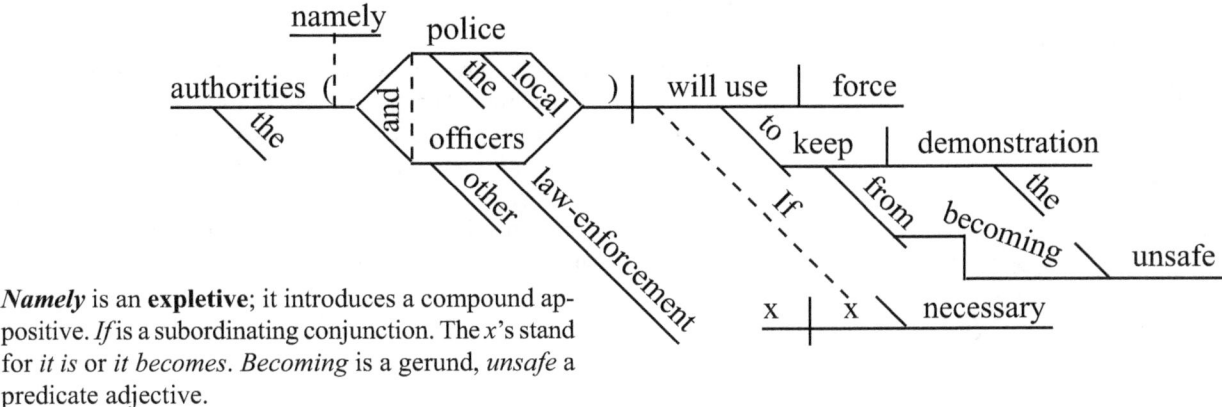

Namely is an **expletive**; it introduces a compound appositive. *If* is a subordinating conjunction. The *x*'s stand for *it is* or *it becomes*. *Becoming* is a gerund, *unsafe* a predicate adjective.

20, 5.

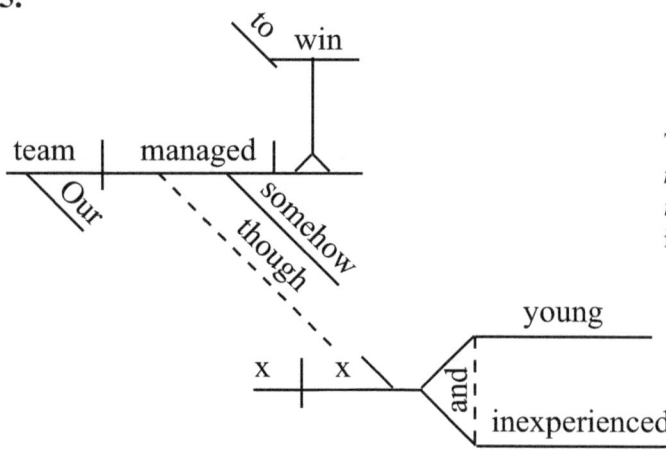

The infinitive *to win* is a direct object. *Though young and inexperienced* is an **elliptical subordinate clause**. The omitted words, *it is*, are represented in the diagram by *x*'s. *Young and inexperienced* is a compound predicate adjective.

20, 6.

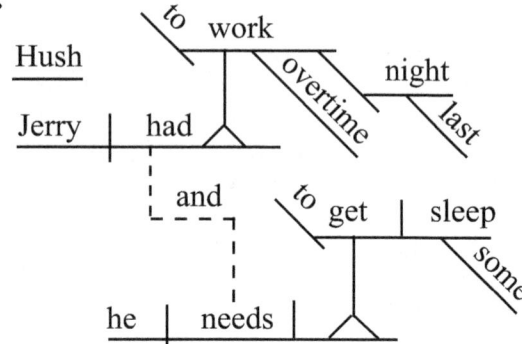

Hush is an **interjection**. The coordinating conjunction *and* connects the two main clauses of this sentence. *To work* is a complementary infinitive. The infinitive phrase *to get some sleep* is a direct object. *Night* is an adverbial objective.

20, 7.

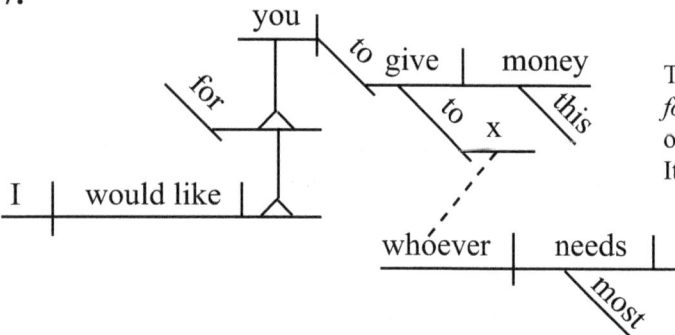

The preposition *for* has little meaning here. In fact, one can omit *for* without altering the meaning of the sentence. *You* is the subject of the infinitive *to give*. *Whoever* is an indefinite relative pronoun. Its **unexpressed antecedent** is represented in the diagram by *x*.

20, 8.

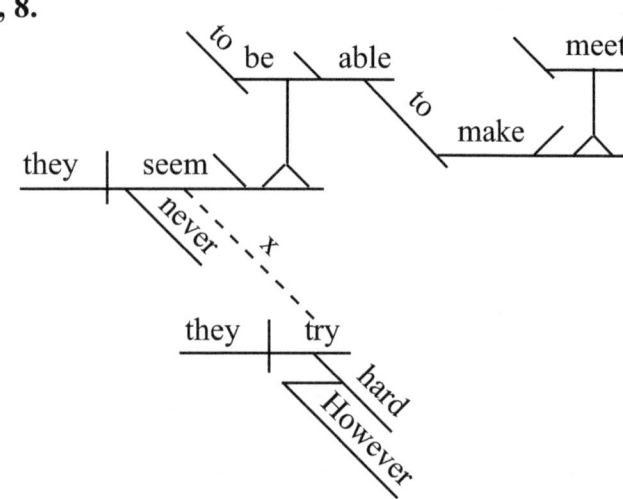

In this sentence, *however* is an indefinite adverb used to introduce a **concessive clause**. The **unexpressed subordinating conjunction** *although* is represented in the diagram by an *x*. The infinitive phrase *to be able* functions here as a predicate adjective. The infinitive phrase *to make ends meet* is the adverbial modifier of the predicate adjective *able*. The "*to*-less" infinitive *meet* is used here as an objective complement.

~ 230 ~

20, 9.

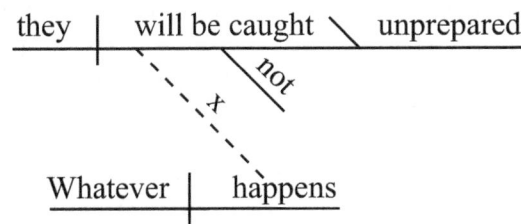

Whatever is an indefinite pronoun used, in this sentence, to introduce a clause that is implicitly **concessive**. An *x* is used in the diagram to represent the **unexpressed concessive conjunction** *although*.

20, 10.

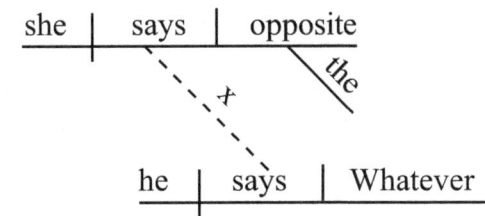

As in 20, 9, *whatever* is an indefinite pronoun used to introduce a **concessive clause**. Once again, *x* represents an **unexpressed concessive conjunction**. In this sentence, *whatever* is a direct object.

21, 1.

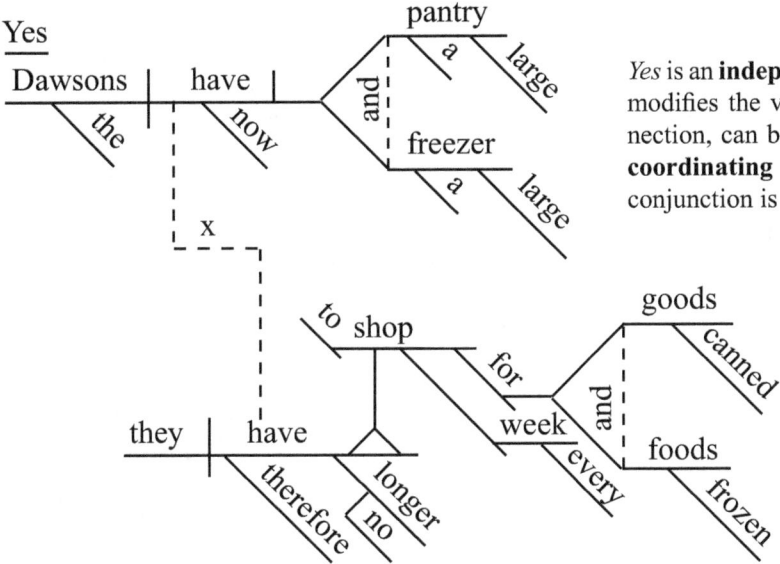

Yes is an **independent adverb**. *Therefore*, a **transitional adverb**, modifies the verb phrase *have to shop*. The transition, or connection, can be shown by an *x* that stands for an **unexpressed coordinating conjunction**; in this sentence, that unexpressed conjunction is *and*.

21, 2.

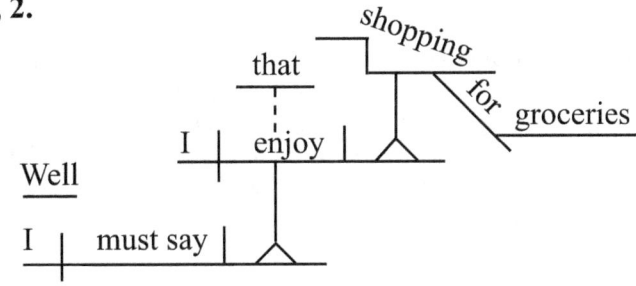

Well, as used in this sentence, is an **independent adverb**. The noun clause *that I enjoy shopping for groceries* functions as the direct object of the verb *must say* and includes, as its direct object, the gerund phrase *shopping for groceries*. The *that* in this clause is an expletive.

21, 3.

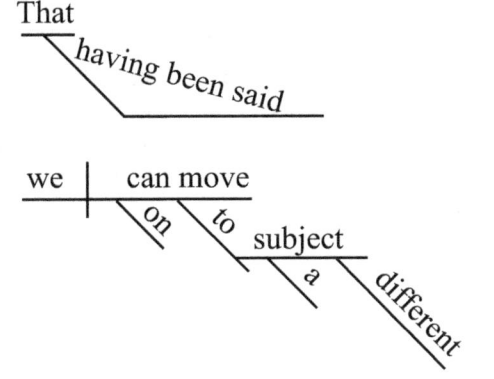

That having been said is an **absolute expression**, specifically, a **nominative absolute**. *Having been said* is a present-perfect passive participle. *On*, often a preposition, is an adverb here.

21, 4.

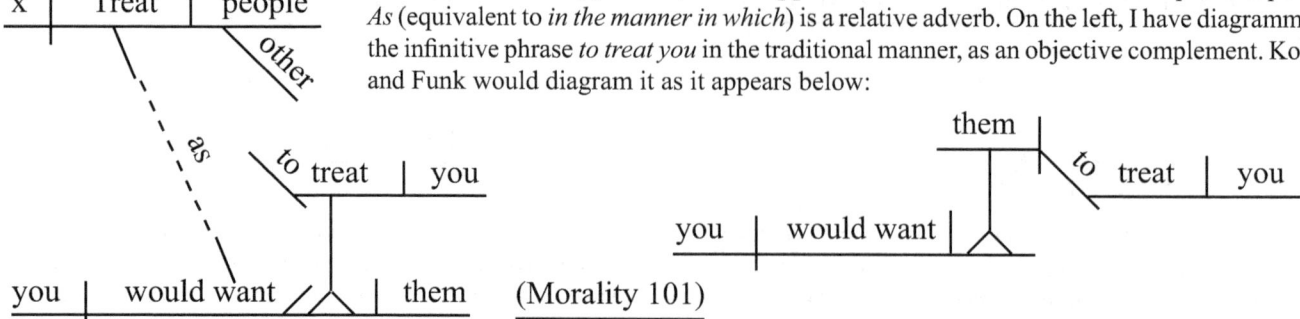

Morality 101 is an appositive; it is **in apposition with the entire sentence** up to that point. *As* (equivalent to *in the manner in which*) is a relative adverb. On the left, I have diagrammed the infinitive phrase *to treat you* in the traditional manner, as an objective complement. Kolln and Funk would diagram it as it appears below:

21, 5.

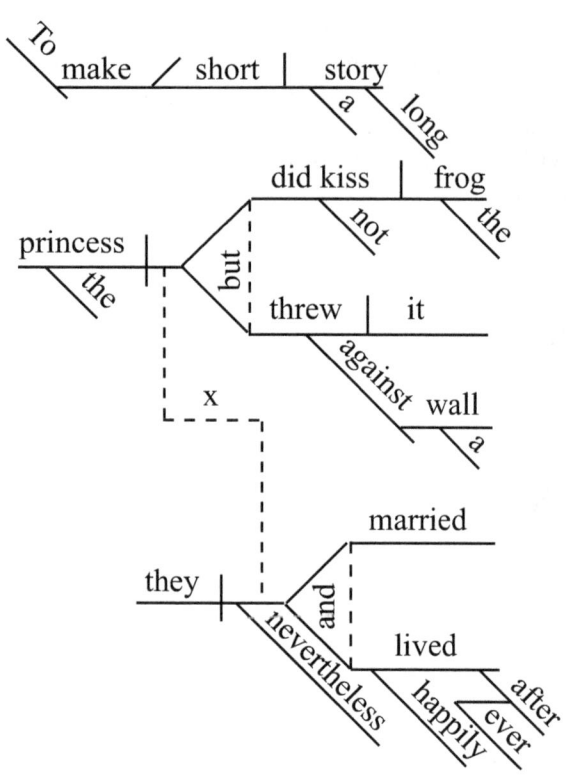

To make a long story short is an **independent infinitive phrase**. *Nevertheless* is a **transitional adverb**. In the diagram, the *x* stands for an unexpressed coordinating conjunction.

21, 6.

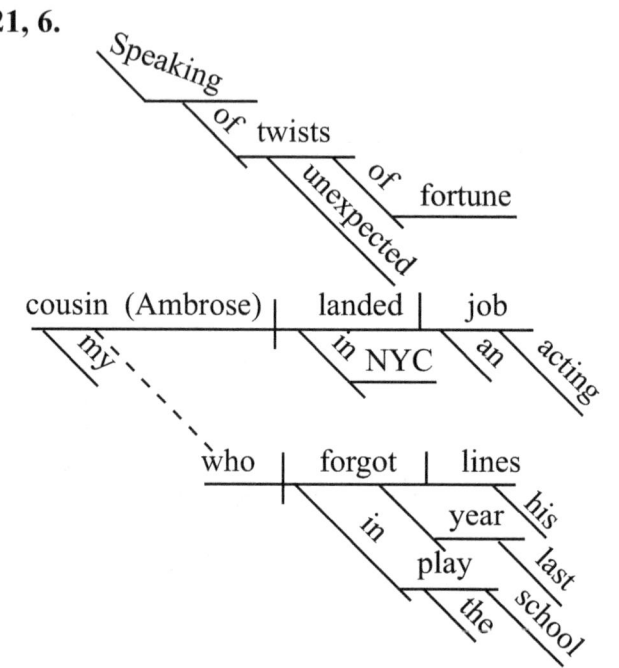

Speaking of unexpected twists of fortune is an **independent participial phrase**. *Ambrose* is in apposition with *cousin*; it a restrictive appositive. *Acting* is not a participle (the job is not doing anything) but a noun (an ordinary noun, not a gerund) used as an adjective. *Who forgot his lines . . . last year* is an adjective clause. The antecedent of the relative pronoun *who* is *cousin*. *Year* is an adverbial objective.

21, 7.

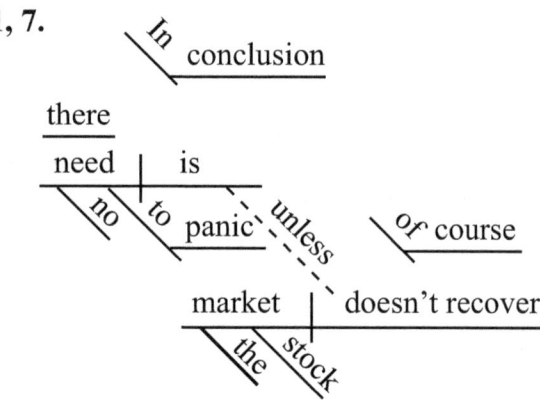

The prepositional phrases *in conclusion* and *of course* are **independent adverbial phrases**. *There* is an expletive; it has no meaning but only a function, which is to announce an inverted word order in which the verb precedes the subject. *Unless* is a subordinating conjunction.

21, 8.

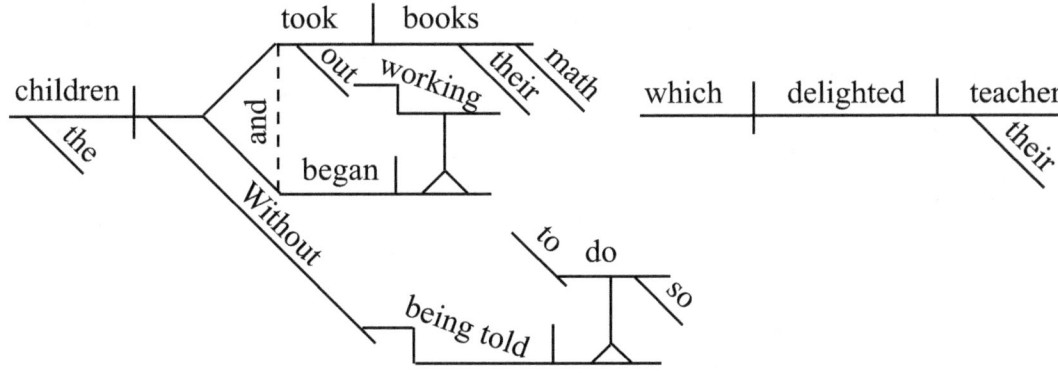

This sentence has a compound predicate. *Out* is an adverb. *Working* and *being told* are gerunds; the former is the direct object of the verb *began*, while the latter introduces a *gerund phrase* that is the object of the preposition *without*. The infinitive phrase *to do so* is the retained object of the gerund *being told*. The **relative clause** *which delighted the teacher* is a **sentence modifier**; therefore, the usual broken line connecting a relative pronoun with a single-word antecedent cannot be used here.

21, 9.

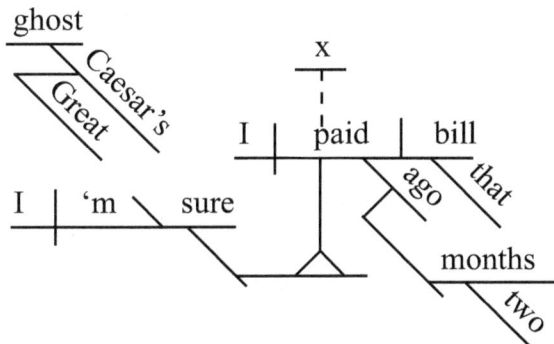

The **independent expression** *Great Caesar's ghost* is an interjection. The noun clause *I paid that bill two months ago* functions as an adverbial objective. Within that adverbial objective there is another adverbial objective, *two months*, which modifies the adverb *ago*. The unexpressed expletive *that* is represented in the diagram by an *x*.

21, 10.

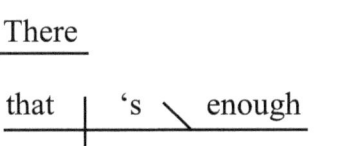

This *there* is not an expletive but an **independent adverb**. *Enough* is a predicate adjective.

22, 1.

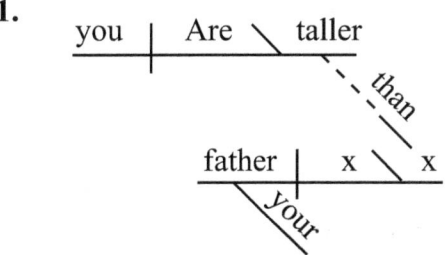

This sentence can be restated in this way: *Are you tall beyond the degree in which your father is tall?* The *x*'s in the diagram stand for the words *is* and *tall*. The relative adverb **than** (equivalent to *in which*) modifies the unexpressed adjective *tall*. To show this, the diagonal line is made solid at the lower end.

22, 2.

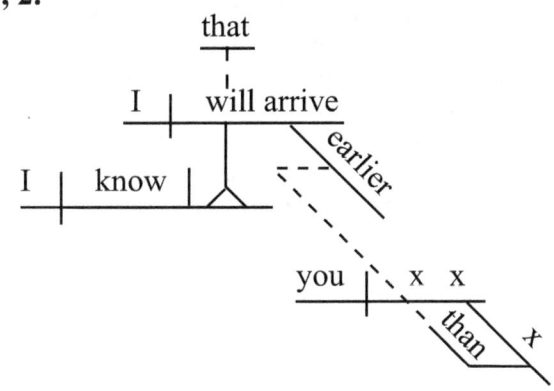

The noun clause *that I will arrive earlier* is the direct object of the verb *know*. *That* is an expletive. From the word *earlier* on, the sentence can be restated as *early beyond the degree in which you will arrive early*. The diagonal line on which the **relative adverb** *than* rests is made solid at the lower end to show that *than* modifies the unexpressed adverb *early*. **Than** is used in **unequal comparisons**.

22, 3.

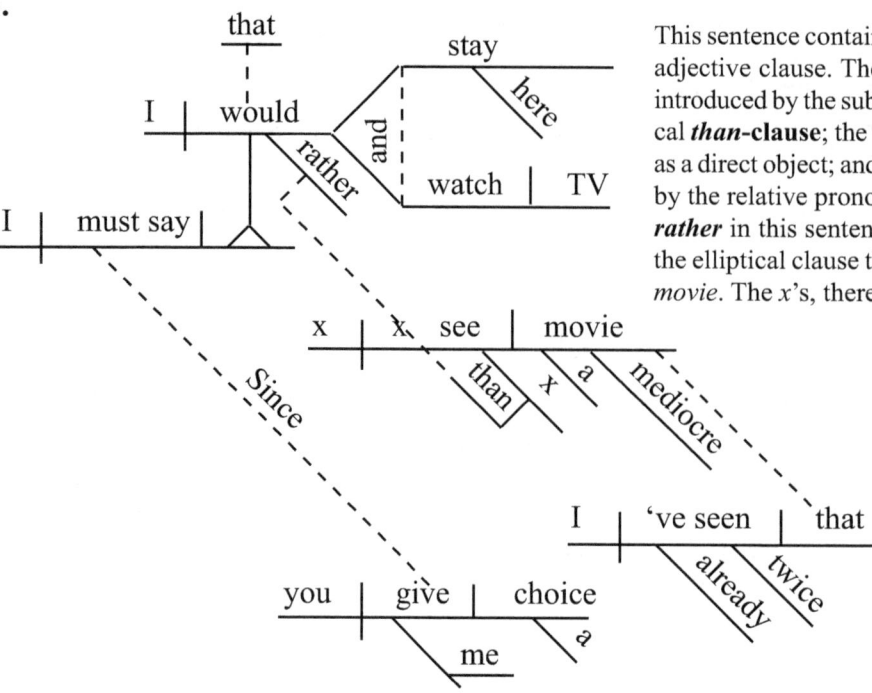

This sentence contains two adverb clauses, a noun clause, and an adjective clause. The adverb clauses are the subordinate clause introduced by the subordinating conjunction *since*, and the elliptical ***than*-clause**; the noun clause is the *that*-clause that functions as a direct object; and the adjective clause is the clause introduced by the relative pronoun *that*: *that I've already seen twice*. Since *rather* in this sentence means *more gladly*, one could complete the elliptical clause this way: *than I would gladly see a mediocre movie*. The *x*'s, therefore, stand for *I would* and *gladly*.

22, 4.

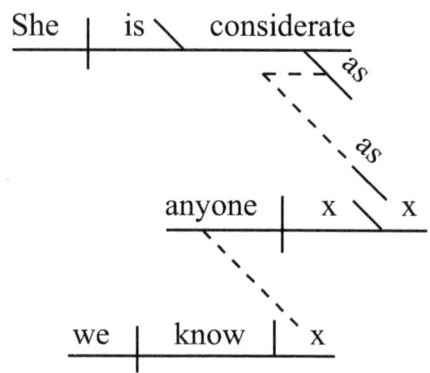

This sentence can be restated as follows: *She is considerate to the extent to which anyone we know is considerate*. The first *as* means *to the extent*, and the second *as* means *to which*. The solid portion at the lower end of the diagonal line shows that the second *as* modifies the unexpressed adjective *considerate*. The *x*'s stand for *is considerate* and the unexpressed relative pronoun *that*. The **correlatives *as . . . as* and *so . . . as*** are used in so-called **equal comparisons**.

22, 5.

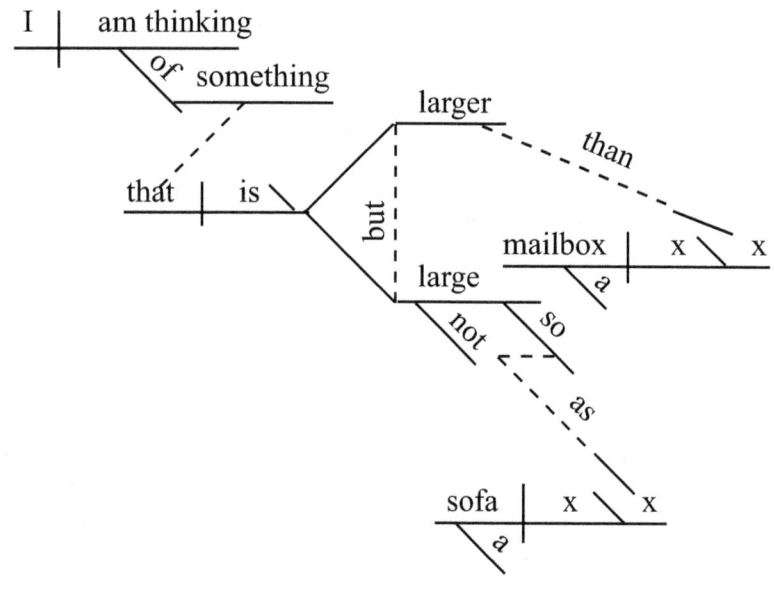

Both pairs of *x*'s stand for the same thing, *is large*. **As and than** are both **relative adverbs**; both are equivalent to *in which* in the following restatement: *large beyond the degree in which a mailbox is large but not large in the degree in which a sofa is large*. The relative pronoun *that* is the subject of its clause. The antecedent of *that* is *something*. The coordinating conjunction *but* connects two adjective phrases.

22, 6.

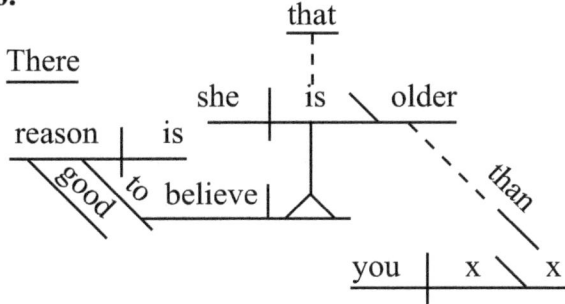

There is an expletive. It signifies that the subject will follow the verb. The infinitive phrase introduced by the infinitive *to believe* is adjectival, a modifier of the noun *reason*. The phrase *older than you* can be restated as *old beyond the degree in which you are old*. Thus the *x*'s stand for *are old*. **Than** is a relative adverb.

22, 7.

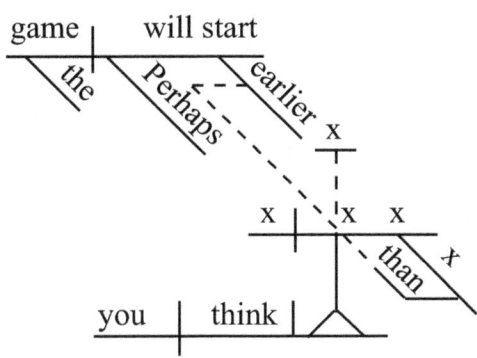

The elliptical adverb phrase is completed as follows: *earlier than you think that it will start early*. The uppermost *x* stands for the unexpressed expletive *that*; the remaining four *x*'s stand for the words *it will start early*. **Than** is a relative adverb.

22, 8.

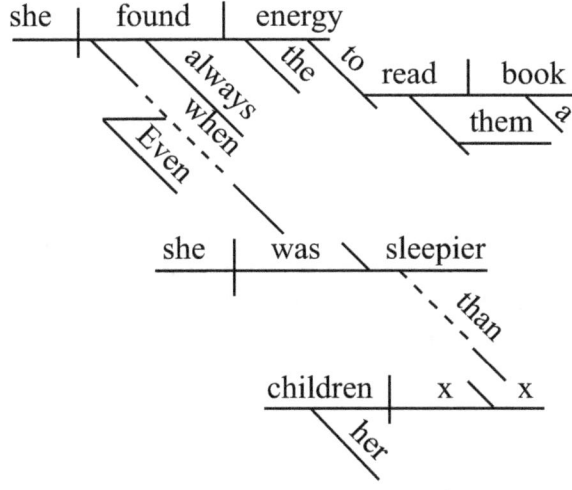

The adverb *even* modifies the relative adverb *when*, which is equivalent in meaning to *at the times at which* and modifies both *found* and *was*. The phrase *sleepier than her children* can be restated as *sleepy beyond the degree in which her children were sleepy*; thus **than** is also a relative adverb. In the diagram, the solid ends of the diagonals show which words the relative adverbs modify. The infinitive phrase *to read them a book* is adjectival; it modifies the noun *energy*. *Them* is an indirect object.

22, 9.

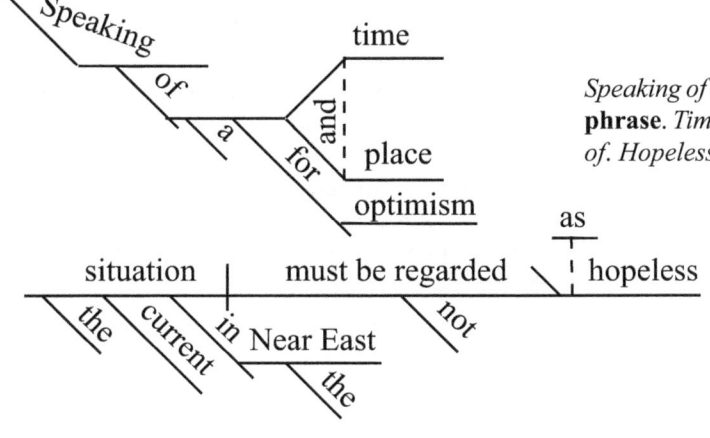

Speaking of a time . . . for optimism is an **independent participial phrase**. *Time and place* is the compound object of the preposition *of*. *Hopeless* is a predicate adjective. *As* is an expletive.

22, 10.

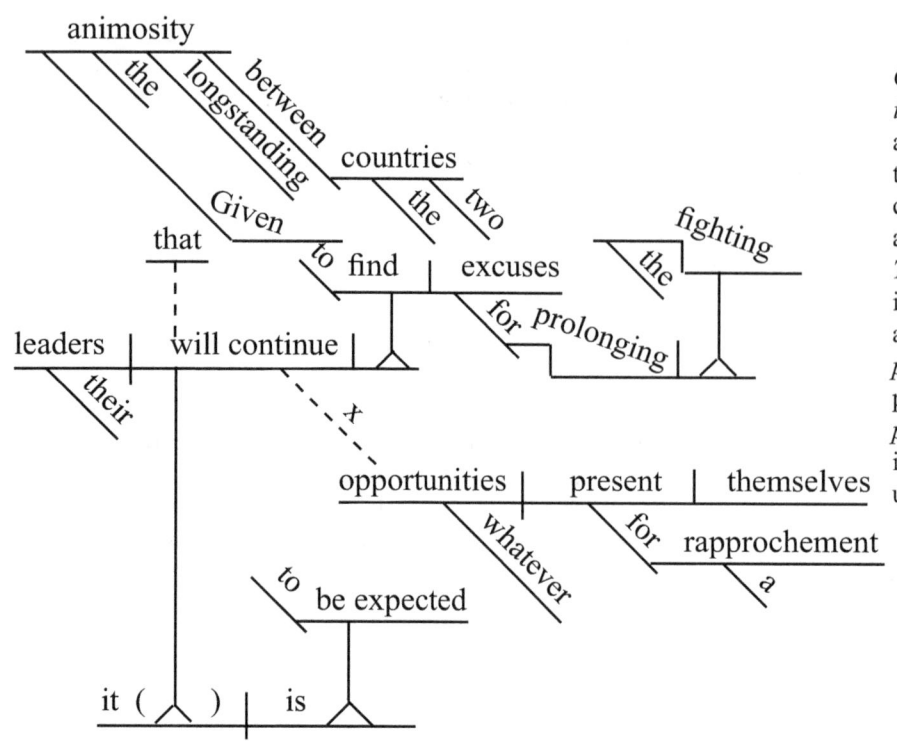

Given is a past participle; it modifies *animosity* (for it is animosity that is given or granted as a basis for argumentation) in a construction called a **nominative absolute**. The noun clause beginning with the expletive *that* is in apposition with the subject of the sentence, *it*. *To be expected* is a complementary infinitive in the present tense, passive voice. *Prolonging* and *fighting* are gerunds. The gerund phrase *prolonging the fighting* is the object of the preposition *for*; *fighting* is the direct object of *prolonging*. The **indefinite adjective whatever** introduces a **concessive clause**; *x* stands for an understood *although*.

23, 1.

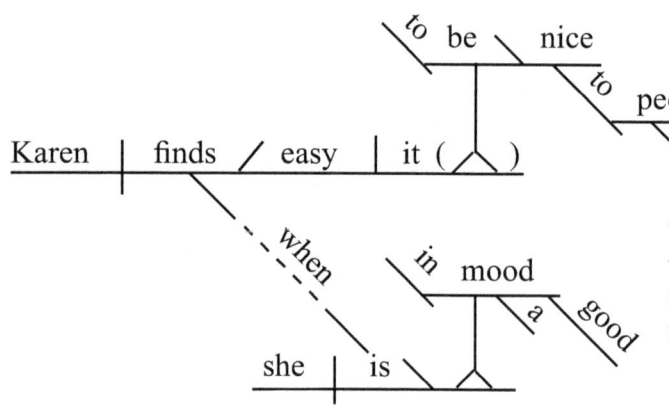

The infinitive phrase *to be nice to other people* is in apposition with the direct object, *it*. *Easy* is an objective complement. *When* (equivalent to *at the time at which*) is a relative adverb. The **prepositional phrase** *in a good mood* functions as a predicate adjective.

23, 2.

The noun clause introduced by the expletive *that* is used as the direct object of the verb *understand*; within the noun clause, the infinitive phrase *to use the phone* is the direct object of the verb *need*. *But* is a coordinating conjunction. The **prepositional phrase** *out of order* is used as a predicate adjective. *Out of* is a **phrasal preposition**. *Ours* is an absolute possessive form of the personal pronoun *we*. It is called absolute because it is never used with a noun; it represents not only the possessor but also the thing possessed.

23, 3.

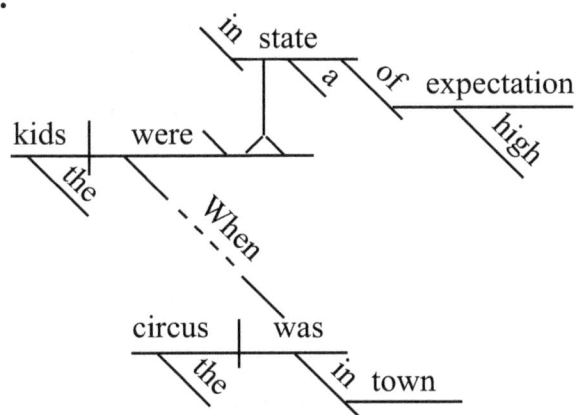

The **prepositional phrase** *in a state of high expectation* describes the kids; on the other hand, the **prepositional phrase** *in town* does not describe the circus but merely tells where it was. *When* is a relative adverb.

23, 4.

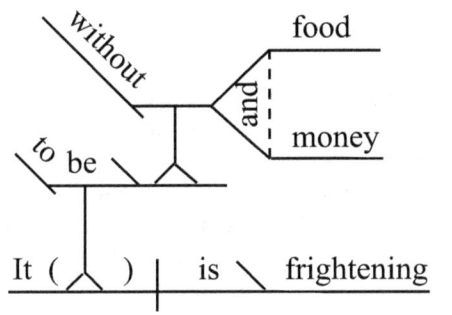

The infinitive phrase *to be without food and money* is an appositive; it is in apposition with the subject of the sentence, *it*. The **prepositional phrase** *without food and money* functions as a **predicate adjective**. *Frightening* is not used here as a participle but as a simple adjective.

23, 5.

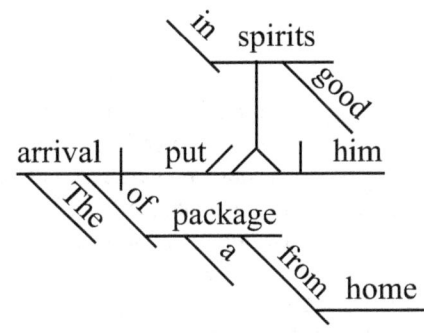

The **prepositional phrase** *in good spirits* functions as an **objective complement**.

23, 6.

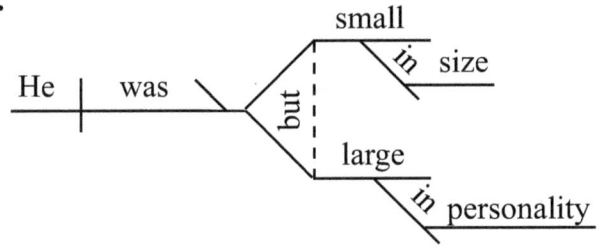

Two predicate adjectives, *small* and *large*, are connected by the coordinating conjunction *but*. Each adjective is modified by a **prepositional phrase**.

23, 7.

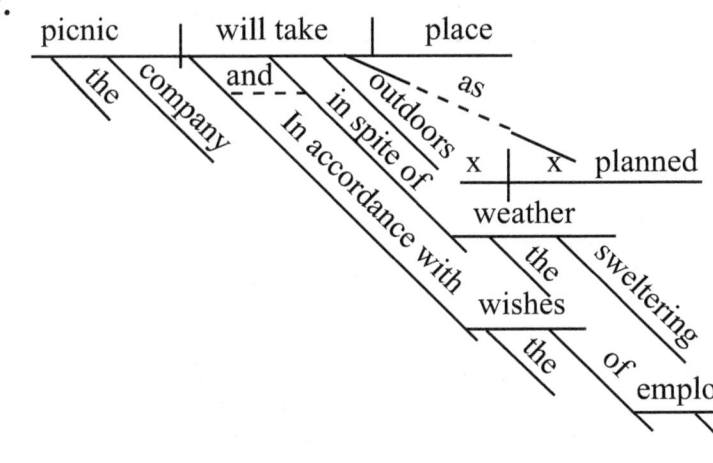

In accordance with and *in spite of* are **phrasal prepositions**. They introduce **prepositional phrases** that are joined by the coordinating conjunction *and* to form a **compound adverbial modifier**. *As planned* is an elliptical clause; the expanded form is *as it was planned*. *As* is a relative adverb. *Sweltering* is not a present participle here, just an adjective.

23, 8.

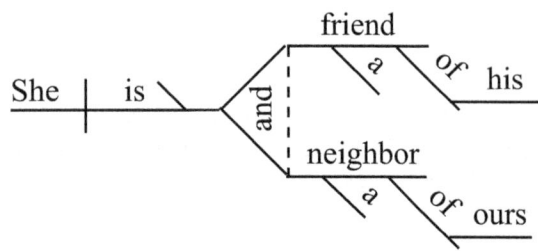

Two predicate nominatives, *friend* and *neighbor*, are connected by the coordinating conjunction *and*. The possessive pronouns *his* and *ours* are used as **objects of the preposition** *of*.

23, 9.

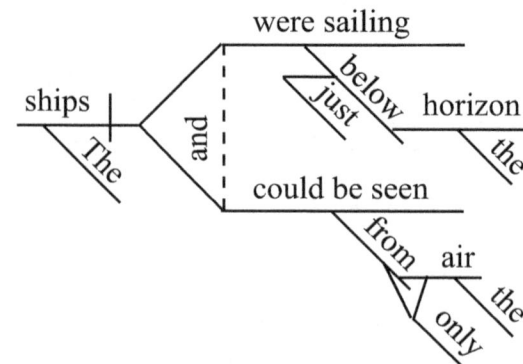

The adverb *just* modifies the **preposition** *below*, whereas the **adverb** *only* modifies the **prepositional phrase** *from the air*. This sentence has a compound predicate; the coordinating conjunction *and* connects its two parts.

23, 10.

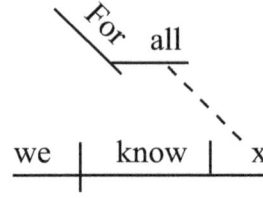

For all we know is an **independent prepositional phrase**; *all*, the object of the preposition *for*, is modified by an adjective clause with an unexpressed relative pronoun. The word *very*, which is usually an adverb, is an adjective in the expression *this very moment*. The noun *planet* and the pronoun *one* are **appositives**; each is in apposition with an **object of a preposition**. Everything in the sentence from the second *from* on, is an adverbial modifier of the adjective *third*. *That comprise the universe* is an adjective clause; the antecedent of the relative pronoun *that* is *stars*.

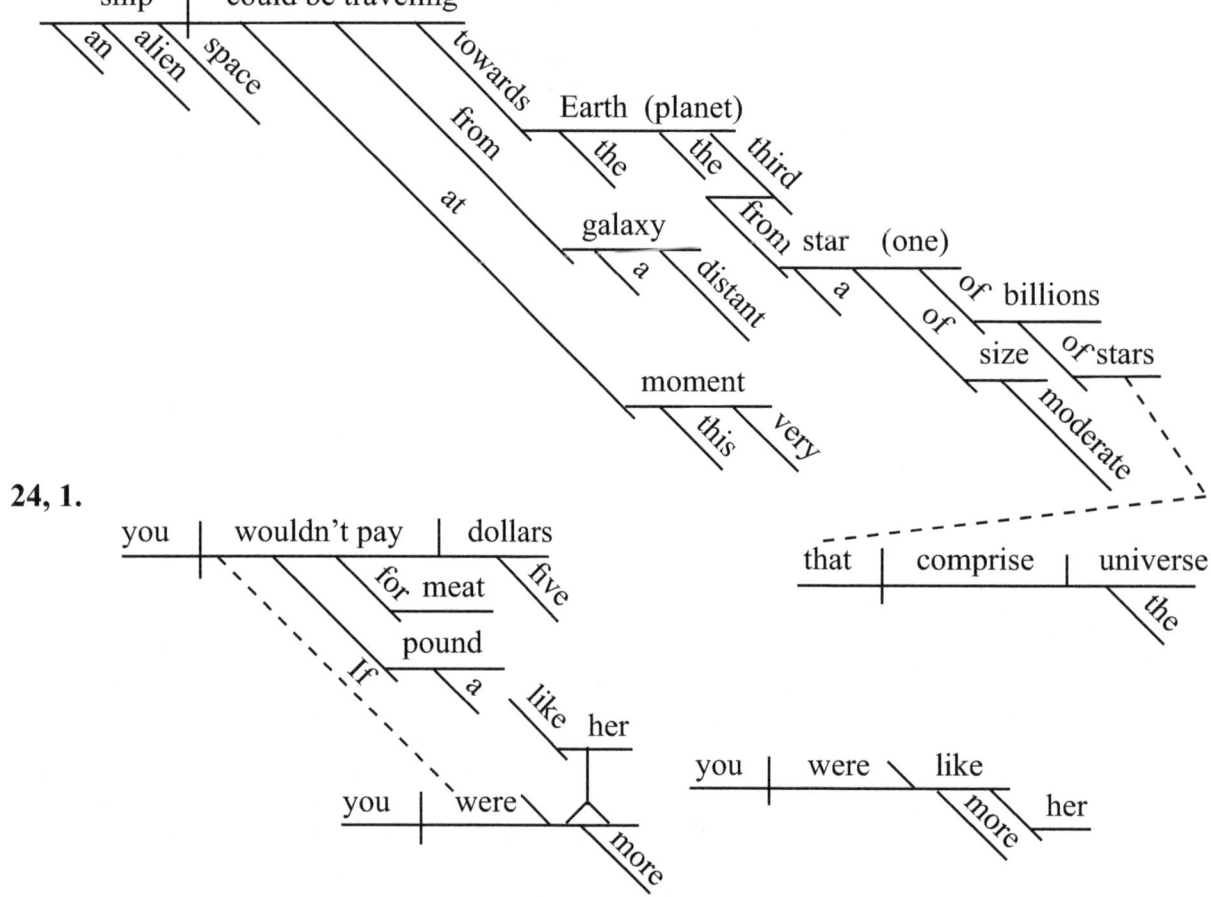

24, 1.

House and Harman would diagram the subordinate clause with *like* as a predicate adjective and *her* as an adverbial objective (above, right). They argue that *like* is inflected (i.e., one can say *more like* and *most like*), and prepositions are not inflected. That's true; however, one can say that someone is more into a game, more with it, or more on the defensive. The adverb *more* modifies the prepositional phrases, not the prepositions *into, with,* and *on*. Likewise, *more* modifies the prepositional phrase *like her*, not the preposition *like*. *Pound* is an adverbial objective.

24, 2.

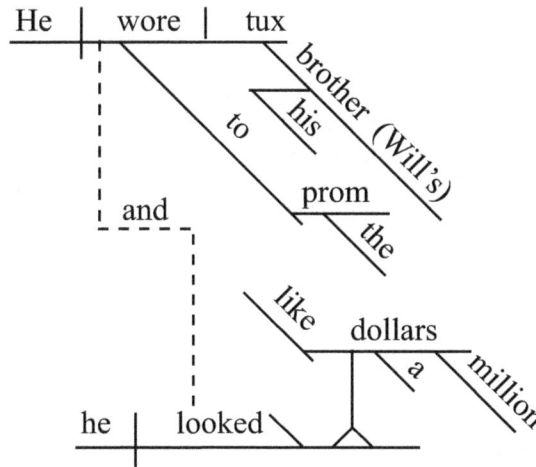

This is a compound sentence; the coordinating conjunction is *and*. If the **appositive** *Will's* were not **possessive** in form, the noun with which it is in apposition, *brother*, would be. The prepositional phrase *like a million dollars* functions in this sentence as a predicate adjective.

24, 4.

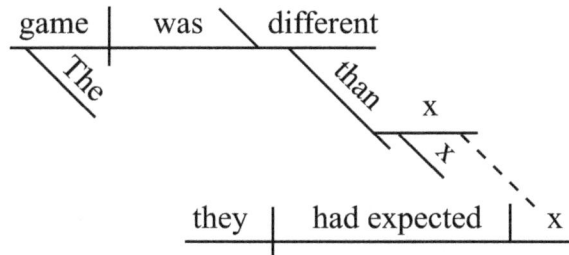

24, 5.

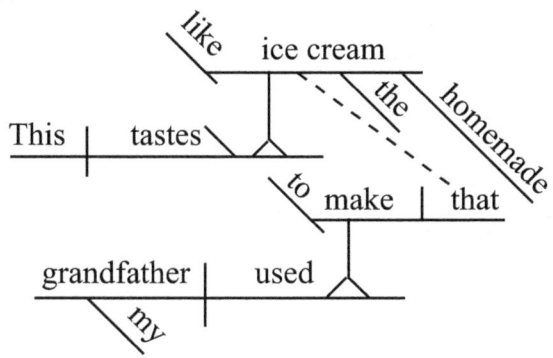

The prepositional phrase *like the homemade ice cream* functions as a predicate adjective. The relative pronoun *that* has *ice cream* as its antecedent. To understand how *tastes* can take a predicate adjective, consider that we say that the ice cream tastes good (adjective), not that it tastes well (adverb).

24, 3.

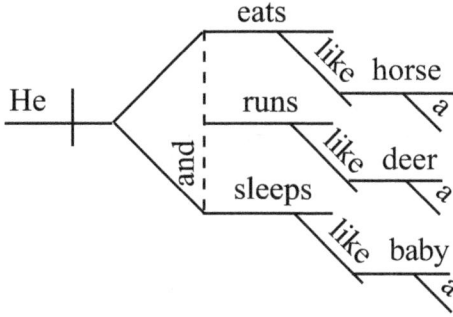

This sentence has a tripartite predicate. House and Harman also accept the following manner of diagramming an adverbial *like*-phrase, according to which *like* is an adverb and *horse* is an adverbial objective:

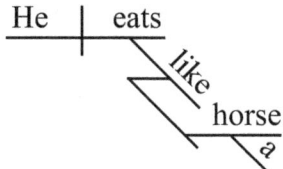

In this elliptical sentence, the words *the game that* are unexpressed. They are represented in the diagram by *x*'s. **Than**, often a relative adverb, is a **preposition** is this sentence.

24, 6.

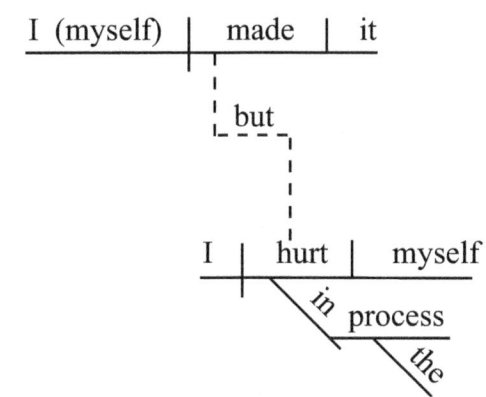

In this compound sentence, the coordinating conjunction is *but*. The first *myself* is an **intensive (or emphatic) pronoun** and is diagrammed as an appositive. The second *myself* is a **reflexive pronoun**; it is a direct object in this sentence.

24, 7.

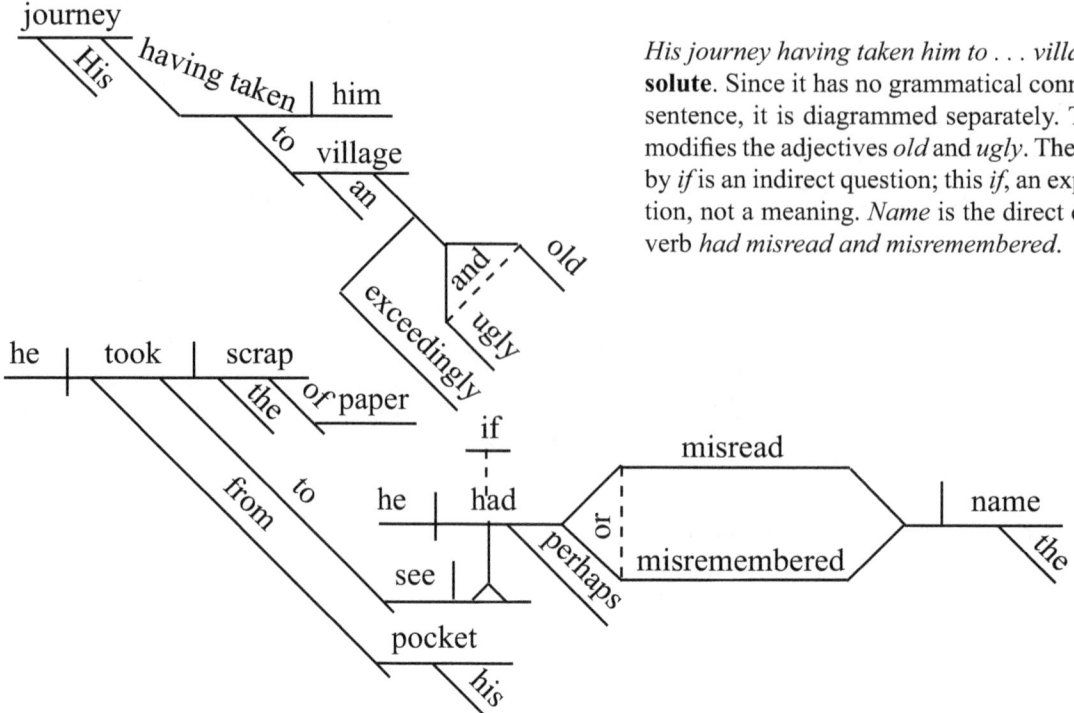

His journey having taken him to . . . village is a **nominative absolute**. Since it has no grammatical connection to the rest of the sentence, it is diagrammed separately. The adverb *exceedingly* modifies the adjectives *old* and *ugly*. The noun clause introduced by *if* is an indirect question; this *if*, an expletive, has only a function, not a meaning. *Name* is the direct object of the compound verb *had misread and misremembered*.

24, 8.

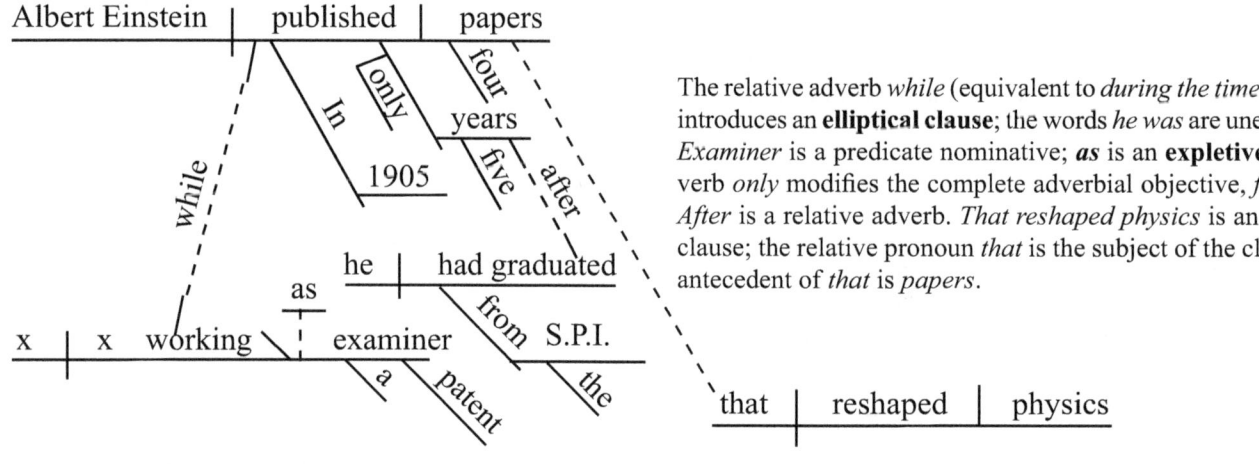

The relative adverb *while* (equivalent to *during the time at which*) introduces an **elliptical clause**; the words *he was* are unexpressed. *Examiner* is a predicate nominative; *as* is an **expletive**. The adverb *only* modifies the complete adverbial objective, *five years*. *After* is a relative adverb. *That reshaped physics* is an adjective clause; the relative pronoun *that* is the subject of the clause. The antecedent of *that* is *papers*.

24, 9.

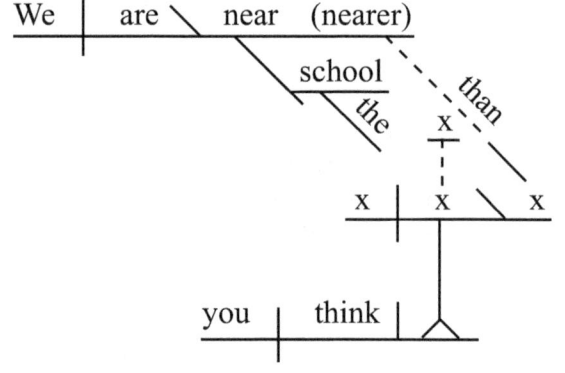

Unlike *like* in previous sentences in this exercise, *near* is unquestionably a predicate adjective. *School* is an adverbial objective. The adjective *nearer* is in **apposition** with the adjective *near*. The relative adverb *than* introduces an **elliptical clause**, which if expressed fully would be *than you think that we are near*. The last four words are represented by *x*'s in the diagram.

24, 10.

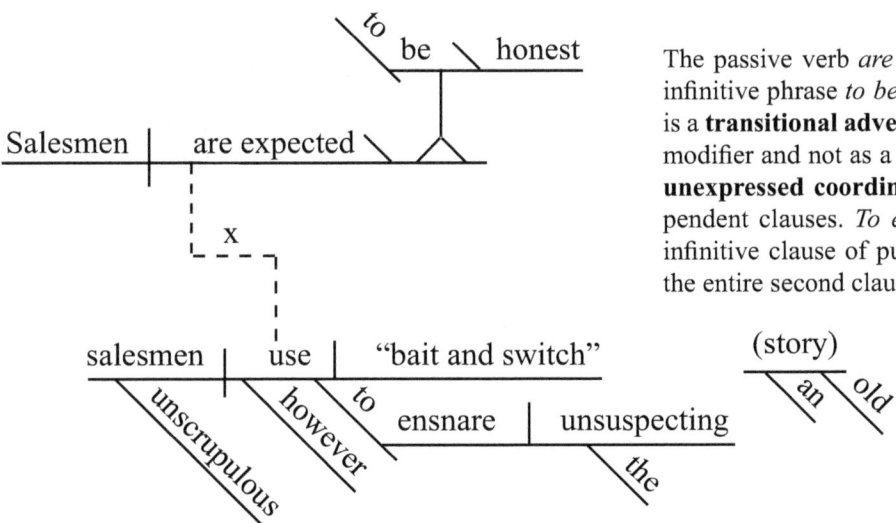

The passive verb *are expected* acts as a linking verb, with the infinitive phrase *to be honest* as a predicate adjective. *However* is a **transitional adverb**. Since it is diagrammed as an adverbial modifier and not as a connecting word, an *x* is used to show an **unexpressed coordinating connection** between the two independent clauses. *To ensnare the unsuspecting* is an adverbial infinitive clause of purpose. *An old story* is in apposition with the entire second clause.

25, 1.

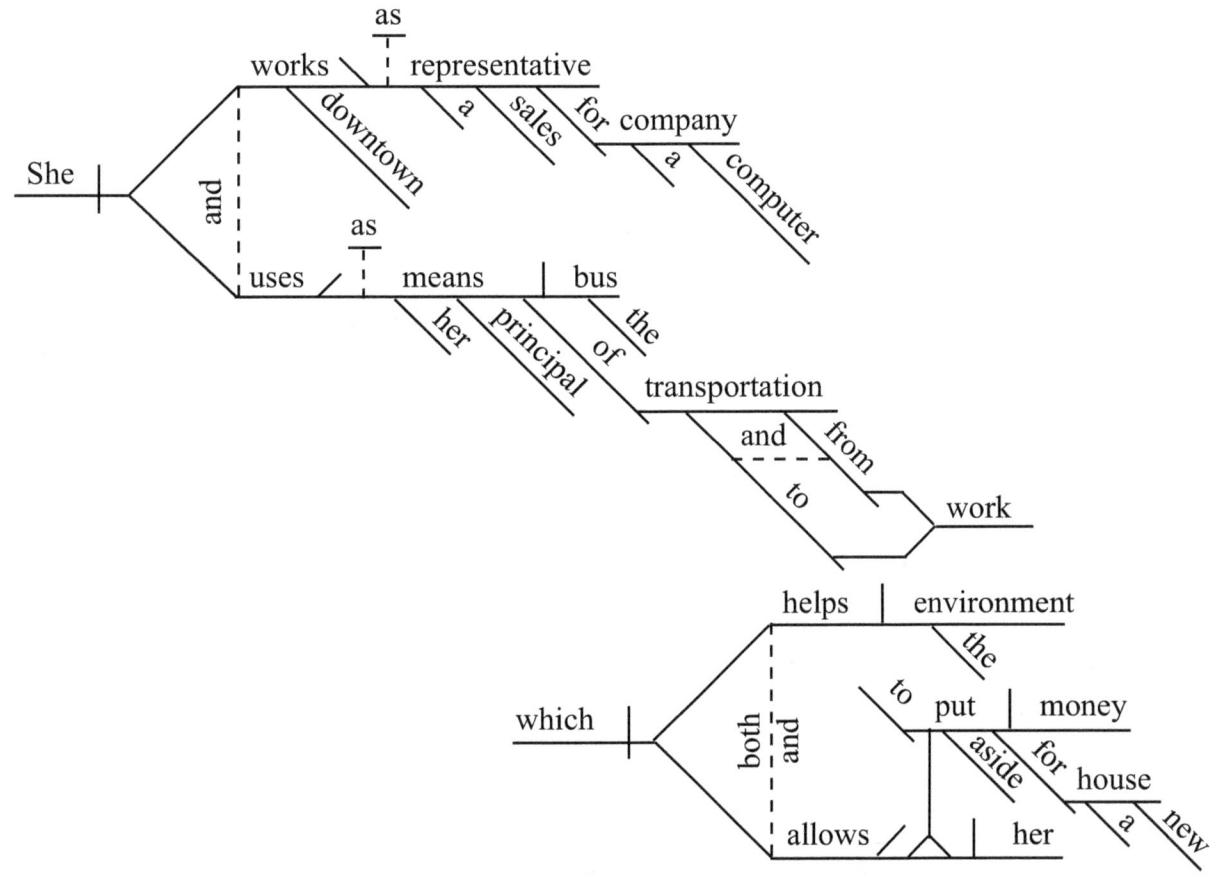

This sentence has a **two compound predicates** and a **compound adjectival modifier**; the latter contains two different prepositions with the same object. *Works*, a **non-linking verb**, functions here as a **linking verb**; *representative*, which repeats the **subject**, is a **predicate nominative**; *as* is an **expletive**. The second *as* is also an **expletive**, and *means* is an **objective complement**. *Which*, a relative pronoun, is a sentence modifier; its antecedent is the second part of the compound predicate. The infinitive phrase that begins with the infinitive *to put* functions as an objective complement. *Both . . . and* are correlative conjunctions.

25, 2.

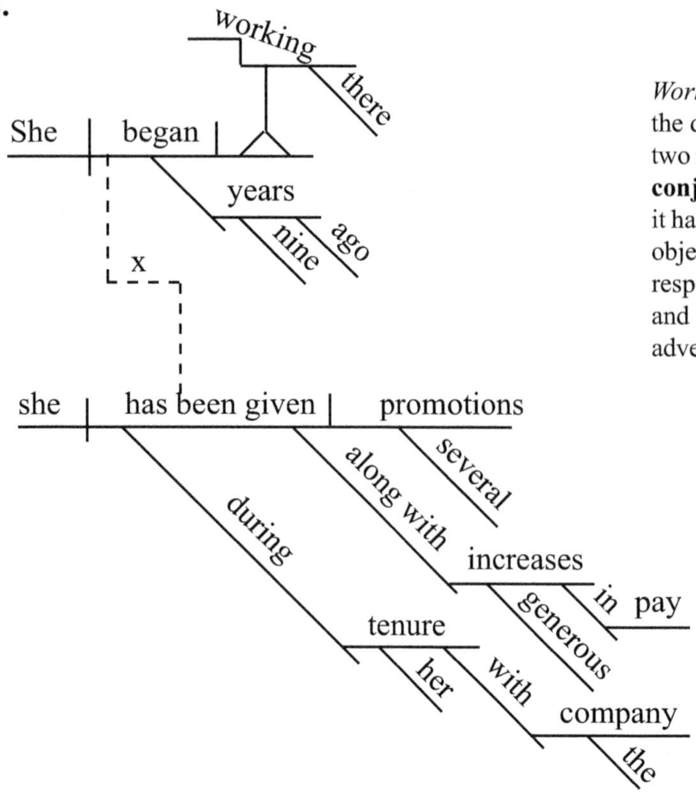

Working is a gerund. The gerund phrase *working there* serves as the direct object of the verb *began*. An *x* is used to show that the two main clauses are connected by an **unexpressed coordinating conjunction**. Even though *has been given* is in the passive voice, it has a direct object, *promotions*. This happens when the indirect object of an active-voice sentence becomes the subject of a corresponding passive-voice sentence. The direct object is retained and is called a **retained object**. *Ago* can also be construed as an adverb modified by the adverbial objective *nine years* (see below)

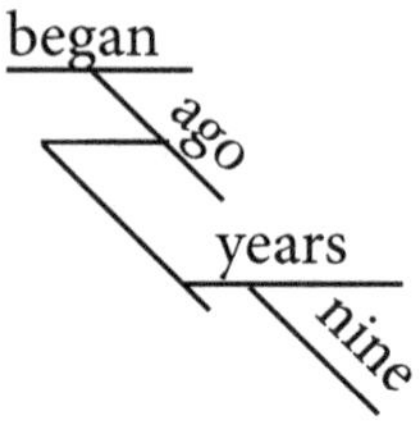

25, 3.

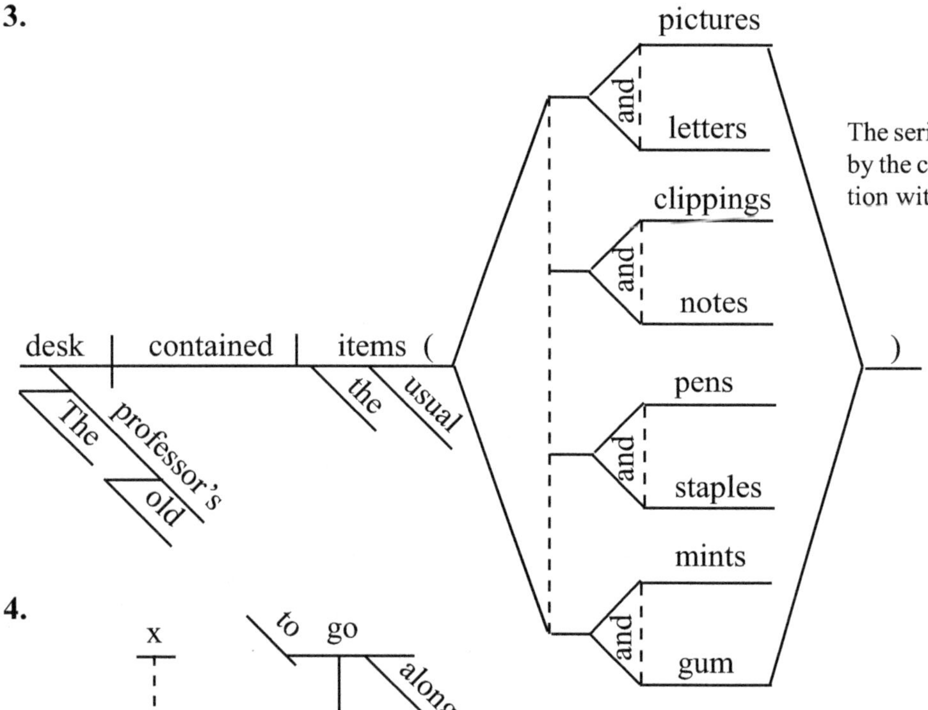

The series of four pairs of items, each connected by the coordinating conjunction *and*, is in apposition with the direct object *items*.

25, 4.

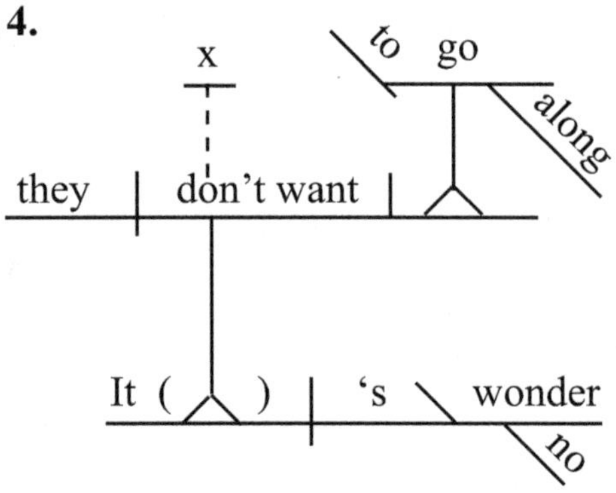

The noun clause *they don't want to go along* is in apposition with the subject of the sentence, *it*. The infinitive phrase *to go along* is the direct object in the noun clause. *Wonder* is a predicate nominative.

25, 5.

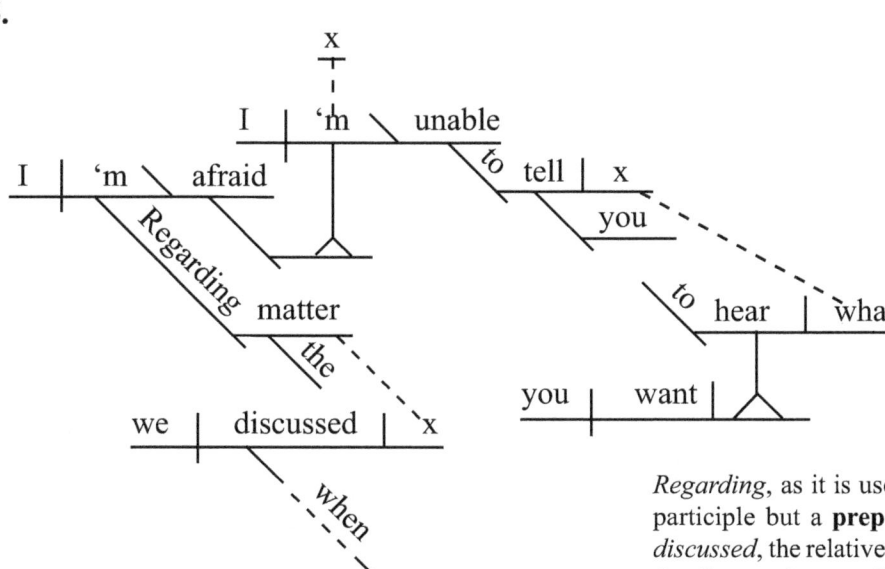

Regarding, as it is used in this sentence, is not a present active participle but a **preposition**. In the elliptical clause [*that*] *we discussed*, the relative pronoun is unexpressed; it is repesented in the diagram by an *x*. *When* is a relative adverb. The **noun clause** following *afraid* functions as an **adverbial objective**; *x* stands for the unexpressed expletive *that*. The infinitive phrase introduced by the infinitive *to tell* is an adverbial modifier of the predicate adjective *unable*. *You* is an indirect object. The adjective clause *what you want to hear* modifies the unexpressed direct object of *tell*. The infinitive *to hear* and its direct object, the **indefinite relative pronoun** *what*, comprise the direct object of *want*.

25, 6.

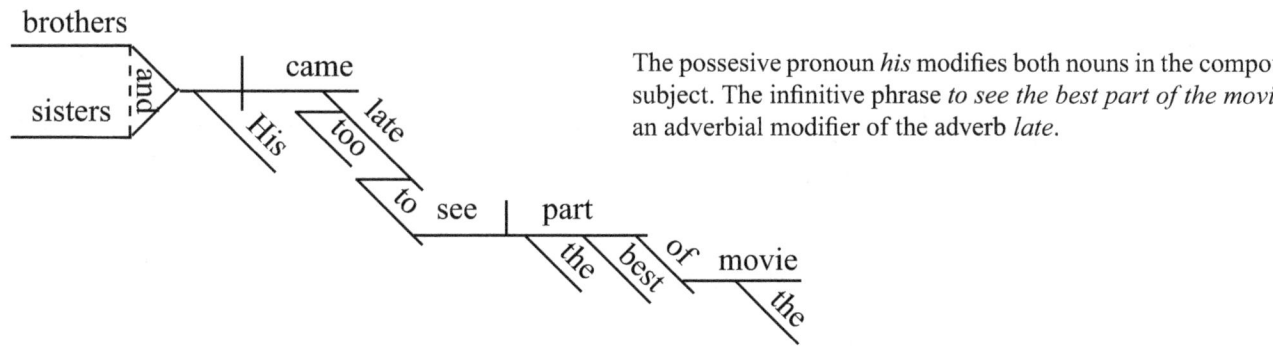

The possesive pronoun *his* modifies both nouns in the compound subject. The infinitive phrase *to see the best part of the movie* is an adverbial modifier of the adverb *late*.

25, 7.

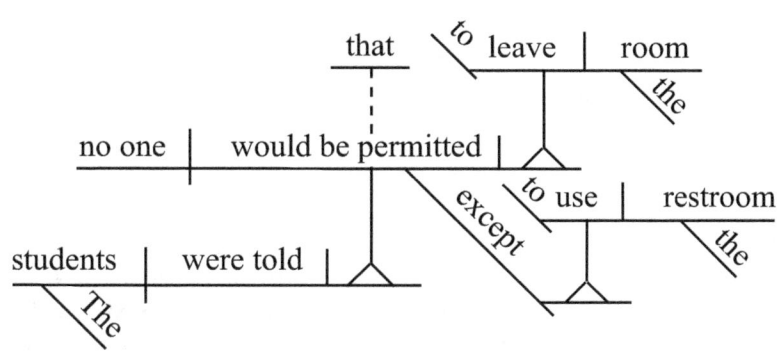

The expletive *that* introduces a noun clause that, with objects and modifiers, is the direct object of the passive verb *were told*; similarly, the infinitive phrase *to leave the room* is the direct object of the passive verb *would be permitted*. Both objects are "retained," although only the first fits exactly the definition of **retained object** if one insists that *no one* is an **objective complement** in the sentence *They permitted no one to leave the room*. I am persuaded that it could be called an **indirect object** with at least equal justification. Consider the sentence *It was permitted <u>to them</u> to leave the room*. The infinitive phrase *to use the restroom* is the object of the preposition *except*.

25, 8.

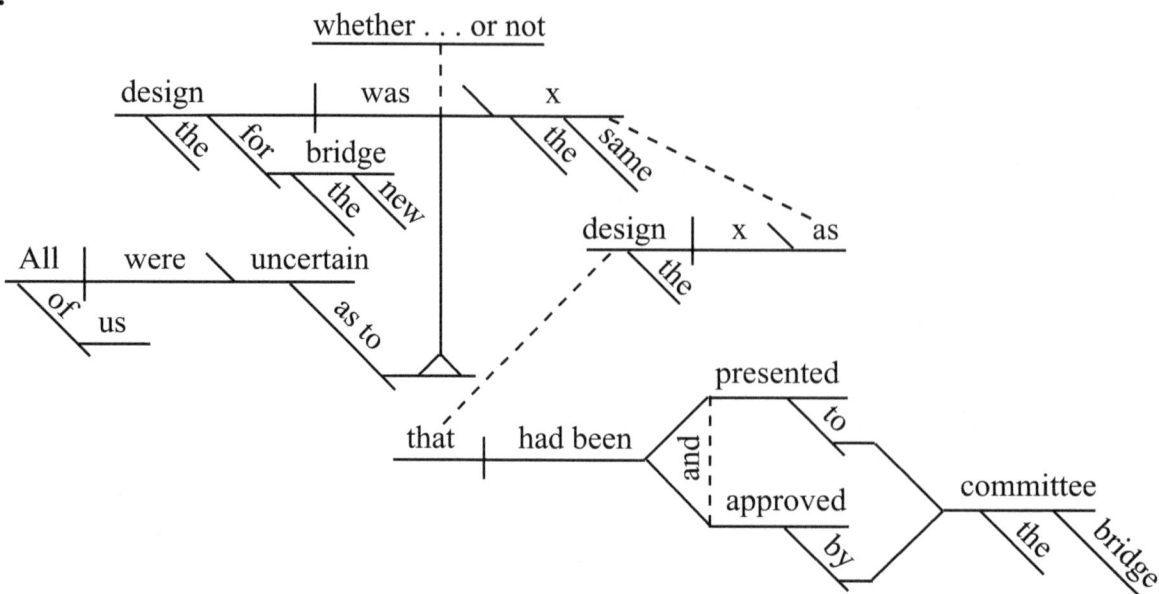

As to is a **phrasal preposition**; *whether . . . or not* is a phrasal expletive. *As* functions as a **relative pronoun** in this sentence (*the design . . . was the same one as the design was that . . .*); its antecedent is an unexpressed *one*. *That* is a relative pronoun whose antecedent is *design*. *Presented* and *approved* share the helping verb *had been*. The prepositions *to* and *by* have the same object, *committee*.

25, 9.

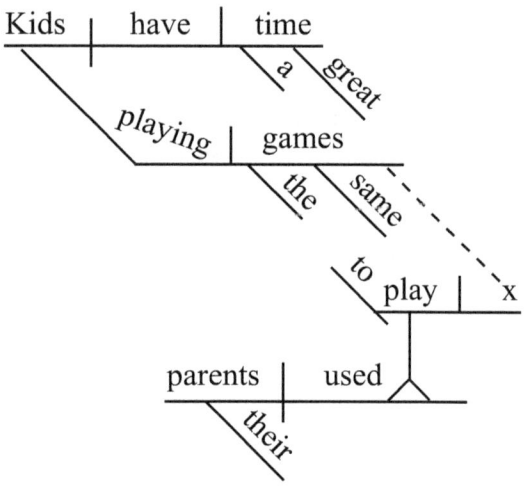

Playing . . . games is a delayed participial phrase. Although it comes after the main verb, it nevertheless modifies the subject of the sentence, *kids*. The relative pronoun *that* has been omitted from the clause *their parents used to play*. The expanded form would be *that their parents used to play*. The **unexpressed relative pronoun**, which is the direct object of the complementary infinitive *to play*, is represented in the diagram by an *x*.

25, 10.

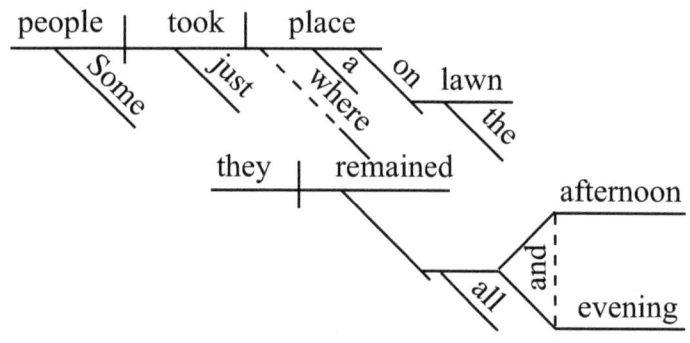

Where is a **relative adverb**, equivalent to the phrase *in which*; it introduces an **adjective clause** that modifies the noun *place*. The solid lower portion of the diagonal line indicates that *where* modifies the verb *remained*. *Afternoon and evening* is a **compound adverbial objective**. The adjective *all* modifies both *afternoon* and *evening*.

26, 1.

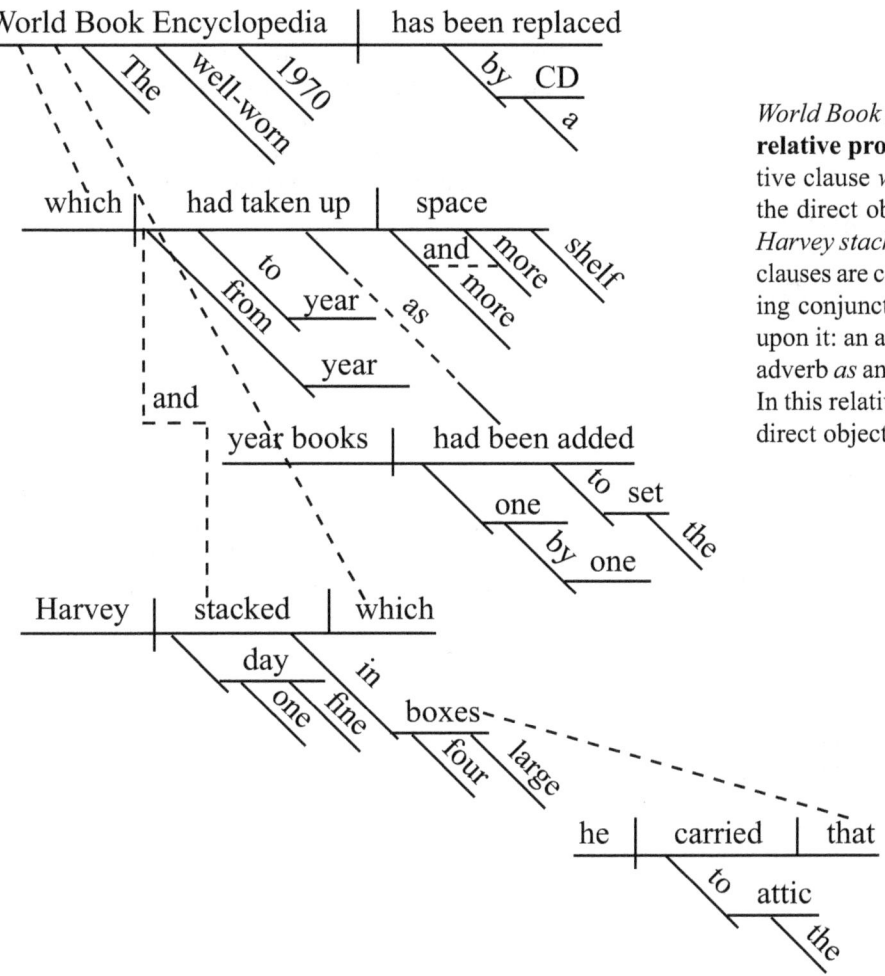

World Book Encyclopedia is the **antecedent of two relative pronouns**: *which*, the subject in the adjective clause *which had taken . . . space*; and *which*, the direct object in the adjective clause *which . . . Harvey stacked in four large boxes*. These adjective clauses are connected to each other by the coordinating conjunction *and*. Each has a clause dependent upon it: an adverb clause introduced by the relative adverb *as* and a third adjective clause, respectively. In this relative clause, the relative pronoun *that* is a direct object; its antecedent is *boxes*.

26, 2.

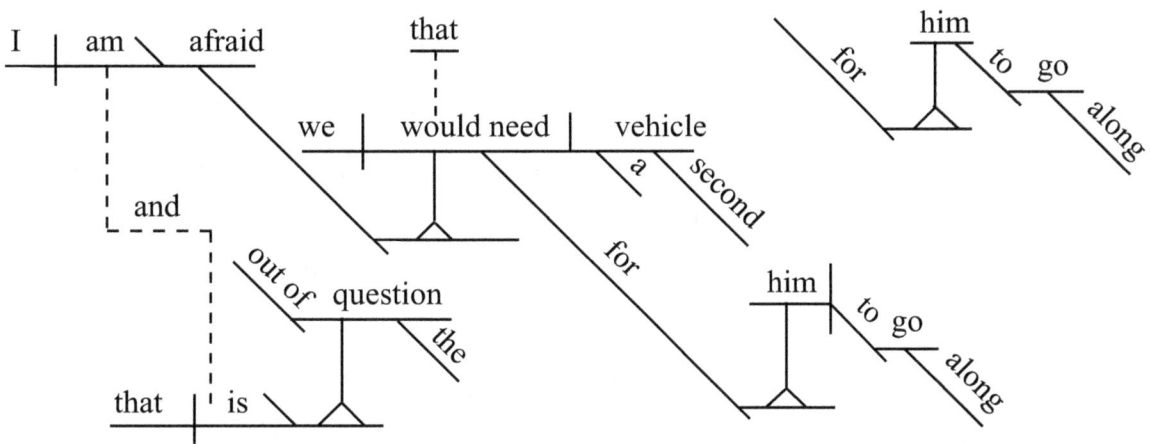

In this compound sentence, the predicate adjective of the second main clause is the prepositional phrase *out of the question. Out of* is a phrasal preposition. In the first main clause, the noun clause (introduced by the expletive *that*) functions as an adverbial objective. The object of the preposition *for* is not *him* alone but the expression *him to go along*, in which *him* acts as a kind of **subject of the infinitive**. House and Harman seem to acknowledge that, in constructions of this kind, a noun or pronoun in the objective case serves as the subject for an infinitive; however, their manner of diagramming such a construction (cf. above right) does not show a subject-verb relationship.

26, 3.

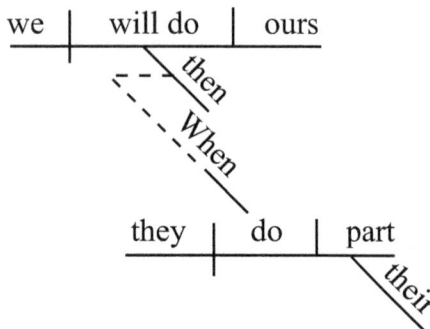

Ours, a possessive pronoun, is a direct object; this is possible because *ours*, like the other **absolute possessive pronouns** (*mine, yours, his, hers, yours, theirs*), consists of a possessive pronoun and an unexpressed noun, in this case, the word *part*. *When* is a relative adverb; *then* is equivalent to *at the time*, and *when* to *at which*.

26, 4.

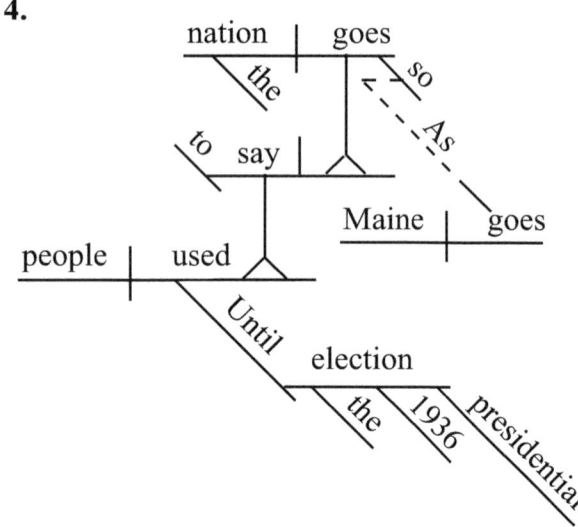

To say is a complementary infinitive. *As* is a relative adverb; *so* means *in the manner* and *as* means *in which*. In the diagram, the line on which *as* is situated is solid at the lower end to show that *as* modifies the lower *goes*. The **direct quotation** is the direct object of the verb *say*.

26, 5.

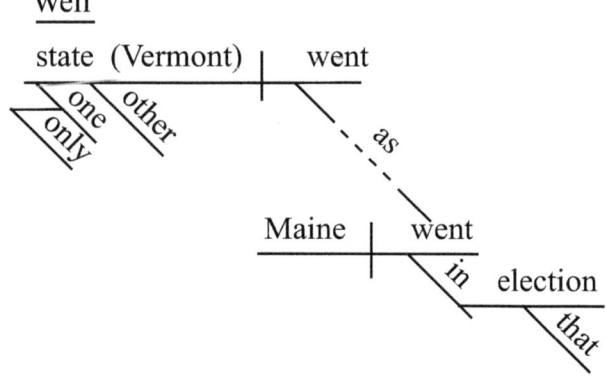

Only is an adverb modifying the adjective *one*. *Vermont* is an appositive; it is in apposition with the subject of the sentence, *state*. *As* is a relative adverb; since it is equivalent to *in the manner in which*, it modifies both *went*s. The diagonal line is solid at both ends to show this. *Well* is an **independent adverb**.

26, 6.

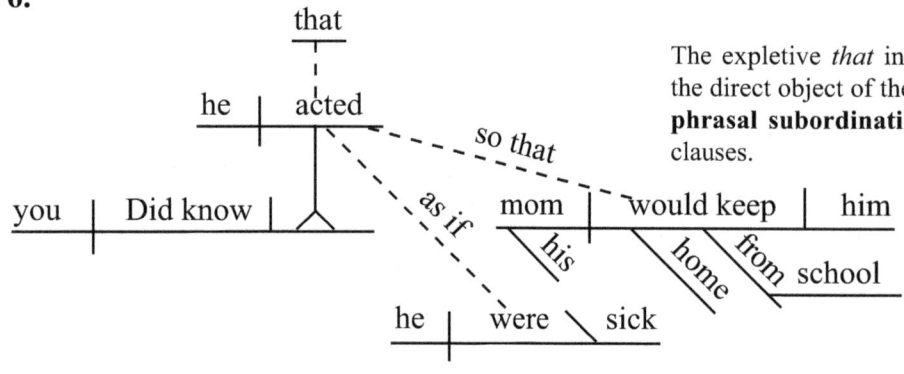

The expletive *that* introduces a noun clause that functions as the direct object of the verb *did know*. *As if* and *so that* are both **phrasal subordinating conjunctions**; they introduce adverb clauses.

26, 7.

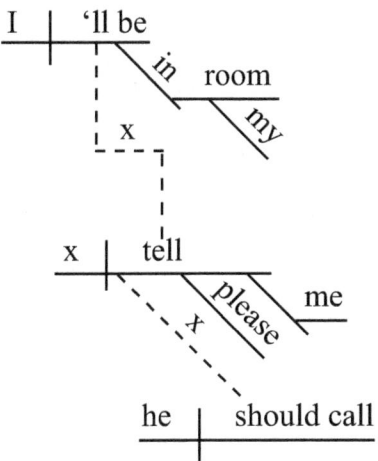

This is a compound sentence; the two main clauses are connected by the unexpressed coordinating conjunction *and* (represented in the diagram by the first *x*). The *x* before the imperative (command) form of the verb *tell* stands for an unexpressed *you*. The subordinate clause is conditional; *x* represents an unexpressed *if*. I take **please** to be an adverb, short for the adverb clause *if you please*. According to House and Harman, *please* should be construed as a main verb and the accompanying verb as a complementary infinitive. If House and Harman are right, the second main clause would be diagrammed as follows:

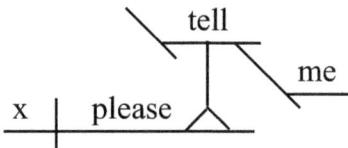

26, 8.

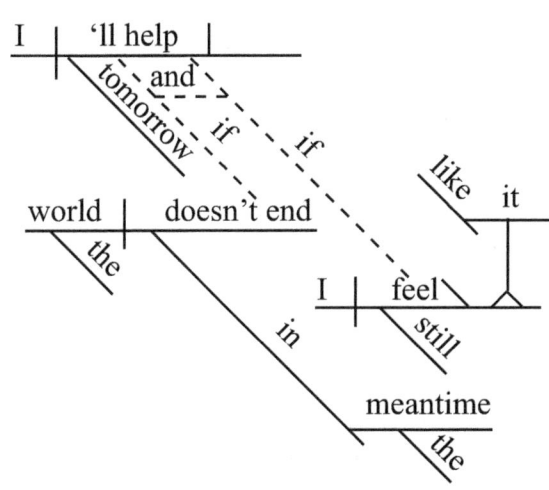

This sentence features two conditional clauses connected by the coordinating conjunction *and*. The prepositional phrase *like it* functions as a predicate adjective.

26, 9.

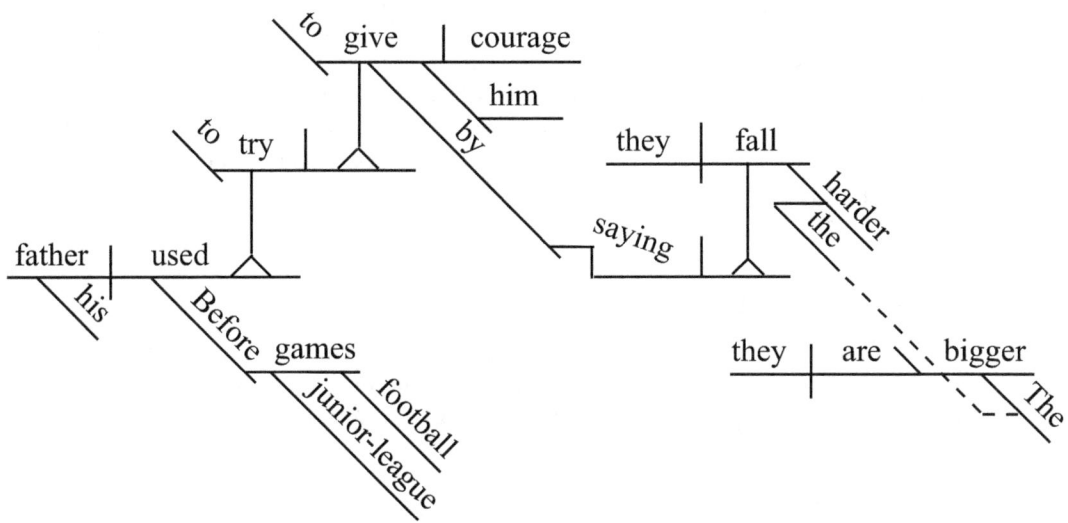

To try is a complementary infinitive. The infinitive phrase beginning with *to give him courage* is the direct object of *try*. The **gerund phrase** introduced by the gerund *saying* is the object of the preposition *by*. The quotation functions as the direct object of *saying*. The *the*s in this sentence are **correlative adverbs**. The first *the* modifies the adjective *bigger*, and the second modifies the adverb *harder*.

26, 10.

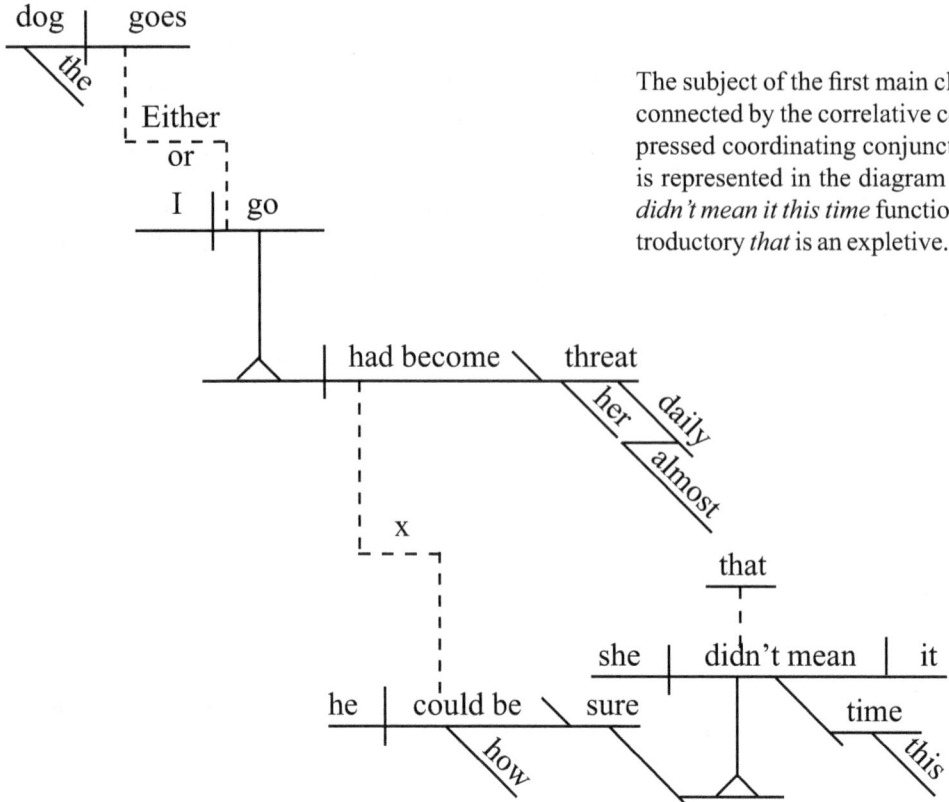

The subject of the first main clause consists of **two noun clauses** connected by the correlative conjunctions *either . . . or*. An unexpressed coordinating conjunction between the two main clauses is represented in the diagram by an *x*. The noun clause *that she didn't mean it this time* functions as an adverbial objective; the introductory *that* is an expletive. *Time* is also an adverbial objective.

27, 1.

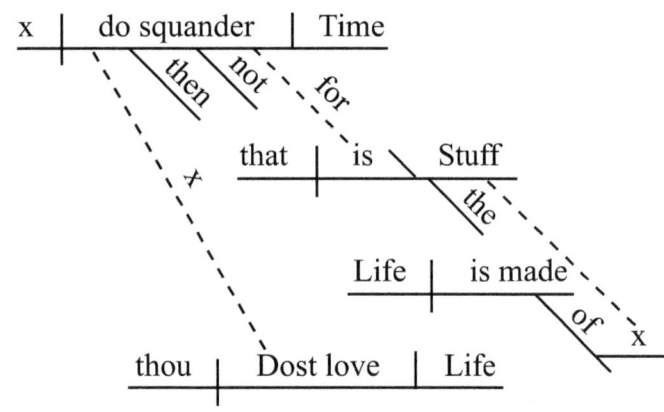

Dost thou love Life is a **conditional clause**; the first *x* in the diagram stands for an unexpressed *if*. *For* can be **a coordinating or a subordinating conjunction**, coordinating if the *for*-clause is equal in importance to the main clause, and subordinating if the *for*-clause is of subordinate importance relative to the main clause. In the adjective clause *life is made of*, the relative pronoun *that* (the object of the preposition *of*) is unexpressed and is represented in the diagram by a second *x*. The antecedent of the relative pronoun is the predicate nominative *Stuff*.

27, 2.

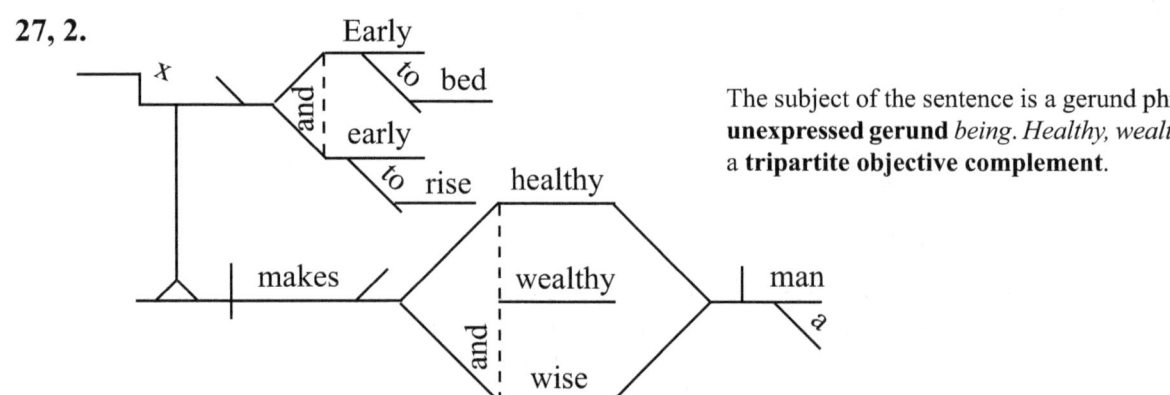

The subject of the sentence is a gerund phrase introduced by the **unexpressed gerund** *being*. *Healthy, wealthy, and wise* constitute a **tripartite objective complement**.

27, 3.

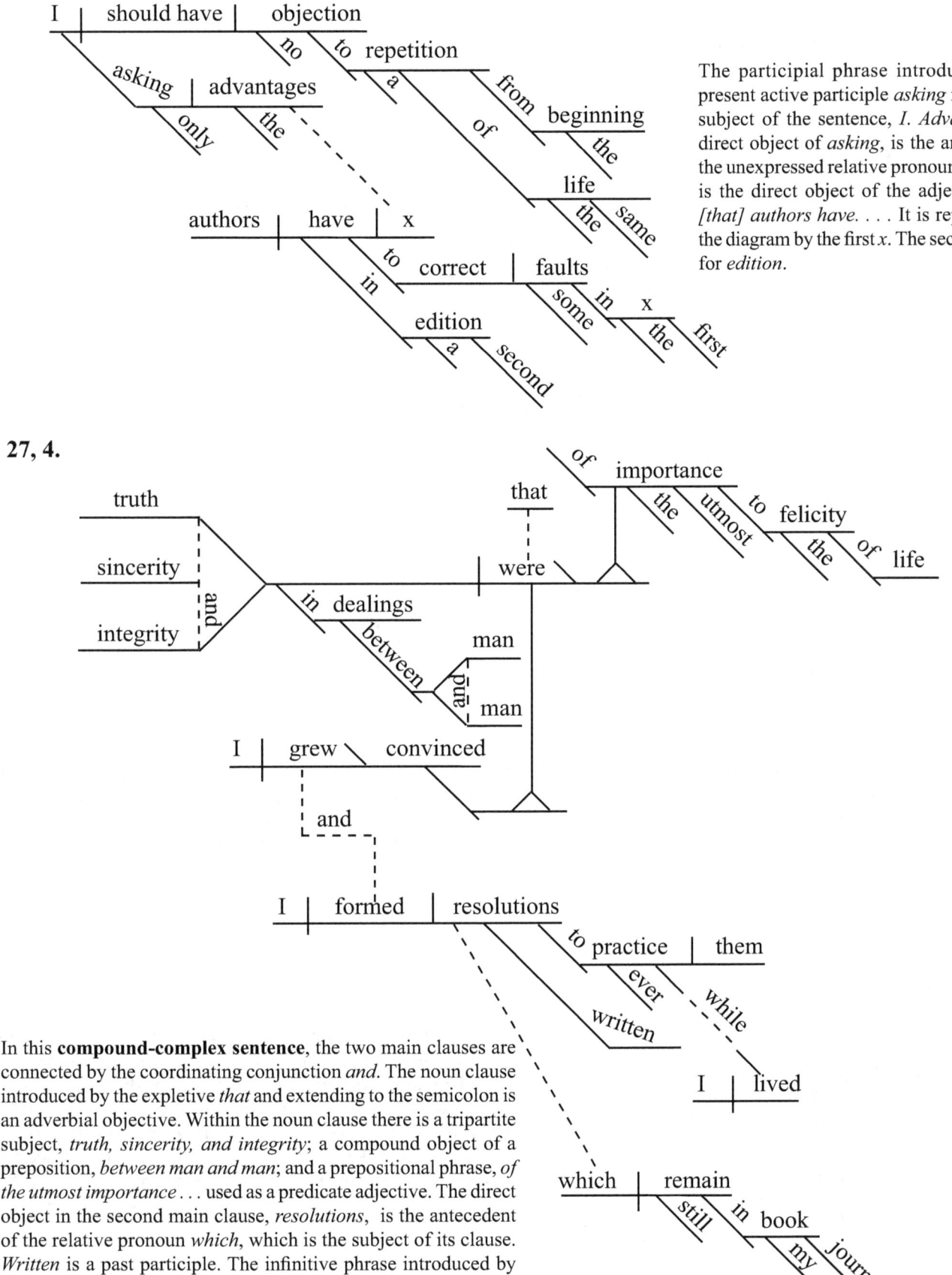

The participial phrase introduced by the present active participle *asking* modifies the subject of the sentence, *I*. *Advantages*, the direct object of *asking*, is the antecedent of the unexpressed relative pronoun *that*, which is the direct object of the adjective clause *[that] authors have*. . . . It is represented in the diagram by the first *x*. The second *x* stands for *edition*.

27, 4.

In this **compound-complex sentence**, the two main clauses are connected by the coordinating conjunction *and*. The noun clause introduced by the expletive *that* and extending to the semicolon is an adverbial objective. Within the noun clause there is a tripartite subject, *truth, sincerity, and integrity*; a compound object of a preposition, *between man and man*; and a prepositional phrase, *of the utmost importance*. . . used as a predicate adjective. The direct object in the second main clause, *resolutions*, is the antecedent of the relative pronoun *which*, which is the subject of its clause. *Written* is a past participle. The infinitive phrase introduced by the infinitive *to practice* modifies *resolutions*. *While I lived* is an adverb clause; *while* is a relative adverb.

27, 5.

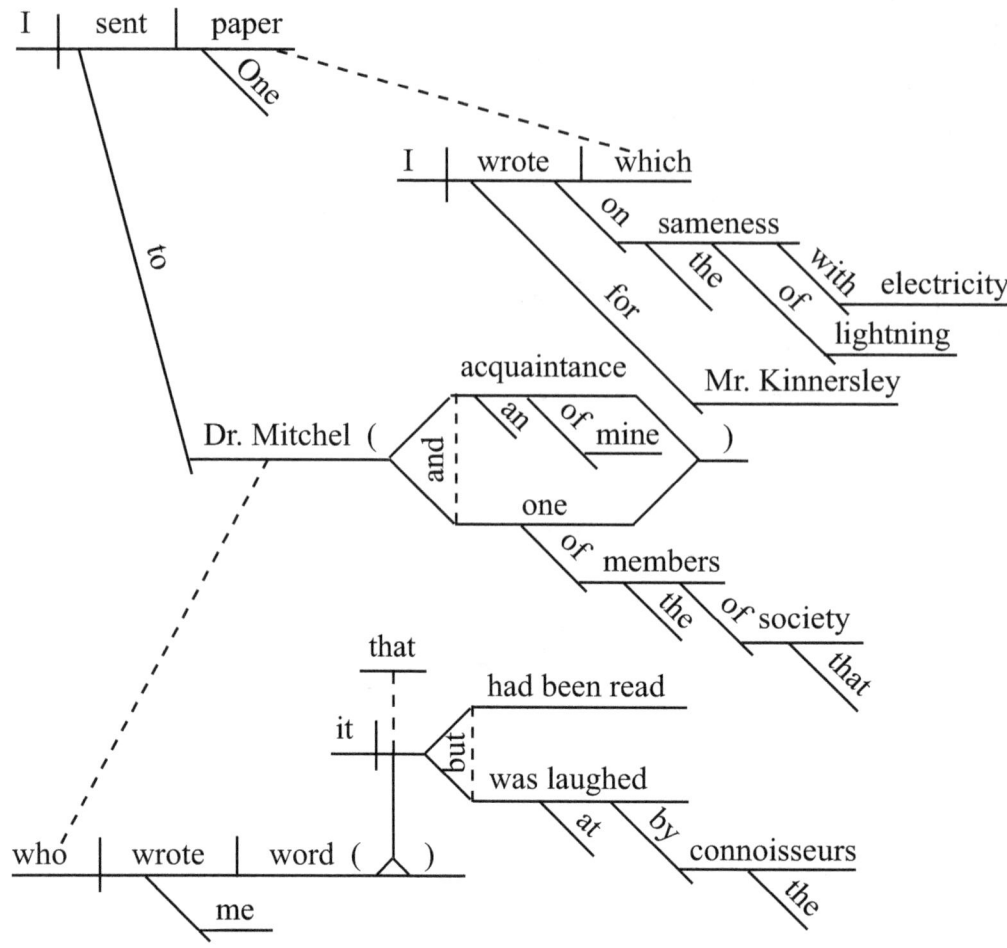

Which and *who* are relative pronouns; their antecedents are *paper* and *Dr. Mitchel*, respectively. *An acquaintance of mine and one of the members of that society* is a compound appositive. The noun clause introduced by the expletive *that* is also an appositive; it is in apposition with the noun *word*. This noun clause has a compound predicate; the coordinating conjunction is *but*. The word *at*, a **preposition** in the sentence *They laughed at it*, becomes an **adverb** when the object of the preposition, *it*, becomes the subject of an equivalent sentence in the passive voice.

28, 1.

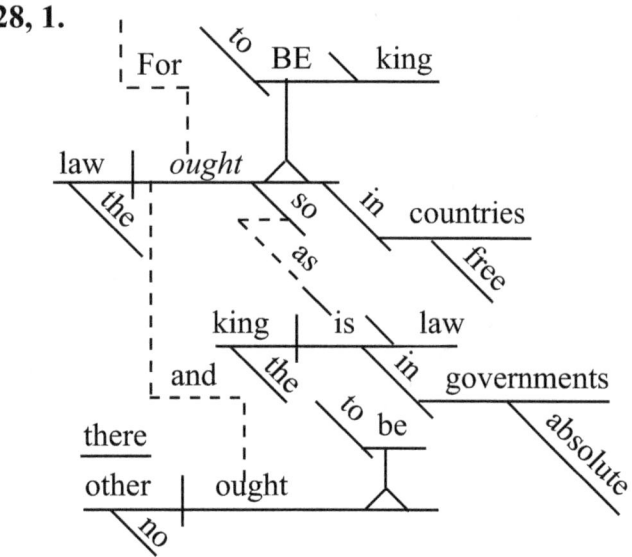

The coordinating conjunction *for* connects this sentence to the previous sentence. The infinitive *to be* is used twice as a **complementary infinitive** following the verb *ought*. *As* is a relative adverb (*so as* is equivalent to *in the manner in which*). The coordinating conjunction *and* joins two main clauses. *There* is an expletive; it does not affect the meaning of the sentence but announces that the subject will follow the verb.

28, 2.

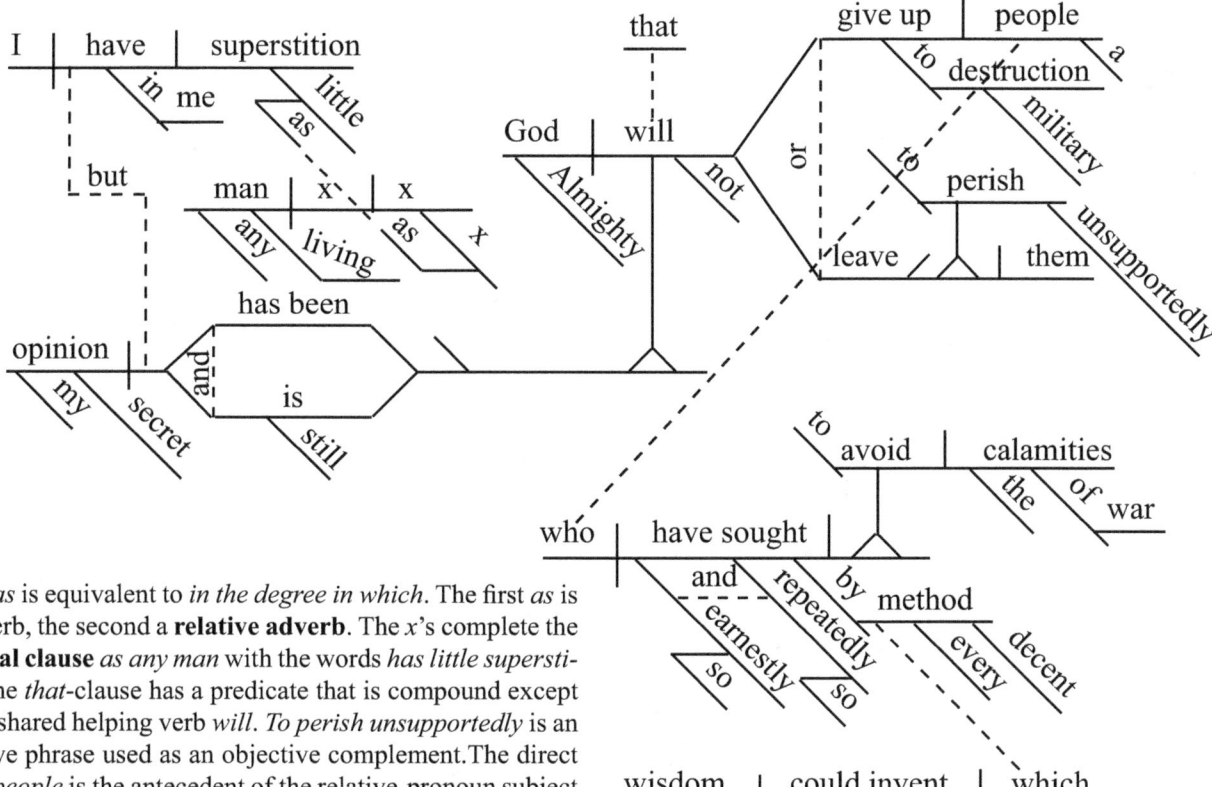

As . . . as is equivalent to *in the degree in which*. The first *as* is an adverb, the second a **relative adverb**. The *x*'s complete the **elliptical clause** *as any man* with the words *has little superstition*. The *that*-clause has a predicate that is compound except for the shared helping verb *will*. *To perish unsupportedly* is an infinitive phrase used as an objective complement. The direct object *people* is the antecedent of the relative-pronoun subject *who*. The direct object of the verb *have sought* is the infinitive phrase *to avoid the calamities of war*. *Method*, the object of the preposition *by*, is the antecedent of the relative pronoun *which*, which is a direct object in its clause.

28, 3.

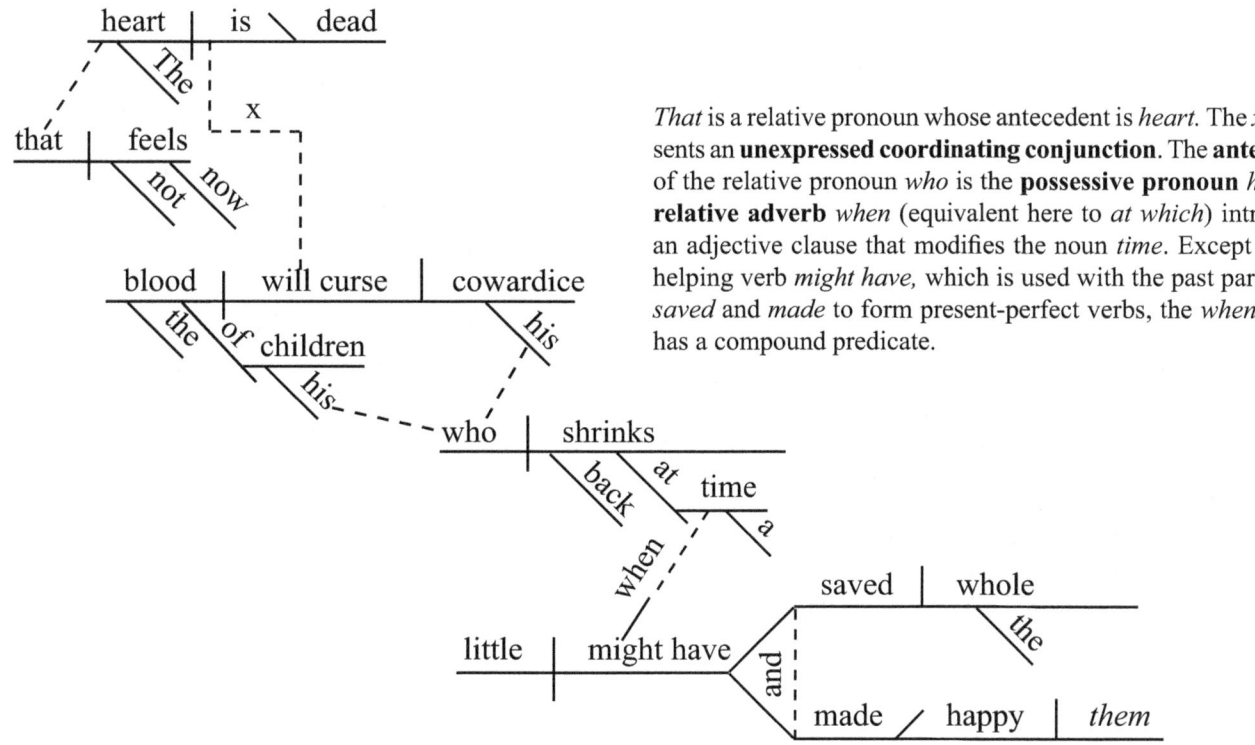

That is a relative pronoun whose antecedent is *heart*. The *x* represents an **unexpressed coordinating conjunction**. The **antecedent** of the relative pronoun *who* is the **possessive pronoun** *his*. The **relative adverb** *when* (equivalent here to *at which*) introduces an adjective clause that modifies the noun *time*. Except for the helping verb *might have*, which is used with the past participles *saved* and *made* to form present-perfect verbs, the *when*-clause has a compound predicate.

28, 4.

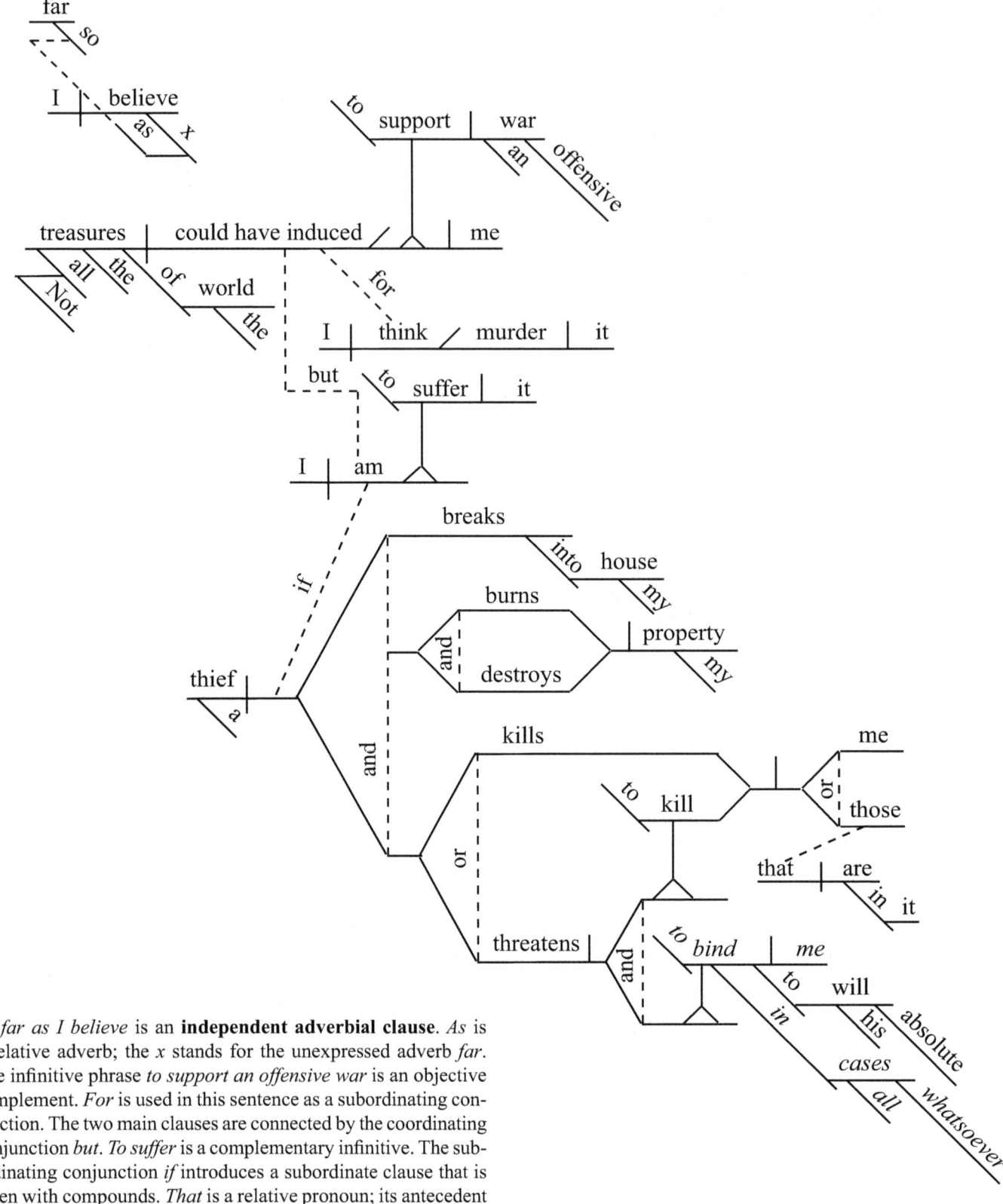

So far as I believe is an **independent adverbial clause**. *As* is a relative adverb; the *x* stands for the unexpressed adverb *far*. The infinitive phrase *to support an offensive war* is an objective complement. *For* is used in this sentence as a subordinating conjunction. The two main clauses are connected by the coordinating conjunction *but*. *To suffer* is a complementary infinitive. The subordinating conjunction *if* introduces a subordinate clause that is laden with compounds. *That* is a relative pronoun; its antecedent is *those*, a demonstrative pronoun.

29, 1.

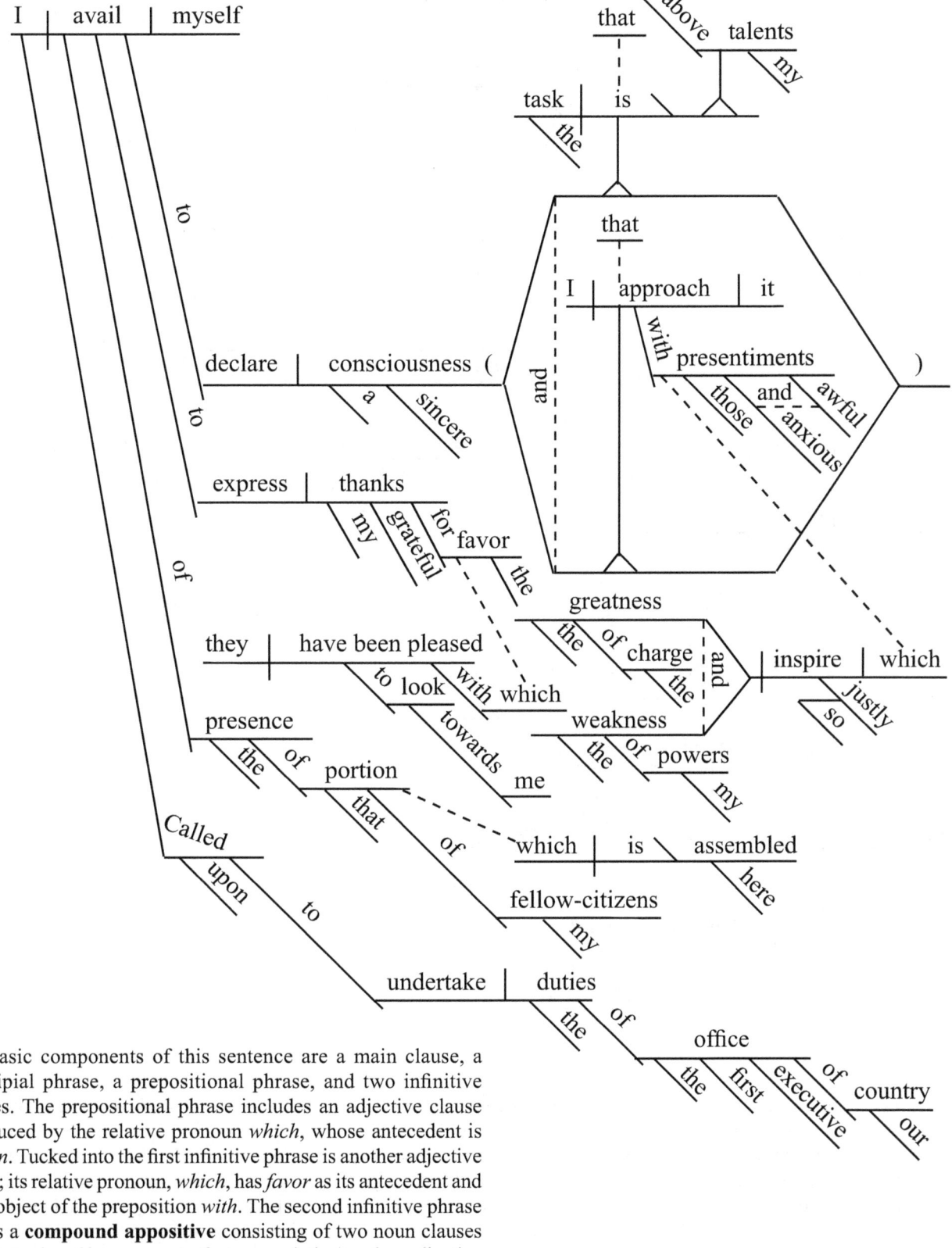

The basic components of this sentence are a main clause, a participial phrase, a prepositional phrase, and two infinitive phrases. The prepositional phrase includes an adjective clause introduced by the relative pronoun *which*, whose antecedent is *portion*. Tucked into the first infinitive phrase is another adjective clause; its relative pronoun, *which*, has *favor* as its antecedent and is the object of the preposition *with*. The second infinitive phrase houses a **compound appositive** consisting of two noun clauses (each introduced by a separate *that*, an expletive) and an adjective clause. The first noun clause includes the prepositional phrase *above my talents* as a predicate adjective. The relative pronoun *which* is a direct object and has *presentiments* as its antecedent.

29, 2.

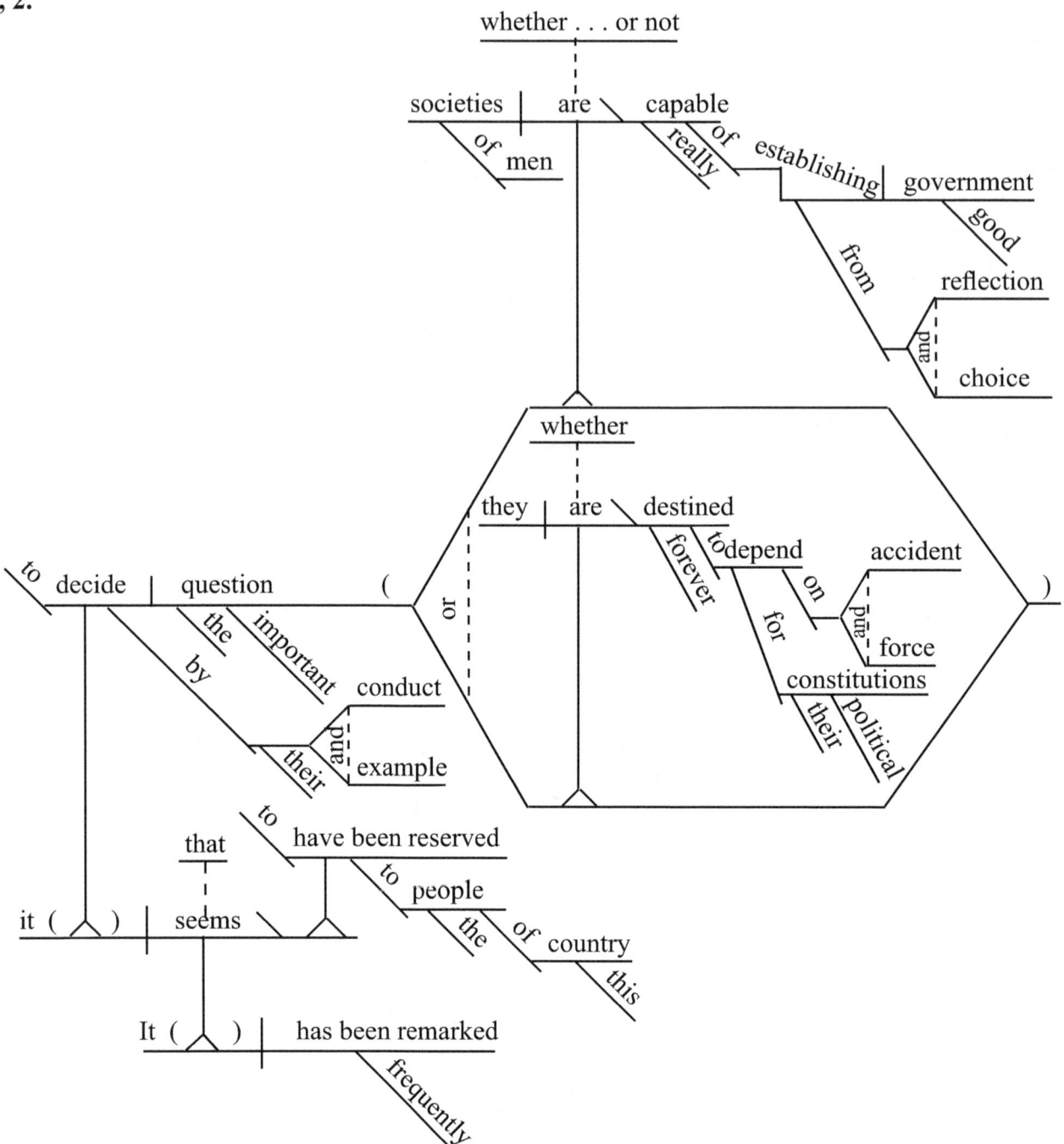

In this appositive-laden sentence, the only words not in **apposition** are the first five: *It has been frequently remarked*. The rest of the sentence is in apposition with the first word of the sentence, *it*; furthermore, everything in the sentence after the seventh word, another *it*, is in apposition with that *it* as well; and, finally, the bulk of the sentence, being in apposition with the word *question*, is in triple apposition. The first appositive is a noun clause introduced by the expletive *that* and containing an infinitive phrase as a predicate adjective; the second is an infinitive phrase; and the third consists of two noun clauses (indirect questions, introduced by the expletives *whether . . . or not* and *whether*, and connected by the coordinating conjunction *or*). The first of these clauses includes a gerund, *establishing*, used as the object of a preposition.

30, 1.

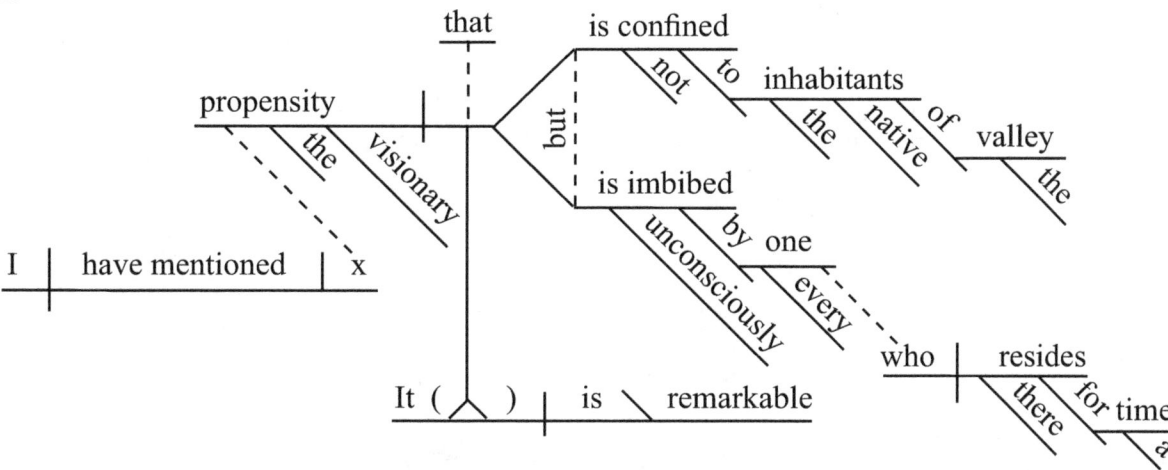

Everything in the sentence after the first three words is in **apposition** with the subject of the sentence, *it*. This appositive is a noun clause with a compound predicate; it is introduced by the expletive *that* and has two adjective clauses dependent on it. The two predicates are connected by the coordinating conjunction *but*. The first relative pronoun, the object of the verb *have mentioned*, is an unexpressed *that*, represented in the diagram by an *x*; its antecedent is *propensity*. The other relative pronoun is *who*, the subject of its clause; its antecedent is *one* (Washington Irving wrote *everyone* as two words).

30, 2.

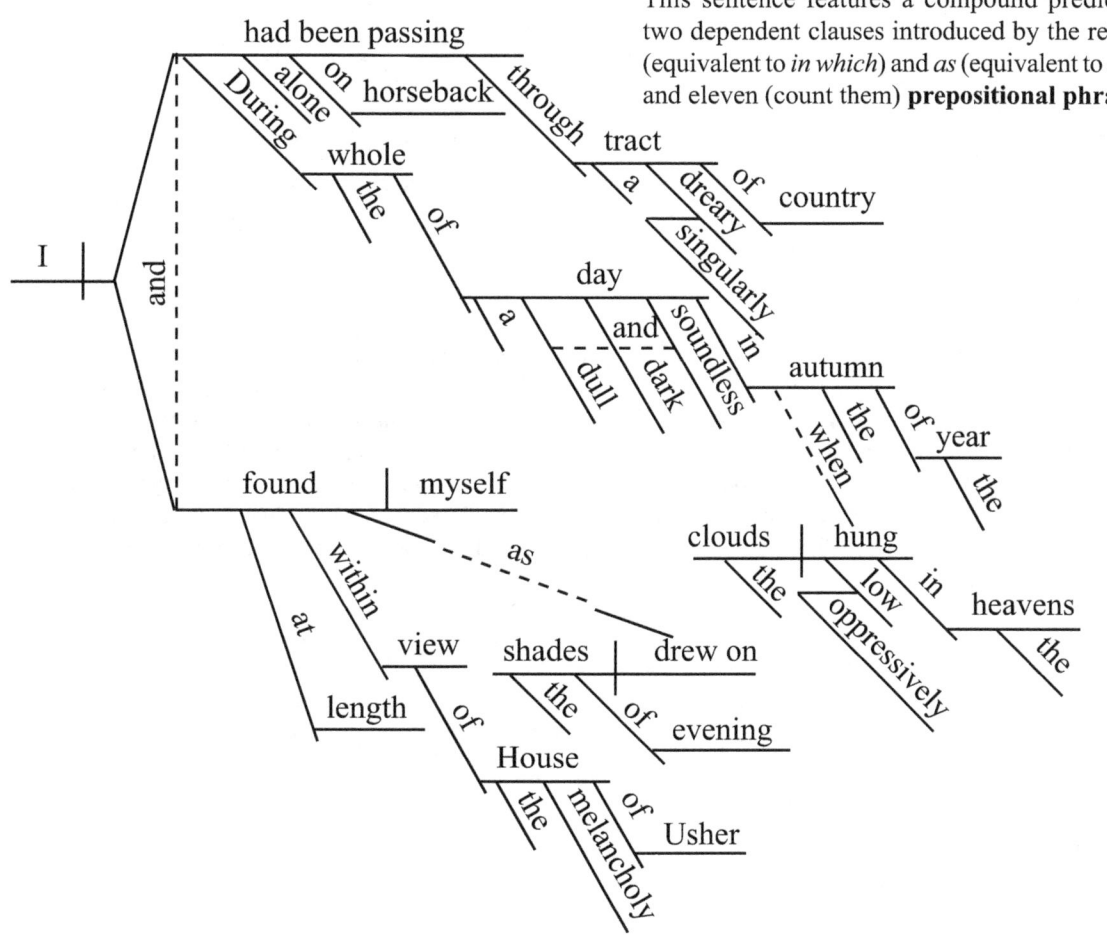

This sentence features a compound predicate joined by *and*, two dependent clauses introduced by the relative adverbs *when* (equivalent to *in which*) and *as* (equivalent to *at the time at which*), and eleven (count them) **prepositional phrases**.

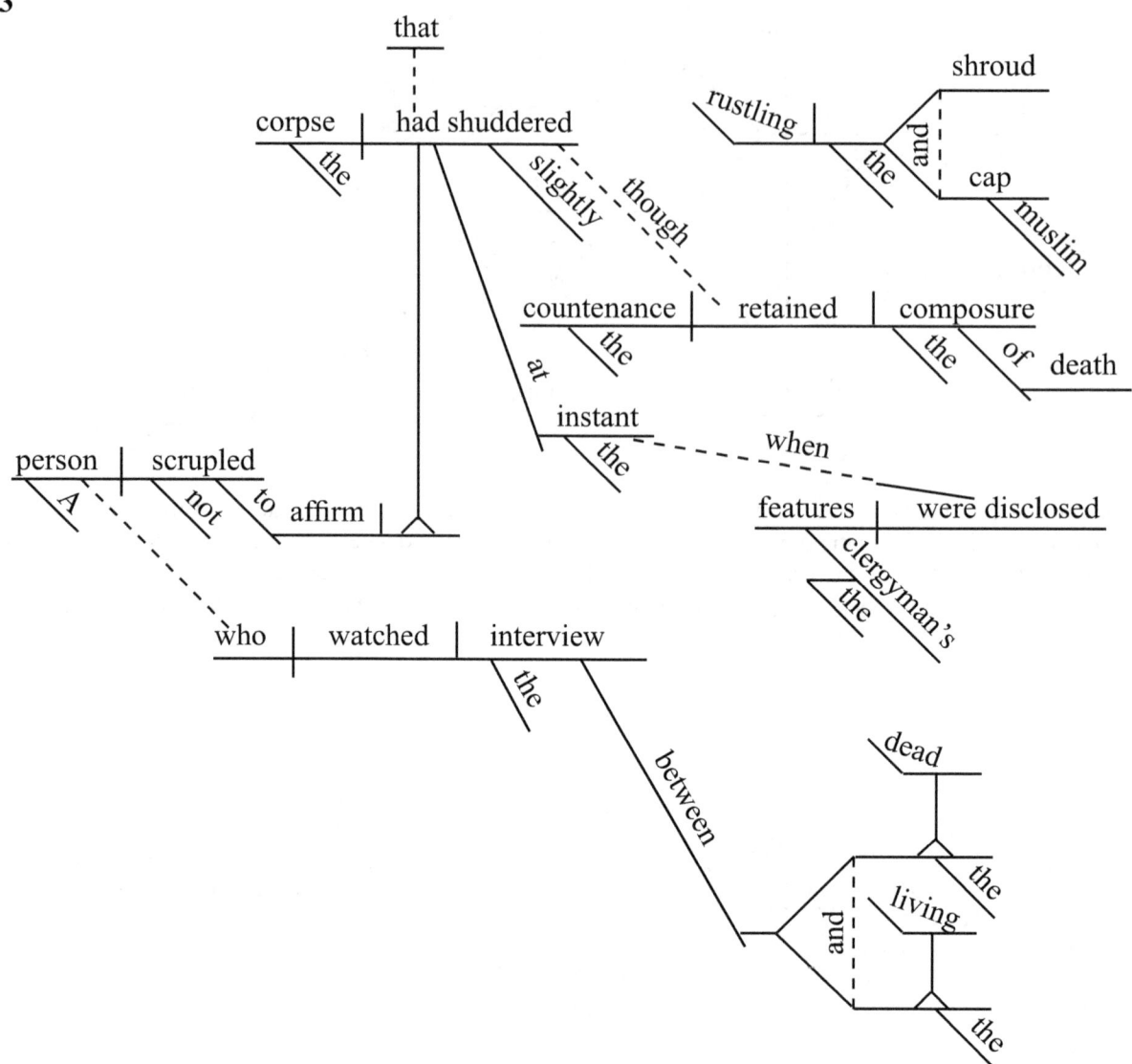

Rustling, dead, and *living* are participles (present active, past, and present active, respectively). *Dead* and *living* function as nouns, while *rustling* introduces a participial phrase, *rustling the shroud and muslim cap*. Whereas most participles and participial phrases modify nouns and pronouns, this phrase **modifies a clause**, *the corpse had slightly shuddered*. One of the ways of diagramming such a modifier is simply to place it next to the modified clause. Additional features of this sentence include a noun clause, two adjective clauses, and an adverb clause. The noun clause is introduced by the expletive *that* and serves as the direct object of the infinitive *to affirm*. One of the adjective clauses is introduced by the relative pronoun *who*; the other is introduced by the relative adverb *when* (equivalent to *at which*) and modifies *instant*. The adverb clause is introduced by the subordinating conjunction *though*.

~ Additional Sentences and Solutions ~

1. The fifteen-year-old twins John and Susan have a younger brother.
2. Their brother's name is Alan.
3. He is twelve years old.
4. Alan not only enjoys reading books, but he also likes to study.
5. Hoping to buy Alan a book, Susan goes into a large bookstore, where there are many books of all kinds.
6. Although she finds the right book, she discovers that she has no money.
7. Then she sees John, who lends her the money that she needs.
8. Susan calls John a lifesaver.
9. It is hard to shop without money, checks, or credit cards.
10. Would you like to be able to buy whatever you want?

11. Allison, a high-school junior, hopes to become the proud owner of a car soon.
12. She wonders if she can afford the insurance and gasoline.
13. "I could do it," she tells Sarah, "if I worked evenings and weekends."
14. "When would you have time to study?" asks Sarah.
15. "However important a car may be, grades are more important."
16. "In other words, being successful in school is more important than owning a car."
17. "There is no doubt about that; nevertheless, it is hard to give up a dream."
18. "Instead of giving up your dream, postpone it, which is what people do all the time."
19. "Holy cow, Sarah, you sound like my mother."
20. "I try to be as helpful as I can, even if my advice is perceived as motherly."

21. Although exciting, the play was different from anything we had imagined.
22. It's understandable that it had the theatergoers scratching their heads as they left the theater.
23. In the play, Stone-Age cavemen live in modern houses, wear modern clothes, and drive modern vehicles.
24. Gradually the audience becomes aware that these modern cavemen still have primitive minds and instincts.
25. For them to function in our society, our society has to be ready to change its rules.
26. A might-makes-right ethic must replace rule by laws based on the rights of each individual.
27. Amazingly, this happens, and the cavemen are given the license to which they are accustomed.
28. When they want something, they take it; as the cavemen go, so goes society.
29. The shocker is that, if one substitutes *powerful* for *primitive*, the new society dominated by cavemen is (*mutatis mutandis*) our twenty-first century society.
30. "The more things change, the more they stay the same."

1.

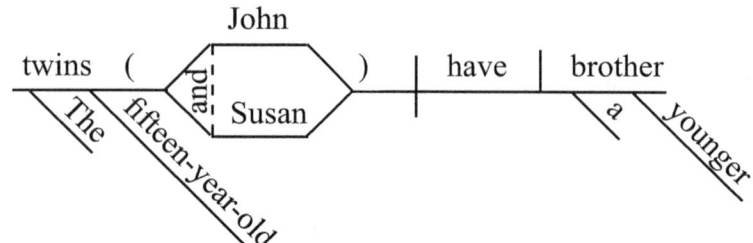

The **compound appositive** *John and Susan* is in apposition with the subject of the sentence, *twins*. *Brother* is a direct object. *Twins* is modified by the definite article, *the*, and the hyphenated adjective *fifteen-year-old*. *Brother* is modified by the indefinite article *a* and the adjective *younger*.

2.

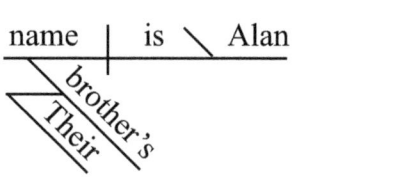

The subject of the sentence, *name*, is modified by the **possessive noun** *brother's*, which in turn is modified by the **possessive pronoun** *their*. *Alan* is a predicate nominative.

3.

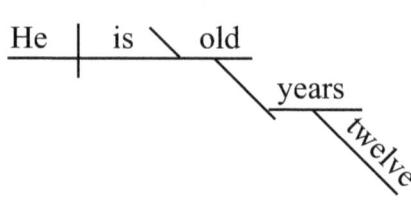

The predicate adjective *old* is modified by the **adverbial objective** *years*.

4.

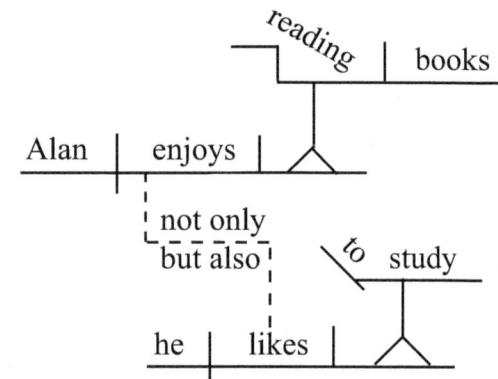

The two main clauses of this **compound sentence** are joined by the correlative conjunctions *not only . . . but also*. *Reading* is a **gerund**, and *books* is its direct object. The **gerund phrase** *reading books* functions as the direct object of the verb *enjoys*. The **infinitive** *to study* is the direct object of the verb *likes*.

5.

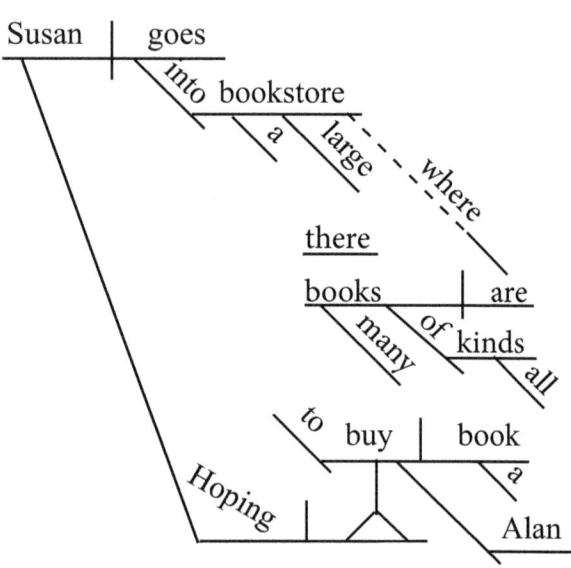

The **participial phrase** *hoping to buy Alan a book* modifies the subject of the sentence, *Susan*. The present active participle *hoping* has the **infinitive phrase** *to buy Alan a book* as its direct object. *Alan* is an indirect object. The **relative adeverb** *where* (equivalent to *at which*) introduces an **adjective clause**. *There* is an expletive.

6.

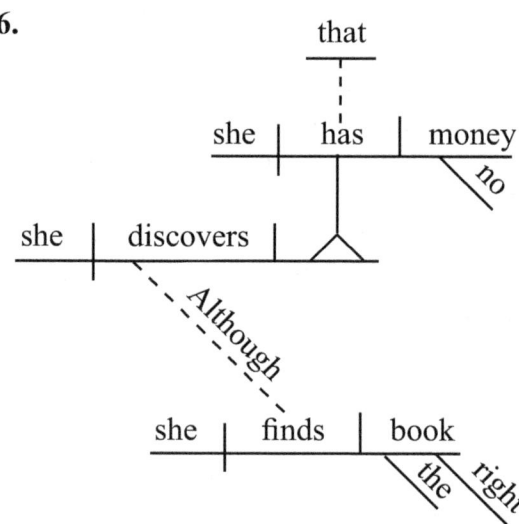

Although she finds the right book is a **subordinate (dependent) clause**; *although* is a **subordinating conjunction**. The **noun clause** *that she has no money* is used as a direct object. *That* is an **expletive**.

~ 258 ~

7.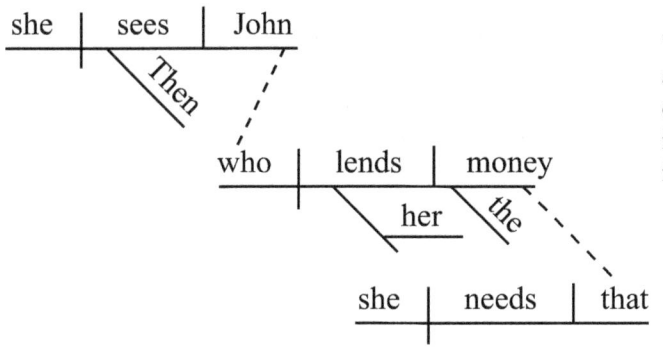

This sentence has two **adjective clauses**, *who lends her the money* and *that she needs*. The **relative pronoun** *who* is the subject of its clause, while the relative pronoun *that* is used as a direct object in its clause. The **antecedent** of *who* is *John*; the antecedent of *that* is *money*. *Then* is an adverb. *Her* is an **indirect object**.

8.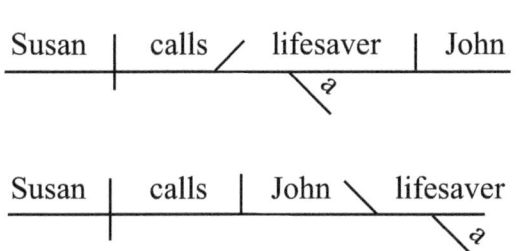

Lifesaver is an **objective complement**. In sentence diagrams, some authorities place the objective complement, preceded by a slash, before the direct object; others place it, with a backslash, after the direct object.

9.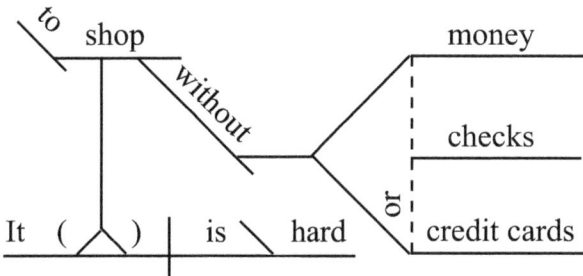

The **infinitive phrase** *to shop without money, checks, or credit cards* is in **apposition** with the subject *it*. *Money, checks, or credit cards* is the **tripartite object of the preposition** *without*. *Hard* is a **predicate adjective**. *Credit cards* is a **phrasal noun**.

10.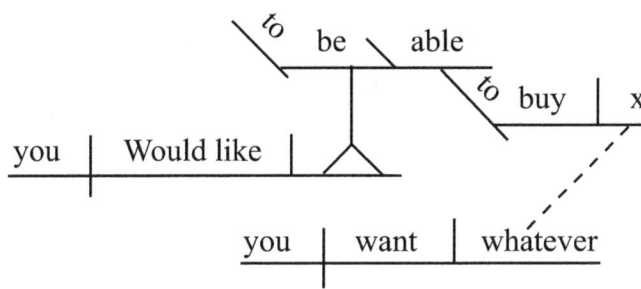

The infinitive phrase introduced by the infinitive *to be* (and, with its modifiers, extending to the end of the sentence) functions as the direct object of the verb *would like*. A second infinitive phrase, introduced by the infinitive *to buy*, is an adverbial modifier of the predicate adjective *able*. In the **adjective clause** *whatever you want*, the **indefinite relative pronoun** *whatever* is a direct object; its **antecedent** is the unexpressed (and unexpressible) direct object of *buy*.

11.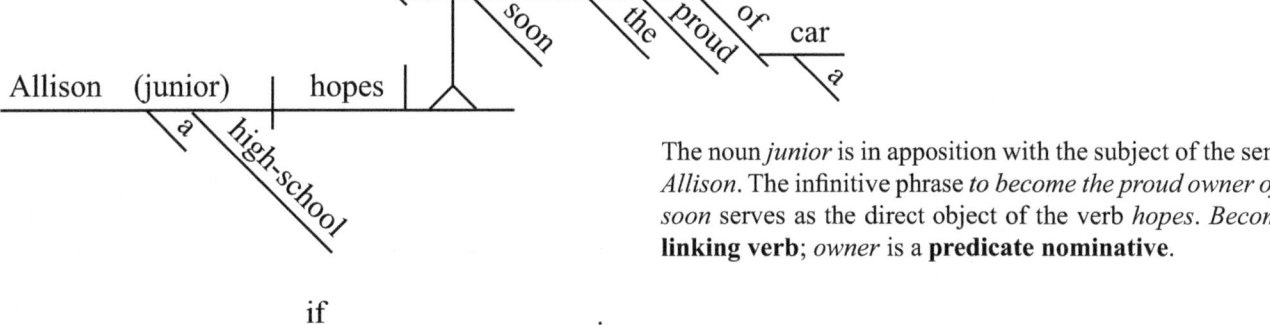

The noun *junior* is in apposition with the subject of the sentence, *Allison*. The infinitive phrase *to become the proud owner of a car soon* serves as the direct object of the verb *hopes*. *Become* is a **linking verb**; *owner* is a **predicate nominative**.

12.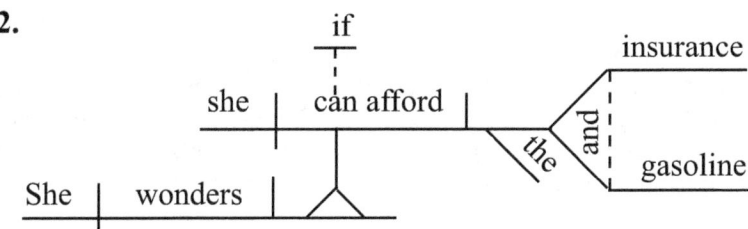

The direct object of the verb *wonders* is the **noun clause** *if she can afford the insurance and gasoline*, which is an **indirect question**. In this sentence, *if* is an **expletive**. *The* modifies both *insurance* and *gasoline*.

13.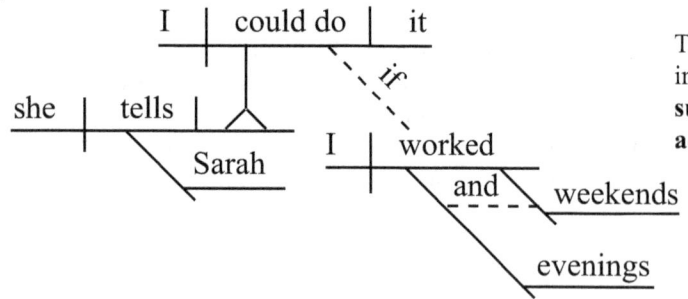

The **quotation** is the direct object of the verb *tells*. *Sarah* is an indirect object. The **subordinating conjunction** *if* introduces a **subordinate (dependent) clause**. *Evenings* and *weekends* are **adverbial objectives**.

14.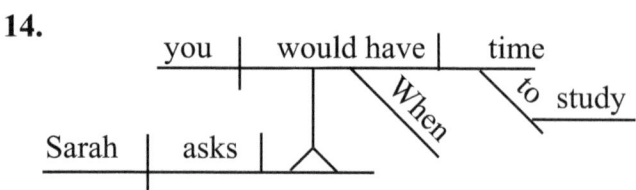

The quotation is the direct object of the verb *asks*. *When* is an **interrogative adverb**. The infinitive *to study* is used here adjectivally, as a modifier of the noun *time*.

15.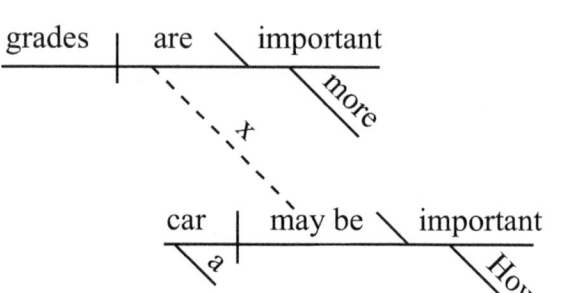

16.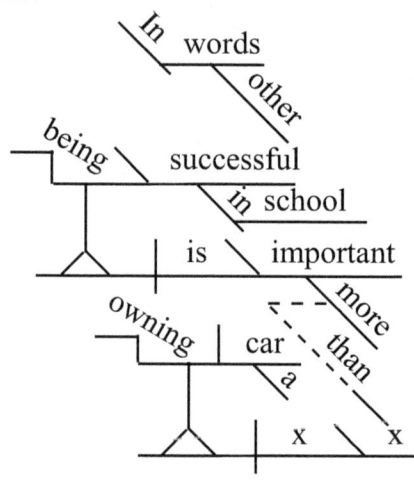

In this sentence, *however* is an **indefinite adverb** used to introduced a **concessive clause**. The **unexpressed subordinating conjunction** *although* is represented in the diagram by an *x*. *Are* and *may be* are linking verbs; *important* is a **predicate adjective** in both clauses.

In other words is an **independent prepositional phrase**. *Being* and *owning* are **gerunds**. Both **gerund phrases** function as subjects. The subordinate clause introduced by the **relative adverb** *than* is **elliptical**; the **unexpressed words** are *is important*.

17.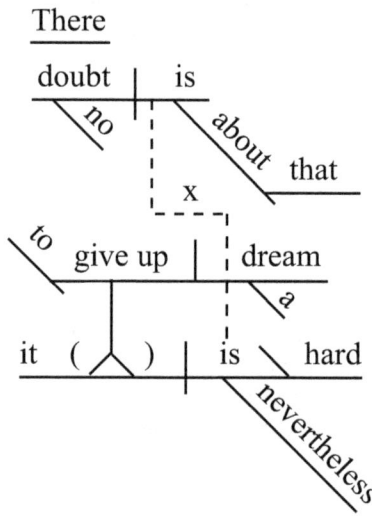

18.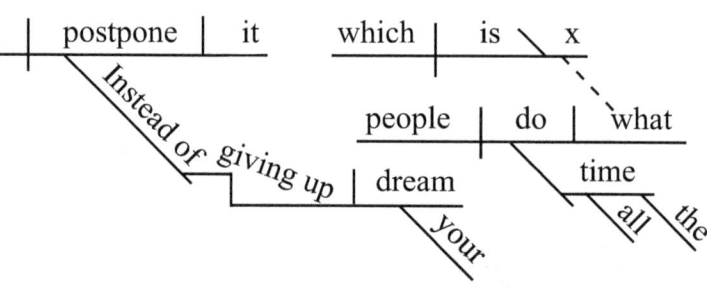

There is an **expletive**. The infinitive phrase *to give up a dream* is in apposition with *it*, the subject of the sentence. *Give up* is a **phrasal verb**. The *x* in the diagram represents an **unexpressed coordinating conjunction**. ***Nevertheless*** is a **transitional adverb**.

In the diagram, the first *x* represents the **unexpressed subject** *you*. The gerund phrase *giving up your dream* is the object of the phrasal preposition *instead of*. The **adjective clause** introduced by the **relative pronoun** *which* is a **sentence modifier**. In diagramming an adjective clause of this kind, one does not draw a connecting line between the relative pronoun and its antecedent, because the latter is a clause, not a particular word. In the other adjective clause, the antecedent of the **indefinite relative pronoun** *what* is an **unexpressed predicate nominative**; this antecedent is represented by the second x in the diagram.

19.

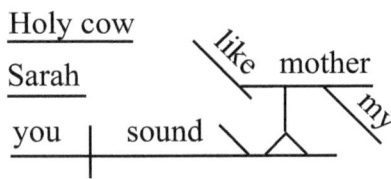

Holy cow is an interjection. *Sarah* is a vocative, i.e., a noun of direct address. In this sentence, *sound* is a linking verb. The prepositional phrase *like my mother* functions as a predicate adjective.

20.

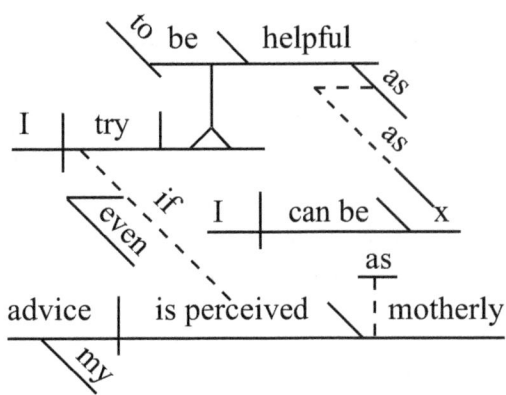

In the **correlative expression** *as . . . as*, the first *as* is an ordinary adverb, the second a *relative adverb*. The infinitive phrase introduced by the infinitive *to be* is used as a direct object. The **subordinating conjunction** *if*, **modified by the adverb** *even*, introduces a subordinate clause. The *x* in the diagram represents the **unexpressed predicate adjective** *helpful* that completes the **elliptical clause** *as I can be*. The final *as* is an expletive.

21.

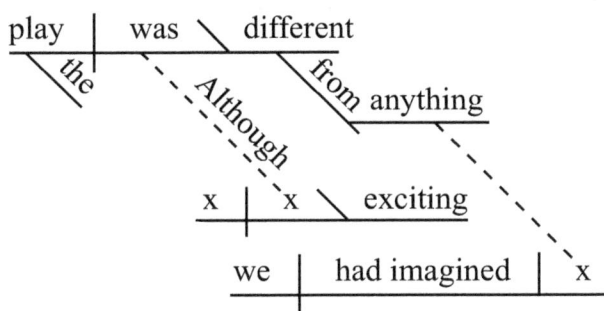

Although exciting is an **elliptical subordinate clause**; the words *it was* are unexpressed. *We had imagined* is an adjective clause from which the relative pronoun *that*, a direct object, has been omitted. The omission of a relative pronoun occurs only in **restrictive adjective clauses** and involves only objects, never subjects.

22.

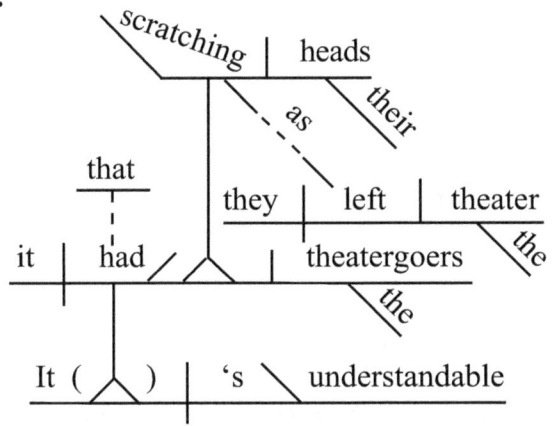

The **noun clause** that begins with the expletive *that* is in **apposition** with the subject of the sentence, *it*. **Contractions** involving a subject and a verb are separated in sentence diagrams; thus *it* is separated from *'s*. *Scratching* is a present active participle. The **participial phrase** *scratching their heads* functions as an objective complement. *As they left the theater* is a subordinate clause. *As*, equivalent to *at the time at which*, is a relative adverb.

23.

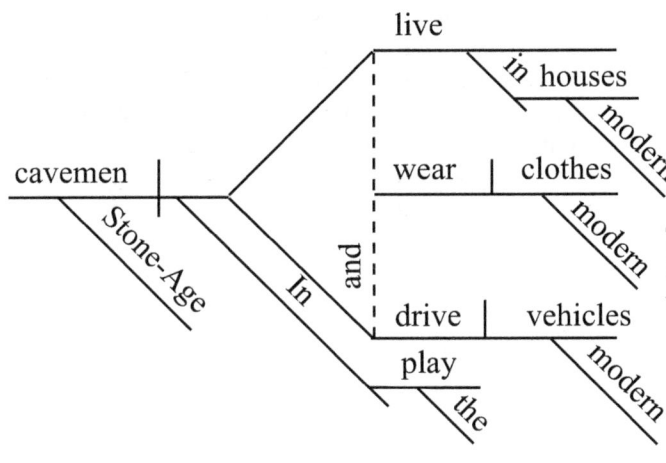

This sentence has a **tripartite predicate**. The prepositional phrase *in the play* modifies all three verbs and must, therefore, be attached to the part of the base line shared by all three.

24.

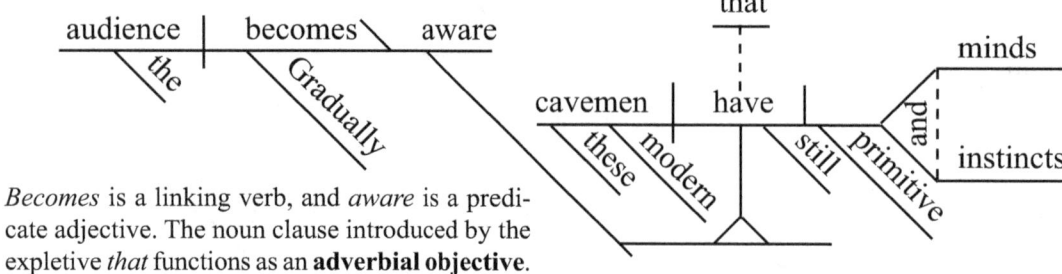

Becomes is a linking verb, and *aware* is a predicate adjective. The noun clause introduced by the expletive *that* functions as an **adverbial objective**.

25.

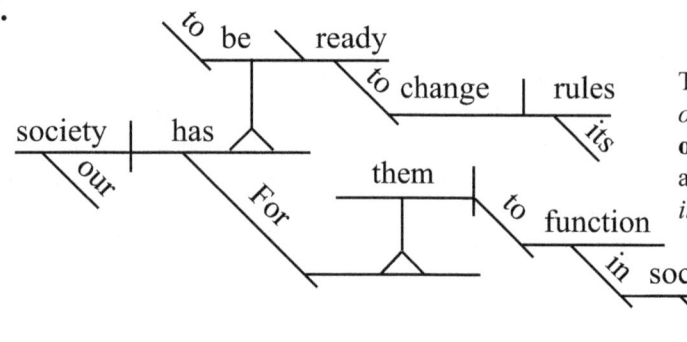

The object of the preposition *for* is the phrase *them to function in our society*, in which the objective-case *them* acts as the **subject of the infinitive** *to function*. *To be* is a **complementary infinitive**, and *ready* is a predicate adjective. The infinitive phrase *to change its rules* modifies *ready*.

26.

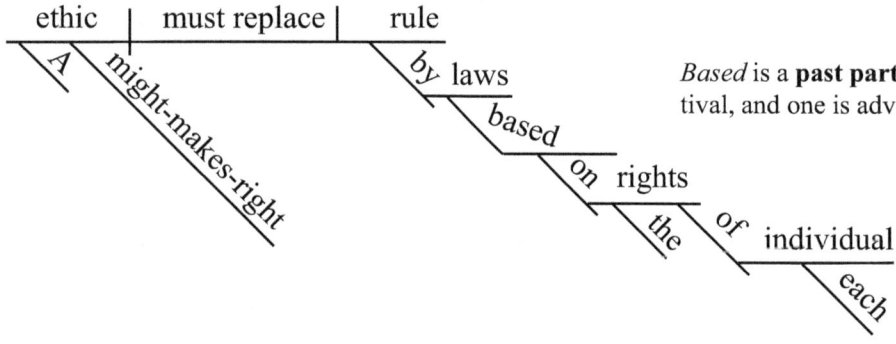

Based is a **past participle**. Two prepositional phrases are adjectival, and one is adverbial.

27.

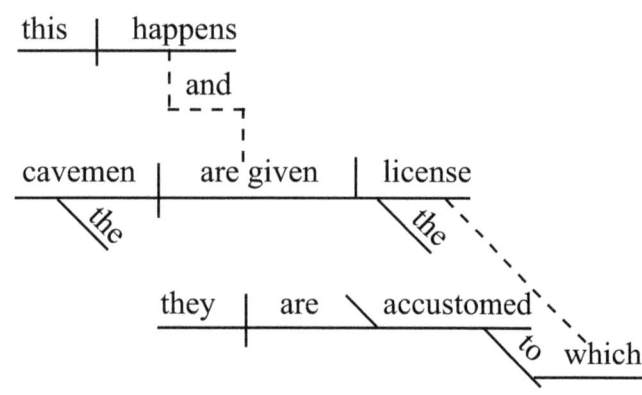

Amazingly (i.e., *to our amazement* or *it is amazing that*) is an **independent adverb**. If it modified *happens*, the meaning would be *this happens in an amazing way*. *License* is a **retained object**. *Accustomed* is neither a **participle** nor the participial component of a passive-voice form. If it were the former, it could not be replaced by the simple adjective *used*; if it were the latter, the meaning would be that the cavemen are being accustomed to the license, which would distort the obvious meaning of the sentence. It is an **ordinary adjective** used as a predicate adjective.

28.

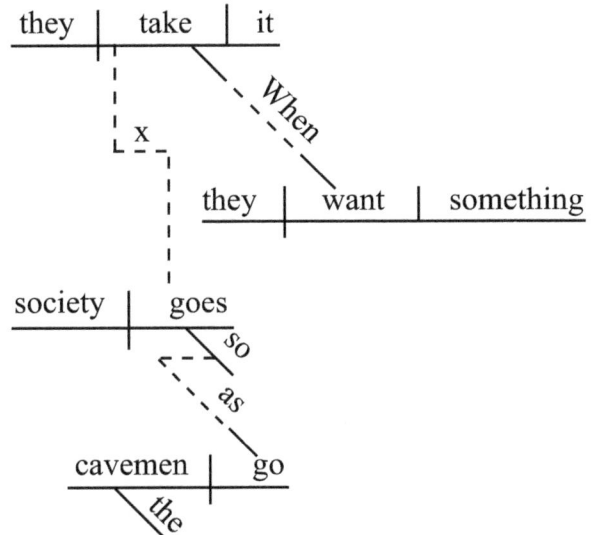

When (*at the time at which*) is a relative adverb. The *x* in the diagram represents an unexpressed coordinating conjunction. In the **correlative expression** *so . . . as* (*in the way in which*), *so* is an ordinary adverb and *as* is a relative adverb.

29.

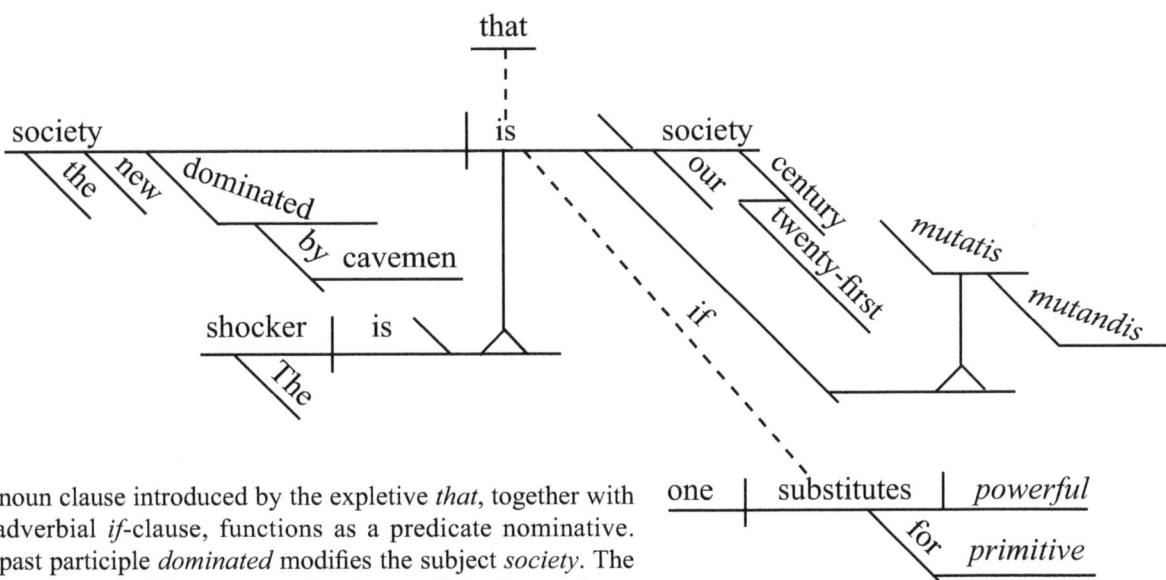

The noun clause introduced by the expletive *that*, together with the adverbial *if*-clause, functions as a predicate nominative. The past participle *dominated* modifies the subject *society*. The **noun** *century*, used here **as an adjective**, modifies the predicate nominative *society*; the adjective *twenty-first* modifies *century*. Although *powerful* and *primitive* are normally adjectives, they function here as nouns; they are words used *as* words.

Mutatis mutandis (meaning: *when those things have been changed that must be changed*) is a Latin ablative absolute. *Mutatis* is a perfect passive participle that functions here as a noun (an adverbial objective); *mutandis* is a future passive participle, a form that English lacks.

30.

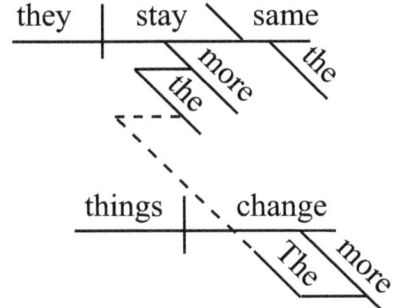

The **correlative expression** *the . . . the* is equivalent to *in the degree in which*. *The*, the first word of the sentence, is a relative adverb; the other *the* is an ordinary adverb.

~ 263 ~

~ Grammatical Terms and Diagramming Symbols ~

Active voice - a characteristic of **transitive verbs** that indicates the relationship of the verb to the subject as doer or performer. A transitive verb is in the active voice when the subject of the sentence is the agent, i.e., when the subject is doing something.

Adjective clause - a clause that functions as an adjective by modifying (qualifying, describing, limiting) a noun, pronoun, or equivalent expression. There are two types of adjective clauses: 1) clauses containing a **relative pronoun** and 2) clauses linked to nouns in other clauses by means of a **relative adverb**.

Adjective - a word that modifies (qualifies, describes, limits) a noun, pronoun, or equivalent expression. One differentiates between **attributive adjectives** and **predicate adjectives** according to their position relative to the modified nouns and pronouns

Adverb - a word that modifies verbs, adjectives, and other adverbs, as well as prepositions, prepositional phrases, conjunctions, clauses, and sentences

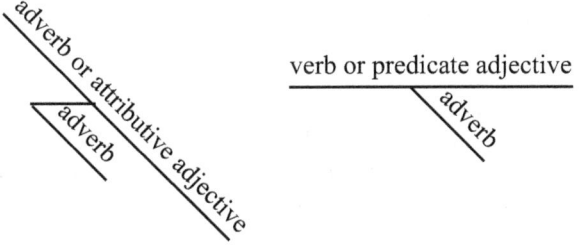

Adverbial objective - a noun or pronoun used as an adverb (indirect objects are included among adverbial objectives)

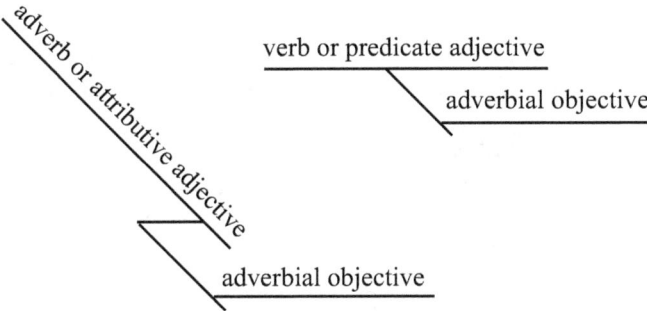

Antecedent - a word, phrase, or clause to which a pronoun refers (for which a pronoun stands)

Appositive - a word or group of words whose purpose is to identify or explain another word or group of words in the same sentence. The appositive usually follows the word(s) with which it is in apposition. Appositives can be **restrictive** or **non-restrictive**. An example of a restrictive appositive is the word *John* in *his brother John* (he has more than one brother; no comma is used between *brother* and *John*); on the other hand, *John* is a non-restrictive appositive in *his brother, John* (John is his only brother; a comma separates the two nouns).

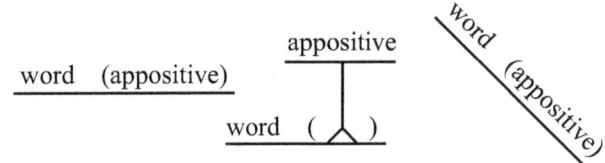

Article - definite (*the*) and indefinite (*a, an*)

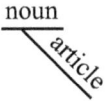

Attributive adjective - an adjective that either precedes the noun or pronoun it modifies (*a pleasant evening, a certain someone*) or comes immediately after it (e.g., *there will be time enough for that tomorrow* or *let's do something different*)

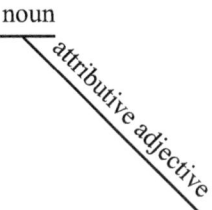

Auxiliary verb - a **helping verb**. Auxiliary verbs help to form such things as tense, voice, emphasis, and mood. They are underlined in the following examples: the present progressive *am seeing, are seeing,* and *is seeing*; the emphatic *do see* and *did see*; the perfect tenses *has seen, had seen,* and *will have seen*; the future *will see* and *shall see,* the passive *is seen, was seen, will be seen,* etc.; and the modal forms *must see, can see, may see,* etc.

Clause - a group of words with a **subject** and **predicate**

Comparative degree - forms of adjectives and adverbs with the suffix *-(e)r* or with a preceding *more*, e.g., *larger, more beautiful, faster, more abundantly*; also *worse*. Comparisons using the comparative degree and the relative adverb *than* are called **unequal comparisons**.

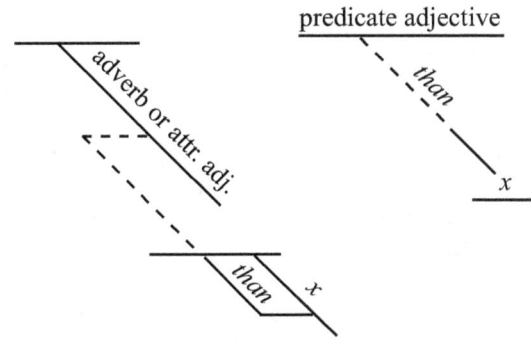

Complement - a term that includes **subjective complement** (predicate nominative and predicate adjective), **direct object**, **indirect object**, **objective complement** and **retained object**

Complementary infinitive - an infinitive used to complete certain verbs. The complementary infinitives are underlined in the following examples: *they ought to study, she used to collect stamps, I have to prepare a speech, he is going to announce the winners, you are to travel to London.*

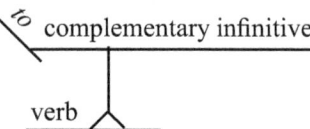

Complex sentence - a sentence containing at least one **dependent (subordinate) clause**

Compound sentence - a sentence containing at least two **independent (main) clauses**

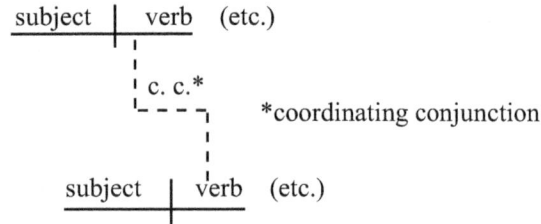

Compound-complex sentence - a sentence containing two or more **independent (main) clauses** and at least one **dependent (subordinate) clause**

Conjunction - a word that connects words, phrases, and clauses. One distinguishes two kinds of conjunctions: **coordinating conjunctions** and **subordinating conjunctions**.

Conjunctive adverb - a word that, like a conjunction, connects and, like an adverb, modifies. There are two kinds of conjunctive adverbs: **transitional adverbs** (*however, moreover, therefore*, etc.) and **relative adverbs** (*when, while, where*, etc.).

Coordinating conjunction - a word that connects words, phrases, and clauses of equal importance. The principal coordinating conjunctions are *and, or, but,* and *nor.* See **compound sentence**.

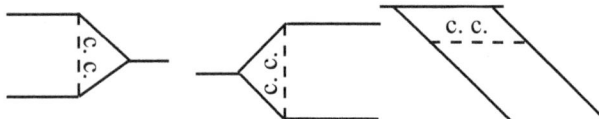

Correlative adverbs - the adverb pairs *as . . . as, so . . . as, so . . . that, then . . . when, there . . . where,* and *the . . . the.* Each of these adverb pairs can be restated as a pair of prepositional phrases, with the second of the two containing a relative pronoun (thus the second adverb is called a **relative adverb**) and the first containing the **antecedent** (e.g., *as . . . as* can be restated as *in the degree in which*).

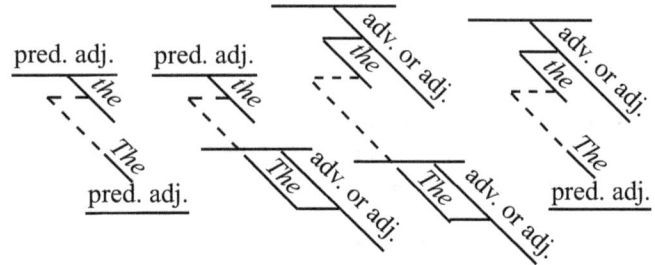

Correlative conjunctions - two-part conjunctions such as *both . . . and, either . . . or,* and *neither . . . nor.*

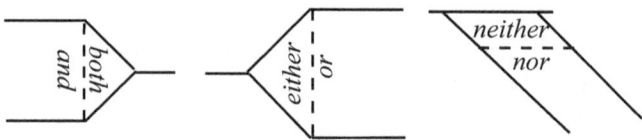

Definite article - English has only one definite article: *the.* It designates the noun it modifies as specific or as previously mentioned.

Demonstrative adjective - *this, that, these, those.* These adjectives are used to point out someone or something.

Demonstrative pronoun - *this, that, these, those.* Like all pronouns, they are used as noun substitutes.

Dependent clause - also called **subordinate clause**. A dependent clause functions as an adverb, an adjective, or a noun; it is dependent upon, or subordinate to, an **independent (main) clause**.

Direct address - a noun or phrase indicating the person(s) spoken to; sometimes called a **vocative**.

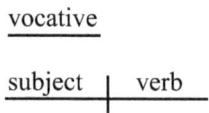

Direct object - a noun, pronoun, or equivalent expression that names the direct recipient of the action of a **transitive verb**. Not all sentences have direct objects. You can identify a direct object by asking *whom?* or *what?* immediately after a non-linking verb. If the sentence provides no answer, it has no direct object.

subject | verb | direct object

Elliptical clause - a clause with an unexpressed, but understood, word or words. In diagrams, *x*'s represent unexpressed words.

Equal comparison - a comparison using the positive degree of the adjective or adverb and the **correlatives** *as . . . as* or *so . . . as.*

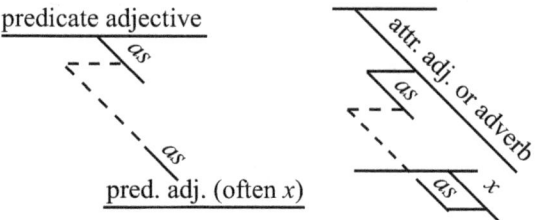

Expletive - a word with a function but with little or no meaning. For example, in the following sentences *there, that,* and *whether* are expletives: *There is a cat on the roof. Did you hear that the game has been canceled? I don't know whether she will be able to attend.*

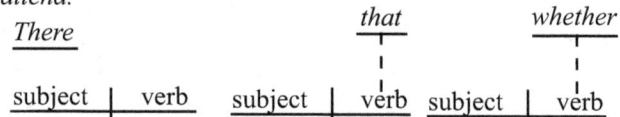

Finite verb - a verb that has person and number. Participles, gerunds, and infinitives are **nonfinite verbs**.

~ 266 ~

Future tense - a tense that is formed by combining the auxiliary verbs *shall* and *will* with the present infinitive (without *to*)

Future-perfect tense - a tense that is formed by combining the auxiliary verbs *shall* and *will* with the present-perfect infinitive (without *to*)

Gerund - a verbal noun; a word ending in *-ing* that is both verb and noun

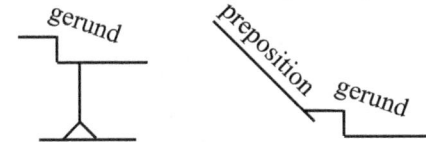

Imperative sentence - a sentence that expresses a command or a request. The subject, *you*, is usually unexpressed.

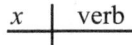

Indefinite article - English has only two forms of the indefinite article: *a* and *an*.

Indefinite pronoun - a word like *each, every, enough, much, any, either*, and *some*

Indefinite relative pronoun - *whoever, whomever, whosever, whichever*, and *whatever*, as well as *whosoever, whomsoever, whosesoever, whichsoever, whatsoever*, and *what*. Indefinite relative pronouns refer to unexpressed indefinite antecedents such as *anyone* or *anything*.

Independent expression - a word or group of words with no grammatical connection to the rest of the sentence. Independent expressions include **vocatives, interjections, nominative absolutes,** and **pleonasms**. Not only nouns, but also adverbs, infinitives, infinitive phrases, participles, participial phrases, and prepositional phrases can be used independently.

Indirect object - a noun or pronoun used with verbs of giving, saying, and showing to indicate *to whom* or *for whom* the direct object is intended. Indirect objects are adverbial objectives.

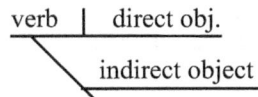

Indirect question - a question expressed as part of a sentence without the use of quotation marks. The following sentences contain indirect questions: *He asked why we were late. She wondered if she had to go to school. The teacher wants to know who said that.*

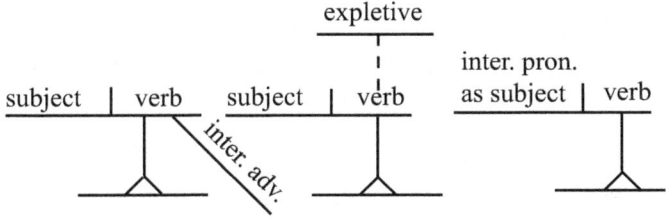

Infinitive - the basic form of any verb (usually preceded by the word *to*). Infinitives have tense and voice (present active, *to call*; present passive, *to be called*; present-perfect active, *to have called*; and present-perfect passive, *to have been called*) as well as progressivity (*to be calling, to have been calling*). Infinitives can function as adverbs (*they are running to win*), as adjectives (*you have nothing to do*), and as nouns (*we all want to succeed*).

Infinitive phrase - an infinitive with its modifiers and objects. Like simple infinitives, infinitive phrases can be used as adverbs, adjectives, or nouns.

Intensive pronouns - pronouns that intensify or identify nouns and other pronouns. In form, they are indistinguishable from **reflexive pronouns**: *myself, yourself, himself, herself, itself, ourselves, yourselves,* and *themselves*. Intensive pronouns are **appositives** and are so diagrammed. Examples: *she herself made the dress* (or *she made the dress herself*), *we met with the manager herself to discuss the problem*.

noun or pronoun   (intensive pronoun)

Interjection - a word or group of words with no grammatical connection to the rest of the sentence, used to express feeling or emotion, e.g., *wow, holy Toledo, for crying out loud, hurrah*

interjection

subject | verb

Interrogative adjectives - adjectives used in direct and indirect questions: *which, what*

Interrogative pronouns - pronouns used to ask **direct and indirect questions**: *who, whom, whose, which, what*

Intransitive verb - a verb that does not need a **direct object**. Some intransitive verbs are *be, seem, go, sleep, grin,* and *travel*. Many intransitive verbs can also be **transitive**; for example, a tent can *sleep three people*, a boss can *grin his approval*, and one can *travel the world*.

Linking verb - an intransitive verb that requires a **predicate nominative** or a **predicate adjective** for completion. The most common linking verb is *be*, including the participles and gerunds *being* and *having been*, and the finite forms *is, am, are, was, were*, etc. Some other verbs that can be linking verbs are *seem, become, feel, look, remain,* and *taste*. **Factitive verbs** (*make, call, elect,* etc.) can function in the **passive voice** as linking verbs: *he was made rich, she is called Kathy, you will be elected president*. Some scholars put the verb *be* in a category of its own and do not include it among the linking verbs. When *be* means *exist*, it is a **non-linking** verb.

Modal auxiliary - a verb used with a main verb to add a note of necessity, possibility, permissibility, or the like: *can, could, may, might, must, should, would*

Nominative absolute - a substantive (noun or noun substitute) modified by a **participle** or a **participial phrase** and having no grammatical connection to the rest of the sentence. The participle *being* is sometimes unexpressed: *His money [being] safely in the bank, he relaxed at last.*

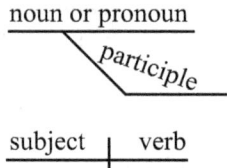

Noun - the name of anything (*Mr. Smith, John, woman, principal, student, Atlanta, country, kindness, hatred, dawn, darkness, sound, loudness, lion, lemur, book, computer, alertness, curiosity, weight, water, wish,* and thousands of others)

Noun clause - a clause that functions as a noun

Noun phrase - a noun and its modifiers (including articles, adjectives, prepositional phrases, relative clauses, and infinitives)

Nouns as adjectives - a noun placed before another noun such that the former modifies the latter, e.g., <u>wastepaper</u> basket, <u>K-Mart</u> special, <u>holiday</u> blues, <u>cabin</u> fever

Number - singular or plural. Nouns and pronouns have number (singular or plural) and so do verbs. The number of the subject of a sentence must agree with the number of the verb. If one says, "They eats later," one makes an agreement error involving number.

Objective complement - a noun, adjective, or equivalent expression (prepositional phrase, infinitive, infinitive phrase, participle, participial phrase, gerund, or gerund phrase) that completes the action of the verb and in some way either repeats (i.e., is identical with) or describes the direct object. Consider these sentences: *They named their baby daughter <u>Estelle</u>. That makes me <u>angry</u>. We found the book <u>difficult</u>. I saw them <u>leaving</u>. The weather forced him <u>to stay at home</u>. She asked him <u>to help with the groceries</u>.* Most authorities agree that the first four sentences contain objective complements; however, there is significant disagreement concerning the last two. In this book, all underlined words above are considered objective complements. One way to recognize an objective complement, when it is a substantive, is this: If a verb seems to have two direct objects and the first of the two is not an indirect object, then the second is an objective complement.

| verb | direct object \ objective complement |
| verb / objective complement | direct object |

Object of a preposition - a noun or other substantive that follows a preposition and completes it. All prepositions have objects.

Participial phrase - a participle with its objects and modifiers

Participle - a verbal adjective. **Transitive verbs** have five different kinds of participles: present active (*giving, speaking*), present passive (*being given, being spoken*), present-perfect active (*having given, having spoken*), present-perfect passive (*having been given, having been spoken*), and past (*given, spoken*). **Intransitive verbs** have fewer participial forms.

Particle - a subordinate word that is uninflected, i.e., doesn't change its form to reflect changes in tense, number, or the like. In English, nouns, pronouns, verbs, adjectives, and adverbs are inflected; prepositions, conjunctions, interjections, articles, and expletives are not. Nowadays many authorities use the word *particle* exclusively for preposition-like words that, together with verbs, form **phrasal verbs**.

Passive voice - a characteristic of **transitive verbs** that indicates the relationship of the verb to the subject as receiver of the action. A transitive verb is said to be in the passive voice when the subject of the sentence is acted upon, i.e., when something is done to the subject. See **active voice**.

Past participle - a verb form used with various tenses of the verb *have* to form the perfect tenses, e.g., *driven, called, gone, seen*

Past-perfect tense - the tense in which verbs use *had* as an auxiliary verb, e.g., *had worked, had been reading, had been planted*

Past tense - This tense is subdivided into three groups: 1) simple past, e.g., *saw, gave, hunted, was (were) seen, was (were) given, was (were) hunted*; 2) past progressive, e.g., *was (were) seeing, was (were) giving, was (were) hunting, was (were) being seen, was (were) being given, was (were) being hunted*; 3) emphatic past, e.g., *did see, did give, did hunt*.

Person - an expression used to distinguish among the speaker (or writer), the person spoken (or written) to, and the person spoken (or written) about: first person (*I, we*), second person (*you*), and third person (*he, she, it, they*). The person of the subject must agree with the person of the verb. If one says, "I likes him," one makes an agreement error involving person.

Personal pronouns - pronouns that denote person (first, second, third) and, in some instances, number (singular, plural), gender (masculine, feminine, neuter), and case (nominative, objective, possessive): nominative forms *I, you, he, she, it, we,* and *they*; objective forms *me, you, him, her, it, us,* and *them*; and possessive forms *my, mine, your, yours, his, her, hers, its, our, ours, their,* and *theirs*

Phrasal prepositions - prepositions that consist of more than one word, e.g., *out of, because of, instead of, along with, as for, by means of, in addition to, in spite of*

Phrasal verb - a verb-particle combination with an idiomatic meaning such that the meaning cannot be known from the separate meanings of the verb and the particle, e.g., *she looked up the word, he carried out the command*. Notice that one cannot say *the word up which she looked* or *the command out which he carried*, which shows that *up* and *out* are not prepositions here.

Phrase - a group of words in a sentence that form a unit but do not have a subject or a predicate

Pleonasm - the deliberate repetition within a sentence of an important element, e.g., *Coney Island, what a magical place it was*.

Possessives - the inflected forms of nouns (*Mary's, the workers', the men's*) and pronouns (*my, mine, your, yours, his, her, hers, its, our, ours, their, theirs*) used to show possession or belonging

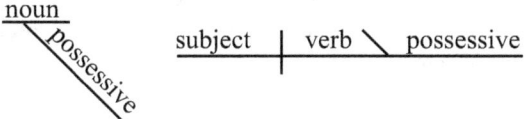

Predicate - the verb together with its modifiers and complements

Predicate adjective - an adjective or equivalent expression that follows a **linking verb** and refers to the subject

subject | linking verb \ predicate adjective

Predicate nominative - a substantive that follows a linking verb and refers to the subject

subject | linking verb \ predicate nominative

Preposition - a particle that requires an object (noun, pronoun, or the equivalent) for completion. Prepositions usually precede their objects.

Prepositional phrase - a preposition with its object (including article and adjectives, if any). Prepositional phrases function as **adverbs** and as **adjectives**. See **object of a preposition**.

Present participle - a verb form ending in *-ing* that can function 1) both as a verb and as an adjective, e.g., *a woman wearing a blue skirt, lovers holding hands*; 2) as a verb only, e.g., *the deer were running through the woods, we are planning a party*; 3) as an adjective only, e.g., *a sinking ship, the loving mother*

Present-perfect tense - the tense in which verbs use *has* or *have* as an auxiliary verb, e.g., *has (have) held, has (have) woven, has (have) been holding, has (have) been weaving, has (have) been held, has (have) been woven*

Present tense - This tense is subdivided into three groups: 1) simple present, e.g., *see, give, hunt, am (are, is) seen, am (are, is) given, am (are, is) hunted*; 2) present progressive, e.g., *am (are, is) seeing, am (are, is) giving, am (are, is) hunting, am (are, is) being seen, am (are, is) being given, am (are, is) being hunted*; 3) emphatic present, e.g., *do (does) see, do (does) give, do (does) hunt*

Progressive verb forms - verb forms in various tenses used to show action going on or state continuing. These forms occur in all six tenses of finite verbs (*is showing, was showing, will be showing, has been showing, had been showing, will have been showing*) and in the present and past tenses of the passive voice (*is being shown, was being shown*). Infinitives have progressive forms in the present and present-perfect tenses (*to be showing, to have been showing*)

Pronoun - a word that takes the place of a noun. There are various kinds of pronouns: **personal pronouns** (*I, you, he, she, it*, etc.), **relative pronouns** (*who, whom, whose, which, that*, among others), **interrogative pronouns** (*who, whom, whose, which, what*), **demonstrative pronouns** (*this, that, these, those*), **reflexive and intensive pronouns** (*myself, yourself, himself, herself*, etc.), **indefinite pronouns** (*someone, anyone*, etc.), **possessive pronouns** (my, your, his, her, its, etc.), and **reciprocal pronouns** (*each other, one another*).

Reflexive pronouns - *myself, yourself, himself, herself, itself, ourselves, yourselves, themselves*. A reflexive pronoun can be used as a predicate nominative, a direct object, an indirect object, or an object of a preposition to refer to the subject of the sentence.

Relative adverb - an adverb that can be restated as a prepositional phrase containing a relative pronoun, or as two prepositional phrases, the second of which contains a relative pronoun. For example, *where* in the expression *the hotel where we are staying* can be restated as *in which*, and *when* in the sentence *We can go when the light turns green* can be restated as *at the time at which*. See **correlative adverbs**.

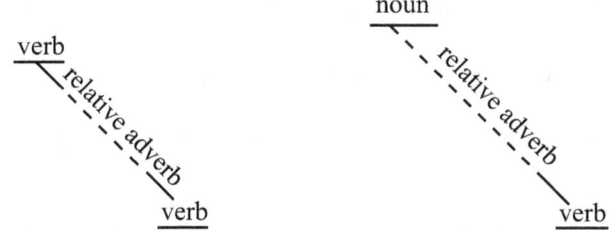

Relative clause - an **adjective clause** (introduced by a **relative pronoun** or a **relative adverb**)

Relative pronoun - a pronoun that introduces an **adjective clause** and has an **antecedent** (a previously mentioned noun, pronoun, or the equivalent to which it refers) within the same sentence. The principal relative pronouns are *who, whom, whose, which*, and *that*. Additional relative pronouns include the indefinite forms *what, whoever, whomever, whosever, whichever, whatever, whosoever, whomsoever, whosesoever, whichsoever*, and *whatsoever*; these have an unexpressed antecedent. *As* can be a relative pronoun (e.g., *he liked the same songs as his parents had liked when they were young*).

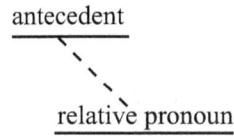

Retained object - a **direct object** that continues to function as a direct object when the **indirect object** of a sentence in the active voice becomes the subject of a corresponding sentence in the **passive voice**. The retained object is underlined in the following ex-ample: *Someone gave the youngster a new baseball glove* (active). *The youngster was given <u>a new baseball glove</u>* (passive).

<pre>
verb in the passive voice | retained object
                           |
</pre>

Sentence - a group of words that begins with a capital letter and ends with a period, a question mark, or an exclamation point, and contains at least one **independent clause**

Sentence modifier - a word, phrase, or clause that modifies an entire sentence or a major portion thereof, like a clause or an entire predicate

Subject - a noun, pronoun, or equivalent word, phrase, or clause about which the sentence says something

<pre>
        subject | verb
                 |
</pre>

Subjective complement - a noun, adjective, or the equivalent of either, that completes a linking verb. Such substantives are called **predicate nominatives**; such adjectives and equivalent expressions are called **predicate adjectives**.

Subjunctive mood - the modification of verbs used for contrary-to-fact conditions (e.g., *if she were here, if I had a million dollars*), unreal wishes (e.g., *I wish I were an astronaut, he wishes he could fly*), and indirect commands and suggestions (e.g., *she insists that he go along*), among others (e.g., *Be it ever so difficult, . . .*)

Subordinate clause - See **dependent clause**.

Substantive - a noun or a noun substitute (such as a pronoun, adjective, phrase, or clause)

Tenses - present, past, future, present perfect, past perfect, future perfect. Tense has a lot to do with time but is not synonymous with it.

Transitional adverb - an adverb used (usually after a semicolon) to join clauses. Examples are *consequently, furthermore, however, moreover, nevertheless, therefore*, among others.

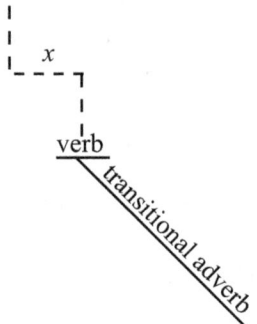

Transitive verb - a verb that needs a direct object for completion (see **intransitive verb**)

Unequal comparison - See **comparative degree**, **equal comparison**.

Verb - a word expressing action or state. Most verbs end in *-s* in the third person singular of the simple (one-word) present tense. An *-ing* ending is used to express verbs as **participles** and **gerunds**. The simple past of most verbs differs in form from the present tense, as does the past participle.

Verbals - nonfinite verb forms: **gerunds**, **participles**, and **infinitives**

Vocative - See **direct address**.

Voice - a term that refers to the relation of the verb to the subject as doer of the action of the verb or as recipient of the action. A **transitive verb** is said to be either in the **active voice** (when the subject of the sentence is acting) or in the **passive voice** (when the subject is acted upon).

~ Diagramming Symbols ~

subject |	| verb	predicate nominative * * Predicate adjectives are also diagrammed this way.
direct object	preposition / object of preposition	objective complement or objective complement
indirect object * * and other adverbial objectives	modifier / adverb * * attributive adjective, adverb	possessive / modifier *** ** or a noun used as an adjective *** article, attributive adjective, or possessive
noun of direct address *	* Interjections and the expletive *there* are also diagrammed in this manner.	(appositive)	c. c. = coordinating conjunction
antecedent relative pronoun	expletive * noun clause * with some noun clauses	verb sub. conj. * verb * subordinating conjunction
verb c. c. * verb compound sentence * coordinating conjunction	gerund participle	to infinitive infinitive
relative adverb	as / as / x	than / than / x

~ 271 ~

~ Index of Boldfaced Words and Phrases ~

~ A ~

absolute possessive pronouns, 246
active voice, 265, 268, 270
adjective clauses, 74, 89, 94, 164, 173, 213-215, 233, 244, 259-261, 265, 270
    as sentence modifier, 260
    restrictive adjective clauses, 261
adjectives, 11, 12, 81, 265, 269
    as appositives, 240
    as modifiers of compounds, 43
    as modifiers of gerunds, 106, 168, 176
    as modifiers of possessive nouns, 32
    attributive adjectives, 11, 23, 43, 155, 156, 173, 198, 199, 265
    compound adjectival modifiers, 41, 43, 167, 173, 203, 204
    demonstrative adjectives, 198, 199
    indefinite adjectives, 236
    interrogative adjectives, 33, 173, 267
    nouns as adjectives, 23, 156, 157, 173, 198, 263, 268
    predicate adjectives, 12, 156, 157, 163, 168, 197, 203, 259, 260, 261, 265, 267, 269, 270 (cf. separate entry)
adverb clauses, 76, 86, 89, 209, 212, 252
adverbial objectives, 42, 159, 161, 170, 175-177, 179, 206, 207, 240, 243, 244, 258, 260, 262, 265
adverbs, 18, 155, 156, 173, 199, 200, 265, 269
    as modifiers of gerunds, 80, 176
    as modifiers of prepositions and prepositional phrases, 178, 238, 265
    as modifiers of subordinating conjunctions, 261
    as modifiers of verbs, adjectives, and other adverbs, 18, 155, 156, 173, 199, 200, 265
    compound adverbial modifiers, 43, 168, 203, 204, 237, 241
    conjunctive adverbs, 266
    correlative adverbs, 171, 234, 247, 261, 263, 266
    difference between adverbs and prepositions, 250
    indefinite adverbs, 260
    independent adverbs, 177, 231, 246, 262
    interrogative adverbs, 33, 85, 157, 158, 173, 260
    relative adverbs, 86, 90, 171, 175-177, 211-213, 234, 265, 266, 269
    transitional adverbs, 109, 175, 232, 241, 260, 266, 270
antecedents, 74, 94, 164, 168, 173, 213-215, 230, 245, 251, 265, 269
    unexpressed antecedents, 165, 168, 230, 259
appositives, 28, 176, 178, 204, 238, 251, 265, 267
    adjectives as appositives, 240
    compound appositives, 173, 205, 253, 258
    infinitive phrases as appositives, 169, 254, 259
    non-restrictive appositives, 265
    noun clauses as appositives, 183, 254, 255, 261
    possessive nouns as appositives, 32, 239
    pronouns as appositives, 28, 208, 267
    restrictive appositives, 265
articles, 7, 265
    as modifiers of compounds, 43
    as modifiers of gerunds, 106
    as modifiers of possessive nouns, 32
    definite article, 7, 155, 173, 198, 265, 266
    indefinite article, 7, 155, 198, 266
as . . . as, 90, 171, 234, 261
as as expletive, 240
as as relative adverb, 86, 90, 175, 177, 211, 234, 251
as as relative pronoun, 244
as for, 101
as if, 101
as though, 101
attributive adjectives, 11, 23, 43, 155, 156, 173, 198, 199, 265
auxiliary (i.e., helping) verbs, 6, 265
    modal auxiliary verbs, 6, 155, 195, 268

~ B ~

both . . . and, 41
but as preposition, 170, 182

~ C ~

cannot, 157
clauses, 265
    adjective clauses, 74, 89, 94, 164, 173, 213-215, 233, 244, 259-261, 265, 270
    adverb clauses, 76, 86, 89, 209, 212, 252
    as antecedents of relative pronouns, 94
    concessive clauses. 183, 230, 231, 236, 260
    conditional clauses, 247, 248
    dependent (i.e., subordinate) clauses, 74, 75, 89, 162, 168, 171, 175, 258, 260, 266
    elliptical clauses, 164, 175, 229, 230, 240, 251, 260, 261, 266
    independent (i.e., main) clauses, 76, 79, 89, 162, 164, 174, 266, 270
    noun clauses, 75, 85, 165, 166, 169-171, 174, 182, 216-219, 243, 248, 259, 261, 268
commands (i.e., imperatives), 21, 174, 267
comparative degree, 265, 270
    equal comparisons, 90, 234, 266, 270
    unequal comparisons, 90, 233, 265, 270
complementary infinitives, 100, 170, 183, 226-228, 250, 262, 266
complements, 265
    direct objects, 16, 38, 157, 158, 173, 196, 265-267, 270 (cf. separate entry)
    objective complements, 38, 163, 168, 174, 177, 178, 208, 209, 221, 226-228, 243, 248, 259, 265, 268
    retained objects, 160, 168, 183, 242, 243, 262, 265, 270
    subjective complements, 265
        predicate adjectives, 12, 156, 157, 163, 168,

197, 203, 259, 260, 261, 265, 267, 269, 270 (cf. separate entry)
    predicate nominatives, 8, 156, 173, 197, 259, 260, 269, 270
complex sentences, 162, 266
compound adjectival modifiers, 41, 43, 167, 173, 203, 204
compound adverbial modifiers, 43, 168, 203, 204, 237, 241
compound adverbial objectives, 244
compound appositives, 173, 205, 253, 258
compound-complex sentences, 89, 266
compound direct objects, 160, 161, 162, 176, 179, 202, 203
compound infinitive phrases, 169, 225
compound objective complements, 208, 209, 248
compound objects of prepositions, 161, 203, 259
compound predicate adjective, 173, 203
compound predicate nominatives, 162
compound predicates, 43, 161, 162, 177, 202, 204, 207, 241, 261
compound sentences, 79, 161, 162, 174, 203, 258, 266
compound subjects, 160, 174, 203
concessive clauses, 183, 230, 231, 236, 260
conditional clauses, 247, 248
conjunctions, 266
    coordinating conjunctions, 41, 43, 79, 173, 203, 266 (cf separate entry)
    correlative conjunctions, 179, 202, 266
    phrasal conjunctions, 101, 246
    subordinating conjunctions, 76, 86, 162, 168, 209, 212, 246, 248, 260, 261, 266
conjunctive adverbs, 266
    transitional adverbs, 109, 266
    relative adverbs, 86, 90, 266
contractions involving a verb and *not*, 21, 104
contractions involving a subject and a verb, 42, 104, 261
coordinating conjunctions, 41, 43, 79, 173, 203, 266
    correlative conjunctions, 179, 202, 266
    unexpressed coordinating conjunctions, 231, 241, 242, 251, 260
correlative adverbs, 171, 234, 247, 261, 263, 266
    correlative conjunctions, 179, 202, 266

~ D ~

definite article, 7, 155, 173, 198, 265, 266
demonstrative adjectives, 198, 199, 266
demonstrative pronouns, 157, 266, 269
dependent (i.e., subordinate) clauses, 74, 75, 89, 162, 168, 171, 175, 258, 260, 266
    adverb clauses, 76, 86, 89, 209, 212, 252
    noun clauses, 75, 85, 182, 268 (cf. separate entry)
    adjective clauses, 74, 89, 94, 164, 173, 213-215, 233, 244, 259-261, 265, 270
direct address (cf. vocatives), 26, 159, 174, 178, 205, 206, 266
direct objects, 16, 38, 157, 158, 173, 196, 265-267, 270
    compound direct objects, 160, 174, 176, 182, 203
direct quotations, 246, 260

~ E ~

either . . . or, 41, 79
elliptical clauses, 164, 175, 229, 230, 240, 251, 260, 261, 266
expletives, 75, 267
    as as expletive, 240
    if as expletive, 105, 170, 259
    namely as expletive, 229
    that as expletive, 75, 85, 99, 165, 258, 266
    there as expletive, 91, 158, 162, 260, 267
    whether, 105, 267

~ F ~

factitive verbs, 267
finite verbs, 267
for, 248

~ G ~

gerund phrases, 80, 167, 168, 175, 179, 223, 224, 247, 258, 260
gerunds, 80, 167, 168, 222, 224, 258, 260, 267, 270
    as objects of prepositions, 80, 171
    forms of gerund, 106
    gerunds as compound direct object, 175
    modified by adjectival modifier, 106, 176, 223
    modified by adverbial modifier, 80, 106, 176, 223
    unexpressed gerund, 248

~ H ~

helping (i.e., auxiliary) verbs, 6, 155, 195, 265, 268
however, 109, 260

~ I ~

if as expletive, 105, 170, 259
imperative sentences, 21, 174, 267
indefinite adjectives, 236
indefinite article, 7, 198, 266
indefinite pronouns, 267, 267
indefinite relative pronouns, 229, 243, 259, 260, 267
independent (i.e., main) clauses, 76, 79, 89, 162, 164, 174, 214, 266, 270
independent expressions, 233, 267
    independent adverbial phrases, 232
    independent adverbs, 177, 231, 246, 262
    independent infinitive phrases, 232
    independent participial phrases, 232, 235
    independent prepositional phrases, 232, 238, 260
    interjections, 31, 204, 205, 229, 230, 267
    nominative absolutes, 177, 231, 236, 240, 268
    pleonasm, 267, 269
    vocatives (cf. direct address)
indirect objects, 37, 42, 159, 174, 178, 206, 207, 226, 243, 259, 265, 267, 270
indirect questions, 105, 170, 171, 174, 216-219, 259, 267
infinitive phrases, 168-171, 174, 178, 224-228, 232, 258, 259, 267
    compound infinitive phrases, 169, 225
infinitives, 84, 96, 100
    complementary infinitives, 100, 170, 183, 226-228, 250, 262, 266
    forms of, 84, 267

subjects of infinitives, 179, 181, 245, 262
"to-less" infinitives, 170
intensive pronouns, 208, 239, 267, 269
interjections, 31, 204, 205, 229, 230, 267
interrogative adjectives, 33, 173, 267
interrogative adverbs, 33, 85, 157, 158, 173, 260
interrogative pronouns, 36, 85, 157, 158, 173, 267, 269
intransitive verbs, 195, 267, 268, 270

~ L ~

like, 238-240
linking verbs, 8, 12, 156, 163, 168, 175, 241, 259, 268, 269

~ M ~

main (i.e., independent) clauses, 76, 79, 89, 162, 164, 174, 214, 266, 270
modal auxiliary verbs, 6, 155, 195, 268
moreover, 109

~ N ~

namely, 229
near, 240
neither . . . nor, 41
nevertheless, 109, 260
nominative absolute, 177, 231, 236, 240, 268
non-linking verbs, 16, 241, 268
noun clauses, 75, 85, 182, 268
    noun clauses as appositives, 183, 254, 255, 261
    noun clauses introduced by expletive, 75, 85, 99, 165, 166, 169-171, 216, 217, 243, 248, 261
    noun clauses introduced by interrogative words, 174, 218, 219
nouns, 195, 268
    nouns as adjectives, 23, 156, 157, 173, 198, 263, 268
    nouns of direct address, 26, 159, 174, 178, 205, 206, 266
    noun phrases, 268
    phrasal nouns, 159, 259
    possessive nouns, 31, 32, 106, 158, 239, 258
number, 268

~ O ~

objective complements, 38, 163, 178, 209, 259, 268
    compound objective complements, 208, 248
    infinitives as objective complements, 226-228
    participles as objective complements, 168, 177, 221, 261
    indirect questions as objective complements, 174
objects of prepositions, 22, 158, 173, 179, 203, 259, 268, 269

~ P ~

participial phrases, 177, 222, 232, 235, 258, 261, 268
participles, 81
    participles and adjectives, 262
    forms of, 81, 166, 168, 176, 177, 183, 195, 220-222, 262, 268
    prepositions resembling participles, 243
particles, 268
passive voice, 183, 195, 268, 270
person, 268
personal pronouns, 155, 173, 269
phrasal nouns, 159, 259

phrasal prepositions, 101, 163, 170, 175, 202, 236, 237, 244, 269
phrasal subordinating conjunctions, 101, 210, 246
phrasal verbs, 95, 163, 260, 269
phrases, 269
    gerund phrases, 80, 167, 168, 175, 223, 224
    independent phrases, 235
    infinitive phrases, 168-171, 174, 178, 224-228, 232, 258, 259, 267
    participial phrases, 177, 222, 232, 235, 258, 261, 268
    prepositional phrases, 22, 27, 104, 158, 173, 175, 200-202, 236, 237, 255, 258, 260, 269
please, 247
pleonasm, 267, 269
possessives, 13, 43, 269
    possessive nouns, 31, 32, 106, 158, 239, 258
    possessive pronouns, 13, 32, 106, 156, 173, 198, 199, 246, 251, 258, 269
predicate, 265, 269
predicate adjectives, 12, 156, 157, 163, 168, 197, 203, 259, 260, 261, 265, 267, 269, 270
    compound predicate adjectives, 173, 203
    prepositional phrases as predicate adjectives, 104, 175, 236, 237
    unexpressed predicate adjectives, 261
predicate nominatives, 8, 156, 173, 197, 259, 260, 269, 270
prepositional phrases, 22, 255, 269
    independent prepositional phrases, 238, 260
    prepositional phrases as attributive adjectives, 27, 158, 173, 200-202
    prepositional phrases as adverbs, 22, 158, 173, 200-202, 258
    prepositional phrases as predicate adjectives, 104, 175, 236, 237
    prepositional phrases modified by adverb, 178, 238, 265
prepositions, 22, 27, 158, 173, 200-202, 243, 269
    but as a preposition, 170, 182
    difference between prepositions and adverbs, 250
    objects of prepositions, 22, 158, 173, 179, 203, 259, 268, 269
    phrasal prepositions, 101, 163, 170, 175, 202, 236, 237, 244, 269
    than as preposition, 239
pronouns, 269
    demonstrative pronouns, 157, 266, 269
    intensive pronouns, 208, 239, 267, 269
    interrogative pronouns, 36, 85, 157, 158, 173, 267, 269
    personal pronouns, 155, 173, 269
    possessive pronouns, 13, 32, 106, 156, 173, 198, 199, 246, 251, 258, 269
        absolute possessive pronouns, 246
    reflexive pronouns, 239, 267, 269
    relative pronouns, 74, 94, 168, 173, 213-215, 229, 243-245, 259, 260, 267, 270

~ Q ~

questions, 17, 33, 36
    direct questions, 105
    indirect questions, 105, 170, 171, 174, 216-219, 259, 267

~ R ~

reflexive pronouns, 239, 267, 269
regarding as preposition, 243
relative adverbs, 86, 265, 266, 269
    after as relative adverb, 86, 213
    as as relative adverb, 86, 90, 175, 177, 211, 234, 251
    as if as relative adverb, 212
    before as relative adverb, 86, 212
    than as relative adverb, 90, 171, 233-235, 260
    until as relative adverb, 86, 212
    when as relative adverb, 86, 211, 251
    whenever as relative adverb, 211
    where as relative adverb, 176, 212, 244
relative clauses, (cf. adjective clauses)
relative pronouns, 74, 164, 259, 270
    antecedents of, 74, 94, 164, 168, 173, 213-215, 230, 245, 251, 265, 269
    clauses as antecedents of, 94
    indefinite relative pronouns, 229, 243, 259, 260, 267
    unexpressed relative pronouns *whom* and *that*, 99, 165, 215, 244
retained objects, 160, 168, 183, 242, 243, 262, 265, 270

~ S ~

sentence modifiers, 233, 256, 260, 270
sentences, 270
    complex sentences, 89, 162, 266
    compound-complex sentences, 89, 249, 266
    compound sentences, 79, 161, 162, 174, 203, 258, 266
so . . . as, 234, 263
subjective complements, 265, 270
    predicate adjectives, 12, 156, 157, 163, 168, 197, 203, 259-261, 265, 267, 269, 270
    predicate nominatives, 8, 156, 173, 197, 259, 260, 269, 270
subjects, 6, 155, 173, 195, 265, 270
    compound subjects, 160, 174, 203
    subjects of infinitives, 179, 181, 245, 262
    unexpressed subject *you*, 21, 159, 174, 229, 260
subordinate clauses (cf. dependent clauses)
subordinating conjunctions, 76, 86, 162, 168, 209, 212, 246, 248, 260, 261, 266
    for as subordinating conjunction, 248
    phrasal subordinating conjunctions, 101, 210, 246
    subordinating conjunction modified by adverb, 261
    unexpressed subordinating conjunction, 183, 230, 231, 260
substantives, 270
suggestions, 21

~ T ~

tenses, 81, 84, 195, 267-270
    tenses of gerunds, 106
    tenses of infinitives, 84, 267
    tenses of participles, 81, 176, 183, 220-222, 262, 268

than as preposition, 239
than as relative adverb, 90, 171, 233-235, 260
that as expletive, 75, 85, 99, 165, 258, 266
the . . . the, 247, 263
there as expletive, 91, 158, 162, 260, 267
therefore, 109
"to-less" infinitives, 170
transitional adverbs, 109, 175, 232, 241, 260, 266, 270
transitive verbs, 81, 265-68, 270

~ U ~

unexpressed words, 90
    unexpressed antecedents, 165, 168, 230, 259
    unexpressed auxiliary verbs, 229
    unexpressed coordinating conjunction, 231, 241, 242, 251, 260
    unexpressed expletive *that*, 99
    unexpressed gerund, 248
    unexpressed predicate adjective, 261
    unexpressed predicate nominative, 260
    unexpressed relative pronouns, 99, 165, 215, 244
    unexpressed subject *you*, 21, 159, 174, 229, 260
    unexpressed subordinating conjunctions, 183, 230, 231, 260
    unexpressed verbs, 229

~ V ~

verbals, 270
    gerunds, 80, 167, 168, 171, 175, 176, 222-224, 258, 260, 267, 270
    infinitives, 84, 100, 170, 179, 181, 183, 226-228, 245, 250, 262, 266, 267, 270
    participles, 81, 166, 168, 176, 177, 183, 195, 220-222, 258, 262, 268
verbs, 6, 16, 155, 173, 195, 270
    auxiliary (i.e., helping) verbs, 6, 265
        modal auxiliary verbs, 6, 155, 195, 268
    emphatic form of, 173, 195
    factitive verbs, 267
    intransitive verbs, 195, 267, 268, 270
    linking verbs, 8, 12, 156, 163, 168, 175, 241, 259, 268, 269
    non-linking verbs, 16, 241, 268
    person, 269
    phrasal verbs, 95, 163, 260, 269
    progressive verb forms, 173, 195, 196, 269
    tenses, 195, 267-270
    transitive verbs, 81, 265-268, 270
vocatives (cf. direct address), 26, 159, 174, 178, 205, 206, 266
voice, 81, 84, 270
    active voice, 265, 268, 270
    passive voice, 183, 195, 268, 270

~ W ~

whether, 105, 267